Tom Stienstra's

Outdoor Getaway Guide

Northern California

Tom Stienstra

Foghorn Press
BOOKS BUILDING COMMUNITY™

ISBN 1-57354-038-2

9 781573 540384 01895

Inquiries and excerpt requests should be addressed to:
Foghorn Press
Rights Department
340 Bodega Avenue
Petaluma, CA 94952
foghorn@well.com

Foghorn Outdoors' guidebooks are available wherever books are sold. To find a retailer near you or to order, call 1-800-FOGHORN (364-4676) or (707) 521-3300 or visit the Fokghorn Press web site at www.foghorn.com. Foghorn Press titles are available to the book trade through Publishers Group West (800-788-3123) as well as through wholesalers.

LIbrary of Congress ISSN Data:
August 1998
Tom Stienstra's Outdoor Getaway Guide for Northern California
Third Edition
ISSN: 1099-4726

AUTHOR'S NOTE

Dear Readers,

The best part of the great outdoors is now right in the palms of your hands. As part of a three-year effort, *Getaways* has been completely rewritten and redesigned to make it the most accurate, enjoyable, easy-to-use, and comprehensive guidebook to outdoor activities in Northern California available anywhere.

Every listing was checked, faxed, and reviewed by resource experts. In the end hundreds of people were involved in polishing the final product. I also incorporated dozens of suggestions made by readers like you.

Your comments are always welcome. Write to me at Foghorn Press, 340 Bodega Avenue, Petaluma, CA 94952.

—T.S.

ACKNOWLEDGEMENTS

This book would not have been possible without the support of the *San Francisco Examiner,* Jim Sevrens, Phil Bronstein, Glenn Schwarz, Dave Dayton, Larry Yant, Rick Nelson, and Kevin Casey.

—Tom Stienstra

For Mom and Dad

"Out in Luckenbach, Texas, there ain't nobody feelin' no pain."
—*Waylon Jennings*

PREFACE

Let me tell you how you can get the shock of your life: Go for a ride in an airplane, then look down and take in the view of the Bay Area and beyond—and all the secret places to go and have fun.

You see, despite strips and pockets where the cars are jammed and the housing is crowded, about 90 percent of the land here is wild, unsettled, and beautiful, sprinkled with lakes and streams galore. That's right: Hundreds of hidden spots remain for hiking, camping, fishing, boating, and many other outdoor getaways. The purpose of this book is to share my favorite of these. There are hundreds of them.

The Bay Area, for instance, has 125 significant parks, 5,000 miles of hiking trails, 50 lakes, beautiful stretches of coast, mountains with lookouts, and a bay dotted with islands. If you expand your adventures, you'll find the state has 20 million acres of national forest, 17.5 million acres of land under the Bureau of Land Management, 373 drive-to lakes, 483 significant lakes you can hike to, and 185 streams, each with many tributaries. The land has no limits—and neither do you.

As a full-time outdoors writer, I can live anywhere I want, but guess what? I choose to live here. I've ventured across much of North America and have learned that there is no better place, day after day, for year-round adventure, diversity, and beauty than right here in Northern California.

The outdoors is good for the soul. Adventure can refresh the spirit. So go for it, and don't be surprised if you run into me out there. It's my home, too.

—*Tom Stienstra*

• TABLE OF CONTENTS •

Chapter 1: HIKING

• TOM'S RATINGS •

• FEATURED TRIPS •

Chapter 2: CAMPING

• TOM'S RATINGS •

• FEATURED TRIPS •

Chapter 3: BACKPACKING

• Tom's Ratings •

• Featured Trips •

Chapter 4: ROMANTIC GETAWAYS

• Tom's Ratings •

• Featured Trip •

Chapter 5: TOURING

• Tom's Ratings •

• Featured Trips •

Chapter 6: WILDLIFE WATCHING

• Tom's Ratings •

Chapter 7: BICYCLING

Chapter 8: SNOW GETAWAYS

Chapter 9: BOATING AND WATER SPORTS

Chapter 10: FISHING

Chapter 11: BONUS GETAWAYS

• TOM'S RATINGS •

• FEATURED TRIPS •

Chapter 12: RESOURCES

Parks and Recreation Areas

Nature Preserves

Midpeninsula Open Space Preserve

SEE LAST PAGE FOR NORTHERN CALIFORNIA AND BAY AREA FOLDOUT MAPS.

1
HIKING

• Tom's Ratings •

• Featured Trips •

See last page for Northern California and Bay Area foldout maps.

• TOM'S RATINGS •

THE TOP 25 HIKES

In the San Francisco Bay Area

The top 25 hikes in the Bay Area are highlighted by hidden waterfalls, gorgeous views, and one of the last secret spots in the region. But while all 25 hikes hold different appeal, each provides an extended tour into a land of charm that makes the Bay Area the number one metropolitan region in North America for outdoor recreation.

The hikes are rated on five factors: natural beauty, quality of destinations, views, diversity of flora, and tranquillity. For the most part, difficult climbs didn't make the list, except for one, the little-known but first-class butt-kicker to Rose Peak in remote Alameda County.

These trails will lead you to the finest panoramas California can offer. They include the grandest waterfall, lookout, and beach in the Bay Area, truly secluded redwood forests, a fern-walled canyon on the North Coast, and high Sierra lakes.

What you invest is a little time and a little energy, walking to a place where machines are not allowed. In return, you get an experience that will stay with you for a long time. It is what some people call "the power of place." It's difficult to explain, but you know it when you feel it. And when you feel it, you don't forget it.

In the past several years, I have ventured to about 50 Bay Area parks and hiked some 75 different trails in an ongoing quest to visit every park in the Bay Area and the rest of Northern California. Previous to that, my adventures include a week-long, 125-mile hike around SAN FRANCISCO BAY, and explorations to every little secret spot I can find in the region, about 150 trails in all.

Here are my ratings:

1. COAST TRAIL

The Coast Trail offers the closest thing to a religious experience for Bay Area hikers. It's that good, as if each of your steps were divinely blessed. The landscape is dramatic, diverse, and beautiful, featuring the rebirth of the western slopes below Inverness Ridge, burned in the wildfire of October 1995. But there are also great lookouts of the PACIFIC OCEAN, ocean bluff camps, Sculptured Beach and its rock formations and tide pools, an extraordinary bluff-top waterfall, and even small freshwater lakes for swimming.

The Coast Trail is 15 miles one way, perfect for an overnight trip with a shuttle car waiting at the end of the trail. The best route is north to south, starting at the Point Reyes Hostel so the wind will be at your back. For a day hike, a better strategy is to start from the southern Palomarin Trailhead, located just north of BOLINAS, then make the 8.5-mile round-trip hike to ALAMERE FALLS and back. Only dense fog or howling winds can ruin the deal, but catch it right and you'll be granted temporary entry into heaven.

Contact: Point Reyes National Seashore, (415) 663-1092. **Locator:** POINT REYES NATIONAL SEASHORE (E1a). **See featured trip pages:** 67, 166, and 262.

2. BERRY CREEK FALLS

If I ever go a year without hiking to Berry Creek Falls, I figure I just wasted that year. I made the trip yet again recently, and just like always, I feel like the experience has realigned my senses for the coming months. Woods and water have a way of doing that, and you get the best of both here, with a vast and beautiful redwood forest and a series of three drop-dead gorgeous waterfalls, Berry Creek, Silver, and Golden Falls.

From park headquarters, it's 4.7 miles to Berry Creek Falls, first making the short climb out to the Big Basin Rim, then continuing with an easy 600-foot descent over the course of four miles to the falls. Just upstream is Silver Falls, a pretty free fall with the trail stair-stepped right aside it. Above that is Golden Falls, a stunning spot where clear water cascades over gold-tinged, iron-based rocks polished slick by the rushing water. Though a danger sign on the trail warns that this is a six-hour hike, most make it in 4 1/2 to 5 hours, including a half hour for a snack.

Contact: Big Basin Redwoods State Park,(831) 338-8860; California State Parks, Santa Cruz District, (831) 429-2851. **Locator:** BIG BASIN REDWOODS STATE PARK (E1d). **See featured trip page:** 136.

3. TRAIL CAMP LOOP

Can any trail take hikers into a wider variety of spectacular settings than the Trail Camp Loop? None that I know of. In the course of a 5.5-mile loop, you get the best of everything: a secluded canyon, a waterfall, views, and honeycombed sandstone formations, all of it dramatic. This is what makes CASTLE ROCK STATE PARK, located on Skyline Boulevard just south of the junction of Highways 9 and 35, so special.

The trip starts on the Saratoga Gap Trail (toward Trail Camp) by dropping down into a tree-covered canyon, then in less than a mile, emerges at an edge-of-the-world viewing area of Castle Falls, a 50-foot waterfall, and across the SANTA CRUZ MOUNTAINS and a sea of conifers. This alone is spectacular. But you continue on, taking in the views of Big Basin and MONTEREY BAY, occasionally passing these strange rocks filled with holes, as if a rock-eating gopher had been digging tunnels. Eventually you loop back on the Ridge Trail, passing Goat Rock, the king of sandstone, with another incredible view from the top, looking down at MONTEREY BAY.

Contact: Castle Rock State Park, (408) 867-2952; California State Parks, Santa Cruz District, (831) 429-2851. **Locator:** CASTLE ROCK STATE PARK (E1d).

4. MONTARA MOUNTAIN TRAIL

On my first visit to SAN PEDRO VALLEY COUNTY PARK, in 1980, my first impression was that if a trail was built past Brooks Falls to San Pedro Ridge, then linked to MONTARA MOUNTAIN, this would be one of the best parks for hiking in California. Well, that is exactly what they did, and yep, it is. This is a seven-mile round-trip, gaining nearly 1,900 feet on the way up. Recently, excellent signs were added and brush was cleared out, making for better views.

The hike starts by heading up through a eucalyptus forest, then lateraling along the north flank of Brooks Canyon, where there is a good view of wispy, three-tiered Brooks Falls and surrounding granite outcrops. Shortly after, you turn left at a junction and hike up to San Pedro Ridge for a picture-perfect view of the coast, looking north. Eventually, the hike reaches the North Peak of MONTARA MOUNTAIN (1,898 feet), with long-distance views of the PACIFIC OCEAN and the FARALLON ISLANDS on one side and of the off-limits San Francisco Fish and Game Refuge to the other.

Contact: San Pedro Valley County Park, (650) 355-8289. **Locator:** SAN PEDRO VALLEY COUNTY PARK (E1b). **See featured trip page:** 80.

5. STEEP RAVINE TRAIL

This is one of the few trails anywhere that is best experienced in the rain or during a heavy, dew-dripping fog. That is because when wet, the entire setting comes to life, and if you get soaked by a surprise spring rain, like I did on one trip, it can feel as if you are being baptized by nature.

From the trailhead at Pantoll on the western slopes of MOUNT TAMALPAIS, the trail drops into a lush, deep, extraordinarily beautiful canyon. There are towering redwoods, a closed treetop canopy, and a rich undergrowth of sword ferns, mosses, and a diversity of greenery, with pretty Webb Creek running right down the center. Over the course of two miles, the trail descends 1,100 feet and crosses over the creek eight times. On the return trip, looking upstream, you'll get framed views of the creek and the surrounding canyon. This is one of my favorite places on Earth.

Contact: Mount Tamalpais State Park, (415) 388-2070; California State Parks, Marin District, (415) 893-1580. **Locator:** MOUNT TAMALPAIS STATE PARK (E1a). **See featured trip page:** 62.

6. LAND'S END TRAIL

One small trick can turn San Francisco's greatest lookout into its greatest walk. That trick is to get here early, at sunrise if possible, especially on Sundays, well before the tourists and the rest of humanity inundate the place. Add a clear day and you'll discover, right from your first steps, why this is a world-class destination. In one 180-degree turn of the head from right to left, you can see the GOLDEN GATE BRIDGE, the MARIN HEADLANDS, the mouth of the bay, and crashing breakers. Beyond and out to sea are passing ships and fishing boats, with long-distance views of POINT REYES and the FARALLON ISLANDS.

The trail starts at Land's End, near the Cliff House, then is routed along the SAN FRANCISCO HEADLANDS toward the GOLDEN GATE BRIDGE. In the process, you peek in and out of cypress trees while walking on nearly level ground for 2.5 miles to the overlook of CHINA BEACH. Get here late and the parking is difficult and the trail is often crowded. Get here early and there's no better flat, easy walk in the Bay Area.

Contact: San Francisco Headlands, (415) 556-8371; Golden Gate National Recreation Area, (415) 556-0560. **Locator:** SAN FRANCISCO HEADLANDS (E1b).

7. SAN PABLO RIDGE

When I hiked the 31-mile EAST BAY SKYLINE NATIONAL TRAIL, it was San Pablo Ridge that provided the most memorable moments of the trip. Nowhere can you get more quickly to remote land with great views. From the ridge looking west, SAN FRANCISCO BAY and beyond to the San Francisco waterfront is simply stunning, while to the east, there is nothing but untouched rolling foothills, with SAN PABLO and BRIONES RESERVOIRS tucked in canyons like sapphires.

From the trailhead at WILDCAT CANYON REGIONAL PARK, the trail climbs 700 feet in 2.5 miles to gain the ridge. From here, you continue along the ridge for as long as you want (the trail eventually links to TILDEN REGIONAL PARK); the farther you go, the fewer the people, the more remote the land, and the better the views. This hike provides glimpses of Contra Costa County's prettiest areas.

Contact: East Bay Regional Park District, (510) 635-0135 extension 2200. **Locator:** WILDCAT CANYON REGIONAL PARK (E1c). **See featured trip pages:** 87 and 100.

8. BLACK ROCK FALLS TRAIL

This can be a stunning surprise, with five waterfalls and several smaller cascades packed into a 3.5-mile round-trip hike. I was first attracted to Uvas Park by the good fishing at UVAS RESERVOIR, but my hiking partner told me that there is another world here that you can access by striking out on the Black Rock Falls Trail, adding to it by looping out to Alec Canyon and Alec Creek.

The first waterfall you come to is Black Rock Falls on Swanson Creek, named for the crystal-clear water flowing over black rocks, unusual and radiant. As you go on, you come upon one waterfall after another, including Basin Falls, Upper Falls, and Triple Falls. Each is beautiful in its own way. This park is the best reason there is to venture down to south Santa Clara County, or when heading to the southland on U.S. 101, to stop and take time out for a great, short adventure.

Contact: Uvas Canyon County Park, (408) 779-9232. **Locator:** UVAS CANYON COUNTY PARK (F1).

9. THREE LAKES TRAIL

There are no prettier lakes in the Bay Area than LAGUNITAS, BON TEMPE, and ALPINE, set on the north slope of MOUNT TAMALPAIS. And there is no better easy loop hike than this one, which links a series of trails over the course of 5.5 miles and allows you to soak in the beauty of all three. All the while, Mount Tam's East Peak looms above. Note that there is no officially named "Three Lakes Trail," that the trail does not border the shore of all three lakes, and that you must have a map to get it right, available at the kiosk at the Sky Oaks entrance station.

All three lakes are on the Lagunitas Creek watershed and can be very pretty when full, surrounded by green. Start at the Lagunitas Picnic Area, where you'll find the first lake, little Lagunitas Lake, covering just 22 acres. At sunrise, the scene is quiet and pristine, with steam often rising from the still surface. Lagunitas feeds water down into BON TEMPE, 140 acres and just as pretty, often with a variety of wildfowl exploring about. Below BON TEMPE is 224-acre ALPINE; bordered to the south by forest, it's one of the prettiest lakes anywhere. Of the nearly 50 lakes in the Bay Area, few have stellar walks that let you explore them. This is the best.

Contact: North Marin Water District, (415) 924-4600; Sky Oaks Ranger Station, (415) 459-5267. **Locator:** MOUNT TAMALPAIS (E1a). **See featured trip page:** 62.

10. OHLONE WILDERNESS REGIONAL TRAIL (ROSE PEAK)

The Bay Area's worst butt-kicker just had to make the top 10, and it de–serves it. From the trailhead at SUNOL/OHLONE REGIONAL WILDERNESS (390 feet elevation), the Ohlone Wilderness Regional Trail climbs 3,427 feet over the course of 10 miles to reach Rose Peak (3,817 feet). In the process, you rise across the foothills of the north end of the Mount Hamilton Range, entering the wildest and most remote land remaining in the East Bay hills. To see it, your butt will be thoroughly kicked.

The flora features grasslands peppered with oak and bay trees, with good numbers of deer and hawks. As you climb and make the ridge, there are views to the west of SAN FRANCISCO BAY and beyond, and to the east of the SIERRA NEVADA. It's little known that Rose Peak is only 32 feet lower than MOUNT DIABLO to the north. To do this right, most hikers will split the trip into two days and set up a backpack camp at Maggie's Half Acre, which is located half a mile from Rose Peak; reservations and wilderness permits are required.

Contact: Sunol Regional Wilderness, (9 25) 862-2244; East Bay Regional Park District, (510) 635-0135 extension 2200. **Locator:** SUNOL/OHLONE REGIONAL WILDERNESS (E1d). **See featured trip pages:** 99 and 168.

11. MATT DAVIS/SUNSET TRAIL

Contact: Mount Tamalpais State Park, (415) 388-2070 or (415) 893-1580. **Locator:** MOUNT TAMALPAIS STATE PARK (E1a). **See featured trip page:** 62.

12. NORTH RIDGE/SUNSET TRAIL

Contact: Angel Island, (415) 435-1915 or (415) 893-1580. **Locator:** ANGEL ISLAND (E1a).

13. WHITTEMORE GULCH TRAIL

Contact: Purisima Creek Redwoods, Half Moon Bay, (650) 691-1200. **Locator:** PURISIMA CREEK REDWOODS (E1b). **See featured trip page:** 78.

14. ESTERO TRAIL

Contact: Point Reyes National Seashore, (415) 663-1092. **Locator:** POINT REYES NATIONAL SEASHORE (E1a). **See featured trip pages:** 67 and 166.

15. SWEENEY RIDGE

Contact: Golden Gate National Recreation Area, San Bruno, (415) 556-8371 or (415) 556-0560. **Locator:** SWEENEY RIDGE (E1b). **See featured trip page:** 85.

16. ROCK SPRINGS TRAIL

Contact: Mount Tamalpais State Park, (415) 388-2070 or (415) 893-1580. **Locator:** MOUNT TAMALPAIS STATE PARK (E1a). **See featured trip page:** 62.

17. AÑO NUEVO LOOKOUT

Contact: Butano State Park, Pescadero, (650) 879-2040 or (415) 330-6300. **Locator:** BUTANO STATE PARK STATE PARK (E1d). **See featured trip page:** 137.

18. LONG RIDGE LOOP

Contact: Midpeninsula Regional Open Space District, (650) 691-1200. **Locator:** LONG RIDGE LOOP (E1b).

19. FRANKLIN RIDGE LOOP TRAIL

Contact: Carquinez Strait Regional Shoreline, (510) 635-0135 extension 2200. **Locator:** FRANKLIN RIDGE LOOP TRAIL (E1c). **See featured trip page:** 89.

20. LOCH LOMOND LOOP

Contact: Loch Lomond County Park, (831) 335-7424. **Locator:** LOCH LOMOND COUNTY PARK. (E1d).

21. BAY VIEW TRAIL

Contact: Point Pinole Regional Shoreline, Richmond, (510) 237-6896 or (510) 635-0135 extension 2200. **Locator:** POINT PINOLE (E1c).

22. PILLAR POINT

Contact: Half Moon Bay, no phone. **Locator:** HALF MOON BAY (E1b). **See featured trip pages:** 224, 365, and 401.

23. AGAVE TRAIL

Contact: Golden Gate National Recreation Area, (415) 556-8371 or (415) 556-0560. **Locator:** ALCATRAZ ISLAND (E1b). **See featured trip page:** 221.

24. Volvon Loop Trail

Contact: Morgan Territory, north of Livermore, (635) 634-0135 extension 2200 **Locator:** MORGAN TERRITORY (E1c). **See featured trip page:** 92.

25. Golden Gate Bridge

Contact: San Francisco, (415) 556-8371 or (415) 556-0560. **Locator:** GOLDEN GATE BRIDGE (E1b).

• TOM'S RATINGS •

The Top 50 Parks

In the San Francisco Bay Area

Can you imagine canoeing in quiet lagoons, walking on an earthquake fault, or combing miles of untouched beach, secret tide pools, and strange sea tunnels and rock stacks set along a wilderness coastal trail?

Or what about meeting up with elk sporting antlers so tall that they practically poke holes in the clouds? Or standing at a lighthouse and spotting dozens of whales blowing their spouts? Or hiking to a rare waterfall that actually pours over an ocean bluff and into the sea?

The only place on Earth where these visions come true is POINT REYES NATIONAL SEASHORE, which is rated as the number one park in my personal survey of some 200 parks in the Bay Area. POINT REYES is the only parkland that is first-class in every respect, from its backcountry wilderness camps and drive-to lookouts to the free trail maps and courteous rangers. The park even has its own radio frequency so drivers can tune in and get oriented as they near the area.

I rated the parks for scenic beauty, wildlife habitat, size, and recreational opportunities such as hiking, fishing, boating, and mountain biking, as well as for dispersal of visitors and the helpfulness of rangers. Ironically, the Bay Area has so many superb parks that many fine places did not make the final cut.

Here are the results, the complete list of the Bay Area's top 50 parks:

1. Point Reyes National Seashore

Some places project a special aura, and POINT REYES is one of those places. It often casts a spell on visitors, not just because it offers more diverse recreation than anywhere within 150 miles, but because of the feeling people get when visiting. There are 65,000 acres of wildlands, miles and miles of ocean frontage, remote wilderness, and, of course, that remarkable herd of giant elk near TOMALES POINT. The rangers and information assistants are by far the most helpful and friendliest of those in any single Bay Area park.

Contact: Point Reyes National Seashore, (415) 663-1092. **Locator:** POINT REYES NATIONAL SEASHORE (E1a). **See featured trip pages:** 132, 166, and 262.

2. Big Basin Redwoods State Park

The hike to Berry Creek Falls at BIG BASIN REDWOODS STATE PARK is the number one hike in the Bay Area. It is a 5.5-hour round-trip that is routed through redwoods, up the Big Basin Rim, then down a canyon and finally to the remarkable 70-foot waterfall, framed in a mountain canyon. Nearby Silver Falls and Golden Falls make this place as special as any in California. The park has excellent camping facilities, both drive-to sites and wilderness backpack camps, mountain bike routes on fire roads, and a wildlife paradise along WADDELL CREEK as it runs to the PACIFIC OCEAN.

Contact: Big Basin Redwoods State Park, (831) 338-8860; California State Parks, Santa Cruz District, (831) 429-2851. **Locator:** BIG BASIN REDWOODS STATE PARK (E1d). **See featured trip pages:** 136 and 270.

3. HENRY W. COE STATE PARK

A good pair of hiking boots and plenty of ambition is your ticket to the 70,000 acres of wildlands that comprise HENRY W. COE STATE PARK. This is the Bay Area's backyard wilderness, a place for someone who wants solitude and quality pond-style bass fishing and isn't averse to finding it through extremely rugged hiking. The park has dozens of ponds, but Kelly Lake (10.5 miles in), Coit Lake (12 miles in), and Paradise Lake (33 miles in) occasionally can even provide a bass per cast on warm spring evenings. Don't try to explore this park in a day, and instead plan on at least two days or more with backpack camps. The park is so big that you can take a week to hike the Rooster Comb Loop, a 70-miler, the longest continuous trail in the Bay Area.

Contact: Henry W. Coe State Park, (408) 779-2728; California State Parks, Four Rivers District, (209) 826-1196. **Locator:** HENRY W. COE STATE PARK (E1d). **See featured trip page:** 139.

4. ANGEL ISLAND STATE PARK

The trip starts with a ferry ride from TIBURON or SAN FRANCISCO that transports you to a little slice of heaven in the center of SAN FRANCISCO BAY. The hike on the Perimeter Trail is like a walk through history as you pass old barracks and abandoned military buildings before heading through eucalyptus forests and finally topping 781-foot Mount Livermore. This is the number one lookout in the Bay Area, where you are circled by world-class landmarks. When camping here, you can feel like you are the luckiest person in the world. And maybe you are.

Contact: Angel Island State Park, (415) 435-1915; California State Parks, Marin District, (415) 893-1580. **Locator:** ANGEL ISLAND (E1a).

5. MOUNT TAMALPAIS STATE PARK

There is no better place to watch the sun set than from the 2,571-foot-high East Peak of MOUNT TAMALPAIS. You are above the fogline, and when the sun dips into that low stratus to the west, orange light is refracted for hundreds of miles. It is but one of dozens of great destinations and hikes. Hiking the Steep Ravine Trail is like being baptized by the divine spirit of nature, and O'Rourke's Bench, set on a knoll at 2,071 feet, provides a Pacific panorama. There are so many unique features—Cataract Falls, West Point Inn, Mountain Theater . . . no wonder it was John Muir's favorite place to hike during the winter.

Contact: Mount Tamalpais State Park, (415) 388-2070; California State Parks, Marin District, (415) 893-1580. **Locator:** MOUNT TAMALPAIS STATE PARK (E1a). **See featured trip page:** 62.

6. SAN PABLO RESERVOIR RECREATION AREA

SAN PABLO RESERVOIR is the only lake in the Bay Area that provides first-class beauty, boating, fishing, and bird-watching, with opportunities for hiking and biking. It is a large lake, covering 850 acres in an East Bay canyon, a divine sight amid hills glowing with green in spring. SAN PABLO RESERVOIR is best known for its trout fishing, offering the most successful urban fishing program in America, where funds from the daily $3 fishing permits are used to buy hatchery-raised rainbow trout. This is among the best-stocked lakes in the western U.S. The only thing missing is a campground.

Contact: San Pablo Reservoir Recreation Area, (510) 223-1661. **Locator:** SAN PABLO RESERVOIR (E1c). **See featured trip page:** 375.

7. Butano State Park

Redwoods, ferns, a pretty stream, and views of the PACIFIC OCEAN await hikers who visit BUTANO STATE PARK. There isn't a bad hike in the park, and if you look closely in spring, you may see rare wild orchids blooming in the moist redwood understory. The best view is from the lookout on the Año Nuevo Trail, while the densest forest is on the Jackson Flats Trail. In addition, the park has good drive-to and walk-in campgrounds (reservations advised) and, for backpackers, a remote environmental camp on an 11-mile hike that loops the park.

Contact: Butano State Park, (415) 879-2040; California State Parks, Bay Area District, (415) 330-6300. **Locator:** BUTANO STATE PARK (E1d). **See featured trip page:** 137.

8. Grant County Park

Here is the Bay Area's great undiscovered wild playland. It covers 9,000 acres and has a campground, outstanding routes for mountain bikes and hikers, and a lake with catfish, bluegill, and bass. Best of all, it has just about no people. You can make a 1,500-foot climb on the Pala Seca Trail to the park's highest point (2,987 feet) for a great overlook of the Santa Clara Valley. The Hotel Trail provides a route to remote Eagle Lake, with a short side trip available to San Felipe Creek, the prettiest stream in the park.

Contact: GRANT COUNTY PARK, (408) 274-6121. **Locator:** GRANT COUNTY PARK (E1d). **See featured trip page:** 103.

9. Marin Headlands

The most spectacular photographs of the GOLDEN GATE BRIDGE are taken from the MARIN HEADLANDS—you know, the classic shots with SAN FRANCISCO in the background. At night, it is even more dramatic, with the bridge and city glowing charmingly. The MARIN HEADLANDS is also an excellent destination for hiking, biking, and bird-watching, with more than 10,000 raptors flying over Hawk Hill during the five-month migration season. Old Nike missile launch sites, military buildings, and the Point Bonita Lighthouse make every trip memorable.

Contact: Marin Headlands Visitor Center, (415) 331-1540; Golden Gate National Recreation Area, (415) 556-0560. **Locator:** MARIN HEADLANDS (E1a). **See featured trip page:** 59.

10. Mount Diablo State Park

No matter how fouled up things get, you can't foul up the view from the top of MOUNT DIABLO. At 3,849 feet, it towers over the East Bay, with 360-degree views that can include the GOLDEN GATE BRIDGE (66 miles away), MOUNT LASSEN (165 miles), and even a piece of Half Dome (135 miles) sticking out of YOSEMITE VALLEY. You can drive nearly to the top and take the Summit Loop (also called the Fire Interpretive Trail), an easy and short (0.7-mile) hike. The park has a campground and also a great little-known trailhead near Clayton heading to remote Mitchell Canyon.

Contact: Mount Diablo State Park, (925) 837-2525; California State Parks, Bay Area District, (415) 330-6300. **Locator:** MOUNT DIABLO STATE PARK (E1c). **See featured trip page:** 93.

11. Loch Lomond County Park

What is the prettiest of the 44 lakes in the Bay Area? The answer is LOCH LOMOND RESERVOIR, complete with a little wooded island. The water is deep blue and the shoreline is bordered by redwoods and firs, set in a canyon near BEN LOMOND in the SANTA CRUZ MOUNTAINS. The trout and bass fishing is often good. Hikers will find an excellent loop trail routed up to the mountaintop above the lake, a great viewpoint. Great lake, great hike, great park.

Contact: Loch Lomond County Park, (831) 335-7424. **Locator:** LOCH LOMOND COUNTY PARK (E1d).

12. Marin Water District Lands

A series of pretty lakes on the northern slopes of MOUNT TAMALPAIS makes a picturesque backdrop for hikes and picnics. LAGUNITAS, BON TEMPE, and ALPINE are the prettiest and best known lakes, and trails can be linked to hike past all three of them in a loop. Little Phoenix Lake and giant KENT LAKE are good weekend destinations. The district's vast holdings include a small, hidden waterfall. Rules allow you to bring your dog along for the fun.

Contact: Marin Water District, (415) 924-4600; California State Parks, Marin District, (415) 893-1580. **Locator:** MOUNT TAMALPAIS (E1a). **See featured trip pages:** 60 and 62.

13. San Francisco Headlands

Some of America's most striking landmarks are included in this national parkland, including the GOLDEN GATE BRIDGE walk, Land's End (at the Cliff House) at the mouth of SAN FRANCISCO BAY, the Golden Gate Promenade along the bay shoreline, and SWEENEY RIDGE in San Bruno. All feature magnificent views, with miles of sunlit wonder in all directions. It is one of the most popular national parks in the nation, with local residents joined by visitors from throughout the world to walk, jog, and ride bikes. Well, if that's true, then why doesn't it rank at least in the top 10? Because there are too many vagrants around these parts, that's why.

Contact: Land's End Visitor Center, Cliff House, (415) 556-8642; Fort Funston, (415) 556-8371; Golden Gate National Recreation Area, (415) 556-0560. **Locator:** FORT FUNSTON (E1b). **See featured trip pages:** 70 and 85.

14. Año Nuevo State Reserve

Touring AÑO NUEVO STATE RESERVE to see the giant elephant seals has become one of the most curious yet popular winter adventures in the Bay Area. Reservations in a tour group are required from December through early March. You walk along roped-off trails and wind your way amid the creatures, some reaching nearly 20 feet in length and weighing 5,000 pounds. Pups are born there in early spring, with an average weight of 75 pounds. The rest of the year, when the elephant seals have headed to Baja, the reserve still offers a quiet beach walk.

Contact: Año Nuevo State Reserve, (650) 879-2025; California State Parks, Bay Area District, (415) 330-1580. **Locator:** AÑO NUEVO STATE RESERVE (E1d). **See featured trip page:** 265.

15. Memorial/Sam McDonald County Parks

The Iverson Trail is one of the prettiest hikes on the Peninsula, routed along Pescadero Creek amid redwoods and riparian vegetation. It is the highlight of 50 miles of trails available at this park complex. Fishing is illegal; steelhead spawn in the creek within park boundaries. Bonuses include campgrounds and remote fire roads that provide good mountain biking opportunities.

Contact: Sam McDonald County Park, (650) 879-0238; San Mateo County Parks, (650) 363-4020. **Locator:** Pescadero Marsh (E1d).

16. Mount Madonna County Park

A chance to see rare white deer, something you will never forget, lifts Mount Madonna County Park into the top 20. These deer are similar to black-tailed deer, the most common deer in California, except that they are larger and are white, completely white. They are kept in a large pen that is about a 100-yard walk from park headquarters. The park has great scenic beauty, good hiking trails, camping, horseback riding, and views of Monterey Bay on the Bayview Trail.

Contact: Mount Madonna County Park, (408) 842-2341. **Locator:** Mount Madonna (F1). **See featured trip page:** 104.

17. Castle Rock State Park

Two rare honeycombed sandstone formations, Castle Rock and Goat Rock, are prime destinations for rock climbers honing their craft. But they are just fine to look at as well on the 5.5-mile Camp Loop Trail, along with scenic views to the west of Big Basin and Monterey Bay. The park is semiwilderness, covering 3,600 acres, with 50 miles of hiking trails, including the first section of the 38-mile Skyline-to-Sea Trail.

Contact: Castle Rock State Park, (408) 867-2952; California State Parks, Santa Cruz District, (831) 429-2851. **Locator:** Castle Rock State Park (E1d).

18. Portola Redwoods State Park

The Sequoia Trail provides a one-mile route that will lead you to the Shell Tree. This giant redwood has been charred by fire but it's still alive, now 17 feet in diameter. It is the most striking feature in a remote, pristine forest of redwoods and Douglas fir. The park covers about 1,000 acres, including one route (the Summit Trail) that ventures to remote land on the eastern border. A campground and the headwaters of Pescadero Creek are nice bonuses.

Contact: Portola Redwoods State Park, (650) 948-9098; California State Parks, Santa Cruz District, (831) 429-2851. **Locator:** Portola Redwoods State Park (E1d). **See featured trip page:** 143.

19. Purisima Creek Redwoods Open Space Preserve

This 2,500-acre redwood preserve is one of the Bay Area's newest parks, and already it is one of the best. There are access points along Skyline Boulevard (Highway 35), as well as in the Half Moon Bay foothills, allowing a one-way trip downhill (with a shuttle car waiting at the bottom). The views of the coast are exceptional from Skyline, but it is exploring this surprising redwood forest and the surrounding Purisima Creek watershed that will give you a glow that can stay with you for weeks.

Contact: Midpeninsula Regional Open Space District, (650) 691-1200. **Locator:** PURISIMA CREEK REDWOODS (E1b). **See featured trip page:** 78.

20. DIABLO FOOTHILLS REGIONAL PARK

Many Bay Area residents have gazed at giant MOUNT DIABLO for years without a clue about the China Wall rock formation, yet it is one of the most fascinating areas on the mountain's slopes. What you see on this hike is a line of prehistoric-looking sandstone formations that resemble the Great Wall of China in miniature (well, kind of). Look closely because you also get a good chance to see golden eagles, hawks, and falcons, all of which nest here. It is only a 1.5-mile hike to China Wall, with a good view to the east of Castle Rocks.

Contact: East Bay Regional Park District, (510) 635-0135 extension 2200. **Locator:** MOUNT DIABLO (E1c). **See featured trip page:** 93.

21. HENRY COWELL REDWOODS STATE PARK

This park gets heavy use by Highway 1 vacationers, but it still rates near the top 20 because of its scenic beauty, highlighted by redwoods, the SAN LORENZO RIVER, and a unique lookout platform. You can reach the latter with a 0.3-mile hike from Campground 49. It is the highest point in the park and furnishes great views of SANTA CRUZ and MONTEREY BAY when the fog hasn't shrouded the area. The River Trail, which runs adjacent to the SAN LORENZO RIVER, provides an inspiring walk.

Contact: Henry Cowell Redwoods State Park, (831) 335-4598; California State Parks, Santa Cruz District, (831) 429-2851. **Locator:** HENRY COWELL REDWOODS STATE PARK (E1d).

22. STEEP RAVINE

Who ever heard of rustic cabins overlooking the PACIFIC OCEAN available for rent? Only the few who know of Steep Ravine, where cabins at Rocky Point on the Marin coast are available for $30 per night. They include a wood stove, picnic table, and a flat wood surface for sleeping; you bring everything else. It is one of the most dramatic camp settings on the Pacific coast, with passing whales, pelicans and murres, freighters and fishing boats. Two beach trails are available, routed to Redrock Beach and a pretty cove.

Contact: Mount Tamalpais State Park, (415) 388-2070; California State Parks, Marin District, (415) 893-1580. **Locator:** MOUNT TAMALPAIS STATE PARK (E1a). **See featured trip page:** 62.

23. MUIR WOODS

Redwood Creek is completely surrounded by giant redwoods, providing rare cathedral-like beauty. It has become the destination for the thousands of tourists who are bused in from SAN FRANCISCO every year. The main trail follows Redwood Creek, then climbs up a grade and is routed back through the redwoods, an easy two-mile tromp. The beauty is entrancing, but the high number of hikers can be like a parade. Much of the trail in the valley along the creek is paved.

Contact: Muir Woods National Monument, (415) 388-2596. **Locator:** MUIR WOODS (E1a). **See featured trip page:** 64.

24. AUDUBON CANYON RANCH

This is the best place on the Pacific coast to view herons and egrets as they court, nest, mate, and rear their young. It is open only on weekends and holidays, spring through summer. From headquarters, a short but steep hike will take you to the viewing area. Here you will find spotting scopes that can be used to peer across the valley and zero in on the giant nests in the redwoods. It is a wildlife spectacle like no other in the Bay Area.

Contact: Audubon Canyon Ranch, (415) 868-9244. **Locator:** AUDUBON CANYON RANCH (E1a). **See featured trip page:** 260.

25. Del Valle Regional Park

DEL VALLE REGIONAL PARK is best known for its big, long reservoir, good fishing and boating, and a large campground. That alone could rate it in the top 50. But a little-known trailhead to the Bay Area's highest waterfall puts it in the top 25. That waterfall is Murietta Falls, 100 feet high and secreted away in a canyon, little known and rarely seen. Getting to it requires a 5.5-mile hike one way, including a climb of 1,600 feet in just 1.5 miles that will leave you seriously sweating. The trailhead is also the start to the OHLONE WILDERNESS TRAIL, which runs 28 miles westward over Mission Peak to FREMONT.

Contact: Del Valle Regional Park, (925) 373-0332; East Bay Regional Park District, (510) 635-0135 extension 2200. **Locator:** DEL VALLE REGIONAL PARK (E2). **See featured trip page:** 168.

26. San Francisco Bay National Wildlife Refuge

This is a giant slice of marshland paradise, 23,000 acres in all, set on the edge of south SAN FRANCISCO BAY, just below the eastern foot of the DUMBARTON BRIDGE. The Tidelands Trail pours right through the best part of it, amid salt marsh and tidewaters. It is common to see egrets, ducks, sandpipers, and herons, while over the course of a year, some 250 species use the refuge as a resting stop. Bonuses include an excellent fishing pier that extends to the main channel of the South Bay, as well as the start of a great bicycle route over the DUMBARTON BRIDGE.

Contact: San Francisco Bay National Wildlife Refuge, (510) 792-4275 or (510) 792-0222. **Locator:** SAN FRANCISCO BAY NATIONAL WILDLIFE REFUGE (E1c). **See featured trip page:** 263.

27. Fitzgerald Marine Reserve

One of the best tidepool reefs on the Pacific coast is here at FITZGERALD MARINE RESERVE, where you will find a 30-acre tidal basin filled with all manner of tiny marine organisms. During minus low tides, the ocean rolls back and exposes hundreds of tidal pockets and crevices where visitors can view crabs, sea anemones, sculpins, starfish, snails, and many plants in various colors. Take special care not to walk on fragile sea plants and remove nothing—this is a preserve.

Contact: Fitzgerald Marine Reserve, (650) 728-3584. **Locator:** FITZGERALD MARINE RESERVE (E1b). **See featured trip page:** 266.

28. Black Diamond Mines Regional Preserve

The Prospect Tunnel is a 400-foot tunnel that was bored into the side of MOUNT DIABLO by miners in the 1860s, and 200 feet of it is now accessible to hikers. There is nothing like it anywhere else in the Bay Area. To reach the Prospect Tunnel, you hike 1.5 miles one way on the Stewartville Trail. You will cross grasslands and foothills, fresh green in spring, often dotted with wildflower blooms. Whatever you do, bring a flashlight with fresh batteries or else you might wind up like Tom Sawyer and Becky Thatcher.

Contact: East Bay Regional Park District, (510) 635-0135 extension 2200. **Locator:** MOUNT DIABLO (E1c).

29. CHABOT REGIONAL PARK

CHABOT is best known for its beautiful lake with good trout fishing, a few giant but elusive bass, and large numbers of crappie. The giant largemouth bass caught here include one that weighed 17 pounds, 2 ounces, the record for Northern California. The park also has a campground, stables, and bike trails, but my favorite place here is Bort Meadow in Grass Valley, where you get an instant passport to tranquillity. It is a divine sight in the spring, a meadow lined on each side by miniature mountains and glowing from fresh grasses and blooming blue-eyed grass.

Contact: East Bay Regional Park District, (510) 635-0135 extension 2200; Chabot Marina, (510) 582-2198. **Locator:** CHABOT REGIONAL PARK (E1c). **See featured trip page:** 230.

30. HUDDART/WUNDERLICH COUNTY PARKS

The Peninsula has few places better than this for clearing out the brain cobwebs. Between the two parks, now linked by a section of the Bay Ridge Trail, there are 2,000 acres of wildlands and 45 miles of trails. This parkland sits on the mountain slopes above WOODSIDE, where a second-growth redwood forest is flourishing. The trails weave in and out of the woods, occasionally providing glimpses of the South Bay, at times ranging through meadows and oak woodlands. A little-known bonus is that HUDDART has a backpack camp.

Contact: Huddart County Park, (650) 851-7570; Wunderlich County Park, (650) 851-7570; San Mateo County Parks, (650) 363-4020. **Locator:** HUDDART/WUNDERLICH COUNTY PARK (E1b). **See featured trip pages:** 72 and 86.

31. BRIONES REGIONAL PARK

Here is a 5,700-acre sanctuary of peace, one of the best parks for hiking in the East Bay. Your goal should be Briones Peak, at 1,483 feet, a 2.5-mile hike (one way) on the Alhambra Trail. From here, you get panoramic views of the East Bay's quiet and tranquil rolling hillsides. Many people consider this their favorite place in the East Bay. Another attraction at Briones is a huge, beautiful lake where the water is often a deeper blue than any lake in the Bay Area; alas, it is off-limits to hiking, fishing, and boating.

Contact: East Bay Regional Park District, (510) 635-0135 extension 2200. **Locator:** BRIONES REGIONAL PARK (E1c).

32. LONG RIDGE OPEN SPACE PRESERVE

When you first see the beautiful little pond hidden in a canyon at Long Ridge Open Space Preserve, you may think you have discovered a divine setting. And maybe you have. It is a private, little-known Zen center called the Jikoji Retreat, where visitors are allowed to quietly seek their peace, then head off down the trail. The park covers more than 1,000 acres and provides excellent hiking in a variety of settings, from moist canyons with small streams to lookouts over BIG

Basin Redwoods and the Pacific Ocean.

Contact: Midpeninsula Regional Open Space District, (650) 691-1200. **Locator:** Santa Cruz Mountains (E1d).

33. Redwood Regional Park

It is always a surprise to newcomers that a beautiful grove of redwood trees can be found here in a canyon in the Oakland foothills, but even after the shock wears off, the experience can give you a lasting glow. In addition, a trout stream flows down the center of the canyon. This is where a native strain of rainbow trout swim upstream from San Leandro Reservoir, then jump up a fish ladder and spawn. It's the only place in the Bay Area to witness such a spectacle.

Contact: East Bay Regional Park District, (510) 635-0135 extension 2200. **Locator:** Oakland (E1c).

34. San Pedro Valley County Park

This is a very special place. San Pedro Park is set on the edge of southern Pacifica, literally bordering very developed urban neighborhoods, yet within minutes of entering you feel far removed from everybody else. The park is clean, quiet, and pretty, preserving its native habitat. There is a large meadow that attracts deer in the evening and a great trail routed up the northern flank of Montara Mountain. In addition, the headwaters of San Pedro Creek are found here, where a remnant steelhead population still spawns each winter.

Contact: San Pedro Valley County Park, (650) 355-8289. **Locator:** San Pedro Valley County Park (E1b). **See featured trip pages:** 74 and 80.

35. Pescadero Marsh

Watching a giant blue heron lift off and fly away can be one of the most spectacular experiences in nature. These are huge birds, often four feet tall with a wingspan of seven feet, and their labored wing beats make them seem like prehistoric creatures. This scene is one of the classic sights that can be witnesses at Pescadero Marsh, a 600-acre wetland that attracts hundreds of species of birds each year. A dirt path is routed amid pampas grass and bogs along the edge of wetland habitat, providing excellent viewing opportunities. State park volunteers conduct guided nature walks most weekends.

Contact: California State Parks, Half Moon Bay District, (650) 726-8819. **Locator:** Pescadero Marsh (E1d). **See featured trip page:** 268.

36. Hayward Regional Shoreline

Cogswell Marsh is the heart of an 800-acre marsh and wetland on the Hayward Regional Shoreline. Here you can typically count on seeing peregrine falcons and may have a chance to see white pelicans and merlins. A trail borders the edge of San Francisco Bay, providing a wonderful view looking north toward the Oakland Bay Bridge. The park has a sense of remoteness as well, with two sections of trail bridged across soggy tidal marshland.

Contact: East Bay Regional Park District, (510) 635-0135 extension 2200. **Locator:** Hayward Regional Shoreline (E1c).

37. McNee Ranch State Park

On a clear day from the top of Montara Mountain, the Farallon Islands seem close enough to touch and Mount Diablo across the bay appears within leaping distance. The Montara Summit is the highlight of an undeveloped wilderness park north of HALF MOON BAY. Reaching the top is a killer climb for many, aerobic much of the way, but it's a four-hour round-trip for the well-conditioned. On clear days, the views are all the compensation desired.

Contact: California State Parks, Half Moon Bay District, (650) 726-8819. **Locator:** MCNEE RANCH STATE PARK (E1b). **See featured trip pages:** 73 and 74.

38. SUNOL/OHLONE REGIONAL WILDERNESS

This is one of the hidden parks that can make a visitor feel like they have discovered their own secret paradise. It is a 6,500-acre wilderness that has many striking spots: Little Yosemite, a miniature canyon with a pretty stream; Cave Rocks, a series of natural, gouged-out rock formations; Cerro Este, the highest point in the park at 1,720 feet. Few get farther than Little Yosemite, but it is beyond the canyon where you will find the park's most remote and least-visited areas.

Contact: East Bay Regional Park District, (510) 635-0135 extension 2200; Sunol Regional Wilderness, (925) 862-2244. **Locator:** SUNOL/OHLONE REGIONAL WILDERNESS (E1d). **See featured trip pages:** 99 and 168.

39. SAMUEL P. TAYLOR STATE PARK

SAMUEL P. TAYLOR has a two-for-one offer for hikers—and for many it's an offer they can't refuse. The Pioneer Tree Trail provides a simple, quiet walk through the park's grove of coastal redwoods, while the Barnabe Trail, a steep service road, rises 2.5 miles to Barnabe Peak (1,466 feet), a scenic lookout over POINT REYES and the PACIFIC OCEAN. A good campground, a hidden waterfall, excellent ranch roads for mountain biking, and steelhead spawning habitat on Lagunitas Creek round out the park's highlights.

Contact:Samuel P. Taylor State Park, (415) 488-9897; California State Parks, Marin District, (415) 893-1580. **Locator:** SAMUEL P. TAYLOR STATE PARK (E1a).

40. MONTE BELLO OPEN SPACE PRESERVE

MONTE BELLO encompasses more than 2,600 acres of the most natural scenic lands on the western slopes of the Peninsula foothills. It includes the 2,700-foot Black Mountain Ridge, the headwaters of Stevens Creek, and the San Andreas Fault. A pretty nature trail drops into a ravine where you will discover the headwaters of Stevens Creek, a quiet, special place where moss grows on trees and the scent of spicy bay leaves fills the air.

Contact: Midpeninsula Regional Open Space District, (650) 691-1200. **Locator:** MONTE BELLO OPEN SPACE PRESERVE (E1b).

41. POINT PINOLE REGIONAL SHORELINE

A long cobble beach on the shore of SAN PABLO BAY offers a quiet setting with great views and a park that is overlooked by many. The Bay View Trail provides waterfront lookouts over MOUNT TAMALPAIS and, on clear days, MOUNT ST. HELENA to the distant north. An excellent fishing pier is a bonus. No vehicles are allowed past the main parking area. Instead, you take a shuttle bus to the shoreline, then roam around at any pace you desire.

Contact: Point Pinole Regional Shoreline, (510) 237-6896; East Bay Regional Park District, (510) 635-0135 extension 2200. **Locator:** POINT PINOLE (E1c).

42. MISSION PEAK REGIONAL PRESERVE

To reach the top of MISSION PEAK (elevation 2,517 feet), you must climb 2,100 feet over the course of just 3.5 miles. It's one of the steepest hikes in the Bay Area, but you will be well rewarded, especially in the spring when the grasslands are such a bright green that the hills seem to be gleaming, sprinkled everywhere with blooming wildflowers. The views are also outstanding, especially looking west toward the South Bay and the SANTA CRUZ MOUNTAINS. The Bay Area is quite crowded, but it is extremely rare for you to have to share this mountaintop with anybody.

Contact: East Bay Regional Park District, (510) 635-0135 extension 2200. **Locator:** MISSION PEAK (E1c).

43. TILDEN REGIONAL PARK

One of the best pieces of the 31-mile EAST BAY SKYLINE NATIONAL TRAIL is at TILDEN REGIONAL PARK, starting at Inspiration Point and then heading onward for six miles to San Pablo Ridge. The first four miles of trail are paved with mileage markers, making it ideal for joggers, bikers, and even wheelchair users. Hikers should continue on past the gate, where the trail turns to dirt, then offers stunning views in all directions, particularly to the east of BRIONES and SAN PABLO RESERVOIRS and to the west of SAN FRANCISCO BAY and the city's skyline.

Contact: Tilden Nature Area, (510) 525-2233; East Bay Regional Park District, (510) 635-0135 extension 2200. **Locator:** TILDEN REGIONAL PARK (E1c). **See featured trip pages:** 87.

44. TOMALES BAY STATE PARK

When viewed from the nearby ridge, TOMALES BAY appears cobalt blue, beautiful and soft, unlike most saltwater bays, which look green and harsh. Up close, its docile nature makes it perfect for wading, playing in the water, hand-launching small boats, and, during low tides, clamming. Hiking trails are highlighted by the Johnstone Trail from Heart's Desire Beach to Shell Beach, a four-mile, one-way trip that passes beaches, forests, meadows, and fields.

Contact: Tomales Bay State Park, (415) 669-1140; California State Parks, Marin District, (415) 893-1580. **Locator:** TOMALES BAY (E1a). **See featured trip page:** 220.

45. SIERRA AZUL/MOUNT UMUNHUM OPEN SPACE PRESERVE

From anywhere in the Santa Clara Valley, MOUNT UMUNHUM (elevation 3,486 feet) is the most prominent landmark on the western horizon—the big mountain with the radar station atop it. A trail here provides a half-mile route to BALD MOUNTAIN, a hilltop knoll with sweeping views of the Almaden Valley and across SAN JOSE to MOUNT HAMILTON, the highest drive-to point in the Bay Area. Because access is sharply limited, the Midpeninsula Regional Open Space District requests a phone call prior to all visits.

Contact: Midpeninsula Regional Open Space District, (650) 691-1200. **Locator:** MOUNT UMUNHUM (E1d).

46. MARTIN LUTHER KING REGIONAL SHORELINE

Arrowhead Marsh is one of the best bird-watching areas in the East Bay, with 30 species common here. It is set along the shore of SAN LEANDRO BAY, covering 1,220 acres, and includes some of the bay's most valuable remaining wetland habitat. Rails, which are more often heard than seen, are often spotted here. A trail leads for a mile along the marsh, with a fishing pier also available.

Contact: East Bay Regional Park District, (510) 635-0135 extension 2200. **Locator:** SAN LEANDRO BAY (E1c).

47. Palo Alto Baylands

There is no walk in the Bay Area quite like this one, where you hike on an elevated wood walkway called a "catwalk" across tidal marshland. The habitat is ideal for egrets, coots, and ducks, as well as ground squirrels and jackrabbits. An excellent observation deck juts out over South Bay waters and can be reached with only a 10-minute jaunt. An option is to walk for over a mile northward, where eventually the catwalk reaches water, a fair fishing spot for sharks during high tides and an excellent lookout across the South Bay.

Contact: Palo Alto Baylands Interpretive Center, (650) 329-2506; Palo Alto Recreation Center, (650) 329-2261. **Locator:** BAYLANDS TRAIL (E1b). **See featured trip page:** 283.

48. Skyline Ridge Open Space Preserve

Two hidden lakes, Alpine Pond and Horseshoe Lake, provide destinations for hikers exploring this popular regional preserve. The lakes are quite pretty, like mountain farm ponds, but they are for looking only, not for touching and, alas, that means no fishing. On the short SKYLINE RIDGE TRAIL, you play peek-a-boo in and out of woodlands, with occasional views of plunging canyons to the west. The trail skirts the flank of the highest point in the park at 2,493 feet.

Contact: Midpeninsula Regional Open Space District, (650) 691-1200. **Locator:** SKYLINE RIDGE OPEN SPACE PRESERVE (E1d). **See featured trip pages:** 82 and 84.

49. Arastradero Lake Park

A truly hidden lake on the Peninsula offers an opportunity for hiking, fishing, bird-watching, and picnicking. It's within a 10-minute walk of the parking lot and comes as something of a surprise when you clear the rise and see this pastoral little farm pond circled by tules in the foothill country. The area is home to lots of squirrels, rabbits, hawks, and songbirds. There always seem to be ducks or other waterfowl on the little pond.

Contact: Foothills Park, (650) 329-2423. **Locator:** ARASTRADERO LAKE (E1b). **See featured trip page:** 69.

50. San Bruno Mountain County Park

SAN BRUNO MOUNTAIN is best known as that "big ol' hill" west of U.S. 101 near Candlestick (3Com) Park. Not only is it a landmark, it's a unique island of open space amid the Peninsula's urban sprawl. It is quite pretty in the spring as the hills turn green and have good numbers of wildflowers. Many hiking trails provide access to the park's hilly terrain, offering expansive views of the South Bay. The main drawback is the legendary wind, which can really howl through here on its way from the ocean to Candlestick Point.

Contact: San Mateo County Parks, (650) 363-4020 or (650) 355-8289. **Locator:** SAN BRUNO MOUNTAIN (E1b).

• TOM'S RATINGS •

THE TOP 4 MARIN COUNTY HIKES

One day while I was being interviewed on the radio, a caller asked, "If you had just one place to go hiking within a 45-minute drive of SAN FRANCISCO, where would it be?"

Well, I know a place where, in the span of just a few miles, hikers will find a series of stellar walks that provide a glimpse of much of the best of what the Bay Area has to offer—waterfalls, beautiful streams, four lakes, and MOUNT TAMALPAIS, the prettiest mountain in the Bay Area.

Here is a synopsis of what awaits on the Bolinas-Fairfax Road:

1. THREE LAKES TRAIL

As you drive west on Bolinas-Fairfax Road, you will come to a turnoff on the left that says, "LAGUNITAS LAKE." Turn left and you'll arrive shortly at the Sky Oaks Ranger Station. From here, it is a short drive to the parking area and trailhead.

While there is no officially named Three Lakes Trail, one of my favorite hikes in the Bay Area is linking a series of trails to make a 5.5-mile loop and hike past LAGUNITAS, BON TEMPE, and ALPINE LAKES. Park at the Lagunitas Picnic Area and start hiking on the Bon Tempe Shadyside Trail. You must eventually link three other trails, detailed on the map for the Marin Water District.

This hike provides an intimate glimpse of three of the prettiest lakes in the Bay Area, including a two-mile jaunt along the pristine southern edge of ALPINE LAKE. The outlets of LAGUNITAS LAKE and BON TEMPE LAKE are like spilling cascades, quite beautiful.

2. CARSON FALLS

Carson Falls in season is absolutely drop-dead gorgeous, a series of five decks over the course of about 75 feet, pool-and-drop, in a boulder-lined canyon. Even when the flow is down to a trickle, though, it's still a very pretty setting.

After driving past the Lagunitas Lake turnoff and the golf course, continue for a few miles to a parking area on the left side of the road, marked best by a blue Porta Potty. After parking, cross the road and look for the billboard; this is the trailhead for Pine Mountain Road, a district service road.

The hike is a pleasant one, climbing 400 feet on Pine Mountain Road over the course of a mile to a junction with another service road, Oat Hill Road. Turn left and walk a little over a quarter mile. On your right, keep a lookout for the power lines and the narrow hiking trail that leads down the canyon. Bingo: This is it, a quarter-mile walk down to Carson Creek.

The waterfalls here are best seen by crossing over the creek above the falls, left to right, then dropping down to the plunge pool of the fourth fall and looking upstream. Bring your camera.

3. ALPINE PUMP TRAIL

If you want something easy, but still desire an idyllic setting, then the Pump Trail is the answer. It features an easy walk down to a pretty stream.

To get here, continue west on Bolinas-Fairfax Road past ALPINE LAKE to Alpine Dam. Park just before reaching the dam, then look for the sign for the Pump Trail and the trailhead on the right side of the road.

It takes only a minute to reach a view of the spillway of Alpine Dam. From here, hike on, dropping down on the Pump Trail along Lagunitas Creek. In just 10 or 15 minutes, you can take a cutoff trail to the left that leads down right along the stream in a gorgeous canyon lined with boulders below a forest canopy. This is a perfect picnic spot.

If you want more, you can continue on the Pump Trail for several miles, eventually leading to KENT LAKE, the biggest lake in Marin County. But most people turn back and return to Alpine Dam, then try yet another hike, to see Cataract Falls.

4. CATARACT FALLS

These are among the prettiest waterfalls in the Bay Area, a long series of different cascades, chutes, and small drops and pools. It is set on the northwest slopes of MOUNT TAMALPAIS in a lush canyon that after heavy rains can remind some of a tropical rain forest. Like Carson Falls, it, too, can dwindle to a trickle but is still very special.

The trailhead is just past Alpine Dam on the left side of the road at the hairpin turn. Parking space is limited and the heavy rains of recent winters have made this one of the most popular destinations in Marin, so be forewarned about scarce parking.

The hike is steep and challenging, a 750-foot climb over the course of just a mile, what for many turns out to be a butt-kicker. But when you start seeing the falls, the reward eases the challenge. And you will discover that the farther you go, the better the falls get. They come one after another, lush, white, each a bit different, but all framed in greenery.

Note that to avoid the steep climb, you can instead visit the falls from the Laura Dell Trail on MOUNT TAMALPAIS and walk less than half a mile with a drop of 240 feet. But do that and you miss the three other great hikes along Bolinas-Fairfax Road.

No doubt about it, if I had to pick one trip to make within 45 minutes of SAN FRANCISCO, this is where I'd head.

Directions (for all listings): From U.S. 101 in Marin, take the Sir Francis Drake exit and drive six miles west to the town of Fairfax. Turn left at the first gas station in Fairfax on Pacheco Road and then make an immediate right onto Broadway Avenue. Drive one block, turn left on Bolinas Road, and head west about 1.5 miles to the Mount Tamalpais State Park entrance.
Contact: Sky Oaks Ranger Station, (415) 459-5267; Marin Water District, (415) 924-4600; Mount Tamalpais State Park, (415) 388-2070; California State Parks, Marin District, (415) 893-1580.
Locator: MOUNT TAMALPAIS (E1a). **See featured trip pages:** 60 and 62.

• TOM'S RATINGS •

THE TOP 10 HIKES ON POINT REYES

From our hiding place behind a bush atop Inverness Ridge, we slowly rose and peered down into White Gulch. TOMALES BAY came into view, peaceful and cobalt blue, and as we looked closer at the gulch, we spotted dozens and dozens of curious brown specks.

We snuck closer, creeping, sometimes crawling, on animal trails through the low brush. We again snuck a peek over the top, and just 40 yards away were two elk, their noses high, their senses on alert—they had smelled us, but not seen us.

My partner, Doug McConnell of the TV show *Bay Area Backroads,* looked at me like I had antlers growing out of my head.

"Look at 'em all down there," he said. "Dozens and dozens of them."

Those brown specks down in White Gulch were actually elk, more than 75 in all, some grazing, some drinking from a small watering hole, some even swimming along the shore of TOMALES BAY.

The hike to see the tule elk near Tomales Point is the number one hike at POINT REYES NATIONAL SEASHORE, one of the best places for hiking or short walks among the Bay Area's 150 parks.

Regardless of where you go here, it really does seem like a world apart from the Bay Area, with rare geologic phenomena (the San Andreas Fault), secluded waterways (Drakes and Limantour esteros), and long, solitary beaches (Point Reyes Beach). And there is so much more: You get wildlife viewing (Pierce Ranch), whale watching (Point Reyes Lighthouse), secluded camping on an ocean bluff (Wildcat Camp), and a waterfall that flows into the sea (Alamere Falls). Add a trail with a mountain lookout (Mount Vision), another with seclusion (Bear Valley), and a series of small lakes (Lake Ranch Trail) and you have the most diverse parkland in California.

Here is a list of my 10 favorite hikes at POINT REYES and what you get when you take them:

1. COAST TRAIL

What? Point Reyes has lakes? That's right, six in all: Bass Lake, Pelican Lake, Crystal Lake, Mud Lake, Ocean Lake, and Wildcat Lake. They provide quite a surprise for coastal hikers. The best access point is the Palomarin Trailhead (see the trailhead directions for Alamere Falls, above), taking the Coast Trail for 3.1 miles to Bass Lake. The trail skirts right aside the northern edge of the lake.

2. PIERCE RANCH TRAIL

There is no better place to see wildlife than at Pierce Ranch near TOMALES POINT, where a herd of 200 tule elk roam. The bulls are in full plumage from midsummer through fall, with huge antlers that practically poke holes in the clouds. They are often seen right near the parking area at the end of Pierce Point Road, but you can add a lot of excitement by hiking and stalking them for closer views. The round-trip hike to TOMALES POINT and back is eight miles.

3. PALOMARIN TRAILHEAD

After a good rain, Alamere Falls is a sensation, a waterfall that actually pours onto a beach and then tumbles a short way into the ocean. The best way to view it is from below, rather than from atop. It is best reached from the Palomarin Trailhead, located right on the coast on Mesa Road, a five-mile drive north of BOLINAS. The hike covers about four miles on the Coast Trail.

4. BEAR VALLEY TRAIL

One of the most popular first-time hikes in the park is the easy route down Bear Valley. The trail starts at Bear Valley Park Headquarters and is routed to Divide Meadow, a 1.6-mile round-trip, gentle enough for nearly all hikers. For the more ambitious, there is another series of trails that link up with the Bear Valley Trail, allowing a loop hike back to headquarters.

5. POINT REYES LIGHTHOUSE TRAIL

POINT REYES is the westernmost point along the central California coast, with migrating whales often passing quite close by. The fenced cliff area at the Point Reyes Lighthouse, a 0.4-mile hike from the parking lot at the end of Sir Francis Drake, is the best land-based whale viewing area in the greater Bay Area. Scan the ocean and look for the little "puffs of smoke," which are actually whale spouts.

6. Inverness Ridge Trail

The Inverness Ridge Trail traces the highest points in the park, including Point Reyes Hill (1,336 feet) near the trailhead at the end of Mount Vision Road. A great loop hike heads south on the Inverness Ridge Trail, cutting west on the Bayview Trail, then looping back on the Buckskin Trail, in all a distance of 6.8 miles. The views of Drakes Bay to the west are astounding. 'Nuff said.

7. Estero Trail

A series of protected, tranquil estuaries/bays called esteros provide quiet spots for hiking, as well as canoeing and kayaking. For hiking, park at the Estero parking lot; the turnoff is on Sir Francis Drake Highway two miles west of the Pierce Ranch turnoff. The trail is routed down a valley and along the east side of Drakes Estero, a 3.9-mile hike (one way) to a secluded beach.

8. Elephant Rock Trail

The Point Reyes Beach, extending from Elephant Rock on south to the Point Reyes Lighthouse, is a 15-mile stretch of pristine coast where sand dunes meet the sea. There are five access points, two off Pierce Point Road and three off Sir Francis Drake Highway. My favorite is Abbotts Lagoon Beach. The trailhead is on Pierce Point Road, exactly 4.4 miles after turning north off Sir Francis Drake. The trail is 1.6 miles to the beach, including a short climb to a 265-foot ridge, then a descent to Abbotts Lagoon and a short hop to the beach.

9. Five Brooks Trailhead

There are four hike-in environmental camps in Point Reyes National Seashore and my favorite is Wildcat, perched on an ocean bluff on a grassy meadow above Wildcat Beach. To reach it requires a five-mile circuitous backpack hike from the Five Brooks Trailhead, or a more direct six-mile hike from the Bear Valley Trailhead. Several good side trips are available, including one to nearby Wildcat Lake and another to the Sea Ranch lakes to the south. Camping is free, but reservations must be made through park headquarters.

10. Rift Zone Trail

The Rift Zone Trail starts at Bear Valley Park Headquarters and follows the San Andreas Fault southward for four miles. It provides the best views in the park of watersheds formed along the fault, which continues to jolt and shift with every earthquake. Much of the trail roughly parallels Olema Creek, tracing the earthquake fault rift zone, which has moved 370 miles over the past 60 million years.

Directions for all listings: From San Francisco, drive north on U.S. 101 to San Rafael and take the Sir Francis Drake Highway exit. Drive to the town of Olema and look for the flashing red light. Turn right and head north on Highway 1, then take the first left, Bear Valley Road, and drive half a mile. Turn left at the Point Reyes National Seashore information sign and drive to the parking lot at park headquarters. **Fees:** Access is free. **Maps:** A free trail map is available at park headquarters. **Special rules:** Dogs are banned on all trails and many beaches. Check specifics with park rangers at headquarters. **Contact:** Point Reyes National Seashore headquarters, Point Reyes National Seashore, Point Reyes, CA 94956, (415) 663-1092. **Locator:** POINT REYES NATIONAL SEASHORE (E1a). **See featured trip pages:** 67, 132, 166, and 262.

• TOM'S RATINGS •

THE TOP 4 WALKS IN SAN FRANCISCO

The most spectacular easy strolls anywhere are in SAN FRANCISCO, along trails that are routed along the bay, the mouth of the Golden Gate, and the PACIFIC OCEAN.

There are four excellent starting points, each providing many side trip options and near-flat terrain for easy adventures and great views.

1. BAY PROMENADE

This is a paved trail along the bay's shoreline from Marina Green to Fort Point. It is virtually flat, yet the views are magnificent, with the GOLDEN GATE BRIDGE, ALCATRAZ, TIBURON, and SAUSALITO providing a backdrop. The entire trail is popular with joggers and walkers. For people looking for a fitness workout, an option here is one of the Bay Area's most popular par courses, located along the route at Marina Green.

Side trips include visiting the Presidio, which runs alongside much of the route, and the old Muni Pier. Fishing for kingfish and jacksmelt can be very good there.

Directions: From U.S. 101, take the Marina Boulevard exit near the southern foot of the Golden Gate Bridge and drive on Marina Boulevard toward Fisherman's Wharf. Parking lots are available off Marina Boulevard at Fort Mason, Marina Green, Crissy Field, and near the St. Francis Yacht Club. **Locator:** SAN FRANCISCO (E1b). **See featured trip page:** 228.

2. GOLDEN GATE BRIDGE

Though this is the number one tourist walk in the world, surprisingly few locals ever get around to trying it out.

The view is incomparable, of course. If you look eastward from the center of the bridge, you'll see ALCATRAZ, ANGEL ISLAND, and the bay framed by the San Francisco waterfront and the East Bay hills. On weekends, the pathway on the eastern side of the bridge is for walkers only, while the one on the west side is reserved for bicyclists.

Directions: Parking is available at either the north end of the bridge at Vista Point, or at the south end of the bridge, just west of the toll stations. To reach the bridge after parking at the latter, walk under a short tunnel that runs under U.S. 101, then loop up to the pathway entrance. **Locator:** SAN FRANCISCO (E1b).

3. LAND'S END BLUFF

The Coastal Trail provides one of San Francisco's greatest lookouts. The trailhead is at Land's End (near the Cliff House restaurant), and from there you meander eastward.

It is a dirt trail sprinkled with pine needles, set near bluffs topped with cypress trees. In one glance, you take in the mouth of the bay, crashing breakers, the GOLDEN GATE BRIDGE, and the MARIN HEADLANDS in the foreground, and the PACIFIC OCEAN, the FARALLON ISLANDS, and POINT REYES in the background.

Directions: From the south, take Skyline Boulevard (the Great Highway) north past Lake Merced and continue to the Cliff House. From the east, take Geary Boulevard until it deadends at the ocean and the Cliff House. Parking is available along Geary, Skyline, and in a dirt lot across from Louis' Restaurant. **Locator:** SAN FRANCISCO (E1b).

4. OCEAN BEACH

SAN FRANCISCO has a unique stretch of beach that provides a wide variety of hiking and jogging trails. OCEAN BEACH is set along the coast's Great Highway, and here you will discover a long expanse of beach, a paved jogging trail, and miniature parks at FORT FUNSTON and Thornton Beach.

The beach ranges about three miles, and its huge expanse makes it popular for jogging on the hard-packed sand at low tide. A paved jogging trail is located just east of the Great Highway. FORT FUNSTON has trails along ocean bluffs, including the coast's first wheelchair-accessible path on the three-quarter-mile Sunset Trail. A bonus in this area is the most popular hang gliding spot in the Bay Area, and those daredevils are something else to watch. Thornton Beach is located less than a mile to the south of FORT FUNSTON and offers a beach where sand dollars seem abundant, as well as a protected valley for hiking and picnicking.

Directions: Parking is available on the west side of the Great Highway at the intersections with Fulton Avenue or Sloat Boulevard, and also at Fort Funston at Thornton Beach along Highway 35. **Contact:** For more information about these walks, phone the Pacific West Region, National Information Center, (415) 556-0560. **Locator:** FORT FUNSTON (E1b). **See featured trip page:** 70.

• TOM'S RATINGS •

THE TOP 12 HIKE-TO STREAMS

In the San Francisco Bay Area

For many, it just plain feels good to watch water flow past, like a stream of consciousness. Taking a hike and finding these hidden creeks is a special experience, made even more unique when they are flowing like fountains after a big siege of rain. Here are my 12 favorite hike-to creeks in the Bay Area:

1. CARSON CREEK

A week of rain creates a set of waterfalls that tumble into granite pools, hidden on the north slope of MOUNT TAMALPAIS. You park at the first trailhead adjacent to the head of Alpine Lake, then walk about three miles; a map is required.

Contact: Marin Municipal Water District, (415) 924-4600. **Locator:** MOUNT TAMALPIAS (E1a). **See featured trip pages:** 60 and 62.

2. LAGUNITAS CREEK

You get peace and solitude for the minimal physical investment here. After parking at the Alpine Dam, walk downhill on the Pump Trail for about 10 or 15 minutes, then take a cutoff route to the adjacent creek on your left. You get absolute beauty, a divine stream pouring over boulders as it runs toward KENT LAKE, all underneath a dramatic forest canopy.

Contact: Marin Municipal Water District, (415) 924-4600. **Locator:** MOUNT TAMALPAIS (E1a). **See featured trip pages:** 60 and 62.

3. Lagunitas Creek

Woods and water make the half-mile walk on the service road next to Lagunitas Creek a memorable trip. Towering redwoods and a tumbling stream are the highlights, with a chance to see rare coho salmon or steelhead, which still spawn in this stretch of river.

Contact: Samuel P. Taylor State Park, (415) 488-9897. **Locator:** Samuel P. Taylor State Park, (E1a). **See featured trip pages:** 60 and 62.

4. Alameda Creek

Several miniature pool-and-drop waterfalls pour through the granite floor of Little Yosemite, the winter highlight at Sunol/Ohlone Regional Wilderness. Getting there entails a pleasant hike on the Canyon View Trail, taking a cutoff route down to the valley floor.

Contact: Sunol/Ohlone Regional Wilderness, (925) 862-2244. **Locator:** Sunol/Ohlone Regional Wilderness (E1c) **See featured trip pages:** 99 and 168.

5. Pine Creek

Pine Creek is a genuine secret in Castle Rocks/Diablo Foothills Regional Park. You hike on the Stage Road Trail, climb a short but steep grade, pass a flood-control dam, then head on into Pine Canyon. There you will discover this pretty creek, running amid live oak and bay woodlands, with an impressive, craggy sandstone formation called Castle Rocks towering above.

Contact: Diablo Foothills Regional Park, administered by Las Trampas Park, (510) 837-3145. **Locator:** Mount Diablo (E1c). **See featured trip page:** 93.

6. Redwood Creek

This is a treasure in the Oakland hills, a short hike that provides a lasting glow. Redwood Creek, set in the center of a redwood forest, comes complete with a fish ladder for trout arriving to spawn from San Leandro Reservoir. The fish start jumping up the ladder in late January, a rare but sensational sight.

Contact: East Bay Regional Park District, (510) 635-0135 extension 2578. **Locator:** Oakland (E1c).

7. Wildcat Creek

A very short walk at Wildcat Canyon Regional Park will lead visitors to this creek and its bridge overlook, where you'll discover this small stream running through a canyon tumbling over boulders, the banks lined with bay and buckeye. Despite being right next to Richmond, it looks like wilderness.

Contact: Wildcat Canyon Regional Park, (510) 236-1262. **Locator:** Wildcat Canyon Regional Park (E1c).

8. Brooks Creek

Brooks Falls is one of the best-kept secrets around, a 175-foot waterfall that cascades in three long tiers. It is hidden in San Pedro Valley County Park in southern Pacifica, requiring a hike of about a mile on the Montara Mountain Trail to the viewpoint. Brooks Creek is a tributary to San Pedro Creek, which still attracts steelhead upstream to spawn every winter. The falls often require a fresh rain.

Contact: San Pedro Valley County Park, (650) 355-8289. **Locator:** San Pedro Valley County Park (E1b). **See featured trip page:** 80.

9. Pescadero Creek

The Iverson Trail at Portola Redwoods State Park near La Honda is routed along Pescadero Creek, a beautiful stream in the SANTA CRUZ MOUNTAINS. Over the years, the creek has cut a deep chasm, edged by forest, and after strong rains it can power forward with surprising force.

Contact: Portola Redwoods State Park, (650) 948-9098; Portola Creek Park Complex, (650) 879-0238. **Locator:** PORTOLA REDWOODS STATE PARK (E1d). **See featured trip page:** 143.

10. PURISIMA CREEK

This is more of a babbling brook, clean and pristine, set amid redwoods, ferns, and sorrel—a highlight of the PURISIMA CREEK REDWOODS OPEN SPACE PRESERVE. The creek is a short walk from the Higgins-Purisima parking area, just southeast of HALF MOON BAY.

Contact: Midpeninsula Regional OpenSpace District, (650) 691-1200. **Locator:** PURISIMA CREEK REDWOODS OPEN SPACE PRESERVE (E1b). **See featured trip page:** 78.

11. SAN ANDREAS CREEK

Heavy rains turn a mere rivulet of water, San Andreas Creek, into a streaming course—beautiful, small, and pure. The creek connects the upper and lower San Andreas lakes on the Peninsula near Interstate 280, with the best hiking access at the Sawyer Camp Trailhead along Highway 35 (Skyline Boulevard).

Contact: San Mateo County Parks and Recreation Department, (650) 363-4020. **Locator:** HALF MOON BAY (E1b). **See featured trip page:** 79.

12. SAN FELIPE CREEK

Not many people know about San Felipe Creek, which is not only the prettiest stream in GRANT COUNTY PARK, but my favorite in all of Santa Clara County. The trailhead is right along the road to the Mount Hamilton Observatory. From there you hike a few miles out on the Hotel Trail, then turn right on the Cañada Depala Trail, dropping down one-half mile into the pretty canyon that hides this waterway.

Contact: Grant County Park, (408) 274-6121. **Locator:** GRANT COUNTY PARK (E1d). **See featured trip page:** 103.

• TOM'S RATINGS •

THE TOP 4 EARTHQUAKE TRAILS

In the San Francisco Bay Area

Years ago in college, a professor in environmental science took me aside and said, "Whatever you do, don't let school interfere with your education." Instead, he advised me to "attend the University of Nature."

Well, considering how earthquake-prone California is, every Bay Area resident might want to sign up for a course at one of four hiking trails that provide some of the world's best examples of an earthquake fault line.

We're talking about the San Andreas Fault, of course. The big one. The fault that roared in 1906 and reduced much of the Bay Area to rubble. It has been building up force stress ever since, maybe jostling a bit now and then, just as it has throughout time.

The movement of two geologic plates in opposite directions created the San Andreas Fault and with it many hidden curiosities in the Bay Area. They can be best seen by taking two hiking trails in MARIN, the Olema Valley Trail and the Rift Zone Trail, and two more on the San Francisco Peninsula, the SAN ANDREAS FAULT TRAIL and the Stevens Creek Nature

Trail. After a weekend hike, you might qualify for a degree from the University of Nature.

Here are the details:

1. Olema Valley Trail

The phenomenon of two parallel creeks running in opposite directions is the main feature of the Olema Valley Trail, an easy but great hike in the Point Reyes National Seashore. It is a strange marvel, with Olema Creek running in one direction and the adjacent Pine Gulch Creek running the other. There is nothing like it anywhere else in the Bay Area. This is an unchallenging walk, starting at the Five Brooks Trailhead, which is located just off Highway 1 about five or six miles north of Bolinas. From the trailhead, it is a 1.3-mile walk to the headwaters of Pine Gulch Creek. From there, you can hike onward (south) for four miles, a pretty walk, most of it along the creek, before the trail ends at Highway 1. Most hikers turn back long before that, but with a partner and a shuttle car, it makes a great one-way hike, 5.3 miles in all.

Contact: Point Reyes National Seashore, (415) 663-1092. **Locator:** Point Reyes National Seashore (E1a). **See featured trip pages:** 67, 132, 166, and 262.

2. Rift Zone Trail

This hike ranges along Olema Creek, where horizontal movement of 21 feet was recorded during the 1906 earthquake. There are many examples of earthquake activity on this trail, including parallel ridges, but the most obvious sign is the clear difference in vegetation types on each side of the earthquake fault. The Rift Zone Trail has become one of the most popular hikes in the Bay Area, an easy walk starting near the Bear Valley Visitor Center at the Point Reyes National Seashore Headquarters. The trail has no difficult grades, and most visitors just walk along for 30 or 40 minutes then turn and go back. However, the trail does continue for 5.2 miles to the Five Brooks Trailhead, allowing for an excellent one-way walk using a shuttle car.

Contact: Point Reyes National Seashore, (415) 663-1092. **Locator:** Point Reyes National Seashore (E1a). **See featured trip pages:** 67, 132, 166, and 262.

3. San Andreas Fault Trail

This is a self-guided tour of an "earthquake trail," with 13 numbered signposts along the half-mile path that correspond to explanations in the park brochure. It includes several examples of fault movement. If you don't want a geology lesson, there are good views of the Peninsula from the 2,000-foot ridgeline. This is the featured walk at Los Trancos Open Space Preserve, located along Page Mill Road in the Palo Alto foothills. If you hike down into the hardwood forest, you will find the air is always fresh and scented with bay leaves and damp woods. Most hikers will connect the San Andreas Fault Trail to the Lost Creek Loop Trail, a pleasant and easy bonus trip that is routed into secluded spots along a pretty creek.

Contact: Midpeninsula Regional Open Space District, (650) 691-1200. **Locator:** San Andreas Trail (E1b). **See featured trip page:** 79.

4. Stevens Creek Nature Trail

The Monte Bello Open Space Preserve encompasses more than 2,600 acres of the most natural and scenic lands on the Peninsula, set on Page

Mill Road in the Palo Alto foothills. At the heart of it is the 3.5-mile Stevens Creek Nature Trail, which follows the San Andreas Fault. It traces along the headwaters of Stevens Creek and includes a view of the 2,700-foot Black Mountain Ridge. The trail starts by traversing a grassland bluff, then drops 450 feet into the wooded headwaters of the creek. As you descend through the forest, you will smell spicy bay leaves and notice the cool dampness, as well as the moss growing on so many trees. The trail emerges from the forest and is routed back along the San Andreas Fault, where you'll see two starkly contrasting images: on one side, to the west, are dense woodlands, yet to the east are grass- lands and chaparral. This is a product of the differences in soil composition, the result of the two earth plates moving in opposite directions for eons.

Contact: Midpeninsula Regional Open Space District, (650) 691-1200. **Locator:** MONTE BELLO OPEN SPACE PRESERVE (E1b).

• TOM'S RATINGS •

THE TOP 15 SURPRISE HIKES IN THE RAIN

In the San Francisco Bay Area

In the winter, the weather report for the Bay Area and the rest of California can sometimes sound like a broken record: "Rain, heavy at times." Heard that before? Rains turn forgotten creeks into rivers, make spillways at several dams into waterfalls, and fill hundreds of ponds and lakes in the foothills. Adventuring to streams and spillways around the Bay Area at such a time can provide an extraordinary glimpse of what is possible when it starts raining and won't quit. For a list of the Bay Area's 20 best hike-to waterfalls, see page 187.

Here is a synopsis of the best spots:

1. ALPINE DAM

A must-do trip is the drive out of Fairfax on Bolinas Road to Alpine Dam. When water is plunging over the dam's spillway, an awesome cascade waterfall is the result.

Contact: Marin Water District, (415) 924-4600. **Locator:** MOUNT TAMALPAIS (E1a). **See featured trip pages:** 60 and 62.

2. STEVENS CREEK RESERVOIR

Though nearly 10 lakes are off-limits to the public on the Peninsula, there are still a few that are primary attractions. Peninsula residents became so accustomed to seeing STEVENS CREEK bone-dry from 1988 to 1992 that watching it fill is now quite an event.

Contact: Midpeninsula Regional Open Space District, (650) 691-1200. **Locator:** MONTE BELLO OPEN SPACE PRESERVE (E1b).

3. ALAMEDA CREEK

Another stream to watch is ALAMEDA CREEK. It can run so low most of the summer that it is rendered nothing more than a series of small pools set amid boulders in the bottom of Little Yosemite in SUNOL REGIONAL WILDERNESS. Then, when heavy rains come, the water tumbles over the tops of those boulders, creating a series of mini waterfalls at the bottom of the canyon, absolutely gorgeous.

Contact: For maps or general information, phone the East Bay Regional Park District, (510) 635-0135 extension 2200. For trail information, phone park headquarters, (925) 862-2244. **Locator:** SUNOL/OHLONE RE-

GIONAL WILDERNESS (E1c). **See featured trip pages:** 99 and 168.

4. Brooks Creek

Contact: San Pedro Valley County Park, (650) 355-8289; San Mateo County Parks and Recreation Department, (650) 363-4020. **Locator:** PACIFICA (E1b). **See featured trip page:** 80.

5. Pump Trail

If you want to see more; wear your rain gear and hike the adjacent Pump Trail, which traces along Lagunitas Creek—something of a babbling brook most of the year, but in heavy rain it can run bank-to-bank. This streams pours into giant KENT LAKE.

Contact: Mount Tamalpais State Park, Pantoll Ranger Station, (415) 388-2070; California State Parks, Marin District, (415) 893-1580. **Locator:** MOUNT TAMALPAIS (E1a). **See featured trip pages:** 60 and 62.

6. Purisima Creek

Contact: For information or a trail map of Purisima Creek Redwoods, contact the Midpeninsula Regional Open Space District, 330 Distel Circle, Los Altos, CA 94022; (650) 691-1200. **Locator:** PURISIMA CREEK REDWOODS (E1b). **See featured trip page:** 78.

7. Donner Creek

Contact: Mount Diablo State Park, (925) 837-2525. For Diablo Foothills Regional Park information, phone the Las Trampas Wilderness Office, (925) 837-3145. **Locator:** MOUNT DIABLO STATE PARK (E1c). **See featured trip page:** 93.

8. Redwood Creek

Contact: For a brochure and map of the East Bay Skyline National Trail, or individual maps of each regional park, phone the East Bay Regional Park District, (510) 635-0135 extension 2200. **Locator:** REDWOOD REGIONAL PARK (E1c).

9. San Gregorio Creek

Contact: Memorial County Park, (650) 879-0212. **Locator:** MEMORIAL COUNTY PARK (E1d).

10. Pescadero Creek

Contact: Half Moon Bay State Beach and Park, (650) 726-8819; California State Parks, Bay Area District, (650) 330-6300. **Locator:** PESCADERO MARSH (E1d). **See featured trip page:** 268.

11. San Felipe Creek

Contact: Grant County Park, (408) 274-6121. **Locator:** GRANT COUNTY PARK (E1d). **See featured trip page:** 103.

12. Pine Creek

Contact: Mount Diablo State Park, (925) 837-2525. For Diablo Foothills Regional Park information, phone the Las Trampas Wilderness Office, (925) 837-3145. **Locator:** MOUNT DIABLO STATE PARK (E1c). **See featured trip page:** 93.

13. Wildcat Creek

One of the biggest surprises to newcomers to the Bay Area is how dry and hot the Diablo Range and nearby foothills can be in the summer, and how many secret and beautiful streams await discovery during peak storm runoff in the winter. The best streams to check out are Wildcat Creek at Wildcat Canyon Regional Park near RICHMOND

Contact: East Bay Regional Park District, (510) 635-0135 extension 2200. **Locator:** TILDEN REGIONAL PARK (E1c).

14. San Andreas Creek

The Peninsula foothills are loaded with creeks, several reservoirs, and a few waterfalls. For most of the year, the creeks are small and gentle, and in some years, they even dry up completely by summer.

The most easily accessible is San Andreas Creek, which connects upper and lower San Andreas Lakes on the Peninsula (just north of Crystal Springs Reservoir) along Interstate 280. It is small and beautiful, running with force and character as the series of lakes in the San Francisco Peninsula Watershed are filled.

Contact: Midpeninsula Regional Open Space District, 330 Distel Circle, Los Altos, CA 94022; (650) 691-1200. **Locator:** SAN ANDREAS TRAIL (E1b).

15. LAGUNITAS/BON TEMPE LAKES

The outlets of LAGUNITAS LAKE and BON TEMPE LAKE have also been known to run like waterfalls. In fact, the entire Lagunitas Creek drainage, from high on MOUNT TAMALPAIS on through LAGUNITAS, BON TEMPE, ALPINE, and KENT LAKES, is a stunning setting during and after heavy rains, right on through SAMUEL P. TAYLOR STATE PARK on Sir Francis Drake Boulevard near POINT REYES.

Contact: Mount Tamalpais State Park, Pantoll Ranger Station, (415) 388-2070; California State Parks, Marin District, (415) 893-1580. **Locator:** MOUNT TAMALPAIS (E1a). **See featured trip pages:** 60 and 62.

Say, has it rained lately?

• TOM'S RATINGS •

THE TOP 7 HIKES WITH A DOG

In the San Francisco Bay Area

Can you imagine being able to take your best friend hiking with you any time you want?

Dream on, right? I've heard all the excuses, too: "Not available." "I've got other plans." Or they just plain don't like you right now. That never happens when your best hiking friend happens to be a doggy. Especially if you have a dog bone in your pocket.

The Bay Area has 250 parks that provide great hiking destinations, but it requires a little inside knowledge to know the best ones where you can take your best pal. There are a good 100 that permit dogs on trails, according to author Maria Goodavage (The California Dog Lover's Companion), but she warns that there is a huge difference between the quality of experience available.

"My dog Joe likes wide-open land where he can roll around on the wild grasses with lots of trees for shade," said Goodavage. "He doesn't like crowds and he doesn't like mountain bikes." My dog Bart feels the same way. That's why we list whether or not dogs are permitted at all 1,000 trails in my book *California Hiking*.

Joe explained this to Maria one Sunday after a bad experience hiking on the PENINSULA. He told her, "Don't ever do this to me again," Maria remembers, "and furthermore, I want an extra dog bone. Next time, take me someplace where a dog can be a dog. Woof!"

Well, as it turns out, Maria's search led to the creation of her book, which details where to go hiking with doggies, as well as where you can eat (cafes, restaurants), sleep (hotels, bed-and-breakfasts), travel (trains, ferries), tour (wineries, festivals), and shop (clothing stores, etc.) together.

My best pal, Bart-Dog, and I hike all over the Bay Area. Here are Bart and Joe's picks for the best hikes in seven Bay Area counties:

1. Sunol Regional Wilderness

Joe and Bart both picked Sunol Regional Wilderness, with Redwood Regional Park getting tail wags. Sunol Regional Wilderness covers 6,400 acres, big enough for any dog to discover many secret spots. Joe's favorite is Little Yosemite, where Alameda Creek provides a pretty setting. "I like to view it from the top of the gorge," said Joe, "then I take Maria down to the creek for a little drink, but I never get my paws wet. I leave that to Bart and the other dogs."

Contact: Sunol Regional Wilderness, (925) 862-2244; East Bay Regional Park District, (510) 635-0135 extension 2200. **Locator:** Sunol/Ohlone Regional Wilderness (E1c). **See featured trip pages:** 99 and 168.

2. Point Isabel Regional Shoreline

Both Joe and Bart really like bayfront views, such as at the Point Isabel Shoreline near Berkeley. Bart tells me how much he likes dreaming of chasing all those birds, but he knows that he can't because it would mean he is a "bad dog." Joe, meanwhile, likes to sit on the shoreline, then sniff at the breezes flowing off the briny green. Point Isabel features a 21-acre park with an easy shoreline walk, ideal for a 30-minute evening jaunt. It seems like there are lots of dogs here, so Joe asked the ranger for some specific numbers; turns out that 784,000 dogs visit here annually, and they bring 558,000 people with them.

Contact: East Bay Regional Park District, (510) 635-0135 extension 2200. **Locator:** Berkeley (E1c).

3. Marin County Open Space District

There are many hikes in Marin County that Joe and Bart would put in the Doggy Hall of Fame, especially those on the Marin Water District lands where a pooch can peruse the fire roads without a leash; leashes are required on all trails, however. The best hike, according to Bart, who likes being on a leash because he feels more secure with Dad, is the trail to beautiful Cascade Falls, part of the Marin County Open Space District. It's an easy mile hike to the falls, where doggies are rewarded with a swim and a drink to cool off. "Been there, done that," said Joe, "and no thanks, but I'll enjoy the view and keep my feet dry."

Contact: Marin County Parks, (415) 499-6387. **Locator:** Mount Tamalpais (E1a). **See featured trip page:** 60.

4. Alston Park

Every once in a while, Joe explained, you just plain have to feel the breeze running past your ears. "I can do that," he said, "at Alston Park in Napa." This park covers 157 acres, but it seems to stretch out forever because of its wide-open spaces with prune trees sprinkled about. Dogs are permitted here without a leash, though they must be kept under control. "I like the lower flat section of the park because that's where most of the prune trees are," Joe said. "I've rarely had so much fun sniffing."

Contact: Napa County Parks, (707) 257-9529. **Locator:** Napa (D1).

5. Fort Funston

Fort Funston gets the top rating, a five-paw headliner. What a place: "I can run up and down the trails on the sand dunes without a care in the world," said Joe. "I don't even give a passing thought to where my next dog bone is coming from." Fort Funston is located just west of Lake Merced on the San Francisco coast, where dogs are permitted to roam without a leash as long as they remain under your complete control. "The only downer for me," said Joe, "are all the hang gliders here. People like watching them, but for me, it's scary, and it can be quite embarrassing when I put my tail between my legs and hide behind Maria, especially if that cute little poodle Sophi shows up."

Contact: Fort Funston, (415) 239-2366; San Francisco Headlands, (415) 556-8371; Golden Gate National Recreation Area, (415) 556-0560. **Locator:** FORT FUNSTON (E1b). **See featured trip page:** 70.

6. McNee Ranch State Park

The only state park that allows dogs on the trails is McNEE RANCH STATE PARK, located on the northern slopes of MONTARA MOUNTAIN. My late pal Rebel hiked to the summit, an elevation of 1,898 feet, more than 500 times, often getting ahead and looking back, asking, "What's the holdup, bub?" It can be a steep, demanding tromp for humans, three very steep sections and a 7.6-mile round-trip, but your dog will usually put up with you anyway. "I was here Tuesday and noticed that if there are bikes, that I can always take Maria on one of the spur trails," noted Joe, pausing only to lick a nice, long slobber from his chin.

Contact: California State Parks, Bay Area District, (415) 330-6300 or (650) 726-8800. **Locator:** McNEE RANCH STATE PARK (E1b). **See featured trip pages:** 73 and 74.

7. Almaden Quicksilver County Park

This was a tough call, with Joe leaning in favor of ALMADEN QUICKSILVER COUNTY PARK, and Bart's memories favoring Arastradero Preserve. "Fair enough," says Joe. "I like all the squirrels." This is a hiking and biking park, set in the foothills covering 613 acres, and features a beautiful pond, six miles of trails, and lots of birds and wildlife to pant at. "When you first lead your person here, you get the rolling, open grasslands," Joe said with a woof, "then you walk past the pond, where I pause to let Maria catch her breath, and head into the shaded woodlands and all those squirrels on the Acorn Trail. After that, it's time to go back and get a dog bone."

Contact: (408) 268-3883. **Locator:** ALMADEN QUICKSILVER COUNTY PARK (E1d).

• TOM'S RATINGS •

The Top 6 One-Way Hikes Using Public Transportation

In the San Francisco Bay Area

The ability to use public transit to visit Bay Area parks for hiking, picnicking, and exploring can open up a whole new world—and not just for people who don't own cars.

Using BART, buses, or both, visitors can gain access to 47 parks in the Bay Area, one of the great hidden benefits of the transit system. At the same time, great one-way trips are possible, because when you go by bus, you don't always have to return to the trailhead where you started.

There are many benefits to using public transit, and only a few drawbacks.

You don't have to deal with traffic, parking, the price of gas, and the vehicle access fee that many parks charge. Even though it is a rare occurrence, you don't have to worry about your vehicle being vandalized at the trailhead. It also can make even longtime residents feel like carefree tourists. For city residents who don't own cars, it provides access to dozens of outstanding adventures; and those who do can experience several stellar one-way hikes that are not possible if you go by car.

The drawbacks are obvious. Trips take longer, for one thing, and waiting for late buses can be tormenting. You also can't bring your dog, or your pet Bigfoot either, although neither are permitted on state park trails anyway.

To make it easier for Bay Area residents to use the transit system as a gateway to adventure, a free Transit Outdoors Map produced by the Bay Area Open Space Council is now available. The foldout map shows the parks, transit connections, and some trails, and describes how to reach 47 parks that are accessible by public transit. There is also a listing of phone numbers that you can call to obtain park and transit publications.

A single copy of the map is available for free by contacting the Bay Area Open Space Council, 116 New Montgomery Street, Suite 640, San Francisco, CA 94105; (800) 543-GREEN/543-4733.

"Transit Outdoors (map) is exciting because it opens up the greenbelt to urban, low-income, and senior communities with high numbers of people who don't drive," said Jim Sayer, executive director of the Greenbelt Alliance. "The secret of how to get there without a car is now out of the bag."

According to John Woodbury of the Bay Area Open Space Council, most people who don't drive haven't even gotten past trying to figure out what's possible.

"Most people have never taken public transit to the great outdoors," Woodbury said. "For those thinking, 'This is all very nice, but when I'm going hiking I don't have time to sit on a bus,' consider all the trips you haven't done because with a car you have to return to the same place you start. As a transit user, you can go places the automobile-dependent hiker cannot."

One of the best examples is a one-way hike that I've always wanted to complete but haven't, from SAN PEDRO VALLEY COUNTY PARK in southern PACIFICA, up to the top of MONTARA MOUNTAIN, then down the other side to MCNEE RANCH STATE PARK in MONTARA, a seven-mile trip. Instead, like most everybody else, I've had to drive to both of the parks, hiking on separate days.

But with a bus as a shuttle, you can instead rise out of San Pedro Valley, hike past Brooks Falls, then continue climbing to the sweeping coastal lookouts on MONTARA MOUNTAIN. Instead of doubling back, you can instead continue your tromp southward into MCNEE RANCH, where the steep drop-offs and views of PILLAR POINT, MOSS BEACH, and the PACIFIC OCEAN can make one stretch out their arms, palms up, and feel as if they are grabbing the entire world.

Here is a list of the best one-way trips possible using a transit bus as a shuttle, rated 1 through 6. I have hiked all of these but No. 6.

1. Mount Tamalpais to Stinson Beach

Start at Mountain Home, or to shorten the trip, the Pantoll ranger station and trailhead at MOUNT TAMALPAIS STATE PARK, then make the beautiful downhill glide to the beach.

Contact: (415) 893-1580 or (415) 388-2070. **Locator:** MOUNT TAMALPAIS (E1a). **See featured trip page:** 62.

2. Pacifica to Montara

Start at SAN PEDRO VALLEY COUNTY PARK, climb over the top of MONTARA MOUNTAIN, then sail downhill to MCNEE RANCH STATE PARK and the bus stop at adjacent Montara State Beach.

Contact: (650) 355-8289 or (650) 726-8800. **Locator:** SAN PEDRO VALLEY COUNTY PARK (E1b). **See featured trip pages:** 73, 74, and 80.

3. Marin Headlands to the Spencer Bus Pad

This hike features dramatic views of the entrance to the GOLDEN GATE, the PACIFIC OCEAN, and the SAN FRANCISCO HEADLANDS.

Contact: (415) 331-1540 or (415) 556-0560. **Locator:** MARIN HEADLANDS (E1a). **See featured trip page:** 59.

4. San Bruno to Pacifica

Start at Skyline College and hike the Sweeney Ridge Trail to Mori Ridge on lands managed by the GOLDEN GATE NATIONAL RECREATION AREA, with views of the South Bay and Crystal Springs Reservoir to the east, the PACIFIC OCEAN to the west.

Contact: (415) 556-0560 or (415) 561-4323. **Locator:** SWEENEY RIDGE (E1b) **See featured trip page:** 85.

5. Oakland hills to the Richmond hills

From TILDEN REGIONAL PARK, hike on the East Bay Skyline National Trail to San Pablo Ridge (incredible views to the west of SAN FRANCISCO BAY and the surrounding landmarks), then continue down to WILDCAT CANYON REGIONAL PARK.

Contact: (510) 635-0135 extension 2200. **Locator:** TILDEN REGIONAL PARK (E1c). **See featured trip page:** 100.

6. Moraga to Oakland

You'll cross the foothills along the border of Contra Costa and Alameda Counties. This is possible by taking trails that lead through watershed lands managed by the East Bay Municipal Utility District, REDWOOD REGIONAL PARK, and BLACK DIAMOND MINES REGIONAL PRESERVE.

Contact: (510) 635-0135 extension 2200. **Locator:** MORAGA (E1c).

• TOM'S RATINGS •

The Top 4 One-Way Hikes Using a Shuttle Car

In the San Francisco Bay Area

What goes down, as hikers always discover, must go up. Even the most relaxed downhill glide on a trail is often shadowed by visions of the climb that must follow.

But can you imagine a hike where there is no up at all? Just down? Nothing awaiting you, that is, but a nice, relaxing saunter, a downhill breeze that will have you laughing all the way?

It turns out that there is a hidden handful of trails throughout the Bay Area where you can get just that. With a partner and a shuttle car, you can hike these trails downhill one way. You and your partner leave a car at the trail's end, then drive to the other end of the park to the trailhead and start hiking, relaxed and happy all the way.

Here are my four favorite one-way hikes, each in a different part of the Bay Area:

1. West Mount Tamalpais

If nature is your way of getting religion, the Steep Ravine Trail can provide a descent into heaven. The hike starts on the west side of Mount Tamalpais, then drops 1,100 feet over a span of two miles down to the coast at Highway 1. In the process, you are routed down into a lush gulch, hiking along pretty Webb Creek (with eight stream crossings), at times bordered by redwoods with a flourishing understory. It is one of the prettiest yet easiest hikes in the Bay Area, about a one-hour, one-way trip. By the way, if you prefer sweeping coastal views to a redwood canyon, the nearby Matt Davis Trail (from the Pantoll Trailhead to Stinson Beach) is the route for you.

Contact: Mount Tamalpais State Park, (415) 388-2070; California State Parks, Marin District, (415) 893-1580. **Notes:** Start at the Pantoll Trailhead in Mount Tamalpais State Park; end at Highway 1 near Rocky Point. **Locator:** MOUNT TAMALPAIS STATE PARK (E1a). **See featured trip page:** 62.

2. PURISIMA CREEK REDWOODS

There is no better way to see the pristine PURISIMA CREEK REDWOODS than on this one-way hike that links Skyline Boulevard out westward to the foothills on the outskirts of HALF MOON BAY. The trail is about 4.5 miles one way, starting at 2,000 feet and descending 1,600 feet. Imagine going the other way, eh? You drop in elevation steeply for the first mile on the Harkins Fire Road, then turn left on the Soda Gulch Trail and hike out to the Higgins Staging Area. This route will take you through a beautiful redwood forest and along a creek with giant ferns and sorrel.

Contact: Midpeninsula Regional Open Space District, (650) 691-1200. **Notes:** Start at the Whittemore Gulch Trailhead on Skyline Boulevard; end at the Higgins Staging Area near Half Moon Bay. **Locator:** PURISIMA CREEK REDWOODS (E1b). **See featured trip page:** 78.

3. TILDEN REGIONAL PARK

The one-way route through TILDEN REGIONAL PARK is highlighted by far-reaching views of the East Bay's most untouched foothills, lush green and popping with wildflowers in spring, with hawks often seen floating about on the afternoon's rising thermals. The trail covers three miles and drops 860 feet in the process, the easiest and one of the prettiest sections of the 31-mile East Bay Skyline National Trail. From the trailhead adjacent to Vollmer Peak (elevation 1,913 feet), the highest point on the Skyline Trail, the trail meanders through TILDEN to Inspiration Point. When I hiked it, I didn't see another person the entire way.

Contact: East Bay Regional Park District, (510) 635-0135 extension 2200; Tilden Nature Area, (510) 525-2233. **Notes:** Start at the Lomas Contadas Staging Area; end at Inspiration Point. **Locator:** TILDEN REGIONAL PARK (E1c). **See featured trip page:** 100.

4. BIG BASIN REDWOODS STATE PARK

The 12-mile hike from park headquarters to the coast at Rancho del Oso is an ambitious trip, but the payoff is a chance to explore the Bay Area's prettiest and most inspiring scenery. It is the premier section of the 38-mile Skyline-to-Sea Trail. The route passes the magnificent giant redwoods of BIG BASIN and 70-foot Berry Creek Falls, then runs alongside WADDELL CREEK out to the coast. While it includes a short climb from the trailhead over the Big Basin Rim, the rest is downhill to the coast. If you need more than a day, primitive overnight camps are available along the route, but reservations are required. When I hiked this one, I took a weekend to do it, which allowed plenty of time to meander by the waterfalls and also to work the shuttle ride without being rushed.

Notes: Start at Big Basin Redwoods State Park headquarters; end at Rancho del Oso on Highway 1. **Contact:** Big Basin Redwoods State Park, (831) 338-8860. **Locator:** BIG BASIN REDWOODS STATE PARK (E1d). **See featured trip page:** 136.

• TOM'S RATINGS •

THE TOP 10 TRIPS INTO THE REDWOODS

In the San Francisco Bay Area

A walk through a redwood park in the Bay Area can not only restore the human spirit, it can simplify the ongoing war over the Headwaters Forest in the Redwood Empire.

A single old-growth redwood tree is worth $20,000 to $30,000 to loggers, according to the Pacific Lumber Company. The bigger ones are worth $40,000, and the colossal giants, the 300-footers with gargantuan trunks, can be worth as much as $100,000 each. On the other hand, many hikers consider the experience of walking among these ancient trees to be priceless.

The Bay Area is the only metropolitan region in the world with redwood parks sprinkled about its outskirts. Their ongoing protection shows exactly what people believe the old-growth redwoods are really worth: Thumbs down on a single truckload worth $25,000, because no price is high enough to merit cutting them down.

Here, rated from 1 through 10, are places where you can go to hike among the redwoods in the Bay Area:

1. BIG BASIN REDWOODS STATE PARK

By my best estimate, there are 10,000 miles of hiking trails in the Bay Area. My favorite 11 miles are in BIG BASIN, hiking out from park headquarters to 70-foot Berry Creek Falls, continuing on to Silver Falls and Golden Falls, then looping back to headquarters. It is the one place that has it all: old-growth giants, dense second-growth trees, beautiful waterfalls, and a huge variety of trails, 80 miles in all, from a short loop among the ancient trees at headquarters to long traipses to remote ridges. The park is huge and makes an outstanding destination for off-season camping, with tent cabins, backpack trail camps, walk-in camps, and drive-to camps.

Contact: BIG Basin Redwoods State Park, (831) 338-8860; California State Parks, Santa Cruz District, (831) 338-6132. **Locator:** BIG BASIN REDWOODS STATE PARK (E1d). **See featured trip page:** 136.

2. MUIR WOODS NATIONAL MONUMENT

The valley floor of MUIR WOODS is home to the mammoth ancients, and a beautiful stroll here will take you among them. Walking along Redwood Creek, every pore in your body seems to open in order to absorb the magic energy of the place. It is one of the most popular walks at any park in North America, and though it's paved for a mile because of the heavy use it receives, you can link into an excellent three-mile loop trail by taking the Hillside Trail up the west side of the canyon.

Contact: Muir Woods National Monument, (415) 338-2596. **Locator:** MUIR

WOODS (E1a). **See featured trip page:** 64.

3. BUTANO STATE PARK

This is a great destination for hiking and biking (potential user conflicts have been resolved, and trails are well signed), picnics, and camping. It's also ideal for lookouts and look-ins, that is, looking out from ridgetop viewpoints or heading into the forest for a look inward at yourself. The 2,713-acre state park encompasses the redwood-filled Butano Canyon as well as the U-shaped ridgeline that frames it. A great network of trails offers many different ways of hiking through the redwoods and then up to the ridge for views, including glimpses of the PACIFIC OCEAN. I've hiked every trail in the park and would rate all of them as first-rate.

Contact: Butano State Park, (650) 879-2040; California State Parks, Bay Area District, (415) 330-6300. **Locator:** BUTANO STATE PARK (E1d). **See featured trip page:** 137.

4. PURISIMA CREEK REDWOODS

For newcomers, this 2,500-acre preserve can be stunning in its beauty and scope, extending from Skyline Ridge all the way down to the outskirts of the town of Half Moon Bay. It features a redwood forest, a pretty creek, riparian habitat, and wild berries in the lowlands, and if you climb out on the Whittemore Gulch Trail, a 1,600-foot climb, you will gain sweeping lookouts of the PACIFIC OCEAN and PILLAR POINT HARBOR. There are three access points, two on Skyline Boulevard and one on Higgins Canyon Road southeast of HALF MOON BAY.

Contact: Midpeninsula Regional Open Space District, (650) 691-1200. **Locator:** PURISIMA CREEK REDWOODS (E1b). **See featured trip page:** 78.

5. SAMUEL P. TAYLOR STATE PARK

The campground here has a classic woods-and-water setting, surrounded by a deep, dark redwood forest and with the headwaters of Papermill Creek (also called Lagunitas Creek) running nearby. A picnic area is set in a beautiful redwood grove, and from there, the Pioneer Tree Trail provides a short, easy indoctrination to the park. If you want more, you can seek out a secret waterfall, always a surprise (ask a ranger for specific directions to the trailhead). A paved wheelchair-accessible trail is now available along Papermill Creek.

Contact: Samuel P. Taylor State Park, (415) 488-9897; California State Parks, Marin District, (415) 893-1580. **Locator:** SAMUEL P. TAYLOR STATE PARK (E1a).

6. PORTOLA REDWOODS STATE PARK

This park is a favorite of mine not only for hiking, camping, and poking along the headwaters of PESCADERO CREEK, but for its several hidden meadows and pretty views of the coastal foothills. Trails are linked to nearby MEMORIAL and Sam McDonald County Parks. The road in is quite twisty, which is just perfect because it means that the only people who get here are those who love it and earn it.

Contact: Portola Redwoods State Park, (650) 948-9098; California State Parks, Santa Cruz District, (831) 429-2851. **Locator:** PORTOLA REDWOODS STATE PARK (E1d). **See featured trip page:** 143.

7. MEMORIAL COUNTY PARK

This county park set in a pocket of redwoods between LOMA MAR and LA

HONDA has 50 miles of trails, a pretty stream (PESCADERO CREEK), and hiking links to two adjacent parks. The Iverson Trail along PESCADERO CREEK is a sure-bet winner for newcomers.

Contact: Memorial/Sam McDonald County Parks, (650) 879-0238; San Mateo County Parks, (650) 363-4020. **Locator:** PESCADERO CREEK (E1d). **See featured trip page:** 143.

8. REDWOOD REGIONAL PARK

Rain is a magic tonic here, giving life not only to the surprising grove of redwoods, but to Redwood Creek and its wild strain of rainbow trout. When the creek fills with water in winter, trout will migrate upstream from UPPER SAN LEANDRO RESERVOIR and spawn here, with an excellent fish ladder constructed to help them make the trip over obstacles. The fish ladder and the surrounding redwoods make the Stream Trail one of the top five hikes among hundreds in Alameda and Contra Costa Counties.

Contact: East Bay Regional Park District, (510) 635-0135 extension 2200 or 2578. **Locator:** REDWOOD REGIONAL PARK (E1c).

9. HUDDART COUNTY PARK

This park sits on the western slopes of the Peninsula foothills, covering 1,000 acres and featuring several groves of redwoods, mostly well-established second-growth trees. The park has 45 miles of trails, and with many junctions, visitors with maps in hand can custom-tailor any kind of hike they desire. That makes it one of the top parks for hiking on the Peninsula.

Contact: Huddart County Park, (650) 851-7570; San Mateo County Parks, (415) 363-4020. **Locator:** HUDDART COUNTY PARK (E1b). **See featured trip page:** 72.

10. WUNDERLICH COUNTY PARK

While WUNDERLICH does not provide an expansive redwood forest, there are pockets of redwoods dotting canyons amid hills supporting tan oak and madrone, with 45 miles of trails weaving in and out from one habitat to another. The result is a bit of everything for hikers, with occasional views of the Peninsula foothill country and beyond providing a nice bonus.

Contact: Wunderlich County Park, (650) 851-7570; San Mateo County Parks, (415) 363-4020. **Locator:** WUNDERLICH COUNTY PARK (E1b). **See featured trip page:** 86.

• TOM'S RATINGS •

THE TOP 5 STEEP HIKES

In the San Francisco Bay Area

It's amazing how much money people will spend to get in good physical condition. But instead of shelling out hundreds of dollars on equipment or a fitness club membership, there's another way to do the job that is a lot more fun, and it's free.

On a mission to get your butt in shape, I have searched out the worst butt-kicker hikes in the Bay Area. Yes, there are stretches where you'll be sweating like Charles Manson's cell mate, and at trail's end you'll generally feel like a horse that's been rode hard and put away wet. But it will do the job.

If you check out America's greatest hikers—John Muir, Joe Walker, and Kit Carson—you'll discover that they were the skinniest guys you've ever seen. Kit Carson, for instance, often described as our country's number one mountain man, weighed all of 140 pounds. To get that body, he never signed up at a Linda Evans Fitness

Center.

If you need more incentive, there are many other reasons to get in great shape. For one thing, you will feel a lot better, waking up each day with real zest. For another, you'll look a lot better. It will also give you the ability to explore California's most beautiful areas this summer without being too exhausted to savor the experience.

Of course, anybody who has not hiked, biked, or otherwise exercised in some time should see a doctor for a physical examination prior to setting out on these hikes or undertaking any other aerobic activity. After all, all you want kicked is your butt. Here are the five best hikes that can do the trick:

1. Peak Trail

Steep? Oh yeah, it's a 2,100-foot climb in 3.5 miles to the top of Mission Peak (elevation 2,527 feet), a heart-thumper on the way up, a toe-jammer on the way down. This is not only the steepest day hike in the Bay Area, but it also provides sweeping views and maybe a decent wildflower bloom, with a few poppies sprinkled in the grasslands. The round-trip is seven miles.

From the trailhead at the end of Stanford Avenue in Fremont (there's an easier trailhead, Spring Valley Trail, at Ohlone College), the hike rises quickly up the mountain, eventually climbing to the top along the northern flank. On the way up, there are great views of the South Bay and the Santa Clara Valley, and from the top on crystal-clear days, you can see San Francisco, the Santa Cruz Mountains, and across the Central Valley to the Sierra crest.

Contact: East Bay Regional Park District, (510) 635-0135 extension 2200. **Locator:** Mission Peak (E1c). **See featured trip page:** 168.

2. Coyote Creek

You have to be partially insane for this trip, and that is what makes it a favorite. The worst section is a drop-dead descent that I estimated at 1,400 feet over 2.5 miles, with one half-mile section straight out of hell: straight down to the creek, straight up to get back. Coyote Creek is quite pretty, small but running cold and clear. Bring a water filtration pump for drinking water, and figure on a round-trip of eight miles.

The trip starts at the main entrance for Coe State Park east of Morgan Hill. After parking, hike out on the Northern Heights Route over the top of Pine Ridge (elevation 2,800 feet), continue past Little Coyote Creek (dropping 600 feet), then head onward past Frog Lake, a beautiful rest spot. From here, it's up and over Middle Ridge and finally you face the deathlike descent to Skeel's Meadow and Middle Fork Coyote Creek, bottoming out at 1,600 feet, a drop of 1,000 feet in a mile. The climb out to return is a genuine killer, especially on a hot day. Perfect, right?

Contact: Henry W. Coe State Park, (408) 779-2728. **Locator:** Henry W. Coe State Park (E1d). **See featured trip page:** 139.

3. Rocky/Wauhab Ridge

Just don't say you weren't warned. This can be a hot, dry, grueling climb and the sole rewards are having nobody else around and a view of some of the Bay Area's wildest, most remote lands. The worst stretch is right off, climbing 1,600 feet in 1.3 miles to gain Rocky Ridge (elevation 2,400 feet). Yeah, this is bad. From here, it's another 7.5 miles to Wauhab

Ridge (3,490 feet), making a roundtrip of over 16 miles, long enough to test anybody. Of course, most everybody turns around earlier.

The trailhead is at the southern end of Del Valle Regional Park south of Livermore. Suddenly, you start the climb, and you may wonder why you are doing this. Just when you reach Rocky Ridge, you may figure that better times are ahead, and sure enough, they are. From here, you hike out on the Ohlone Wilderness Trail, rising through fields of grasslands and oaks. A regional park wilderness permit is required.

Contact: East Bay Regional Park District, (510) 635-0135 extension 2200. **Locator:** Sunol/Ohlone Regional Wilderness (E1d). **See featured trip page:** 168.

4. Giant Loop

There is no better way to see Mount Diablo than on the Giant Loop, an 8.6-mile hike that provides the most intimate glimpses of this old mountain, along with great views and two sustained climbs. The worst of it is an 1,800-foot climb up to Deer Flat, steep enough to keep you pumping in aerobic rhythm.

The trailhead for the Giant Loop is located at the end of Mitchell Canyon Road out of Clayton (a good map is available here), not at the state park headquarters at the summit. From the trailhead, the hike up to Deer Flat (and a side trip to Eagle Peak at 2,369 feet) is a steady grind, challenging in hot weather. The return trip is a delight, though, heading down Donner Canyon, with pretty Donner Creek running down the center.

Contact: Mount Diablo State Park, (925) 837-2525. **Locator:** Mount Diablo (E1c). **See featured trip page:** 93.

5. Montara Mountain

The rewards are panoramic coastal views and a glimpse of the off-limits San Francisco Fish and Game Refuge (just east of the peak). It is a true untouched wildland, and right, the hike is a steep sucker.

The trailhead is located along the east side of Highway 1, just south of Devil's Slide. Park at the little yellow pipe gate on the east side of Highway 1 in northern Montara, or across the highway at Montara State Beach. From here, it is 3.8 miles to top of the mountain (1,898 feet), including three stretches of up, including one 20-minute stretch that is as bad as anything anywhere. In other words, just right.

Contact: Half Moon Bay State Park, (650) 726-8800. **Locator:** McNee Ranch State Park (E1b). **See featured trip page:** 73.

• Tom's Ratings •

The Top 10 Strolls

In the San Francisco Bay Area

Based on scenic beauty, adventure, and lack of people, I have selected the Bay Area's 10 best easy walks, most requiring just 10 to 15 minutes to reach the promised destination. They range from a secluded beach that is often sprinkled with abalone shells to a 2,000-foot coastal lookout at Mount Tamalpais, from which mountaintops can resemble islands poking holes through a sea of fog. All are ideal for winter, when a short trip to a beautiful spot can make for a perfect afternoon venture.

Here they are:

1. Point Bonita Lighthouse

All you need is a clear, fog-free day to discover one of the easiest-to-reach paradises in the Bay Area. From the parking area, it is just a half mile to the lighthouse, perched on a cliff's edge at Point Bonita at the mouth of San Francisco Bay. But in that half mile, the walk includes a trip through a handmade tunnel, followed by a stretch across a suspension bridge where hiking becomes an act of faith. Then you reach the old lighthouse, first constructed in 1855, providing a perfect lookout of the Golden Gate, the entrance to the bay, Bonita Cove, and the Pacific.

Note: After being closed due to a landslide, the trail has now been reopened for public access on Saturdays and Sundays from 2:30 to 3:30 p.m. **Contact:** Marin Headlands Visitor Center, (415) 331-1540. **Locator:** Marin Headlands (E1a). **See featured trip page:** 59.

2. O'Rourke's Bench

With its sweeping coastal views, there may be no better place for a picnic lunch than O'Rourke's Bench. It sits on a knoll at 2,071 feet on Mount Tamalpais, a short walk from the Rock Springs Trailhead. After parking at Rock Springs, cross Ridgecrest Boulevard and take the O'Rourke's Bench Trail for three-tenths of a mile. After just 10 or 15 minutes, you will come upon this little bench next to a plaque that reads: "Give me these hills and the friends I love. I ask no other heaven." Way back in 1927, the bench and plaque were dedicated to "Dad O'Rourke" by his friends and family—who were grateful, no doubt, that he shared this spot with them—on the occasion of his 76th birthday.

Contact: Mount Tamalpais State Park, (415) 388-2070. **Locator:** Mount Tamalpais State Park (E1a). **See featured trip page:** 62.

3. Whaler's Cove

This is the best beach I know of to cob for abalone shells. They come in all sizes, from the massive seven-inchers down to little one-inch shells that make for a perfect necklace, as well as all sizes in between. Park about one mile south of Pigeon Point Lighthouse (located just off Highway 1 about five miles south of the Pescadero turnoff). Then hike down to the beach directly to the south and enjoy the walk to the north towards the lighthouse. It leads to Whaler's Cove, with Shag Rock just offshore and tidal waters in between, a prime abalone ground. It can only be visited during winter's minus low tides.

Contact: Pigeon Point Hostel, (650) 879-0633. **Locator:** Pigeon Point (E1d).

4. Cogswell Marsh

Cogswell Marsh is the heart of an 800-acre marsh and wetlands on the Hayward shore of the South Bay, a great place for taking short nature hikes and identifying many rare birds. It is always a good place to see shorebirds, with the bonus of peregrine falcons typically either hovering over the marsh or perched on a power pylon. You can spot as many as 200 white pelicans here, along with the occasional merlins. From the parking area, the walk starts with a 0.4-mile hike across landfill, then enters the marshland, with a loop trail circling the most vital habitat. The loop is best hiked clockwise, so you will be facing the Bay Bridge and the San Francisco skyline, an outstanding view, when you walk along the water's edge of the South Bay.

Contact: Hayward Regional Shoreline, (510) 783-1066. **Locator:** HAYWARD REGIONAL SHORELINE (E1c).

5. Redwood Trail

The quarter-mile REDWOOD TRAIL provides an opportunity for anybody to experience the grandeur of redwoods. Anybody? People with baby strollers, wheelchairs, or walkers, and even those recovering from poor health, can make this walk. It starts at 2,000 feet on the Peninsula's Skyline Boulevard (Highway 35) and is routed north under a canopy of giant redwoods. At the end of the trail, there are picnic tables and a rest room facility. Most people don't really hike this trail. They just kind of mosey along, enjoying the sensation of being surrounded by old redwoods.

Contact: Midpeninsula Regional Open Space District, (650) 691-1200. **Locator:** PURISIMA CREEK REDWOODS (E1b). **See featured trip page:** 78.

6. Jake's Island Trail

Even though this is a short (0.8-mile) walk, it is rare to find one so unique. It is also rare to find a trail that provides such an intimate glimpse of wetlands, marshes, tidal waters, and the waterfowl that live there. The trailhead is on the SAN PABLO BAY side of San Pedro Road at CHINA CAMP STATE PARK, east of SAN RAFAEL. After parking, you follow the trail along the east side of Turtle Back Point. Tidal wetlands are all about, and during low tides they become exposed mudflats. The trail then crosses a wetlands bridge to reach Jake's Island, a small land mass encircled by marshland.

Note: Because of the fragile nature of this habitat, the trail may be closed at certain times. **Contact:** China Camp State Park, (415) 456-0766. **Locator:** CHINA CAMP STATE PARK (E1a).

7. McClures Beach Trail

In the divine panorama of Point Reyes, McClures Beach is one of the easy-to-reach spots that often gets overlooked. It sits in the shadow of nearby Pierce Ranch with its 200-strong elk herd, and most visitors never take the quarter-mile drive to road's end, except perhaps to use the rest rooms and telephone there. But an easy half-mile walk will lead you to McClures Beach, featuring tide pools to the south and beachfront to the north. This area is always best visited during minus low tides, when you can survey the tide pool life. Also during low tides, beachcombing along McClures and Driftwood Beaches (to the immediate north) can often unveil unusual finds.

Contact: Point Reyes National Seashore, (415) 663-1092. **Locator:** POINT REYES NATIONAL SEASHORE (E1a). **See featured trip pages:** 67 and 262.

8. Baylands Catwalk

Now, you say, what the heck is the Baylands Catwalk? As you will discover, it is an old wooden walkway that crosses tidal marshland and is routed under a series of giant electrical towers. In recent years, the catwalk has been improved and extended, now sporting an observation deck on the edge of South Bay waters. You start your walk here at the Baylands Interpretive Center, which provides explanatory exhibits of the marshland habitat. From there, you can make the short walk straight east out to the observation deck, about a 10-minute trip. You can also take a dirt trail that leads across the tidal marshlands, where there are egrets, coots, ducks, and ground squirrels.

Contact: Palo Alto Baylands Interpretive Center, (650) 329-2506; Palo Alto Recreation Department, (650) 329-2261. **Locator:** BAYLANDS TRAIL (E1c). **See featured trip page:** 283.

9. FALSE GUN VISTA TRAIL

A little-known lookout over San Francisco Bay is the highlight of MILLER-KNOX REGIONAL SHORELINE, located west of Richmond. Getting there requires only a short hike and climb. From the parking area, you walk about half a mile up Old Country Road, making a right turn on the Crest Trail to reach False Gun Vista Point, in the process climbing 300 feet to the lookout (elevation 322 feet). On clear days, you get picture-perfect views of SAN FRANCISCO BAY and its many surrounding landmarks.

Contact: Miller-Knox Regional Shoreline, (510) 235-1631. **Locator:** RICHMOND (E1c).

10. GRASS VALLEY TRAIL

There's a hidden spot in the East Bay hills near CASTRO VALLEY, a simple paradise. Called GRASS VALLEY, it consists of a long valley sprinkled with wild grasses and wildflowers, and is bordered to the north by Bort Meadow, framed by the rims of miniature mountains on each side. After winter rains, it glows with the varied greens of wild grasses, along with blooming wild radish, blue-eyed grass, and golden poppies. The Grass Valley Trail is one of the quickest routes to tranquillity, starting at the Bort Meadow Staging Area on Redwood Road and then heading south through GRASS VALLEY and on to Stone Bridge, for a distance of 1.5 miles.

Contact: Chabot Regional Park, (510) 635-0135 extension 3402 or 3400. **Locator:** CHABOT REGIONAL PARK (E1c). **See featured trip page:** 230.

• TOM'S RATINGS •

THE TOP 5 WALKS AT LOW TIDE

In the San Francisco Bay Area

As Christmas Eve approaches, children dream of Santa Claus making his journey across the night skies amid the glow of a beautiful full moon. Meanwhile, lovers of the great outdoors can look forward to an extra special present that they can enjoy through Christmas.

In the winter, full moons result in minus low tides, when the lunar forces exert their full powers on oceans and bays across the planet. In the Bay Area, that makes it one of the best times of the year for an easy tidelands walk, whether at coastal tide pools or along the bay's wetlands.

It also means that Santa will have an easier time spotting chimneys on Christmas Eve. That's a good thing, because a full moon can affect people in strange ways, and often the first thing to go is any semblance of intelligence while driving (or flying sleighs). There might actually be a scientific explanation for this: Since the percentage of water on the surface of the Earth is exactly the same as the percentage of water in a human body, 71 percent, some say that full moons can cause voluble mood swings in people, much as full moons cause big swings in tides. That could explain the sudden appearance of so many lousy drivers.

So take caution when the moon nears filling, but also take the time to plan a low-tide walk. Check the almanac and note that precision isn't that important; prime time usually lasts at least four hours.

Here are my 5 favorite places along the coast and bay shoreline to walk and explore during minus low tides:

1. Fitzgerald Marine Reserve

There's no better place to go tide pool hopping than this amazing 30-acre reef where hundreds of tidal pockets are exposed during low tides. They feature hermit crabs, rock crabs, sea anemones, sculpins, starfish, and more. As you walk and enjoy, be certain not to crush the fragile sea plants.

Contact: Fitzgerald Marine Reserve, (650) 728-3584. **Locator:** FITZGERALD MARINE PRESERVE (E1b). **See featured trip page:** 266.

2. McClures Beach

This secluded beach is located within a half-mile walk of the parking lot near Pierce Ranch, known better for its giant herd of elk. But this pretty beach features tide pools to the south and a great beachfront to the north for excellent beachcombing.

Contact: Point Reyes National Seashore, (415) 663-1092. **Locator:** POINT REYES NATIONAL SEASHORE (E1a). **See featured trip pages:** 67 and 262.

3. Fort Funston

One of the biggest expanses of beach anywhere is on the San Francisco coast at Fort Funston, making for nonpareil beachcombing walks during minus tides. It's the best place I know of to find sand dollars, not to mention one of the best places anywhere to bring a dog.

Contact: Fort Funston, (415) 239-2366; San Francisco Headlands, (415) 556-8371; Golden Gate National Recreation Area, (415) 556-0560. **Locator:** FORT FUNSTON (E1b). **See featured trip page:** 70.

4. Cogswell Marsh Loop

A 2.8-mile walk will take you through Cogswell Marsh, the heart of an 800-acre wetland. There are two bridged sections amid the wetlands, where, if you are lucky, you can occasionally see rafts of white pelicans. This is always a good spot to view a variety of shorebirds.

Contact: East Bay Regional Park District, (510) 635-0135 extension 2200. **Locator:** HAYWARD REGIONAL SHORELINE (E1c).

5. Point Pinole

A shuttle ride to the trailhead, an extraordinary long cobble beach, and beautiful views of SAN PABLO BAY, Marin, and MOUNT TAMALPAIS make this a real find. You can walk for miles along the shore and see nothing but passing ships and feeding birds on the flats.

Contact: Point Pinole Regional Shoreline, (510) 237-6869. **Locator:** POINT PINOLE (E1c).

• TOM'S RATINGS •

The Top 5 Hikes on the Peninsula

In the San Francisco Bay Area

The Peninsula is one of California's classic paradoxes. It holds some of the state's prettiest parkland and open space, yet it also has that hellish commuter trap, U.S. 101, one of the ugliest roads anywhere.

Because of the latter, many folks forget about the former. But there are refuges on the Peninsula that are set in landscapes that seem very distant from the highway's stream of brake lights. If you haven't visited lately, you might be surprised not only by the beauty of some of these spots, but by the lack of people and sense of peace there.

There are many places like this, yet they typically attract relatively few visitors, especially on weekdays. Here is a synopsis of five of my favorite hikes:

1. Skyline Trail

Huddart and Wunderlich Parks are two of the Peninsula's prettiest redwood retreats. This trail connects the two, for a one-way distance of about seven miles. It is ideal for a shuttle, and since most people don't like taking the trouble, you've got a beautiful trail with few folks on it.

Your best bet is to start at the north entrance of Huddart County Park on Kings Mountain Road, then hike south to Wunderlich, losing about 1,000 feet in elevation in the process. The trail generally parallels Highway 35, but you will feel very far from any road.

Contact: San Mateo County Parks Department, (650) 363-4020; Huddart County Park or Wunderlich County Park, (650) 851-1210. **Locator:** Huddart County Park (E1b). **See featured trip pages:** 72 and 86.

2. Sweeney Ridge

Everybody's heard of Sweeney Ridge, right? Well, you might think so until you actually get out and hike it. Often, you won't see another soul. The trailhead from the south parking lot at Skyline College is routed up to the Bay Discovery Site, about a 45-minute walk. From there, you get some of the best views anywhere, the Pacific Ocean on one side and the South Bay on the other.

Contact: Golden Gate National Recreation Area, (415) 556-0560. **Locator:** Sweeney Ridge (E1b). **See featured trip page:** 85.

3. Mills Canyon Park

City and county parks frequently get overlooked by out-of-towners, and such is the case here. Mills Canyon is a 40-acre city park set just east of Skyline Boulevard off of Arguello. The highlight is Mills Creek, a pretty stream with pools and short cascade drops. Figure on about an hour to hike the loop trail along the creek. This is a wildlife refuge, with no formal park headquarters, entrance station, or even a telephone. A trail map is available; call the number below.

Contact: Burlingame City Parks, (650) 696-7245. **Locator:** Burlingame (E1b).

4. Purisima Creek Redwoods

This area sits beside Highway 35 (Skyline Boulevard), four miles south of the junction with Highway 92. Here you will find untouched wildlands with redwoods and ferns, ocean views, and if you hike in, a beautiful little stream. It is an open space preserve, a do-it-yourself special not a developed park. The best trailhead is near Skyline Boulevard mile marker SM 16.65, where you can make a four-mile downhill trip amid redwoods. With a companion, you can park another vehicle at trail's end (at Higgins Canyon Road near Half Moon Bay, CA), allowing for a one-way hike with no uphill grunt. A trail map is available; call the number below.

Contact: Midpeninsula Regional Open Space District, (650) 691-1200. **Locator:** Purisima Creek Redwoods (E1b). **See featured trip page:** 78.

5. Arastradero Lake Trail

It takes about a 10- or 15-minute walk from the parking area to reach the lake, and it is always a refreshing sight to top the rise and see this nice little pond. Arastradero is usually full, ringed by tules, with ducks and coots paddling about. There are also ground squirrels, rabbits, hawks, and owls in the surrounding hills. The park covers about 600 acres; a trail map is available at the parking area. There is no formal entrance station or telephone, but the rangers at nearby Foothills Park manage the preserve.

From Interstate 280, take the Page Mill Road exit, then turn right at Arastradero Road. The parking area is just two miles up the road on the right.

Contact: Foothills Park, (650) 329-2423; Palo Alto Parks and Recreation Department, (650) 329-2487. **Locator:** ARASTRADERO LAKE (E1b). **See featured trip page:** 69.

• TOM'S RATINGS •

The Top 7 Shoreline Walks

In the San Francisco Bay Area

If you have never taken a walk along the shore of the East Bay, you are likely to be stunned by the beauty here, particularly on a stellar morning or during an orange-flecked sunset.

On the other hand, if you are familiar with these beautiful settings, then you probably also know that there is no better time to savor them than when winter gives way to spring, when north winds clear the air and the wetlands are filled with birds.

From RICHMOND to NEWARK, there are seven shoreline parks along the bay, from little 21-acre Point Isabel Regional Shoreline to the mammoth 23,000-acre San Francisco Bay National Wildlife Refuge, but each has its own charm.

Most all provide sweeping views of the bay, easy shoreline walks, and destinations for picnicking, bird-watching, and kite flying. Three of them, Crown Memorial State Beach, Martin Luther King Regional Shoreline, and Coyote Hills Regional Park, are also ideal for low-speed family bike trips. Here is the lowdown on each, listed from north to south:

1. Miller-Knox Regional Shoreline

This 260-acre parcel at POINT RICHMOND offers a great lookout of SAN FRANCISCO BAY, excellent kite flying, and one of the best places anywhere to bring a dog. It's a half-mile hike and a 300-foot climb to False Gun Vista Point for a view of the bay, often picture-perfect at sunrise. Keller Beach is ideal for a romp with the dog, and strong afternoon winds make the entire park good for kite flying. Access is free.

Contact: East Bay Regional Park District, (510) 635-0135 extension 2200. **Locator:** RICHMOND (E1c).

2. Point Isabel Regional Shoreline

This 21-acre park is located just north of the Golden Gate Fields Racetrack. The highlight is a half-mile-long trail that extends to Point Isabel along the shore of San Francisco Bay, where the bayfront views are outstanding. The hike then returns along Hoffman Channel and Hoffman Marsh, where there is good bird-watching. Add it up: You get an easy shoreline walk, great views, lots of birds, and free access.

Contact: East Bay Regional Park District, (510) 635-0135 extension 2200.
Locator: BERKELEY (E1c).

3. Crown Memorial State Beach

The trail here is a paved bicycle path running right along the shore of the bay, perfect for a low-speed family bike trip. It runs 2.5 miles (five-miles round-trip) to an overlook of a bird sanctuary, with lots of sandpipers and the occasional egret at low tide, and ducks, grebes, and coots at high tide. This is also one of the best spots around for windsurfing. When the kiosk is attended, a parking fee is charged.

Contact: East Bay Regional Park District, (510) 635-0135 extension 2200.
Locator: ALAMEDA (E1c).

4. Martin Luther King Regional Shoreline

A paved trail for hiking, jogging, and biking extends along Arrowhead Marsh for a round-trip distance of 3.5 miles to Garretson Point and back. You'll stroll along San Leandro Bay, out along the Airport Channel, and across San Leandro Creek. It's a pretty setting with decent bay views, but the stunner is the variety of birds: more than 30 species are typically present here at one of the best bird-watching spots anywhere along the bay's shoreline. Access is free.

Contact: East Bay Regional Park District, (510) 635-0135 extension 2200.
Locator: OAKLAND (E1c).

5. Hayward Regional Shoreline

The 2.8-mile Cogswell Marsh Loop is a first-class gem of a hike, particularly on calm evenings and stellar mornings. Always walk the loop in a clockwise direction, so you are hiking north along the shoreline of the South Bay, getting views every step of the way of the bay, Candlestick Point, the Bay Bridge, and a piece of the San Francisco skyline, especially on clear evenings with the backdrop of a sunset. The trail loops through vital marsh habitat, and two sections are bridged to keep your feet from getting wet. Birdlife flourishes in the marsh, and birders will see lots of shorebirds, with high odds of spotting a peregrine falcon and even a rare opportunity at times to see flocks of white pelicans. Access is free.

Contact: East Bay Regional Park District, (510) 635-0135 extension 2200.
Locator: HAYWARD (E1c).

6. Coyote Hills Regional Park

There is no better park for views of the South Bay. Though this park sits directly along the shoreline, there's a series of small hills that you can climb to find a spot to enjoy sweeping views, both north and south of the DUMBARTON BRIDGE. Just take the Bayview Trail, a three-mile loop that circles the park, then climb a short distance to the top of one of the four hills in the park. To extend the adventure, an additional trail is available out of the parking area, a short walk across a wooden walkway that leads to an excellent waterfowl area called the North Marsh. A parking fee is charged when the kiosk is attended.

Contact: East Bay Regional Park District, (510) 635-0135 extension 2200.
Locator: FREMONT (E1c).

7. San Francisco Bay National Wildlife Refuge

The best way to see the wildlife refuge is to plan a long hike, extending your trip on the Shoreline Trail out along the levee that borders South Bay waters. That is where you will get the best views. On clear days, it can seem as if you could take a running start and jump right across the water to PALO ALTO. The refuge consists of a series of large ponds edged by levees, and while not visually spectacular, the wetlands do provide habitat for dozens of species of birds. Guided walks are available on weekends, usually following a short seminar in the adjacent visitor center. Access is free.

Contact: San Francisco Bay National Wildlife Refuge, (510) 792-4275. **Locator:** SAN FRANCISCO BAY NATIONAL WILDLIFE REFUGE (E1b). **See featured trip page:** 263.

• FEATURED TRIP •

MOUNT EDDY

Rated: One of the Top Hikes in California

If you had time for one trip into the mountains, where would you go? Someplace remote and quiet with no people, only pretty lakes, forests, pure air, clear skies, and views?

The answer to this question once took me 300 miles north of SAN FRANCISCO to MOUNT SHASTA, where I turned left and drove a half hour west into the Eddy Range to the Parks Creek Trailhead, set at an elevation of 6,854 feet on the back flank of MOUNT EDDY. Yes, this would be perfect.

Bart-Dog, my little bear cub of a pooch, led the first steps out on the trail, with views to the west of the Trinity River Canyon and beyond to the TRINITY ALPS and its Sawtooth Ridge. In the valley, a sea of green conifers was sprinkled with the orange and yellow hues of turning oak, aspen, and dogwood leaves.

The Mount Eddy Trail is one of the best hikes in California, starting out as an easy three-mile saunter to beautiful Middle DEADFALL LAKE, a popular spot for visitors of all ages. Everything is turned up a notch, and so is the hike when you start the climb to the summit. Your senses are sharpened by the perfect clarity of the air, the absolute quiet, and the taste of each breath, cool and clean.

MOUNT EDDY tops out at 9,025 feet and lies directly west of MOUNT SHASTA (14,162 feet), with Interstate 5 (at 3,200 feet) running right down the middle between them. From the trailhead, reaching the top of MOUNT EDDY requires a climb of about 2,200 feet over the course of 5.5 miles, for a round-trip of about 11 miles.

The adventure starts easily enough, hiking above a deep valley and meadow, contouring along the mountain slope, the trail nearly flat. The route peeks in and out of fir and pine on a gentle grade, just a 450-foot gain over three miles. You cross little Deadfall Creek, a pretty brook that's often crystal clear, then take a short cutoff over the rise. There, coming into view, is the full expanse of DEADFALL LAKE. It is a beautiful lake, pristine, cold, holding plenty of small trout, with a few campsites at each end.

This is as far as most visitors go. After all, how could you top such an easy hike with such a gorgeous destination? Keep walking and you'll find out.

From here, the trail begins to climb, first 500 feet to Upper DEADFALL LAKE, then another 400 feet to the ridge overlooking the Deadfall Lakes Basin. Suddenly, you start puffing. Just above you looms the peak of MOUNT EDDY, giant, orangish, and craggy.

The final push is a huff-and-a-puff all the way. The trail loops to the south flank of the mountain, then climbs

900 feet with seven switchbacks. As you get higher and higher, the views get better and better, first with sapphire-like LAKE SISKIYOU just below to the east and beyond to MOUNT LASSEN on the distant horizon, and with the spiked rim of CASTLE CRAGS below to the nearby south.

What could be better? Well, keep walking. Trail builders designed this route in a way that at no time can hikers see MOUNT SHASTA until they actually reach the Eddy summit. So no one cuts the trip short.

Gaining the summit is a dramatic moment, and the view is one of the most stunning and beautiful anywhere in America. With a few final steps, you make it to the top on Eddy's south side and, suddenly, there in full view is giant MOUNT SHASTA, California's most beautiful mountain, rising 14,162 feet from the valley floor like a giant diamond.

Of some 25 significant peaks in California that I have climbed, I'd rate the view third behind only Glacier Point on the rim of Yosemite Valley (first) and MOUNT WHITNEY with its 11,000-foot drop into the Owens Valley to the east and a panorama of 12,000-foot peaks to the north (second).

After enjoying a late lunch on the summit and soaking up the views in all directions for more than an hour, we finally started down. The quiet was absolute. This must be God's country because no one else could have thought of it.

Contact: Shasta-Trinity National Forest, (530) 926-4511. **Locator:** MOUNT EDDY (B2).

• FEATURED TRIP •

✶ LASSEN VOLCANIC NATIONAL PARK

Rated: The Top 50 Base Camps, 110

When I first set eyes on Paradise Meadow, it was like a symphony was playing in my heart. The trail topped a ridge, we walked a few steps forward, and were suddenly surrounded by acres of lush and brilliant flora, one of nature's most exotic gardens.

The meadow sits in a mountain bowl at elevation 7,100 feet, an incandescent green backed by a stark, glacial-carved wall, sprinkled with violet lupine, corn lily, and yellow mule's ear, and cut by a pretzel-like creek. It is so pristine that no one ever walks across Paradise Meadow, as if their footsteps would defile a mountain temple; instead, people either sit on a log or a rock at its edge, or climb the adjoining ridge for a better look, soaking in the beauty.

On the hike in, just 30 minutes from the parking lot, you pass through an old forest of pine and cedar, two waterfalls, with the smell of pine duff in the air until you pass through a garden of lupine, the fragrance sweeter than any perfume. In the background, you can hear the happy calls of meadowlarks and the rush of pure waters.

It was here that I saw a vacationer wearing a T-shirt that said, "Expect A Miracle." But at Paradise Meadow and elsewhere in LASSEN VOLCANIC NATIONAL PARK, the miracle has already happened, a place where everything fits together perfectly . . . streams, meadows, waterfalls, volcanic peaks, pristine wilderness lakes, sulfur vents, boiling volcanic pots, deer and bear, hawks and quail. There is nothing more to expect.

LASSEN PARK is located about 50 miles east of RED BLUFF. Many vacationers cruising Interstate 5 spot the old volcano known as MOUNT LASSEN (10,457 feet) and make a mental note to visit the park someday. But it is often overlooked as a destination in California among travelers in the face of YOSEMITE, TAHOE, MOUNT SHASTA, BIG SUR, MAMMOTH, MOUNT WHITNEY, and the coastal redwoods. That means there are usually plenty of campsites available at the park's five campgrounds, relatively few hikers on the 150 miles of trails, and often virtually nobody backpacking across the 80,000 acres of wilderness or camping at the sites near the 46 wilderness lakes.

For short hikes spanning a few miles or less, this is one of the best parks in California, making it an outstanding choice for vacationers of all ages and all levels of physical conditioning. Of the trails I have hiked, here is a synopsis of my favorites:

PARADISE MEADOW

From the Hat Lake parking area, it is a 1.5-mile hike along a creek to Paradise Meadow, with a climb of 600 feet. Highlights along the way include two small waterfalls, spectacular wildflower blooms along the creek, and a first look at the meadow so pretty that it can take your breath away. You can extend the trip to the nearby ridge, or beyond two miles to Terrace Lake, a decent climb.

KING'S CREEK FALLS

One of the most popular hikes in the park, this trip descends 700 feet over the course of 1.5 miles, including a stair-stepped section that takes you along a 300-foot cascade and ends at the bottom of a 30-foot freefall. On one visit, this is where I had a staredown with a deer at 25 feet, after which she walked as close as 10 feet and kept looking straight at me while nibbling on manzanita buds.

BUMPASS HELL

Walking here you get the sense that at any minute a dinosaur might come out and start eating people. In just a few miles, the trail feeds you into Hell's Half Acre, where sulfur vents, boiling mud pots, and hot springs amid volcanic rock provide evidence of the park's volcanic past and the horrific explosion of Lassen volcano in 1914. This hike is easy and unusual, and has become the most popular in the park.

LASSEN PEAK TRAIL

The ascent to the top is a 2.5-mile zigzag of a hike on a hard, flat trail, climbing just over 2,000 feet to a perfect pinnacle at the top. It is an extraordinary summit, a huge volcanic flume with hardened lava craters and crags, and an awesome view to the north of MOUNT SHASTA. Start this hike early, by 7:30 a.m., when the temperatures are cool, and bring plenty of water to drink on the way or face serious dehydration.

MILL CREEK FALLS

The sight is just plain drop-dead gorgeous: two creeks join together in a slot to form one that freefalls into a 30-foot gorge and, after landing with a pounding splash, spills over into another 45-foot fall, 75 feet in all. The viewing area is one of the most perfect for any waterfall in the state. In addition, just 15 minutes from the parking area, the trail is routed through the bottom of a deep valley filled with blooming mule's ear, literally a wall of green spanning miles. At dusk it was one of the prettiest places I'd seen all year.

Devil's Kitchen

This is the only hike on the list whose trailhead isn't right off Highway 89, the main route through the park. The trailhead for Devil's Kitchen is at Drakesbad, in the remote Warner Valley, best reached out of Chester. The hike is easy but adventurous, a two-mile tromp one way into a barren, volcanic pocket of steaming vents and boiling pots. Hike another quarter mile up Hot Springs Creek to discover a small, pretty waterfall.

Directions: From the Bay Area, take Interstate 80 north to Interstate 505, then go north to Interstate 5. Follow Interstate 5 north about 95 miles to Red Bluff and take the Highway 36/Lassen Park exit. Drive east on Highway 36 for 47 miles to Highway 89. Continue 4.5 miles north on Highway 89 to the park entrance. **Fees:** A $5 national park entrance fee is charged. Campsite fees are $8 to $12 per night. **Pets:** Leashed pets are permitted in developed areas only (campgrounds, parking lots, park roads). Pets are not permitted on trails, in meadows, streams, lakes, or campfire areas. **Maps:** Get a complimentary map at the park entrance or by writing to the front desk, Lassen Volcanic National Park, at the address below. To obtain a topographic map of the area, ask for Lassen Peak from the USGS. **Contact:** Lassen Volcanic National Park, P.O. Box 100, Mineral, CA 96063; (530) 595-4444 or fax (530) 595-3262. **Locator:** Lassen Volcanic National Park (B3-C3).

• Featured Trip •

★ Annadel State Park

Rated: The Top 5 Areas to Mountain Bike, 281

An example of an ideal spot rarely visited by the masses, especially in the fall, is Annadel State Park. It offers a 35-mile network of trails for hikers and equestrians and good black bass fishing, yet it's only an hour's drive north of San Francisco, just east of Santa Rosa.

The park spans almost 5,000 acres of rolling hills, meadows, and woodlands, and is cut by several creeks. A secret is that two miles inside the park border is Lake Ilsanjo, a good spot for bass and bluegill fishing that will always remain that way because you have to hike for an hour to reach it. Most people are not willing to hike to fish, and that's just fine for those who are. They know that the lake record here for bass is a nine-pounder, and that every spring, anglers tangle with bass of similar proportions.

If you like to explore by foot or horseback, then this park is for you. My favorite hike here is the Lake Trail to Lake Ilsanjo (2.5 miles), where I stop to fish, then return via steep Steve's Trail (three miles). Horses are allowed on the trails, and although the creeks do not flow year-round, there is usually plenty of water available for the animals. Be sure to carry a canteen for yourself.

While camping is not allowed in Annadel State Park, if you want to make a weekend trip out of it, there are some nearby campgrounds available. The western edge of the park is bordered by Spring Lake (which is stocked with trout) and its 30-site campground.

The rangers here say that a few herds of wild pigs run loose at the park, rooting, snorting, and doing what wild pigs do. Their reputation as fighters is overblown; I've been face to face with several wild boars and, given a choice, they always run. Just don't box them in. This wild country is also home to deer and fox, although sightings are infrequent.

The terrain varies, so use care in selecting a hike. How much sun each respective area receives determines the kind of plant and tree growth it can sustain, so in just a few hours, you can hike through forests of Douglas fir to meadows and chaparral areas. A dozen plant communities thrive here, as do the bass in the lake. Arriving at Ilsanjo after an early morning hike seems like a perfect way to start a day.

Directions: Drive north on U.S. 101 to Santa Rosa and take the Highway 12 exit. Head east on Highway 12, which eventually becomes Farmers Lane, until you reach Montgomery Drive. Turn right on Montgomery Drive and continue southeast. Stay on Montgomery when it merges with Mission Drive. Go past the Spring Lake Dam to Channel Drive. Turn right and proceed to the park. **Fees:** A $2 per vehicle day-use fee is charged. Maps can be purchased for a nominal fee from a machine at the park. **Pets:** Horses are allowed on trails, but dogs are not. **Fishing tip:** Purple plastic worms are tops for the bass at Lake Ilsanjo, and bluegill prefer small bait like mealworms or red worms. **Hours:** Annadel is open from sunrise to sunset. **Camping:** Campsites are available at adjacent Spring Lake Park Campground on a first-come, first-served basis for a fee of $14 per night. For information, phone (707) 539-8092. **Contact:** Annadel State Park, 6201 Channel Drive, Santa Rosa, CA 95409, (707) 539-3911 or (707) 938-1519. California State Parks, Silverado District, (707) 938-1519. **Locator:** ANNADEL STATE PARK (D1).

• FEATURED TRIP •

ARMSTRONG REDWOODS STATE RESERVE

Rated: Some of the Tallest Trees in California

Ever wish you were seated in the middle of a cool redwood forest, away from the madness of the city? If you're willing to drive 90 minutes north from SAN FRANCISCO, you can get exactly that.

ARMSTRONG REDWOODS STATE RESERVE is the answer, a jungle of some of the tallest trees remaining in California, including several that have lived for more than a thousand years. The reserve sits adjacent to the Austin Creek Recreation Area, so you can turn your sojourn into a full-scale camping and hiking expedition.

This area is tucked away just northwest of SANTA ROSA, a relatively short distance from the Bay Area. Yet despite the relative ease of getting here, you can still capture the sense of total privacy that comes from being in the midst of giant redwood trees. Some 5,000 acres of wildland, filled primarily with redwoods, tan oaks, and madrone, provide just that.

The area was designated as a redwood reserve way back in the 1890s by a logger, of all people. While other timber interests were cutting wide swaths through California's giant redwoods, logger James Armstrong set this area aside. Armstrong was one of the few loggers who recognized the beauty and natural value of the forests, as well as the lumber value, and that is why this reserve bears his name.

Campers will find two choices: 24 drive-in sites at tiny Redwood Lake, and four prime hike-in areas. The drive-in family campground near the lake sits at the end of a steep, winding two-laner that climbs to 1,000 feet and cannot be negotiated by trailers or RVs. The other alternative is to head to the primitive campsites at Gilliam Creek, Mannings Flat, and Tom King Campground, all accessible via short hikes on the park's trail system.

A bonus is that the trails follow the streams that cut through the park. Austin Creek, Gilliam Creek, Schoolhouse Creek, and Fife Creek provide water sources for backpackers (boil or filter all water before drinking). In addition, horses are allowed on the trails so equestrians can share in the redwood beauty with their steeds doing all the puffing. Austin Creek, a tributary to the RUSSIAN RIVER, is home to a wide variety of animals and birds. In the fall, when water is a bit scarce, deer, raccoons, and squirrels are likely to be seen near the watersheds. On rare occasions, bobcats and wild pigs have been spotted.

Tiny REDWOOD LAKE, which can be reached by car and has an adjacent campground, provides bass and bluegill fishing, but the fish tend to be runts.

Not the trees. The redwoods that grow in the ARMSTRONG REDWOODS STATE RESERVE are among the tallest anywhere.

Directions: The easiest route from San Francisco is to head north on U.S. 101, exiting on River Road, five miles north of Santa Rosa. Head west on River Road for 20 miles to Guerneville and take a right on Armstrong Woods Road. **Fees:** A $5 access fee is charged per vehicle. Walk-in access is free. There is a $12 fee for drive-in camping and a $7 fee for backcountry camping. Please obtain a backcountry permit. **Dogs:** Dogs are permitted in Armstrong Redwoods State Reserve, but they must be leashed. **Supplies:** Last-minute shopping can be done in Guerneville. **Contact:** Armstrong Redwoods State Reserve, 17000 Armstrong Woods Road, Guerneville, CA 95446, (707) 869-2015. California State Parks, Russian River–Mendocino District, (707) 865-2391. **Locator:** ARMSTRONG REDWOODS STATE RESERVE (D0).

• FEATURED TRIP •

MOUNT ST. HELENA

Rated: The Top 10 Chances for Bay Area Snow, 288

You could search across America in early spring and not find a better hike than at MOUNT ST. HELENA, just north of the Bay Area.

It's the complete package, a mountain experience with incredible views, yet the trail up is nothing like the buttkicker effort required to reach most mountaintops. The entire hike can be pulled off in four hours. The air is cool and fresh, and when there are light winds out of the north, the views are spectacular in all directions. On a perfect day, you can even see MOUNT SHASTA to the north, 192 miles away.

In fact, it's a good idea to bring binoculars and a map of Northern California with you, then see how many distant spots you can identify. The most obvious peaks are MOUNT TAMALPAIS and MOUNT DIABLO to the south, and Snow Mountain to the north (located north of CLEAR LAKE), but that's only a start. To the east, it is possible to make out the Sutter Buttes near COLUSA, and on good days, the Sierra Buttes, Mount Round Top, and the adjoining white-flecked Sierra Crest on the horizon. Looking north, the outline of MOUNT LASSEN is within range.

MOUNT ST. HELENA is located at the northern head of the Napa Valley, and many people make the hike as a side trip while visiting CALISTOGA for the weekend. But the trip provides enough rewards to make it a focus point.

The hike up requires a climb of 2,068 feet over the course of five miles, topping out at the summit at 4,343 feet. Most hikers can make the round-trip in about four hours, that is, 2.5 hours to the top, and 1.5 hours for the return back down. Some choose to take longer, but the point is that the gradient doesn't require what feels like an endless ascent to nowhere land.

Much of the trail is an abandoned ranch road, graded for a steady ascent, with just two steep sections. The latter of the two is right near the summit, where the payoff is so close that you don't mind the investment in sweat equity. When you get near the summit, the last part of the route does require a good huff and a puff, but it's short and before you know it, you'll be standing on top, enjoying one of the best views available anywhere.

The trailhead is located about eight miles north of CALISTOGA on the left side of Highway 29. The road is quite twisty as it rises out of the Napa Valley, but even then, the trailhead is obvious on the left side of the road.

From here, the route starts out as a standard hiking trail through the woods, and no mountain bikes are permitted on this section. Here's an insider's note: If you drive a quarter mile north on Highway 29, bikers will find a fire road that provides legal access to the mountain slopes.

For hikers, the trail starts climbing, then rises above the woods and meets a fire road. From here on up, the habitat is primarily brush and chaparral, and while it isn't pretty, the immediate surroundings are not a primary concern. What is of note, however, are the views. With each step, they get better and better.

Since the views are the payoff, it is critical to go only when they are a sure thing. That means in late winter and spring, from February through early May, when north winds between storms often blow through California and clear the skies of clouds, haze, and smoke. By summer, haze reduces visibility a great deal, obliterating the distant scenes, and by winter, rising smoke from Central Valley farmers burning off rice stubble often does the same.

It is also critical to pack all the water you will need for the entire trip. None is available anywhere along the route. I recommend carrying a two-quart canteen, and plan on drinking all two quarts. You'll need it.

In addition to plenty of water, be certain to carry a daypack with high-energy food, a change of shirts, and a windbreaker. What often occurs is that during the hike up to the summit, people start sweating, drenching their shirts. Then once on top, they face a surprise cold breeze and are chilled to the bone in their wet shirts. Such discomfort quickly eliminates the joy and wonder that a spectacular lookout can provide.

Another factor in timing are temperatures. Often in the late winter and early spring, the weather on the mountain is ideal between storms, ranging from lows in the 40s to highs in the 60s. In the summer, it gets hot here, commonly in the high 80s and 90s, and with virtually no shade on most of the route, you need to be a human camel to even have a shot at enjoying yourself.

Even as late as March, there is a chance for a rare bonus of snow if a cold front sweeps through Northern California. For the most part, it takes a temperature of 47 or 48 degrees during a rainstorm in San Francisco for there to be a possibility of snow on the summit at Mount St. Helena. If the temperature drops to 44 or 45 degrees during a rain in San Francisco, then the top thousand feet of Mount St. Helena can get a dusting.

But snowstorms here are rare events. What you get at Mount St. Helena is a great mountain hike with glorious views. The experience can make you glow for weeks.

Contact: Robert Louis Stevenson State Park c/o Bothe–Napa Valley State Park, (707) 942-4575; California State Parks, Silverado District, (707) 938-1519. **Locator:** Mount St. Helena (D1).

• FEATURED TRIP •

Grouse Lakes Area

Rated: Best One-Day Trip in the Sierra

A lot of people complain about this planet, but if you look at the options, hey, it's still the best one around.

If you have any doubts, let me tell you about a special place in the heart of the Sierra Nevada, where anybody of any age can visit and experience the full exhilaration of the great outdoors.

It is called the Grouse Lakes Area, an 18,000-acre wildland in Tahoe National Forest, featuring 125 lakes sprinkled in a mountain landscape of granite and pine. It is located 40 miles east of Auburn off Interstate 80 near Yuba Gap, with elevations ranging from 5,000 to 7,500 feet, all of it sculptured in the classic Sierra style.

It is accessible to anybody for hiking, camping, boating with a raft or canoe, biking, backpacking, fishing, or just driving in for a picnic, leaning against a big pine and watching the chipmunks. It is a great destination for stellar day hikes, heading to excellent drive-to campgrounds, or strapping on a backpack and venturing to the beyond, discovering lake after lake on trails that are as easy as any in the Sierra.

On one recent visit, after pulling into camp, the first thing I noticed was the scent of pine duff in the air, and it took me back to my first visit here 25 years ago. It was just the same then, and I remembered the initial excitement of the chance of discovering so many beautiful places within such close reach.

The drive in provides dozens of options for starting your trip. From Interstate 80 at Yuba Gap, you take the Highway 20 exit and drive to Bowman Road. From here, it's a right turn and then entry into your destined wonderland. Bowman Road and its spur roads provide drive-to access to a series of lakes, including Weaver Lake, McMurray Lake, Bowman Lake, Sawmill Lake, Faucherie Lake, Catfish Lake, Jackson Lake, French Lake, Meadow Lake, Fuller Lake, Lindsey Lake, Carr Lake, and Feeley Lake.

Many of these lakes are small, beautiful, and perfect for plopping in an inflatable raft or kayak, or a canoe, and just paddling around or fishing a bit for trout. Most also have small campgrounds, as well as trailheads that offer easy access for hiking or biking to many other nearby lakes.

After parking at Carr Lake, we chose to hike past Feeley Lake and Hidden Lake for a picnic at Island Lake, a clear, deep blue lake set in a mountain bowl of sheet-smooth, glacial-carved granite. Guess how long it took to get there? Three days? Twelve hours? Wrong. Would you believe about 45 minutes? Yep. This is how it is out here. This is the best destination for newcomers who desire easy hiking in beautiful surroundings.

There are a lot of bonuses as well. Unlike land governed by the state or national park systems, you can walk with your dog here, and for my little bearlike pup, Bartolius Fluffbucket Snowpuff Bart-Dog, it was his first hike in the Sierra. Unlike the south Sierra, known for its dramatic canyons and high ridges, the trails here are relatively flat, making the trip pretty easy, especially for multiday backpack trips. And there is no beauty like that of the pristine lakes of the Sierra.

Many stellar hiking trips are possible in the area. Hiking Grouse Ridge, for instance, provides access to a series of small but gorgeous lakes—Sawmill Lake, Rock Lake, Middle Lake, Crooked Lakes, and Milk Lake—and sweeping views of the Sierra's high granite beauty. Milk Lake is an awesome sight, as deep a blue as LAKE TAHOE, but many of the lakes are tinted azure blue due to their extreme clarity.

While the area is not a designated wilderness, it does have wilderness qualities. For backpackers, one of the better trips is to take off from Grouse Ridge and hike east on Sand Ridge for about five miles to the Five Lakes Basin, which is sprinkled with a series of tiny but gorgeous little lakes.

For the most part, the fishing is okay for small brook trout and rainbow trout across the GROUSE LAKES AREA. It's not great, not bad, with the best prospects in the region at Bowman Lake, Fuller Lake, and Faucherie Lake. Since insects, not minnows, provide the primary forage in these stark, clear lakes, fly-fishing or using a fly with a bobber gets far better results than using small lures or bait.

For families, what often works best is just playing on the water, especially with inflatables or cartop boats at one of the drive-to lakes. Since there are no boat ramps, it is ideal for those looking for quiet waters where they can float and paddle around without having to worry about any Jet Ski–type personal watercraft or ski boats.

But when you're out amid this kind of beauty, with so many pretty lakes and easy hiking trails nearby, it can be difficult to worry about anything.

Directions: From Interstate 80 at Yuba Gap, take the Highway 20 exit and drive to Bowman Road. Turn right on Bowman Road and note signs on the spur roads leading to a series of lakes. **Maps:** The U.S. Forest Service has published a map detailing all fishing waters, campsites, Forest Service roads, and backpack trails. Ask for the map of Tahoe National Forest from the Office of Information, U.S. Forest Service, 630 Sansome Street, San Francisco, CA 94111. **Contact:** To obtain recreation flyers on the area, contact

Tahoe National Forest, Nevada City Ranger District, P.O. Box 6003, Nevada City, CA 95959, (530) 265-4538 or fax (530) 478-6109. **Locator:** GROUSE LAKES AREA (D3).

• FEATURED TRIP •

★ STEVENS TRAIL

Rated: Best Hike in the Sierra Foothills

For most people in the Bay Area, the Central Valley foothill country is the black hole of California recreation, a place you have to drive past in order to reach TAHOE and the SIERRA NEVADA.

I have found, however, that the grind on Interstate 80 can be broken up by a stellar walk, and it is located right where most people are ready to take a break from the drive and stretch their legs while en route to North Tahoe.

Called the STEVENS TRAIL, it is located near COLFAX, where the valley oak woodlands give way to the alpine zone, and the surprise trailhead is only a one-minute drive from the highway. The hike features a waterfall, drop-dead gorgeous views of a river canyon, tons of wildflowers in season, and once the water warms up a bit, a chance to go swimming in the remote SOUTH FORK AMERICAN RIVER.

Every region of California has many recreation secrets, and so it is in the Central Valley. The foothills are loaded with a series of great lakes for boating, camping, and fishing, several deep river canyons, and the most diverse wildflower blooms in the state. There are also scads of deer still here, loading up on the wild grasses and budding plants and trees, waiting for summer before commencing their annual migration to the Sierra.

Most people cruising I-80 enjoy the views of the green foothills every spring, but that is as far as it gets. They drive the highway hard and fast, and grind out the hours as a required payment in order to get to TAHOE. But next time you're up this way, when you reach COLFAX and see the North Canyon Way exit on the right, go ahead and take it. Turn left at the stop sign, drive less than a mile to the trailhead on the left side of the road, and prepare to take one of the best driving breaks you've ever had.

You have three great choices: 1) An hour round-trip walk to a surprise waterfall; 2) A 90-minute round-trip hike to an overlook of the river canyon; or 3) A 9.5-mile round-trip tromp to the bottom of the canyon and the banks of the secluded SOUTH FORK AMERICAN RIVER.

Most trails that enter the deep river canyons of the foothills, such as the nearby South Fork American and Middle Fork Feather, are so steep that you practically need to bring an oxygen tank. That's because they were constructed 150 years ago by gold miners who believed the shortest distance between two points is a straight line, and in turn, made the trails virtually straight up and straight down. Not so with the STEVENS TRAIL.

It was built just a few years ago under the direction of the Bureau of Land Management with hiking in mind, not gold. That is why it has the easiest gradient of any of the extensive canyon hiking trails in the foothills, a great plus.

The parking area is a simple dirt lot with a BLM trailhead sign, and access is free. A one-page map brochure of the STEVENS TRAIL can be obtained from the BLM, but none were available at the trailhead.

When you first park, the ominous roar of passing cars on the nearby interstate might quell your hopes a bit, but the sounds of the highway are left completely behind in just 10 minutes of walking. The trail starts by running downhill at a moderate grade, entering a mixed forest of oak, fir, and pine with a lush understory, so thick that you are boring a hole through the vegetation, shaded and lush. It's easy and fun, and you soon arrive at a small stream. As you cross it with a few hops over rocks, Interstate 80 will seem a million miles away.

After about 15 minutes, you cross another stream, then emerge from the forest and intersect with a dirt road. Here you turn right and walk on the road for a short distance, reaching a canyon ridge. The trail then breaks off to the left, and the real adventure begins.

Part 1

The Stevens Trail starts a traverse down the canyon, and as you go, the variety of wildflowers is astonishing. Poppies, paintbrush, blue dicks, buttercups, wallflowers, monkey flowers, lanterns, blue-eyed grass, wild radish, redbud, dogwood . . . and you don't need to be a botanist to enjoy them.

After about a quarter mile (1.5 miles from the trailhead, about 30 minutes of walking from your car), keep a lookout for a small stream that crosses the trail. Though it may not look like much, if you explore upstream on a spur trail for about 100 feet you will find a surprise waterfall. This is a thin, silvery cascade that runs through a rock crevice and into a small pool. You can't see it from the trail because it is completely secreted by vegetation.

Returning to the parking area from here entails a 600-foot climb over 1.5 miles, a 30- to 45-minute walk for most.

Part 2

If you keep walking, it is another half hour or so with an additional 200-foot descent to a dramatic lookout of the South Fork American River Canyon. From above, the river is gorgeous, filled with fresh white, oxygenated white-water rapids tumbling into deep, azure blue pools.

As you forge onward, you will find a series of lookouts, best discovered by looking downriver. The canyon walls here rise about 2,000 feet above the river, and being surrounded by wild and untouched country will make you feel two million miles away from Interstate 80.

Part 3

As long as you've started, you might as well finish—that's right, walk it out, all the way to the bottom to find a beautiful streamside setting for a picnic. There are several deep pools in the South Fork American that can make for good swimming holes in warm weather, but the water can be so cold that just putting your big toe in will turn it instantly into an ice cube. Regardless, you will now feel three million miles away from Interstate 80.

To return to the parking area requires a 1,200-foot climb over 4.5 miles. For the most part, the trail gradient is outstanding, allowing you to set a good pace, with just two stretches that are short enough to get hearts thumping. Most people take 3 1/2 to 4 hours for the entire trip.

When you get back in your car and continue down the interstate, you might notice that your driving has slowed a bit, that the urgency is gone. Why hurry? No matter what you have planned for the rest of your trip, it will be tough to beat what you've already experienced.

Directions: From Interstate 80 in Colfax, turn right at the North Canyon Way exit. Turn left at the stop sign and drive less than a mile to the trailhead on the left side of the road. **Contact:** For a one-page brochure with a map, write Stevens Trail, Bureau of Land Management, 63 Natoma Street, Folsom, CA 95630, or phone (916) 985-4474. **Locator:** STEVENS TRAIL (D3).

• FEATURED TRIP •

MARIN HEADLANDS

Rated: The Top 50 Parks, 7; The Top 6 One-Way Hikes Using Public Transportation, 32; The Top 10 Strolls, 40; The Top 9 Doggy Getaway Ideas, 196; The Top 14 Places to Fly Kites, 389

Somewhere in the course of time, you see this amazing film clip or photograph—an overhead view of the GOLDEN GATE BRIDGE with a backdrop of the SAN FRANCISCO skyline. It makes the Bay Area look like a world apart, and as you stare at the picture, you eventually figure out the photographer could only be standing in one place: the MARIN HEADLANDS.

This stirs your curiosity, and from there comes the inspiration to make that first trip—the desire to stand in the same place as the photographer who snapped that picture. Then it takes only a few hours to discover that the MARIN HEADLANDS is an easy-to-reach destination where there are so many ways to spend an afternoon that you'll find yourself coming back again and again.

Most of these adventures are available year-round: hawk watching on hilltops; hiking along pristine bluffs, valleys, and beaches; exploring former missile-launching sites; fishing for free at a pier where no license is required; visiting a museum with hands-on exhibits for children; watching sea lions and harbor seals play tag at POINT BONITA; picnicking at a wheelchair-accessible picnic site; camping with a spectacular ocean sunset for a backdrop—and there are many other options.

You can always just tromp up to a lookout, maybe that famous one, and bring your camera along to record the event.

To make your trip easier, the Park Service has completed a new Headlands Visitor Center at Fort Barry Chapel. Hiking maps, field guides, and event schedules are available, as well as rangers who will answer questions or provide directions to your chosen venture.

Here is a guide to the best of them:

MISSILE SITE

During the Cold War, the MARIN HEADLANDS was chosen as a missile-launching site because of its strategic defensive position at the entrance of SAN FRANCISCO BAY. Now it is a popular visitor attraction, with two underground concrete pits, missile assembly buildings, and guard dog kennels. On the annual Headlands Day, park volunteers and Army veterans conduct simulated missile raisings each hour.

BIRDS OF PREY

Each fall, Hawk Hill is one of California's top viewing areas for raptors, as thousands of hawks and other raptors pass by during their migrations.

HARBOR SEALS AND SEA LIONS
Harbor seals play games at POINT BONITA, jumping in and out of the water. In the coves, such as those just east of POINT BONITA, sea lions will sometimes swim about the shallows and play peek-a-boo with beach strollers.

HORSES AND HORSESHOES
Mi-Wok Stables is open for self-guided tours. Any stray horseshoes can be kept as good luck charms. Guided trail rides are available from the private concessionaire there. For information, phone (415) 383-8048.

GREAT HIKE
The walk to the Point Bonita Lighthouse is easy, yet it has great views of the mouth of SAN FRANCISCO BAY and the ocean. The sight is spectacular at night under a full moon.

FAMILY MUSEUM
Hands-on exhibits are ideal for children, including a demonstration on marine life in SAN FRANCISCO BAY and a crawl-through underbay tunnel.

WEEKEND PICNIC
A picnic area is available near what is called Battery Wallace. The views of the GOLDEN GATE BRIDGE and passing ships are fantastic. The picnic area includes a windbreak and tables designed so visitors in wheelchairs can sit right at the table.

SUNSET CAMPING
Hawk Camp is a primitive setting located just above Gerbode Valley. It is surrounded by a small stand of trees, yet there are views of both SAN FRANCISCO and ocean sunsets. Camping is free, but reservations are required; phone (415) 331-1540.

FREE FISHING AND BOATING
Both a free fishing pier and a free boat ramp are available at Fort Baker. In the fall months, salmon are sometimes caught from the pier as they migrate past on their journey from the ocean to points upstream.

Directions: From U.S. 101 just north of the Golden Gate Bridge, take the Alexander Avenue exit, loop underneath the highway, heading west, and take the wide paved road to the right (look for the sign that says Marin Headlands). Continue for one mile, take a right on the downhill fork, and follow the direction signs for two miles to the Marin Headlands Visitor Center. **Maps:** To obtain maps, write to the Golden Gate National Recreation Area, Marin Headlands, Building 1056, Fort Cronkite, Sausalito, CA 94965. **Fees:** Entrance and use of all facilities are free. **Contact:** Marin Headlands Visitor Center, (415) 331-1540. **Locator:** MARIN HEADLANDS (E1a).

• FEATURED TRIP •

MARIN'S HIDDEN ROAD TO THE OUTDOORS

Rated: The Top 50 Parks, 7; The Top 4 Marin County Hikes, 19; The Top 12 Hike-to Streams, 24; The Top 15 Surprise Hikes in the Rain, 28; The Top 7 Hikes with a Dog, 30; The Top 20 Hike-to Waterfalls, 187; The Top 9 Doggy Getaway Ideas, 196; The Top 10 Scenic Back Roads, 198; The Top 14 Places to Fly Kites, 389

The Bay Area has plenty of unique, hidden back roads, but the best just might be a little winding two-laner in Marin County, west of SAN RAFAEL. It's Marin's Hidden Road to the Outdoors—we're talking about a road that provides access to three lakes, 15 trailheads for secluded hikes, a golf course, and much, much more.

The route is called Bolinas-Fairfax

Road. It's pretty enough to enjoy on a Saturday evening drive or a Sunday morning bike cruise, but you can take things one giant step forward by using it as a jump-off for hiking or fishing trips.

Getting there is simple enough: From U.S. 101, take Sir Francis Drake Boulevard west into FAIRFAX, then turn left onto Bolinas-Fairfax Road.

That is where your journey starts. After leaving FAIRFAX and passing the Meadow Club Golf Course after two miles, the road twists its way up to a 600-foot elevation. Another mile and you will start seeing little turnouts dotting the side of the road. Look closer. Each of those turnouts marks a hiking trail, with the trail-head nearby.

There are 15 trails between FAIRFAX and BOLINAS. You can just head down the trail for a little in-and-outer, or manufacture a longer trip by hooking up with the network of trails that are linked in the Marin backcountry.

It can make for very quiet and secluded hiking. If there are no other cars parked at a turnout, you will know that there is no one on the trail but you.

Your mission, should you decide to accept it, can be made easier by obtaining a detailed map of the area.

Two of the best hikes in the late summer and fall months start on either side of ALPINE LAKE, which is about a five-mile drive west of FAIRFAX. You should park at the dam, then take your pick.

The easier hike heads north and follows a gentle grade downhill along the section of Lagunitas Creek that connects Alpine Lake to Kent Lake. Having a picnic at creekside, amid the big oaks, you might feel like you're in Tennessee wilderness, not just five miles from the Marin suburbs.

If you want more of a challenge and some good views of ALPINE LAKE, cross the dam, and right where the road takes a hairpin turn, look for the trailhead for the Cataract Trail. You can put together a loop hike that zigzags its way to almost 1,700 feet, then drops back down along the southeast shore of ALPINE LAKE.

In the fall and spring, after the rains come, another good hike can take you to a little-known series of waterfalls. The trail starts about a mile past the golf course at the first large parking area on the left side of the road. Cross the road from the parking area, and with map in hand to help you make the proper turns, you can arrive at Carson Falls in an hour's walk.

If hiking is not for you, there are three lakes along Bolinas-Fairfax Road. The most impressive is ALPINE, a long, deep lake bordered by forest. Fishing, however, is often poor. No boats are allowed, either.

The other lakes, which are reached by taking the Sky Oaks Road turnoff, are BON TEMPE and LAGUNITAS. BON TEMPE is stocked with rainbow trout in the fall and winter, and LAGUNITAS has been converted to a special wild trout lake.

No boats, rafts, float tubes, or water contact of any kind are permitted at the lakes, which is something of a ripoff. Marin Water District officials have told fishers that they fear the spread of a water plant called hydrilla, but that is absolute nonsense.

Hydrilla can only be spread by boats if it is somehow stuck on the bottom of somebody's watercraft, then comes off and starts growing in a lake.

It's a potential problem at every lake, but the chances are so infinitesimal that other water districts virtually ignore it. At Contra Loma Reservoir near ANTIOCH, which is part of the State Water Project, a sign has simply been posted asking boaters to please clear their boats and propellers of any weeds. That warning has been sufficient since Contra Loma was constructed in 1969. Enough said.

The Marin lakes are all pretty, primarily because they are hidden among forested hillsides. The entire area is like that, hidden and secluded. Driving along Bolinas-Fairfax Road helps unveil these secrets.

Directions: From U.S. 101 in Marin, take the Sir Francis Drake exit and drive six miles west to the town of Fairfax. Turn left at the first gas station in Fairfax on Pacheco Road and then make an immediate right onto Broadway Avenue. Drive one block, turn left on Bolinas Road, and head west about 1.5 miles to the Mount Tamalpais State Park entrance. **Maps:** The best map of the area can be purchased from the Olmsted Brothers Map Company. It details all roads, trails, creeks, and lakes, and includes contour lines. **Contact:** Olmsted Brothers, P.O. Box 5351, Berkeley, CA 94705; (510) 658-6534. **Locator:** FAIRFAX (E1a).

• FEATURED TRIP •

MOUNT TAMALPAIS

Rated: The Top 25 Hikes, 2; The Top 50 Parks, 7; The Top 4 Marin County Hikes, 19; The Top 12 Hike-to Streams, 24; The Top 15 Surprise Hikes in the Rain, 28; The Top 6 One-Way Hikes Using Public Transportation, 32; The Top 4 One-Way Hikes Using a Shuttle Car, 34; The Top 10 Strolls, 40; The Top 6 Coastal Camps, 115; The Top 10 Spots for a First Kiss, 180; The Top 10 Spots to Go on a Date, 182; The Top 10 Overnight Locations, 185; The Top 10 Chances for Bay Area Snow, 288; The Top 14 Places to Fly Kites, 389; The Top 4 Places to Sky Watch, 394

A mantle of fog hangs like a cape most days off the western slopes of MOUNT TAMALPAIS. But once you get above the fog near the summit, you'll discover a heaven-like setting for sunsets, beautiful drives, and short hikes.

I have witnessed one of the most breathtaking sunsets imaginable from near the summit. Looking off to the west, I saw cloud layers, a layer of broken cumulus out to sea at 10,000 feet, and a layer of stratus (fog) at 2,000 feet streaming in from the ocean. Late evening sunbeams were boring rays through the cumulus like something out of *The Ten Commandments,* and when they hit the fog, the light refracted gold for miles.

As each minute passed and the sun dropped, the color changed as if by command from a great artist, with a giant brush painting yellows, then oranges, then pinks, and finally grays, as the sun disappeared in the fog layer on the horizon on nature's greatest canvas. No wonder John Muir named this his favorite place in all the Bay Area.

MOUNT TAMALPAIS (2,571 feet) is the big mountain in Marin, of course, and the silhouette of its peak against the sky can be spotted from many parts of the Bay Area. Although three peaks in the Bay Area are taller—MOUNT HAMILTON, MOUNT DIABLO, and MISSION PEAK—it is MOUNT TAM that provides the most wondrous experiences by far, the best views, and the best hikes of them all.

The experience starts with the drive, climbing on the Panoramic Highway on the south flank of the mountain, leaving behind the typically sunny climate of the North Bay and disappearing under the leading edge of the coastal fog. At this point, newcomers can be terribly disappointed, thinking the fog will ruin the day by blocking the views and making it cold and damp, sometimes even downright wet. Nope.

Keep driving up the mountain, and usually between 1,500 and 2,000 feet, you will suddenly pop above the fog layer. It often looks like a pearlescent sea, calm, soft, and always a gorgeous sight. Once above the fog, you can pick one of the trailheads along the road, often anywhere from Pantoll on up, but the mandatory trip is all the way to the top, with the road leading right up to the base of the summit, dead-ending at a parking area at the trailhead (there's a $5 parking fee).

From here it is a 15- or 20-minute walk to the top, very short, less than a quarter mile, but the trail climbs 330 feet, steep enough to get most anybody puffing. An old lookout station is perched right on top of the summit, and most visitors will try to find a spot to sit as close to the top as possible, then be still, absorb the setting, and watch the colors change out to the west during sunsets.

But the views are spectacular most any time. When there is no fog, unbelievable miles of ocean come into view, an expanse so wide that when you hold your arms out, palms up, you swear you are both taking it all in and sensing the curvature of the earth on the horizon.

Looking in other directions, it is just as spectacular. SAN FRANCISCO BAY, below to the south and west, appears much more blue than from any other lookout, and the number of islands often comes as a surprise. From here, you can see why some people say it reminds them of the Mediterranean Sea. At night, the sparkling lights of the bridges and cities around the darkened bay can sometimes make the setting seem like an apparition.

Many hikes on MOUNT TAMALPAIS can match even this sight. There are hundreds of miles of hiking trails in the area, crossing land managed by MOUNT TAMALPAIS STATE PARK, the Marin Municipal Water District, Golden Gate National Recreation Area, and MUIR WOODS.

The best for views on clear days are the easy walks on the Matt Davis Trail and to O'Rourke's Bench, and on foggy days, to the summit, with a possible side trip to Inspiration Point.

The Matt Davis Trail, which overlaps with the Coastal Trail for a short stretch, starts at the Pantoll Trailhead and extends for a mile or so across open foothill grassland country, with the ocean off to the west for as far as you can see. The elevation is about 1,000 feet, and the views are truly stellar on clear days. The walk is easy, more of a stroll than a hike.

If this is fogged in, the answer is to head higher, then see where the fog line ends. The drive to nearby Rock Springs Trailhead usually provides an answer, which is to take the easy 0.3-mile walk out to O'Rourke's Bench (with five other trails available at Rock Springs). O'Rourke's Bench is set on a knoll at 2,071 feet, usually above the fog. It's a dramatic overlook, and next to the bench you will find a plaque that reads: "Give me these hills and the friends I love. I ask no other heaven. To our dad O'Rourke, in joyous celebration of his 76th birthday, Feb. 25, 1927. From the friends to whom he showed this heaven."

At times the fog line is right exactly at O'Rourke's Bench, and it seems almost eerie as it undulates above and below you.

Drawn by East Peak Summit, many folks bypass this stroll and instead head straight to the East Peak Summit parking area. A popular option here is making the 1.3-mile walk out on a dirt road to Inspiration Point (2,040 feet), with jaw-dropping views of San Pablo Bay and beyond. Many people make this short hike in the early evening, then return and climb the short distance to the East Peak Lookout to soak in the sunset.

Whatever you choose to do, you will discover why so many believe the MOUNT TAMALPAIS highlands to be the prettiest spot in the Bay Area. It has the most profound sense of place.

Directions: From U.S. 101 in Marin, take the Stinson Beach/Highway 1 exit. Drive west to the stoplight at the T intersection. Turn left and drive about 2.5 miles uphill to Panoramic Highway. Turn right and drive 5.5 miles to the Pantoll Ranger Station (this is the parking area for the Bootjack Trailhead). Turn right on Pantoll Road and go 1.5 miles to the T intersection (this is the parking area for the Rock Springs Trailhead to reach O'Rourke's Bench). Turn right on Ridgecrest and continue to the East Peak. The road deadends at the parking area at the base of the summit. **Maps:** Maps can be obtained for $2 by contacting the Marin Municipal Water District, Sky Oaks Ranger Station, P.O. Box 865, Fairfax, CA 94978; (415) 459-5267. Complimentary maps or brochures are also available at the Pantoll Ranger Station in the state park or by calling the Golden Gate National Recreation Area at the number below. A premium, color trail map can be purchased from the Olmsted Brothers Map Company, P.O. Box 5351, Berkeley, CA 94705; (510) 658-6534. **Contact:** Mount Tamalpais State Park, Pantoll Ranger Station, (415) 388-2070; California State Parks, Marin District, (415) 893-1580; Golden Gate National Recreation Area, (415) 331-1540. **Locator:** MOUNT TAMALPAIS (E1a).

• FEATURED TRIP •

✷ MUIR WOODS NATIONAL MONUMENT

Rated: The Top 50 Parks, 7; The Top 10 Trips into the Redwoods, 36

There are two MUIR WOODS and they are about as far apart as the North and South Poles. One of them seems to have more people than trees. The trail is so heavily used that it is paved with asphalt—and your chance of seeing a deer is about as good as sighting Bigfoot. The whole place seems about as peaceful as a bowling alley.

The other MUIR WOODS, however, is a sanctuary, a cathedral of redwoods and ferns. It is a place where people are few and the only sound is that of a light breeze brushing through tree limbs. By the time you leave, the world feels fresh and clean again.

Both of these MUIR WOODS are in Marin County, tucked in a canyon on the slopes of MOUNT TAMALPAIS. Your approach to the park determines which one you visit.

For example, consider a typical visit on a summer day. When I arrived at noon, the two parking lots were jammed full, including four tour buses that were shooting people out like popcorn from a popper. The information stand and small store were crowded with visitors. The Bootjack Trail, the paved loop hike that travels along Redwood Creek on the valley floor, was more of a parade than a nature walk.

But then I turned right, taking the Ocean View/Panoramic Trail. While this trail is listed as the Ocean View Trail, most people call it the Panoramic Trail. It is listed as both on various maps and signs. Ironically, there is almost no ocean view. However, hike this trail and in less than a minute, you'll enter a different world. This is the Muir Woods where you can find peace and serenity.

The Ocean View/Panoramic Trail is one of the best-kept secrets in what is one of the West's most popular parklands. It can provide solitude and a good hike. From the valley floor of Muir Woods, the trail veers right and heads up the east side of the canyon. It is a steady grade, just enough to get most hikers puffing in a natural rhythm as they make the climb.

It is three miles before you clear the treetops and get a lookout over the entire valley—a sea of conifers—and glimpses of the Pacific Ocean to the southwest. In the meantime, you walk a trail that gets little traffic. Your worries begin to fall away, and no matter what your problems, all seems simple and pure.

There is another attraction as well. When you reach the canyon rim, you can take a quarter-mile detour to the town of Mountain Home, or turn right on the connecting trail that leads to the Tourist Club. Both serve ice-cold drinks, and nothing tastes better after the three-mile climb to the lookout. The Tourist Club is a premium destination because it has a redwood deck and offers a great view of Marin's wildlands.

The other trail option that provides a degree of solitude in Muir Woods is the Dipsea Trail, although it is a famous route among Bay Area hikers. This trail runs all the way to Stinson Beach, about four miles. The hiker follows a series of "ups and downs," passing a network of connecting trails on Mount Tamalpais.

August often seems the coldest month of the year here. When the Central Valley burns in 100-degree temperatures, nature's built-in air-conditioner fogs in the coast and sends chilly breezes eastward.

A unique feature of Muir Woods is that headquarters can be something of a United Nations. People from all over the world touring the Bay Area find the old-growth redwoods a special attraction.

There are two Muir Woods. You decide which one you want to visit.

Directions: From San Francisco, drive north on U.S. 101 to the Highway 1 exit. Continue to the stoplight and turn left on Shoreline Highway (Highway 1). Continue for a few miles and take the right fork on Panoramic Highway. From there, drive one mile and take the left lower road. Drive one mile to the Muir Woods parking area. All turns are well signed. **Maps:** Maps are available for a nominal fee. **User groups:** Hikers only are permitted. No mountain bikes, motorcycles, horses, or dogs (except seeing-eye dogs) are allowed. **Fees:** Entrance costs $2. **Contact:** Muir Woods Ranger Station, Muir Woods National Monument, Mill Valley, CA 94941, (415) 388-2596. **Locator:** Muir Woods (E1a).

• FEATURED TRIP •

★ OWL TRAIL

Rated: Best Walk to the Hidden Marin Coast

A short, easy hiking trail on the Marin coast is a perfect testimonial to why the Bay Area is the best metropolitan region in America for people who love the outdoors.

It's called the OWL TRAIL, and in the course of a few miles it provides incredible ocean views, an easy walk, a chance to see wildlife, a guarantee of spotting farm animals, access to a secluded rocky beach with tide pools—and one short, tricky section, great for kids and easy for adults, where you let yourself down a slick, steep 25-foot piece of trail by using a rope fixed into position.

What has kept the Bay Area great despite huge increases in population are its 250 parks and dedicated open-space areas and the thousands of hiking trails available at them. Many of these trails, the OWL TRAIL among them, are unsigned and remain secret.

The trailhead is located at the Muir Beach Overlook on Highway 1, about a half-hour drive from SAN FRANCISCO. After parking (access is free and two rest rooms are available), most all visitors make the five-minute walk on the trail out to the overlook, once a gunnery site and now one of the best lookouts on the Marin coast. On clear days, it provides a panoramic view of the ocean and nearby rocky coast, with the chance to see passing whales, ships, and fishing boats.

For most folks, that's the end of the trip. Little do they know that on the north side of the parking area is an obscure little footpath that starts out routed through coastal scrub, unsigned and unofficial-looking. After all, with such a dramatic view at the MUIR BEACH Overlook, how can you do any better? Just start walking, that's how.

According to my altimeter watch, the trail starts at 440 feet. Then, as you lateral down the hillside, the open ocean on your left descends 240 feet over the course of a mile to Slide Ranch. Views are excellent all along this section of trail. Hikers should wear long pants, not shorts, because portions of the trail have been narrowed a bit by the bordering chaparral.

At Slide Ranch, the sideshows begin. First you arrive at a row of giant coastal cypress trees, about 90 to 110 years old by my best estimate. It is here that two-foot-tall great horned owls reside and base their nightly patrols, though it is extremely unusual to see one in the daytime. The reason is because their feathers camouflage them almost perfectly against the bark of the cypress. I once saw a big owl land in a cypress, then sit motionless, but I could not actually spot it until I was within 10 feet.

The trail continues through Slide Ranch, a hamlet of wood houses and miniature farms, complete with goats, chickens, and even ducks bobbing around in a tiny pond. Youngsters new to such close-up encounters with animals will be fascinated by the experience.

From here, it is another three-quarters of a mile down to the beach. To prevent erosion, some of the path has been sprinkled with hay. As you head down, you will suddenly come to a short, steep section of trail that is more like a chute. Here's where the fun begins: You grab on to a rope, set in a fixed position to aid hikers, then work your way down. It takes just a moment, and there is nothing else like it on any trail in the Bay Area. Be sure to allow only one person to use the rope at a time; with two people at once, the actions of one could upset those of another.

The rope descends to the beach, a rock-strewn piece of coast with stacks, tide pools, and hiding spots. As we sat watching the ocean, it suddenly seemed as if the rocks were alive. We looked closer and saw why: hundreds of little rock crabs were crawling about and climbing up on a boulder, only to get washed off by small waves.

The trip back is easy, a gentle grade all the way, making it a 3.5-mile round-trip. The entire time, you feel quite distant from the rest of the Bay Area, the traffic, and all the people.

It's hikes like this that make living here worth it.

Directions: From U.S. 101 in Marin, take the Stinson Beach/Highway 1 exit and drive to the coast. Turn left at the Muir Beach Overlook and continue a short distance to the parking area. **Contact:** Golden Gate National Recreation Area, (415) 331-1540. **Locator:** OWL TRAIL (E1a).

• FEATURED TRIP •

POINT REYES NATIONAL SEASHORE

Rated: The Top 25 Hikes, 2; The Top 4 Earthquake Trails, 26; The Top 10 Strolls, 40; The Top 5 Walks at Low Tide, 43; The Top 50 Base Camps, 110; The Top 10 Easy Backpack Trips, 150; The Top 10 Hikes on Point Reyes, 20; The Top 10 Spots for a First Kiss, 180; The Top 10 Spots to Go on a Date, 182; The Top 9 Places to Bird-Watch, 252; The Top 3 Places to Whale Watch, 256; The Top 22 Water Adventures, 311; The Top 14 Places to Fly Kites, 389; The Top 10 Swimming Holes, 395

Some places project a special aura, and some places do not. MOUNT SHASTA has it, for instance, but MOUNT WHITNEY does not. LAKE TAHOE has it, while LAKE BERRYESSA doesn't. In the Bay Area, POINT REYES definitely has it. Sure, the area offers more recreation potential than anywhere else within 150 miles, but that is not what you remember when you leave. What you remember is the feeling you get when you're there.

For one thing, there is a sense of total separation from the Bay Area, even though it's actually very close. For another, there are hundreds of little hideaways to be explored. After awhile, some of them start to feel like your own secret spots.

POINT REYES is gigantic, bordered by the wide-open ocean to the west, with a unique and varied terrain inland. The coast itself has miles of untouched beach just north of the lighthouse, and to the south, it offers miles of little bays, inlets, and sea tunnels.

Inland, there is even more diversity. The coastal bluffs are sprinkled with wildflowers and chaparral, the rolling hills with wild grasses and poppies, and the mountain interior is heavily wooded, with little creeks following the earth's fissures. With that kind of diversity, weekenders are given a huge number of recreation choices. And POINT REYES is one of the few popular destinations able to handle weekend traffic.

You can pick an easy walk or a rugged stomper, look for a migrating whale or a resident tule elk, stay just a few hours or overnight. You can canoe or kayak, study the geology, or simply enjoy the ocean lookouts.

Two things don't fit in, though. Mountain bikes seem out of place on the trails because any form of mechanization is intrusive in a park preserved in its natural state. I've done some biking myself, but Wild America and Machine America just don't mix. The other thing that strikes you are the cows, the good ol' bovines. They're nice enough creatures, but there are just too many of them. In some areas, you have to remain alert to keep from planting your Vibram soles in the middle of a fresh meadow muffin.

Aside from that, the area is among the best in California for day hikes. There are some 30 trails covering 65,000 acres of wildlands. The easier hikes are on the northern end of the national seashore, where easy, rolling hills lead to the ocean.

The more rugged trails are in the southern end of the park, in the coastal mountains. The Bear Valley Trail, which extends along much of Coast Creek all the way to the ocean, is one of the better hikes in the park. If you want something more rugged and remote, four other trails intersect the Bear Valley route, all of them involving steep climbs. You know the old adage: If you want to be alone, just start walking up.

If a day hike isn't your game, there are a number of very short walks that can provide excitement. My favorite is at the tip of Point Reyes, where a five- to 10-minute walk from the parking lot will take you right to the lighthouse. This is the best shoreline lookout on the Pacific coast for spotting migrating whales. Because the point extends so far west into the sea, the whales often pass within a few hundred yards of the lookout. They can be identified by their telltale spouts. Because it is easy to reach, however, the lookout is often crowded.

The Tomales Peninsula is just as easily accessible, yet is far less crowded. It is here that POINT REYES' herd of tule elk roams. The herd, several dozen strong, often hangs out near the parking lot. You can take short walks from here, or go for a three-miler to TOMALES POINT.

At TOMALES POINT, there is an area that slid more than 16 feet during the 1906 earthquake, providing a fascinating look into the area's unique geology. The entire Point Reyes Peninsula is a dislocated land, set just west of the San Andreas Fault. It's a rift zone that is steadily moving north at an average of three inches per year. The rocks of Point Reyes match those from the Tehachapi Mountains, more than 300 miles to the south.

The area has both natural history and a special feel. When you leave, that's what you will remember. The place just feels good.

Directions: There are two possible routes from San Francisco. The shortest is to drive north on U.S. 101 to San Rafael and take the Sir Francis Drake Boulevard exit. Turn west on Sir Francis Drake Boulevard and drive about 35 miles to the tiny town of Olema. You will see a red flashing light; turn left and drive a short distance to the Point Reyes National Seashore entrance on the right. A longer, more scenic route is to drive north of San Francisco on U.S. 101 and take the Highway 1 cutoff. Turn west and continue to Point Reyes. The park is located on the left side of the highway, along the western shore of Tomales Bay. **Fees:** Access, maps, and camping are free.

Camping: There are four primitive, hike-in campsites. Permits are required and may be obtained free of charge at the Bear Valley Visitor Center. Reservations can be made by calling (415) 663-8054 between 9 a.m. and noon Monday through Friday. **Contact:** Point Reyes National Seashore headquarters, (415) 663-1092. For free maps, write to the Superintendent, Point Reyes National Seashore, Point Reyes, CA 94956. **Locator:** POINT REYES NATIONAL SEASHORE (E1a).

• FEATURED TRIP •

ARASTRADERO LAKE

Rated: The Top 50 Parks, 7; The Top 5 Hikes on the Peninsula, 44; The Top 22 Water Adventures, 311; The Top 43 Lakes to Fish, 333

A truly hidden lake on the Peninsula offers an opportunity for hiking, fishing, bird-watching, and picnicking. Open since 1987, ARASTRADERO LAKE is the only lake that allows public access between SAN FRANCISCO and SAN JOSE. It is set in the foothill country above PALO ALTO as part of a 600-acre nature preserve.

There are some 60 lakes around the Bay Area, but Peninsula residents have long been frustrated by the "No Trespassing" signs set up by the public agencies that are supposed to serve them. The Peninsula has several magnificent lakes—Crystal Springs, Pilarcitos, Felt, Searsville, Boronda—but they are all off-limits to the public at large.

Belmont has a tiny, squarish reservoir that is open to the public, but it provides few recreational opportunities and can't be called a lake by any definition.

Park rangers are stretching things a bit, too, calling ARASTRADERO a lake, but the recreational opportunities here make for a worthwhile visit anyway. The best time to visit is on a warm summer evening, when the birds are feeding and the fish are jumping.

The lake looks more like a farm pond, circled by tules and nestled in the foothill country. It was created by a small earth dam built across the canyon, and is filled with the winter runoff from a small creek.

It's a 10-minute walk from the parking area to the lake, and even though you know the lake is there, it is still a surprise when you top the rise and see it for the first time. It is prettier than you might anticipate. The birdlife is abundant, and on a quiet evening, it makes an idyllic setting.

The area is a good one for a short walk, say just to the lake and back. If you have kids, it's short enough to keep their attention and long enough to get the ants out of their pants.

But the area is worth exploring on a longer trip. The Perimeter Trail connects to both the Acorn Trail and the Corte Madera Trail, and from those you can visit most of the preserve. It is mostly flat; the highest rise is 300 feet, so it is comfortable for hikers of all ages.

My favorite piece of trail is the Corte Madera Trail above the lake, where it borders the Arastradero Creek watershed. A map that shows all the trails is available for free in a box at the parking lot.

Birds and wildflowers provide a good sideshow. In the foothill country, there are a lot of hawks circling around, looking for prey. As you near the lake, there is more diversity, with both songbirds and waterfowl. In less than an hour, I spotted more than a dozen species of birds.

The area is exceptionally pretty as spring gives way to summer. The hills are still green, though fading, and there are blooms of lupine, blue-eyed grass, and California poppies to give the hillsides some close-up color.

If there is a frustrating aspect to the trip, it is that fishing should be great at ARASTRADERO LAKE. It isn't. Why? Because of overregulation and poor management by the Palo Alto Department of Recreation. The lake is set in an area where climate, food production, and cover make for abundant populations of largemouth bass and bluegill. The lake is fed by a creek, so it is full (another plus). The fish are in there, including some big ones—I know, because I have seen them. But fishing for them is virtually impossible, which is a shame, especially for the kids in the area who have no other place to try.

The fishing problems are shoreline access, weed growth, and a rule that makes fishing from a raft or float tube illegal. There are just a few breaks in the tules along the shoreline where a kid could try to fish. But even if you are lucky enough to get a spot that isn't taken, the heavy weed growth in the shallows makes every retrieve a frustrating experience.

The solution would be to fish from a raft or float tube, as is so much fun at farm ponds in the Central Valley. But, alas, the city of PALO ALTO has deemed that illegal. As a result, they have screwed up the one public freshwater fishing spot between SAN FRANCISCO and SAN JOSE. What's left is a chance to catch a small bluegill or two if, that is, you can get them through the weeds.

Regardless, the ARASTRADERO LAKE area provides a good adventure for visitors. It is hidden away, known only by a few local residents, and is pretty, warm, and peaceful.

And you won't find any signs that proclaim "No Trespassing." That's the best news of all.

Directions: From San Francisco, drive south on Interstate 280 for about 30 miles. Take the Page Mill Road exit and turn west. Turn right on Arastradero Road. A signed parking lot is on the right side of the road. **Fees:** Admission and parking are free. A trail map is available for free in a box at the parking lot. **Pets:** Dogs are permitted year-round and must be leashed at all times. Horseback riding is allowed on the trails. **Restrictions:** No boats, flotation devices, or swimming are permitted at Arastradero Lake. Camping and bicycles are prohibited on the Perimeter Trail. **Contact:** Foothills Park, (650) 329-2423. **Locator:** ARASTRADERO LAKE (E1b).

• FEATURED TRIP •

FORT FUNSTON

Rated: The Top 50 Parks, 7; The Top 4 Walks in San Francisco, 23; The Top 7 Hikes with a Dog, 30; The Top 5 Walks at Low Tide, 43; The Top 9 Doggy Getaway Ideas, 196

All it takes to turn an easy adventure into a great one is natural beauty and a surprise or two along the way, and that is exactly what you get at FORT FUNSTON on the SAN FRANCISCO coast.

FORT FUNSTON is set on a bluff and offers a short, easy hike with ocean views. That alone can make it an attractive destination, but then—ah hah!—come the surprises.

Look up and you are likely to see daredevil hang gliders rising in the afternoon coastal breezes; this is the most popular hang gliding spot on the Bay Area coast. Take a stroll on the adjacent beach and look down—you are likely to see sand dollars; this is the best spot I know of to find them.

A bonus is that compared to nearby Ocean Beach to the north, FORT FUNSTON gets relatively light use. That is because you can't see this park from the adjacent access road, Highway 1, since a small hill blocks the view, so thousands of people drive right on by every day without a clue as to what lies so close.

Natural beauty, an easy hike, a chance to see hang gliders and find sand dollars, and the option of adding miles to a beach walk or jogging trip make FORT FUNSTON an ideal and easy getaway for many in SAN FRANCISCO and beyond. In addition, it is one of the best places in the Bay Area to take your dog for a walk.

From this blufftop spot you have the ocean on one side and LAKE MERCED on the other. Most people are first attracted by the sight of the hang gliders floating about. When the breezes off the ocean hit the coastal bluffs here, the air is sent skyward, providing rising thermals to keep the hang gliders aloft.

While hang gliding was once extremely dangerous, major advances in equipment, instruction, and certification have made the sport much safer. Once a test of faith, it is now more like a euphoric joy ride. As you watch these folks, they really do look kind of like human kites, just hovering about, appearing to float more than glide.

A pal of mine recently tried hang gliding for the first time. As he described it, words like "ecstatic," "spine-tingling," and "incredible" kept popping into the conversation. He called hang gliding the "second best feeling" of his life. "Landing," he explained, "was even better."

To make watching the hang gliders more enjoyable, a viewing deck is available adjacent to the parking area. This is also where the Sunset Trail starts, the most popular hike in the park.

The Sunset Trail is a 1.5-mile round-trip, which means it can make a great, easy evening walk at—right, you got it—sunset. It is routed through the coastal bluffs on north, just above the sand dunes, for three-quarters of a mile to the park's border. Along the way there are many prime lookouts to enjoy the sunsets over the ocean.

If you want to extend the trip, head down to the beach. From here, you can walk for a mile south to Thornton Beach, which is beyond the walking range of most of the beach visitors parking to the north at Ocean Beach. That means there are typically relatively few people here. In addition, with the ocean bluffs on one side and the open sea on the other, the sweeping sand dunes provide a sense of privacy.

The beach walk offers two bonuses. One is during low tides, when you are apt to find sand dollars on the moist, hard-packed sand. The second is during incoming tides, when anchovies arriving for the summer often roam near the surf line, attracting pelicans and other shorebirds that hover and then dive into the baitfish with a tremendous crash, a spectacular scene.

At one time, this was a sure sign that a school of striped bass had arrived, corraling the anchovies against the back of the surf line. While the striped bass have become more rare, surf fishers will still send long casts toward the diving birds, remembering the good old days when striped bass were the kings of the SAN FRANCISCO coast every summer.

FORT FUNSTON, a part of the Golden Gate National Recreation Area, is designed to appeal to as many people as possible. There is good access for hikers, joggers, and horseback riders, and partial access from the parking lot for wheelchair users.

This is also a great spot for walking dogs, especially if they enjoy playing tag on the beach with the ocean waves. For many years, this has been one of the few spots where dogs are not required to wear leashes if they are under voice control; however, leashes may be mandated in the future, so call ahead for current regulations.

Directions: From the Peninsula, take Interstate 280 to Daly City. Turn west on Highway 1. Drive two miles to Highway 35 and turn right (north). Continue on Highway 35 (Skyline Boulevard) for about four miles and look for the signed Fort Funston parking area. If you pass Lake Merced, you've gone too far. In San Francisco, take Geary Boulevard to the Coast Highway (at the Cliff House). Follow the road south along Ocean Beach until intersecting with Highway 35 at Lake Merced. Turn right and drive half a mile to the signed parking area. **Fees:** Parking and access are free. A complimentary map is available from the Golden Gate National Recreation Area. **Rules:** No mountain bikes are permitted. **Contact:** Fort Funston Ranger Office, (415) 556-8371 or (415) 239-2366. Golden Gate National Recreation Area, Fort Mason, Building 201, San Francisco, CA 94123. **Locator:** FORT FUNSTON (E1b).

• FEATURED TRIP •

★ HUDDART COUNTY PARK

Rated: The Top 50 Parks, 7; The Top 10 Trips into the Redwoods, 36; The Top 5 Hikes on the Peninsula, 44

HUDDART PARK is a perfect example of an attractive, hidden woodland that, though located near thousands of residents, goes almost unused from October to May. A lot of folks just don't seem to know it's here, even on the crackling fresh weekends of spring.

But it is here—some 1,000 acres of redwoods, tan oak, and madrone cut by miles of trails that can take you on an easy walk to a picnic site or on a good puffer of a hike that rises to the 2,000-foot Skyline Ridge.

A bonus is that the SKYLINE TRAIL connects HUDDART PARK to WUNDERLICH COUNTY PARK, which sits just below the town of Sky Londa. The resulting 20-mile hike provides a good close-to-home weekend backpacking trip for Bay Area hikers who don't want to wait until summer for the Sierra Nevada icebox to defrost. Combined with WUNDERLICH COUNTY PARK, hikers have access to nearly 2,000 acres of mountain vistas. In all, there are about 45 miles of trails, enough to keep you coming back for more.

Every time you return to HUDDART, you see something different. This makes it probably the best hiking park on the Peninsula, and a worthwhile destination for people from all over the Bay Area.

During the summer, the park is quite popular, especially for family picnics. There's a variety of short loop trails that are well suited for little kids and make for a good family trip. One of the best is the Redwood Trail, little more than half a mile long, which starts from the Redwood Picnic Area. However, because much of it is such an easy walk amid redwoods, this trail gets heavy use, and by midsummer it's what backpackers call a "highway." For hikers who yearn for solitude, there are several excellent options, all good half-day adventures.

My favorite is a route that circles the park, about a five-mile trip that takes you through redwood forests, along stream-bedded canyons to skyline ridges, and eventually back to your starting point. With a map in hand, you should start on the Dean Trail from the Werder Picnic Area and eventually connect to the Richard Road's Trail, Summit Springs Trail, and Archery Fire Trail to complete the circuit. Because several trails intersect at HUDDART PARK, you can tailor a hike to suit your desires.

WOODSIDE was originally named for the stands of native redwoods on the nearby mountain slopes. However, just over 100 years ago, there was hardly a redwood tree left. Loggers went wild here after the 1849 gold rush, cutting down practically anything in sight. The giant stumps you see today beckon back to that era, but the present second-growth forest, now thick and lush, is a testimonial to how our best work involving nature is often just to do nothing.

Directions: From Interstate 280, take the Woodside Road exit west, then turn right on King's Mountain Road and drive two miles to the main entrance. **Fees:** A $4 entrance fee is charged. **Camping:** Backpack camping is permitted by reservation only; phone (650) 363-4021. No drive-in camping is allowed. **Contact:** Huddart County Park, (650) 851-0326 (at times the phone is unattended); San Mateo County Parks and Recreation Department, (650) 363-4020. **Locator:** HUDDART COUNTY PARK (E1b).

• FEATURED TRIP •

McNEE RANCH STATE PARK

Rated: The Top 50 Parks, 7; The Top 7 Hikes with a Dog, 30; The Top 6 One-Way Hikes Using Public Transportation, 32; The Top 4 One-Way Hikes Using a Shuttle Car, 34; The Top 5 Steep Hikes, 38; The Top 9 Doggy Getaway Ideas, 196

Let's get right to the point: You've never heard of McNEE RANCH STATE PARK, right? That's one of the best reasons why this is the place you should visit this weekend. Nobody else seems to know about it either.

One of California's newest parks, McNEE is only 25 miles from SAN FRANCISCO and can provide one of the Bay Area's best lookouts from the top of MONTARA MOUNTAIN. It's a primitive setting, with no camping or piped water, but it's perfect for short walks or longer gut-thumpers to the ridge. Best of all, you can bring your dog.

McNEE PARK is located on the San Mateo County coast between MONTARA and PACIFICA.

You'll find it is a remarkably peaceful place with many good walks or hikes, and with them some of the best coastal views anywhere. Most of the trails are actually long-abandoned ranch or country roads. They connect to enough footpaths to provide endless options for weekend walks.

But no matter how many different routes you take, eventually you will want to head to the top, the peak of MONTARA MOUNTAIN.

It's not far, but it's a challenge,

climbing from sea level to about 2,000 feet. The distance from the entrance gate at the park to the summit is 3.8 miles. A round-trip requires nearly four hours. But in that short time, you can experience many of the elements of a wilderness mountain trip.

The trail follows the ridgeline of San Pedro Mountain until it connects to the MONTARA COASTAL RANGE, and has three "serious ups." One of the serious ups is three-quarters of a mile and can get you puffing like a locomotive for several minutes.

Then suddenly, the trail nearly flattens on a mountain saddle and a 30-yard cutoff to the left provides a perch for a dazzling view of the Pacifica coast and, on clear days, POINT REYES. My dad, Robert G. Stienstra Sr., made the hike to this great lookout when he was in his 60s. You can make it, too.

Another 45 minutes of "steady up" will take you all the way to the top. You'll look around as if you had just discovered the Bay Area for what it is—miles of open range and mountains, with only the flatlands jammed with people.

On a clear day, the FARALLON ISLANDS—30 miles offshore—can look close enough to be plucked right out of the ocean, and the peak of MOUNT DIABLO to the east can seem within leaping range. Some 10 miles to the north and south lies nothing but mountain wilderness connecting to SWEENEY RIDGE and an off-limits Fish and Game refuge.

More than 150,000 people jam into HALF MOON BAY for the annual Pumpkin Festival. Virtually all of them drive right past MCNEE RANCH STATE PARK. This weekend, if you'd like a nice quiet walk, stop here and go for it.

Directions: From San Francisco, drive south on Highway 1 for about 17 miles, passing Pacifica. Continue up through Devil's Slide and down to the base of the hill. Look for a small pullout area on the left. A small yellow gate with a state park property sign marks the access point. There is enough space to accommodate only a few cars, so if you can't fit, continue down Highway 1 a short distance and park at the lot for Montara State Beach. **Note:** Because of landslide problems, Highway 1 is sometimes closed at Devil's Slide. An alternate route is to take Interstate 280 to Highway 92 in San Mateo. Turn west and drive to Highway 1 and Half Moon Bay. Turn right and drive about nine miles to the Montara State Beach parking area. **Fees:** The parking fee is $5 per day. There's a $1 pet fee. **Trip tips:** Strap on a small daypack filled with lunch and drinks. If you plan to reach the top, it's a good idea to bring a change of shirts so you can stay dry and warm as you enjoy the views. Bring a quart of water and a small drinking dish for your dog, as well as plenty of water for yourself. **Contact:** Ranger station at Half Moon Bay, (650) 726-8819; California State Parks, Bay Area District, (415) 330-6300. **Locator:** MCNEE RANCH STATE PARK (E1b).

• FEATURED TRIP •

MONTARA MOUNTAIN

Rated: The Top 50 Parks, 7; The Top 7 Hikes with a Dog, 30; The Top 6 One-Way Hikes Using Public Transportation, 32; The Top 10 Chances for Bay Area Snow, 288; The Top 4 Places to Sky Watch, 394

The future of MONTARA MOUNTAIN has generated a lot of controversy over the years, but now that it is guaranteed to remain a recreation paradise, it is capturing the daydreams of Bay Area hikers, bikers, and explorers.

For years now, MONTARA MOUNTAIN has been a political football, with CalTrans booting around plans to build a four-lane highway right through the middle of MCNEE RANCH STATE PARK, topping a flank of the mountain.

The concept made sense to engineers, who desired a bypass to the troubled Devil's Slide section of Highway 1, which has been closed repeatedly by slides, washouts, and drops in the road. Engineers say that Devil's Slide will eventually fall right into the ocean, and they have set up sensory equipment on the most volatile section of Highway 1 to monitor any new movement.

But the bypass did not make sense to residents of local communities, who passed a ballot measure mandating that CalTrans instead build a tunnel to solve the problem on Highway 1 at Devil's Slide. Not only will this keep the integrity of MONTARA MOUNTAIN and its two parks intact, but the success of the ballot measure and the attention it drew to the mountain have revived its reputation as a stellar getaway.

MONTARA MOUNTAIN is located on the San Mateo County coast about 20 miles south of SAN FRANCISCO, and has long been one of my most treasured places to hike in the Bay Area. I have hiked to the North Peak (1,898 feet) hundreds of times, and I keep going back to the old mountain.

What makes the place so special are the panoramic coastal views, with several picture-perfect lookouts from every trail, and the fact that it is a true, untouched wildland for 50 square miles, like a huge wilderness island amid the Peninsula's sprawl. There are two great parks that provide access, MCNEE RANCH STATE PARK in MONTARA and SAN PEDRO VALLEY COUNTY PARK in PACIFICA.

MCNEE is the most primitive state park in California, not to mention the only one with free access, and allows leashed dogs and bikes on the trails. There are no facilities of any kind, just old gravel roads that contour up ridgelines to a radio transmitter at the North Peak.

To enter MCNEE, you park at the little yellow pipe gate on the east side of Highway 1 in northern MONTARA, or across the highway at Montara State Beach. From the entrance gate, I measured the distance as exactly 3.8 miles to the top of the mountain. That includes three stretches of trail that will get you puffing, including one 20-minute wheezer of a section to San Pedro Ridge that is an outright butt-kicker.

Like any hike that goes up, your rewards are the views. In clear weather, they can been absolutely breathtaking here, especially from the summit.

Looking west, the FARALLON ISLANDS, about 30 miles out to sea, look so close that it seems you could reach out and pluck them right out of the water. To the north are miles of coastline, from PACIFICA on to SAN FRANCISCO and all the way to POINT REYES. To the south and east are miles of wildlands, including the 23,000-acre state Fish and Wildlife Refuge, the last untouched land in the Bay Area.

The coastal beauty is also divine on Montara Mountain's northern slopes, which are accessible from SAN PEDRO VALLEY COUNTY PARK in southern PACIFICA. The $3 entrance fee there allows you to use a patrolled parking lot, a clean rest room, a visitor center, a map/brochure, and signed trailheads and junctions. No bikes or dogs are permitted.

On my latest visit, I found that trail crews have done an outstanding job adding new trail signs and clearing away brush, so hikers know where they are going; in the process, the views have become better than ever. The trail up the mountain is a dirt pathway that is routed up to San Pedro Ridge, where it intersects with a service road at McNee Ranch State Park, for a final 1.1-mile push to the summit.

You start by hiking through a grove of big eucalyptus, then enter a wilderness canyon, a gentle climb all the way, for a lookout of Brooks Falls. This is a three-tiered waterfall, and the surrounding canyons and their rock outcrops are gorgeous. From here, it is a 10-minute walk to a fantastic view of Pacifica and the coast, then onward to the peak. If you don't want to make the huff-and-puff to the summit, the trip can also be shortened to a loop hike back to the parking lot.

Note that it can be cool and breezy on the top. If you sweat a lot, consider bringing a spare shirt for a quick change so you can stay dry and warm and enjoy the views for as long as you wish.

For me, it never seems long enough. That's why I keep going back again and again. And with protections in place to forever protect the mountain from the intrusion of a highway, I know I can always return to the same special place.

Directions: From San Francisco, drive south on Highway 1 for about 17 miles, passing Pacifica. Continue up through Devil's Slide and down to the base of the hill. Look for a small pullout on the left. There is a small yellow gate with a state park property sign; that is the access point. There is room enough to accommodate only a few cars, so you might have to continue down Highway 1 a short distance and park at the lot for Montara State Beach. **Note:** Because of landslide problems, Highway 1 is sometimes closed at Devil's Slide. An alternate route is to take Interstate 280 to Highway 92 in San Mateo. Turn west and drive to Highway 1 and Half Moon Bay. Turn right and drive about nine miles to the Montara State Beach parking area. **Contact:** McNee Ranch State Park, (650) 726-8800; California State Parks, Bay Area District, (415) 330-6300; San Pedro Valley County Park, (650) 355-8289. **Locator:** Montara Mountain (E1b).

• Featured Trip •

Princeton by the Sea

Rated: The Top 10 Spots to Go on a Date, 182; The Top 10 Places to View Wildlife, 257

Princeton by the Sea is not on the same plane as the rest of the Bay Area, but when you combine a great walk there with a trip to one of the nearby restaurants, it can seem out of this world.

What makes Princeton so different from the rest of the region are its natural barriers, Devil's Slide to the north, Skyline Ridge to the east, and the Pacific Ocean to the west. That means nobody gets here by accident, that a visit is always a choice, putting up with Highway 1 at Devil's Slide to the north and clogged-up Highway 92 to the east over to San Mateo and

HAYWARD.

So over time, the residents here have evolved into an independent lot, doing everything out of personal conviction, and the entire San Mateo County coast reflects this. The experiences that are available are just as unique.

The best way to get the full flavor is to drive straight to Pillar Point Harbor at PRINCETON. At the signal, turn toward the harbor and drive about half a mile through Princeton Village, then turn left and drive about a mile toward the big radar station on top of Pillar Point. Near the radar station, you'll discover a small parking lot on the left side of the road. This is where your adventure begins.

A flat trail for easy hiking and great views starts here. It begins on the west side of the harbor, a hard, dirt surface on a bluff over a quiet beach that gets overlooked by all the tourists trying to find a parking spot along Highway 1. This is one of the best spots on the entire coast to throw sticks in the water for dogs.

It is also adjacent to a large wetland that attracts dozens of species of waterfowl and marine birds throughout the year. We've seen plovers, cormorants, and grebes; in early summer, brown pelicans begin to arrive.

It's only a 10-minute walk to the PRINCETON jetty, the rock breakwater for the harbor, and from here, you turn right and find another secluded beach. If you look close, just offshore, you may see the black heads of sea lions poking out of the water in the kelp beds, where they often play peek-a-boo with visitors. The beach extends west to the tip of Pillar Point, where at minus low tides, you can explore tide pools for more than a hundred yards out.

At low tides, you can also turn right at Pillar Point and discover more tide pools and tidal crevices, all filled with hermit crabs, sea snails, green anemones, and just a few starfish and purple urchins. One problem is that some unethical numskulls have removed the starfish and other sea creatures and taken them away, even though this is technically part of the FITZGERALD MARINE RESERVE and all take is prohibited. Since starfish average 15 to 20 years in age and are slow to replenish themselves, they can be wiped out when they are removed from their homes.

If you choose to walk around Pillar Point and explore the remote tidal crevices, be certain to pay close attention to the tides. It can be very easy to head out during a low tide, then get marooned when the high tide comes in. In fact, after several visits, it finally happened to me when I lost track of time getting caught up in all the beauty. My partner had to wade knee-deep to make it back, while I tried to rock climb just above the water, but slipped when a rock gave way and went kerplunk into the drink anyway. Heh, heh.

For many, this is enough of an adventure, finishing off the day with a meal at one of the restaurants in PRINCETON; reservations are an absolute must, especially on weekends. But there is more to do, for those so inclined.

After returning to the parking area, there is another trail directly adjacent, just across the access road, that climbs a 150-foot hill. It rises to a bluff-top view of the ocean and a drop-dead gorgeous beach, then follows a trail north, with sweeping views every step of the way of the ocean to the west and MONTARA MOUNTAIN to the northeast.

It's common to look down from the bluffs and spot sea lions sleeping on the rocks or playing in the shallows. From here you can continue to walk north for about 20 minutes, coming eventually to a small road that leads right to the Moss Beach Distillery. This is a first-class spot with a dramatic beachfront porch where you can sip drinks, slurp oysters, or munch salads, calamari, and the like. We saw a passing whale from here, a nice moment.

A few words of warning before heading out: If you go to PRINCETON on a weekend, it is best to get there either early or late, because in the middle of the day, from 11 a.m. to 6:30 p.m., the place is often inundated with people, especially when it's not foggy, and the roads, restaurants, and parking areas can get jammed to capacity.

That noted, take your time when you get here, because as you enjoy the rugged beauty, the magic can be in every moment, over and over again.

Directions: From San Francisco, drive south on Interstate 280 for 19 miles to the Highway 92 cutoff. Drive west on Highway 92 to Highway 1, then turn north and continue to Princeton by the Sea. **Marine Reserve:** The Fitzgerald Marine Reserve is located in Moss Beach, with a well-signed turnoff on Highway 1. Access is free. For information, phone (650) 728-3584. **Contact:** Half Moon Bay Chamber of Commerce, (650) 726-8380. **Locator:** PRINCETON (E1b).

• FEATURED TRIP •

PURISIMA CREEK REDWOODS

Rated: The Top 25 Hikes, 2; The Top 50 Parks, 7; The Top 12 Hike-to Streams, 24; The Top 15 Surprise Hikes in the Rain, 28; The Top 10 Trips into the Redwoods, 36; The Top 10 Strolls, 40; The Top 5 Hikes on the Peninsula, 44

PURISIMA CREEK REDWOODS is the kind of place many people in the Bay Area constantly yearn for—but don't even know exists. This is one of the truly great secret spots that the Bay Area has to offer. A giant preserve with redwood forests, creeks, glens, and fantastic lookouts, this place seems as if it is in a secluded Northern California forest, 350 miles away.

But it isn't. It is located on the western slopes of the San Francisco Peninsula ridgeline, about a 30-minute drive from SAN FRANCISCO or HAYWARD, even closer for Peninsula residents.

There are three access points, with two on Skyline Boulevard (Highway 35) about four miles south of the Highway 92 junction. The other is off Higgins Canyon Road, a four-mile drive from Main Street in HALF MOON BAY. The southern Skyline Boulevard entrance (located near road marker SM 16.65) is accessible to wheelchairs.

Between those three points is a vast area—some 2,500 acres—that will be preserved forever by the Midpeninsula Regional Open Space District. Because it is a newer parkland, having opened in 1988, not many people know about it.

The centerpiece of the preserve is Purisima Creek Canyon and its classic redwood forests, bedded with ferns, wild berries, and wildflowers. But the area also offers great views of the PACIFIC OCEAN and HALF MOON BAY to the west and, from the ridgetop on Skyline Boulevard, of SAN FRANCISCO BAY to the east. That combination of woods and ocean views makes it feel like BIG SUR, MOUNT TAMALPAIS, and the HUMBOLDT coast all in one.

This is a do-it-yourself trip. There is no ranger station, park kiosk, or information center. If you have a good memory, there are permanent wood trail maps mounted at the trailheads.

A better bet is to obtain the one-page trail map of the park by writing to headquarters. The map details 10 miles of trails for hikers, along with fire roads for mountain bikes. The southern side of the park is more heavily wooded than the northern side. So if you want views, start from the northern access point on Skyline Boulevard, located near road marker SM 18.36. If you want woods, start at the southern access point near Skyline road marker SM 16.65.

For the ideal walk, start at the southern SKYLINE RIDGE access point. You can make the beautiful four-mile walk downhill to the western end of the park at Higgins Canyon Road. With a companion, you can park another vehicle at trail's end to use as a shuttle. That way you can get a one-way hike with almost no uphill walking, perfect for people planning their first walk of the summer.

The trail is a beauty, following along much of Purisima Creek. At times it is a lush watershed, heavy with redwoods and ferns. In some of the more open areas, you can spot all kinds of wildflowers including large patches of blue forget-me-nots.

Like other lands managed by the Midpeninsula Regional Open Space District, this is an open space preserve, not a developed park. That means there are no barbecues, ball fields, campsites, or developed recreation areas.

What you find instead is a big chunk of Bay Area land protected in its natural environment. It is one of the best secrets you might uncover this year.

Directions: From San Francisco, drive south on Interstate 280 for about 15 miles to the Highway 92 cutoff. Head west toward Half Moon Bay, then turn south on Skyline Boulevard (Highway 35). There are two access points off Skyline. The northern access point is a 4.5-mile drive at road marker SM 18.36, the other a 6.5-mile drive at road marker SM 16.65. Parking areas are provided. Access from Half Moon Bay: From Main Street in Half Moon Bay, drive south through town and turn east on Higgins-Purisima Road. Continue on the winding road for four miles to the park. A small parking lot is on the left side of the road. **Fees:** Access and parking are free. **Contact:** For information or a trail map of Purisima Creek Redwoods, contact the Midpeninsula Regional Open Space District, 330 Distel Circle, Los Altos, CA 94022, (650) 691-1200. **Locator:** PURISIMA CREEK REDWOODS (E1b).

• FEATURED TRIP •

SAN ANDREAS TRAIL

Rated: The Top 12 Hike-to Streams, 24; The Top 4 Earthquake Trails, 26

The SAN ANDREAS TRAIL overlooks Crystal Springs Reservoir and winds through wooded foothills. It is minutes away by car for Peninsula residents, can be reached by bus, and provides access to the edge of a special fish and game refuge where eagles still fly. The air is fresh and clean up here, and the wide trail is suitable for jogging, hiking, and bicycling.

The trail sits on the eastern edge of Crystal Springs Reservoir, just off Skyline Boulevard (Highway 35) in MILLBRAE. All you have to do is show up, park your car, and go for it. The only irritation is that a few miles of the trail run fairly close to the road and the traffic noise is within earshot. A wall of trees provides a buffer in some areas, and south of the access point at Hillcrest Boulevard the trail meanders away from the road and cuts along the edge of the south end of the lake.

Whether you run, walk, or bike, at some point you will come to a complete halt and just gaze at the wonders this country holds. The eastern slope of MONTARA MOUNTAIN is true wilderness, untouched by mankind, and the sparkling lake below might trigger visions of giant fish. But don't get any ideas about bringing a rod and reel. Fishing or trespassing on the lake or the wooded refuge to the west is illegal and doing so will quickly land you in the pokey. The area is patrolled around the clock.

The SAN ANDREAS TRAIL starts near the northern end of the lake, where a signed trailhead marker sits on Skyline Boulevard, which runs parallel to the trail. It goes about three miles and is fairly level until the next access point at Hillcrest Boulevard.

A good option for well-conditioned runners is to start at the Hillcrest Boulevard access point, then head south. The trail connects to the Sawyer Camp Trail, which cuts six miles along the lake, away from the road. It provides the quiet that you might miss on the SAN ANDREAS TRAIL, but you pay for this serenity with a longer distance and a steeper grade (a drop of 400 feet). You can count on some huffing and puffing on the return trip.

If you want to bicycle here, then plan on going slow. Street speed limits are enforced by rangers, sometimes using radar.

During the winter, this area is remarkably cool, green, and fresh. On summer evenings, you can witness the spectacle of rolling fogbanks cresting MONTARA MOUNTAIN to the west. Regardless of whether you hike, run, or bike, this is a great spot to bust loose.

Directions: From the north, take Interstate 280 to the Skyline Boulevard (Highway 35) exit. A signed trail entrance is on the west side of the road. From the south, take Interstate 280 to the Millbrae Avenue exit and head north on what appears to be a frontage road (Skyline Boulevard) to Hillcrest Boulevard at the trailhead. **Mass transit:** SamTrans runs a bus line that stops at Hillcrest and Skyline Boulevards. For route information, phone SamTrans at (800) 660-4BUS/4287. **Trip tip:** If you plan to run, bring a friend along so you can shuttle using cars rather than having to double back on the trail. **Contact:** Midpeninsula Regional Open Space District, 330 Distel Circle, Los Altos, CA 94022; (650) 691-1200. **Locator:** SAN ANDREAS TRAIL (E1b).

• FEATURED TRIP •

SAN PEDRO VALLEY COUNTY PARK

Rated: The Top 25 Hikes, 2; The Top 50 Parks, 7; The Top 12 Hike-to Streams, 24; The Top 15 Surprise Hikes in the Rain, 28; The Top 6 One-Way Hikes

Using Public Transportation, 32; The Top 20 Hike-to Waterfalls, 187; The Top 10 Chances for Bay Area Snow, 288

Just 20 minutes south of SAN FRANCISCO is a secluded setting where visitors are few, the coastal beauty is divine, and hikers can carve out their own personal slice of heaven.

Yet when I entered SAN PEDRO VALLEY COUNTY PARK, there were so few visitors that the entrance station had been vacated and there were only two cars parked at the lot adjacent to headquarters. What a paradox: It seems that everybody in the Bay Area complains about having "no place to go"—yet here, so close to so many, is a backyard wilderness that is often overlooked.

That is why this park is one of my favorite places to find both adventure and solitude. It features a hidden three-tiered waterfall, sweeping coastal views, the highest mountain on the San Francisco Peninsula, and frequent wildlife sightings. That makes it one of the best hiking parks in the Bay Area.

The park is located in southern PACIFICA, stretching from San Pedro Valley up the slopes of MONTARA MOUNTAIN, with trails available for hikers (no mountain bikes allowed) to the top destinations. Because it sits in an inland coastal valley shielded by a mountain ridge, the temperatures are 10 to 15 degrees warmer here than just a few miles away at the beach and the skies are often clear, even when the coast is fogged in.

My favorite trail here is the Montara Mountain Trail, which takes you by the best viewing area for Brooks Falls. This is the newest trail in the park.

You hike about a mile, climbing several hundred feet, until suddenly the waterfalls appear in a surprising cascade down a canyon. The falls are connected in three giant tiers, falling 175 feet in all. These are the least-known falls in the Bay Area, yet they are among the most impressive. One reason it attracts so little attention is that it doesn't flow year-round. As a tributary to San Pedro Creek, Brooks Creek runs only in late winter and spring, best of course after several days of good rain.

The hike continues all the way to the North Peak of MONTARA MOUNTAIN (1,930 feet), 3.5 miles one way, including a 1.1-mile push on a fire road to reach the summit. On a clear spring day, the views are absolutely stunning in all directions, highlighted by the PACIFIC OCEAN and the FARALLON ISLANDS, as well as SWEENEY RIDGE and the San Francisco Fish and Game Refuge.

Completed a few years ago, this trail provides one of the few great one-way hikes (with a shuttle) in the Bay Area. From the top of MONTARA MOUNTAIN, you enter MCNEE RANCH STATE PARK and hike 3.8 miles to Montara State Beach, descending all the way, with glorious views along the entire route. With a car parked at each end of the trail, you can hike 7.3 miles one way from SAN PEDRO VALLEY COUNTY PARK, up MONTARA MOUNTAIN, and down to Montara State Beach.

When spring arrives, the views close up are as pleasant as those on the distant horizon. The coastal hills are aglow in greens and wildflowers are just starting to bloom. A few golden poppies are sprinkled about as well.

At the same time, wildlife is emerging to nibble on the budding plants and fresh grasses. The most common sightings are of rabbits and deer, according to park ranger Dennis Hanley.

"I've seen mountain lions, bobcats, coyotes, fox, deer, rabbits, raccoons, possum, skunks," he told me. One reason for the abundance of wildlife is that the park abuts miles and miles of wildlands, McNee Ranch State Park, and the San Francisco Fish and Game Refuge.

The best way to see wildlife here is to arrive on a warm spring evening and take the easy walk on the wide, flat trail that starts at park headquarters and heads east through the valley floor to a large meadow. This trail is wheelchair accessible and is perfect for people with disabilities as well as for children not ready for ambitious hikes to lookouts.

"Children in wheelchairs love it because they can get down and feel the grass in the meadow, and they often see deer and other animals," Hanley said. "Too often, people with disabilities don't get the opportunity to have this kind of experience."

The park is so pretty and litter-free and the trails are in such good condition in part thanks to the efforts of a group called the San Pedro Volunteers, folks who have learned not only to love this place but to volunteer their time to take care of it. In addition, mountain bikes are prohibited on the hiking trails, which keeps the pace tranquil and carefree, and dogs are prohibited as well, which keeps the wildlife docile.

There are about 200 parks in the Bay Area. San Pedro Valley County Park could serve as a prime example to those who run the others of how to do something right.

Directions: From San Francisco, take Highway 1 south into Pacifica and continue to Linda Mar Boulevard. Turn east on Linda Mar and continue until it deadends at Oddstad Boulevard. Turn right; the park entrance is located about 50 yards ahead on the left. **Fees:** Parking is $4 per day. Many visitors opt to park at the nearby Safeway lot or in the overflow lot at the adjacent church to avoid paying the fee. **Special rules:** No mountain bikes or dogs are allowed. Horses are permitted. **Contact:** San Pedro Valley County Park, (650) 355-8289; San Mateo County Parks and Recreation Department, (650) 363-4020. For information about the San Pedro Volunteers, phone (650) 599-1306. **Locator:** San Pedro Valley County Park (E1b).

• Featured Trip •

Skyline Ridge

Rated: The Top 50 Parks, 7; The Top 9 Doggy Getaway Ideas, 196; The Top 14 Places to Fly Kites, 389

A glow seems to take over the land come late September and October. As the sun's azimuth lowers with the arrival of fall, the refracted light can cast a golden sheen over miles of grasslands in the Bay Area foothills.

The prettiest area from which to see this phenomenon is on the Peninsula's Skyline Ridge, whether you're driving or hiking. Sweeping views of the coast and the South Bay, a beautiful drive on a country two-laner amid miles of open space, and some 25 trailheads in the span of 20 miles make the Skyline Ridge one of the best weekend excursions in the Bay Area during fall.

The skyline is easily reached from San Francisco, the East Bay, and, of course, the Peninsula itself. The northern end of Highway 35 junctions with Highway 92 right at Skyline, and there are other access roads at WOODSIDE (Highway 84), PALO ALTO (Page Mill Road), and SARATOGA (Highway 9).

SKYLINE RIDGE is a beautiful drive in any vehicle, and is a special favorite among motorcyclists, especially those with the big fat bikes that rumble slow and easy. At its northern starting point, Highway 35 provides views of HALF MOON BAY to the west and the South Bay and MOUNT DIABLO to the east. From here, the road heads south into redwoods, becoming twisty at times, then emerges north of SKY LONDA and straightens out atop the ridge again, skirted by grasslands.

It runs south all the way past the junction with Highway 9 and the Castle Rock Ridge, providing view after view on each side along the way, with miles of rolling foothills, glimpses of the ocean to the west, and a panorama of the Santa Clara Valley and beyond to MOUNT HAMILTON to the east. Besides nearly a dozen excellent pullouts in which to park and enjoy the views, there are several designated Vista Points.

The road runs all the way to Highway 17, though it degenerates into a curvy, 15 mph test a few miles south of CASTLE ROCK STATE PARK. What most do is turn west at Highway 84 or Highway 9, drive to the coast, and return via Highway 1 to make one of the preeminent loop drives anywhere.

You can make it even better by not only stopping to take in the views on Skyline, but adding in a short hike. There are more hiking trails off Skyline than any other road in the Bay Area, some 25 in all, and they feature many stellar walks, most of them short and easy on lands managed by the Midpeninsula Regional Open Space District. Access is free, and most have one-sheet trail maps available in holders at the trailheads. Here are the best hikes:

WHITTEMORE GULCH TRAIL

After turning south from Highway 92 to Highway 35, the first major trailhead and parking area will be on your right after 4.5 miles, the access point for PURISIMA CREEK REDWOODS OPEN SPACE PRESERVE. For a great short hike with a view, take the Whittemore Gulch Trail; it drops about 400 feet to a rocky overlook with a gorgeous view of HALF MOON BAY, PILLAR POINT HARBOR, and the PACIFIC OCEAN.

SKYLINE TRAIL

This hike parallels much of Highway 35 along the east side of the ridge, featuring views of the South Bay, second-growth redwoods, and some giant tree stumps. It extends eight miles one way to SKY LONDA as part of the Bay Ridge Trail, though most people just walk in for 20 minutes, then turn around and head back. The trailhead is located 6.5 miles south of the junction of Highway 92 and Highway 35, adjacent to the blue sign for the Bay Ridge Trail.

REDWOOD TRAIL

An even easier hike, just a half-mile round-trip, is available down the road at the parking area at mile marker 16.65. This is where you will find the Redwood Trail, an easy trail that's accessible to anybody, including those in wheelchairs or with baby strollers. It enters a beautiful redwood forest, with a few picnic tables and a rest room available.

WINDY HILL TRAIL

From the 1,900-foot summit, hikers can see miles and miles in all directions, yet getting there requires only a 0.7-mile hike on the Anniversary

Trail. The trailhead is located 2.3 miles south of SKY LONDA (at the junction of Highway 35 and 84).

BOREL HILL TRAIL
Borel Hill tops out at 2,572 feet, the highest point in the Russian Ridge Open Space Preserve. But because it is surrounded by lower grasslands, visitors get sensational, unblocked views. From the parking area, the hike involves a climb of only 250 feet in less than a mile. The trailhead is located just north of the intersection of Highway 35 and Page Mill Road.

LONG RIDGE TRAIL
A two-hour loop hike covering 4.6 miles will take you down a canyon and up a wooded slope, then emerge on the ridge for breathtaking views of coastal foothills and the ocean. The trailhead is located at a dirt pullout parking area on the west side of the road, about three miles south of the junction of Highway 35 and Page Mill Road.

SARATOGA GAP TRAIL
This is one of the main attractions of CASTLE ROCK STATE PARK, a great three-hour loop hike. The trail starts by dropping into a canyon with a beautiful forest canopy, emerges at an overlook of a dramatic waterfall, then leads to the top of Goat Rock, a honeycombed sandstone formation with an incredible view of BIG BASIN and MONTEREY BAY. The trailhead is adjacent to a large dirt parking area with a rest room, 2.5 miles south of the junction of Highway 35 and Highway 9.

Directions: From San Francisco, drive south on Interstate 280 about 30 miles. Take the Page Mill Road exit and turn west, then continue until you reach the intersection with Skyline Boulevard. **Contact:** Midpeninsula Regional Open Space District, (650) 691-1200. **Locator:** SKYLINE RIDGE (E1c).

• FEATURED TRIP •

★ SKYLINE RIDGE OPEN SPACE PRESERVE

Rated: The Top 50 Parks, 7

Skyline Ridge Preserve is a quiet place that offers classic ridgetop vistas from secluded trails routed near both a lake and a pond. The preserve is perched above PALO ALTO on Skyline Boulevard, convenient to thousands of Peninsula residents. This is a good place to go if you want some peace and quiet.

December is one of the best times to visit, since a good Christmas tree farm, the Skyline Ranch Tree Farm, borders an edge of the preserve. You can take in the view, then take home a tree you cut down yourself, a good two-for-one offer.

Skyline spans about 1,100 acres and is bordered by open space. HORSESHOE LAKE, located in the southeastern region, is the focal point of the preserve. It can be reached by a number of trails that connect and border the western edge of the lake.

Another hike will take you to the highest point in the preserve at 2,493 feet. When you look down from here, the canyon seems to plunge thousands of feet below you.

Most of the trails are actually more like old dirt roads, but they provide a good walking surface. Combined with a network of old paths, they can take you to a wide variety of scenic spots. The trails cut through woodlands filled primarily with Douglas fir, madrone, and oak, as well as prairie-like grasslands.

In December, you can drive right up to the Christmas tree farm on Skyline Boulevard, cut your tree, and then continue your day by exploring the SKYLINE RIDGE PRESERVE. In fact, the trail that will get you most quickly to HORSESHOE LAKE starts at the tree farm.

The other access point is just south of the intersection of Skyline Boulevard and Page Mill Road.

One note: The preserve could become one of the best in the Bay Area if fishing was allowed in both HORSESHOE LAKE and the nearby pond. But the Midpeninsula Regional Open Space District currently prohibits fishing here, and that seems like a crime committed by a public agency against the public. HORSESHOE LAKE ranges up to 40 feet deep and is lined with tules. It would support an excellent largemouth bass fishery. What a shame! The people who run the Open Space District are smart folks, so perhaps they will be persuaded by common sense in the near future.

Directions: From San Francisco, drive south on Interstate 280 approximately 30 miles. Take the Page Mill Road exit and turn west. Continue until you reach the intersection with Skyline Boulevard. You can gain access to the preserve at the southeast corner of the Page Mill Road/Skyline Boulevard intersection, or through the Christmas tree farm located two miles south of the intersection. **Fees:** Access is free. **Contact:** For maps and information, phone the Midpeninsula Regional Open Space District, (650) 691-1200. **Locator:** SKYLINE RIDGE OPEN SPACE PRESERVE (E1d).

• FEATURED TRIP •

★ SWEENEY RIDGE

Rated: The Top 25 Hikes, 2; The Top 50 Parks, 7; The Top 6 One-Way Hikes Using Public Transportation, 32; The Top 5 Hikes on the Peninsula, 44; The Top 10 Spots for a First Kiss, 180; The Top 9 Doggy Getaway Ideas, 196; The Top 14 Places to Fly Kites, 389

You practically need a head that can rotate 360 degrees when you're perched atop SWEENEY RIDGE, one of the most spectacular viewpoints in the Bay Area. Way back in 1769, explorer Don Gaspar de Portola first viewed SAN FRANCISCO BAY from this spot, and they say his neck still hurts. Millions of people have since moved to the Peninsula, yet just a few can tell firsthand of the sights from SWEENEY RIDGE. They're the ones with the neck braces.

It is just a 40-minute walk from the trailhead at the Skyline College campus, located on the ridge that splits SAN BRUNO and PACIFICA atop the San Francisco Peninsula. A bonus is that the trail is easily accessible using mass transit, with SamTrans buses providing the connecting link at the DALY CITY BART station.

On clear mornings, the entire Bay Area seems to be at your feet. With binoculars or a spotting scope, even the most distant sights will seem within your grasp.

SWEENEY RIDGE provides remarkable glimpses of three of the largest mountains in the Bay Area. To the north is MOUNT TAMALPAIS, to the east is MOUNT DIABLO, and to the south is MONTARA MOUNTAIN. You get the proper sense of perspective when you realize how long the mountains have been here—compared to your own lifespan.

Just below is PACIFICA, from Mussel Rock to Pedro Point, where the ocean appears like a giant lake lapping at the beach. To the west, the FARALLON ISLANDS jut out from the PACIFIC OCEAN, looking as if you could reach them with a short swim. They are actually 25 miles away. That expanse of curved blue horizon spanning hundreds of miles will remind you that the earth isn't flat after all.

To reach SWEENEY RIDGE, you hike up a moderate grade that takes you through coastal grasslands that sprout with green after the first rains of fall. In the spring, there are lots of wildflowers.

From the SAN BRUNO entrance, figure on about an hour for a round-trip hike, not including viewing and a picnic. The ideal time for a hike is the morning after a good rain, which leaves the air sparkling fresh and clear. Summer evenings can often be the worst times, because thick fog powered by 25 mph winds can reduce visibility to zero and make your hike about as cold as an expedition to the Arctic.

Directions: From points south, take Interstate 280 to Hickey Boulevard and head west. Turn left on Highway 35 (Skyline Boulevard), then turn right on College Drive. From the north, take Interstate 280 to the Skyline Boulevard exit, turn left on College Drive, and proceed to the south end of parking area No. 2. **Mass transit:** SamTrans runs buses that will take you to the Skyline College campus. For route information, phone (800) 660-4BUS/4287. **Trailhead:** The trail starts on the southeast end of the Skyline College campus, near parking area No. 2. Walk east past the maintenance yard and then right to the service road—a sign marks the trail. **Fees:** Access is free. **Contact:** Golden Gate National Recreation Area, (415) 556-0560. **Locator:** SWEENEY RIDGE (E1b).

• FEATURED TRIP •

★ WUNDERLICH COUNTY PARK

Rated: The Top 50 Parks, 7; The Top 10 Trips into the Redwoods, 36; The Top 5 Hikes on the Peninsula, 44

What most people want from a park is a sense of remoteness without actually being far from home. WUNDERLICH PARK offers just that, with 25 miles of secluded trails that cut quiet pathways through forest and meadow, located on the San Francisco Peninsula above WOODSIDE.

This park is one of the best around for cleaning the cobwebs out of your brain, offering a variety of trails from short strolls to all-day treks. Take your pick. I hiked here all day with a companion and we did not see a single other hiker. Now that's what I call solitude. The trail cuts through lush ravines to mountainsides strewn with redwoods. That's called beauty. It's the combination you may be seeking.

First get a map of the park, which details all of the trails. You will discover that because the network of trails intersects at several points, you can tailor your hike to fit the amount of time you have as well as your level of ambition. A good hike for first-timers is a loop trip from the main park entrance to "The Meadows," or to Alambique Creek and Redwood Flat. If you don't want to spend all day hiking, this is a good compromise.

But if you want to challenge yourself, your goal should be the SKYLINE RIDGE at 2,200 feet. A 10-mile, five-hour round-trip to the ridge can be a highlight. You gain almost 2,000 feet, which can get you puffing like a locomotive, but most of the grade is a gentle, steady climb. In the process you cross through a wide variety of plant and tree communities—and also reach some classic vistas OF SAN FRANCISCO BAY and the East Bay hills.

It's at these lookouts where the rewards of hiking become clear. Here you are on the edge of the Bay Area, on the outside looking in.

A few notes, however. Poison oak can be prevalent in some areas. If you're vulnerable, wear long-sleeved shirts, wash your clothes right after your hike, and, of course, stay on the trails. The latter can do more than anything to protect you. In addition, no drinking water is available on the trails, so bring a small daypack with a lunch and drinks, or at least a canteen.

Directions: The most direct route from Interstate 280 is to take the Sand Hill Road exit, then head west to Portola Road. Turn right and continue just past the junction with Highway 84. The park entrance is on the left; a large sign is posted. **Fees:** A $4 fee per car is charged. **Maps:** For a free map, send a stamped, self-addressed envelope to the San Mateo County Parks and Recreation Department, 590 Hamilton Street, 4th Floor, Redwood City, CA 94063. **Pets:** No pets are allowed. **Contact:** San Mateo County Parks and Recreation Department, (650) 363-4020; Wunderlich County Park, (650) 851-7570. **Locator:** WUNDERLICH COUNTY PARK (E1b).

• FEATURED TRIP •

★ EAST BAY SKYLINE NATIONAL TRAIL

Rated: The Top 25 Hikes, 2; The Top 50 Parks, 7; The Top 9 Doggy Getaway Ideas, 196

A 31-mile trail along the East Bay's skyline offers a unique opportunity for a long-distance hike that can be chopped into many little segments over the course of days or weeks.

The trail extends from the CASTRO VALLEY foothills northward to the ridgeline behind RICHMOND, in the process crossing six regional parks, including some of the region's prettiest and wildest lands. Called the EAST BAY SKYLINE NATIONAL TRAIL, it is the Bay Area's longest single continuous trail.

I once hiked the route south to north in two days, but you can divide the trip into seven sections using the different access points available at parking areas. Bicycles and horses are permitted on the roughly 65 percent of the trail that is wide enough to accommodate them.

It is a great trip, whether for a weekend or over several weeks, taking it a little at a time. No permits are needed, leashed dogs are allowed, and access is free. The only drawbacks are the lack of campgrounds along the route, which makes backpacking and overnights impossible, and the lack of piped drinking water. Water is available at only four points over 31 miles of trail, at Lomas Cantadas, SIBLEY PRESERVE, Skyline Gate, and Bort Meadow. Come prepared for each day of hiking with a full canteen of water per person, along with a hat and sunscreen.

My two favorite legs of the trip are from Inspiration Point in TILDEN RE-

GIONAL PARK north along San Pablo Ridge and the steep, dense section of trail in Huckleberry Regional Preserve.

On the remote areas of San Pablo Ridge, the views are sweeping in all directions, with Briones and SAN PABLO RESERVOIRS to the east and San Francisco Bay and the city to the west, yet there is almost nobody out on this section of trail. At Huckleberry Preserve, there are also few visitors to a very steep, densely wooded section of trail at the southern end of the park. You'll find squirrels, foxes, and a variety and abundance of birdlife, including a resident eagle, but because it is so steep, only rarely will you encounter another hiker. Bicycles are banned from this section.

Of course, there are many divine settings. The redwoods are a heavenly vision in Redwood Regional Park, where a thick forest lines a canyon wall for miles, enclosing a small, beautiful trout stream. Bort Meadow at the northern end of Chabot Regional Park is a perfect picnic site; after rains, the adjacent Grass Valley seems vibrant with life.

Another one of my favorite sections of the trail is the two-mile hike from SIBLEY PRESERVE over the Caldecott Tunnel and on to Lomas Cantadas at the southern end of TILDEN PARK. For one reason, the section is wild and infrequently traveled, a place to go slow, and it seems a paradox that below you in the tunnel are so many in a hurry, driving somewhere fast. Another reason is that from Lomas Cantadas it is about a 20-minute walk up to Vollmer Peak (1,913 feet), the highest point on the EAST BAY SKYLINE NATIONAL TRAIL.

Following my preferred route from south to north, here is a synopsis of each of the seven major sections of trail:

PROCTOR GATE TO BORT MEADOW

The trail starts next to a golf course and is routed up a ridge, then meanders on a ranch road in CHABOT PARK. At Stone Bridge (don't turn left at the trail junction!), the trail leads into Grass Valley and on to Bort Meadow.

Distance: 6.5 miles, climbing 600 feet, then dropping 320 feet. **Locator:** CHABOT REGIONAL PARK (E1c).

BORT MEADOW TO MACDONALD GATE

The trail climbs steeply out of Bort Meadow. At the ridge, turn and look south for the great view of Grass Valley. This is an open face, hot and dry in the afternoon, that is best hiked in the early morning. From the ridge, the trail proceeds through a hardwood forest, with some chaparral in the mix, then drops into a canyon, crosses Redwood Road, and puts you at the entrance to REDWOOD REGIONAL PARK.

Distance: 2.7 miles, climbing 300 feet, then dropping 500 feet. **Locator:** CHABOT REGIONAL PARK (E1c).

MACDONALD GATE TO SKYLINE GATE

Hikers have two options here. My preference is to split off at the French Trail in order to hike up the canyon bottom, enveloped by redwoods. In addition, bikes are banned from this section of trail. The alternative, a must for bikers, is to take the West Ridge Trail, a steep climb routed to the canyon rim, which then drops to the junction at Skyline Gate.

Distance: 5 miles, dropping 200 feet, then climbing 400 feet via the French Trail; climbing 900 feet, then dropping 200 feet via West Ridge. **Locator:** REDWOOD REGIONAL PARK (E1c).

Skyline Gate through Huckleberry Preserve to Sibley Preserve

Here is a choice hike for nature lovers, with an abundance of birdlife and other wildlife, especially in the early morning and late evening. The trail passes through a deciduous woodland habitat, with a short but quite steep climb after entering Huckleberry Preserve.

Distance: 3 miles, dropping 200 feet, then climbing 480 feet. **Locator:** Sibley Volcanic Regional Preserve (E1c).

Sibley Volcanic Regional Preserve to Lomas Cantadas

This unique section of trail crosses over the Caldecott Tunnel, a relatively unpeopled stretch. The area has many hawks, a nice bonus. Sibley is best known for its volcanic past, with a side trip available to Mount Round Top, a one-time volcano that blew its top off. No bicycles are permitted.

Distance: 3.4 miles, dropping 300 feet, then climbing 600 feet. **Locator:** Tilden Regional Park (E1c).

Lomas Cantadas to Inspiration Point

This section of trail starts at a major access area off Grizzly Peak Boulevard, with an adjacent side trip available to Vollmer Peak, the highest point on the East Bay Skyline National Trail. The trail is then routed north to Inspiration Point at Wildcat Canyon Road, another well-known access point, losing elevation most of the way. Hikers enjoy many sweeping views of the East Bay's wildest lands on this portion of the trail.

Distance: 3 miles, dropping 860 feet. **Locator:** Tilden Regional Park (E1c).

Inspiration Point to Wildcat Canyon Regional Park

The last stretch starts at the most heavily used section of the entire trail, then crosses its most dramatic and unpeopled area. From Inspiration Point, the trail is actually paved for four miles, ideal for bicycles and wheelchairs. Beyond that, it to turns to dirt and traces San Pablo Ridge, with inspiring views in all directions, before dropping very steeply into Wildcat Canyon Park in the Richmond foothills.

Distance: 7.2 miles, dropping 800 feet. **Contact:** For a brochure and map of the East Bay Skyline National Trail, or individual maps of each regional park, phone the East Bay Regional Park District, (510) 635-0135 extension 2200. **Locator:** Richmond (E1c).

• FEATURED TRIP •

Franklin Ridge

Rated: The Top 14 Places to Fly Kites, 389

Timing can be everything when it comes to love, business, and adventures. When it comes to dusk at a place called Franklin Ridge, the timing is better than money in the bank. In fact, it will make you fall in love with the place.

What happens at dusk here is that even harsh features take on a soft glow, and the beautiful highlights can seem almost surreal. Franklin Ridge overlooks Carquinez Strait, the gateway to the Delta, where sunsets are gorgeous with yellow and orange hues cast across both the hills and the water. As darkness takes over, lights from boats, bridges, and piers can reflect off the water, mirrored and beautiful.

It gets even better when you stop, stretch out your arms, and soak in the surroundings with a full turn. The views from the top are highlighted by miles of waterfront and the East Bay foothills, all of it changing color minute by minute at dusk, as the sunlight diminishes.

FRANKLIN RIDGE is easy to reach, less than a 10-minute drive from MARTINEZ; in fact, I was cruising through the Bay Area when I decided to get away from some lunatic drivers and made the short detour to regain my sanity. The trailhead is on Carquinez Scenic Drive (for directions, see below), and as you drive in, you can clearly see FRANKLIN RIDGE, set on the hilltop overlooking MARTINEZ. Even when you first spot it from a distance, it looks like an intriguing place with great views. No lie.

At the staging area, the East Bay Regional Park District often has a small brochure/map available for free; you can also obtain one by phoning (510) 635-0135 extension 2200. Rules set by the park district allow your dog to join you on your adventure, providing he is kept under control at all times. Bikes are also allowed, but mountain bikers should be prepared for a climb that is easy enough on foot but on a bike can seem to the unconditioned like running into a wall.

The trailhead and parking area for FRANKLIN RIDGE is called the Carquinez Strait East Staging Area. From here, the hike starts up the California Riding and Hiking Trail, where you will generally be heading toward FRANKLIN RIDGE, climbing all the way. As you go, including up a few short, steep spots, the views start getting better and better. It then connects to the Franklin Ridge Loop, an old ranch road.

The loop circles the ridge, with great views most of the way and with one section dropping into a ravine filled with live oak and bay. But there are very few trees on the top, so you get a clear, sweeping view of CARQUINEZ STRAIT. I can't imagine this region looking prettier than at dusk, brought to life by the lights of MARTINEZ, BENICIA, and the MARTINEZ-BENICIA BRIDGE.

After finishing the Franklin Loop, you will again intersect with the Riding and Hiking Trail, and return to the parking area. In all, the trip covers 3.1 miles and takes about two hours to complete on foot, including 15 minutes or so to stop and enjoy the views.

On top of FRANKLIN RIDGE, visitors often experience a moment of total irony. Nearby, within 10 miles, are three major highways—Interstates 80 and 680, and Highway 4—each of which has its share of drivers who can seem crazed, dodging around each other, taking bizarre high-speed cuts, trying to save time. Yet up there on that ridge, there isn't a care in the world, other than the beautiful view that evolves each moment as you turn to a new vantage point, the colors changing as day gives way to dusk.

At that moment, time doesn't matter. And it's all because you had great timing.

Directions: From Martinez, take Highway 4 to the Alhambra Avenue exit and drive north on Alhambra for two miles (toward Carquinez Strait). Turn left on Escobar Street and drive three blocks to Talbart Street. Turn right and drive about half a mile (Talbart Street becomes Carquinez Scenic Drive) to the parking area on the left side of the road. **Fees:** Parking and access are free. **Contact:** For a free map/brochure or other information, contact the East Bay Regional Park District, 2950 Peralta Oaks Court, P.O. Box 5381, Oakland, CA 94605, (510) 635-0135 extension 2200. **Locator:** FRANKLIN RIDGE (E1c).

• FEATURED TRIP •

MARTINEZ SHORELINE

Rated: Renovation Makes It a First-Class Harbor

One of the surprise stories of the great outdoors is how the Martinez Marina, along with the adjacent MARTINEZ REGIONAL SHORELINE PARK, has suddenly become one of the top destinations in the Bay Area.

How big of a surprise? Well, people from as far away as the Peninsula, MARIN, and the DELTA are making the trip on weekends, and they keep coming back, giving a local hot spot some regional prominence.

The primary reason is the fishing access, with a renovated marina, boat ramp, pier, party boats, bait shop, and added parking, as well as sturgeon fishing.

But it goes beyond that. The adjacent parkland was cleaned up and now offers first-class picnic sites, shoreline walks with beautiful views of CARQUINEZ STRAIT, excellent bird-watching, and even a lagoon with geese and coots and grassy areas with tons of pigeons. For families with youngsters, this is the best place around to feed geese and pigeons.

Best of all, everything is fresh and clean, with no litter. On one visit, I saw a crew of youngsters raking and picking up any refuse they could find. Perhaps they were being trained by CalTrans, because all were wearing orange coats, one person was working, and seven others were watching. Heh, heh.

MARTINEZ has been a well-known fishing spot for years, and the nearby mothball fleet of old ships is legendary among longtime anglers. A party boat out of MARTINEZ, the *Happy Hooker*, came home one winter day with 23 sturgeon, the highest one-day score in Bay Area history, and MARTINEZ was back on the map.

New owners have renovated the bait shop and attracted new party boats to the marina. In addition, it is an easy place to park, launch a boat, then make the short cruise to the mothball fleet. But with its location in CARQUINEZ STRAIT, MARTINEZ is also an easy jump-off spot for boaters to reach not only the mothball fleet, but Grizzly Bay and Montezuma Slough to the east as well as SAN PABLO BAY to the west, all good spots.

The fishing is what has attracted people from significant distances. But those who prefer walking, bird-watching, sight-seeing, and picnicking will discover that the adjacent MARTINEZ REGIONAL SHORELINE is just as attractive.

Newcomers will find a lagoon located within 40 yards of the parking lot. It is loaded with geese and coots, well fed and always eager to eat handouts. These are usually supplied in ample portions by youngsters tossing out bits of bread.

During a feeding binge, you will not only find yourself surrounded by geese but by pigeons, with dozens and dozens of them begging for a handout along the grassy shore. Judging by their demanding comportment, perhaps they were trained by the panhandlers in SAN FRANCISCO.

Most visitors either go for a walk on the shoreline Pickleweed Trail or have a picnic. The Pickleweed Trail is a great little walk, spanning about a mile of waterfront. It takes about an hour, even walking slowly, but can be expanded east along CARQUINEZ STRAIT.

From the parking area, the trail crosses pretty Arch Bridge (over muddy Alhambra Creek), where you get a great view of the waterfront. It then runs along the shoreline, passing an old wooden hull of a schooner. This is a popular spot for birds, because of the nearby mouth of the creek, and on one visit there was a virtual raft of canvasback ducks, and a few mallards, with some white egrets poking along the shore.

The walk is easy and flat, with CARQUINEZ STRAIT on one side, marshland on the other. The trail extends to the western boundary of the 343-acre park, then links with another trail that runs beside railroad tracks for miles, heading west along the shore.

Most visitors will explore the marina instead or head to the picnic area. The latter is well maintained and pretty, set in a grassy area near the park entrance. On good weather weekends, all the tables are usually taken for lunch and dinner picnics.

Directions: From Highway 4 in Martinez, take the Alhambra Drive exit and head north, following signs to the parking area next to the pier. **Fees:** Access is free. **Contact:** For a brochure of Martinez Regional Shoreline, phone (510) 635-0135 extension 2200. Martinez Bait and Tackle, (510) 229-9420; *Happy Hooker,* (510) 223-5388. **Locator:** MARTINEZ (E1c).

• FEATURED TRIP •

★ MORGAN TERRITORY REGIONAL PRESERVE

Rated: The Top 25 Hikes, 2; The Top 10 Scenic Back Roads, 198

MORGAN TERRITORY is the Bay Area's mystery park. Not many people have heard of it, fewer know where it is, and just a handful of know-hows realize that in the spring, this is one of the area's best-kept recreation secrets.

It is just far enough out there to make a visit special and is remote enough to feel as if you have left the Bay Area behind. Miles of greenery are loaded with blooming wildflowers in the spring and summer, adding some sparkle to dramatic views from the ridges.

Where? Where? Where? This hidden park is located in remote eastern Contra Costa County, in the eastern foothills of MOUNT DIABLO, about 10 miles north of LIVERMORE. Though a trip to LIVERMORE might sound about as exciting as a vacation in GILROY, the idea that some place secret actually exists near LIVERMORE can actually add to the intrigue.

You can bring your dog and do not even have to keep him on a leash, as long as he is under control. Imagine that.

The best trail here is the Volvon Loop, a 5.7-mile trip that takes about three hours of hiking on a trail that undulates through the foothills but has little elevation gain.

The parking area and trailhead are set at about 2,000 feet in elevation. From here, you hike northward along Walker Ridge, rising and dropping amid the park's hills and sandstone outcrops. To your northwest is MOUNT

DIABLO; to the east you can see the vast expanse of the Central Valley and, on clear days, the Sierra crest and its snowpack gleaming in the sun.

The best route is to hike the Volvon Trail to an unnamed peak (1,977 feet), then circle the peak on the Volvon Loop. You can then return the way you came, or take either the Blue Oak Trail (fairly level) or Coyote Trail (which drops into a valley to Marsh Creek and then requires a climb back out). All of them return to the parking area.

Once you hike out to the peak, the preferred route back is to take the Blue Oak Trail, because it is routed through a pretty stand of blue oaks and buckeyes. Though a bit longer than the Volvon Trail, it is just as easy to hike.

Spring is one of the best times to visit, for the surrounding hills are bright green and loaded with wildflowers. Where the Volvon Trail junctions with the Volvon Loop, there might be a hillside filled with bird's-eye gilia and, in various places, fully blooming ceanothus (a bush loaded with light violet blooms) and tons of buttercups. And then there are all the usuals, including golden poppies and brodiaea (a blue flower on long stalks that is better known as "blue dick").

Morgan Territory also is filled with history. It is located within the traditional homeland of the Volvon, one of five historical Indian nations in the MOUNT DIABLO area. The Volvon Trail, named after the first people of the area, is the feature hike in the park.

You can see further evidence of this on the Coyote Trail. In an area along Marsh Creek, best found by looking for an adjacent single live oak, there is a rock once used for acorn grinding by the Volvon people. Look for a rock with a series of bowl-like pits carved into it. This is where the Volvon mashed the acorns into flour, then leached the tannic taste out of the flour using water from the adjacent creek.

According to legend, this activity would always draw a large crowd of squirrels in the nearby trees, watching in envy.

Directions: From Oakland, drive east on Interstate 580 to the North Livermore Avenue exit, then head north on North Livermore Avenue for four miles to Highland Road. Turn left and drive a short distance, then turn right on Morgan Territory Road. The road twists and climbs out of the Livermore Valley, rising into the Diablo foothills, then narrows, climbing a ridge. After topping a hill, look along the right side of the road for a dirt parking area with a wood sign that says, "Morgan Territory Regional Preserve." **Contact:** For a brochure/map, contact the East Bay Regional Park District, 2950 Peralta Oaks Court, P.O. Box 5381, Oakland, CA 94605 (510) 635-0135 extension 2200. The naturalists at nearby Black Diamond Mines Regional Preserve lead guided hikes at Morgan Territory; phone them at (510) 757-2620. **Locator:** MORGAN TERRITORY REGIONAL PRESERVE (E1c).

• FEATURED TRIP •

★ MOUNT DIABLO STATE PARK

Rated: The Top 50 Parks, 7; The Top 12 Hike-to Streams, 24; The Top 15 Surprise Hikes in the Rain, 28; The Top 5 Steep Hikes, 38; The Top 20 Hike-to Waterfalls, 187; The Top 9 Places to Bird-Watch, 252; The Top 10 Chances for Bay Area

Snow, 288; The Top 4 Places to Sky Watch, 394

Anytime is a good time to visit MOUNT DIABLO, the old 3,849-foot-high mountain in the East Bay hills that seems to tower over everything. The hikes, bike trips, driving tours, and views are year-round attractions, and then there are the seasonal waterfalls, wildflowers, and greenery. MOUNT DIABLO is actually the second highest mountain in the Bay Area; MOUNT HAMILTON is the highest at 4,062 feet, but DIABLO has the most imposing presence.

There are really two MOUNT DIABLOS. The familiar summit is one of the West's greatest lookouts. Not so well known is the other DIABLO, even though it features the mountain's most fascinating geological characteristics, the China Wall and Castle Rocks.

Every season brings its own experience of the mountain, but I like to visit in the spring when the rain saturates the ground. The hidden waterfalls and wildflowers are sensational, and it's vibrant green all the way to the top. When March winds leave the air crystal pure, you can see to forever from the summit.

Put together, all of these elements make MOUNT DIABLO one of the prime one-day getaways in the Bay Area.

Here is a synopsis of the best of it:

DRIVING TOURS

The drive to the top of MOUNT DIABLO is long and curvy, but it makes a great tour on a clear day. You can drive right to the summit, and in the process you will pass several pullouts along the road where you can stop and enjoy the views, often with hawks hovering in the rising thermals, or either take a short walk or start a bike trip from roadside trailheads.

At the summit, an outstanding visitor center is perched on the top of the mountain, where Diablo's exact tiptop actually pokes through the floor of the building and is circled by a short enclosure. There are also displays that detail the mountain's views, flora, and wildlife, and a miniature replica of the mountain that shows the different trails for hiking and biking.

It was at the visitor center where we spotted a photograph of Donner Creek Falls and were inspired to embark on a great hike to see Diablo's five hidden waterfalls. There was also a surprise hatch of friendly ladybugs, hordes of them, that covered everything on the summit within 200 yards. Never seen anything like it.

VIEWS

The distant views from the mountain are remarkable, like nothing else in California, even though they are not as breathtaking as the ocean and bay vistas from MOUNT TAMALPAIS.

On clear days, looking west, you can see across SAN FRANCISCO BAY to the GOLDEN GATE BRIDGE (66 miles), the PACIFIC OCEAN, and 25 miles out to sea, the FARALLON ISLANDS. To the east you can see the snow-covered Sierra crest, and on a perfect day with binoculars, it is possible to see a piece of Half Dome sticking out from YOSEMITE VALLEY 135 miles away.

To the north, you can see well up the Central Valley and spot MOUNT LASSEN 165 miles distant. To the south lie many miles of rolling foothills/mountains extending toward the Livermore Valley. Even on less than pristine days, the overlook to the Delta and Central Valley is unmatched.

Waterfalls

Finding Diablo's hidden waterfalls is a great fortune hunt, in which the rewards of a 6.5-mile hike are views of a series of five falls.

Do not attempt this hike without a detailed park map. Many of those who try without a good map end up missing a key turn and never find the falls. Also note that the trailhead for Donner Creek Falls is nowhere near the summit, but rather at the end of Regency Drive, which is located off of Clayton Road (which becomes Marsh Creek Road) out of CLAYTON.

Don't let this warning scare you off. This is my favorite hike in the East Bay counties, featuring a walk along Donner Creek, then rising amid pretty rolling hills peppered with oaks. You cross a stream and, after climbing a short series of switchbacks, walk along a pretty trail on the left side of a canyon. Then, one by one the falls come into view.

The first is a 20-foot cascade, across the other side of the canyon. Moments later, you see another straight ahead, more of a chute. You keep on and two more come in view, including one short but pretty free fall. Then, scanning across the slopes, you can see yet another, a smaller cascade. After a spring rain, they are gorgeous.

Hiking

Most newcomers to DIABLO head straight to the summit, drop in to the visitor center, and are ready for a short hike. When you're ready, drive back down about a quarter mile to a pullout along a deep bend in the road, where an unsigned trailhead is located.

From here, it is a delightful walk for a little over a mile down to Prospector's Gap, with more than a dozen kinds of wildflowers providing color along the way in the spring and excellent views of the Delta and Central Valley. Once at the Gap, you can add another mile, climbing 500 feet in the process, to reach Diablo's North Peak, which rises 3,557 feet into the sky and affords more sweeping views.

If the Diablo Summit is crowded, as is commonly the case on spring weekends, this hike allows you the great option of going to a more isolated lookout. For those who want an even more secluded venture, there is a lesser-known park on the northwestern slopes of Diablo. Diablo Foothills Regional Park is not well known, yet for many who do wind up there, it becomes their favorite spot on the mountain.

The featured hike here is the China Wall Loop, a 3.3-mile route that explores both China Wall and a lookout to the Castle Rocks. Note that this is my own name for the trail; you won't find a sign that reads "China Wall Loop," but you will know what I'm talking about when you see the distinctive line of sandstone rocks. To hike it, start at the Borges Ranch Trailhead in Diablo Foothills Regional Park. It's a 1.5-mile hike, heading off on the Briones-to–Mount Diablo Trail. Turn right at the trail junction (Alamo Valley Trail), which runs half a mile along the base of China Wall. Along the way, you'll get glimpses to the east of Castle Rocks, prominent sandstone outcrops located just outside the park boundaries. Bring binoculars, since you'll have a chance of seeing golden eagles, hawks, and falcons, all of which nest here. To complete the loop hike, turn right again on Hanging Valley Trail and hike back to the parking area.

Directions (Mount Diablo State Park)**:** From Danville on Interstate 680, take the Diablo Road exit and drive a short distance. Turn east on Black Hawk Road and go to South Gate Road. Turn left and proceed to the park. **Directions** (Diablo Foothills Regional Park): From Walnut Creek on Interstate 680, drive north to the Ignacio Valley Road exit. Turn east and drive to Walnut Avenue. Turn right on Walnut Avenue, which runs into a Y at Oak Grove Road. Veer to the right on Oak Grove. A short distance later, Oak Grove becomes Castle Rock Road. Follow that road to its end, where there is a well-signed parking area and trailheads. **Contact:** Mount Diablo State Park, (925) 837-2525. For Diablo Foothills Regional Park information, phone the Las Trampas Wilderness Office, (925) 837-3145. **Locator:** MOUNT DIABLO (E1c).

• FEATURED TRIP •

★ MURIETTA FALLS

Rated: The Top 5 Steep Hikes, 38; The Top 20 Hike-to Waterfalls, 187

The Bay Area's highest waterfall is little known and rarely seen. It is not in the SANTA CRUZ MOUNTAINS, nor is it in MARIN. Rather, it is hidden away in the southern Alameda County wilderness, where few venture.

I'm talking about MURIETTA FALLS, named after the legendary outlaw of the 1800s, Joaquin Murietta. It is set in the OHLONE WILDERNESS, where a free-flowing creek runs through a rocky gorge then plunges 100 feet over a cliff, landing in the rocks below. Upstream, there is an additional series of small pools and cascades, which, with MURIETTA FALLS, creates a destination like nothing else in the East Bay.

Why do so few people even know about it? Why is it rarely visited?

The answer is not blowing in the wind. The answer is because it takes a butt-kicker of a hike to get there, 5.5 miles each way, most of it up a steep ridge.

MURIETTA FALLS is a beautiful silver-tasseled stream after winter rains. It makes the hike well worth the effort, though only those in good physical shape should try.

The best trailhead is at DEL VALLE REGIONAL PARK, located south of LIVERMORE. When you enter the park, be certain to obtain an Ohlone Wilderness Trail Permit, which costs $2 per person and includes a map. You also pay a park entrance fee of $3 to $5, depending upon the season. Park at the south end of Del Valle Reservoir, which is close to the trailhead.

Are you ready? Are you in good shape? Are you prepared to inflict pain on yourself? You'd best be, because you're going to have to work before you can get the payoff.

Take the trailhead for the Ohlone Wilderness Trail. In less than a mile, you will reach a posted information panel, where there is a sign-in register. The panel includes details about how steep a hike you are about to undertake—and, by the way, you will likely be puffing pretty good already by this time.

But it gets worse. The steepest section of the entire 28-mile Ohlone Wilderness Trail starts here, climbing 1,600 feet in just 1.5 miles. This is as steep as anything I've come across in mountain wilderness, including the Kalmiopsis Wilderness in southern Oregon, which is known for having the steepest wilderness trails in the western United States.

It tops out at Rocky Ridge, drops into Williams Gulch, then climbs again toward even higher Wauhab Ridge. You reach as high as 3,300 feet, before turning right on the Springboard Trail (signpost 35, not 36). From there, it's one mile to the waterfall.

Walk along a ridge about a quarter mile, then turn left on the Greenside Trail, which descends into a valley and to the falls. When MURIETTA FALLS first comes into view, it presents an astonishing contrast with the East Bay hills, a grassland and oak habitat where you wouldn't expect to see steep cliffs and a waterfall.

But here it is, pouring 100 feet, framed by often green hills, a remarkable refuge of tranquility only a few miles from suburbia, concrete, and traffic jams.

Although MURIETTA is the Bay Area's highest waterfall, taller even than the spectacular 70-foot Berry Creek Falls in BIG BASIN REDWOODS STATE PARK, it rarely sees visitors. The most frequent ones are the occasional marathon runner who uses the Ohlone Wilderness Trail as a mode of self-torture and decides to make the short side trip. Even on a late winter weekend, after rains have the waterfall flush and cascading, it is likely to be flowing in isolation.

Late winter or early spring is the time to visit. Even in big rain years, the creek is reduced to a trickle by summer and sometimes even goes dry. In addition, it gets hot out here, really smokin': 100 degrees is typical come summer. By July, the hills are brown, the waterfall disappears, and only the ghost of Murietta remains to laugh as you struggle to make that 1,600-foot climb.

Even in winter, always take at least two full canteens of water, as well as a daypack with food and spare clothing. In addition, always tell at least one person where you are going. A solo hiker could get stranded out here and, without a trip plan, not be found for several days. If you want to stay overnight in the wilderness, a trail camp (Stewart's Camp) is available about half a mile from MURIETTA FALLS; reservations are required.

My favorite time to visit is in March, when the soil has been saturated by rains and the first warming days of spring inspire wild grass and wildflowers to sprout forth. The wildflower displays can be spectacular, a sea of blooms, and you'll see many birds soaring in the thermals, including eagles, hawks, and, alas, vultures.

Yes, it's you they're interested in. You see, they, too, realize just how difficult the hike is to MURIETTA FALLS.

Directions: From eastbound Interstate 580 at Livermore, take the North Livermore Avenue exit. Turn south and travel on North/South Livermore Road (this will turn into Tesla Road) to Mines Road. Turn right and drive about three miles south to Del Valle Road. Turn right and continue for three miles to the entrance to Del Valle Regional Park. Park at the south end of Del Valle Reservoir, which is near the trailhead for Murietta Falls. **Fees:** Del Valle Regional Park charges an entrance fee of $3 from December through February, $4 from March through November, and $5 on weekends and holidays throughout the year. **Maps, permits:** To obtain a map and permit for the Ohlone Wilderness Trail, send a check for $2, payable to East Bay Parks, to Reservations Department, East Bay Regional Park

District, 2950 Peralta Oaks Court, P.O. Box 5381, Oakland, CA 94605-0381. **Camping:** For information about backcountry camping, phone (510) 562-CAMP/2267. **Contact:** Del Valle Regional Park, (925) 373-0332 or (925) 373-0405; East Bay Regional Park District, (510) 635-0135 extension 2200. **Locator:** MURIETTA FALLS (E1d).

• FEATURED TRIP •

Sibley Volcanic Regional Preserve

Rated: The Top 10 Spots to Go on a Date, 182

Have you ever wanted to walk on the side of a volcano? Well, you don't have to go to Mount St. Helens in Washington, not with ol' Mount Round Top sitting above OAKLAND. And you don't have to worry about getting your toes fried either. Round Top, now named the Sibley Volcanic Regional Preserve, is extinct. It's a unique part of the East Bay Regional Park District.

It's an ideal half-day hike or evening jaunt for explorers and geologists alike. From the old quarry site at the eastern border of the park, hikers can get a first-class view of the East Bay hills and MOUNT DIABLO.

Spring is the best time to go because the area is fresh with newly sprouted grass and wildflowers, and the park is cooled by northwesterly breezes off SAN FRANCISCO BAY. Avoid the summer, particularly September, when it can get so hot here that you'll think you could fry an egg on a rock. You'd swear a cauldron of lava was getting ready to blast out of Round Top.

But a close look at the mountain allays those fears. Round Top has already shot its steam. In fact, after it blasted out its lava contents, the interior of the mountain collapsed into the void left by the outburst. Blocks of volcanic stone are scattered everywhere around the flanks of the peak.

Some of these have been dated at almost 10 million years old. When you pick up a rock that is 10 million years old, it has a way of making your stay on Earth seem a little bit short.

About half a mile northwest of Round Top, a quarry operation has made a large cut into the side of the extinct volcano. This allows hikers to view the roots of the volcano, as well as a major volcanic vent. If you want to explore the unusual geology of the mountain, a self-guided tour brochure that marks the key spots is provided free at the East Bay Regional Park District office. One sector, on the northern edge of the park, shows one of the most spectacular volcanic outcrops in the Bay Area.

If geology is not your game, no problem. The park still provides a good half-day hike, especially if you want to bring your dog. Park rules allow you to let your pooch run free in open space and undeveloped areas of parkland, provided he remains under your control. Considering that state parks do not even allow leashed dogs on trails, this is quite a bonus for dog owners.

A section of the EAST BAY SKYLINE NATIONAL TRAIL cuts across the western border of the park and connects to a road that circles the park. It makes for a few hours of puffing. For the ambitious, the SKYLINE TRAIL can connect you to the town of EL SOBRANTE, 12 miles by trail to the north, or to CASTRO VALLEY, 17 miles to the south.

Other volcanic areas in California

include the Pinnacles near HOLLISTER, the Sutter Buttes in the Sacramento Valley, and MOUNT LASSEN in the SHASTA area.

Mount Round Top is right in the backyard of a million East Bay residents, yet is known by only a few.

Directions: From Interstate 580 to the west or Interstate 680 to the east, drive to Highway 24. Proceed to just east of the Caldecott Tunnel and take the Fish Ranch Road exit west to Grizzly Peak Boulevard. Continue south to the park entrance. **Fees:** Access and brochures are free. **Trip tip:** If long hikes are not for you, you can drive within a quarter mile of the peak of Mount Round Top for spectacular views of the Bay Area. **Pets:** Your dog is allowed to run free in open spaces and undeveloped areas, but must be under control at all times. **Contact:** For more information, phone the East Bay Regional Park District, (510) 635-0135 extension 2200. **Locator:** SIBLEY VOLCANIC REGIONAL PRESERVE (E1c).

• FEATURED TRIP •

SUNOL REGIONAL WILDERNESS

Rated: The Top 25 Hikes, 2; The Top 50 Parks, 7; The Top 12 Hike-to Streams, 24; The Top 15 Surprise Hikes in the Rain, 28; The Top 7 Hikes with a Dog, 30; The Top 50 Base Camps, 110; The Top 5 Winter Backpacking Trips, 156; The Top 10 Spots for a First Kiss, 180

There are unique, hidden places in the Bay Area that can feel like secret spots known only to you. That's how Little Yosemite is. Now wait a minute. Little Yosemite? Isn't that the park where four million campers a year look at Half Dome and get their food raided by Smokey the Bear? No, that's big YOSEMITE.

Its little brother is situated east of FREMONT near Interstate 680. There is no El Capitan or Cathedral Rocks here, but neither is there a Curry Village. In other words, there is usually nobody around. Little Yosemite is part of the SUNOL REGIONAL WILDERNESS, a 6,500-acre wilderness area in the East Bay hills. You say you've never been there? Join the club.

The centerpiece of the park is Little Yosemite, a hidden canyon edged by craggy rock outcrops and cut by a little trout stream. The stream is just a trickle in late summer, but when the rains come the river forms a nice waterfall around a giant boulder.

Visiting makes for a prime half-day adventure. The park is only a short drive away for most Bay Area residents. If you have a dog, by all means bring him along because this is one of the few places where dogs are allowed on the trails.

There are six trails in the SUNOL REGIONAL WILDERNESS. For your first trip, the best choice is the Canyon View Trail, about a 3.5-mile round-trip that sweeps above the valley to the canyon rim above Little Yosemite. It offers a fine view from the top of the cliffs. (A wide, flat trail in the bottom of the valley makes Little Yosemite wheelchair accessible.)

For a good loop hike from the parking area, take the Canyon Rim Trail to the Yosemite Valley Overlook. From there, you will spot a gated cutoff trail that drops down to the floor of Little Yosemite.

Like much of the East Bay hills, Little Yosemite is owned by the San Francisco Water District. The East Bay Regional Park District has taken the lead in working out a few special deals for the water district land—opening not only Little Yosemite, but the 28-mile Ohlone Wilderness Trail as well. In the process, it has proved that recreational access can be provided to the public without risking any environmental impact.

In fact, the biggest impact to this area is not from the few people who visit, but from the numerous wild boars that live here. You can see evidence of their rooting and digging, and if you're lucky, you might even spot one deep in a shaded canyon.

Little Yosemite is also an ideal habitat for a variety of birds. In a morning, you might spot 20 species. It's a result of the riparian habitat of the Alameda Creek setting, which supports alder, willow, and sycamore trees.

Out here, you can see red-tailed hawks cruising for their next meal. In addition to boar, deer sightings are common. There are also a few skunks in the hills, so if you bring a dog, keep her on a leash—or she might chase the "black and white cat with the big tail" and end up getting a skunk blast.

Regardless of whether you're here for an overnighter, or just to take the short half-day loop through Little Yosemite, you'll remember this park as a hidden spot—one that you'll wish you knew about years ago.

Directions: From Interstate 680, take the Calaveras Road turnoff just south of the town of Sunol. Turn left at Calaveras Road and continue to Geary Road. Turn left and follow Geary to the park entrance. **Fees:** A $3 per vehicle parking fee is charged. Campsite fees are $11 per night. **Special law:** No alcohol is permitted in the park. **Camping:** There are a few campsites near the parking area, as well as backcountry hike-in camping. A backpacking camping permit is required in advance. For reservations, phone (510) 636-1684 ($5 reservation fee). **Contact:** For maps or general information, phone the East Bay Regional Park District, (510) 635-0135 extension 2200. For trail information, phone park headquarters, (925) 862-2244. **Locator:** SUNOL/OHLONE REGIONAL WILDERNESS (E1c).

• FEATURED TRIP •

TILDEN REGIONAL PARK

Rated: The Top 25 Hikes, 2; The Top 6 One-Way Hikes Using Public Transportation, 32; The Top 4 One-Way Hikes Using a Shuttle Car, 34; The Top 10 Spots for a First Kiss, 180; The Top 16 East Bay Lakes, 205; The Top 5 Bike Rides, 278; The Top 14 Places to Fly Kites, 389; The Top 10 Swimming Holes, 395

When you're perched atop Inspiration Point in the East Bay hills during the early evening, the beautiful views can sweep away all your daily gripes.

This quiet spot is roosted above BERKELEY in TILDEN REGIONAL PARK. The best thing about this park is that it offers a number of different activities, including hiking, bicycling, horseback riding, weekend backpacking, cross-country jogging, and even a scenic trail for those who do their walking in a wheelchair. And you can bring your dog along to join in the adventure, a bonus most state parks don't allow.

One of the Bay Area's most dramatic lookouts is on the western border of TILDEN PARK, where the entire SAN FRANCISCO BAY and its skyline unfold before you.

For impressive vistas to the east, take Nimitz Way, a 4.5-mile trail that winds its way from Inspiration Point to Wildcat Peak, overlooking SAN PABLO and Briones Reservoirs. To the west, you get views of wooded parklands and beyond to SAN FRANCISCO BAY. Since this stretch of trail is gentle terrain and also paved, it is well suited for wheelchairs, bicycles, and even baby strollers.

Most of the East Bay Regional Park System is joined by the EAST BAY SKYLINE NATIONAL TRAIL, a 31-mile hike for backpackers. To the north from Inspiration Point, hikers can extend their walks into WILDCAT CANYON REGIONAL PARK, where a gorge has been cut by Wildcat Creek and is lined by riparian vegetation. To the south, you can hike onward through SIBLEY VOLCANIC PRESERVE, Redwood Park, and ultimately to LAKE CHABOT just east of SAN LEANDRO, all connected by the SKYLINE TRAIL.

Within TILDEN PARK are two of the highest points in the East Bay hills—Vollmer Peak (1,913 feet) at the southern tip of the park and Wildcat Peak (1,250 feet) at the northern end. Wildcat Peak is tucked away in a stand of trees, and is a popular two-hour hike from Inspiration Point.

Directions: From Interstate 580 to the west or Interstate 680 to the east, drive to Highway 24. Proceed to just east of the Caldecott Tunnel and take the Fish Ranch Road exit west to Grizzly Peak Boulevard. Turn right on Grizzly Peak Boulevard and drive to the southern entrance of the park. **Fees:** Access is free. **Best times to visit:** Evenings are prime, especially to cool off after a hot day. Expect company on weekends, although long trails still provide seclusion. **Contact:** For tips, maps, or brochures, call the East Bay Regional Park District, (510) 635-0135 extension 2200. **Locator:** TILDEN REGIONAL PARK (E1c).

• FEATURED TRIP •

BERRY CREEK CANYON

Rated: The Top 50 Parks, 7; The Top 12 Hike-to Streams, 24; The Top 10 Scenic Back Roads, 198

Where will you find the most beautiful spots in the great outdoors within reach of the entire Bay Area?

I spend quite a bit of time searching for such places, first flying over the entire region, carefully scanning for any hideaways I may have missed in the past, then driving, hiking, and exploring the most promising prospects. In the SANTA CRUZ MOUNTAINS my favorite is BERRY CREEK CANYON, deep in BIG BASIN REDWOODS STATE PARK.

Over the course of a mile, this canyon holds a series of three waterfalls, and exploring here is like entering a gateway to nature's paradise. It ranks right up there with Steep Ravine at MOUNT TAMALPAIS STATE PARK, the summit view at night from Mount Livermore at ANGEL ISLAND, and Alamere Falls at POINT REYES NATIONAL SEASHORE.

The most famous of the three waterfalls is Berry Creek Falls, but the other two, Silver Falls and Golden Falls, can be just as spectacular after heavy rains. Berry Creek Falls is the most classic of the 20 waterfalls in the Bay Area, 70 feet high, with a silver cascade and undercurrents that fall to a pool that seems like perfect artwork. It is surrounded by a high redwood canopy and bordered by moss, swordtail ferns, and sorrel. Visiting it each spring can be a baptism for some Bay Area hikers. There are two perfect viewing areas, and most people take considerable time to absorb the moment before hiking back, refreshed for weeks.

Yet, if you spend an extra hour exploring farther up the canyon, taking in Silver and Golden Falls, you'll have an opportunity to be transported about as close to heaven as you can get in the Bay Area.

Reaching Silver Falls requires about a 20-minute traipse past Berry Creek Falls, with a moderate climb along the pretty stream (on your left) at the bottom of the narrow canyon. The first view is just a glimpse of falling silver, but in moments, hiking toward it, you get a full-on look: a 50-foot cascade with silver tassels falling across rock that is colored bright orange from its iron content.

Hikers can hop across a few boulders and a log and walk right to the base of the falls, a perfect place for a photograph. There is also a downed tree adjacent to the falls that provides an ideal perch from which to take in this dramatic scene.

But it gets even better. From Silver Falls, the trail is built into the rock, and you hike up steps right aside the falls, with a single cable rail on your left for safety. You top the crest, just a foot away from the water, then hike onward for a few minutes to Golden Falls, a waterfall like no other in Northern California.

Golden Falls looks like a giant golden water slide that could have been built for river otters. About 125 feet long, it consists of a series of short slides, chutes, and pools coursing over golden iron-tinged rock, hence the name. A short way up the falls, right beside the trail, is a small but perfect area where you can view the spectacle and enjoy a picnic.

If this sounds like the kind of place that every Bay Area resident should see at least once, well, you are right. But it is just distant enough that visitors must earn the privilege.

BIG BASIN REDWOODS STATE PARK is located in the SANTA CRUZ MOUNTAINS, about 10 miles from Boulder Creek, so it is a considerable drive (about two to three hours, depending on traffic) from many Bay Area cities. Once you reach park headquarters, you face a 4.7-mile hike on the Skyline-to-Sea Trail to Berry Creek Falls. My partner and I have hiked it in one hour, 40 minutes, taking time to note three banana slugs, a few blooming sorrel and wild iris, a newt swimming in a small pool in the creek, and the freshly sprouted chutes of swordtail ferns and several mammoth redwoods. Most hikers reach the falls in two hours.

Even then, most visitors should allow five hours for the hike, adding in an hour for the side trip up BERRY CREEK CANYON to see Silver Falls and Golden Falls. A loop trip is possible, returning instead on the Sunset Trail, but that makes it a 12-mile trip. For this reason, park rangers caution visitors that the round-trip is a six-hour hike; we timed it, taking the long loop back from Golden Falls, and it took us exactly 2.5 hours for the return trip.

From park headquarters, the hike out to Berry Creek Falls starts by taking you past many of the park's biggest redwoods, old-growth giants that are more than 600 years old. It's about a 20-minute climb to the Big Basin Rim, reaching an elevation of 1,200 feet. From here, the trail descends 900 feet over a four-mile span to Berry Creek Falls, according to my Avocet altimeter watch. It's a steady grade, and if you return this way (rather than by the longer loop), you can get into a good, aerobic rhythm and march out the climb.

Throughout the park, there is a sense that this is as pristine as it gets in the Bay Area, and most visitors are aware of the sensation. Only a handful of idiots ever litter on the trail, and most others quickly pick up any trash they see in order to keep the place as clean as a church. For the same reason, most people are very happy here and keep their noise down; shouting is like sacrilege. After all, you wouldn't do that during a prayer at church, right?

One tip is to leave early on weekends, as the incoming traffic is very light before 9 a.m. then grows exponentially heavier each following hour. If the trip is too distant for you to complete in a day, some excellent campgrounds are available, including drive-in camps, tent cabins, walk-in camps, and wilderness-style backpack camps.

Directions from San Francisco: Drive south on Highway 1 to Santa Cruz, turn east on Highway 9, then turn left on Highway 236 and continue to Big Basin Redwoods State Park. **Directions from the Peninsula:** Drive south on Highway 9 from Los Gatos over the ridge, then turn right on Highway 236 and drive to Big Basin Redwoods State Park. **Fees:** A $5 state park access fee is charged. Campsites are $17 to $18 per night with a $1 pet fee. **Contact:** Big Basin Redwoods State Park, (831) 338-8860. **Locator:** BERRY CREEK CANYON (E1d).

• FEATURED TRIP •

★ GRANT COUNTY PARK

Rated: The Top 15 Surprise Hikes in the Rain, 28

Sometimes you just can't figure it. GRANT PARK provides exactly what so many people yearn for, yet it gets less use than any other large park in the Bay Area. To learn why, I decided to visit for myself, but after a day here I'm just as confounded as when I'd started.

You see, this park is the Bay Area's suburban wilderness, covering a vast area (9,000 acres) in the foothills of MOUNT HAMILTON in rural Santa Clara County. The land is perfect for hiking, biking, and fishing, and even offers a campground that is open daily, spring through fall, and on weekends in March and November. Yet there's just about nobody here.

And it isn't all that hard to reach either, with a parking area and entrance right along the road to MOUNT HAMILTON, about 10 miles east of SAN JOSE. You pull up, park, put a couple of dollars in a little envelope, deposit it in a metal receptor, and you're on your way. And what a way to go.

There are about 50 miles of old abandoned ranch roads and hiking trails, the former perfect for mountain bikes. Hikers can create their own routes, heading off the trail, down canyons and over rims into unpeopled valleys. There is also a 40-acre lake, GRANT LAKE, which has bass and catfish.

It is a classic oak woodland habitat, and with no pressure from nearby development, wildlife thrives here. My buddy and I had walked less than 10 minutes when we spotted a bobcat near the trail. There are flocks of wild turkeys, 25 to 30 in all, that are commonly seen, and more rarely, herds of wild pigs for those adventuring into the canyons. By the way, there are also some bovines in the area; if you come across them, give the bulls plenty of leeway.

The hills turn lush green from the

first good rains of fall and stay that way well into May. In summer, the warm evenings seem perfect for a walk or bike ride. My favorite time is spring, when the lake is full and several Canadian geese are nested down. The creeks pour down the center of canyons, creating many beautiful little waterfalls.

Many parks are not well suited for both mountain biking and hiking, but Grant is an exception. The abandoned ranch roads are ideal for bikes, with the roads wide enough, hard, and routed well into the backcountry. Meanwhile, hikers can either share the ranch roads (there typically are not many bikes out here), or head off on their own across the countryside.

We chose the latter, hiking past the lake and down into Hall's Valley. We reached a creek at the bottom of the valley, then headed upstream in search of little waterfalls. We found a procession of them, all flowing strong.

There are many good lookout points, too. For a view, we clambered up to a craggy point at the canyon rim where we could see clear to the South Bay, with miles of wildlands in between. People? What people?

Other prime destinations at the park are Deer Valley, which is huge and tranquil; the crest (2,956 feet) on the Washburn Trail above Hall's Valley; and in the spring, the remote habitat around EAGLE LAKE in the southern reaches of the park.

Grant Lake has some promise for anglers, too. The lake is much larger than you might first expect, and has good cover for bass and catfish. The fishing is just fair, but with the recovery from the drought and the chance for some stocks to jump-start the fishery, the prospects could be decent in the near future. The park has four other ponds—McCreery, Bass, Rattlesnake, and EAGLE LAKES—all nice picnic settings during the cool months.

If this sounds like a place where you can have a good time, you should give it a go. As for why there is almost nobody else here, well, after completing my research, I still can't figure it.

Directions: Drive south on U.S. 101 to San Jose, then turn east on Interstate 680. From there, take the Alum Rock exit and head east on Alum Rock Avenue. Turn right on Mount Hamilton Road and drive eight miles to the park entrance. **Fees:** A $4 entry fee is charged on weekends and holidays. **Locator:** GRANT COUNTY PARK (E1d).

• FEATURED TRIP •

★ MOUNT MADONNA COUNTY PARK

Rated: The Top 50 Parks, 7

MOUNT MADONNA COUNTY PARK provides great scenic beauty, good hiking, camping, and horseback riding. It is located between GILROY and WATSONVILLE, and surrounds the highest peak in the southern range of the SANTA CRUZ MOUNTAINS. A three- or four-hour visit here, capped by dinner at one of nearby MONTEREY BAY'S fine restaurants, can make for a classic day.

In late summer, this area can be like a hot volcano, but the temperate days of spring and early summer provide ideal weather for hikes and picnics. In the spring, the grasslands bloom in color from brilliant wildflower displays.

The park covers more than 3,000 acres, and if you take the time to hike and explore it, you will find surprising diversity. Imagine redwoods near GILROY. No way? Look closer. The park's major canyons not only shelter redwoods and tan oaks, but are also cut by streams gurgling over rocks and submerged limbs. Redwoods up to 100 feet tall can be found at the top of Mount Madonna, as well as on the west slopes. There are also some rare white deer in a pen.

A network of 18 miles of trails weaves throughout the park, intersecting in several spots and allowing you to custom-tailor your hike. Be sure to obtain a trail map from park headquarters, since the best hikes are combinations of different trails. My favorites are the Redwood and Blackhawk Canyon Trails. At 1,897 feet in elevation, the peak of MOUNT MADONNA may not seem like much, but since most of the surrounding land is near sea level, the peak can provide a lookout with impressive views. To the west, you can see the Salinas Valley unfold to MONTEREY BAY, and to the east, the vast Santa Clara basin.

Some of the better vistas can be seen without even leaving your car. Pole Line Road and Summit Road lead to near the summit. But don't be content with that. This park has many secrets, none of which can be discovered by car. The most unusual find is the pen rangers built in 1993 to house a few rare white deer. If you have never seen white deer, this is a must-do hike.

If MOUNT MADONNA PARK sounds like the kind of place where you'd like to spend more than an afternoon, there are some 115 campsites available on a first-come, first-served basis. Unlike at state parks, reservations are not necessary. Why? Because most folks have never even heard of this place. It is a well-kept secret.

Directions: From the Bay Area, take U.S. 101 south to Gilroy. Turn west on Highway 152 and proceed to Pole Line Road. Turn north and continue to the park. For the slow, winding, scenic route from Gilroy or Watsonville, take the Old Mount Madonna Road to the Summit Road entrance. **Fees:** A $4 entrance fee is charged. Campsite fees are $10 to $20 per night. **Maps:** A good map detailing 18 miles of trails can be obtained at park headquarters for a small fee. **Pets:** You can bring your dog along for the ride, but it is not permitted on trails. **Camping:** Campsites are first come, first served. Group camping reservations can be obtained by phoning (408) 358-3751. **Contact:** Mount Madonna County Park, (408) 842-2341 (the phone line is sometimes not attended). **Locator:** MOUNT MADONNA COUNTY PARK (E1c).

2
CAMPING

• TOM'S RATINGS •

• FEATURED TRIPS •

See last page for Northern California and Bay Area foldout maps.

• TOM'S RATINGS •

THE TOP 5 PLACES TO BEACH CAMP

In Northern California

Beach camping can add up to the time of your life: cruising down the highway, watching ocean sunsets, fishing practically from your tent, and playing hide-and-seek with all the little tidepool creatures. It goes on: waking up to the sound of the sea, playing tag with the waves, beachcombing at low tide, and going on long walks with someone special.

But, alas, if you are unprepared, just making it through a weekend can turn into an endurance test.

My first beach camping trip was just like that. I arrived late one evening at a state beach in MONTEREY, with no reservations; the campground was full. So I had to strike out on my own, laying my sleeping bag down on a piece of secluded beach and going to sleep with the sound of waves in my ears.

Everything seemed great, right? Hey, the ocean was just waiting for me to pass into slumberland. At about 4 a.m., a thunderous wave cascaded over me. Are we having fun yet?

The following 10 hours were a disaster: turning into a human icicle in a wet sleeping bag, trying to sleep in the truck, a cold morning fog making the beach feel like the North Pole, eating a breakfast marinated in sand, getting hit in the arm with a seagull dropping, and snagging up on every cast while trying to fish. By noon it was time to surrender.

Well, that was long ago, but you might have the same experience today if you head off unprepared.

For starters, camping reservations are a necessity. Coastal state beaches are among the most popular campgrounds in California, especially in the summer. It is recommended that you call the campground of your choice to ask about projected availability, then call the toll-free reservation line to lock up a spot: (800) 444-7275.

The next step is getting your gear together. Always have a list. At the very least, it will keep you from forgetting the toilet paper.

Then be prepared to deal with two key elements: the weather and the sand.

When many people across the country envision this coast, they think of warm, sun-swept days. The truth is that at Northern California beaches in the summer, about half the days are foggy and cold.

On warm days in the Central Valley, inland damp fog will cloak the coast during the night, then break up by mid-morning. This fog brings with it a penetrating cold, the kind that goes right to the bones. Therefore, a tent is mandatory. And if you plan to camp on sand, make sure you have the kind of tent that doesn't need stakes. The pegs usually won't hold.

Also make certain that you have a warm sleeping bag and some kind of ground pad for insulation, either a lightweight Ensolite pad or a Therm-A-Rest. If you lay a sleeping bag directly on the ground or beach, the cold earth will suck the warmth right out of you. By 2 A.M. you will feel like you are sleeping in a freezer, regardless of the air temperature.

Another key factor in an enjoyable trip is to concentrate on playing on the beach, rather than eating a good portion of it with every meal. At state park beaches, picnic tables and food lockers are provided. Use them. If you are freelancing it in a remote area, this becomes more difficult.

One answer is to have all of your food in separate airtight containers. This will allow you to set your food down at your picnic site without worrying about it tipping over and filling with sand.

Of course, sometimes a disaster seems fated. One time I dropped a roasted hot dog on the beach, and it was so completely coated with sand that even my dog wouldn't eat it. Smart fellow.

For the most part, however, beach camping is a unique and fun experience. But do remember to bring a tide book. It just might keep you from getting a surprise dunking some night.

Here are some places to get you started, listed from north to south:

1. Patricks Point State Park

This park near Trinidad is a real favorite, with campsites set amid Sitka spruce, trails that tunnel through thick fern vegetation, and an agate beach. There are several ocean lookouts where visitors can spot migrating whales. It's often foggy and damp here, but always beautiful.

There are 124 sites for tents or RVs up to 31 feet long, with picnic tables, fireplaces, and piped water provided. Rest rooms are also available.

Contact: Patricks Point State Park, (707) 677-3570; California State Parks, North Coast Redwoods District, (707) 445-6547. **Locator:** Patricks Point State Park (B0). **See featured trip page:** 124.

2. Van Damme State Park

This park near Mendocino is ideally situated for year-round adventures. You get ocean frontage on one side and forest on the other. In the winter, the nearby Noyo and Navarro Rivers can provide steelhead fishing.

The park has 74 sites for tents or RVs up to 35 feet long. All facilities are available at the park or nearby.

Contact: Van Damme State Park, (707) 937-5804; California State Parks, Russian River–Mendocino District, (707) 937-5804. **Locator:** Van Damme State Park (C0).

3. Salt Point State Park

Located north of Jenner, this park is just far enough from the Bay Area to give visitors a feeling of total separation from mass humanity. It is a great spot for abalone diving in season, beachcombing, and quiet walks. Horses are available for riding.

The park has 109 sites for tents or RVs up to 31 feet long, 20 walk-in sites, and 10 hiker/bicyclist sites, all with facilities provided at the park or in nearby Jenner.

Contact: Salt Point State Park, (707) 847-3221; California State Parks, Russian River–Mendocino District, (707) 865-2391. **Locator:** Salt Point State Park (D0).

4. Half Moon Bay State Beach

A pretty and popular spot, Half Moon Bay State Beach offers tent campsites on a grassy area instead of sand. It is a prime spot for a long beach walk, especially during low tides. A bonus is nearby Pillar Point Harbor, located seven miles to the north, with a boat launch, sportfishing operations, and quality restaurants.

The park has 56 sites for tents or RVs, with piped water and rest rooms provided.

Contact: Half Moon Bay State Beach, (650) 726-8820. **Locator:** Half Moon

BAY STATE BEACH (E1b). **See featured trip pages:** 224 and 401.

5. SUNSET STATE BEACH

Sunsets often look like they are imported from Hawaii at this park. SUNSET STATE BEACH, on the shore of south MONTEREY BAY near WATSONVILLE, is a favorite for vacationers and a good alternative to BIG SUR to the south. There are several good trails for short walks, and clamming can be good during low tides.

There are 90 sites for tents or RVs up to 31 feet long. Each comes with a picnic table.

Contact: Sunset State Beach, (408) 763-7062; California State Parks, Santa Cruz District, (408) 429-2851. **Locator:** SUNSET STATE BEACH (F1). **See featured trip page:** 244.

• TOM'S RATINGS •

THE TOP 50 BASE CAMPS

In Northern California

To people who know that simple pleasures can bring the most happiness, there is nothing better than sharing an evening campfire, a trout for dinner, and a night looking at the stars with the people you care for most.

That is part of what makes camping so popular in California, especially when combined with a favorite activity, such as hiking, boating, fishing, or backpacking. There is no better place to do it than right here, with more variety—mountains, lakes, streams, coast, and desert—and many of the world's most beautiful natural places, among them Emerald Bay at LAKE TAHOE, the YOSEMITE backcountry, BIG SUR, and the redwoods. Hundreds of first-class destinations await.

In fact, there are some 1,600 campgrounds in California that can be reached by car and hundreds more that are accessible on short walks. According to reservation services, advance camp bookings are now the highest they've ever been. But don't worry about not being able to find a spot, not with hundreds of stellar destinations available, some well known, some largely secret, all waiting to be explored and savored. The Forest Service alone has more than 800 campgrounds, highlighted by many small, beautiful sites near remote lakes and streams.

The best suggestion is to plan well in advance and make reservations (if possible), obtaining as much information as you can, and to keep alternate sites in mind. In the past several years, I have visited about 900 of the campgrounds in the state, and here are my favorites for the best of the best:

These are listed on a region-by-region basis and not by my personal ranking.

1. TUOLUMNE MEADOWS

No campground in America lies at the threshold of more stellar hikes than Tuolumne Meadows. YOSEMITE's biggest camp, with 314 drive-in sites, it is set high in the backcountry at 8,600 feet near Tioga Pass. To the north is a pristine day hike on the PACIFIC CREST TRAIL along the TUOLUMNE RIVER, an easy walk that passes two gorgeous waterfalls; in addition, nearby Lembert Dome provides breathtaking views after an 800-foot climb. Heading south from camp is an easy hike of a few miles on the John Muir Trail, nearly flat along Lyell Fork, with good fishing for brook trout. Backpackers can continue onward for miles, including a great one-way, five-day trip over Vogelsang Pass, down to Half Dome, past Vernal and Nevada Falls en route to Yosemite Valley. Note: only 50 percent of the campgrounds are available by reservation, with the rest first come, first served.

Contact: Yosemite National Park, (209) 372-0200. **Locator:** YOSEMITE NATIONAL PARK (E4). **See featured trip page:** 239.

2. Big Basin Redwoods State Park

Secluded campsites amid redwoods, a rare opportunity to stay in a tent cabin, 10 backpack sites, and an outstanding trail system make BIG BASIN one of the best state parks in California. Hiking destinations feature four waterfalls, some mammoth redwoods, and the Bay Area's best one-way trip, from park headquarters to Rancho del Oso on the Skyline-to-Sea Trail. The waterfalls include a close one, Sempervirens Falls (1.5-miles round-trip on the Sequoia Trail) and three that are more distant, Berry Creek, Silver, and Golden Falls, my favorite place in the Bay Area. To see the latter, most hikers should figure on five hours round-trip.

Contact: Big Basin Redwoods State Park, (408) 338-8860. **Locator:** BIG BASIN REDWOODS STATE PARK (E1d). **See featured trip page:** 136.

3. Lakes Basin Recreation Area

Locator: PLUMAS NATIONAL FOREST (C3).

4. Sinkiyone Wilderness State Park

Locator: SINKIYONE WILDERNESS STATE PARK (C0).

5. Agnew Meadows

Locator: INYO NATIONAL FOREST (E4). **See featured trip page:** 237.

6. Castle Crags State Park

Locator: CASTLE CRAGS STATE PARK (B2). **See featured trip page:** 127.

7. Emerald Bay

There is no more beautiful place on Earth to run a boat or paddle a canoe than Emerald Bay at LAKE TAHOE, a place of divine beauty with its cobalt blue waters and the surrounding spectacular mountain ridges. Though the natural setting at TAHOE is often devastated by high numbers of cars and visitors, the 20 boat-in campsites at Emerald Bay provide remarkable serenity. Boaters can add to the adventure by slipping out the narrow mouth of Emerald Bay to gain access to the main lake. At 6,200 feet, newcomers may find their breath comes up a little short—but the views alone are enough to take your breath away.

Contact: Emerald Bay State Park, (530) 541-3030 or (530) 525-7277. **Locator:** LAKE TAHOE (D4). **See featured trip page:** 232.

8. Englebright Lake

If you own a boat and haven't camped at Englebright, well, that's like owning a baseball bat and never getting to use it in a big game. Englebright is the perfect lake for boaters, with 100 boat-in sites (and other than a group camp, no drive-in sites for cars) and rules that solve user conflicts. It's very pretty, long and narrow like a giant water snake and almost always full of water. At 520 feet in elevation, the place gets a lot of warm weather, and the lower end of the lake is outstanding for waterskiing. The upper end of the lake, on the other hand, receives cold water from the YUBA RIVER and is good for trout fishing; waterskiing is prohibited in the fishing area. How can you improve on perfection?

Contact: Englebright Lake, (530) 639-2342; Skipper's Cove, (530) 639-2272. **Locator:** MARYSVILLE (D3).

9. Stone Lagoon

Locator: STONE LAGOON (A0).

10. Bullards Bar Reservoir

Locator: BULLARDS BAR RESERVOIR (C3).

11. Lake Sonoma

Locator: LAKE SONOMA (DO). **See featured trip page:** 322.

12. Lake Oroville

Locator: LAKE OROVILLE (C2).

13. Shasta Lake

Locator: SHASTA LAKE (B2).

14. Trinity Lake

Locator: TRINITY LAKE (B1).

15. Deadfall Lakes

You can hike all 1,700 miles of the PACIFIC CREST TRAIL in California and not find a prettier lake with an easier walk than Deadfall Lake. It's a sapphire, deep and peaceful, tucked on the western slope of Mount Eddy in a mountain bowl at 7,300 feet in elevation. This is the kind of place backpackers might walk for days to reach. Yet it's only a 2.5-mile jaunt on a mostly flat trail, and a steady cruise of an hour or so will deliver you to the lake's shoreline with nary a huff or a puff.

Contact: Shasta-Trinity National Forest, Mount Shasta Ranger District, (530) 926-4511. **Locator:** SHASTA-TRINITY NATIONAL FOREST (B2). **See featured trip page:** 48.

16. Winnemucca Lake

Here is a small but beautiful high mountain lake that, along with nearby Round Top Lake and Fourth of July Lake, provides a perfect introduction to backpacking for families with young children or those who do not desire a long, grueling hike. After departing from CARSON PASS, elevation 8,580 feet, it is only two miles to Winnemucca Lake, another mile to Fourth of July, and another two miles from there to Round Top, all easy but beautiful destinations in the MOKELUMNE WILDERNESS.

Contact: Eldorado National Forest, Information Center, (530) 644-6048. **Locator:** ELDORADO NATIONAL FOREST (D4).

17. Glen Aulin

Locator: YOSEMITE NATIONAL PARK (E4). **See featured trip page:** 239.

18. May Lake High Sierra Camp

Locator: YOSEMITE NATIONAL PARK (E4). **See featured trip page:** 239.

19. Wilderness Falls out of Young's Valley

Locator: SISKIYOU WILDERNESS (A0).

20. Mill Creek

Locator: SOUTH WARNER WILDERNESS (B4).

21. Sunset Camp

What a trip! You start at park headquarters and hike through mammoth redwoods to the Big Basin Rim, down a canyon to 70-foot Berry Creek Falls, upstream past a pair of stunning falls (Silver and Golden), then finish the romp up to Sunset Backpack Camp. It's a 5.7-mile trip, one-way, to the camp, my favorite hike in the Bay Area. As with all backpack trips, it is critical to bring a water purification pump, so you can get drinking and cooking water from Berry Creek, a five-minute walk from camp.

Contact: Big Basin Redwoods State Park, (408) 338-8860. **Locator:** BIG BASIN REDWOODS STATE PARK (E1d). **See featured trip page:** 136.

22. Wildcat Camp

In just 5.1 miles of hiking from the Palomarin Trailhead to Wildcat Camp, you will pass great coastal lookouts, hidden lakes, a stunning waterfall, coastal rock formations, and a pretty beach. The crowning feature is Wildcat Camp, a backpack site perched on an ocean bluff. From there you can access an additional network of trails that link to routes that explore the hills to the east. At night you'll feel the giant, calming presence of the sea, and it has way of making you feel that all is right with the world.

Contact: Point Reyes National Seashore, Bear Valley Visitor Center, (415) 663-1092. **Locator:** Point Reyes National Seashore (E1a). **See featured trip pages:** 67, 132, 166, and 262.

23. Trail Camp

Locator: Castle Rock State Park (E1d).

24. Sunol Regional Wilderness

Locator: Sunol Regional Wilderness (E1c). **See featured trip page:** 99.

25. Henry W. Coe State Park

Locator: Henry W. Coe State Park (E1d). **See featured trip page:** 139.

26. Angel Island Environmental Sites

When the last ferryboat of the day departs Angel Island, the handful of people camping suddenly have a chance at a rare and unforgettable experience. Imagine having the trails, lookouts, beaches, coves, hey, the whole darn island . . . all to yourself! It can make the Bay Area seem like a new world, especially when you take an evening walk to 781-foot Mount Livermore for the 360-degree view of San Francisco Bay and all its landmarks. Reaching your assigned campsite requires a two-hour walk, and visitors should note that the southern end of the island is undergoing extensive removal of non-native trees and plants.

Contact: Angel Island State Park, (415) 435-1915; California State Parks, Marin District, (415) 893-1580. **Locator:** Angel Island (E1a).

27. Hell Hole Reservoir

Hell Hole Reservoir is a mountain shrine with azure blue water. This camp is near the rim of the gorge at Buck Meadow, not far from an overlook of Hell Hole, a three-mile hike from the trailhead at the southwest corner of the lake. The Granite Chief Wilderness is to the immediate east. It's a long, twisty drive just to reach the trailhead, but there is nothing like it anywhere.

Contact: Eldorado National Forest, Information Center, (530) 644-6048. **Locator:** Eldorado National Forest (D3, D4). **See featured trip page:** 146.

28. Andrew Molera State Park

Locator: Big Sur (F1). **See featured trip page:** 242.

29. Pantoll

Locator: Mount Tamalpais State Park (E1a).

30. Pomo Canyon

Locator: Sonoma Coast State Beach (D0).

31. Surfwood

Locator: MacKerricher State Park (C0).

32. Lake Earl Walk-In

Locator: Lake Earl State Park (A0).

33. Lassen View Resort

This one of the few classic "fish camps" in California, designed from start to finish with fishing in mind. It has cabins, RV sites, a tackle shop, a fish cleaning station, boats, a ramp, guides—and one of the best fishing spots on the lake, Big Springs, only a five-minute boat ride away. This is where salmon and trout often congregate to feed on the lake's population of pond smelt. How good can it get? Once I caught a five-salmon limit here that weighed 22 pounds, and no one raised an eyebrow.

Contact: Lassen View Resort, (530) 596-3437. **Locator:** LAKE ALMANOR (C3). **See featured trip page:** 351.

34. Convict Lake Resort

This magical place of pure waters and big fish lies in the high country of the eastern Sierra, elevation 7,583 feet. CONVICT LAKE is deep and blue-green, set below high, sheer mountain walls and granite peaks. It is an inspiring sight, and so is the fishing, with excellent catch rates for rainbow trout and sometimes even a giant brown, some ranging 15 pounds and up. There are 23 cabins, a small marina, boat rentals, a ramp, a store, and a small high-quality restaurant, but best of all, there are often lots of fish.

Contact: Convict Lake Resort, (760) 934-3803 or (800) 992-2260. **Locator:** CONVICT LAKE (E5). **See featured trip page:** 239.

35. Bucks Lake Cabins

Locator: BUCKS LAKE (C3).

36. Lakeview Terrace

Locator: LEWISTON LAKE (B1).

37. Caples Lake Resort

Locator: ELDORADO NATIONAL FOREST (D4).

38. Four Seasons Cabins

Locator: JUNE LAKE (E5).

39. Eagle Lake Cabins

Locator: EAGLE LAKE (B4).

40. Jim's Soda Bay Resort

Locator: CLEAR LAKE (D1).

41. Lake Davis Cabins

Locator: LAKE DAVIS (C4).

42. Mary Smith

LEWISTON is a jewel, and the lakeside campsites at Mary Smith can make you feel as if you have discovered something very precious. That's because you have. The lake is always full, often with a tourmaline tint to it, and from a boat, the TRINITY ALPS provide a fantastic backdrop. Bird-watching is excellent and trout fishing is usually decent, but every once in a while it is incredible, always at the head of the lake when the Trinity Powerhouse is running.

Contact: Shasta-Trinity National Forest, Weaverville Ranger District, (530) 623-2121. **Locator:** LEWISTON LAKE (B1). **See featured trip page:** 128.

43. Emerald Bay State Park

The campground here is a big one, 100 sites in all, but they are sprinkled amid pines at Eagle Point, near the mouth of Emerald Bay. That presents campers with a spectacular setting, with several short hiking trails available to take it all in. Dramatic Emerald Bay and LAKE TAHOE are among the world's most beautiful places, but add in the chance to camp at the edge of this paradise in a forest and you've got it all.

Contact: Emerald Bay State Park, (530) 525-7277; California State Parks, Sierra District, (530) 525-7232. **Locator:** LAKE TAHOE (D4). **See featured trip page:** 232.

44. Wrights Lake

Locator: ELDORADO NATIONAL FOREST (D4).

45. Union Valley Reservoir

Locator: ELDORADO NATIONAL FOREST (D3).

46. Tioga Lake

Locator: Inyo National Forest (E5). **See featured trip page:** 237.

47. Gull Lake

Locator: Inyo National Forest (E5). **See featured trip page:** 237.

48. June Lake

Locator: Inyo National Forest (E5). **See featured trip page:** 237.

49. Scotts Flat Reservoir

Locator: Nevada City (D3).

50. D. L. Bliss State Park

Locator: Lake Tahoe (D4). **See featured trip page:** 232.

• Tom's Ratings •

The Top 5 Drive-to Camps on Streams

In Northern California

1. Agnew Meadows

Timing is everything, but it is difficult to time a bad trip to the upper San Joaquin. This is a perfect camp from which to launch a hiking trip into the Ansel Adams Wilderness, heading south for six miles on the John Muir Trail to gorgeous Thousand Island Lake below Banner and Ritter Peaks. It is also excellent for fishing—the stream is stocked near camp—and fly fishers who hike upstream on the River Trail will find a good evening surface rise for trout.

Contact: Inyo National Forest, Mammoth Lakes Ranger District, (760) 924-5500. **Locator:** San Joaquin River (E4). **See featured trip page:** 237.

2. Ah-Di-Na Campground

Ah-Di-Na is one of the true gems among the 800 drive-to camps operated by the Forest Service. The camp is set along the McCloud River, a beautiful stream with big boulders, deep pools, and a few limestone gorges. Trout fishing is often a great challenge, but can be rewarding just the same with beautifully colored fish and streamside beauty. The Pacific Crest Trail runs through the area, providing access to several miles of river.

Contact: Shasta-Trinity National Forest, McCloud Ranger District, (530) 964-2184. **Locator:** McCloud River (B2). **See featured trip page:** 349.

3. South Fork Rubicon

Location: Eldorado National Forest (D4).

4. Wild Plum

Location: Tahoe National Forest (C3).

5. Big Flat

Location: Six Rivers National Forest (A0).

• Tom's Ratings •

The Top 6 Coastal Camps

In Northern California

1. Andrew Molera State Park Walk-in Sites

If you can just hit this place during the week, when the fewest campers are here, you will discover why some consider Big Sur to be something akin to heaven. The Big Sur landscape is the most dramatic on the Pacific coast, featuring deep canyons, giant rock stacks, and sweeping ocean views. The camp can provide a sense of intimacy, however, with easy, flat trails that lead out to secluded beaches, where visitors can often view sea lions and otters; rangers often have a printed sheet that details the best places to see them.

Contact: Andrew Molera State Park, (408) 667-2315; California State Parks, Monterey District, (408) 649-2836. **Lo-**

cator: BIG SUR (F1). **See featured trip page:** 242.

2. SURFWOOD WALK-IN

The Mendocino coast has many beautiful camps, but the best is Surfwood Walk-in, where campers can find seclusion to go with all that coastal beauty. The best sites are numbers 7 through 10, which are set amid coastal forest yet provide glimpses of the ocean—all just a five-minute walk from the parking area. You can access the Headlands Trail right from camp and follow it to a seal watching station (no kidding) and tidepools, about a 15-minute walk. Want more? Got more: A secluded ocean cove and beach, and Lake Cleone (trout fishing and rafting for youngsters) are both within a five-minute walk.

Contact: MacKerricher State Park, (707) 937-5804; California State Parks, Russian River–Mendocino District, (707) 865-2391. **Locator:** MACKERRICHER STATE PARK (C0). **See featured trip page:** 214.

3. ENVIRONMENTAL CABINS

Locator: MOUNT TAMALPAIS STATE PARK (E1a). **See featured trip page:** 62.

4. SUNSET STATE BEACH

Locator: MONTEREY BAY (F1). **See featured trip page:** 244.

5. NICKEL CREEK WALK-IN

Locator: REDWOOD NATIONAL PARK (A0). **See featured trip page:** 125.

6. SALT POINT STATE PARK

Locator: SALT POINT STATE PARK (D0).

• TOM'S RATINGS •

THE TOP 6 LAKESHORE CAMPS

In Northern California

1. SPRING LAKE

SANTA ROSA's backyard fishing hole is unknown to most people who don't live in the area. The lake is stocked with rainbow trout and has a resident population of bluegill and largemouth bass. It's located about five miles outside of SANTA ROSA. The campground has 30 sites for tents or RVs; during the summer season, 20 of them are first come, first served and 10 are available by reservation. There's good fishing in the morning and evening, especially from March through early May.

Contact: Spring Lake County Park, (707) 539-8092. For reservations, phone (707) 539-8082. **Locator:** SANTA ROSA (D1).

2. LAKE CHABOT

This is the centerpiece of the East Bay Regional Park District, a pretty lake that gets heavy stocks of rainbow trout and hard-to-catch largemouth bass that reach 10 pounds and up. Boat rentals are available.

The park, which is four miles west of Castro Valley, has 53 campsites for tents or RVs. On weekends, the camp either fills up or comes close to it. Reservations are required.

Contact: East Bay Regional Park District, (510) 635-0135 extension 2200; Anthony Chabot Regional Park, (510) 881-1833 extension 2570. For reservations, call (510) 562-2267. **Locator:** LAKE CHABOT (E1c). **See featured trip page:** 230.

3. DEL VALLE RESERVOIR

A lot of people have no idea that a big, cool lake is tucked in the golden hills south of LIVERMORE. But DEL VALLE RESERVOIR is. It is stocked weekly with rainbow trout, supports populations of bluegill and smallmouth bass, and has some big striped bass as well. A full marina with boat rentals and a launch is available.

The campground has 129 sites for tents or RVs, of which 21 have full hookups. The campground is typically full on weekends, but space is almost always available during the week. Reservations are required.

Contact: East Bay Regional Park District, (510) 635-0135 extension 2200; Del Valle Regional Park, (925) 373-0332. For reservations, call (510) 562-2267. **Locator:** DEL VALLE RESERVOIR (E2).

4. Uvas Reservoir

Of the eight lakes in Santa Clara County, UVAS has the best fishing. Set about 10 miles south of SAN JOSE, it can provide good fishing for largemouth bass and crappie, and for trout after the late winter stocks. The best strategy is to sneak up on coves in the backwaters during the evening, then cast a white crappie jig. Nonmotorized boating is permitted.

The campground has 15 sites for tents and 15 spaces for tents or RVs. All are provided on a first-come, first-served basis.

Contact: Uvas Canyon County Park, (408) 779-9232; Santa Clara County Parks Reservations, (408) 358-3751; Coyote Discount Bait and Tackle, (408) 463-0711. **Locator:** UVAS CANYON RESERVOIR (E2).

5. Coyote Reservoir

You'll find this long, narrow lake in the oak and grass-covered hills east of GILROY. Anglers with boats can catch largemouth bass, primarily during the early morning and late evening.

The park has 74 campsites for tents or RVs. No reservations are taken. A boat launch is located a quarter mile from the campground.

Contact: Coyote Lake Ranger Station, (408) 842-7800; Coyote Discount Bait and Tackle, (408) 463-0711. **Locator:** COYOTE RESERVOIR (E1d).

6. Pinto Lake

You say you never heard of Pinto Lake? Neither have a lot of folks. Set just outside of WATSONVILLE, the lake is shaped like a horseshoe—and it's good luck for fishing for rainbow trout, bluegill, catfish, and in some years, crappie.

There are two campgrounds for tents or RVs: Marmo's Resort has 50 sites, and Pinto Lake Park has 28 sites. Reservations are accepted.

The lake is often full, but the campgrounds are often not, except on three-day weekends.

Contact: Pinto Lake, (408) 722-8129. **Locator:** WATSONVILLE (F1).

• TOM'S RATINGS •

The Top 10 Remote Camping Spots

In Northern California

If you want solitude, your best bet is to hop on Interstate 5, kick it up north for about five hours, and settle in at an unimproved Forest Service campground. While researching my book *California Camping,* we discovered 240 campgrounds in some of the state's most remote counties: Shasta (56), Siskiyou (42), Trinity (48), Modoc (14), Lassen (19), Tehama (16), and Del Norte (45). Here are 10 suggestions to get you started:

1. Deadlun Campground

Most people have never heard of Iron Canyon Reservoir. Go to Deadlun Camp and you'll get a taste of it, with good swimming and boating by day and fishing in the early morning and late evening. It's a good idea to bring along your own drinking water. The campground has 30 spots, all first come, first served with no fee charged. It's located at an elevation of 2,750 feet, surrounded by SHASTA-TRINITY NATIONAL FOREST.

Directions: From Redding, drive 37 miles east on Highway 299. Turn left on Big Bend Road and go 15 miles to Big Bend. Continue for five miles to the lake, veering right at the T, then go two miles to the campground turnoff on the left. Turn and travel one mile to the camp. **Contact**: Shasta-Trinity National Forest, Shasta Lake Ranger District, (530) 275-1587. **Locator:** IRON CANYON RESERVOIR (B2).

2. MADRONE CAMPGROUND

This camp is out there in the boondocks, between nothing and nothing, nestled in a forest of fir and pine. It's adjacent to Squaw Creek, which is okay for swimming and trout fishing, too, if you walk upstream a ways. The camp has 13 campsites; no fee is charged and no reservations are taken. It is set at a 1,500-foot elevation, about 50 miles northwest of REDDING.

Directions: From Redding, take Highway 299 east for 40 miles, then follow Fenders Ferry Road, a gravel road, west for 20 miles. **Contact:** Shasta-Trinity National Forest, Shasta Lake Ranger District, (530) 275-1587. **Locator:** PIT RIVER (B2).

3. TRAIL CREEK

Here's a beautiful spot far from everything. It's set between Callahan and Cecilville near the SALMON RIVER at a 4,700-foot elevation. The gurgling of nearby Trail Creek will lull you to sleep each night. The campground has 15 sites; a small fee is charged but reservations are not accepted.

Directions: Turn west off Highway 3 at Callahan and drive about 15 miles to the camp. **Contact:** Klamath National Forest, Scott River Ranger District, (530) 468-5351. **Locator:** TRINITY ALPS WILDERNESS (B1).

4. SHADOW CREEK

This is a good alternative to the Trail Creek Camp, located about five miles east. It has space for 10 campers available for a small fee. The peaceful, out-of-the-way spot offers good swimming in the South Fork of the SALMON RIVER. The closest amenities are about five miles away in Cecilville, population 25. For hiking trails, a map of KLAMATH NATIONAL FOREST details the possibilities.

Directions: Turn west off Highway 3 at Callahan and drive about 20 miles to the camp. **Contact:** Klamath National Forest, Scott River Ranger District, (530) 468-5351. **Locator:** TRINITY ALPS WILDERNESS (B1).

5. JACKASS SPRINGS CAMPGROUND

Here's an isolated campground that gets very little attention, even though it's right on one of California's favorite reservoirs, TRINITY LAKE. The camp has 21 campsites and is free. Just show up with your gear. It is set at a 2,500-foot elevation, beneath the towering TRINITY ALPS. You can camp right along the east shore of the lake.

Directions: From Redding, head west on Highway 299 to Weaverville. Turn right on Highway 3 and drive 29 miles to Trinity Center. Continue five miles to County Road 106, turn right, and go 12 miles to the Jackass Springs turnoff (County Road 119). Turn right and proceed four miles to the camp.

Contact: Shasta-Trinity National Forest, Weaverville Ranger District, (530) 623-2121. **Locator:** TRINITY LAKE (B2).

6. Big Flat Campground

The South Fork of the SALMON RIVER and Coffee Creek provide a beautiful setting for this little-known spot at elevation 5,000 feet. It is right on the edge of the TRINITY ALPS WILDERNESS and is a premium jump-off spot to the Caribou Lakes (a nine-mile hike) for a backpacking trip. There are three tent sites.

Directions: From REDDING, drive east on Highway 299 to WEAVERVILLE. Turn north on Highway 3 and go just past the north end of TRINITY LAKE to Coffee Creek Road (Road 104), adjacent to a ranger station. Turn left and drive 21 miles west to the camp. **Contact:** SHASTA-TRINITY NATIONAL FOREST, Weaverville Ranger District, (530) 623-2121. **Locator:** TRINITY RIVER (B1).

7. Cave Lake Campground

Here's a spot out in the sticks. This lake is located very close to the Oregon border in northeastern California and, along with adjoining Lily Lake, provides a double-barreled fishing opportunity. Both lakes contain eastern brook trout and rainbow trout. The campground has six spots, with no fee charged (heck, if they charged, somebody would have to hang out for a couple of years to collect enough money just to pay for one dinner). The elevation is 6,600 feet.

Directions: From Alturas, drive north on U.S. 395 for 40 miles to Forest Service Road 2 (if you reach the town of New Pine Creek on the Oregon border, you have gone a mile too far). Turn right on Forest Service 2 (a steep dirt road—trailers are not recommended) and go six miles east to the camp entrance on the left. **Contact:** Modoc National Forest, Warner Mountain Ranger District, (530) 279-6116. **Locator:** MODOC NATIONAL FOREST (A4).

8. Crater Lake Campground

And you thought Crater Lake was in Oregon? Well, there's another Crater Lake that nobody's heard of on the eastern side of MOUNT LASSEN. It has pretty good fishing, primarily for rainbow trout and brook trout, but don't expect anything huge. An option is to place a piece of bacon or chicken on a hook and get yourself a pot full of crawdads. There are 17 campsites; the fee is about $10 per night.

Directions: From the Bogard Ranger Station on Highway 44 east of LASSEN VOLCANIC NATIONAL PARK, turn east on a dirt road and drive nine miles to the camp. **Contact:** Lassen National Forest, Eagle Lake Ranger District, (530) 257-2151. **Locator:** LASSEN VOLCANIC NATIONAL PARK (B3).

9. Beegum Gorge Campground

This hidden, obscure spot has only two campsites, but it's free, quiet, and there's some fair evening trout fishing on nearby Beegum Creek. It's set at an elevation of 2,200 feet, beneath the Yolla Bolly Mountains. Expect hot weather and bring all your own supplies.

Directions: From Red Bluff, turn west on Highway 36 and drive to Platina. Turn south on Forest Service Road 29N06 and go 6.5 miles to the campground. **Contact:** Shasta-Trinity National Forest, Yolla Bolly Ranger District, (530) 352-4211. **Locator:** SHASTA-TRINITY NATIONAL FOREST (B2).

10. Big Flat Campground

Here is a nice little spot along Hurdy Gurdy Creek, close to the South Fork of the SMITH RIVER. I have had some good trout fishing success here, searching out spots on the river where rapids tumble into pools, and then casting a blue/silver Kastmaster into the white water. The fish bite where the water flattens out. There are 30 campsites and vault toilets, but no piped water. A small fee is charged.

Directions: From U.S. 199 just east of Gasquet, turn south on South Fork Road and drive 25 miles to the camp. **Contact:** Six Rivers National Forest, Gasquet Ranger District, (707) 457-3131. **Locator:** SIX RIVERS NATIONAL FOREST (A0).

• TOM'S RATINGS •

THE TOP 10 CAMPS FOR KIDS

In Northern California

Here are my recommendations for the top camps for families with children in Northern California, listed from north to south:

1. PRAIRIE CREEK REDWOODS STATE PARK

This is the best park in California for viewing wildlife, including a tremendous herd of Roosevelt elk. It has a beautiful campground set amid redwoods, good biking and hiking trails, and nearby access to miles of untouched beach.

Contact: Prairie Creek Redwoods State Park, (707) 488-2171; California State Parks, North Coast Redwoods District, (707) 445-6547. For reservations, phone (800) 444-7275. **Locator:** PRAIRIE CREEK REDWOODS STATE PARK (A0). **See featured trip page:** 125.

2. LASSEN VIEW RESORT

It's rustic and down-home, but comfortable and fun, with something for everyone: cabins, RV sites, tent sites, a play area, boat rentals, and one of the best fishing spots on the lake, Big Springs, only a five-minute boat ride away.

Contact: Lassen View Resort, (530) 596-3437 or fax (530) 596-4437. **Locator:** LAKE ALMANOR (C3). **See featured trip page:** 351.

3. MACKERRICHER STATE PARK

No park has more variety for kids, with little Lake Cleone available for trout fishing and floating around in a raft, a seal watching station within a 15-minute walk, tidepools galore, a great bike trail, and a secluded ocean cove.

Contact: California State Parks, Mendocino District, (707) 937-5804; for reservations, phone (800) 444-7275. **Locator:** FORT BRAGG (C0). **See featured trip page:** 214.

4. ENGLEBRIGHT LAKE

The weather is hot, the lake is warm—perfect for water play, swimming, and boating—and if you've got a boat, this is the place to come, with 100 boat-in campsites (first come, first served). Boating rules solve user conflict, with fast boats kept out of fishing and swimming areas.

Contact: Englebright Lake, (530) 639-2342; Skipper's Cove, (530) 639-2272. **Locator:** ENGLEBRIGHT LAKE (D3).

5. BIG BASIN REDWOODS STATE PARK (TENT CABINS)

BIG BASIN has these great tent cabins that can make any child feel safe and secure at night. The park is home to mammoth redwoods and lots of squirrels, butterflies, and deer, as well as pretty waterfalls and a network of trails for easy walks or hikes.

Contact: Big Basin Redwoods State Park, (408) 338-8860; for cabin reservations, phone (800) 874-8368. **Locator:** BIG BASIN REDWOODS STATE

PARK (E1d). **See featured trip page:** 136.

6. WINNEMUCCA LAKE

Here is the perfect introduction to backpacking for families, a two-mile hike from CARSON PASS on Highway 88 to a small but beautiful high mountain lake in the MOKELUMNE WILDERNESS. Good side trips are nearby Round Top Lake and Fourth of July Lake. Sites are first come, first served, but a permit is required; call the Amador Ranger District, (209) 295-4251.

Contact: Eldorado National Forest Information Center, (530) 644-6048. **Locator:** ELDORADO NATIONAL FOREST (D4).

7. TUOLUMNE MEADOWS

No campground in the country puts you at the threshold of more stellar hikes than Tuolumne Meadows, YOSEMITE'S biggest camp with 314 drive-in sites. It's set high in the backcountry at 8,600 feet near Tioga Pass. Lots of bears, chipmunks, and good fishing for small trout in Lyell Fork add sizzle. Half of the campgrounds are available by reservation, with the rest first come, first served.

Contact: Yosemite National Park, (209) 372-0200. **Locator:** YOSEMITE NATIONAL PARK (E4). **See featured trip page:** 239.

8. CONVICT LAKE RESORT

CONVICT LAKE is deep and blue-green, set below high, sheer mountain walls and granite peaks at 7,583 feet in elevation. Bonuses include good fishing, boat rentals, horseback riding, and hiking, with both campsites and cabin rentals available.

Contact: Convict Lake Resort, (760) 934-3803 or (800) 992-2260. **Locator:** CONVICT LAKE (E5). **See featured trip page:** 237.

9. ANDREW MOLERA STATE PARK WALK-IN SITES

The BIG SUR landscape is the most dramatic on the PACIFIC coast, featuring deep canyons, giant rock stacks, and sweeping ocean views. What is better for kids are the easy, flat trails that lead out to secluded beaches, where you can often spot sea lions and otters; rangers may provide a printed sheet that details the best places to see them. Camping is first come, first served.

Contact: Andrew Molera State Park, (408) 667-2315; California State Parks, Monterey District, (408) 649-2836. **Locator:** BIG SUR (F1). **See featured trip page:** 242.

10. LAKE NACIMIENTO

There's no better lake anywhere to catch scads of white bass, like 40 to 50 in a few hours, feisty little fellows that average a pound. This is also a great lake for swimming, boating, and water sports.

Contact: Lake Nacimiento Resort Marina, (805) 238-1056; for reservations, phone (800) 323-3839. **Locator:** LAKE NACIMIENTO (G1).

• TOM'S RATINGS •

THE TOP 5 SIERRA NEVADA LAKES

In Northern California

Interstate 80 is the route that will zip you up to one of six prime camping, fishing, and hiking areas near Truckee. The drive takes about four hours from the Bay Area. You don't need a four-wheeler, just four wheels and an engine, to discover Donner Lake, Martis Creek Lake, and Boca, Stampede, and Prosser Reservoirs. The air has the crackling fresh scent of pines up here on a pure mountain morning.

1. Donner Lake

Here is a good choice for a family camping trip. The lake sits directly adjacent to Interstate 80 just west of Truckee, all facilities are provided, and the area is well developed with cabins and roads. However, it is for those same reasons that many serious anglers bypass this spot. Donner Memorial State Park at the east end of the lake is for weekend campers, and reservations are advised. A public boat ramp is available at Donner Village Resort, where trout fishing is good in the summer. But if you hope to tangle with something big here, like a 15-pound Mackinaw or brown trout, then you'd better be on the water at daybreak in a boat, trolling a Countdown Rapala or J-plug near the northern shore.

Locator: Truckee (D4).

2. Martis Creek Lake

This small lake has been set aside by the Department of Fish and Game as a special fishing refuge. There are wild trout, but all fish are released and only the use of artificial lures or flies with a single barbless hook is allowed. It's definitely not for family campers. But for proficient fly fishers, there is no better place to tangle with 18- to 24-inch wild trout, brown or lahontan cutthroat. Boat motors are not permitted on the lake, so fishing from a float tube or small raft is ideal. The Sierra View Campground has hookups for RVs and provides fair sites for tent camping.

Directions: To get here, turn south on Highway 267 at Truckee, drive six miles, then turn east on the first turnoff to the lake. **Locator:** Truckee (D4).

3. Boca Reservoir

Boca Camp, on the far side of the lake, is the best spot to camp and is close to a boat ramp. RV hookups are available nearby. A few giant, elusive brown trout and a good sampling of stocked rainbow trout make Boca Reservoir a good lake for trollers.

Directions: To get here, turn north on Stampede Meadow Road, six miles past Truckee. **Locator:** Truckee (D4).

4. Prosser Reservoir

Prosser is tucked away just five miles north of Truckee, so supplies can be obtained within a very short drive. A 10 mph speed limit on the lake keeps water-skiers off, and with steady trout fishing, the lake is a favorite of local anglers. Prosser Campground, a great spot, is perched on a wooded lake overlook. However, many campers don't discover it, since they usually stop at the first campground they see here, Lakeside Camp.

Directions: Five miles north of Truckee off Highway 89. **Locator:** Truckee (D4).

5. Stampede Reservoir

If you want the classic Sierra experience, this is a good choice. Tucked away at 6,000 feet, Stampede offers some 250 postcard-pretty campsites and consistent trout fishing year-round. A bonus is a chance at big brown trout; troll a large Rapala directly across from the boat launch along the northern shoreline, and be on the water at dawn.

Directions: Stampede is 14 miles from Truckee and eight miles off Interstate 80 from the Stampede Road turnoff. **Locator:** Truckee (D4).

Maps for all listings: The U.S. Forest Service publishes a map that details all fishing waters, campsites, Forest Service roads, and backpack trails.

Ask for the map of Tahoe National Forest from the Office of Information, U.S. Forest Service, 630 Sansome Street, San Francisco, CA 94111. **Fishing for all listings:** For fishing tips, call Tahoe Truckee Sports, (530) 587-9000, or Mountain Hardware, (530) 587-4844. **Camping/lodging for all listings:** For information, contact the Truckee-Donner Chamber of Commerce, 12036 Donner Pass Road, Truckee, CA 96160, (530) 587-2757. **Contact for all listings:** Tahoe National Forest, Supervisor's Office, (530) 265-4531.

• FEATURED TRIP •

Jedediah Smith Redwoods State Park

Rated: The Top Outdoor Tourist Draw

Disneyland, San Francisco, and the North Coast redwoods are California's primary tourist draws, but it is only in the sanctuary of the redwoods that you can find peace as well as adventure.

Jedediah Smith Redwoods State Park is the northernmost of 30 redwood state parks scattered along the coast from Monterey to the Oregon border. It is my favorite because of the variety of adventures that await explorers. The kicker is that the summer climate is far warmer there than in most areas that harbor coastal redwoods.

The park lies in the northwestern corner of California off Highway 199, just on the edge of the Smith River, California's largest undammed river. In the spring and summer, the South Fork provides good fishing for rainbow and cutthroat trout. In the fall and winter, the main Smith River draws runs of giant salmon and steelhead, although they can prove to be quite elusive.

The park is an ideal base station for fishing adventures on the nearby river, and a good stopover for vacationers heading north as well. For hikers, the park has 23 miles of trails that wind through a countryside filled with giant redwoods, and it is located on the edge of the vast Six Rivers National Forest, which contains more than one million acres of wildlands.

The trails at Jedediah Smith are varied enough that you can match a hike to your physical condition. Of the 11 trails, six are rated "easy" and follow relatively flat terrain. A good example is the Stout Grove Trail, where you walk half a mile to reach the awesome Stout Tree, which measures 340 feet tall and 20 feet in diameter. Ask the ranger for directions.

A good two-hour hike, rated "moderate," is the Hiouchi Trail, which takes you along the west bank of the Smith River and right through a hole in a giant burned-out redwood tree.

All the nearby diversity magnifies the appeal of the park, so even with 108 campsites, you can expect camping reservations to be necessary, particularly during the summer.

But for people who hear the call of giant trees, this place beats Disneyland by a mile.

Directions: From San Francisco, head north on U.S. 101 for approximately 325 miles, past Crescent City, to the Highway 199 turnoff. Turn east and drive nine miles to the park entrance on the right. **Fees:** A $5 state park entrance fee is charged. Campsite fees range from $12 to $16 per night. **Camping:** Each of the 108 campsites has a table, stove, and cupboard. Rest rooms with hot showers are nearby. No RV hookups are available. If you want a more remote campsite, you should contact the Smith River National Recreation Area, (707) 457-3131, for camping spots in Six Rivers National Forest. For camping reservations at Jedediah Smith State Park, phone (800) 444-7275. **Contact:** Jedediah Smith Redwoods State Park, (707) 458-6101 extension 5064; California State Parks, North Coast Redwoods District, P.O. Drawer J, Crescent City, CA 95531, (707) 445-6547; Humboldt Lagoon Visitor Center, (707) 488-2041. **Locator:** JEDEDIAH SMITH REDWOODS STATE PARK (A0).

• FEATURED TRIP •

PATRICKS POINT STATE PARK

Rated: The Top 5 Places to Beach Camp, 108; The Top 10 Overnight Locations, 185

PATRICKS POINT STATE PARK is a remarkable chunk of land on California's North Coast. You get the best of two worlds: It's lush and green with a classic fern undergrowth, yet bordered by the rock-strewn PACIFIC, where you can go tidepool-hopping and whale watching.

But what makes PATRICKS POINT unique is the virtual wall-to-wall plant growth within the park's 625 acres. The trails are often nothing more than tunnels through vegetation. Hikers can become completely sheltered and isolated by the mammoth walls of ferns. The first time I stopped here was back in 1978, and like most folks, it was more by accident than intent. I just wanted a campsite for the night, but I got much more.

The park sits adjacent to U.S. 101, and from the road, you have little idea of the beauty hidden within. Always a stunner for first-timers, it's like a rain forest jungle, where the dense undergrowth can only be explored by foot. The Rim Trail, an easy two-miler, follows the edge of the bluff around three sides of the park. Short yet steep cutoffs can take walkers to the best vistas in the park—Wedding Rock, Palmer's Point, Patricks Point, and Agate Beach. From these lookouts, it is common to spot migrating gray whales.

You can find adventure here nearly year-round. Spring and fall are best for whale watching, however, because the air is crystal clear and the migration is peaking. During the summer, dense fog can cover PATRICKS POINT, as well as the tourists within. Water droplets trickle from the ferns and tourist's noses, and many folks think it is raining. It isn't; it's just fogging. This drip-drip, low-visibility stuff almost never envelops PATRICKS POINT in spring and fall. The muggy days of Indian summer are the warmest days of the year here.

Three campgrounds offer 124 campsites, and like most state parks, they come with a sturdy table, a barbecue stove, and a cupboard. Water faucets and rest rooms with hot showers are provided within short walking distance of each campground. Play it safe and get a reservation.

It is a good idea to plan your trip for when a low tide will roll back the PACIFIC and unveil tidepools. Tiny marine organisms will conduct their little wars at your feet as you hop from one pool to another. Anglers will discover good prospects for lingcod, cabezone, and sea trout during low tides, because you can walk to the outer reaches of the tidal basin. During high tides, on the other hand, you will be casting into a shallow, rocky seafloor where a snag per cast is the likely result.

A side trip to Agate Beach is a must. Here you will find a shoreline loaded with semiprecious stones polished by centuries of sand and water action.

Pick one up and put it in your pocket. Someday when you're enduring a particularly frustrating day, touching the smooth rock will bring you back to calmer days spent at this state park.

Directions: From U.S. 101 at Trinidad, drive five miles north to the park entrance. **Fees:** A $5 state park entrance fee is charged. Campsite fees range from $12 to $16 per night. **Reservations:** For camp reservations, phone (800) 444-7275. **Contact:** Patricks Point State Park, (707) 677-3570; California State Parks, North Coast Redwoods District, (707) 445-6547; Humboldt Lagoon Visitor Center, (707) 488-2041. **Locator:** PATRICKS POINT STATE PARK (A0).

• FEATURED TRIP •

PRAIRIE CREEK REDWOODS STATE PARK

Rated: The Top 6 Coastal Camps, 115; The Top 10 Camps for Kids, 120

The first time you stare at a giant animal eye-to-eye, it can make your backbone tingle. It doesn't have to be something that can eat you—it just has to be big. You have a sudden recognition that the critter standing before you is one huge fellow, and whether he knows it or not, he could do the Bigfoot Stomp all over your body. The funny thing is, though, he usually doesn't seem to know it.

This is how it is with the Roosevelt elk, a monstrous-sized animal that stands five feet at the shoulder. The bulls have long, pointed antlers that look like they could turn you into an instant shish kebab. But unless you try to pet one on the nose and say, "Nice elky," this animal is more likely to maintain an air of gentle indifference, rather than behave like a Doberman attack dog.

Visitors at PRAIRIE CREEK REDWOODS STATE PARK on California's northern coast gain a quick understanding of this behavior, even after the initial shock of seeing something so huge, so close. The elk here are wild, not tame, but are domesticated to the point where they will allow various forms of humanoids, even Southern Californians, to view them from a certain distance.

When the big bulls look up and freeze you with a stare, that means "Close enough, buddy." Most people seem to understand this language.

If you have never seen a huge elk in its native habitat, PRAIRIE CREEK REDWOODS is the spot. It is located about 50 miles north of EUREKA, where the two-lane U.S. 101 cuts right through the park. Often the elk will herd up just beyond the old wooden rails that line each side of the road.

Sometimes all you have to do is pull over on the road's shoulder, which has been enlarged for parking, and you'll have what may be your first significant wildlife sighting outside of a zoo. As many as 50 to 75 elk will often mill around in the large meadow right along the highway. It can make for some remarkable photographs.

One time while I was studying a big bull through binoculars, I saw a family of tourists cruising by in a motor home. The driver accidentally turned his head and spotted all the elk in the adjacent meadow. He braked hard, jerked the RV over to the side of the road, and jumped out. "Look at that! Look at that!" he shouted to his family.

Ten minutes later, as he was calming down, he said to his wife, "Wendy, those are the biggest deer I've ever seen in my life. We sure don't have anything like that in Oklahoma. Did you get a picture? Howie back home won't believe this."

If you've never ventured up here, there are a lot of other things you and Howie won't believe—like the redwood forests, the secluded campgrounds, the scenic drives, and some of the prettiest day hikes in the country. You've got PRAIRIE CREEK REDWOODS as a good base camp with 75 campsites, one of the best day hikes in California at nearby Fern Canyon, and, of course, there are the elk—who will play hide-and-seek for as long as you want.

The redwoods here average more than 200 feet tall and 12 to 13 feet in diameter. They aren't as big around as the sequoias in YOSEMITE's Mariposa Grove, but they are taller. Put thousands of them together, most of them 1,000 years and older, and you get the feeling that this place has been here a long while without anybody fooling with it.

It's even more special in Fern Canyon. This canyon has 50-foot-high walls that are masses of ferns and flora, and the redwoods tower above. Most people have never seen anything like it.

The walks are not difficult, with little elevation gain or loss. There are many shorter options to the Fern Canyon Trail available right from the parking lot at PRAIRIE CREEK REDWOODS. A good trail map is available at the park's headquarters.

PRAIRIE CREEK is one of four contiguous parklands on California's North Coast that stretch for miles and miles. That provides camping options and plenty of alternatives if you want to extend your stay. If the 75-site or 25-site campgrounds in the park are full, you can camp at DEL NORTE COAST REDWOODS STATE PARK (145 campsites) or in adjacent SIX RIVERS NATIONAL FOREST.

But if you want to see elk, PRAIRIE CREEK is the spot.

Several years ago, a fellow decided he wanted a special picture of an elk, that is, a close-up head shot. The ambitious photographer did not have a zoom lens, so he innocently walked right up in front of an elk to take the picture.

Well, Mr. Elk did not like that. In fact, Mr. Elk snorted and chased that fellow right up a tree. At last look, the fellow was perched on a limb, with the elk standing below, looking up at him.

As far as I know, he's still up there, and with pictures to be developed that are far more interesting than he ever imagined.

Directions: From San Francisco, drive north on U.S. 101 for approximately 330 miles. About six miles north of Orick, take the Newton B. Drury Scenic Parkway and follow it straight to the park. **Camping:** Campsites in the park can be reserved by phoning (800) 444-7275. Camping options outside the park include Del Norte Coast Redwoods State Park; call (707) 464-6106. Also try Jedediah Smith Redwoods State Park east of Crescent City at (707) 464-6101, and Six Rivers

National Forest north and east of the park at (707) 442-1721. **Fees:** A $5 state park access fee is charged. Campsite fees range from $12 to $16 per night. **Side trips:** Two excursions are suggested; both are well signed. To get to the Fern Canyon Trail, take the Davison Road off U.S. 101. To get to Lady Bird Johnson Redwood Grove, take the Bald Hill Road off U.S. 101. **Contact:** Prairie Creek Redwoods State Park, (707) 464-6101 extension 5301; California State Parks, North Coast Redwoods District, (707) 445-6547; Humboldt Lagoon Visitor Center, (707) 488-2041. **Locator:** PRAIRIE CREEK REDWOODS STATE PARK (A0).

• FEATURED TRIP •

CASTLE CRAGS STATE PARK

Rated: The Top 50 Base Camps, 110; The Top 10 Easy Backpack Trips, 150; The Top 5 Winter Backpacking Trips, 156

One of the world's truly awe-inspiring views can be seen at CASTLE CRAGS STATE PARK, where soaring spires of ancient granite seem to lift above even giant MOUNT SHASTA. At the base of the crags, Castle Creek tumbles, a classic babbling brook. The surroundings are miles of forested mountain wildlands, and it's just 25 miles north of Shasta Lake.

Many people have glimpsed CASTLE CRAGS while heading up Interstate 5; the ridge sits just west of the highway. But by driving on, they are missing one of California's geologic wonders, as well as a darn good place to spend a weekend. You can camp, hike, and picnic—and the inspired can backpack into adjoining wild country to find a series of hidden lakes that provide good trout fishing.

For car campers, there are 64 well-spaced campsites, most of them large enough to accommodate trailers, although no hookups are provided. As at most state parks, each site comes with a table, barbecue stove, and storage locker, with a nearby rest room/shower available.

Elevations range from 2,000 feet at the campsites to 6,000 feet at the top of the crags, so although it can be quite warm in the day, the temperature can get downright chilly at night, unexpectedly so in spring and autumn. Campers should come prepared for a wide range of temperatures.

The best hike at CASTLE CRAGS is a 3.7-mile climb from the Crags' lookout up to Castle Dome. It is well worth the effort, with great views of MOUNT SHASTA and the Sacramento River Valley and many good picnic sites.

CASTLE CRAGS sits on the edge of wildlands filled with pines, firs, and cedars, along with a number of alders, maples, and oaks. Do not be surprised if you see wildlife, particularly if you come in the uncrowded off-season. The fewer tourists there are, the less apt deer and bears are to be spooked. Year-round, however, the park attracts squirrels, chipmunks, raccoons, and countless lizards; all seem to be looking for a handout.

No matter where you go here, you are always in the shadow of the dramatic landscape. To the north, dominating the countryside for a hundred miles, is the 14,162-foot MOUNT SHASTA, always huge, always covered with snow.

But the crags themselves provide a fascinating attraction. The giant rock chutes and clusters jut upward for thousands of feet, looking like something out of a science fiction movie. But CASTLE CRAGS is real, not make-believe.

Directions: From Redding, drive north on Interstate 5 about 45 miles. Take the Castle Crags Park exit and follow signs to the park entrance. **Fees:** A $5 state park access fee is charged. Campsite fees are $7 to $14 per night. **Camping:** For reservations, phone (800) 444-7275. **Lodging:** If you do not wish to camp, contact the Shasta Cascade Wonderland Association, 1699 Highway 273, Anderson, CA 96007, for a list of available lodgings and for maps and information on Siskiyou, Shasta, Trinity, Lassen, Modoc, and Tehama Counties. **Contact:** Castle Crags State Park, (530) 235-2684; Shasta Cascade Wonderland Association, (800) 474-2782. **Locator:** CASTLE CRAGS STATE PARK (B2).

• FEATURED TRIP •

LEWISTON LAKE

Rated: The Top 50 Base Camps, 110; The Top 16 Lakes with Cabin Rentals, 177; The Top 10 Overnight Locations, 185; The Top 25 Lakes, 307

When you roll out of your sleeping bag at your campsite alongside LEWISTON LAKE, you may rub your eyes a few extra times to make sure you're still on Earth and not in heaven.

This jewel of a lake laps quietly at the bank, and a few trout rise to the surface just a few feet from your campsite. You rub your eyes some more. Thickly wooded mountains rise around you, and in the distance, the snow-covered peaks provide a backdrop. Is this Montana? Canada? Switzerland? Hardly. You're having yet another adventure in our own California: LEWISTON LAKE, tucked away 30 miles west of REDDING in Northern California, snuggled below the TRINITY ALPS.

It's a unique place that provides quality camping, fishing, boating, and hiking, yet is far enough from the Bay Area—a five-hour drive—to keep it from becoming a zoo of summer vacationers.

Four campground facilities provide 100 campsites, and if tents are not for you, there's a private resort along the northwest end of the lake that offers cabins and hookups for RVs. But a tent is all you need at Mary Smith Campground, a truly idyllic spot at the lake's edge. It has 18 sites for tent camping and is the first campground you reach as you drive along the lake.

With 15 miles of shoreline, the lake is just big enough so that it remains uncrowded both for camping and boating. A 10 mph speed limit on the lake makes it ideal for canoes and small aluminum boats, and keeps high-powered boats out. You don't have to contend with water-skiers, only with the fish. And there are plenty of the latter.

As at any lake, the fishing runs in cycles, but you may find rainbow trout and a few giant but elusive brown trout here. A key is that LEWISTON is actually the afterbay for TRINITY LAKE—and that means that its water is cold year-round, since it comes from the bottom of Trinity Dam.

Some of the best fishing in the summer is right before sunset at the upper end of the lake, particularly upstream of Lakeview Terrace, just where you can start to see the current on the surface. This is the haunt for rainbow trout, most averaging 13 to 14 inches, sometimes bigger. By boat, you should anchor in this area and let a night crawler flutter in the current, testing different depths.

If you're without a boat, bring chest waders and from above the Lakeview Terrace area, wade outside the tules and either cast a threaded night crawler with splitshot for weight, or fly-cast. Spin fishers might also try using a bubble-and-fly combination. Evening bites can be quite good.

Typical daytime fishing is not as good, but trollers using flashers and a needlefish lure or a night crawler can take rainbow trout in the 10- to 12-inch class, sometimes bigger. The exception is when the Trinity Dam Powerhouse is running. Anchor in the current and let a night crawler or PowerBait flutter near the bottom. That can be dynamite.

Boat and motor rentals are available at Pine Cove Marina in Lakeview Terrace for guests only.

A good option, especially for families, is to rent a boat for a half-day trip and fish the evening bite. Spend the morning and midday exploring a trail around neighboring Trinity Lake. A good suggestion is the three-mile trail that runs from Clark Springs Campground to Cedar Stock Resort.

If you're roughing it, and need supplies while you're here, there are small grocery stores at Lewiston (on the southern end of the lake) and at Pine Cove Trailer Park.

That leaves little to worry about. You can just show up, kick back, and try to remember that you're not in some far corner of the world, but still in California. Then again, maybe you don't even need to remember that.

Directions: From the Bay Area, take Interstate 80 north to Interstate 505, then travel north to Interstate 5. Drive north on Interstate 5 about 125 miles to Redding and take the Highway 299 West exit. Drive west on Highway 299 for 23 miles, then turn on Lewiston Road and drive to the lake. **Camping:** Campsites are operated on a first-come, first-served basis by Shasta-Trinity National Forest; for information, phone (530) 623-2121. RV hookups are available as well; phone Pine Cove Resort, (530) 778-3838, or Lakeview Terrace Resort, (530) 778-3803. **Cabins:** Lakeview Terrace offers cabins of various sizes for rental. For information, phone (530) 778-3803. **Boat rentals:** Boat and motor rentals are available at Pine Cove Marina, (530) 778-3770. **Contact:** For free maps, brochures, directions, and fishing tips, contact the Shasta Cascade Wonderland Association, 1699 Highway 273, Anderson, CA 96007; (800) 326-6944. **Locator:** Lewiston Lake (B1).

• FEATURED TRIP •

Lake Siskiyou

Rated: The West's Best Camp near Interstate 5

From Mexico to Canada on the Interstate 5 corridor, there is no better place for a one-night layover than Lake Siskiyou, set literally at the foot of 14,162-foot Mount Shasta.

It is one of the prettiest lakes you can drive to in the West, always full and azure blue, with awesome Shasta providing sweeping background scenery. And get this: It is only a five-minute drive from Interstate 5.

But that alone is not what makes this an ideal vacation stop. It's a model for other areas because the entire complex is designed for vacationers making a quick stop and go. No matter what you decide to do, you don't have to spend a few days trying to figure out the right way to go about it.

The features include a protected swimming beach (cordoned off by marker buoys and ropes), excellent trout and bass fishing (a speed limit keeps the water quiet), and a campground in the pines with 225 tent sites, 127 RV sites with hookups, and 60 additional sites for either tents or RVs. There is also a marina with a variety of low-speed boat rentals (including foot-powered paddleboats) and "cabins" (actually mobile homes) for people without tents, as well as a restaurant that specializes in barbecue.

LAKE SISKIYOU is located in Northern California, about an hour's drive north of REDDING, some 280 miles from SAN FRANCISCO. The elevation is about 3,400 feet, so the temperature is typically about 12 degrees cooler than in REDDING, hot enough to feel like summer, but not the valley inferno that can make you feel burned to a crisp.

Most visitors arrive late in the afternoon, hoping for a good time in the midst of a vacation trip. They usually find it—and quick.

When leaving Interstate 5 and making the quick drive over to the lake, the first thing most people notice is that SISKIYOU is always full. That is because the lake was created for the sole purpose of providing recreation, so it is always brimming with water. (A hydro unit was added to the dam in the late 1980s, but it doesn't spoil the lake's natural beauty a bit.)

The next thing that sets the place apart is that all visitors must register at an entrance kiosk, much like what you would find at a state park, with day users required to pay a $1 fee. Since it is one of the only lakes in Northern California where a day-use fee is charged, the riffraff go elsewhere.

Then, in a matter of minutes after entering the park, you will find yourself quickly en route to your chosen adventure. I timed it. In 10 minutes, I was on the lake in my canoe trolling for trout, and two minutes into it—15 minutes after taking the turnoff from Interstate 5—my companion was tussling with a 12-inch rainbow trout. It was the first of seven trout caught in little over an hour.

And there was nothing to it, just trolling along during the evening bite, as slowly as possible, with a Rebel crawdad lure, Bingo Bug, Triple Teaser, or gold Z-Ray. A fish cleaning station is provided near the boat ramp, so you don't need to make a mess at your campground. A small tackle shop is located at the dock. The fishing is best typically in May, June, and early July. It slows in August, then often gets good again from mid-September through October.

Boat and motor rentals are available, including patio boats and aluminum fishing boats, but the paddleboats often seem to be most in demand. These are those little plastic boats where the occupants pedal as if on a bicycle. Pedaling powers the boat onward, sometimes in the strangest directions imaginable, often by choice.

The campground is one of the largest in Northern California, but the pine forest prevents visitors from feeling too squished together and a noise ordinance keeps it pretty quiet. In summer, sunset arrives at about 8:30 p.m. Dusk continues to 9 p.m. and it is typically another hour before campers start quieting down for the night. Too many fish stories to tell.

There are many other attractions

in the area, the most compelling, of course, being MOUNT SHASTA. A beautiful car tour of the mountain is available on the Everitt Memorial Highway, which is routed up to 8,000 feet (where the snow starts) and a hiking trailhead.

If you instead head up into the Mount Eddy Range, making a right turn from the exit from LAKE SISKIYOU, you can access several alpine lakes and many good hiking areas. Gumboot Lakes, Heart Lake, and the Mumbo Basin are the top hiking areas. The view of MOUNT SHASTA from Heart Lake is probably the best available anywhere.

But most visitors are here for a long stay. After all, they're cruising Interstate 5 on vacation and simply want a premium layover spot. And that is what LAKE SISKIYOU provides.

Directions: From the Bay Area, take Interstate 80 east to Interstate 505, then head north to Interstate 5. Continue on Interstate 5 past Redding and Dunsmuir. At the town of Mount Shasta, take the Central Mount Shasta exit and drive to the stop sign. Turn left, cross the highway, and continue to another stop sign at W. A. Barr Road. Turn left and proceed over Box Canyon Dam at Lake Siskiyou. Two miles farther, turn right at the entrance road for Lake Siskiyou Campground and Marina and proceed a short distance to the entrance station. **Facilities:** You'll find a campground, RV hookups, a boat ramp and dock, boat rentals, a swimming beach, marina tackle, a snack shop, and a barbecue restaurant. **Special rules:** A $1 day-use fee is charged at the entrance station. A speed limit on the lake prohibits high-speed boating and waterskiing. Campers are asked to keep noise levels down. **Contact:** For a brochure, call the Shasta Cascade Wonderland Association, (800) 474-2782. For a campsite reservation or information, phone Lake Siskiyou Camp Resort, (530) 926-2610. **Locator:** LAKE SISKIYOU (B2).

• FEATURED TRIP •

★ BOTHE–NAPA VALLEY STATE PARK

Rated: Best Redwoods near Napa Valley

Most people think of the Napa Valley as a 20-mile stretch of wineries and tourists, but nearby BOTHE–NAPA VALLEY STATE PARK offers a spot for camping and picnicking, as well as hiking trails that wind through the easternmost stands of coastal redwoods in California.

Now wait a minute. Redwoods in the Napa Valley, you say? Sure thing, and that's not all that will surprise Bay Area residents who are accustomed to driving past this area rather than walking through it. BOTHE–NAPA VALLEY STATE PARK is cut by Ritchey Creek at the bottom of a canyon and is bordered by mountains that climb from 300 to 2,000 feet. It provides habitat for squirrels, foxes, deer, raccoons, and coyotes.

One tip is to be sure to get a reservation if you plan on camping, because the park has just 50 campsites, including 10 walk-in sites. Reservations can be made by calling the number shown at the end of this story, and rangers advise allowing a minimum of four weeks lead time. Each campsite offers a table, cupboard, and barbecue stove. Rangers ask that no downed wood be used for fires, but they often sell firewood at the park entrance.

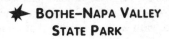

Barbecue chips are advised for cooking.

Many of the park's visitors are folks who have just taken a tour at one of the nearby wineries. They're just looking for a shade tree to sit underneath and sample the contents of a recent purchase, and usually find the park by accident. However, on subsequent trips, most of these people return, and that's no chance occurrence. Not with walks available that range from an easy stroll on the Loop Trail to a rugged hike that takes you up to ridges for panoramic views. The best moderate hike is the Coyote Peak Trail, an hour-long jaunt that climbs to a lookout offering views of the park's back canyon and glimpses of the Napa Valley.

One of the most popular hikes at the park is the Ritchey Canyon Trail, an easy walk that borders Ritchey Creek and is hidden by redwoods, firs, and ferns. This cool spot is a special refuge during the summer, when temperatures elsewhere often reach 90 to 100 degrees.

One key tip is to stay on the trail. The park is loaded with poison oak. Remember that poison oak always grows in clumps of three leaves, and turns from a shiny green in the spring to rich orange and red in the summer and fall.

Directions: From San Francisco, take Interstate 80 north to the Highway 29 cutoff to Napa. Turn north and continue on Highway 29, past St. Helena. Turn left at the park entrance, just past Bale Lane. **Fees:** A $5 state park access fee is charged. Campsite fees are $15 to $16 per night. A $1 fee is charged for pets, and another $1 for access to the swimming pool at park headquarters. **Reservations:** For camping reservations, phone (800) 444-7275. **Pets:** Dogs must be kept on a leash and have proof of rabies vaccination. While dogs may enter the park, they are not allowed on the trails. **Contact:** Bothe-Napa Valley State Park, (707) 942-4575; California State Parks, Silverado District, 3801 St. Helena Highway North, Calistoga, CA 94515; (707) 938-1519. **Locator:** BOTHE-NAPA VALLEY STATE PARK (D1).

• FEATURED TRIP •

★ POINT REYES NATIONAL SEASHORE

Rated: The Top 50 Parks, 7; ; The Top 4 Earthquake Trails, 26; The Top 50 Base Camps, 110; The Top 10 Easy Backpack Trips, 150; The Top 10 Spots for a First Kiss, 180; The Top 10 Places to View Wildlife, 257

Many people miss the best of POINT REYES NATIONAL SEASHORE simply because of one little thing: they aren't willing to hike a little and spend the night.

But do that one little thing and you will discover that there are four hike-in trail camps set at the threshold of the Bay Area's greatest land of adventure. The highlights are well worth the effort, with divine bluff-top views of the ocean, hilltops with yet more views, secluded beaches, surprise lakes where you can swim, beautiful coastal rock formations and tidepools, and, yes, small campsites perfectly situated to enjoy it all. All you have to do is walk a little and camp.

All four camps—Coast, Sky, Glen, and Wildcat—are hike-in sites, but none is difficult to reach: Coast Camp is the easiest, a flat, 2.8-mile walk, followed by Sky (3.0 miles), Glen (4.6 miles), and Wildcat (5.6 miles).

There is no better time to enjoy this trip than early fall, when the Marin coast gets its best weather of the year. The coastal winds tend to be down (no northerners in your face!), the nights are usually clear (for great stargazing), and the temperatures are mild to warm (perfect for hiking).

October also marks the anniversary of the 1995 POINT REYES fire, when a wildfire raked the hillsides from Inverness Ridge on west all the way to the ocean; today, watching the land and its vegetation renew themselves has become one of the biggest ongoing spectacles in the Bay Area. The best camps to witness this process are Coast Camp and Sky Camp, both of which sit right on the edge of the burned area.

These four camps are called "environmental camps," meaning they are primitive, but provide piped water, pit toilets, and flat areas for tents. All cooking must be done on backpacking stoves, and no campfires are permitted. The cost is $10 per night per individual site, with reservations available up to two months in advance by calling (415) 663-8054. Naturally, they tend to fill up quickly on Saturday nights.

What follows is a description of each camp, the hikes to reach them, and the nearby adventures available:

COAST CAMP

This is the perfect camp for people who love quiet, expansive beaches with few people around. Coast Camp is in an open, bluff setting, about a five-minute walk from a beautiful beach. In addition, it is the only camp at POINT REYES, and one of the few camps in the Bay Area, that is accessible by bike. It is best reached by parking at the lot near the Point Reyes Hostel, then taking the COAST TRAIL. On the way in, a 2.8-mile hike, you will have a panoramic view to your left of the foothills leading up to Inverness Ridge, once burned and now reborn. Coast Camp was somehow spared by the '95 fire, when the blaze burned right up to the edge of the campground, then suddenly made an arcing turn right around it. Once you've set up camp, a great side trip is hiking (no bikes allowed) south on the Coast Trail for 1.4 miles to Sculptured Beach and its rock towers, caves, and tunnels.

SKY CAMP

You get a sense of drama at Sky Camp. It lies near Inverness Ridge on the western flank of Mount Wittenberg (1,407 feet), providing a sweeping view of the burned area, the Marin coast, and beyond to the ocean. In fact, the '95 fire partially burned Sky Camp, necessitating some renovation work. To get here, start at park headquarters, the Bear Valley Visitor Center, and take the Bear Valley Trail for one mile to the turnoff for the Meadow Trail. Turn right (north) on the Meadow Trail and climb for 1.5 miles to Inverness Ridge and the four-way junction with the Sky Trail. Do not turn on the Sky Trail. Go straight across and continue for another half mile to the campground. When the foothills and coast come into view, be sure to stop at least once, spread out your arms palms up, and soak it all in.

GLEN CAMP

The most secluded of the four camps at POINT REYES, Glen Camp is in the foothills well south of the burned area and provides the best chance for hikers to get away from it all, even on a weekend. The nearby hilltop views of the coast are divine, and the best side trip is the 2.8-mile hike down to the ocean to Sea Tunnel and Arch Rock. To start the trip, park your car at the Bear Valley Visitor Center and hike out on the Bear Valley Trail (more of a road) for 3.2 miles, which involves an easy climb to Divide Meadow and then heads onward through Bear Valley to the turnoff for the Glen Camp Trail. Here you turn left and hike through two small canyons for 1.4 miles to reach the campground.

Wildcat Camp

It's a fantastic adventure: You enjoy a great hike to a beautiful campsite where you spend the night, then you have a choice of many side trips, including one to a gorgeous beach. The camp is set in the southern reaches of the park, best accessible at the Palomarin Trailhead, located north of Bolinas off Mesa Road. It's a 5.6-mile walk on the Coast Trail to the camp. The trail in crosses a canyon and climbs 500 feet to a short hill (great ocean views), then turns left and over the next three miles passes Bass Lake, Pelican Lake, Ocean Lake, and Wildcat Lake, often good for swimming. The trail also passes the cutoff to Alamere Falls, beautiful when the creek is running full, a 40-foot waterfall that cascades over a bluff and lands right on the beach. Want more? Adjacent to the camp is secluded Wildcat Beach, out of distance for most day hikers.

Contact: For camping reservations and information, including space available on specific dates, phone Point Reyes National Seashore, Backcountry Camping, (415) 663-8054. To reach the Bear Valley Visitor Center, phone (415) 663-1092. **Locator:** Point Reyes National Seashore (E1a).

• Featured Trip •

★ The East Bay Regional Park District: Camping with Kids

Rated: East Bay Hills Top Spots

The magic is always in the moment. Nobody remembers days, and weeks are a blur. But what children and their parents will always treasure most about campouts are the special moments: roasting marshmallows, when the fish finally decided to bite, the owl hooting in the night . . .

"I remember going camping when I was eight years old, and looking up that first night and seeing all the stars," Kathy Small, who now leads camping trips for parents and children, told me. "I remember seeing shooting stars and how bright they were. It was incredible for me. I remember laying there and trying to count them all, and never wanting to go to sleep."

Small is the recreation coordinator for the East Bay Regional Park District, the director of a new program that offers camping opportunities that are ideal for single parents, first-time campers, and families looking for a re-introduction to the great outdoors.

"The way this works is that we do everything, so parents can relax, have fun, and learn, right along with their kids," Small said. "They have this experience, and then they can go camping on their own. They gain the ability and the confidence."

At one campout at Chabot Regional Park, 73 parents and children participated. There were 25 tents, including 15 provided by the parks district, as well as a variety of programs and activities. The naturalist programs featured reptile and insect identification, and covered the park's wildlife and wildflowers. Activities included boating, fishing, hiking, and horseback riding. Saturday night was capped by a ranger-led program, goodies, and campfire stories.

But what seemed to fascinate the youngsters most was this unexpected moment from an unexpected visitor. In the grassy area adjoining the campsites, a gopher suddenly appeared, burrowing a hole, throwing tufts of grass and dirt, and the kids were glued to this scene as if they were watching an action thriller. They talked about it for hours.

"This was an excellent program to introduce my children to camping," said Dionne Libran of RICHMOND. "As a single parent, such opportunities are rare."

"My son Brandon and I had a great time," said Cynthia Bulat of FREMONT. "We'll definitely look into joining another camping event in the near future."

The East Bay Regional Park District has sponsored such camps at DEL VALLE REGIONAL PARK south of LIVERMORE, TILDEN REGIONAL PARK in the BERKELEY hills, and REDWOOD REGIONAL PARK in the OAKLAND hills. The price is $20 per adult, $15 per child, and includes the cost of the campsite, three meals, and naturalist-led activities; 15 tents are available for free on a first-come, first-served basis.

The way it works is that participants arrive on Saturday morning, and then program staffers help people set up their tents. After that, they form a welcome circle followed by lunch.

"Some people might be a little wary at first, but by lunch they warm up and join other families for activities," Small said.

What the kids like best are exploring and finding new things, such as a lone stink beetle, a big banana slug, or a newly hatched butterfly. Seeing their kids discover the wonders of camping and the outdoors has a way of touching something deep in most parents, as if they themselves are reliving their own childhood.

At night, the kids often have difficulty getting to sleep, not so much from being scared, but rather from the exhilaration of the new experience. Many see their first shooting star, and with that, drift off to never-never land.

At the first glimpse of dawn on Sunday, the kids are up and about, while their parents attempt (and usually fail) to snooze away. Suddenly, the youngsters are aware of how much there is to do in the outdoors, that they don't need television to have fun, and that they can hardly wait for the next adventure.

At CHABOT and DEL VALLE, two parks with beautiful lakes, kids have an opportunity to catch fish, many for the first time.

"A lot of kids have never caught a fish," Small said. "When they get their first bite and set the hook, they can be shocked, an absolute happy shock." Some small children are secretly worried that the fish could pull them into the lake, but their parents are always there to assure them that everything is fine, that they can reel the big one in, even if it is just a four-inch bluegill.

"To them, it is the big one," Small said.

The youngsters depart with their parents on Sunday afternoon, happy, a bit tired, but with some of the most memorable moments of their lives fresh in their minds. The parents suddenly realize that, while it is a lot of fun, the true reward of camping is that it can be the tie that binds.

Contact: For information, phone Kathy Small, (510) 635-0135 extension 2521. To register, call (510) 636-1684. **Locator:** (E1c).

• FEATURED TRIP •

★ BIG BASIN REDWOODS STATE PARK

Rated: The Top 25 Hikes, 2; The Top 50 Parks, 7; The Top 4 One-Way Hikes Using a Shuttle Car, 34; The Top 10 Trips into the Redwoods, 36; The Top 50 Base Camps, 110; The Top 10 Camps for Kids, 120; The Top 5 Winter Backpacking Trips, 156; The Top 10 Spots for a First Kiss, 180; The Top 10 Overnight Locations, 185; The Top 20 Hike-to Waterfalls, 187

Imagine a short Sunday morning drive from the Bay Area, a two-hour walk, mostly downhill, then lunch beside a magnificent 70-foot waterfall in a fern-lined canyon. It's a scene that looks like something out of YOSEMITE.

When you visit BIG BASIN REDWOODS STATE PARK in the SANTA CRUZ MOUNTAINS, you will discover that this image is not a product of your imagination. BIG BASIN became California's first state park in 1902, and after you hike it you will understand why. It is a place of special calm, with thousands of acres of redwoods, ferns, moss-lined canyons, and a series of waterfalls that make prime destinations for hikers.

Spending time in the mountains here can give you a fresh perspective. A few drops of water caught by a spiderweb look like crystals in midair. A blooming trillium alone in a bed of ferns catches your eye as you stroll amid huge redwoods, some more than 2,000 years old. When you leave, you'll feel as if your batteries have been recharged.

BIG BASIN is an ideal place for a one-day hike, with some 80 miles of trails to choose from. But you may choose to visit the park for weeklong camping trips, since then you won't squander your time driving long distances. Some 145 drive-in campsites, 43 walk-in sites, and 38 tent cabins are available. Each camp is in a redwood setting and includes a picnic table and food locker.

BIG BASIN also offers unique options for backpackers either in training for a Sierra expedition, or just in need of a good two-day pull. You'll find one of the best weekend hikes in the Bay Area here. It's part of the Skyline-to-Sea Trail, a 12-miler from headquarters at BIG BASIN to the PACIFIC OCEAN. I have always enjoyed this hike. However, this is not a loop trail, so you will need to arrange for shuttle service with a friend in order to return to your car.

If you have a little of the adventuring spirit in you, then consider hiking the entire Skyline-to-Sea Trail, a 38-mile foot-stomper. It starts at CASTLE ROCK STATE PARK on Highway 35, set at 2,700 feet just south of the Highway 9 junction. It's a good three-day jaunt, most of it downhill as the trail descends to the shores of the PACIFIC. Several backcountry camps are available for overnight stays. In order to be certain that wildlife and the forest habitat are not damaged, park rules mandate no fires (use a camp stove), and bedding down is allowed only in designated sites.

The strict rules have left most of the native animals undisturbed. Gone are the grizzly bears (one killed logger William Waddell in 1875) and the eagles, but deer, coyotes, raccoons, bobcats, opossums, and the like remain. Also, more than 250 species of birds have been observed in Waddell Valley. The most common is the Steller's jay, mistaken by most for a blue jay; the Steller's jay has a crested head while the blue jay does not. These birds arrive promptly when you start eating lunch, hoping for a handout, and leave just as quickly when you are finished.

The centerpiece of BIG BASIN is Berry Creek Falls. The entire loop from park headquarters requires five to six hours hiking time. If you take the direct route on your return trip, you can cut it to about four and a half hours. If you have never seen it, then a Sunday drive and hike should be at the top of your priority list.

Directions: From San Francisco, take Highway 1 south to Santa Cruz, turn east on Highway 9, then turn left on Highway 236 and continue to the park. From the San Francisco Peninsula, take Highway 9 from Los Gatos over the ridge, then turn right on Highway 236 and continue to the park. Signs to the park are posted. **Fees:** A $6 state park access fee is charged. Campsite fees are $17 per night. **Camping:** For drive-in campsite reservations, phone (800) 444-7275. Reservations for backpacking sites must be made through park headquarters, (831) 338-8860. **Contact:** Park maps can be obtained for a small fee by writing to the Santa Cruz Mountains Natural History Association, 525 North Big Trees Parks Road, Felton, CA 95018. Or phone Big Basin Redwoods State Park, (831) 338-8860, or California State Parks, Santa Cruz District, (831) 429-2851. **Locator:** BIG BASIN REDWOODS STATE PARK (E1d).

• FEATURED TRIP •

BUTANO STATE PARK

Rated: The Top 25 Hikes, 2; The Top 50 Parks, 7; The Top 10 Trips into the Redwoods, 36; The Top 50 Base Camps, 110; The Top 10 Spots for a First Kiss, 180

The mountain biker vs. hiker controversy has been solved at a Bay Area state park where you can get the best of both worlds—just not at the same time.

I'm talking about BUTANO STATE PARK near PESCADERO, one of 12 redwood parks in the Bay Area, but the only one where the hiker/biker affair has been completely resolved. It has become an ideal destination for both activities, with 12 miles of fire roads perfect for biking and 20 miles of narrow paths perfect for hiking.

All of it is scenic. The trails are routed through a dense redwood forest and the fire roads traverse Butano Ridge, with great lookouts of the PACIFIC OCEAN and a redwood-filled canyon.

It is a great place to visit, but if you go, remember that the name is pronounced "BUTE-uh-no" and not "bew-TAH-no." Of the 150 parks in the Bay Area, BUTANO is the favorite of the few who know it well—and you can tell the difference immediately by how they pronounce it. In fact, BUTANO is the number one hiking destination for Don Murphy, the former director of the California State Parks Department.

When you first drive up, you may wonder what could possibly inspire such devotion. The area is pretty, primarily coastal foothills and grasslands, but hey, the number one favorite of the parks chief? Then you turn left on the park access road and find out why, entering a canyon that is a universe apart from the rest of the Bay Area.

The Butano Canyon grows redwoods, creating a classic forest habitat, complete with stream, giant ferns, sorrel, trillium, and even wild orchids. The hiking trails weave among this dense vegetation, which provides a quiet and pristine setting.

Above the canyon is Butano Ridge, where a good fire road is routed completely around the outskirts of the park. It provides outstanding views of the canyon below and west to the PACIFIC OCEAN, rising to the highest point in the park at 1,713 feet.

The park covers 2,700 acres and has a picnic area, 21 drive-in campsites, 18 walk-in sites, and an environmental trail camp. The camps are available on a first-come, first-served basis during the winter, cost $14 per night, and usually fill up each weekend. During summer, you can reserve a site by calling (800) 444-7275. The trail camp, however, must be reserved year-round.

Here are three of the park's great routes:

AÑO NUEVO LOOKOUT TRAIL (HIKERS ONLY)

Just pick a clear day, tighten your boots, and this trail will reward you with a good climb and a great view. Park at the entrance station, then start the 2.7-mile round-trip hike at the trailhead directly to the right. The trail climbs 730 feet in less than a mile to reach the southern canyon rim, and with it, the great Año Nuevo Lookout.

From the lookout point, Año Nuevo Island to the south, as well as the PACIFIC OCEAN, seems framed perfectly by conifers. There is a park bench here where many a couple has had their first kiss. To complete a loop, continue on the Año Nuevo Trail, follow the Olmo Fire Road, then return on the Doe Ridge/Goat Hill trails. This route provides a good climb, a great lookout, then a trek through redwoods for the return descent. There and back should take about 1.5 hours.

BUTANO LOOP (PRIMARILY FOR BIKERS)

While hikers are permitted on this trail, the route is too long to complete in a day, covering an estimated 14 miles, including a 1,500-foot ascent. The smooth, hard-packed fire road traces the Butano Rim, with continuous lookouts much of the way.

Park at the entrance station and ride into the park on the main access road—look for the Ox Mill Trailhead on the left and a gated service road on the right. This is the starting point. Turn right and start climbing Goat Hill, turning off on the Olmo Fire Road. The latter continues to the most remote sections of the park, climbing most of the way. If you are not in good condition, you will be reminded of it on this climb.

Turn left at the Butano Fire Road, still climbing, and you will come to an abandoned airstrip at 1,713 feet, the highest point in the park. From here, the trail descends on the Butano Rim for six miles, a great ride, often with ocean views. It emerges back on the valley floor at Cloverdale Road, which requires a left turn and a short ride back to the park's entrance station to complete the loop.

MILL OX LOOP (PRIMARILY FOR HIKERS)

If you love redwoods and ferns, but also love the sun and warm afternoons, the Mill Ox Loop is a perfect choice. Why? Because here you get all of the above in good doses. The trailhead is about half a mile past the park entrance on the left side of the road, where there is a pull-out area to park.

The Mill Ox Loop Trail (no bicycles permitted) starts by crossing a small creek in a dense redwood forest, then heads up a very steep grade on switchbacks, emerging at the top of the canyon on the Butano Fire Road (where bikes are allowed—see the Butano Loop description above).

Here you turn right and begin a more gradual climb as you head toward the park's interior. The fire road gets plenty of sun, and plenty of shirts come off on the climb en route to 1,138 feet. There are also excellent views of the PACIFIC OCEAN along the way, if you turn and look back to the west.

When you reach a junction with the Jackson Flats Trail, turn right. The trail descends quite steeply for a quarter mile, with switchbacks over rock face, then drops into the Butano Canyon and the surrounding redwood forest. The rest of the hike is beautiful and pleasant, a meandering walk past ferns, trillium, redwoods, and, occasionally in the spring, blooming wild orchids, one of my favorites.

Directions: From the junction of Highways 1 and 92 in Half Moon Bay, drive 18 miles south on Highway 1 to the Pescadero Road junction. Turn east on Pescadero Road and drive past the town of Pescadero. Turn right (south) on Cloverdale Road and continue until you see the signed park entrance turnoff on the left side of the road. **Fees:** There is a $7 day-use access fee per vehicle. **Camping:** Campsites cost $16 per night and are available on a first-come, first-served basis during the winter. From spring through fall, phone (800) 444-7275 for reservations. There will be an additional charge for the service. **Dogs:** Dog owners must show proof of current vaccinations. Dogs are allowed on leashes in the campgrounds, but are not permitted on trails. **Mountain bikes:** Bikes are permitted on 10 miles of fire roads, but not on hiking trails. **Contact:** Butano State Park, P.O. Box 9, Pescadero, CA 94060, (650) 879-2040. If there is no answer at the park, phone California State Parks, Bay Area District, (415) 330-6300. **Locator:** BUTANO STATE PARK (E1d).

• FEATURED TRIP •

HENRY W. COE STATE PARK

Rated: The Top 50 Parks, 7; The Top 5 Steep Hikes, 38; The Top 50 Base Camps, 110; The Top 5 Winter Backpacking Trips, 156; The Top 10 Places to Fish with Kids, 332

Great solitary spots are like $100 bills—the supply never seems to equal the demand. But such a place exists just a short drive from the San Francisco Bay Area, a hidden wildland that you can use as your personal fishing reserve.

Imagine catching and releasing dozens of black bass in a weekend, chasing scads of bluegill, and locating fat crappie and sunfish.

That's what you'll find at HENRY W. COE STATE PARK, which sits on the edge of the Bay Area southeast of SAN JOSE in the Gavilan Mountains. COE PARK encompasses over 117 square miles of wildlands, some 79,000 acres, with more than 80 lakes and ponds, more than half of which support fisheries. The prime fishing areas can be found on the 100-plus miles of trails and long-abandoned ranch roads. It is a place for the person who wants solitude and quality fishing in the same package and who isn't averse to rugged hiking or mountain biking. If there's a catch, that's it—the lakes and ponds can be reached only by trail, not by car, and the routes in are long and rugged.

For starters, you should obtain a map of the park. With the map in hand, you can plan your route. Without a map, you can wander around to many of the lakes and risk missing much of the quality fishing.

The best bets for bass are Coit Lake, Hoover Lake, Kelly Lake, and the distant ponds in the Orestimba and Red Creek drainages.

"In the spring, there are times when you can catch and release 200 bass in a weekend at Coit Lake," ranger Barry Breckling told me. "I told this one guy that he could catch a bass per cast here. He came back from his trip a few days later and said he did even better than that—he caught two bass at once on the same lure." That guy was me.

Most of the largemouth bass at Coit Lake are in the 10- to 13-inch range, with an occasional one even larger. Hoover, Kelly, and Paradise Lakes have bass ranging to larger sizes, and Kelly has the bonus of some big crappies as well, including fish in the 14-inch class.

The lakes are virtually untouched, and in some cases the fish are even stunted in size from overpopulation. How is it that few people have taken advantage of the fishing here over the years? The answer lies in the history of the park. Much of the land was once owned by rancher Marvin Coit, who built most of the ponds and reservoirs some 35 to 60 years ago, then stocked them with fish for his personal use. This property was added to Coe Park in the late 1980s; thus, some of the lakes have been fished very lightly in the last 50 years.

One of the park's prettiest settings is Mississippi Lake, an 11-mile hike from headquarters and a haven for the few who know of it. The lake is home to a small number of wild trout with a remarkable growth rate—reaching 16 inches in as little as two years. All should be released, given that there are so few.

The park is about an hour's drive from San Jose. If you're planning on taking advantage of the fishing, I suggest calling or stopping at Coyote Discount Bait and Tackle, located five miles south of San Jose off U.S. 101. Owner Denise Bradford is a good source for up-to-date information on fishing tips in the area. Another good idea is to call park headquarters for fishing and camping conditions.

Once you reach the park, you should get a wilderness permit for overnight backpacking from the rangers. For drive-in campers, there are only 20 campsites at headquarters, each with a picnic table and barbecue. It's on a first-come, first-served basis, with no reservations accepted. A more appealing plan is to obtain a backpack permit from park headquarters, then hike or mountain bike into one of the many wilderness camps. They are spaced apart so that you can hike for five days without having to camp twice in the same area. In the process, you can sample the wide variety of fishing the park provides. The Coyote Creek Trailhead can cut the distance to Coit, Kelly, and Mississippi Lakes in half.

Since open fires are not permitted in the park, a lightweight backpacking stove should be taken along.

A water purification system is a necessity; dehydration can be a problem for some hikers on California's warm spring days. And since thoughts of outstanding fishing can set off ambitious plans, you should be sure to wear a quality pair of hiking boots.

Most hikers travel light, and that includes their fishing equipment. Five- or six-piece backpack rods, micro spinning or lightweight fly reels, and tiny boxes that will fit into your shirt pocket are the most practical equipment. I take a six-piece graphite pack rod—which can be used for spin or fly-fishing—along with a spinning reel filled with four-pound test line, and a Plano "macromagnum" tackle box. The latter fits into a shirt pocket, yet will hold many lures and flies.

What to use? The wise angler would do well to listen to scientist Jerry Smith of San Jose State University, who has studied the feeding patterns of trout at Mississippi Lake.

According to Smith, the major source of food for trout there is the water flea, a tiny swimming crustacean. Fly fishers casting small dark patterns, particularly nymphs, can do quite well in the spring months. Small midge, mosquito, and gnat patterns should be included in your box. At times, it can be necessary to use fly patterns as small as a no. 16 in order to match the size of insects the trout like to eat. Pinch down the barb on your hooks to make it easier to release your catch without injury.

The bass are less picky about what they strike. Some of the lakes have golden shiners as forage fish, and anglers should take a tip from that. In the spring, shad-type plugs in the one- to three-inch range are the most effective. I use the floating Rapala in blue/silver, Countdown Rapala in black/silver, and the black/silver Shad Rebel Shorty. For fly-fishing, small bass poppers gently laid along lines of tules with floating fly lines can inspire strikes from bass and bluegills alike. Crappies hit best on small white jigs.

In addition to the fishing, springtime at Coe Park is highlighted by explosions of wildflowers. In some areas, entire hillsides change color when the shooting star blooms. Your hike can take you to summits of 3,000 feet and along hillsides studded with oak, madrone, buckeye, and pine. The valleys are bright green from the crackling fresh grasslands.

Black-tailed deer and ground squirrels are common sights; you will likely see far more of them than people. If you spend enough time exploring, you may see wild pigs, coyotes (or at least hear one), or a golden eagle. Mountain lions and bobcats are widespread, but their cautious nature makes sightings rare. Often, footprints from many of these species can be found in the mud at the edge of lakes.

"This is one of the best parks in California, but few know of it," said Harry Battlin, District Superintendent of the Gavilan Mountain District. "It offers solitude, yet is close to an urban area. People who spend all week cooped up in an office can set out for Coe Park when they get off work on Friday, camp at headquarters, then head for the hills Saturday morning."

The best time to visit the park is from February to May, before the furnace-like heat of summer sets in. In the spring, the lakes are full to the brim and the fish are awakening from their annual winter slowdown. They are hungry and will do their best to prove it to you. It won't take much proving before you'll draw the conclusion that this place is your own private fishing wonderland.

With 80 lakes and several streams at COE STATE PARK, you could spend more time searching for the perfect spot than fishing here. Some 35 to 45 of the lakes and ponds in the park provide fisheries, according to biologist Tom Taylor. Here's a guide to the top prospects, in order of hiking distance:

FROG LAKE

Since it is just a 1.5-mile hike from park headquarters, this pond gets more fishing pressure than many of the others. It has bass that top out at 18 inches, although most are smaller, along with bluegills and some catfish.

BASS POND

Golden shiners provide an excellent forage fish for the bass and bluegill in Bass Pond. Two miles out, it's a good resting stop on your way to the outback.

MAHONEY PARK

This pond (you can cast across it) was originally stocked with just six bass and two bluegill. It now supports an abundant fishery, although most of the fish are stunted. Figure on about a six-mile hike.

MIDDLE FORK OF COYOTE CREEK

The upper stretches of the stream are fair for rainbow trout. Eight-inchers are common in good years.

HOOVER LAKE

Eager bass fishers often stop to hit Hoover en route to Coit Lake. Eight miles out, you can't blame them, with largemouth bass in the 12- to 14-inch range.

COIT LAKE

A long hike, 11 miles with an elevation gain of 1,600 feet, will bring you to a lake where a bass per cast is possible on spring evenings. Most of the fish are in the 10- to 12-inch range, with some larger. A bonus is the large green sunfish that hit bass plugs.

MISSISSIPPI LAKE

This is the promised land for many. Rainbow trout grow fast here, to 16 inches in just two years, and fish ranging to 26 inches have been caught. A one-fish, 18-inch minimum size limit is in effect. Expect a rugged hike, almost 12 miles from headquarters with a 2,000-foot elevation gain.

KELLY LAKE

A good dose of large crappies in this lake makes it a winner, although at a distance of 13 miles from headquarters, it is rarely fished. Bass and green sunfish are also present.

PARADISE LAKE

Like most lakes in the Orestimba drainage, Paradise provides larger bass than elsewhere in the park. It is best in the spring and should usually be avoided after mid-May, when it's too hot for the long hike in.

HARTMAN RESERVOIR

Located close to Paradise Lake, Hartman is quite similar in the fishery it provides. You'll find larger bass than at Coit Lake, which is the benchmark for bass fishing in the park.

Directions: From San Jose, drive south on U.S. 101 for seven miles to Morgan Hill. Take the East Dunne Avenue exit and head east, past Lake Anderson, for 13 miles to the park entrance. **Maps:** A map of the park is available for $2 from Henry W. Coe State Park, P.O. Box

846, Morgan Hill, CA 95038. Hikers may be interested in a newer, more detailed map, which shows elevation gains and losses; it's sold at park headquarters. **Fishing:** All anglers should possess a valid California fishing license, available at most tackle shops. For fishing conditions and campsite availability, call the park at (408) 779-2728 or phone California State Parks, Four Rivers District, (209) 826-1196. **Camping:** Drive-in campers will find 20 campsites at headquarters, each with a picnic table and barbecue. It's first come, first served, with no reservations taken. With a backpacking permit, you can hike into one of the many wilderness camps. **Fees:** A $5 state park access fee is charged. Campsite fees are $8 per night. **Wilderness permits:** As soon as you reach the park, you should go to headquarters to acquire a wilderness permit for overnight backpacking. **Contact:** Henry W. Coe State Park, (408) 779-2728; California State Parks, Four Rivers District, (209) 826-1196. **Locator:** HENRY W. COE STATE PARK (E1d).

• FEATURED TRIP •

PORTOLA REDWOODS STATE PARK

Rated: The Top 50 Parks, 7; The Top 12 Hike-to Streams, 24; The Top 10 Trips into the Redwoods, 36; The Top 20 Hike-to Waterfalls, 187; The Top 10 Scenic Back Roads, 198

If explorer Don Gaspar de Portola were to see the suburbia sprawling across the San Francisco Peninsula today, he'd probably do exactly what thousands of Bay Area residents do every year—seek the refuge of PORTOLA REDWOODS STATE PARK.

The area from SAN FRANCISCO to MORGAN HILL can seem like one long chain of houses and cars, but just over SKYLINE RIDGE, behind the outskirts of PALO ALTO, you still can find an asylum of peace. It looks much as it did when Portola first set foot in the area in 1769. Peters and Pescadero Creeks wind through rugged country studded with redwoods, Douglas firs, and oaks. It's an ideal spot for the weekender who is ready to escape the grip of city life but who doesn't want to drive far.

PORTOLA REDWOODS STATE PARK is best known for its natural beauty; hiking, camping, and communing with the quiet are the prime attractions. Some 14 miles of hiking trails lead through varied terrain. Some hikers head up the ridge through redwoods and into chaparral, while others follow the streams and the forest floor of azaleas and lush ferns.

Campers have 53 drive-in campsites to pick from, each with a picnic table, barbecue pit, and wood food locker to protect your eats from raccoons making their nightly raids. There are also four group sites, seven walk-in sites (which means you walk your equipment in 10 to 100 yards), and six trail campsites. Always phone ahead for campsite availability.

In the spring, a special bonus awaits streamside explorers. Steelhead can be seen spawning in the gravel riverbeds after a long journey from the ocean to the high reaches of the streams. But don't bring your fishing rod. All fishing is illegal year-round here, and has been for years. In the winter, the big steelhead are protected so they can spawn, and in the summer, so are the steelhead smolt. In the past, kids catching those "little trout" in the summer were actually killing baby steelhead that were trying to grow large enough to head out to sea.

PORTOLA REDWOODS is a good destination for a family outing on a weekend or for a quiet retreat during the week.

Directions: From Interstate 280 near Redwood City, take Highway 84 east to Highway 35 (Skyline Boulevard). Turn south and drive about seven miles, then turn west on Alpine Road. Follow this road 3.5 miles, then veer left on Portola Park Road. You will come to the visitor center in 3.6 miles. The turns are well signed. An alternate route is to start at Palo Alto, taking the twisting Page Mill Road southwest to the park. **Fees:** A $6 state park access fee is charged. Campsite fees are $14 to $18 per night. **Camping:** Sites are first come, first served in the winter. Reservations can be made for the period from May through September; phone (800) 444-7275. **Pets:** Dogs must be licensed, leashed, and kept off the trails. **Contact:** Portola Redwoods State Park, Box F, Route 2, LA HONDA, CA 94020; (650) 948-9098. California State Parks, Santa Cruz District, (831) 429-2851. **Locator:** PORTOLA REDWOODS STATE PARK (E1d).

• FEATURED TRIP •

★ LAKE ALPINE

Rated: The Top 25 Lakes, 307

One of the Sierra Nevada's great jewels is LAKE ALPINE. With its cabins, campsites, and lodge, it's the ideal destination for an extended stay spent hiking, fishing, and taking advantage of many other nearby adventures.

Though hardly a secret, LAKE ALPINE still gets missed by many of those who would love the place, simply because it is located on Highway 4, near BEAR VALLEY/Mount Reba, rather than on the Interstate 80 or U.S. 50 corridors to Reno and TAHOE.

The first time visitors see the lake, they are usually surprised by the stunning mountain beauty. You round a bend in the two-lane highway, and suddenly, there it is, rising up to road's edge on the right, full and pretty, complete with a mountain backdrop. The lake is set at an elevation of 7,320 feet and covers 180 surface acres; in other words, it's high enough in the mountains to capture the best of the Sierra, small enough to keep the setting quiet and intimate, big enough for low-speed boating and for trout to grow.

But what really makes the place work is Lake Alpine Lodge and its cabins, as well as a series of four campgrounds operated by the U.S. Forest Service. All the cabins have lake views, are within a few minute's walk of the lake, have at least two beds, and are priced from $65 to $90 per day, depending on their size. Most include outdoor barbecue stands, refrigerators, cookware, and showers, and all have decks. It's not quite like finding your own Golden Pond, because the cabins are on a sloping hillside on the opposite side of the highway from the lake; but that is actually a bonus, since the distance provides privacy and quiet, a buffer zone from the activity at the lake.

There are four campgrounds at the lake, Pine Marten (33 sites), Silver Valley (25 sites), Alpine (27 sites), and Silver Tip (24 sites), along with an overflow area called Lodgepole. All are run on a first-come, first-served basis, no reservations, with a $13.50 fee per night.

The lodge, meanwhile, provides a small store, a bar, and a restaurant, so once you arrive, your vacation has started and you're here for keeps; you don't have to retreat back down the mountain to ARNOLD for supplies.

Once you do settle in, it isn't long until all your cares begin to fall away and you focus instead on hiking, fishing, and exploring the region.

Hiking in the area is outstanding. Most visitors will take two hours and hike completely around the lake, a flat four-miler, but there are better trails available. One is the 1.3-mile climb up to Osborne Ridge (the trailhead is located just east of Silver Tip Campground), where you get a gorgeous view of the lake, as well as into the Carson-Iceberg Wilderness. If you like views, this one is a must.

Another must is the 1.5-mile tromp to Duck Luck (the trailhead is at Silver Valley Campground), a tiny, pretty setting with some old pioneer cabins along the route. The ambitious can extend the hike into the adjacent Carson-Iceberg Wilderness to Rock Lake, a pristine lake with clear blue water set in granite, an eight-mile roundtrip.

As for the fishing, it often seems that youngsters catch more trout than anybody else here, fishing from shore, using chartreuse glitter Power Bait. Sometimes the kids will line up along the shore, and all that bait in the water in one area seems to attract the fish right in to them. All the pictures that have been posted on the wall at the lodge seem to prove it, shot after shot of kids holding up their prize catches.

Older, more experienced anglers often fish out of boats or float tubes. It's an ideal lake for a small boat, with a good boat ramp and a 10 mph speed limit guaranteed to keep the lake quiet. In other words, there are no jet skis or similar personal watercraft, no water-skiers, no big, fast boats. Just folks out putting around, trolling, and sometimes paddling canoes or oaring small inflatable rafts.

After a day or two, your curiosity will begin to grow for the other wonders the region holds. A drive up Highway 4 to Ebbetts Pass will reward you along the way with a beautiful distant view to the south of the Dardanelles (rocks shaped like castle tops and towers), a drive out to gorgeous Highland Lake, pristine meadows in Hermit Valley, and a trailhead for the PACIFIC CREST TRAIL.

My recommendation is to try at least one of the following two day trips. The best is to drive out to Highland Lake, then hike the steep, two-mile trail to Wolf Creek Pass and the junction with the PACIFIC CREST TRAIL. Here you get breathtaking sweeping views of the entire region, including three plunging valleys.

The other is to drive to Ebbetts Pass, park, then hike north for two miles. This entails a 45-minute climb, but you gain access to three pretty lakes, Sherold Lake and Upper and Lower Kinney lakes.

Directions: Lake Alpine is located on Highway 4, near Bear Valley/Mount Reba. From Highway 99 at Stockton, turn east on Highway 4 and drive to Angels Camp at the junction of Highways 4 and 49. Drive east on Highway 4 for about 51 miles to the lake.

Contact: For information on Lake Alpine Lodge, contact them at P.O. Box 5300, Bear Valley, CA 95223; (209) 753-6358. For campground information, phone Stanislaus National Forest, Cala-

veras Ranger District, (209) 795-1381.
Locator: LAKE ALPINE (E4).

• FEATURED TRIP •

★ HELL HOLE RESERVOIR

Rated: The Top 50 Base Camps, 110

HELL HOLE RESERVOIR is so named for being set in a 400-foot-deep granite gorge, through which the RUBICON RIVER enters from snowmelt in the Sierra Nevada west of TAHOE. A beautiful lake in any condition, it is ringed by ponderosa pines and old cedars above the rocky shore and is filled with clear, cobalt blue water. Even during a drought, when the water level falls hundreds of feet, this lake still provides a spectacular setting, with sheer granite walls rising from the water's edge.

Getting here requires about a two-hour drive east of AUBURN, turning right at Foresthill and traveling 49 miles out via Mosquito Ridge Road. You'll end up at a primitive boat ramp near the dam at French Meadows Reservoir, at an elevation of 4,580 feet. No people. We parked, walked across the dam, then started hiking east on the Hell Hole Trail, which skirts above the southern shore of the lake, rising and falling in 40- to 60-foot spurts, nothing serious, for 3.5 miles. No people. The trail rises past a granite outcrop, where there are great views of the upper end of the lake, then drops down to a beautiful little campground, accessible only by trail or boat. Still no people.

Once here, many adventures are possible. By boat, the lake's craggy shoreline can be explored in detail, with the opportunity to discover a great swimming spot on a granite point on the south shore, as well as unusual geologic formations upstream in the narrows. Fishing can be good, and not for the little planted rainbow trout found at most lakes, but for Mackinaw trout, brown trout (sometimes quite large), and kokanee salmon.

The hiking is excellent, too. A trail is routed to the east up along the RUBICON RIVER and into the spectacular Granite Chief Wilderness, named for its huge, glacial-sculpted granite face, where dozens of small lakes are set in rock depressions, filled each spring from melting snow. After our hike, we flew a plane over the wilderness, scanned the lakes, and saw virtually no one. It does get a lot of use in good weather on summer weekends, but we hit it just right.

Nearby French Meadows Reservoir is a beautiful spot with excellent camping, boating, and fishing.

The huge lake covers nearly 2,000 acres, circled by conifers, with five campgrounds (including one great boat-in site).

California has 300 mountain lakes and 185 streams with campgrounds that are accessible by car, many of them largely devoid of people. Instead of watching television at home, buy a case of VCR tapes, ask a friend to tape your favorite shows, and get out there right now, camping, boating, fishing, and hiking.

Directions: In Auburn on Interstate 80, take the Foresthill exit at the north end of town and drive 20 miles northeast on Foresthill Road to the town of Foresthill. Turn east on Mosquito Ridge Road (the route to French Meadows Reservoir) and drive 36 miles to French Meadows Reservoir Dam. Cross the dam and turn south on Forest Service Road 48 and travel 13 miles to the primitive boat ramp near the dam. **Contact:** Eldorado National Forest Information Center, (530) 644-6048. For a map of Eldorado National Forest, send $4 to Maps, Office of Information, U.S. Forest Service, 630 Sansome Street, San Francisco, CA 94111. **Locator:** HELL HOLE RESERVOIR (D3).

• FEATURED TRIP •

Pinnacles National Monument

Rated: California's Smallest Mountain Range; The Top 10 Cave Explorations, 380

If you've ever wanted to stop the world and jump off, PINNACLES NATIONAL MONUMENT is a good place to do it, at least for a weekend. For one thing, it looks like a different planet. For another, it is completely out of the way, located in obscure San Benito County, about an hour from HOLLISTER. Nobody comes here by accident.

Add those factors together and the PINNACLES provides an ideal hideaway for an overnight trip, whether you just want to get away from it all or you want a chance to explore the strange caves and huge volcanic clusters that cover much of the 16,000-acre park.

Winter and, even more so, early spring are the best times to make the trip. In the summer and fall, it's hot, dry, and sticky down here. It can get extremely hot, in the 90s and 100s, just about every day of the summer. You might as well plan a trip to Mercury.

This is a place for secrets, and the two extensive cave systems hold many of them. The Bear Gulch Cave is approximately four-tenths of a mile long, and the Balconies Cave extends about three-tenths of a mile.

These are not subterranean tunnels, like the old gold mines of the Sierra Nevada, but talus caves. They were created over time in canyons and crevices where rocks have slipped or fallen and storm runoff has removed the softer volcanic material. The result is a unique series of connected spaces under a rocky canopy.

Once you enter the cave system, you feel like you are entering a new world. If you turn your flashlight off, it gets as dark as the sockets of a skull. Wave your hand in front of your face and you can't see it.

As you probe on, you need to keep the light roaming the darkness, not just where you're walking. Do the latter and you are liable to ram your head into a stalactite, a different way of adjusting your thought patterns than what you originally planned for this trip.

All the cave walks are self-guided, which adds a lot to the adventure. (At the Oregon Caves, only guided group tours are permitted.) If you forget your flashlight, rangers sell them. If you remember to bring you own, be certain your bulb and batteries are fresh.

The caves are subject to closure if there are earthquakes or heavy rains, either of which can loosen material. What the heck, finding it closed is better than having a five-ton volcanic block fall on your big toe. However, when rain is light, the caves can be open all winter without closure.

The rest of the park is as unique as the cave system. The PINNACLES consist of a huge rock mass that suddenly rises in chutes from the valley floor. It was created from a volcanic blast, similar to the one that formed the Sutter Buttes north of SACRAMENTO. Hawkins Peak, a vertical barren spire at 2,720 feet, is what remains of the volcano's flume.

Trails can take you to the canyon ridges, which provide great lookouts onto the surrounding valley. The High Peaks Trail is one of the best. Because this is a primitive area with no piped water, be certain to bring a full canteen or a day pack with your favorite liquid refreshment.

Two campgrounds are available, one primitive and isolated (located on the west side of the park), the other privately developed with full facilities (located just outside the east side of the park). Because no road extends through the park, you can't just hop over to the other camp if your first choice is filled. It is strongly advised that you phone ahead for space availability.

The east side gets more visitation because it has a better access road and full facilities, and is closer to the Bear Gulch Caves. Pinnacles Campground, the privately run camp there, has 125 sites, including space for motor homes, but even so, it can fill up on weekends. To assist with the growing number of visitors, rangers have arranged a shuttle system to carry day visitors from a parking area to the caves.

A good time to plan a trip is during March or early April. That is when the valley's wildflowers begin to bloom, and with the greened-up hills as a backdrop, you can see the most colorful scenes of the year here.

Camping: Pinnacles Campground is a privately operated, 125-site campground with full facilities on the east side of the park. Camping is on a first-come, first-served basis, and it is often full on winter and spring weekends. For more information, phone (831) 389-4462. The primitive camp on the west side has 18 sites, with water and toilet facilities available nearby. Sites are first come, first served; contact rangers at (831) 389-4485. **Fees:** A $5 day-use fee is charged. Fees for primitive sites are $10 per night. The private campground charges $6 per night. **Directions:** To enter from the east from the Bay Area, drive south on U.S. 101 to Gilroy and take Highway 25 to Hollister. Continue south on Highway 25 for about 30 miles, then turn west on Highway 146 and proceed to the park. To enter from the west, drive south on U.S. 101 to the Soledad exit. The exit will bring you out onto Front Street. Follow Front Street into Soledad and go left on Monterey Road until you come to a four-way stop. Turn right on Metz Road and drive three miles to Highway 146. Take a left on Highway 146 (a narrow, winding road) and continue to the primitive camp. **Contact:** Pinnacles National Monument, (831) 389-4485. **Locator:** PINNACLES NATIONAL MONUMENT (F2).

3
BACKPACKING

• Tom's Ratings •

• Featured Trips •

See last page for Northern California and Bay Area foldout maps.

*The area code for all phone numbers followed by an asterisk (*) will change to 559 as of November 14, 1998. Also, area code 805 is scheduled to split on February 13, 1999. The new area code is yet to be introduced. Call Pacific Bell for a list of prefixes that will receive the new area code.

• TOM'S RATINGS •

THE TOP 10 EASY BACKPACK TRIPS

In Northern California

Here's the question: What I want is a backpacking camping trip without the long hike. Where's a place I can go camping and hiking that is real pretty but not too difficult to reach?

Over and over again, I get asked this question. It's coming from people of various backgrounds: From parents with young children for whom a longer trip is impossible, from adults in their 40s and 50s who have neither the time nor the physical energy for an expedition, and from camping newcomers of all ages who desire the pleasures of a wilderness trip on an introductory level.

Turns out there are dozens of answers, that is, beautiful wilderness-style campsites throughout much of Northern California that are a relatively short distance from the trailhead. They often make great home bases for adventuring, without having to use up all your energy getting there.

Here are my 10 favorites:/

1. BOULDER LAKE, TRINITY ALPS WILDERNESS

This beautiful lake sits in an awesome granite bowl with two peaks towering nearby, Yctapom Peak (7,596 feet elevation) and Sugar Pine Butte (8,033 feet). The hike to get here is just two miles from the trailhead near Goldfield Campground, extremely short for such a sensational destination. The lake is perfect for swimming and fishing, with many excellent day hikes available as well. A wilderness permit is required.

Contact: Shasta-Trinity National Forest, Weaverville Ranger District, (530) 623-2121. **Locator:** TRINITY ALPS WILDERNESS (B1).

2. TOAD LAKE, SHASTA-TRINITY NATIONAL FOREST

Can you imagine an alpine lake at the base of a mountain bowl that offers great swimming and hiking yet requires backpacking only 15 minutes? Toad Lake, set on the flank of Mount Eddy at 6,950 feet, can fulfill that vision with shoreline campsites, the perfect water temperature for swimming, and a great side-trip hike to Porcupine Lake. What's the catch? The drive in features a bone-jarring 10-mile ride on Forest Service roads.

Contact: Shasta-Trinity National Forest, Mount Shasta Ranger District, (530) 926-4511. **Locator:** SHASTA-TRINITY NATIONAL FOREST (B2).

3. MILL CREEK, SOUTH WARNER WILDERNESS

There is no more remote wilderness than the SOUTH WARNERS, located in the northeastern corner of the state. That's why so few people visit, making the 1.5-mile jaunt to Mill Creek a joy. Then you venture through Mill Creek Meadow for easy walks and trout fishing. This area is pristine and quiet, with side trips available to see a waterfall or continue on into the interior ridge of the SOUTH WARNERS. One word of warning: The drive here seems endless, as much as 10 hours from SAN FRANCISCO. A wilderness permit is required.

Contact: Modoc National Forest, Warner Mountain Ranger District, (530) 279-6116. **Locator:** SOUTH WARNER WILDERNESS (B4).

4. Fern Canyon, Van Damme State Park

While Fern Canyon and Van Damme are hardly unknown to anybody who has been to Mendocino, the hike-in campsites on the Fern Canyon Trail remain a relative secret. Getting there requires a 1.75-mile backpack hike, in the process passing through a beautiful redwood forest and along a pretty stream. Once you have established your base camp, several other hikes are available, including one to the nearby Pygmy Forest, which is like visiting a bonsai festival, and others that explore the Little River and the adjacent redwoods.

Contact: California State Parks, Mendocino District, (707) 937-5804. **Locator:** Van Damme State Park (C0). **See featured trip page:** 214.

5. Pomo Canyon, Sonoma Coast State Beach

Tons of people stream up and down Highway 1 every summer and virtually all of them miss this spot, hidden in a canyon just over the first ridge east of the highway. But here it is, located south of the mouth of the Russian River, with campsites scattered amid the redwoods anywhere from 30 yards to a quarter mile from the parking area. There are some great hikes here, the best being to a ridge with breathtaking views of the coast (a 40-minute hike), as well as down to Shell Beach (2.5 miles).

Contact: Sonoma Coast State Beach, (707) 875-3483. **Locator:** Sonoma Coast State Beach (D0).

6. Wildcat Camp, Point Reyes National Seashore

The Coast Trail is the number one hike in the Bay Area, and its Wildcat Camp is the number one camping spot. Reaching the camp takes a 5.1-mile hike on the Coast Trail, departing from the Palomarin Trailhead north of Bolinas. Your reward is spending the night on an ocean bluff, as well as passing a series of hidden lakes (good swimming here), Alamere Falls (which runs over an ocean bluff and to the beach), a pretty beach, and coastal rock formations. Reservations are required.

Contact: Point Reyes National Seashore, (415) 663-8054; Bear Valley Visitor Center, (415) 663-1092. **Locator:** Point Reyes National Seashore (E1). **See featured trip pages:** 67, 132, and 166.

7. Trail Camp, Castle Rock State Park

A 2.8-mile one-way hike will take you to Trail Camp, at the threshold of one of the Bay Area greatest lands of beauty. The hike on the Saratoga Trail drops into a wooded canyon, emerges at a lookout for a waterfall (beautiful in the winter and spring, often dry at other times), then passes a series of honeycombed sandstone formations as well as lookouts over miles of forest and to Monterey Bay. You then turn left at the junction with the Ridge Trail and tromp for 15 minutes to the campsites. On the way back, make it a loop by taking the Ridge Trail, enjoying a spectacular lookout of Monterey Bay from the top of Goat Rock.

Contact: Castle Rock State Park, (408) 867-2952. **Locator:** Castle Rock State Park (E1d). **See featured trip page:** 127.

8. Winnemucca Lake, Eldorado National Forest

This great spot is just a two-mile hike from Carson Pass. The hike is easy, a short climb through a forest of lodgepole pine, on the way skirting Round

Top Peak (10,380 feet), the highest point in the Mokelumne Wilderness. Two other lakes are nearby, Fourth of July Lake and Round Top Lake, making for excellent side trips, though Round Top requires a 1,000-foot climb. A wilderness permit is required.

Contact: Eldorado National Forest Information Center, (530) 644-6048. **Locator:** ELDORADO NATIONAL FOREST (D4).

9. Cathedral Lake, Yosemite National Park

From any shoreline campsite at Cathedral Lake it is easy to see how the lake was named, with Cathedral Peak (10,911 feet) looming overhead, a perfect spired pinnacle. The lake is easy to reach from Tuolumne Meadows, hiking out on the John Muir Trail toward Yosemite Valley then taking a cutoff trail, a total of 3.7 miles one way. The fishing is very poor and the water a little cold for most swimmers, but the beauty of the surrounding landscape and the possible day hikes make it a winner. A wilderness permit is required.

Contact: Yosemite Wilderness Center, (209) 372-0740; Yosemite National Park, (209) 372-0200. **Locator:** YOSEMITE NATIONAL PARK (E4). **See featured trip page:** 239.

10. Lyell Fork, Yosemite National Park

The four-mile walk out of Tuolumne Meadows (8,600 feet) and south on the John Muir Trail is nearly flat and provides access to Lyell Fork and its excellent fishing for brook trout. The beauty is spectacular, with nearby Mammoth Peak and Kuna Crest, and side trips are available to Ireland Lake (10,735 feet), Donohue Pass (11,056 feet), and Vogelsang. The camps along Lyell Fork include hang wires so you can hang your food using the counterbalancing system, well out of the reach of bears. A wilderness permit is required.

Contact: Yosemite Wilderness Center, (209) 372-0740; Yosemite National Park, (209) 372-0200. **Locator:** YOSEMITE NATIONAL PARK (E4). **See featured trip page:** 239.

• TOM'S RATINGS •

The Top 3 Peaks to Climb

In Northern California

Some places seem to have a quality to them, something you feel rather than see.

Tenaya Lake, tucked in granite in Yosemite's high country, is one of the few places that has it. LAKE BERRYESSA does not. An ancient redwood forest on the north coast? Like a sacred cathedral. A few oaks in the foothill grasslands? Sorry, they don't seem to have the magic. The KLAMATH RIVER? Yep. The much bigger Columbia? Nope.

California's three best-known mountains qualify: WHITNEY, SHASTA, and LASSEN. All three hold something of mystery and challenge, of fire and ice, giant rocks and hidden spirits. Sure, you can enjoy them by simply looking. WHITNEY at 14,494 feet, SHASTA at 14,162 feet, and LASSEN at 10,457 feet stand apart from surrounding ranges. In the western hemisphere, there are only a few places that can project the power that these mountains do.

But you can share that power by taking it a step further and climbing one. Maybe even all three.

"What? Me? I've never climbed anything in my life. I don't even like climbing a ladder. I'd never do that."

Well, you'd be surprised at where you might walk after you start taking a few steps. My brother Rambob and I, for instance, never figured we'd climb any mountaintops. Then, in 1985, we climbed WHITNEY because it is the official start of the 211-mile John Muir Trail. Up on top, we felt the power of the high country and were drawn to it. We climbed SHASTA a year later and had the kind of special feeling that stays with you for months. The next year, we tackled SHASTA again, following that up a day later with LASSEN. Now it's in our blood.

Newcomers can make the climb, too. My friend Robyn Schlueter had never climbed mountains before, and she made it to the top. Once you get started, the steps come easier than you might think, and the reward is something that lasts.

1. MOUNT LASSEN—10,457 FEET

This is a good introduction to mountain climbing. The Summit Trail is a 2.5-mile zigzag of a hike that just about anybody with a quart of water can handle, yet it provides access to one of the most spectacular peaks anywhere.

In LASSEN VOLCANIC NATIONAL PARK, 50 miles east of RED BLUFF, you can drive to the trailhead at the base of the mountain. The trail surface is hard and flat, so you can get into a nice hiking rhythm, and with a 15 percent grade, it isn't a killer. Most people take under two hours to reach the top, about a 2,000-foot elevation gain. In the process, newcomers often ask themselves, "Why am I doing this?" When they reach the crest, they find out.

The view is superb, with awesome MOUNT SHASTA 100 miles north appearing close enough for you to reach out and grab a hunk of it. To the east are hundreds of miles of forests and lakes, with LAKE ALMANOR a surprise jewel; to the west, the land drops off to several small volcanic cones and the Central Valley.

The peak itself is the top of a huge volcanic flume, and you can spend hours probing several craters and hardened lava flows. Lassen last blew its top in a series of eruptions from 1914 to 1921, which in geologic time is like a few minutes ago.

It's a prime first mountain experience. We met people of all ages and in all kinds of physical shape. If you bring water, something a number of hikers curiously forget to do, you'll make it. It's that simple.

Directions: Take Interstate 80 north to Interstate 505, then proceed to Interstate 5. Drive approximately 95 miles north to Red Bluff and take the Highway 36/Lassen Park exit. Continue east for 47 miles to the Highway 89 cutoff, then turn north and proceed to the park entrance. **Notes:** Bring at least a quart of water, a windbreaker, sunglasses, sunscreen, and a hat, and get an early start to beat the heat. During peak summer months, the Park Service may choose to establish a quota on hikers on the Summit Trail. **Contact:** For a map and general information, phone Lassen Volcanic National Park, (530) 595-4444. **Locator:** LASSEN VOLCANIC NATIONAL PARK (B3). **See featured trip page:** 209.

2. MOUNT SHASTA—14,162 FEET

The true king of California mountains, this giant volcano rises alone 10,000 feet above the surrounding hills in Northern California. Along with Mount Rainier in Washington and Alaska's McKinley, it is among the most majestic and powerful mountains in the western hemisphere.

You feel that power every step of the way to the top. But to get there, you must have the right equipment, and that means crampons on your boots and an ice ax, which makes hiking up the glacier fields enjoyable rather than a slip-and-slide deal. The more snow there is, the easier and more fun the climb.

The hike is a scramble of a trail across small rocks, then when you hit snow, it becomes an easier walk with the help of crampons. The ice ax becomes important when you reach Red Banks, a steep, massive, ice-bordered rock outcrop at 11,500 feet. You can either climb the Red Banks Chute, a rock and ice-laden crevice, or circle around it.

The peak is astounding, a relatively small volcanic flume on which you can climb. On clear days, you feel like you are on top of the earth, with hundreds of miles visible in all directions. Steaming sulfur vents at the foot of the final 300-foot summit climb give rise to the memory of John Muir, who spent an icy night trapped on the peak, hugging a vent to keep warm.

Shasta is also a mountain of mystery, with tales of Lemurians and Yaktavians, elfin creatures said to live in its interior. Even its creation is legend: In Native American lore, the mountain was created when gods stuck a hole through the clouds and built a giant tepee from the broken pieces.

The best strategy is to hike in to the tree line at 8,000 feet and set up a base camp at Horse Camp, where a natural spring provides unlimited water. The next morning, start walking by 4:30 a.m. and figure on seven to eight hours to the top. It's a seven-mile trip, rising more than 6,000 feet in the process. Every step can be a memorable one.

Directions: Take Interstate 80 north to Interstate 505, then proceed north to Interstate 5. Drive approximately 180 miles north to the town of Mount Shasta. Take the Central Mount Shasta exit and head west on Lake Street, which turns into Everett Memorial Highway, and drive about 15 miles to the parking lot at Bunny Flat. It's about an hour hike from there to Horse Camp. **Notes:** Bring pain reliever for high altitude headaches, good hiking boots, warm weather gear in a daypack, along with high energy snacks, sunglasses, sunscreen, and a hat. Also bring crampons, an ice ax, warm clothing, and at least two quarts of water. The Forest Service requests that all climbing parties obtain a wilderness permit and sign a register prior to their trip; this can be accomplished at the ranger station in Mount Shasta. **Contact:** For equipment rental and weather information, phone The Fifth Season, (530) 926-3606, or House of Ski, (530) 926-2359. For maps and general information, phone the Shasta Cascade Wonderland Association, (800) 474-2782 or (800) 326-6944, or the Shasta-Trinity National Forest, Mount Shasta Ranger District, (530) 926-4511. **Locator:** SHASTA TRINITY NATIONAL FOREST (B2). **See featured trip page:** 163.

3. MOUNT WHITNEY—14,494 FEET

Here is the Big Daddy, the highest point in the lower 48. It's a long, steep hike from the trailhead at Whitney Portal, climbing 6,100 feet in 10 miles. But a decent trail takes you to the top, so no mountaineering equipment is necessary.

WHITNEY is located in the southern

Sierra at the foot of Lone Pine on U.S. 395. It is a giant rock cut by glaciers, not formed from a volcano like SHASTA and LASSEN, and the peak reflects its origins, with sheer rock outcrops on the edge of dramatic, plunging canyons.

Nothing can prepare you for the lookout. It is absolutely astonishing. To the west is the entire Western Divide, to the north are rows of 11,000- to 13,000-foot peaks, and to the east the mountain drops straight down—11,000 feet in just 15 miles—to the Owens Valley. The top itself is oval with a jagged edge, and has a little rock house to protect hikers from storms.

The hike is a genuine heart-thumper yet is inspiring at the same time. It includes 100 switchbacks on the ascent to Wotan's Throne, and in the final miles, the ridge is cut by notch windows in the rock. You look through and the bottom drops thousands of feet at your boot tips. Some people try the 20-mile round-trip in one day, but that makes for an exhausting rush. A better strategy is to hike in and set up a base camp at 10,000 feet, getting acclimated to the altitude. The next day, you can hit the top and return, carrying a minimum of equipment for the ascent.

Directions: There are several possible routes, but the most direct is to head south from Reno or Carson City (via Tahoe) and drive approximately 200 miles to the town of Lone Pine on U.S. 395. Turn west on Whitney Portal Road and drive 13 miles to the trailhead and campgrounds. **Notes:** Bring pain reliever for high altitude headaches, good hiking boots, warm weather gear in a daypack, along with plenty of water, high-energy snacks, sunglasses, sunscreen, and a hat. A wilderness permit is required to climb and can be obtained at the ranger station in Lone Pine. **Contact:** Inyo National Forest, Mount Whitney Ranger District (for maps and information), (760) 876-6200. **Locator:** MOUNT WHITNEY (F5).

• TOM'S RATINGS •

THE TOP 7 BUTT-KICKER BACKPACK HIKES

In Northern California

1. GUITAR LAKE, MOUNT WHITNEY WILDERNESS

Butt-kicker? This hike is the definition of the term. Nobody makes the hike without getting their butt kicked, heh, heh. You start at Whitney Portal, then climb more than 6,100 feet over the course of 10 miles, including the inevitable snow crossing below Wotan's Throne, to reach the WHITNEY summit at 14,494 feet. It is an awesome view, not only 10,000 feet below to the town of Lone Pine in the Owens Valley, but northward with Sierra peaks as far as you can see. From the summit, you then tromp down the west side, switchbacking to Guitar Lake. Though often cold and windy, it's the best camp within range of the summit. Finally, you get in your sleeping bag and surrender.

Contact: Inyo National Forest, Mount Whitney Ranger District, (760) 876-6200. **Locator:** INYO NATIONAL FOREST (E5).

2. MOUNT SHASTA, SISKIYOU COUNTY

One of the greatest adventures in the West is climbing the great SHASTA, which rises 14,126 feet from the forests like a diamond in a field of coal. Alas, you get your butt kicked in the process. The best advice is to hike in a day early and camp at Horse Flat at tree line, 7,800 feet. From there, you face a dramatic hike to the top, sometimes as steep as a 35-degree slope over ice; wear crampons to make the going easier and use an ice ax to help you make your way through an icy chute at Red Bank. In all, it's a 13.6-mile round-trip, with a victory dinner at Horse Flat mandatory, before walking out the next morning.

Contact: Shasta-Trinity National Forest, Mount Shasta Ranger District, (530) 926-4511; The Fifth Season, (530) 926-5555. **Locator:** MOUNT SHASTA (A3).

3. ROOSTER COMB LOOP, HENRY W. COE STATE PARK

Contact: (408) 779-2728. **Locator:** HENRY W. COE STATE PARK (E1d).

4. BEACROFT TRAIL, AMERICAN RIVER, TAHOE NATIONAL FOREST

Contact: Tahoe National Forest, Foresthill Ranger District, (530) 367-2224. **Locator:** TAHOE NATIONAL FOREST (D3, D4).

5. PACIFIC CREST TRAIL, HAT CREEK RIM, LASSEN NATIONAL FOREST

Contact: McArthur Burney Falls State Park, (530) 335-2777. **Locator:** MCARTHUR BURNEY FALLS STATE PARK (B3).

6. HARTMAN BAR NATIONAL TRAIL, PLUMAS NATIONAL FOREST

Contact: Plumas National Forest, Feather River Ranger District, (530) 534-6506. **Locator:** PLUMAS NATIONAL FOREST (C3).

7. BLUE RIDGE TRAIL, CACHE CREEK, YOLO COUNTY

Contact: Bureau of Land Management, Clear Lake Resource Area, (707) 468-4000. **Locator:** CACHE CREEK (D1).

• TOM'S RATINGS •

THE TOP 5 WINTER BACKPACKING TRIPS

In the San Francisco Bay Area

Nothing is quite so charming as snuggling deep in a sleeping bag, good and tired after a day of hiking, secreted away in a tent out somewhere beautiful where the only care is whether or not it will rain.

What, you say? Will it rain? Camping in the winter? Are you crazy? Yep, and before you accuse me of suffering from some rare mental aberration, let me tell you that some of the best times I've ever had have been hiking and camping during winter at several parks in the Bay Area foothills and the nearby SANTA CRUZ MOUNTAINS.

For one thing, almost nobody else is out for the night, which means you'll have a beautiful hike-in camp to yourself. For another, the flora is at its best from midwinter through spring, turning neon green and sprinkled with budding wildflowers, with streams and waterfalls running at peak flows. In addition, some of the best weather of the year arrives between rains in the mountains circling the Bay Area, with the freshest air and clearest skies.

The best winter weekend hiking/camping trips in the Bay Area are the COAST TRAIL at POINT REYES NATIONAL SEASHORE, the OHLONE WILDERNESS TRAIL in the SUNOL-OHLONE REGIONAL WILDERNESS, the Skyline-to-the-Sea Trail in CASTLE ROCK STATE PARK, BIG BASIN REDWOODS STATE PARK, and the Frog Lake Trail in HENRY W. COE STATE PARK. Here is a summary of each, starting with the best:

1. Point Reyes National Seashore

The Coast Trail is the perfect weekend backpack, a 15-miler one way that features camps at ocean bluffs, beaches with sculptured rocks, great views, and Alamere Falls, a drop-dead gorgeous waterfall. It is best hiked from north to south, arriving late Friday and parking near the Point Reyes Hostel, then hiking 2.8 miles to Coast Camp. That is followed by a 6.6-mile trek on Saturday, enjoying Sculptured Beach and spending the night at Wildcat Camp, then hiking out 5.6 miles on Sunday, passing Alamere Falls and several freshwater lakes. With three days, there is plenty of time for side trips, exploring beaches and watching the amazing, ongoing recovery of the area burned in the fall of '95 wildfire. Provided you have a shuttle partner, this can be a perfect trip.

Contact: Point Reyes National Seashore, (415) 663-1092. **Locator:** Point Reyes National Seashore (E1a). **See featured trip pages:** 67 and 166.

2. Big Basin Redwoods State Park

For people with a passion for big woods and big water, there is no better camping trip. From park headquarters, a 12-mile loop is available with a hike-in camp at the halfway point. What a hike, a perfect two-day trip: From park headquarters, you start by hiking past giant redwoods to reach the Big Basin Rim, then enjoy a 900-foot descent over four miles to Berry Creek Falls, one of the most perfect settings in the Bay Area. From here, you climb past two more breathtaking falls, Silver and Golden, then arrive at Sunset Camp. The return loop on the Sunset Trail takes you to the park's most remote reaches.

Contact: Big Basin Redwoods State Park, (408) 338-8860. **Locator:** Big Basin Redwoods State Park (E1d). **See featured trip page:** 136.

3. Castle Rock State Park

Here is a perfect mini-expedition, an easy 2.8-mile romp on the Skyline-to-the-Sea Trail to reach Trail Camp. There's no easier overnight hike in the Bay Area, and the quality is first-class. In little over an hour on the way out to the camp, you will pass a dramatic waterfall and awesome views of the redwood-filled Santa Cruz Mountains. The trail then passes several exotic honeycombed sandstone formations, so many that some visitors call this "Swiss Cheese State Park." After camping, a must-see on the return hike is the lookout from the top of Goat Rock, where miles of charming landscape will beckon your outstretched palms.

Contact: Castle Rock State Park, (408) 467-2952; California State Parks, Santa Cruz District, (408) 429-2850. **Locator:** Castle Rock State Park (E1d). **See featured trip page:** 127.

4. Sunol Regional Wilderness

Only the ambitious need apply for this trip, a 28-miler through the East Bay hills with the kind of climbs and drops that resemble those in the Sierra. It is best done in three days, with trail camps at Sunol and Ohlone Regional Parks, making hiking days of 12, 8, and 8 miles. The trip starts at Del Valle Regional Park with a 1,600-foot climb in 1.5 miles, then traverses some of the most remote areas of Alameda County, greening foothills, and remote canyons. The trail crests Rose Peak (3,817 feet) and Mission Peak (2,517 feet), then closes out the final 3.5 miles with a toe-jamming drop of 2,100 feet to the end of the trail. A shuttle car is required.

Contact: Sunol Regional Wilderness, (925) 862-2244; East Bay Regional Park District, (510) 635-0135 extension 2200. **Locator:** SUNOL REGIONAL WILDERNESS (E1, E2). **See featured trip page:** 99.

5. HENRY W. COE STATE PARK

COE STATE PARK holds a lot of mystery for Bay Area hikers, bikers, and anglers because of its size (100,000 acres), its lakes and ponds (120, many with bass and bluegill), and its network of abandoned ranch roads (210 miles) and hiking trails (35 miles). Reaching the best lakes requires killer long trips with grueling climbs, which makes the 1.6-mile trip from headquarters to Frog Lake the perfect test hike to see for yourself if it is worth the rough stuff. This hike or bike has just one climb, about a 15-minute puff job, then drops through oak woodlands to the camp, just above the pond. You like it? Then first-class destinations such as Coit Lake, Mississippi Lake, the Coyote Creek headwaters, and Rooster Comb—all butt-kickers to reach—will lure you back for future exploration.

Contact: Henry W. Coe State Park, (408) 779-2728; California State Parks, Four Rivers District, (209) 826-1196. **Locator:** HENRY W. COE STATE PARK (E1d). **See featured trip page:** 139.

• TOM'S RATINGS •

THE TOP 4 HIKE-TO LAKES IN THE HIGH SIERRA

In the Southeast Sierra, West of Mammoth

You walk in the footsteps of legends in the high Sierra. With each step, you feel the shadows of ghosts, of Muir, Walker, Adams, Carson, and Bridger. These shadows from the past always seem near, along with the beauty of the present—the untouched, pure crystal mountain streams, forests, and vibrant meadows filled with wildflowers.

My favorite piece of wilderness is in the high country of the southern Sierra, in and around the ANSEL ADAMS WILDERNESS west of MAMMOTH and the nearby JOHN MUIR WILDERNESS to the south. These are among the prettiest backpacking destinations in the world, where John Muir and Ansel Adams got much of their inspiration, with the Minaret Mountains providing a backdrop for some of nature's finest architecture.

The trail system is extensive in the ANSEL ADAMS WILDERNESS, with 250 miles in the Minarets alone, and links to more than a hundred miles of trails in nearby INYO NATIONAL FOREST.

Visitors have the opportunity to drive to a trailhead, venture up to the ridge and connect with the PACIFIC CREST TRAIL (PCT), then use other cutoffs along the PCT to custom route trips to remote lakes or streams, pristine meadows, mountaintops, and canyons that seem touched by divine spirit. Elevations range from a low of 7,200 feet at trailheads to the peak of Mount Ritter at 13,157 feet. As you walk, you will understand why Muir called the Minarets a mountain temple: because it is a rare, special place on this planet.

Dozens and dozens of small lakes speckle the high mountain country, each of them created by glacial action and then filled in the springtime by melting drops of snow. All have trout jumping for hatching insects in the evening and provide perfect campsites for people willing to hike to them.

Access is best to the ANSEL ADAMS WILDERNESS near MAMMOTH, via U.S. 395.

The John Muir Wilderness, located about 20 miles to the south, is a true paradise of mountains, lakes, and meadows. Mountaintops reaching 12,000 feet high poke holes in the heavens, and below are more than a hundred pristine lakes, including 25 that hold rare golden trout. The high mountain meadows are splashed with wildflowers, the most common being violet-colored lupine.

The longer you stay in these wilderness surroundings, the less important your everyday "real world" stresses will seem. Each day's hike is like taking a shower and washing off layers of urban dust caked on from the numbing routine of city life. After awhile, the experience will realign your senses and you will suddenly understand what Muir meant by developing a oneness with your surroundings, because you will have done it.

"When one is alone at night in the depths of these woods . . . every leaf seems to speak," he wrote. "Perfect quietude is there, and freedom from every curable care."

Some people go to school to learn history, and others go to church to get religion. With a good pair of boots, a backback, and inspiration, you can find both on the wilderness trail.

Access is best to the JOHN MUIR WILDERNESS from trailheads at lakes on the western slope of the Sierra, via Highway 168. Many trailheads are available at area lakes that are accessible by car. They are perfectly situated for a jump-off into the mountain wilderness. Here are four of the best:

1. Convict Lake

This is one of the prettiest lakes in the world, fronted by conifers and framed by a back wall of wilderness mountain peaks. Its elevation is 7,583 feet. The trail on the north side of the lake heads up through a canyon along Convict Creek. In the space of five miles, it leads into the JOHN MUIR WILDERNESS and to a series of nine lakes. The biggest is Bighorn Lake, originally a granite cirque sculpted by glacial action.

Contact: Inyo National Forest, Mammoth Ranger Station and Visitor Center, (760) 934-2505; Convict Lake Resort, (760) 934-3800. **Locator:** JOHN MUIR WILDERNESS (E5). **See featured trip page:** 237.

2. Lake Mary

The largest of the 11 lakes in the MAMMOTH LAKES area, Mary is a good place to camp for the night before heading off on a hike the next morning. Camping is on a first-come, first-served basis. A trailhead is on the east side of the lake. From there, the trail is routed along Mammoth Creek to Arrowhead Lake, Skeleton Lake, Barney Lake, and finally to Big Duck Lake. Looming just a mile yonder is the PACIFIC CREST TRAIL, by which you can gain access to the wilderness interior.

Contact: Inyo National Forest, Mammoth Ranger Station and Visitor Center, (760) 934-2505; Crystal Crag Lodge, (760) 934-2436. **Locator:** INYO NATIONAL FOREST (E5). **See featured trip page:** 237.

3. Edison Lake

A trail along the north side of this lake, which is set at 7,650 feet, is routed up Mono Creek and then connects to the PACIFIC CREST TRAIL. From there, you can head south up Bear Mountain, where the trail leads through one of the West's most lush aspen groves and beyond to Trout Creek. The other option is to travel north on the PCT, heading toward Devils Postpile National Monument and the crystal headwaters of the SAN JOAQUIN RIVER.

Contact: Sierra National Forest, Pineridge Ranger District, (209) 855-5360.* **Locator:** SIERRA NATIONAL FOREST (F5).

4. FLORENCE LAKE

This is also a pretty lake, situated at 7,327 feet, with the Great Divide country providing a backdrop. From the inlet of the lake, a trail heads up the SOUTH FORK SAN JOAQUIN RIVER to the PACIFIC CREST TRAIL, about a five-mile trip. From there, you can continue southeast along the SAN JOAQUIN (great evening trout fishing), turning into Evolution Valley. This was one of Muir's favorite places, and it has some of the prettiest meadows and woodlands in the entire high Sierra.

Contact: Sierra National Forest, Pineridge Ranger District, (209) 855-5360*; Florence Lake Resort, (209) 966-3195. **Locator:** SIERRA NATIONAL FOREST (E4).

• FEATURED TRIP •

★ THE LOST COAST

Rated: California's Most Remote Coastline

The LOST COAST and the folks who live here seem to be in a different orbit than the rest of California. And that is exactly why people like to visit.

Different? Yeah, it's plenty different. Some days it's more like Pluto than the Bay Area.

The LOST COAST is located in southwest Humboldt County, a place of unique beauty, a few nice residents, and plenty of adventure. It is one of the state's most remote regions that can be reached without four-wheel drive or a pair of hiking boots; anybody can just drive here.

It is called the LOST COAST because of the way nature has isolated it. The region is circled by natural boundaries, with the PACIFIC OCEAN to the west, the King Mountain Range to the south,the Humboldt redwoods to the east, and Bear River Ridge to the north. It's shielded on all sides; in other words, getting here isn't like driving to GILROY. Over a stretch of 80 miles on U.S. 101, access to the heart of this land is provided by only three slow and twisty roads—and two are gravel jobs.

The most direct route from the Bay Area is to cruise up U.S. 101, the Redwood Highway, passing through Richardson Grove State Park, heading north along the EEL RIVER. At the town of Redway, you turn west on Briceland Road, a perpetually winding little sucker that, after about 20 miles, meets Wilder Ridge Road. You turn north on Wilder Ridge Road and eventually meander to the little town of Honeydew along the MATTOLE RIVER. Much of the roadway is gravel, so you won't go anywhere fast.

As you arrive, the first thing you notice is the beauty of the Mattole River Valley, a combe set in green with the MATTOLE pretzeling through its center. From the highest point at Wilder Ridge, elevation 2,224 feet, you also get an excellent view of the highest peaks in the King Range to the west, a wilderness hiking area.

After dropping into the valley, the road is routed northwest along the

Mattole River, passing another little town, Petrolia, before heading north along the ocean, the starkest, most unpeopled beachfront imaginable. Often there are sheep grazing in the adjacent fields, but that's about it. If you keep driving, ultimately you will reach U.S. 101 again at Fernbridge, about 15 miles south of Eureka.

Some vacationers heading north on U.S. 101 to the redwood parks will take a day to drive the half loop from Redway to Fernbridge, sometimes stopping to explore the area in the process. But if you want to prospect further, you will discover many excellent side trips and hiking trails that can feel like your own private nature reserves.

Near where the Mattole River enters the ocean, there is a free, small campground (five campsites) operated by the Bureau of Land Management. Another camp is located at A. W. Way County Park, which borders the Mattole and is a good place during the winter season to pitch a base camp for a steelhead fishing trip. Other lodging prospects are in Petrolia and, to the south, in Shelter Cove. For information, phone the Eureka Chamber of Commerce at (800) 356-6381.

One of the best side trips is to explore between the mouth of the Mattole River, the Mattole Lagoon, south to the old light station at Punta Gorda. To get there, head west from Honeydew on Mattole Road toward Petrolia, then turn left (toward the ocean) on Lighthouse Road and drive five miles.

Heading south along the coast, an abandoned jeep trail is accessible by foot from the campground at Lighthouse Road. It's a fairly rough hike south all the way to the Punta Gorda Light Tower and back, but many spots along the way are ideal for picnics. A good hiking map may be obtained from the Bureau of Land Management.

If you are more ambitious, one of California's greatest, little-traveled hikes, the Lost Coast Trail, is accessible from here. It spans 24 miles from the mouth of the Mattole River on south to Shelter Cove, tracing the most remote portion of coastline, primarily on bluffs and beach. With two vehicles, one parked at each end of the trail, you can set up your own shuttle, then take the trail as a one-way hike. It is better done from north to south, because of prevailing winds—you want them at your back, not in your face.

This is not a hike to attempt in the rainy season. It is common for this area to get 100 inches of rain during the winter and as much as 150 inches in the wettest years.

The area is isolated, and the people are usually quite friendly. At the Honeydew Store, there is a little bench where you can sit and drink a root beer. There are no stoplights anywhere. Hey, the number of stop signs can be counted on one hand.

Like I said, compared to the Bay Area, you're in a completely different orbit out here.

Directions: Take U.S. 101 past Richardson Grove State Park. Just past Garberville, at the town of Redway, turn west on Briceland Road. After 20 miles, turn north on Wilder Ridge Road and drive to the town of Honeydew. From there, continue west past Petrolia to the ocean. The road eventually will reach U.S. 101 south of Eureka at Fernbridge. **Lodging:** Lodging is available in Petrolia. Contact the Eureka Chamber of Commerce, 2112 Broadway, Eureka, CA 95501; (800) 356-6381 or (707) 442-3738. **Camping:** Two campgrounds are available. A small, free, primitive campground (Mouth of the Mattole) is located near the mouth of the Mattole River and is operated by the Bureau of Land Management. A county park (A. W. Way County Park), where campsites cost $10 per night, is located on the Mattole River between Honeydew and Petrolia. **Hiking:** A map of the King Mountain Range detailing all hiking trails is available from the Bureau of Land Management. Contact the BLM, 1125 16th Street, Room 219, Arcata, CA 95521; (707) 825-2300 or fax (707) 825-2301. The map is also available from the Eureka Chamber of Commerce. **Fishing:** The best fishing is in the winter for steelhead. For reliable reports, phone the Honeydew Store, (707) 629-3310. **Contact:** Humboldt County Chamber of Commerce, (800) 356-6381. **Locator:** HUMBOLDT REDWOODS STATE PARK (B0).

• FEATURED TRIP •

★ MOUNT SHASTA

Rated: The Top 3 Peaks to Climb, 152; The Top 5 Learn-to-Ski Packages, 290; The Top 5 Houseboating Sites, 300

Native American legend has it that MOUNT SHASTA was formed when the Great Spirit poked a hole in the sky and shaped a tepee out of the fallen pieces. From afar, it's almost possible to believe this tale. The great snow-capped volcano is sometimes visible from as far away as 150 miles, rising 14,162 feet above the lowlands.

But MOUNT SHASTA is more than just a colossus that casts its shadow over Interstate 5. It's also the centerpiece of one of the West's great adventurelands. Name the activity, and the 25-square-mile area that encircles MOUNT SHASTA has it: quality stream and lake fishing, boating, hiking, rafting, camping, backpacking, and, in the winter, both alpine and cross-country skiing.

Whatever you want to do around MOUNT SHASTA, one of the best places to begin is CASTLE CRAGS STATE PARK. Located about 15 miles from the base of the mountain, the park offers an awe-inspiring view of SHASTA.But Castle Crags is only one of about 50 campgrounds that ring the MOUNT SHASTA area, ranging from places that offer full-hookup facilities for RVs to primitive sites in KLAMATH and SHASTA NATIONAL FORESTS. If you carry a cartop boat or trailer, then head to LAKE SISKIYOU for a prime camping or fishing experience. SISKIYOU glistens in the very shadow of MOUNT SHASTA. The lake's western shore features campsites and a swimming area, and it has plenty of trout and bass. You can rent boats and motors at the Lake Siskiyou Marina.

If you'd simply rather commune with nature, consider spending a few days hiking, rafting, or houseboating. A network of trails crosses the mountain country. One of the best is the PACIFIC CREST TRAIL, which cuts across the southern slope of MOUNT SHASTA, running past CASTLE CRAGS STATE PARK, the SACRAMENTO RIVER, and MCCLOUD RIVER. You can get in some great hiking in this area.

You say that vacations aren't meant for work? Then consider some white-water excitement, riding a raft down the untamed stretches of the SACRAMENTO or KLAMATH RIVERS, a wild but fun way to spend a day or two. Wilderness Adventures is one of many companies in the area offering trips.

The laziest vacation of all could be renting a houseboat on massive SHASTA LAKE, the largest reservoir in California. Though two million people venture to this lake every year, it has the space to handle them all. Figuring you'll need a week on a houseboat to do it right, you can rent one that sleeps six to 14 people for $900 to $2,000.

In winter, skiing down the side of MOUNT SHASTA can beat the heavily used slopes of the Sierra Nevada. Because the skiing operation here was built in the 1980s, the public has not yet discovered how good it is. You'll find short lines at the three lifts and lots of room on the slopes. For cross-country skiing, Bunny Flats is the top spot.

Whatever activity you love, whatever the season, SHASTA could be your perfect outdoors getaway.

Hiking: The Panther Meadows Trail is one of the best on Mount Shasta. For a map of trails on Forest Service land, ask for Shasta-Trinity and send $4 to the U.S. Forest Service, 630 Sansome Street, San Francisco, CA 94111. **Rafting:** For a complete directory of California river outfitters, phone (800) 552-3625. **Lodging:** In Mount Shasta, the Best Western Treehouse, (530) 926-3101, is a quality motel with all the amenities provided. For other lodging possibilities, phone the Mount Shasta Chamber of Commerce, (530) 926-4865. **Contact:** Call the Shasta Cascade Wonderland Association at (800) 326-6944 for information on the entire area, free maps, and brochures. **Locator:** MOUNT SHASTA (B2). **See featured trip pages:** 127 and 129.

• FEATURED TRIP •

TRINITY ALPS WILDERNESS

Rated: The Prettiest Land in the Western United States

The rocky chute rose almost straight up, and from our perch on a narrow ledge, it seemed as if we were trying to climb the backbone of a huge monster. Below was a 1,500-foot wall of rock; above was the Sawtooth Ridge of the TRINITY ALPS. Climbing off-trail as we were, in search of wonders, unknown lakes, and big trout, meant accepting mystery and danger.

Rivers, lakes, and oceans will attack you. Mountains are different. They wait for you to make a mistake.

I reached up and grabbed hold of a rock, and it gave way and went crashing down the talus slope like a bowling ball. My heart shook at the thought that it could be our bodies doing the same.

Then I remembered my old wilderness adage: Don't fight the mountain. Accept it, think it through, and move forward. Deep inside of you, right in your chest, is a window, and when the window opens, the power of the universe will flow through you. Don't let the window shut and lock. Settle down and let it open, and you will move forward and achieve the greatness for which you are meant.

With that thought, and feeling more settled, I grabbed another rock. It held. I pulled myself up, a booted foot lodged in a crevice for support. A light breeze coming up the canyon made the sweat tingle on the back of my neck. The next foot came easier. Made it through a tough spot, just like that.

We scrambled to the mountain rim and peered from a ridge notch as if we were standing on the edge of the earth. Below us was the TRINITY ALPS WILDERNESS, northwest of REDDING, immense wildlands with 585,000 acres, 82 lakes, 50 mountain peaks, and 550 miles of trails.

The biggest mountain-bred rainbow trout of the West live here in remote, little-known lakes. But to reach them, you must leave the trail. One such lake, Little South Fork Lake, is said to have trout that average 15 to 18 inches. But in a guidebook for the area, author Wayne Moss called reaching this lake "a task for deranged souls."

Three likely candidates for such a title are Jeff Patty, Michael Furniss, and myself. Over the years, we have gone off-trail in search of Bigfoot, hiked the entire John Muir Trail, and climbed SHASTA, WHITNEY, and Half Dome, among many other adventures. Patty, a wilderness explorer/photographer, and Furniss, a scientist, aren't quite over the edge, but they are a bit crazy. And the idea of giant rainbow trout in remote wildlands was enough to inspire another trip.

The TRINITY ALPS may be the prettiest land in the western United States. The granite chutes on the mountain rims conjure images of the Swiss Alps. The lakes sit in classic granite bowls. Every deep canyon looks like a sea of conifers.

From the trailhead at Coffee Creek, we hiked in about 10 miles to the Caribou Lakes Basin, spent the night, then stared hard at our map, studying the terrain and slope.

"There's no easy way in to Little South Fork Lake," Patty said. "No easy way out."

"Perfect for three deranged souls," answered Furniss.

There would be an altitude drop of 2,500 feet, then a climb of 3,500 feet without the benefit of a trail. In our way were two mountains and we decided to lateral around them, taking bear paths and deer trails to do it. It wasn't long until we ran into a massive brush field, and one after the other, we three deranged souls disappeared into it.

We'd grapple with the branches, scramble for toeholds, fall down, and curse the brush. After several hours, our forearms were scratched up like we'd waged a losing fight with a pack of bobcats.

"Getting caught in that brush makes you feel like a bug in a spiderweb," Furniss said.

But there's no fighting it, I thought to myself. You lose every time. Remember the window in your chest. Let it open and you can move on.

Later, after dropping elevation and heading through a forest, Patty spotted what looked like a bear trail, and we were able to take one good step after another for the first time in hours. The air smelled of pines and we could faintly hear the sound of a small stream. I took a deep breath and felt like I was back in the 1830s when the first trailblazers came west.

Suddenly, right then, there was a terrible stinging sensation on my right hand. Then bang! Again, in my arm. And again right in the butt. I looked down at my arm and hand and saw bees swarming around me.

I let out a howl, and in a flash, I unhitched my pack and went running through the forest, then stopped to see if I had outrun them. No such luck.

Some 20 bees were clamped onto my pants, trying to sting my legs. Others were circling.

"They've marked you, they've marked you," shouted Furniss. "Run, run!"

In a panic-stricken rush, I swept them off my legs and went running through brush and around trees. I would have given a million dollars for a lake to jump in, but there was no lake. A minute later, after being chased by the swarm, it was over.

Patty, certified for emergency medical treatment, immediately grabbed me.

"Do you have allergic reactions to bee stings?"

"No," I answered, and then he slid the stingers out, taking care not to break the poison sacks.

"You must have stepped on a hive," Furniss said. "You're lucky you didn't get stung a hundred times. One time they got me in the head, but they only got me three times."

"A lot of people get hurt when they're running from a swarm of bees," Patty added. "In a panic, they don't watch where they're going and break an ankle or leg. Then, while they lie there, the bees get them anyway."

Later, we dropped down the canyon stream, hoping to rock-hop straight up the river, eventually reaching the lake. The plan was working well until we ran head-on into a surprise, a 100-foot waterfall. We named it Crystal Falls, because the falling water droplets refracted by sunlight looked like crystals.

But as pretty as it was, that waterfall blocked our route. To get around it required backtracking, then scrambling up a 120-degree talus slope to gain altitude on the canyon wall, lateraling across thick brush and climbing our way to a rock basin. It had taken us 10 hours to travel under two miles—but we could finally see it, Little South Fork Lake.

It was just before sunset. Little South Fork is a particularly beautiful lake—small but deep blue and surrounded by steep, glaciated granite. Even from a distance, we could see the insects hatching and the trout rising.

After a night of recovery, we made our first casts. In my first seven casts, I had five strikes and landed rainbow trout measuring 12, 13, and 16 inches. The biggest catch of the trip was 17.5 inches. I had another one that ripped off 20 feet of line in two seconds before splitting the hook.

Yes, the fish were as big as we'd been told. And there is a logical explanation for it.

Even though the TRINITY ALPS look like the top of the world, the elevations are 5,000 to 6,000 feet, much lower than the Sierra Nevada or the Rocky Mountains.

"That's why there is more terrestrial productivity here than in the high Sierra," said Furniss, who is a soil and water scientist. "There is more soil, more trees, more algae in the bottom of lakes, and more insect hatches."

In other words, there is more life in general, including fish. Big ones. There was no "evening rise," like at most lakes. The fish were feeding continuously. A gold Z-Ray and small Panther Martin spinner were the lures that enticed the most bites.

At night, a remarkable calm settled on this remote lake. Deer, sometimes 15 at a time, could be seen idling in the bright moonlight within 100 yards of the camp.

Patty pointed to the granite rim above the lake. "When it's time to get out of here, let's climb that," he said. "No way do we want to fight the brush, the bees, and that waterfall again."

He smiled and started suggesting possible routes. Nearby, a big trout jumped and landed with a splash. Fifty yards away, a deer started at the surprise visitors, the three deranged souls.

Furniss sized up the ridge, bright in the moonlight, and smiled.

"It looks just about impossible to climb," he said with a laugh.

A minute later, he spoke again.

"Perfect."

Contact: For a map of the Trinity Alps Wilderness, send $4 to U.S. Forest Service, Office of Information, 630 Sansome Street, San Francisco, CA 94111. For information about trail conditions and wilderness permits, phone Shasta-Trinity National Forest headquarters, (530) 246-5222. **Locator:** TRINITY ALPS WILDERNESS (B1).

• FEATURED TRIP •

★ POINT REYES COAST TRAIL

Rated: The Top 25 Hikes, 2; The Top 50 Parks, 7; The Top 10 Hikes on Point Reyes, 20; The Top 4 Earthquake Trails, 26; The Top 50 Base Camps, 110; The Top 10 Easy Backpack Trips, 150; The Top 5 Winter Backpacking Trips, 156; The Top 10 Spots for a First Kiss, 180; The Top 10 Spots to Go on a Date, 182; The Top 20 Hike-to Waterfalls, 187; The Top 22 Water Adventures, 311; The Top 10 Swimming Holes, 395

Of the handful of overnight hiking trips available in the Bay Area, the COAST TRAIL provides the most extended tour into a land of charm.

It is located north of BOLINAS on the remote Marin coast and includes camps at ocean bluffs, great ridge lookouts, coastal lakes, a beach with sculptured rocks and tidepools, and a rare coastal waterfall. The continuous backcountry route is 15 miles, long enough for lingering hikers to spend a weekend strolling it, Friday evening through Sunday, and short enough for the ambitious to tackle in a single day. Among the Bay Area's other backpack hikes, you'll find the 11-mile Butano Rim Loop in BUTANO STATE PARK, the 28-mile OHLONE WILDERNESS TRAIL in remote Alameda County, and the 38-mile Skyline-to-Sea Trail in the SANTA CRUZ MOUNTAINS. The East Bay Skyline National Trail spans 31 consecutive miles, but it's impossible to canvas in one stretch because there are no campgrounds on the trail; only one at CHABOT REGIONAL PARK is even remotely close.

Of these, it is the COAST TRAIL that ventures from civilization and goes on to provide the most continuous route into an enchanting, scenic landscape. There are only a few catches: You need a hiking partner who will double as a shuttle driver, since you will have to leave a car at each end of the trail. While camping is free, you must make a reservation through the headquarters of POINT REYES NATIONAL SEASHORE. Come planning to cook with a small backpack stove, as campfires are not allowed. Tents are also recommended, because the coastal weather is the Bay Area's most unpredictable: clear, calm, and warm one day, then suddenly foggy, windy, and clammy the next. A key solution is to hike when the wind is down.

That is why the best trailhead is at the Point Reyes Hostel, from which you set off hiking north to south, thus keeping the wind at your back and out of your face. The first camp, Coast Camp, is an easy 2.8 miles out from the trailhead, an ideal destination for a Friday evening after getting off work; the sound of ocean waves will lull you to sleep.

The next day, you will continue hiking south, along the way getting glimpses of Sculptured Beach, which is comprised of magnificent rock stacks and tunnels. There is a 0.2-mile marked cutoff that drops down to the beach, allowing you to explore its unique geologic formations and tidepools.

Sculptured Beach is best visited during low tides, of course, especially minus low tides. When the ocean rolls back during a minus low tide, seawater is left behind in countless rock pockets and gorges, where tiny marine organisms play and do battle. In addition, at low water the sea tunnel becomes completely exposed.

When you continue on, the COAST TRAIL eventually turns inland, ventures along the coastal foothill ridges, then skirts a canyon and drops down to Wildcat Camp, set on a bluff overlooking the ocean. Thus ends a 6.6-mile day (or seven miles, if you take the cutoff to Sculptured Beach).

If you luck into a clear, calm evening, and odds are good you will in the fall, hikers will find that the sunsets, camping, and stargazing are extraordinary at Wildcat Camp. In addition to the ocean views, a bonus is an 0.3-mile side trip to Wildcat Lake, the first of five surprise freshwater lakes along the route, north to south.

From Wildcat Camp, it is a 5.6-mile hike to the end of the trail, which means you will have plenty of time to make side trips and explore. That's a good thing, because there is much to see. After leaving camp, you will start hiking past the coastal lakes, creeks, and a rare waterfall. First comes Wildcat Lake, then little Ocean Lake, and soon thereafter, Alamere Falls.

This is a surprising waterfall that tumbles down Alamere Creek and over an ocean bluff. It falls 40 feet right down to the beach and then runs into the PACIFIC OCEAN, one of the few ocean bluff waterfalls anywhere. The key for newcomers is that it is best viewed from about a quarter mile away, not from right on top of it. Of course, it is prettiest after winter runs have refilled Alamere Creek.

After passing the falls, you will climb a short ridge and skirt above Pelican Lake. A mile later, you will come to another lake, Bass Lake, and hike along its northern shore before forging on to the top of a coastal ridge, about a 550-foot elevation. Always take a moment here to just stare at the PACIFIC OCEAN. On clear days, you may be able to get a sense of the curvature of the earth by slowly scanning the blue horizon.

The trail then drops down a canyon back to the ocean bluffs, turns left, and ends a mile later at a parking area known as the Palomarin Trailhead. Provided you have a shuttle car waiting, this is one of the Bay Area's greatest hikes.

While this is the official, signed route, other circuits can be created by connecting to a network of trails that link four backcountry camps in this area. In addition to Coast Camp and Wildcat Camp, you can access Sky Camp on the western flank of Mount Wittenberg (elevation 1,407 feet) near the park headquarters at Bear Valley, and also Glen Camp, which is located about midway between the Point Reyes Hostel and the Palomarin Trailhead. It's on a ridge about 1.5 miles inland, so it requires an extra climb.

Regardless of which side trips you choose, this is the classic coastal backpack trip. Exploring the bluffs and ridges along the Pacific coast will give you a new perspective on the Bay Area and the adventures it holds.

Point Reyes Hostel Trailhead: From SAN FRANCISCO, drive north on U.S. 101 to SAN RAFAEL and take the Sir Francis Drake exit. Drive to the town of OLEMA and look for the flashing red light. Turn right and head north on Highway 1, then take the first left, Sir Francis Drake Highway, and drive two miles to Limantour Road. Turn left and drive six miles, then turn left at the sign for the Point Reyes Hostel and drive two-tenths of a mile to the parking area and trailhead.

Bear Valley Visitor Center: To reach park headquarters from OLEMA, drive seven-tenths of a mile north on Sir Francis Drake Boulevard, then turn left on Bear Valley Road at the Seashore Information sign and drive to the parking lot.

Palomarin Trailhead: From SAN FRANCISCO, drive north on U.S. 101 to SAN RAFAEL and take the Sir Francis Drake exit. Drive to the town of OLEMA and look for the flashing red light. Turn left on Highway 1 and drive nine miles south to Olema-Bolinas Road. Turn right and drive 2.1 miles to Mesa Road. Turn right and drive past BOLINAS toward the ocean, then continue 4.8 miles to the parking area and trailhead.

Camping: Campsite reservations and a backcountry permit are required from the Bear Valley Visitor Center. For reservations, phone (415) 893-1580. Camping is free and there is a four-day stay limit. **User groups:** Only hikers are allowed on this trail. No mountain bikes, dogs, or horses are permitted. **Maps:** For a map of Point Reyes National Seashore, send $7.95 to Superintendent, Point Reyes National Seashore, Point Reyes, CA 94956. For three topographic maps that detail the route, send $4 per map, plus $4.50 for shipping and handling, to U.S. Geologic Survey, Map Sales, P.O. Box 25286, Denver, CO 80225. Ask for map file Nos. 01111/Inverness, 00673/Double Point, and 00219/Bolinas. **Contact:** Point Reyes National Seashore, (415) 663-1092. **Locator:** POINT REYES NATIONAL SEASHORE (E1a).

• FEATURED TRIP •

★ OHLONE WILDERNESS TRAIL

Rated: The Top 25 Hikes, 2; The Top 50 Parks, 7; The Top 12 Hike-to Streams, 24; The Top 15 Surprise Hikes in the Rain, 28; The Top 7 Hikes with a Dog, 30; The Top 5 Steep Hikes, 38; The Top 10 Chances for Bay Area Snow, 288

Some of the East Bay's most unspoiled backcountry is accessible to hikers along a spectacular 28-mile trail. The trail is in the wilderness between FREMONT and LIVERMORE, cutting a path through fields of wildflowers and forests of oak, and rising to 3,000-foot summits. Among the latter is Rose Peak, one of the highest spots in the Bay Area at 3,817 feet.

This hike, the OHLONE WILDERNESS TRAIL, links four parklands in the East Bay Regional Park District. It offers Bay Area hikers a superb close-to-home alternative to mountain backpacking, as well as shorter day hikes that can be taken year-round.

A special bonus is your chance to see rare birds and wildlife. This region is home to bald and golden eagles, as well as a herd of wild goats near the top of Mission Peak. Tule elk are occasionally spotted along the trail as well.

The OHLONE WILDERNESS TRAIL can be an ideal three-day backpacking destination, with hikers able to make trail camps at SUNOL and OHLONE regional parks. Both are spaced perfectly for a three-day expedition. The opening of the Ohlone Camp solves what was previously a logistics problem. You can now break the distances down to a 12-mile trip the first day, followed by two days of about eight miles each.

Because of the design of the OHLONE WILDERNESS TRAIL, portions of it can provide a one-day hike, or what I call an "in-and-outer."

If you want to feel a real sense of accomplishment here on a weekend, plan on a gut-thumping hike, traveling 12 miles the first day, and 16 the second. It might be a little crazy, but you must have a little of that in you anyway to be a backpacker.

The steepest section of the trail, located near DEL VALLE REGIONAL PARK, has an elevation change of 1,600 feet in just 1.5 miles. If you plan on going up, we're talking serious business, but why kill yourself in the process? By traveling west to east, from Mission Peak Regional Preserve to DEL VALLE PARK, you will be going down, not up, in this steep section of trail.

However, don't expect anything easy. From the western trailhead in FREMONT, you will climb from an elevation of 400 feet to Mission Peak at 2,517 feet in 3.5 miles. If you are not in good physical condition, you will find out quickly here. In the spring, this trail is one of the best hikes in the Bay Area. With panoramic views of SAN FRANCISCO, the SANTA CRUZ MOUNTAINS, and, on crystal clear days, even the Sierra Nevada, it won't stay a secret for long.

Directions: To reach the trailhead at the western end of the Ohlone Wilderness Trail from Interstate 680, take the Mission Boulevard exit, near Fremont, and turn east on Stanford Avenue. At the end of Stanford Avenue, there is a parking lot, an information panel, and the trailhead. **Permits and maps:** Since the trail passes through land leased from the San Francisco Water District, a trail permit is required. Purchase one by mail from the East Bay Regional Park District. Maps and brochures are available as well. For information, phone (510) 635-0135. **Camping:** Camping is permitted by reservation only at the Sunol backpack loop and at Del Valle Regional Park; you can book a spot by calling (510) 636-1684. **Day hikes:** For information on one-day hikes, call the Sunol Regional Wilderness, (925) 862-2244*, or Del Valle Regional Park, (925) 373-0405.* **Contact:** For general information, phone the East Bay Regional Park District, (510) 635-0135 extension 2200. **Locator:** SUNOL REGIONAL WILDERNESS (E1, E2). **See featured trip page:** 99.

• FEATURED TRIP •

★ RUSH CREEK

Rated: One of My Favorite Places

Some places will never change until the end of time. People are drawn to them because they have a sense of permanence that can be found nowhere else.

The remote SIERRA NEVADA is home to such places, ageless and eternal, with the kind of natural beauty that makes you believe the entire region glows from some divine force. This is the way it is at the headwaters of Rush Creek, created from drops of melting snow near the Sierra crest at elevation 10,500 feet, then running downhill for miles into forest, rolling like a swirling emerald green fountain. Mountain shrines such as this become accessible to visitors in mid-July, when the snow finally gives way to the summer sun. Spring arrives late, and long after much of California has been baked gold, hikers can finally explore, camp, and fish among one of the most pristine, untouched areas left in America.

Many of these mountain havens can be difficult to reach, and so it is at Rush Creek. A short visit requires a long drive to the trailhead followed by a demanding hike with a backpack, in the process contending with a 10-mile climb out, ice-cold stream crossings, and afternoon thunderstorms in which lightning bolts and thunderclaps rattle off the canyon rims.

But as difficult as it can seem to reach the high country, it is a physical challenge that can be met. For many, leaving becomes more difficult than getting there. Why would anyone want to leave a place that exists in perfect harmony with nature?

Rush Creek starts well above the tree line as a mere trickle, then starts to build in size and force in a matter of miles, heading east down the Sierra slope. By the time it enters a pine forest at 9,500 feet, the stream is about 25 feet wide, quite deep, and bordered by lush grasses and lilies, rolling on with a gentle surge.

The closest trailhead is at Silver Lake, elevation 7,200 feet, located in the June Lake Loop in the southeast Sierra, six miles off U.S. 395. After departing Silver Lake on foot, hikers follow the trail adjacent to Lower Rush Creek upstream toward the Ansel Adams Wilderness. After three miles, you arrive at beautiful Gem Lake, elevation 8,052 feet, then seven miles on you reach Waugh Lake at 9,424 feet.

Many visitors never get farther than that, content to camp, swim, and fish at Gem and Waugh. But it is upstream of Waugh Lake where you can discover the headwaters of Rush Creek, along with the flawless beauty of the untouched high country.

Most people find this spot by accident, just like I did years ago while hiking 250 miles on the Pacific Crest Trail. About five miles from the southern border of Yosemite National Park, we reached a pretty stream late in the day. Ragged and lean from 20 days on the trail, we decided to set up camp rather than cross the river and head for the park.

That evening, we scouted about, up and down the beautiful river. Downstream, golden trout, the prettiest trout in the world, were leaving little swirls on the surface, rising to feed. Every summer day, they are doing the same, as if the place were in a time capsule. Upstream, above the tree line, drops of melting snow were sliding off rocks and forming little dribbles, gravity taking them downhill, feeding the stream. The tundra was mushy, with shaded areas still loaded with snow.

That is typical early in the summer, where above 10,000 feet, you'll still find quite a bit of snow, as much as five to 10 feet in shaded areas, depending on sun exposure. Below 7,500 feet, there is typically no snow at all, but as you climb, you start to see more and more, and from 9,000 feet on up, areas are covered anywhere from 60 to 100 percent. By the end of July, it is all but gone.

Some trails are sloppy, especially in the tundra above the tree line, and the creek crossings are wet, with some of the little streams running too high to cross just by hopping from rock to rock. Never go barefoot, as the cold water will numb your feet, making a fall likely. At the least, wear your boots sockless for traction when crossing streams.

A better strategy is to try a little invention of mine. Cut two strips of skin-diving suit material and glue Velcro to the ends of each piece. Then when it is time for a stream crossing, wrap each boot top. You'll be able to walk right across the stream without getting water down your boot.

Another factor to consider when visiting in summer is the presence of bears. After such a long winter, they are hungry, active and eager to get into your food stash in order to lap up the Tang. (Guess how I know?) The first order of any new camp is to find a sturdy limb on a tall tree for a bear-proof food hang. A woodman's trick is to search for pieces of old rope hanging from limbs, a sure sign that a bear has already made a successful raid at that spot.

Contending with the bears, the stream crossings, and the short but intense afternoon thunderstorms are just part of nature's challenge. When some campers talk of them, you don't know whether they are complaining or bragging. In any case, they don't usually turn out to be the focal point of the adventure.

What stays with you instead, you see, are the feelings you get when you visit a wilderness, a place out of reach of the touch of mankind. Those feelings all start when one senses the "power of place."

The high Sierra has it. For me, sometimes there is nothing better than sitting on a boulder along RUSH CREEK, watching that pure water run past. It will stay this way forever, and I will always return.

Contact: For more information, send $4 for a map of Inyo National Forest (also ask for a free wilderness brochure) to the U.S. Forest Service, Office of Information, 630 Sansome Street, San Francisco, CA 94111; or phone the Inyo National Forest, Mammoth Ranger Station and Visitor Center, (760) 934-2505. **Locator:** INYO NATIONAL FOREST (E5).

• FEATURED TRIP •

PACIFIC CREST TRAIL

Rated: America's No. 1 Hiking Trail

The PACIFIC CREST TRAIL is America's greatest hike, crossing a land spiked by 13,000-foot granite spires, untouched sapphire lakes filled with trout, and canyons that drop as if they were at the edge of the earth.

Every day you are surrounded by the ultimate natural beauty the world can offer: the sound of bubbling, crystal mountain streams. Their symphony recharges both you and the mountain with energy. The high meadows are flooded with wildflowers, mostly violet-colored lupine, their stalks bending to a light breeze. Deer, bears, and marmots are your companions, and you are just a temporary visitor to their wilderness home.

After a few weeks, you'll cast off concerns about the physical challenge of the hike and surrender to the natural untouched beauty of the high country wilderness.

The trail spans 2,627 miles, starting at the California-Mexico border and heading north through the Sierra Nevada and Cascade ranges, finally ending at the Canadian border.

The trail has 1,682 miles in California, 441 miles in Oregon, and 504 miles in Washington. The lowest point is at 400 feet near Palm Springs, and the highest is 13,180 feet at Forester Pass in the southern Sierra Nevada. In addition, there's a short, steep cutoff trail that hikers can take to Whitney Summit, at 14,496 feet in elevation the highest point in the lower 48.

If hikers do not have the time, energy, or equipment to complete the entire trail, hundreds of connector links to the PACIFIC CREST TRAIL are available that allow hikers to customize shorter trips. The trail passes through 24 national forests, seven national parks, three Bureau of Land Management districts, and five state parks. All of these provide easy access links to the trail. In fact, according to a survey by the Forest Service, only 1 percent of the people hiking the trail manage to complete it in a single summer. But members of the 99 percent club keep coming back.

While the route has been established for years, always known simply as the PCT, the trail was officially completed just a few years ago when the Bureau of Land Management designated the final link across a stretch of Southern California desert. Its completion has helped to inspire the proposal of the American Discovery Trail, a byway crossing the country from west to east. Along with the 2,109-mile Appalachian Trail, they are the world's most ambitious hikes.

Hikers from across the United States are attracted by the glacial-cut high Sierra range, the volcano-sprouted mountains of the Cascades, and the lakes and streams filled with the purest water in the world. Most visitors traverse a 50- or 60-mile section of it in a week, only rarely covering the entire length. The complete hike is a five-month trip requiring exceptional physical stamina, complicated logistics for stashing food bags at key locations, and most importantly, the time to do it.

My longest hike on the PCT was a 250-mile thump, including side trips, from Mount Whitney to Yosemite Valley. It took 20 days, more than half of which were spent at elevations over 10,000 feet. I have also explored several other sections in Northern California, Oregon, and Washington. In the process, I have met hikers from throughout the country, all out for the same reasons: to experience pristine beauty, to accept the physical challenge, and to walk in the footsteps of legends.

Jim Penkusky and Susan Day of Columbia, Maryland, both in their mid-20s at the time, completed the entire route, leaving Mexico in March and arriving at the Canadian border in mid-October. I met them at Little Gladys Lake near Devils Postpile National Monument.

"The rangers in northern Washington said that they usually get their first big snow before or after the first week of November," Penkusky said. "We're aiming to finish a little ahead of that. That's when the weather window shuts down."

"Why do it?"

"I feel like I've been called to these mountains for years."

The diversity of habitat is the trail's most striking feature. You get it all:

mountain peaks carved by glacial action; hardened volcanic flumes; seas of conifers in dense, forested valleys; untouched meadows and wetlands; and austere deserts sprinkled with tiny wildflowers.

The natural beauty can be overwhelming for newcomers. From Mount Whitney looking north, you can see rows of mountain peaks spanning nearly 100 miles, all of them 11,000 to 14,000 feet high. In the Sisters Wilderness in central Oregon, there are divine freestone streams and small emerald green lakes. The Pasayten Wilderness in Okanogan National Forest in northern Washington has sections of forest and vegetation so thick that they are virtually impenetrable.

The longer you stay out in these surroundings, the greater your sense of oneness with the natural beauty around you. Eventually, this feeling bonds all hikers.

But even in perfect beauty you must confront frustration, sometimes danger. This is true on the PCT as well and it comes in the form of icy passes. Between WHITNEY and YOSEMITE alone there are 10 passes, all situated at over 11,000 feet. The optimal time to brave these passes is in early July or August. If you time this portion of your trip too early in the season, say late May or early June, or after a snowy winter, they can be loaded with miles of snow and ice. The worst is 13,180-foot Forester Pass, located in Southern California east of Sequoia National Park.

The best strategy for traversing these high mountain passes is to camp at the base the night before. Then climb them in the morning, fresh from a night's rest. After just a few ascending steps, the thin air at such a high altitude forces you into a rhythmic cadence, as if you were running a marathon. Steep trails at high altitudes can do that to you quick.

The ice field at Forester might stop you even quicker. Its steep slope can make it a formidable crossing, and in the morning, when temperatures are still cold, its surface is slick and hard. You try to dig your boot into the ice for grip, but there is little grip available. Some hikers bring ice axes; most others are prisoners of hope for whom hiking becomes an act of faith. Slowly, with the caution of a surgeon, you work your way across the iced slope, positioning each step in the frozen bootprints of previous hikers. Finally, you make it safely to the top. Maybe not completely sane, but on top.

Trail experience, you discover, often has less to do with intelligence than with your ability to learn a lesson. The same can also be true of fishing, of course, but those lessons can come quite a bit more easily.

At one pool along the KERN RIVER where I dunked a sore ankle, a trout actually bit me on the foot. At Rae Lakes, located just north of Glen Pass (11,978 feet), I caught 10 trout in 20 minutes using a bare hook—the only problem was the fish kept hitting the split-shot sinker instead of the hook. In 75 nights of camping on the PACIFIC CREST TRAIL, I've never gone a night without trout for dinner (that will probably jinx me on my next trip).

Rainbow and brook trout are abundant at thousands of lakes along the trail, brown trout are big but rare, and in the high-elevation lakes in the southern Sierra, golden trout are a special prize. The golden may be the most beautiful of all trout, with a crimson stripe and many dark discs in a line along the side, a bright gold band along the belly, and the top of its body lightly spotted.

The hundreds of streams along the way are fresh with pure, cold, oxygenated water, healthy native trout, and an evening bite that makes for a lifetime of memories.

Wildlife viewing is also exceptional. This is because relatively few roads provide direct access to the trail, which means visitors must first hike in on a connecting link before hooking up with the PCT. The final result is that hunting pressure during the fall season is low in many areas, since such a demanding hike is required to reach the high country.

So deer, bears, marmots, squirrels, and other little furry things are abundant and unafraid. One evening while I was camping in the Marble Mountain Wilderness in Northern California, three deer, including a magnificent four-point buck in velvet, sauntered right through camp. It was the perfect end to a day in the mountain wilds.

All along the PACIFIC CREST TRAIL, you'll find pristine spots. Near Tawny Point in the high plateau country north of WHITNEY, for instance, there are acres of wildflowers, what John Muir called "bee pastures," and being among them can make you feel remarkably content.

The lookouts are the best in America, with 100-mile vistas common along any ridge, offering everything from views of snow-covered volcano tops to canyons that drop 7,000 feet. Sometimes you'll find yourself sitting in a vibrant meadow above a lake, scanning the scenery while nibbling on a stick of beef jerky. It is something you never forget.

Then there is the good, tired feeling you get at the end of each day's hike, a sense that you have asked the best of your body and received it.

At the end of every trip is a certainty that some part of you belongs in this wilderness.

Contact: For a free brochure called The Pacific Crest Trail—Washington, Oregon, California, write to the Office of Information, U.S. Forest Service, 630 Sansome Street, San Francisco, CA 94111, or call (415) 705-2874 or (888) 728-7245. **Locator:** See Northern California map for PACIFIC CREST TRAIL (PCT) access points.

4
ROMANTIC GETAWAYS

See last page for Northern California and Bay Area foldout maps.

• TOM'S RATINGS •

THE TOP 4 ISLANDS

In the San Francisco Bay Area

If you ever forget how special the Bay Area is, all you have to do is visit one of the islands in SAN FRANCISCO BAY and you'll remember.

ALCATRAZ, ANGEL ISLAND, TREASURE ISLAND, and the BROTHERS ISLANDS all offer unique adventures and great views. From start to finish, these trips are just plain fun and, in some cases, unforgettable and spectacular.

Each island offers something special. On ALCATRAZ, rub shoulders with Al Capone's ghost. On ANGEL ISLAND, take the most scenic hike in the Bay Area. On TREASURE ISLAND, find a view of San Francisco that makes it look like Oz. On the EAST BROTHERS ISLAND, stay at the most secluded, romantic inn imaginable.

Just getting to these islands makes for an adventure. Except for TREASURE ISLAND, which can be reached by car, each requires taking a boat—a ferry to ANGEL ISLAND, a cruise boat to ALCATRAZ, and a private yacht to the BROTHERS.

1. ALCATRAZ ISLAND

A trip to ALCATRAZ can resemble an eerie walk through history. The feature attraction, of course, is the former prison, where the ghosts of Al Capone and other infamous prisoners cast a spell over visitors. The trip starts with a ride on a Red and White Fleet cruise boat from SAN FRANCISCO and includes a tour of the prison and the opportunity to walk around the island. (If you act nice, they might even bring you back.) You get great views of the bay and an excellent nature walk. There is an abundance of bird life here, with a large population of night herons, friendly fellows that look like their heads are sitting on their shoulders.

Ferry departures: From Pier 41 in SAN FRANCISCO with the Blue and Gold Fleet, departing daily at 9:30 a.m. and every half hour thereafter until 4:15 p.m.

Fees: Tickets cost $11 for adults, $9.25 for seniors, and $5.75 for children. This includes a ferryboat ride, a tour of the prison, and an audio tour. Tours without the audiotape are available for $5.75. Tickets can be charged by phone with all major credit cards; call (415) 705-5555. **Contact:** Blue and Gold Fleet, (415) 705-5555; National Park Service, (415) 556-0560. **Locator:** ALCATRAZ ISLAND (E1b). **See featured trip page:** 221.

2. ANGEL ISLAND

The top of Mount Livermore, the highest point on ANGEL ISLAND, is probably the best lookout in the entire Bay Area. Here you are at the virtual center of the bay, surrounded by dramatic scenery in all directions—the GOLDEN GATE BRIDGE, the SAUSALITO waterfront, the SAN FRANCISCO skyline . . . you need a swivel on your neck to see it all.

The trip starts with a ferry ride from TIBURON or SAN FRANCISCO. Once on the island dock in Ayala Cove, you're on your own. The five-mile Perimeter Trail is most popular, but the climb to the summit is the choicest adventure. A small campground is also available; for reservations, call (800) 444-7275.

Ferry departures: On the weekend, the Angel Island Ferry departs from TIBURON at the top of every hour from 10 A.M. to 5 P.M. For return trips, the ferry departs the ANGEL ISLAND dock at 20 minutes past each hour, from

10:20 A.M. to 5:20 P.M. On weekdays, trips depart at 10 a.m., 11 a.m., 1 p.m., and 3 p.m., with return trips at 20 minutes after the hour.

Contact: Tiburon Ferry, (415) 435-2131; Angel Island State Park, (415) 435-1915; California State Parks, Bay Area District, (415) 330-6300. **Locator:** ANGEL ISLAND (E1a).

3. EAST BROTHERS ISLAND

This is the least known of the islands in SAN FRANCISCO BAY, one of a set of big rocks located just off Point Richmond, north of the RICHMOND BRIDGE. On the east island there's a Victorian-style inn, one of the most unusual bed-and-breakfast lodges anywhere. Three rooms are available for individual couples, and dining is family style. You get a tour of the lighthouse, and on rare occasions the hosts will even sound the foghorn for you.

This is a great trip from beginning to end, starting with a private boat ride from Point San Pablo Harbor in RICHMOND out to the island's docking area.

Day trips are available for $10; overnight rates are $235 per individual or $295 per couple, breakfast and dinner included.

Contact: East Brother Light Station, Inc., (510) 233-2385. **Locator:** EAST BROTHERS ISLAND (E1c).

4. TREASURE ISLAND

Few views match the one from the western shore of TREASURE ISLAND, especially at night when the glow of lights makes SAN FRANCISCO look like it glistens with emeralds. The island is easy to reach, just a short ride on the BAY BRIDGE. Right in front of the gate is a turnaround area—that is where the views are best.

Until recently, a military facility was based here, leaving most of the island off-limits. In addition to the view, the other attractions are a fine restaurant called the Fogwatch (reservations advised) and a museum located in Building 1, just inside the gate.

Contact: Public Affairs, Naval Station, (415) 395-5012 or (415) 395-5292; museum, (415) 395-5067. **Locator:** TREASURE ISLAND (E1c).

• TOM'S RATINGS •

THE TOP 16 LAKES WITH CABIN RENTALS

In Northern California

When all you do is do, then maybe it's time to just do nothing. Take a seat in front of a cabin beside a lake, gaze out at the water, maybe sip a drink, and just enjoy breathing again. Take a boat out and cruise around, possibly fish a little, but for the most part, do nothing.

In my travels across Northern California, I've found 16 lakes where you can do just that, lakes where you can rent a little self-contained cabin or a unit overlooking the water. They range from upscale cottages beside DAVIS LAKE in the Sierra Nevada to cabins with lookouts of TRINITY LAKE in Northern California.

Here's a selection of the possibilities:

1. LEWISTON LAKE

A jewel of a lake, LEWISTON sits below TRINITY LAKE and is surrounded by SHASTA-TRINITY NATIONAL FOREST. Units are available near some of the best trout fishing spots.

Contact: Lakeview Terrace Resort, HC01 Box 250, Lewiston, CA 96052;

(530) 778-3803. **Locator:** LEWISTON LAKE (B1). **See featured trip page:** 128.

2. Shasta Lake

This is the largest reservoir in California, with 365 miles of shoreline. Each lake arm is like a separate lake. There are four lakeside resorts that offer cabins or rooms with a view of the water.

Contact: Shasta Cascade Wonderland Association, 1699 Highway 273, Anderson, CA 96007; (800) 474-2782. **Locator:** SHASTA LAKE (B2).

3. Lake Shastina

This lake is just north of MOUNT SHASTA near WEED. Town houses and chalets overlooking the water are available.

Contact: Carol Richardson, Lake Shastina Accommodations, 6030 Lake Shastina Drive, Weed, CA 96094; (530) 938-4111. **Locator:** LAKE SHASTINA (A2).

4. Trinity Lake

Cedar Stock Resort offers cabins that overlook this giant reservoir. At 2,300 feet in elevation, the lake sits at the gateway to the TRINITY ALPS; summer arrives here around July.

Contact: Cedar Stock Resort, Star Route 510, Lewiston, CA 96052; (530) 286-2225. **Locator:** TRINITY LAKE (B1).

5. Lake Almanor

ALMANOR, a big lake with 52 miles of shoreline, has offerings ranging from exclusive lakeside cabins on the Almanor Peninsula to rustic cabins and motels with individual units.

Contact: Plumas County Visitors Bureau, P.O. Box 4120, Quincy, CA 95971; (530) 283-6345 or (800) 326-2247. **Locator:** LAKE ALMANOR (C3). **See featured trip page:** 351.

6. Eagle Lake

This huge lake is known for its giant cutthroat trout, stark beauty, and spring winds. EAGLE LAKE is located in distant Lassen County, which has only a couple of stoplights. The Lakeview Inn at Eagle Lake Lodge offers lakeside accommodations, and there are cabin rentals at Spaulding Tract.

Contact: Eagle Lake Lodge, (530) 825-2110; Lassen County Chamber of Commerce, 84 North Lassen Street, P.O. Box 338, Susanville, CA 96130; (530) 257-4323. **Locator:** EAGLE LAKE (B4). **See featured trip page:** 358.

7. Lake Berryessa

This is the Bay Area's backyard lake, offering a close-to-home spot for boating, waterskiing, and good trout fishing for those who troll deep enough. There are several lakeside resorts, including Putah Creek, which has cabins at the north end of the lake, and Steele Park, which has apartments overlooking a lake arm.

Contact: Sugarloaf Park, 5100 Knoxville Road, Napa, CA 94558; (707) 966-2347. **Locator:** LAKE BERRYESSA (D1). **See featured trip page:** 359.

8. Blue Lakes

Four resorts sit aside this pretty lake that is often lost in the shadow of its nearby big brother, CLEAR LAKE. If you want bass, go to CLEAR LAKE. If you want trout fishing in a quiet setting, try Blue Lakes.

Contact: Lake County Visitor Information, 875 Lakeport Boulevard, Lakeport, CA 95453; (800) 525-3743. **Locator:** CLEAR LAKE (D1).

9. Clear Lake

Dozens of privately operated resorts offer units with lake views. This is one of the West's best fishing lakes for bass and catfish. As a natural lake, not a reservoir, the water level stays near full through summer.

Contact: Lake County Visitor Information, 875 Lakeport Boulevard, Lakeport, CA 95453; (800) 525-3743. **Locator:** CLEAR LAKE (D1). **See featured trip page:** 362.

10. Lake Pillsbury

PILLSBURY is located within MENDOCINO NATIONAL FOREST, northeast of UKIAH. Evening trout fishing is often good. Lake Pillsbury Resort, the only resort on the lake, offers lakeside lodging and a small marina.

Contact: Lake Pillsbury Resort, P.O. Box 37, Potter Valley, CA 95469; (707) 743-1581. **Locator:** LAKE PILLSBURY (C1).

11. Bucks Lake

This lake is known as one of the best places to catch trout in Northern California. There are two lodges with cabins, but note that each has only a few units with lake views.

Contact: Plumas County Visitors Bureau, P.O. Box 4120, Quincy, CA 95971; (530) 283-6345 or (800) 326-2247. **Locator:** BUCKS LAKE (C3).

12. Davis Lake

DAVIS LAKE, located north of TRUCKEE, has several upscale cabins within walking distance of the lakeshore. This is a favorite spot for evening trout rises near creek inlets.

Contact: Plumas County Visitors Bureau, P.O. Box 4120, Quincy, CA 95971; (530) 283-6345 or (800) 326-2247. **Locator:** DAVIS LAKE (C4).

13. Lakes Basin Recreation Area

This is one of the more beautiful areas you can drive to in California, complete with mirror-like lake settings in the northern end of the Sierra. Cabins are available at Salmon Lake, Packer Lake, Gold Lake, and Sardine Lake.

Contact: Plumas County Visitors Bureau, P.O. Box 4120, Quincy, CA 95971; (530) 283-6345 or (800) 326-2247. For fishing information, call the Sportsmen's Den, (530) 283-2733. **Locator:** PLUMAS NATIONAL FOREST (C3).

14. Bear River Reservoir

Bear River Lodge offers lakeside units, including a few with very nice views. The lake is set at 5,800 feet elevation along Highway 88 in the Sierra Nevada and receives bonus stocks of trophy-size trout in the summer.

Contact: Bear River Lake Resort, 40800 Highway 88, Pioneer, CA 95666; (209) 295-4868. **Locator:** PIONEER (D3).

15. Camanche Lake

About 20 cottages are available on this lake located in the Mother Lode. The bass fishing is excellent in the spring; the weather gets hot in July and August.

Contact: Camanche Recreation, 2000 Camanche Road, Ione, CA 95640; (209) 763-5121. **Locator:** CAMANCHE LAKE (E3).

16. Lake Tahoe

You name it and it's here, from do-it-yourself private cabins to resorts that provide everything for you.

Contact: Lake Tahoe Visitors Authority, 1156 Ski Run Boulevard, South Lake Tahoe, CA 96150; Tahoe Visitors Bureau, (800) 288-2463 (press 0, then ask for the "Tahoe Travel Planner"); South Lake Tahoe Chamber of Commerce, (530) 541-5255. **Locator:** LAKE TAHOE (D4). **See featured trip page:** 232.

• TOM'S RATINGS •

The Top 10 Spots for a First Kiss

In the San Francisco Bay Area

The best thing to do on a first date is take a good hike, with neutral turf and plenty of space, yet surrounded by nature. I'm going to let you in on those rare, special spots where one can steal a kiss on the first date, secure in knowing the odds of not getting slugged in the stomach are relatively good.

Every now and then in the Bay Area's 150 parks and along some 10,000 miles of hiking trails, you'll come across a perfect spot for such a moment—the kiss, that is, not getting slugged for trying.

Alas, there are many spots that might seem perfect but are not. Among these, count the East Peak of MOUNT TAMALPAIS, the center span of the GOLDEN GATE BRIDGE, Land's End in SAN FRANCISCO, the POINT REYES LIGHTHOUSE, and the lookout at TREASURE ISLAND, for instance. All provide beautiful views, but they are often too cold and have too many people around. After all, you don't want the whole world watching if you end up taking a right cross to the midsection. You want seclusion. You want a bench, if possible. And in most cases, it shouldn't take hours and hours of hiking to get there, unless you want to determine whether or not your partner is in shape. Short hikes are usually best because they retain the option of a fast getaway should you start to feel like a flounder on the bottom of a boat.

Here are the 10 best spots to try for that first kiss:

1. Chimney Rock Lookout

While the crowd marches like penguins to the nearby Point Reyes Lighthouse, a popular destination, you can demonstrate your insider wisdom by instead strolling for a half hour on the Chimney Rock Trail to land's end. Here you can see a series of coastal rocks and a sweeping view of the ocean, yet without all the people. A guardrail keeps you from falling off the bluff, but you might want to get your hands on your partner to steady yourself—the old "I'm a bit dizzy" maneuver.

Contact: Point Reyes National Seashore, (415) 663-1092. **Locator:** POINT REYES NATIONAL SEASHORE (E1a). **See featured trip pages:** 67, 132, 166, and 262.

2. Heart's Desire Beach

POINT REYES draws huge numbers of visitors, especially on weekends, but nearby TOMALES BAY STATE PARK often gets overlooked in the crush. That can make it special, particularly to visitors taking the Johnstone Trail to Heart's Desire Beach. TOMALES BAY just sort of laps at the shore, quiet and green, the aptly named beach shielded from north winds by Inverness Ridge. It is a gentle waterfront, just the right setting for a kiss.

Contact: Tomales Bay State Park, (415) 669-1140; California State Parks, Marin District, (415) 893-1580. **Locator:** TOMALES BAY STATE PARK (E1a). **See featured trip page:** 220.

3. Lagunitas Creek

Just a 15-minute walk from the trailhead at Alpine Dam (the Kent Pump Trail) will take you down into a secluded canyon, complete with a redwood and tan oak canopy, where you will discover a beautiful little stream running over boulders and into pools.

It's the kind of place you won't want to leave, ideal for the mission at hand. Few spots provide this kind of peace and solitude for such a minimal hiking investment. The trailhead is located on the right side of Alpine Dam, with parking space for only a few cars.

Contact: North Marin Water District, (415) 897-4133; South Marin Water District, (415) 924-4600. **Locator:** MOUNT TAMALPAIS (E1a). **See featured trip page:** 62.

4. MOUNT LIVERMORE

The trail is steep, a 550-foot climb in just a half mile, but the payoff comes at the 781-foot summit, the highest point on ANGEL ISLAND. Here at the center of SAN FRANCISCO BAY, you are encircled by dramatic scenery in every direction. The picnic bench is a natural stopping point, with its awesome view, hopefully just the inspiration you require. It is best visited as part of the Perimeter Trail, a six-mile loop hike, and crowns a great daylong adventure that also features a ferry-boat ride from SAN FRANCISCO or TIBURON.

Contact: Angel Island State Park, (415) 435-1915; California State Parks, Marin District, (415) 893-1580; Tiburon Ferry, (415) 435-2131; Blue and Gold Fleet, San Francisco, (415) 705-5555. **Locator:** ANGEL ISLAND (E1a).

5. SWEENEY RIDGE

Mountaintops are good romantic destinations because the views provide new perspectives on the world, just what you need with a new partner. The hike here furnishes just that, a great lookout of the South Bay, as well as the surrounding wilderness of the San Francisco Fish and Game Refuge. The best trailhead is at the parking lot of Skyline College. From there, hike 2.2 miles to the 1,200-foot summit.

Contact: Golden Gate National Recreation Area, Fort Funston, (415) 556-8371; National Parks of the West, (415) 556-0560. **Locator:** SAN BRUNO (E1b). **See featured trip page:** 85.

6. ALAMEDA CREEK

One of the features of 6,500-acre SUNOL REGIONAL WILDERNESS is Little Yosemite. While the canyon doesn't really look anything like YOSEMITE, there are still several beautiful spots in the canyon bottom along a little creek. This stream, Alameda Creek, is reduced to several small warm pools in the summer, but when it's running, it provides a few small but pretty pool-and-drop waterfalls. From park headquarters, you can reach it from the Canyon View Trail, taking the short gated cutoff trail that drops down to the valley floor.

Contact: Sunol Regional Wilderness, (925) 862-2244; East Bay Regional Park District, (510) 635-0135 extension 2200. **Locator:** SUNOL REGIONAL WILDERNESS (E1c). **See featured trip page:** 99.

7. LAKE CHABOT

If you feel like a greyhound chasing a rabbit, get off the racetrack and consider renting a paddleboat at LAKE CHABOT. Here, the chase ends before it starts, with your partner right beside you all along. With a little luck, you will be making like a carp mouth with minimal investment. (Paddleboats rent for $9 an hour, plus a $20 deposit.) The lake covers 315 acres amid a 5,000-acre park, set in the foothills near Castro Valley.

Contact: Chabot Marina, (510) 582-2198; East Bay Regional Park District, (510) 635-0135 extension 2200. **Loca-**

tor: Lake Chabot (E1c). **See featured trip page:** 230.

8. Nimitz Way

If you prefer going by bicycle instead by foot, Nimitz Way is an ideal destination. It is a paved route that spans from Inspiration Point out to San Pablo Ridge in Tilden Regional Park, complete with benches positioned along the way for panoramic views of the East Bay hills. The trailhead is on Wildcat Canyon Road. From there, the route is paved for four miles, then passes a gate, turns to dirt, and rises to another ridge for spectacular views of San Francisco Bay. You could do worse.

Contact: Tilden Nature Area, (510) 525-2233; East Bay Regional Park District, (510) 635-0135 extension 2200. **Locator:** Tilden Regional Park (E1c). **See featured trip page:** 100.

9. Año Nuevo lookout bench

Benches with great views make perfect destinations because they are natural stopping points. Hence the chase ends. Such a spot can be found at Butano State Park south of Pescadero, atop a ridge with redwoods framing a postcard-perfect scene of Año Nuevo Island and the coast. The trailhead is next to the entrance station at the park and requires a short but steep hike to the lookout.

Contact: Butano State Park, (650) 879-2040; California State Parks, Bay Area District, (650) 330-6300. **Locator:** Butano State Park (E1d). **See featured trip page:** 137.

10. Berry Creek Falls lookout bench

There may be no prettier spot in the Bay Area than right here in Big Basin Redwoods State Park, but it takes an early start and an all-day adventure to get to Berry Creek Falls and back. The bench sits in a poster-like setting at the foot of the 70-foot falls in a canyon filled with redwoods and ferns, permeated by filtered sunbeams and the sound of moving water. Most hikers take five to six hours for the round-trip from park headquarters, following the Skyline-to-Sea Trail.

Contact: Big Basin Redwoods State Park, (831) 338-8860. **Locator:** Big Basin Redwoods State Park (E1). **See featured trip page:** 136.

• Tom's Ratings •

The Top 10 Spots to Go on a Date

In the San Francisco Bay Area

Okay, so you want to do something really special with someone you are crazy about and you're fresh out of creative ideas. If you don't want to be considered a romantic stick-in-the-mud, check out this list: rental cabins overlooking the Pacific Ocean, a stream filled with wild trout and surrounded by redwoods in the Oakland hills, a secluded beach and boulder-strewn point where you can rock-hop your way to solitude and isolation. . . . What follows are 10 of my favorite secluded and romantic getaways in the Bay Area.

1. Alamere Falls

Here is an extremely rare sight, a waterfall that tumbles over a bluff, onto a beach, then right into the ocean. From a distance, the waterfall looks enormous, but when you get close, you realize it is actually more like a diffused shower. It flows best after heavy rains, of course, and requires a long hike—11 miles round-trip. The best jump-off spot is the Palomarin Trailhead, located north of Bolinas.

Contact: Point Reyes National Seashore Visitor Center, (415) 663-1092. **Locator:** ALAMERE FALLS (E1a). **See featured trip pages:** 67 and 166.

2. Bluff Point

The Golden Gate Vista Point gets deluged with tourists, but just a mile or two away one of the most scenic lookouts in the Bay Area goes unnoticed by many. It is Bluff Point, the first major land point on the Marin shore east of the GOLDEN GATE BRIDGE, south of SAUSALITO. At water level, you get a panoramic view of the GOLDEN GATE, the bay, and the city skyline, and only a few people seem to know about it. For the shortest walk, you can park at Fort Baker, by taking the Alexander exit off U.S. 101, then turning south on East Road. It's especially good for bicycle rides and picnics.

Contact: Marin Headlands Visitor Center, (415) 331-1540. **Locator:** GOLDEN GATE BRIDGE (E1a).

3. Steep Ravine Beach rental cabins

These primitive cabins stand on a bluff at Rocky Point, about a half mile west of Highway 1, providing one of the most dramatic camp settings anywhere. You'll see passing whales, pelicans and murres, freighters and fishing boats, and the sunsets don't get any better. The cabins cost $30 per night, plus a reservation fee of about $7, and include a wood stove, a picnic table, and a flat wood surface for sleeping. You bring everything else. Reservations are required and are available eight weeks in advance by calling (800) 444-7275.

Note: For reservations, select the "environmental site" option using a touch-tone phone. **Contact:** Mount Tamalpais State Park, (415) 388-2070; California State Parks, Marin District, (415) 893-1580. **Locator:** MOUNT TAMALPAIS (E1a). **See featured trip page:** 62.

4. Tourist Club

You want unique? How's this for unique: a short but steep hike at MOUNT TAMALPAIS that leads to a small wood-frame building called the Tourist Club, where you can slake your thirst with a variety of elixirs and, very often, listen to German music. To get there, first park at the lot at Mountain Home along the Panoramic Highway. Hike the Panoramic Trail south for four-tenths of a mile, then take the Redwood Trail cutoff and continue for about three-quarters of a mile (downhill); it feeds right to the spot.

Contact: Tourist Club, (415) 388-9987. **Locator:** MOUNT TAMALPIAS (E1a). **See featured trip page:** 62.

5. Fort Point

This is a well-known landmark to San Francisco joggers who head out regularly on the Golden Gate Promenade, but it's overlooked by most others. Fort Point is located just below the GOLDEN GATE BRIDGE on the SAN FRANCISCO side, one of the better lookouts in the Bay Area. While you can drive right to it, Fort Point is better visited on a bike or in tennis shoes after parking at Crissy Field, the St. Francis Yacht Club, or the Marina Green. The waterfront walkway may offer the most sweeping views for a jogging route anywhere.

Contact: Golden Gate National Recreation Area, (415) 556-0560. **Locator:** SAN FRANCISCO (E1b). **See featured trip page:** 228.

6. Pillar Point Walk

One of the truly great walks along the coast, this venture includes a secluded beach with inshore kelp beds and sea lions playing peek-a-boo. Then during low tide, you can walk "around the corner" at Pillar Point and boulder-hop your way in wondrous seclusion. Watch your tide book, because this area is under water most of the time. Park at the western side of Princeton Harbor, just below the radar station, then start the trip by walking out along the west side of the harbor, turning right at the Princeton jetty.

Contact: There is no phone number to call for information. **Locator:** Princeton (E1b). **See featured trip pages:** 224 and 401.

7. Dumbarton Bridge bike ride

Engineers included a bicycle lane on the southern side of the Dumbarton Bridge, providing a safe ride with dramatic views of south San Francisco Bay. Funny thing is, you just don't see many people taking the ride. Yet when viewed from the center span, the entire South Bay looks much more imposing than from anywhere else. The best place to start your trip is from the visitor center of the San Francisco Bay National Wildlife Refuge at the eastern foot of the bridge.

Contact: U.S. Fish and Wildlife Service, (510) 792-4275. **Locator:** Dumbarton Bridge (E1c). **See featured trip page:** 263.

8. Point Pinole Regional Shoreline

You can walk several miles along the shore of San Pablo Bay without seeing anything but water, passing ships, and birds. The reason is because at Point Pinole, you must stop and park at the entrance station, then take a shuttle bus to the shoreline. There you will find a long, cobblestoned beach and beautiful views of San Pablo Bay, Marin, and Mount Tamalpais. A fishing pier is also available. The shuttle bus costs 50 cents, 25 cents for seniors or youngsters ages 6 through 11. Younger children ride free.

Contact: Point Pinole Regional Park, (510) 237-6896; East Bay Regional Park District, (510) 635-1035 extension 2200. **Locator:** San Pablo Bay (E1c).

9. Mount Round Top

Visitors can explore the remains of the Bay Area's long-extinct volcano, Mount Round Top, at Sibley Volcanic Regional Preserve. What you actually see is exposed volcanic rock. Take a self-guided tour using a pamphlet available at the trailhead. Where? Ol' Round Top is located in the Oakland hills, accessible off Skyline Boulevard, just south of its intersection with Grizzly Peak Boulevard.

Contact: East Bay Regional Park District, (510) 635-0135 extension 2577. **Locator:** Sibley Volcanic Regional Preserve (E1c). **See featured trip page:** 98.

10. Redwood Creek

The Bay Area's only genuine wild trout stream is Redwood Creek, which flows from a redwood-lined canyon into San Leandro Reservoir. When the fall rains arrive, giving life again to the stream, the trout will leave the lake and scurry upstream. In Redwood Regional Park, you can watch them climb a fish ladder and move onward to spawn. There is nothing else like it in the Bay Area.

Contact: East Bay Regional Park District, (510) 635-0135 extension 2200. **Locator:** Oakland (E1c).

• TOM'S RATINGS •

THE TOP 10 OVERNIGHT LOCATIONS

In Northern California

Doesn't everybody yearn for a place they can call their own secret heaven? Well, there are many prospects for fulfilling this wish in Northern California. All you need is someone special to share them with you, and you're off. My 10 favorite overnight dream spots range from the deluxe to the primitive. Some are very close to the Bay Area; others are farther away. Each is a genuine hideaway with great recreational opportunities—the kind of retreat that makes you want to leave behind a piece of your heart.

Tahoe? Yosemite? Big Sur? Kings Canyon? Too many people go there, so they didn't even make my list. Here are the top 10:

1. TRINIDAD COAST

My favorite piece of California coast is located 20 miles north of EUREKA along the little town of TRINIDAD. It is beautiful and remote, with views of rocky and rugged coastline, ocean bluffs, untouched beaches, and spruce forests. There is excellent hiking at PATRICKS POINT STATE PARK, inshore salmon fishing, whale watching from ocean bluffs, beachcombing, and even an agate beach at the park. Lost Whale Inn is a divine place, with private hot tubs overlooking the ocean, and nearby Bishop Pine Lodge offers little log cabins near PATRICKS POINT. A bonus is the Seascape Restaurant at Trinidad Head, which serves the best crab omelette around.

Contact: Lost Whale Inn, (707) 677-3425; Bishop Pine Lodge, (707) 677-3314; Trinidad Chamber of Commerce, (707) 441-9827. **Locator:** TRINIDAD (B0). **See featured trip page:** 124.

2. LEWISTON LAKE

LEWISTON LAKE is one of the prettiest of the hundreds of drive-to lakes in Northern California. It is always full to the brim, ringed by Douglas fir, with the TRINITY ALPS providing a backdrop. Here you will find little Lakeview Terrace, ideal headquarters for folks who don't want to rough it. The fishing for trout is often quite good, especially from Lakeview Terrace on up toward the Trinity Dam Powerhouse; a 10 mph speed limit keeps things peaceful.

Contact: Lakeview Terrace Resort, (530) 778-3803; Shasta Cascade Wonderland Association, (800) 474-2782. **Locator:** LEWISTON LAKE (B1). **See featured trip page:** 128.

3. DRAKESBAD GUEST RANCH

The first time you arrive here it might seem difficult to believe such a dream spot even exists. This is a small but first-class guest ranch, set in a high alpine valley in the little-known and remote southeast corner of LASSEN PARK. The hiking is excellent, with nearby destinations such as Devil's Kitchen (a geothermal area) and Drake Lake (elevation 6,482 feet). Enjoy hot springs, a swimming pool, stream fishing, and horseback riding in virtual seclusion.

Contact: Drakesbad Guest Ranch, (530) 529-1512; Shasta Cascade Wonderland Association, (800) 474-2782. **Locator:** LASSEN VOLCANIC NATIONAL PARK (B3). **See featured trip page:** 209.

4. CLEAR LAKE CABINS

CLEAR LAKE is always big and beautiful in spring, full to the rim and surrounded by lush green hills. While there are a number of mediocre mom-and-pop operations at this giant lake, an exception is Belle Haven Resort, which operates beautiful cabins in an equally beautiful, wooded parklike setting, just below Mount Konocti. Another excellent option is nearby Konocti Harbor Inn, which offers first-class condo-style lodgings with all the trimmings of a private club.

Contact: Belle Haven Resort, (707) 279-4329; Konocti Harbor Inn, (707) 279-4291 or (800) 660-LAKE/5253; Lake County Visitor Information, (800) 525-3743. **Locator:** CLEAR LAKE (D1). **See featured trip page:** 362.

5. Bucks Lake Lodge

BUCKS LAKE is one of the most consistent trout producers anywhere, not just for foot-long rainbow trout but for giant Mackinaw and browns as well. The lake is set at a 5,150-foot elevation, deep in forest about 20 miles west of QUINCY, and is near two lodges. BUCKS is no secret, with popular campgrounds often near full in summer, but during the erratic weather of spring the lake is often overlooked, despite the often great fishing. If BUCKS is full, Lakeshore Resort is a good alternative. For the best fishing information in the area, talk to the folks at the Sportsmen's Den in nearby QUINCY.

Contact: Bucks Lake Lodge, (530) 283-2262; Lakeshore Resort, (530) 283-6900; Plumas County Visitor's Bureau, (800) 326-2247; Sportsmen's Den, (530) 283-2733. **Locator:** BUCKS LAKE (C3).

6. Gold Lakes Basin cabins

This region has high Sierra beauty, much like TAHOE, yet without the tons of people you'll encounter at TAHOE. It's about midway between TAHOE and SHASTA in the north Sierra, where there are dozens of small mountain lakes with excellent hiking, camping, and fishing. The bonus is at Salmon Lake, Packer Lake, Gold Lake, and Sardine Lake, where cabins are available. My favorite is Sardine Lake, one of the prettiest drive-to lakes in California, set in a rock bowl and always full of water, with the Sierra Buttes nearby.

Contact: Sierra County Chamber of Commerce, (800) 200-4949; Sportsmen's Den, (530) 283-2733. **Locator:** PLUMAS NATIONAL FOREST (C3).

7. Big Basin tent cabins

The redwood forest at BIG BASIN REDWOODS STATE PARK provides a rare setting, given it's so close to the Bay Area. Here you can find a sense of seclusion, the kind that comes with big redwoods and pure air, along with some of the best hiking trails anywhere. The latter includes an all-day adventure to 70-foot Berry Creek Falls and back, or taking the Meteor Trail to a little-known lookout over treetops to the PACIFIC coast. The new tent cabins at BIG BASIN provide an easy and secure way to camp overnight, especially for people new to the outdoors.

Contact: Big Basin Redwoods State Park, (831) 338-8860; for reservations, phone (800) 444-7275 and ask for the Big Basin tent cabins. **Locator:** BIG BASIN REDWOODS STATE PARK (E1d). **See featured trip page:** 136.

8. East Point Light Inn

Some 5.5 million people live in the Bay Area and only handful of them know about this idyllic spot. You will discover a Victorian-style inn on little EAST BROTHERS ISLAND, located just north of the RICHMOND BRIDGE. Get this: Access is by shuttle boat from Point San Pablo Harbor. There are three rooms for couples, and the dining is family-style. You don't need to be a rocket scientist to figure out what you do for recreation—and it ain't counting seagulls.

Contact: East Point Light Inn, (510) 233-2385. **Locator:** EAST BROTHERS ISLAND (E1b).

9. STEEP RAVINE CABINS

Here is another virtually unknown gem right in the Bay Area's backyard. Several primitive wood cabins are perched on a bluff at Rocky Point overlooking the PACIFIC OCEAN. It is one of the most dramatic settings along the Bay Area coast, with passing whales, pelicans and murres, freighters and fishing boats. There are good walks down to the beach, and you'll never forget the sunsets here. The cabins are very primitive, however, with only a wood stove, picnic table, and flat wood surface for sleeping; you bring everything else.

Contact: Mount Tamalpais State Park, (415) 388-2070; California State Parks, Marin District, (415) 893-1580. For reservations, phone (800) 444-7275 and ask for the Steep Ravine Environmental Camps. **Locator:** MOUNT TAMALPAIS STATE PARK (E1a). **See featured trip page:** 62.

10. CONVICT LAKE CABINS

People who love untouched mountain beauty can practice their religion in this divine place. CONVICT LAKE is at elevation 7,583 feet in the eastern Sierra, a shrine framed by high wilderness peaks. There's a series of small rental cabins with names like Loch Leven, as well as a great little store, a first-class restaurant, boat rentals, and horseback riding. The lake holds some giant but elusive brown trout, including one I named Horgon. A trail leads along the lake, then rises into the adjoining JOHN MUIR WILDERNESS.

Contact: Convict Lake Resort, (760) 934-3800 or (760) 934-3803. **Locator:** CONVICT LAKE (E5). **See featured trip page:** 237.

• TOM'S RATINGS •

THE TOP 20 HIKE-TO WATERFALLS

In the San Francisco Bay Area

The Bay Area's greatest secret is its 20 hidden waterfalls. Many of them are spectacular, and all provide examples of nature's perfect artwork. Featured in the best Bay Area hikes, they include a 175-foot waterfall in three tiers (Brooks Falls), a cascade over an ocean bluff (Alamere Falls), and even a pristine little chute (Cascade Falls) where visitors are sometimes treated to a mini-symphony by a violinist and classical guitarist who practice there. You should visit any time from early winter through early summer, when winter rains turn creeks from trickles to fountains.

The best of them is Berry Creek Falls in BIG BASIN REDWOODS STATE PARK and its nearby cousin, Silver Falls, located a mile uphill and upstream. You can seek out many smaller ones in Marin County on the flanks of MOUNT TAMALPAIS; Cataract Falls and Carson Falls are my favorites. Alamere Falls, which runs into the ocean at POINT REYES, is unique.

In the East Bay, there are two good falls and lots of little ones. The largest is MURIETTA FALLS (100 feet high in the SUNOL-OHLONE REGIONAL WILDERNESS), along with Abriego Falls in BRIONES REGIONAL PARK. There are numerous other little seasonal falls tumbling down the centers of small canyons throughout the East Bay system, such as in Little Yosemite at SUNOL REGIONAL WILDERNESS, and also in WILDCAT CANYON and TILDEN REGIONAL PARKS.

In the past year or so, I have hiked to all but a few of the following falls, and here is my summary of each:

1. BERRY CREEK FALLS

This comes close to perfection in nature. After hiking for two hours, you round a bend and there it is, Berry Creek Falls, a 70-foot free-fall cascade enclosed in a deep redwood canyon amid a lush grotto of ferns and sorrel. From park headquarters, it's a 4.7-mile hike, one-way, to the falls, passing giant old-growth redwoods, a pristine canyon, and a stream; most hikers allow six hours round-trip, including a picnic lunch at the falls.

Contact: Big Basin Redwoods State Park, (831) 338-8860. **Locator:** BIG BASIN REDWOODS STATE PARK (E1d). **See featured trip page:** 136.

2. ALAMERE FALLS

Here is an amazing sight, a phenomenon of nature in which a wide creek tumbles over a bluff and then cascades 40 feet right down to the beach, one of the few ocean bluff waterfalls anywhere. From the Palomarin Trailhead, it's an 8.4-mile round-trip, a beautiful hike across coastal foothills with surprise lakes and great ocean views.

Contact: Point Reyes National Seashore, (415) 663-1092. **Locator:** POINT REYES NATIONAL SEASHORE (E1a). **See featured trip page:** 166.

3. GOLDEN FALLS

Golden Falls is a cataract topped by a redwood canopy, the most upstream in a chain of three beautiful falls on Berry Creek.

Contact: Big Basin Redwoods State Park, (831) 338-8860. **Locator:** BIG BASIN REDWOODS STATE PARK (E1d). **See featured trip page:** 136.

4. CARSON FALLS

A three-mile round-trip in Marin grasslands takes you to a series of pool-and-drop waterfalls featuring giant boulders and anchored by a spectacular 40-foot silvery chute.

Contact: North Marin Water District, (415) 924-4600. **Locator:** FAIRFAX (E1a). **See featured trip page:** 60.

5. CATARACT FALLS

Cataract Falls is a long, dramatic series of cascades, one after another, a truly precious sight. From the Laura Dell Trailhead, it's a 250- to 500-foot descent over two miles to the falls; from Alpine Dam, it's a climb of 700 to 1,000 feet.

Contact: Mount Tamalpais State Park, (415) 388-2070; California State Parks, Marin District, (415) 893-1580. **Locator:** MOUNT TAMALPAIS (E1a). **See featured trip page:** 60.

6. SILVER FALLS

The pristine cascade of silver fronts a hollowed-out cavern where you can actually dunk your head in the streaming water without getting much of the rest of you wet. It's just upstream from Berry Creek Falls, requiring a tromp up a set of steps.

Contact: Big Basin Redwoods State Park, (831) 338-8860. **Locator:** BIG BASIN REDWOODS STATE PARK (E1d). **See featured trip page:** 136.

7. BLACK ROCK FALLS

Discovering this spot can be an astonishing surprise. It's a 30-foot staircase falls running over black rock, and it requires only a quarter-mile hike.

Three equally spectacular waterfalls are within a mile on the same trail: Basin Falls, Granuja Falls, and Upper Falls.

Contact: Uvas Canyon County Park, (408) 779-9232. **Locator:** Uvas Canyon County Park (F1).

8. Diablo Falls

Hidden on the north flank of Mount Diablo is this series of two falls, a combined 85-foot drop. It can be up to 20 feet wide during major storm runoff, but is reduced to a trickle in dry weather, often as narrow as three feet even in winter. Getting there requires a nine-mile hike, much of it steep, and the latter portion is quite slippery.

Contact: Mount Diablo State Park, (925) 837-2525; California State Parks, Bay Area District, (415) 330-6300. **Locator:** Mount Diablo (E1c). **See featured trip page:** 93.

9. Triple Falls

Triple Falls is a stunning discovery in the Santa Clara County foothills, a series of three cascades, about 40 feet in all. You'll hike 2.5 miles one way to reach it.

Contact: Uvas Canyon County Park, (408) 779-9232. **Locator:** Uvas Canyon County Park (E1c).

10. Castle Rock Falls

Less than a mile of walking on a beautiful trail through a canyon brings you to the viewing platform, where you get a perfect look at 50-foot Castle Rock Falls. This white and pounding waterfall is much more powerful than most expect. Looking westward, you get a panoramic view of the Santa Cruz Mountains.

Contact: Castle Rock State Park, (408) 867-2952; California State Parks, Santa Cruz District, (831) 429-2851. **Locator:** Castle Rock State Park (E1d).

11. Stairstep Falls

Less than a mile of easy, flat trail is routed to this 40-foot stepped fall in three cascades, with giant storm-downed trees sprinkled near its base.

Contact: Samuel P. Taylor State Park, (415) 488-9897; California State Parks, Marin District, (415) 893-1580. **Locator:** Lagunitas (E1a).

12. Maple Falls

Maple Falls is a narrow, 25-foot chute of water, just part of a pretty hike up a streambed with no official trail.

Contact: Forest of Niscene Marks State Park, (831) 763-7063; California State Parks, Santa Cruz District, (831) 429-2851. **Locator:** Santa Cruz (F1).

13. Sempervirens Falls

An easy 1.8-mile walk on the Sequoia Trail is routed to this 25-foot chute/cascade. It's about four feet wide at the top and has an ideal viewing area.

Contact: Big Basin Redwoods State Park, (831) 338-8860. **Locator:** Big Basin Redwoods State Park (E1d). **See featured trip page:** 136.

14. Dawn Falls

Easy to reach and crowded on weekends, this pretty 25-foot cascade entails only a 1.5-mile round-trip hike.

Contact: North Marin Water District, (415) 924-4600. **Locator:** Larkspur (E1a).

15. Brooks Falls

This can be a stunning surprise, a 175-foot waterfall in three tiers, a narrow silver strand that brightens a wilderness canyon on the northern slopes of Montara Mountain. A bonus: Just a short distance beyond on the Montara Mountain Trail is an awesome viewpoint to the north of the Pacifica coast and a huge expanse of ocean.

Contact: San Pedro Valley County Park, (650) 355-8289. **Locator:** San Pedro Valley County Park (E1b). **See featured trip page:** 80.

16. Canyon Creek Falls

This beautiful 25-foot stairstep falls is hidden just off the road in a gorgeous redwood canyon.

Contact: Sugarloaf Ridge State Park, (707) 833-5712; California State Parks, Silverado District, (707) 938-1519. **Locator:** Sugarloaf Ridge State Park (D1).

17. Murietta Falls

At 100 feet, this is the Bay Area's longest free-flowing waterfall, a tall, narrow silver strand. The drawback? You face an 11-mile round-trip hike with a terrible climb, and once there the view is only fair.

Contact: Del Valle Regional Park, (925) 373-0332; East Bay Regional Park District, (510) 635-0135 extension 2200. **Locator:** Murietta Falls (E1c).

18. Cascade Falls

Although only a single cascade of 15 feet, this is a near-perfect piece of nature, with falls sailing over a boulder and into a deep pool surrounded by moss-lined rocks. The hike is only two miles round-trip.

Contact: Marin County Open Space District, (415) 499-6387. **Locator:** Fairfax (E1a).

19. Tiptoe Falls

A trip to this miniature waterfall (just 15 feet) is highlighted by a hike on a pretty trail along Falls Creek.

Contact: Portola Redwoods State Park, (650) 948-9098; California State Parks, Santa Cruz District, (831) 429-2851. **Locator:** Portola Redwoods State Park (E1d). **See featured trip page:** 143.

20. Abriego Falls

This waterfall is in a cavelike setting, where its narrow, 15-foot stream has hollowed out a rock face. An easy 1.5-mile hike gets you there.

Contact: Briones Regional Park, (925) 229-3020; East Bay Regional Park District, (510) 635-0135 extension 2200. **Locator:** Walnut Creek (E1c).

• Featured Trip •

Hope Valley

Rated: The Best Place to Relive the Early Pioneer Experience

Early pioneers traveled more than 2,000 miles before facing the Sierra Nevada, their last barrier to the land of golden dreams in the Sacramento Valley. In the 1990s, "pioneers" from the Bay Area head to South Tahoe with golden dreams of casinos. As with the pioneers, spending a day or two here in nearby Hope Valley can add a degree of reality to your trip.

The remnants and scars of the westward migration of gold seekers can still be seen in Hope Valley, a territory known for its natural beauty, seclusion, historic character, hiking, and trout fishing. Campgrounds beside the Carson River, along with the cabins at Sorensen's Resort, can provide a temporary home, and many folks venture to this area for the hot springs in nearby Markleeville.

Hope Valley is located near Carson Pass, about 20 miles south of Lake Tahoe. Highway 88, a quiet two-laner, divides the valley. Access to the campgrounds and the river is easy.

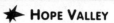

A good day hike, one that most people will find quite easy, is to retrace some of the same steps taken by the pioneers on the Emigrant Trail. Sorensen's Resort, which is more an assemblage of cabins than a resort, offers a guided tour of this trail. Much of the route, which continues over CARSON PASS, was used by the Pony Express.

Come evening, it's time for you and your companion to pull out the fishing rods. The CARSON RIVER provides the classic "babbling brook" setting for trout fishing that armchair anglers like to imagine. Because access to the river is so easy, the fish can be spooked by folks who approach without care. The trout should be stalked. Regardless of your experience, you should move to a new spot after just a few casts. The best fishing here in late summer usually occurs in the last hour of light, with carefully presented fly patterns. The mosquito, abundant in these parts, is a favorite. Stocks are made at the bridges and campgrounds along the stream.

Summer is the most popular time to visit, but my favorite period is in fall, after Labor Day weekend has passed. That's when most of the summer vacationers are back home, the road is no longer clogged up with Winnebagos, and you can see the remarkable change in seasons, from summer to fall. In the Sierra Nevada, the aspens explode in color, and being here in the center of it can make you feel much as the pioneers did nearly 150 years ago.

Directions: From the Bay Area, take Interstate 80 to Sacramento. Turn east on U.S. 50 and drive 90 miles to the Highway 89 turnoff. Turn south and continue for about 15 miles to Hope Valley. **Cabins:** Log cabins are available through Sorensen's Resort; they include two beds and a kitchen. **Camping:** Campsites are first come, first served; the fee is $10 per night. Campgrounds operated by the Forest Service sit at river's edge and are quite popular during the summer. **Contact:** For information regarding fishing, tour guides, or cabin reservations, contact Sorensen's Resort at (800) 423-9949 or (530) 694-2203. For camping information, contact the Eldorado National Forest Information Center at (530) 644-6048. For a brochure on the Emigrant Trail tour and cabin rentals, write to Sorensen's Resort, Hope Valley, CA 96120. **Locator**: HOPE VALLEY (D4).

5
TOURING

• Tom's Ratings •

• Featured Trips •

See last page for Northern California and Bay Area foldout maps.

*Area code 805 is scheduled to split on February 13, 1999. The new area code is yet to be introduced. Call Pacific Bell for a list of prefixes that will receive the new area code.

• Tom's Ratings •

The Top 13 Covered Bridges

In Northern California

Ever since that book came out, followed by the movie, romantics everywhere have been pining away for a covered bridge. You know what I'm talking about, *The Bridges of Madison County*. And right, all you need to make this a compelling adventure is a camera and, while you're at it, maybe a like-minded partner.

It turns out that tracking down the relatively few covered bridges in Northern California does make for great photographs, as well as an extended fortune hunt. That's especially true in the fall, when the yellows and oranges approach peak color, the hardwoods turn and lose their leaves, and the sun's lowering azimuth produces ever-deeper hues of orange late in the day.

In my travels over the past 20 years, I've come across 13 covered bridges in Northern California, usually discovered by accident. According to the folks at the California Division of Tourism, there are actually 14 covered bridges; if anybody out there knows the one that will complete my list, please send me the details.

You'll find the most covered bridges in the Santa Cruz area, with three near Felton in the Santa Cruz Mountains and another one near Aptos. Two of these are landmarks: the Felton Covered Bridge is 34 feet high to the peak of the roof, making it the tallest covered bridge in the United States, and the Roaring Camp Covered Bridge, just 36 feet long, is the shortest covered bridge in the country. But if you're making like Clint and Meryl, you won't really care about that.

Most people find covered bridges by accident, just like I have, in this case, while riding the Roaring Camp steam train, which runs from Felton to Santa Cruz on a narrow-gauge track. The train allows you to see two covered bridges and a beautiful section of the San Lorenzo River and the surrounding redwood forests.

Many of these old bridges have crazy stories behind them. The craziest is the Oregon City Covered Bridge, also called Freeman's Crossing, located north of Nevada City in Yuba County, off Highway 49. This is the oldest bridge in California, built in 1860, and like so many old bridges, it was eventually washed away by a flood. Only in this case, the bridge was not destroyed and was largely intact when discovered downstream. So officials rigged up a team of oxen to drag it back to the original site, where it was reinstalled. But there was one little problem: They placed the bridge backwards.

Another continuing saga is that of the 135-year-old Bridgeport Covered Bridge. The longest single-span covered bridge in existence, its 251 feet cross the Yuba River in the foothills of the Sacramento Valley. The bridge barely escaped destruction one New Year's Day, when floodwaters rose 30 feet and overtook the bridge's base. A 30-inch-diameter tree then rammed it, knocking out a cross brace and almost splitting the bridge in two.

But it didn't collapse. Workers repaired the damage, reinstalling tension cables, and the bridge reopened. It is a centerpiece of Bridgeport State Park, and though it looks much the same as in 1862, its owners no longer charge $1 for a one-horse buggy to cross, or $1.50 for a two-horse buggy.

All of the covered bridges are quite beautiful, an anomaly amid the gray concrete structures so popular in the past 50 years with CalTrans. So it is with the covered bridge near Oregon City and Oroville. "It is one of those sites that is relatively unknown," said Melvin McCray of the Oroville Chamber of Commerce. "We get calls from artists throughout California who come here specifically to photograph that covered bridge."

Here's my list of Northern California's covered bridges, appearing north to south:

1. Berta's Ranch Covered Bridge

Directions: Southeast of Eureka in Humboldt County, off U.S. 101 on Elk Road. **Locator:** Eureka (B0).

2. Zane's Ranch Covered Bridge

Directions: Southeast of Eureka in Humboldt County, off U.S. 101 on Elk Road; located very close to the previous listing. **Locator:** Eureka (B0).

3. Jacoby Creek Bridge

Directions: Six miles north of Eureka in Humboldt County, near Somoa on Somoa Boulevard. **Locator:** Eureka (B0).

4. Honeyrun Covered Bridge

Directions: Seven miles south of Chico, on Humbug/Honeyrun Road. **Locator:** Chico (C2).

5. Oregon City Covered Bridge

Directions: Near Oregon City on Cherokee Road. **Locator:** Oregon City (C2).

6. Freeman's Crossing/ Oregon Creek

Directions: North of Nevada City in Yuba County, off Highway 49. **Locator:** Nevada City (D3).

7. Bridgeport Covered Bridge

Directions: Northwest of Grass Valley, eight miles north of Highway 20 on Pleasant Valley Road on the Yuba River. **Locator:** Grass Valley (D3).

8. Knight's Ferry

Directions: Near Oakdale and Highway 120, on the Stanislaus River. **Locator:** Oakdale (E3).

9. Wawona Covered Bridge

Directions: In south Yosemite National Park. **Locator:** Yosemite National Park (E4). **See featured trip page:** 239.

10. Felton Covered Bridge

Directions: East of Felton in the Santa Cruz Mountains. **Locator:** Felton (E1). **See featured trip page:** 401.

11. Paradise Masonic Covered Bridge

Directions: In a privately owned Masonic park off Highway 9, northeast of Santa Cruz. **Locator:** Santa Cruz (F1).

12. Roaring Camp Covered Bridge

Directions: Near Felton in the Santa Cruz Mountains. **Locator:** Felton (E1). **See featured trip page:** 401.

13. Aptos Creek Covered Bridge

Directions: Off Highway 1 on Soquel Drive at the entrance to Redwood Village. **Locator:** Aptos (F1).

• TOM'S RATINGS •

THE TOP 9 DOGGY GETAWAY IDEAS

In the San Francisco Bay Area

You can find doggy heaven in the East Bay hills, and doggy hell at the state parks. And while national forests in California's mountain country are a paradise for dogs, national parks are more of a purgatory.

After having had my old dog Rebel join me for 17 years of wandering about California, followed by a hollow gap of a few years, my new puppy Bart-Dog is inspiring me to learn all the great places you can take dogs—and the key spots where you cannot.

My new pooch just turned one year old. A purebred black chow, he looks like a little bear cub, and in just a year he's learned to live for the next adventure, to see what's around the bend. Every time I head for my pickup truck and he hears the jingling of the keys, he's right there, ready to jump in.

There are many great places to take dogs in the Bay Area and beyond. In the past year, Bart's joined me on many hikes in the Bay Area foothills, and in the past month, on three backpacking camping trips in mountain wilderness. He's added a lot of pleasure to some great trips. Here is a synopsis of where you can go with your dog—and where you cannot:

1. GOLDEN GATE NATIONAL RECREATION AREA

It can stun out-of-town dog owners to discover that SAN FRANCISCO is a great place to own a dog, with some of the best places in the Bay Area to give your dog a good run and play. My favorites are FORT FUNSTON, Ocean Beach, Baker Beach, the PRESIDIO, and south near Sweeney Ridge, SAN BRUNO.

Contact: Golden Gate National Recreation Area, (415) 556-0560. **Locator:** SAN FRANCISCO (E1b). **See featured trip pages:** 70, 85, and 228.

2. GOLDEN GATE NATIONAL RECREATION AREA

Take your pick: 1) The MARIN HEADLANDS offers gorgeous picture-perfect views of the mouth of the bay and the GOLDEN GATE BRIDGE; 2) Tennessee Valley provides an ideal family-style walk to an ocean view; 3) Fort Baker has a waterfront trail along the shore of the bay from Bluff Point to the northern foot of the GOLDEN GATE.

Contact: Golden Gate National Recreation Area, (415) 556-0560. **Locator:** GOLDEN GATE BRIDGE (E1a). **See featured trip page:** 59.

3. EASY BAY REGIONAL PARK DISTRICT

As summer gives way to autumn and hot days give way to cool nights, the East Bay Regional Park District will be transformed into doggy heaven. The district features 54 parks, 85,000 acres of land, and 1,000 trail miles, plus another 100 miles of trails that link parks. Ol' Rebel's last major hike was here, when at age 14 he joined me on all 31 miles of the East Bay Skyline National Trail. Brochures with small maps are available for almost all of the parks.

Contact: East Bay Regional Park District, (510) 635-0135 extension 2200. **Locator:** EAST BAY SKYLINE NATIONAL TRAIL (E1c). **See featured trip page:** 87.

4. MARIN WATER DISTRICT

A series of great trailheads is available on Bolinas-Fairfax Road (which is routed from FAIRFAX on past Lake

Alpine), providing access to some of Marin's most beautiful areas north of MOUNT TAMALPAIS. The Kent Pump Trail, Pine Mountain, Cataract Falls, and Lily Gulch all provide excellent walks with dogs.

Contact: North Marin Water District, (415) 924-4600. **Locator:** FAIRFAX (E1a). **See featured trip page:** 60.

5. STATE PARKS

State parks are almost a complete washout for dog owners. Dogs are not permitted on any trails, beaches, or even fire roads in state parks throughout California. The one exception is MCNEE RANCH STATE PARK in MONTARA, where dogs are allowed to hike with owners on fire roads, including the great tromp to the top of Montara Mountain. Also note that dogs are permitted at drive-in campsites, provided they are licensed, you provide certification of required shots, and that dogs are never left alone and are kept quiet.

Contact: McNee Ranch State Park, California State Parks, (650) 726-8800. **Locator:** MCNEE RANCH STATE PARK (E1b). **See featured trip page:** 73.

6. MIDPENINSULA REGIONAL OPEN SPACE DISTRICT

This district is highlighted by 30 preserves encompassing more than 50,000 acres of open land, much of it spanning near the beautiful SKYLINE RIDGE (Highway 35). Yet the rules are nonsensical: Mountain bikes are allowed on narrow trails, creating a scenario in which high-speed bikers can terrorize senior slowpokes out for a stroll, while no dogs are permitted on any of the trails here.

Contact: Midpeninsula Regional Open Space District, (650) 691-1200. **Locator:** SKYLINE RIDGE (E1b). **See featured trip page:** 82.

7. NATIONAL FORESTS

There's no better place on Earth for dogs than our national forests. California has 19 national forests that provide virtually unlimited access for dogs and their owners to 20 million acres across the state's mountain country, including 35 stellar wilderness areas. There are 800 drive-to campgrounds, thousands of hike-to trail camps, along with more than 450 lakes with trout fishing. Everywhere you go, your dog can trot right along with you.

Contact: U.S. Forest Service, Pacific Southwest Region, (415) 705-2874.

8. NATIONAL PARKS

Though some people get national forests and national parks confused, you will find that when it comes to dogs, the park system philosophy is the antithesis to that of the forests. The National Park Service strongly discourages anyone from bringing their pets in parks, right down to the way rangers at the entrance stations often wince when they see a dog in a vehicle. Dogs are not allowed on trails or in virtually any open area; while they are allowed at the owner's campsite, they must be under strict control at all times and owners are required to carry all paperwork for shots and licenses. I'd like to see similar restrictions placed on idiots.

Contact: U.S. Department of the Interior, National Park Service, P.O. Box 37127, Washington, D.C. 20013-7127.

9. BLM LANDS

Anything goes on BLM lands, where your dog can roam until all the wag is out of his tail. The Bureau of Land Management is better known in

Southern California, where it manages most of its 17.5 million acres in the state, but BLM lands are also available in remote areas north and east of CLEAR LAKE, southwest of EUREKA on the Lost Coast of the King Range, and in northeastern California.

Contact: Bureau of Land Management, (916) 978-4474.

• TOM'S RATINGS •

THE TOP 10 SCENIC BACK ROADS

In the San Francisco Bay Area

The thing people hate most about driving in the Bay Area is that their speed always seems to be determined by the cars around them. You know how that goes: The driver behind you is rarely patient, but the one ahead of you has all the time in the world. After awhile, you may even feel like giving up, especially if the horizon is filled with brake lights. In the process, you may even remember a time years ago when there weren't so many cars on the highways, when driving in the Bay Area was actually a pleasure.

You say you don't remember? Well, believe me, it used to be that way. And it still is in some special places, the best of the Bay Area's back roads.

You see, one of the great things about the Bay Area is that in an hour or less, you can be driving down a beautiful back road where you can set whatever pace you want and enjoy a ride in a quiet country setting. When you put your foot on the brake, it is because you want to slow down and take in the surrounding beauty, not because some cretin just cut in front of you.

These roads come in all varieties, but by any name, place, or setting, slow always beats fast. Here are my 10 favorite secluded back roads. Several of these rides can be connected for extended adventures:

1. PETALUMA TO BODEGA BAY

If you don't like to drive slow, here is a 50 mph option that can make you feel like you are visiting the rolling dairylands of the Midwest. Shortly after departing PETALUMA, you drive west through old-style country, complete with Jersey cows. The road meanders along, then you climb a hill, pop over a ridge, and find a great view of BODEGA BAY.

Directions: From U.S. 101 at Petaluma, turn west on Bodega Avenue (signed turnoff), drive through Petaluma, and continue west for about eight miles. Turn north (right) on Valley Ford Road, then continue west on the Valley Ford Cutoff/Highway 1 to Bodega Bay. **Locator:** (D0). **See featured trip page:** 212.

2. BOLINAS/FAIRFAX ROAD

If you like to mix in a hike with a drive, this is the best choice in the Bay Area, with access to 15 trailheads for secluded hikes and three lakes. The road leaves Fairfax and climbs a hill, passing a golf course and a series of trailheads, and then traces above ALPINE LAKE, one of the prettiest lakes in the Bay Area. If you take the Sky Oaks turnoff, you can also get access to Bon Tempe and Lagunitas lakes. After crossing the dam at ALPINE LAKE, the road has several hairpin turns (these usually keep the speeders away) and will lead you onto the remote western flank of MOUNT TAMALPAIS.

Directions: From U.S. 101 in Marin, take the Sir Francis Drake Boulevard exit and drive six miles west to the town of Fairfax. Turn left at the first gas station, on Pacheco Road, and then make an immediate right onto Broadway Avenue. Drive one block, turn left on Bolinas Road, and head west about 1.5 miles. Turn left at Sky Oaks Road and drive to the Mount Tamalpais State Park entrance. Continue past the entrance station to Lagunitas Lake. **Locator:** (E1a). **See featured trip page:** 60.

3. Sir Francis Drake Loop

Marin isn't all condos, yuppies, and BMWs, and this trip proves it. Lucas Valley Road is a pretty route that heads west through woodlands, over a hill, and down along Nicasio Creek to Nicasio Reservoir. It dead ends at Petaluma Road, where you turn left, cross the lake, and travel through foothill country—choosing to either head farther out, all the way to Point Reyes if you want, or back south to the metropolis.

Directions: From U.S. 101 north of San Rafael, take Lucas Valley Road west, all the way to Nicasio Reservoir, where the road dead ends at Petaluma Road. Turn left and drive over the bridge at the lake and continue to a Y. To go to Point Reyes, veer right on Point Reyes Road. To return to civilization, turn right on Platform Road, which later turns into Sir Francis Drake Boulevard and runs all the way to U.S. 101. **Locator:** (E1a).

4. Kings Mountain Road/Tunitas Creek Road

Kings Mountain Road departs from Woodside on the Peninsula, winds like a pretzel up and over Skyline Boulevard, then down the other side (where it becomes Tunitas Creek Road) and eventually to Highway 1 and the ocean. In the process, it travels through redwood groves, by mountain lookouts, alongside a stream, past rolling grasslands, and eventually leads to the coast. It is narrow, twisty, and slow. In other words, it's perfect.

Directions: From Interstate 280 on the Peninsula, take the Highway 84 exit and drive west into Woodside. Continue through Woodside, then turn right on Kings Mountain Road and you're on your way. **Locator:** (E1d). **See featured trip page:** 268.

5. Mount Hamilton Road

This is the twistiest road in California, built that way on purpose so that the grade would be easy enough for horses towing wagons to make it to the top. And the top is the highest point in the Bay Area: Mount Hamilton, east of San Jose. At 4,062 feet, it provides a fantastic lookout over both the Santa Clara Valley to the west and miles of wildlands to the east. Once you reach the top, you can extend the trip by heading east on San Antonio Valley Road then continuing (it becomes Mines Road in Alameda County) all the way to Livermore.

Directions: Head south on U.S. 101 into San Jose, then take the Alum Rock turnoff and drive east through San Jose (I know, a real bummer). Turn right on Mount Hamilton Road (Highway 130) and continue 22 miles to the peak and beyond. **Locator:** (E1d). **See featured trip page:** 103.

6. Old Stage Road

This is an old two-laner that connects Pescadero to San Gregorio, about a 20-minute drive through coastal hills and ranches. There is one section where giant eucalyptus trees perfectly frame a straight, 100-yard stretch of road with a beautiful old home at the end, a classic piece of Americana.

Directions: Take Highway 1 south about 20 miles past Half Moon Bay. Turn east on Pescadero Road and drive three miles to Pescadero, then turn left on Old Stage Road. **Locator:** (E1d). **See featured trip page:** 268.

7. Page Mill Road/Alpine Road/ Pescadero Road

Just add some twists and you lose the crowds. That is what this route does, with some beautiful scenery to boot. It climbs out of the PALO ALTO foothills, providing great vistas of the South Bay and passing several parklands, then crosses Skyline Boulevard and passes through a series of redwood forests. At times in the early summer, usually in the evening, fog buries the coastal foothills and this road provides a dramatic lookout above them facing westward. Eventually, the road connects to PESCADERO, where you can take Old Stage Road (see above).

Directions: From Interstate 280 in Palo Alto, take the Page Mill Road exit and drive west. **Locator:** (E1d). **See featured trip page:** 143.

8. Birds Landing/Rio Vista

On a trip out to RIO VISTA, my brother made a wrong turn and we found this back road by accident. Since much of the area borders the Grizzly Island Wildlife Area, there is a chance to view all kinds of critters; in half an hour, we saw pheasant, heron, ducks, hawks, and ground squirrels, but no Bigfoot. Highway 12 to RIO VISTA gently climbs and falls with the foothills, and then the road to RIO VISTA is flat as you explore rural farm country. It feels like you are thousands of miles from the Bay Area, not just 35 miles from VALLEJO.

Directions: From Interstate 80 in Fairfield, take Highway 12 south to Rio Vista and turn right, driving down Main Street, which dead ends at the Sacramento River. Turn right (west) on Montezuma Hills Road and drive about eight miles to Landing Road. Turn left, drive to Birds Landing, then turn right on Collinsville Road and drive one mile. At the Y, veer to the left and take Shiloh Road back to Highway 12. **Locator:** (E2).

9. Clayton Road/Marsh Creek Road/Morgan Territory Road

This trip is a microcosm of the Bay Area, from hell to heaven in one easy lesson. You start by driving from CONCORD to CLAYTON on Clayton Road, and amid the traffic, you may wonder what the heck you are doing here. In CLAYTON, turn right on Marsh Creek Road and you will find out. The road is routed from the base of the northeastern flank of MOUNT DIABLO to some of the most remote sections of the county. From here, turn south on Morgan Territory Road; it travels for nearly 20 miles through wildlands, leading eventually to Livermore and Interstate 580.

Directions: From Interstate 680 in Concord, take the Concord Avenue exit and drive east into Concord, where the road becomes Clayton Road. Drive southeast into Clayton, then turn right on Marsh Road. Drive about four miles, then turn right on Morgan Territory Road and take off for yonder. **Locator:** (E1c). **See featured trip page:** 92.

10. Mines Road

If this road feels like it is out in the middle of nowhere, that's because it is. It is routed south out of LIVERMORE, running in a valley between Crane Ridge to the east and Cedar Mountain

Ridge to the west; much of it follows Arroyo Mocho Creek. It is wild, untouched country, and the farther you go, the wilder it gets. When the road crosses into Santa Clara County, it becomes San Antonio Valley Road and is routed all the way to MOUNT HAMILTON (see above). You may even see a herd of elk way out here.

Directions: Follow Interstate 580 to Livermore, then take the North Livermore Avenue exit and drive south into town. Continue on North Livermore, which becomes South Livermore Avenue, and as you leave town, Tesla Road. Shortly after it becomes Tesla Road, turn right on Mines Road and continue south for 15 miles into San Antonio Valley. **Locator:** (E1d).

• TOM'S RATINGS •

THE TOP 7 LAKES IN THE GOLD LAKES BASIN

The GOLD LAKES BASIN is a chunk of paradise that is just far enough out of the way that it will always remain a special refuge for visitors.

You'll find it in remote Plumas County, located in the northern Sierra about midway between LAKE TAHOE and MOUNT LASSEN. It has the profound beauty of Tahoe's wilderness and the primitive ruggedness of Lassen, yet draws only a sprinkling of people compared to those two famous destinations. On my trips into the Plumas backcountry, I always see more deer than people.

There are 40 natural lakes in the GOLD LAKES BASIN. Many are accessible by car, several others with a short walk, and of course, there are some that require an all-out heart-thumper of a hike. Camping and fishing are superb, but the real appeal of the place is its quiet charm and beauty, two qualities that will stay with you long after your trip is over.

By early June, the snow is usually all but gone here, with just a little patch of the stuff remaining on the highest peaks at the Sierra Buttes above Upper Sardine Lake. The lakes are all full, with the trout jumping every evening. The streams run clear, like crystal fountains. The high meadows are lush green and the little mountain wildflowers are in full bloom.

Visitors will discover a wide variety of available accommodations. You can rent a cabin or stay in a lodge. You can drive right in and set up a tent at a campground near one of the lakes. Or you can lace up your hiking boots, strap on a backpack, and head off into the wilderness without a care in the world.

Many newcomers prefer to stay in a cabin, lodge, or inn. A list of overnight lodgings, part of a free travel packet, is available by contacting the Plumas County Visitors Bureau.

Most families prefer the drive-to campgrounds. In a 10-mile radius near the town of GRAEAGLE (located at the junction of Highways 70 and 89), there are 12 campgrounds, seven lakes, and one stream that can all be reached by car. The favorite for newcomers is Plumas-Eureka State Park. The 5,200-foot elevation there affords a glimpse of what this area is all about: camping, fishing, and hiking amid lakes, streams, and forest.

Visitors requiring solitude can hike into the interior of the GOLD LAKES BASIN. There are so many lakes that you can hike to a different one to camp each night, literally for weeks on end if you wanted. Trailheads for Rock, Wade, Grass, and Jamison Lakes are located in Plumas-Eureka State Park, while trails for more remote lakes, including Smith, Upper Sardine, and Long, are found in Plumas National Forest.

The fellow who introduced me to this area is Al Bruzza, who owns the Sportsmen's Den in QUINCY and who has explored every inch of Plumas County. He can be of great assistance in trip planning, especially when it comes to tips on catching trout. To reach him, phone (530) 283-2733.

Here is a brief synopsis of some of my favorite places:

1. Eureka Lake

This is the most common destination for newcomers to the Plumas mountain country. A beautiful little lake, it is the centerpiece of Plumas-Eureka State Park. A new bonus is that the access road to the lake, which used to be closed from Friday through Sunday, is now open every day of the week.

Locator: GOLD LAKES BASIN (C3).

2. Gold Lake

You can drive right up, with a boat ramp provided and a campground nearby. The lake is at an elevation of 6,400 feet in Plumas National Forest, a beautiful setting. Several trails that start here are routed to nearby wilderness lakes. Another bonus is the big Mackinaw trout, though they often lurk deep. During midsummer, it can be quite windy here, particularly in the afternoon.

Locator: GOLD LAKES BASIN (C3).

3. Long Lake

Of the three lakes in the immediate area (the others being Snake Lake and Big Bear Lake), this is the best. Long Lake is deep and beautiful, very clean, and requires only a half-mile hike in. It is something of a legend for large (up to 18 inches) but elusive trout, along with lots of smaller fish.

Locator: GOLD LAKES BASIN (C3).

4. Packer Lake

This little lake is quiet and pretty, with great views of the Sierra Buttes. It can be reached by car, but there is no piped water at the primitive U.S. Forest Service campground nearby. The fishing is poor to fair, with far fewer fish stocked than at nearby Lower Sardine Lake.

Locator: GOLD LAKES BASIN (C3).

5. Lower Sardine Lake

This is one of the prettiest drive-to lakes in California, a small pool in a rock bowl near the Sierra Buttes. It is also loaded with trout, courtesy of plentiful stocks. A lodge, a restaurant, cabins, and boat rentals make this a unique, although quite popular, destination.

Locator: GOLD LAKES BASIN (C3).

6. Upper Sardine Lake

If the crowds at Lower Sardine scare you off, this nearby alternative may offer the solitude you desire. It's a great spot for hiking and mountain biking, but fishing is poor, as the fish are very small.

Locator: GOLD LAKES BASIN (C3).

7. Wade Lake

You'll hike only two miles to reach Wade Lake, but it's a rugged climb with some rock-hopping. The reward is plenty of brook trout that take Panther Martin spinners during the evening bite.

Contact: For a brochure of Plumas-Eureka State Park, contact park headquarters at 310 Johnsville Road, Blairsden, CA 96103; (530) 836-2380. For detailed travel and fishing information, phone Al Bruzza at the Sportsmen's Den in Quincy, (530) 283-2733. For a map of Plumas National Forest, send $4 to the U.S. Forest Service, Maps, 630 Sansome Street, San Francisco, CA 94111. For a travel packet that includes lodging information, send a self-addressed, stamped envelope and 50 cents to the Plumas County Visitors Bureau, P.O. Box 4120, Quincy, CA 95971, or phone (800) 326-2247. **Locator:** GOLD LAKES BASIN (C3).

• TOM'S RATINGS •

THE TOP 8 MARIN COUNTY LAKES

Marin County has eight hidden lakes, and most people don't know of even one. Ideal for fishing, picnicking, and hiking, they vary widely, from little Phoenix Lake and its spring trout fishing to hidden Soulejule Reservoir, where each evening crappie fishing can provide the spark for anglers of all ages.

The lakes are ideal for a family adventure, as well as for going solo. Several are perfect for an evening picnic, especially Lagunitas, Bon Tempe, and Stafford. Just bring your fried chicken. A number of them also provide ideal jump-off points for hikes. One of the best is Bon Tempe, with trails that connect to several other lakes. One of my favorite areas is the far side of beautiful Alpine Lake, which has an extensive trail system. The hikes here are steep, remote, and provide stunning overlooks.

Here's a capsule look at each of the lakes.

Contact for all listings: For more information on any of the lakes, call Western Boat in SAN RAFAEL at (415) 454-4177, or the Marin Water District, (415) 924-4600.

1. BON TEMPE LAKE

This is headquarters for hikers, picnickers, and shore anglers. A network of outstanding hiking trails starts at BON TEMPE, a pretty lake that is probably the most popular of all the Marin lakes. Why? It seems to get more sun than the others. The Department of Fish and Game stocks it with rainbow trout, and from early winter through late spring, shorefishing can be excellent. There's no secret to it: just bait fish with salmon eggs and marshmallows along the shoreline. It's a good way to spend a pleasant evening.

Directions: From U.S. 101 in Marin, take the Sir Francis Drake exit and drive six miles west to the town of Fairfax. Turn left at the first gas station in Fairfax on Pacheco Road and make an immediate right onto Broadway Avenue. Drive one block, turn left on Bolinas Road, and head west about 1.5 miles to the Mount Tamalpais State Park entrance. Turn left at Sky Oaks Road and continue to the lake. **Locator:** BON TEMPE LAKE (E1a).

2. SOULEJULE LAKE

This is a little-known hike-in lake in northern Marin. You can drive to the base of the dam, and from there a short hike will get you to the lake's edge. It is a hidden spot where crappie and small largemouth bass are abundant. It provides the county's best crappie fishing, with shoreliners using chartreuse and yellow crappie jigs.

Directions: From U.S. 101 in Marin, take the San Marin exit and drive west to Novato Boulevard. Turn right and drive about nine miles. Turn right again on Petaluma–Point Reyes Road and drive one-quarter mile, then turn left on Wilson Hill Road. Drive three miles northwest, then turn left on Marshall-Petaluma Road and drive about five miles to the signed turnoff on the left. Park at the base of the dam. **Locator:** SOULEJULE LAKE (E1a).

3. PHOENIX LAKE

This lake is less accessible than Alpine, Bon Tempe, and Lagunitas, and requires a quarter-mile hike. That's just far enough to keep a lot of people away—and to ensure good fishing for those willing to hoof it. The shore is undeveloped for picnickers, but for hikers it's one of Marin's jewels. A network of trails connects Phoenix Lake to Bon Tempe, Lagunitas, and Alpine Lakes.

Phoenix is a good trout lake from February through May. Try bait fishing from the southern shore. A fly fisher can have some fun here working the mouth of the feeder stream.

Directions: Drive north on U.S. 101 to San Rafael and take the Sir Francis Drake Boulevard exit, heading west. Turn left on Lagunitas Road and continue for a few miles into Natalie Coffin Green Park. You can't see the lake from your car. After parking, hike a quarter mile on the signed trail. **Locator:** PHOENIX LAKE (E1a).

4. ALPINE LAKE

The best known of the Marin lakes, Alpine is a big reservoir in a tree-bordered canyon along Bolinas-Fairfax Road. It is larger and prettier than any first-timer would expect. Trailheads for several excellent hikes can be found here, taking you back into pristine woodlands. The best trailhead is near the dam. This lake has a few large rainbow trout and largemouth bass. It's not stocked, and the fish can be elusive.

Directions: From U.S. 101 in Marin, take the Sir Francis Drake exit and drive six miles west to the town of Fairfax. Turn left at the first gas station in Fairfax on Pacheco Road and make an immediate right onto Broadway Avenue. Drive one block, turn left on Bolinas Road, and head west about 1.5 miles to the Mount Tamalpais State Park entrance. Continue on Bolinas Road, which borders the lake. **Locator:** ALPINE LAKE (E1a).

5. LAGUNITAS LAKE

This lake has a picnic area along the west side, just below the dam. It is located right next to Bon Tempe, and the same hikes are accessible. The little lake gained national attention when the organization California Trout undertook a program in which the lake supports a self-sustaining wild trout fishery with no future stocks. Doing so necessitated a special slot limit, with all 10- to 16-inch fish being released, and a new law mandating the use of artificials with single barbless hooks. Anglers who have the most fun use dry flies and a Cast-A-Bubble, catching and releasing during the evening rise.

Directions: From U.S. 101 in Marin, take the Sir Francis Drake exit and drive six miles west to the town of Fairfax. Turn left at the first gas station in Fairfax on Pacheco Road and make an immediate right onto Broadway Avenue. Drive one block, turn left on Bolinas Road, and head west about 1.5 miles to the Mount Tamalpais State Park entrance. Turn left at Sky Oaks Road and continue to the lake (located directly above Bon Tempe Lake). **Locator:** LAGUNITAS LAKE (E1a).

6. Nicasio Reservoir

You can drive right to this lake because three-quarters of it is accessible by road. There are no picnic tables, so you have to improvise, and that is just how some people like it. It is only fair for hiking, since the area isn't wooded. This lake has been a surprise, providing good bass and crappie fishing during the evening in spring and early summer.

Directions: Drive north on U.S. 101 to San Rafael, take the Sir Francis Drake Boulevard exit, and head west for about seven miles. Turn right on Nicasio Valley Road. Follow that road for another five miles and it will take you directly to the lake. **Locator:** NICASIO RESERVOIR (E1a).

7. Stafford Lake

The lake is open for hiking, which is not spectacular since the surrounding hillsides are sparsely wooded. On the west side of the lake there's a picnic area. The little lake was the site of a local project to improve the fishing for bass and redear sunfish. It was drained to repair the dam, then volunteers completed a habitat-improvement project. Now it is full of water and bass, and bluegill have been stocked and are reestablishing themselves.

Directions: Drive north on U.S. 101 to NOVATO. Take the San Marin exit and continue west to Novato Boulevard. Turn right and drive about five miles to the lake. **Locator:** STAFFORD LAKE (E1a).

8. Kent Lake

When you first see the lake as you hike in, its immense size will come as a surprise. Space for parking is poor along Sir Francis Drake Boulevard, and after you've found a spot you face a half-hour walk to the lake. The area is undeveloped for recreation. It's primitive, with just one trail looping around the lake. And the fishing is not easy, as no stocks are made and the resident trout and bass have taken plenty of smart lessons. One good strategy is to bring a minnow trap, catch your own minnows (bringing foreign minnows to the lake is illegal), then use the live bait with a sliding sinker rigging. The best prospects are to the left of the dam, along the back side.

Directions: From U.S. 101 in Marin, take the Sir Francis Drake Boulevard exit and head west for about 12 miles. Drive through the town of Lagunitas. Just after crossing Shafter Bridge, which spans Paper Mill Creek, park on the side of the road. Look for the locked gate on the left at the entrance to the trailhead. **Locator:** KENT LAKE (E1a).

• TOM'S RATINGS •

The Top 16 East Bay Lakes

Fourteen lakes are open to recreation in the East Bay foothills, and as a group they are a testimonial to how to do something right, especially when compared with the rest of the Bay Area.

In Marin, there are nine public lakes, but boating is allowed at none of them. On the San Francisco Peninsula, there is only one lake with public access and boating, LAKE MERCED; six other beautiful lakes are closed to the public. Santa Clara County has 15 public lakes, but the local water district manipulates the water up and down so much from year to year that not a single fishing program is in place, nor is there a single full marina with boat rentals.

Then there's the East Bay, with its private concessionaires running boating, fishing, and recreation programs at Del Valle, Lafayette, and San Pablo; the East Bay Regional Parks operating at Anza, Chabot, Contra Loma, Cull Canyon, Don Castro, Shadow Cliffs, Shinn, and Temescal; and city programs in place at Bethany, Elizabeth, and Merritt. (Two other beautiful lakes are still off-limits: Upper San Leandro and Briones, both open to hiking.)

Here is a capsule summary of each lake:

1. San Pablo Reservoir

Here is the Bay Area's crown jewel for boating and fishing. San Pablo covers 860 acres, big enough to allow a 25 mph speed limit on the main lake body, yet intimate enough for a 5 mph speed limit along the shore to keep the water quiet for fishing and canoeing. No body/water contact is permitted. A full marina, boat rentals, a boat ramp, and a small store are available.

Contact: San Pablo Reservoir, (510) 223-1661. **Locator:** San Pablo Reservoir (E1c). **See featured trip page:** 375.

2. Del Valle Reservoir

Long, narrow Del Valle is a big lake, 750 acres. Ideal for all boating, it has a strictly enforced 10 mph speed limit to keep things fun for everybody. A good boat ramp, a marina, a tackle shop, a swimming beach, a campground, and a picnic area make this a first-class choice.

Contact: Del Valle Reservoir, (925) 449-5201. **Locator:** Livermore (E1c).

3. Lake Chabot

Chabot covers 315 acres and has many hidden coves and an island, along with a marina that rents out boats (no gas-powered motors), canoes, and paddleboats. Fishing for trout can be sensational at times, with the highest catch of the biggest trout ever documented here. The big downers: No private boats or swimming are permitted.

Contact: Anthony Chabot Park, (510) 582-2198. **Locator:** Lake Chabot (E1c). **See featured trip page:** 230.

4. Lafayette Reservoir

This pretty lake is used only for fishing, canoeing, and sailing, with access restricted to boats that can be hand launched; no motors are permitted. It is a small, round lake, 115 acres, and its deep, clear water creates a gorgeous setting, one of the special places in the Bay Area. Good trout fishing is a bonus.

Contact: Lafayette Reservoir, (925) 284-9669. **Locator:** Lafayette (E1c).

5. Shadow Cliffs Lake

Its clear waters and resident trout make Shadow Cliffs a favorite for anglers in the early morning, while afternoon winds make it a winner for windsurfing. Rowboat, canoe, and paddleboat rentals are available, along with a small boat ramp.

Contact: Shadow Cliffs Regional Recreation Center, (925) 846-3000. **Locator:** Pleasanton (E1c).

6. Lake Temescal

A sandy swimming beach, decent shoreline fishing for small trout, and several great picnic sites make Temescal a local winner. An adjacent hill was devastated by the Oakland fire of 1991, but has revegetated quite nicely. No boating is permitted.

Contact: Temescal Regional Recreation Area, (510) 652-1155. **Locator:** OAKLAND (E1c).

7. Briones Reservoir

When viewed from the ridge above the lake, Briones appears to be the deepest blue of any lake in the Bay Area. That's because it is (as the deepest lake by far in the East Bay). Set among the vibrant greens of the surrounding foothills, it provides one of the most serene hiking spots around. The surrounding park, which covers 5,700 acres, is a sanctuary of peace.

Contact: Briones Regional Park, (925) 229-3020; East Bay Regional Parks, (510) 635-0135 extension 2200. **Locator:** BRIONES RESERVOIR (E1c).

8. Contra Loma Reservoir

This is a great lake on which to learn how to windsurf or sail, with clear, warm water and predictable strong winds each afternoon out of the west. The 70-acre lake is the first stop for freshwater being shipped out of the Delta via the California Aqueduct. There is a large beach and play area, making it ideal for family weekends. Private boats are allowed but may not have gas motors.

Contact: Contra Loma Reservoir, (925) 757-0404. **Locator:** ANTIOCH (E1c).

9. Don Castro Reservoir

Don Castro is just 23 acres, set in the hills east of HAYWARD, but it provides a first-rate swimming lagoon with clear, cool waters and changing rooms for swimmers. Family bonus: A shallow area is roped off for children.

Contact: Don Castro Regional Park, (510) 538-1148. **Locator:** HAYWARD (E1c).

10. Bethany Reservoir

Like its nearby cousin, Contra Loma, this is one of the best places anywhere to windsurf. The lake, which is located in a state park, covers 162 acres and the wind really picks up in the afternoon, so you can get some great rides. Powerboats are restricted to 5 mph. This lake is best known as being the northern trailhead of the California Aqueduct Bike Path.

Contact: Turlock Lake State Recreation Area, (209) 874-2056. **Locator:** BYRON (E1c).

11. Lake Merritt

Located right in downtown OAKLAND, LAKE MERRITT is regardless one of the best spots to learn to sail or windsurf, or spend a few hours in a rented paddleboat, canoe, or rowboat. A boat ramp is available, but no motors are permitted.

Contact: Lake Merritt Boating Center, (510) 444-3807. **Locator:** LAKE MERRITT (E1c).

12. Cull Canyon Reservoir

Cull Canyon is a small lake, just 18 acres, tucked in a canyon. With poor fishing and no boating, it gets overlooked by many. But there is a swimming lagoon and a changing room, a picnic area, a concession operation, and an easy hiking trail along the lake, which is quite pretty on quiet early summer evenings.

Contact: Cull Canyon Reservoir, (510) 537-2240. **Locator:** CULL CANYON RESERVOIR (E1c).

13. Shinn Pond

Little-known Shinn Pond is actually a 23-acre water hole in a gravel pit at Niles Regional Park. The primary appeal is a waterside setting for a picnic, with a needle-in-a-haystack chance of catching a catfish.

Contact: East Bay Regional Parks, (510) 635-0135 extension 2200. **Locator:** FREMONT (E1c).

14. Upper San Leandro Reservoir

The size of this lake is astounding for people who see it from the air. It looks like a giant blue multilegged monster, long and narrow with many arms. It is set in deep canyon walls, a flooded river valley, and is largely off-limits to the public. Only one trail, the King Canyon Trail, provides a glimpse of this body of water.

Contact: East Bay Municipal Utility District, (510) 287-0150. **Locator:** Oakland (E1c).

15. Lake Elizabeth

Fremont's Central Park is home to 80-acre Lake Elizabeth, which provides a respite for many on hot summer days. An adjacent lagoon is good for swimming, but no water contact is allowed in the lake itself; meanwhile, the fishing is terrible. More than anything, this is a good spot for evening picnics.

Contact: Lake Elizabeth Central Park, (510) 791-4340. **Locator:** Fremont (E1c).

16. Lake Anza

The highlights at little Lake Anza, just 11 acres, are a sandy beach, ideal swimming conditions into early summer, a pretty picnic area, and the surrounding parkland. It is set in the Berkeley hills in Tilden Regional Park. No boating is permitted, but hey, the lake is too small for anything but a raft or an inner tube anyway.

Contact: East Bay Regional Parks, (510) 635-0135 extension 2200. **Locator:** Lake Anza (E1c). **See featured trip page:** 100.

• Tom's Ratings •

The Top 5 Bay Boat Tours

In the San Francisco Bay Area

Summer boat tours of San Francisco Bay feature plenty of the old and the new, but from any vantage point, all trips provide a rare perspective on familiar surroundings.

The old favorites are offered by the Blue and Gold Fleet out of Piers 39 and 41 at San Francisco's Fisherman's Wharf. They include the Golden Gate Cruise, the all-time favorite for tourists, and trips to Alcatraz and Angel Island. Also available are charter party/dinner cruises on luxury sailboats and power yachts.

Here is a synopsis of summertime bay boat trips:

1. Alcatraz tour

Many say they feel "ghosts" and "shadows" when walking through the old Alcatraz Prison, and some say the place can even cast a spell. The latter, however, is more likely due to the great views of natural beauty from Alcatraz, rather than the lurking ghost of Al Capone. The trip costs $11 for adults, $5.75 for children, and $9.25 for seniors, and includes a ferry ride, headset/audio cassette, and tour of the prison. Ferries in the Blue and Gold Fleet bound for Alcatraz depart at 9:30 a.m. daily and every half hour thereafter until 4:15 p.m., from Pier 41 in San Francisco; special after-hours tours can be arranged on Thursday through Sunday.

Contact: Blue and Gold Fleet, (415) 705-5555 or (415) 776-1188. **Locator:** Alcatraz Island (E1b). **See featured trip page:** 221.

2. ANGEL ISLAND CRUISE

A ferryboat drops you off at ANGEL ISLAND, where you can spend the day hiking, sightseeing, or picnicking before reboarding in the late afternoon for the return trip. One of my favorite walks is at ANGEL ISLAND, hiking the Perimeter Trail and the cutoff to the top of Mount Livermore, one of the best lookouts anywhere. Ferryboats leave from both the Tiburon Wharf and SAN FRANCISCO at Pier 39 or 41, departing at 10 a.m. on weekends. The price, $10 for adults, includes the park entry fee.

Contact: Tiburon Ferry, (415) 435-2131; Blue and Gold Fleet, (415) 705-5555. **Locator:** ANGEL ISLAND (E1b).

3. GOLDEN GATE BRIDGE CRUISE

Tourists from all over the world take the Golden Gate cruise when they visit SAN FRANCISCO, but it has long been a local favorite as well. In the past 30 years, it has become an institution. When I was 10, I remember taking the trip, staring straight up at the bridge, then having a gust of wind catch the bill of my baseball hat and blow it overboard—a crushing blow at the time. The trips venture past all the major bay landmarks; the price of $16 for adults includes a headset audio program. The boat leaves nine times daily, with the first departure at 10:15 a.m. in the summer, 10 a.m. in the winter.

Contact: Blue and Gold Fleet, (415) 705-5555. **Locator:** GOLDEN GATE BRIDGE (E1b).

4. CHARTER SAILBOAT TRIPS

Here is an opportunity for people who fantasize about sailing around ANGEL ISLAND and maybe out the Golden Gate, but don't have a sailboat to do it. A group of six people can pay about $50 apiece and charter a 35-footer with a captain for a three-hour voyage. (The price will vary with the boat selected.) Other customized trips on luxury sailboats and power yachts are available out of both SAN FRANCISCO and SAUSALITO.

Contact: Five Star Charters, (415) 381-9503. **Locator:** SAN FRANCISCO (E1b).

5. DINNER PARTY CRUISES

These exotic and spectacular trips have become popular for weddings, celebrations, and corporate parties. It is a charter-only proposition, available for as few as six people on a 36-foot luxury sailboat and as many as 700 on the *San Francisco Spirit,* a 150-foot mega yacht. Typical trips include a cruise out in the bay and under the GOLDEN GATE BRIDGE, with cocktails and a full dinner. The cost ranges from $35 to $65 per person and can vary depending upon the menu.

Contact: Five Star Charters, (415) 381-9503. **Locator:** SAN FRANCISCO (E1b).

• FEATURED TRIP •

LASSEN VOLCANIC NATIONAL PARK

Rated: The Top 3 Peaks to Climb, 152; The Top 10 Overnight Locations, 185; The Top 25 Lakes, 307

LASSEN is that spectacular national park in Northern California that you have probably been intending to visit for some time now. Most folks feel the same but never quite get around to it. Sound familiar? To many it does. Lassen has it all—great camping, fishing, hiking, lookouts, and seclusion, in one of America's most beautiful parklands. Yet you've probably never gone.

When I visited, every campground in the park had vacancies. Weekdays are even more empty. Ask campers where home is and they're as apt to say "Cedar Rapids, Iowa" as they are "the Bay Area."

You may have seen LASSEN from a distance as you drove north on Interstate 5. As you near RED BLUFF, look east to the horizon and spot the extinct volcano, the one with its top blown off, rising far above the other mountains. "Oh yeah, that's LASSEN."

That's usually as much as the brain gears engage when you spot Lassen while cruising I-5. But you can get those gears turning, and open up a world of adventure at the same time, by turning east on Highway 36 at RED BLUFF. In 50 miles, you'll rise above the rock-specked foothills and into a forest, come around a bend, and suddenly enter one of the West's greatest parks.

The old volcano is the centerpiece, of course. Mount Lassen peaks out at 10,457 feet, and you can reach the top in a 2.5-mile zigzag of a hike. With a quart of water, you can make the climb in less than two hours. The view is remarkable, with Mount Shasta to the north, miles of forest and lakes to the east, and the Sacramento Valley plunging westward.

As you sit atop LASSEN, you will see why the park is so special. For one thing, it doesn't even look like California, but more like Montana, with 80,000 acres of roadless wilderness. You will spot several jewel-like lakes. And then there is the top itself, a crusty volcano flume with craters, spires, hardened lava flows, and enough hidden trails that you can explore for hours.

The view from the top will likely inspire you to visit what you see. In Lassen Park, that includes 53 lakes. Of those, six can be reached by car, including Manzanita Lake and Summit Lake, where two of LASSEN'S prettiest campgrounds are located.

Manzanita Lake sits just inside the northwest entrance to the park on Highway 89. It's an idyllic setting and a perfect destination for trout anglers. The lake has been converted to a natural fishery, and a special program to protect the wild trout is now in effect. Rules mandate lures or flies only with a single barbless hook and a two-fish limit, none longer than 10 inches.

The campground at Manzanita Lake is the park's largest with 179 sites, though you may want to push on farther since it is right at the entrance. There are several other campgrounds, including two situated alongside lakes—Summit (94 sites) and Juniper (18 sites). See page 211 for descriptions.

To obtain a lakeside campsite, you might figure you'd have to book a reservation several months in advance, right? Wrong. During our visit, we found a fairly secluded spot on the edge of a meadow, not far from Summit Lake. At dusk, several deer suddenly walked out of the forest and into the meadow, grazing yet keeping their ears raised, on alert for intruders. We snuck a bit closer, undetected, and saw a mother with a fawn that hadn't even lost its spots yet.

Along with deer, the park is loaded with ground squirrels, which are always hoping to find a surprise morsel. You'd best not leave anything out for them. That might attract a bear, the masters of the food-raiding business. There are enough bears in the park to cause rangers to advise campers to keep their food well protected.

Tour the park by car to get an overview of its unique places. There are signs of the area's latent volcanic underbase: boiling sulfur vents, huge, hardened mudflows, and fields of volcanic lava balls. LASSEN blew its top in 1914, followed by other eruptions until 1921, and in geological time that's as if it had happened just yesterday.

You can get an even better look by taking a hike or two. Whether you want an easy stroll or a backpacking trip, there are enough trails to find a perfect match. The list starting on page 211 details the best. LASSEN has more than 150 miles of trails, including 17 miles of the PACIFIC CREST TRAIL, which reaches from Mexico to Canada. (See the featured trip on page 171.) Habitat varies from forest to alpine tundra, and trails will take you to hidden lakes and streams.

However, no fishing is permitted at Emerald or Helen Lakes. Since the National Park Service suspended trout plants, the fishing has gone to hell, especially in the backcountry lakes. Since no natural spawning occurs at these lakes, they are either planted or they have no fish. Manzanita, with its special wild trout program, provides the only hope. No powerboats are permitted on any lake in the park, but canoes, rafts, rowboats, and float tubes work perfectly.

The best technique to catch trout here is to offer what they feed on, insects. Fly patterns that imitate insects work the best: No. 14 Calibatis, No. 16 Haystack, No. 14/16 Loop Wing, No. 16 Hare's Ear Nymph, No. 6/8/10 olive or brown Leech.

People from all over America touring California see the big park on the map and head straight for an entrance. At some point in your travels, so should you.

• CAMPGROUNDS •

Lassen National Park operates five campgrounds, with nightly fees ranging from $8 to $10 per site. All campsites are available on a first-come, first-served basis.

JUNIPER LAKE

This is a good spot for those wanting to get away from it all. It is located on the east shore of Juniper Lake, one mile from a ranger station on a rough dirt road. There are 18 campsites, but no piped water is available. The lake is set at 6,792 feet elevation.

MANZANITA LAKE

The park's largest campground (179 sites) is quite popular because of the good fishing and idyllic setting. Concession services are available nearby. It is located at 5,890 feet elevation near the park's northern entrance on Highway 89.

SUMMIT LAKE

There are actually two campgrounds here, one on each side of the lake. The 94 campsites are near the water, where you can swim or fish for trout. Many trails begin in this area. The elevation is 6,695 feet.

WARNER VALLEY

A little-used spot with 18 campsites, Warner Valley is located one mile from the Warner Valley Ranger Station. This is the best choice for hikers who like to stream fish. The nearest supplies are in CHESTER, which is 17 miles away via a dirt road. The camp elevation is 5,650 feet.

• HIKING •

Lassen Park has 150 miles of trails across a great variety of terrain. Here are a few favorite hikes:

Crumbaugh Lake
This hike entails three miles of walking with little elevation gain, taking you through meadows and forests to Cold Boiling Lake and on to Crumbaugh Lake.

Devastated Area
The one-hour breeze of a walk tours the site of a massive mudflow sparked by the 1915 eruption of Mount Lassen.

King's Creek Falls
A three-mile round-trip with a 700-foot descent takes you to King's Creek Falls, just 30 feet high but worth seeing. The trail follows a mountain stream that cuts through both meadow and forest.

Mill Creek Falls
This four-mile round-trip hike leads to Mill Creek Falls, which at 70 feet high is the park's highest waterfall.

Paradise Meadow
It's a three-mile round-trip climbing 600 feet to a beautiful, glacier-carved meadow. Paradise Meadow presents a great wildflower display.

Sifford Lakes
For the adventurous hiker, this four-mile round-trip is all cross country. It leaves the King's Creek Trail, explores a series of beautiful glacier-carved lakes, and has many great lookouts.

Directions: From the Bay Area, take Interstate 80 north to Interstate 505, then proceed north to Interstate 5. Drive approximately 95 miles north to Red Bluff and take the Highway 36/Lassen Park exit. Continue east for 47 miles to the Highway 89 cutoff, then turn north and proceed to the park entrance. **Fees:** A $5 park entrance fee is charged. Campsite fees are $8 to $10 per night. **Maps:** A complete map of the park and the Lassen Trails map can be purchased at the park. **Contact:** Shasta Cascade Wonderland Association, which provides free information on the park at (800) 474-2782. Lassen Volcanic National Park, P.O. Box 100, Mineral, CA 96063; (530) 595-4444. **Locator:** (B3, C3).

• Featured Trip •

Bodega Bay

Rated: The Top 8 Cities with Daily Salmon Trips, 340; The Top 5 Places to Clam Dig, 382

A great getaway destination that anybody can go to on the spur of the moment is Bodega Bay. It's just far enough away to make the trip feel special yet is close enough not to wear you out, with excellent sight-seeing, restaurants, hiking, fishing, and boating. I've always loved this place. I return every year or so, finding it more captivating each time. It features one of the best coastal hikes available anywhere.

The drive in from Petaluma is beautiful and relaxing, especially on an early Sunday morning with no traffic, the two-laner meandering through rolling coastal foothills amid dairy farms and open space. From Petaluma (40 miles north of San Francisco), you take the East Washington Boulevard exit and drive west for about 30 miles to Bodega Bay, finally rising over a small hill as the Pacific coast comes into view. This is always a special moment, and what follows is just as good.

My suggestion is to head north, drive through the little town of Bodega Bay, and scan the restaurants as you go (for later use), but keep on going about a mile north of town to East Shore Road. Turn left here and you can drive all the way around the bay at water's edge, past Spud Point Marina on the west side of the bay, and eventually to Bodega Head.

There are two parking lots here, one overlooking BODEGA BAY, another with a view of the PACIFIC OCEAN. At each, you'll find trailheads for great hikes, one easy and short, the other easy and long.

The short, easy trip is a 1.5-mile loop hike, called the Bodega Head Loop, that starts at the east parking area at Bodega Head. The trail is almost level, traveling in a horseshoe-like route around Bodega Head. Along the way, you get drop-dead gorgeous views to the east of BODEGA BAY and the harbor entrance, to the south of Seal Rock and beyond to TOMALES POINT, and then as you turn north, a full expanse of the PACIFIC OCEAN. At times the trail is routed along clifftops, with one perilous spot that will take your breath away looking at the sheer drop. This is a perfect introduction to the area, providing a vantage point of both the region's beauty and recreational offerings. It is also an easy enough walk for virtually anybody to enjoy.

If you want more, you can get it at the trailhead at the western parking area for Bodega Head, the jump-off for a five-mile round-trip to the Bodega sand dunes and a beach. It's an easy to moderate hike with a 500-foot change in elevation to reach the beach. In the process, you will pass through a U.C. Marine Reserve (you must stay on the trail here), then continue onward to the sand dunes with sweeping ocean views, and turn left to the beach.

This is a great hike, and it would be one of the best anywhere except for the wind and fog that are so common here. Many summer days are foggy, and you lose the views. Then on clear days, the wind often blows out of the northwest. It takes a bit of luck to get a clear, windless day here in the summer.

On either of the above hikes, you will likely look down at BODEGA BAY and notice the steady procession of boats streaming in and out of the harbor. That's because BODEGA BAY has become one of the best ports on the entire Pacific coast for owners of trailered boats, with a six-lane boat ramp, good parking, an excellent marina, and a short cruise to the salmon during July and August.

The short distance to the fish is one of the biggest appeals for boat owners. Often the salmon are just a mile or two west of Bodega Head near a red buoy called "The Whistler." At times the best bite has been four miles west of Bodega Head. Other good spots are just north at the mouth of Salmon Creek, and to the south outside the mouth of TOMALES BAY.

Because of this, the region has become so popular among boaters that Spud Point Marina has turned into one of the best operations on the coast, an example for many other coastal areas of how to do it right. In addition, a small grocery store is available near the boat ramp, so last-minute supplies are always available.

If you don't own a boat but want to get out on the water, Bodega Bay Sportfishing (707) 875-3344) offers party boat trips for salmon, rockfish, and lingcod. The latter entail long-distance trips to Cordell Bank, an offshore reef at the bottom of 300 to 350 feet of water, known for large numbers of huge rockfish. On a typical day at Cordell, a catch sack will be filled with a 15-fish limit of rockfish and lingcod, often weighing 80 to 90 pounds, and if the lings are biting and you catch two or three, sometimes may even range from 110 to 125 pounds.

Regardless of what you do for recreation, most all visitors top off their trip with dinner at one of the restaurants in BODEGA BAY. I've never had a bad meal here. The best is the Bayview Room, and the most popular are Tides Wharf, Lucas Wharf (both a bit cheaper), and a low-cost restaurant called Bodega Bay Grill.

Directions: From San Francisco, drive north on U.S. 101 about 40 miles to Petaluma. Take the East Washington Boulevard exit and drive west about 30 miles to Bodega Bay. **Contact:** For a complimentary information packet, phone (707) 875-3422 or (800) 905-9050, or write to Bodega Bay Chamber of Commerce, P.O. Box 146, Bodega Bay, CA 94923. **Locator:** (D0).

• FEATURED TRIP •

MENDOCINO COAST ADVENTURES

Rated: The Top 10 Scenic Back Roads, 198; The Top 7 Deep-Sea Fishing Trips, 330; The Top 5 Places to Clam Dig, 382

The Mendocino coast is so quiet you can practically hear the flowers bloom. Drive three hours up U.S. 101 and over to the coast on Highway 128, and you'll enter a new world. Instead of concrete and traffic jams, you get redwoods, wildflowers, and miles of untouched Pacific coast.

But more than anything else, you get quiet. It doesn't matter what you choose to do—walk the beaches, watch for whale spouts, hike in redwood forests, or explore little towns such as ELK or MENDOCINO—you get quiet. You can camp in a forest, rent a hotel room for a night, or stay at an expensive coastal inn. No matter which, you get quiet.

It's just what many Bay Area residents need and that makes the Mendocino coast an ideal retreat. Spring is a perfect time to visit because the whale migration is in full swing, all kinds of wildflowers are blooming in the nearby hills, and the air is sparkling clean.

The coast has a different look here than in the south. In many areas, there are giant blocks of rock towering out of the ocean shallows, rocks that look like they have been sculpted by an angry giant with a hammer and chisel, complete with tunnels and cutaways. They give the area a rugged, primitive feel. Ocean and redwoods, you get it all on the Mendocino coast.

Locator for all Mendocino Coast listings: (C0).

VAN DAMME STATE PARK

One of the coast's best hikes is here. It's the Fern Canyon Trail, a gently sloping five-miler that cuts along the bottom of a lush creek. Because the park is located in a perfect setting for car campers heading up Highway 1, many people discover this hike by accident in the summer. You can beat the traffic, though, by going in the spring.

Contact: Mendocino Parks, (707) 937-5804.

WHALE WATCHING

See what looks like a puff of smoke on the ocean surface? Look closer—it's more likely a whale spout. Watching the annual whale migration is one of the area's more popular events. In

April, Fort Bragg hosts the Mendocino Whale Festival, which includes an arts and crafts show and a two-mile run. Big oceangoing boats make whale watching trips from December through March out of Fort Bragg.

Contact: Fort Bragg Chamber of Commerce, (707) 961-6300; Sportsman's Dock, (707) 964-2619.

Fishing

Some of Northern California's best deep-sea fishing is out of Noyo Harbor in Fort Bragg. Fishers catch many species of rockfish, along with lingcod and cabezone. In summer, salmon is king. At times the area gets some of the best salmon fishing on the Pacific coast. Because salmon from the Klamath River migrate as far south as Fort Bragg and salmon from the Sacramento River migrate as far north as Fort Bragg, it's like fishing two runs at the same time.

Contact: Sportsman's Dock, (707) 964-2619.

Hiking

Some 40 of the Mendocino coast's best walks are detailed in the book *The Hiker's Guide to the Mendocino Coast.* Most of the walks suggested are two or three miles long and explore Mendocino County's most beautiful coastal areas. Two of the best are the Lake Cleone Trail and the Falls Loop Trail.

Contact: To order the book, which costs $14, contact Bored Feet, P.O. Box 1832, Mendocino, CA 95460; (707) 964-6629.

Coastal Inns

On the more than 100 miles of coast from Westport to Gualala, there are 70 lodgings, including little country-side inns, more standard hotels in town, and vacation cottage rentals.

Contact: Coast Chamber of Commerce, P.O. Box 1141, Fort Bragg, CA 95437; (707) 961-6300. M-F 9-5

Camping

There are 25 public and private campgrounds along the Mendocino coast. The settings include redwood forests, such as at Russian Gulch State Park (707) 937-5804) near the Point Cabrillo Lighthouse, and beach frontage, such as at Wages Creek (707) 964-2964) at Westport.

Contact: For a listing of campgrounds, write the Coast Chamber of Commerce, P.O. Box 1141, Fort Bragg, CA 95437. Or get my book *California Camping,* which describes 1,500 campgrounds throughout the state, by calling Foghorn Press, 800-FOG-HORN/364-4676.

Ocean Kayaking

Sound crazy to you? Well, it's not. Kayaking is fun, exhilarating, and anybody can do it.

Contact: Catch-a-Canoe, (707) 937-0273.

Horseback Riding

Trails lead either into the redwood forest or to the beach at Ricochet Ridge Ranch, located near Cleone. In addition, special horse packing trips can be booked into the Mendocino mountain wildlands.

Contact: Ricochet Ridge Ranch, (707) 964-PONY/7669.

Even more activities are possible, such as visiting the wine country, photographing the coast, and cruising the craft shops, but you get the idea. After a few days here, you will discover that it's easy to get used to the quiet.

• FEATURED TRIP •

✷ Sonoma Coast Adventures

Rated: The Top 6 Coastal Camps, 115; The Top 10 Camps for Kids, 120; The Top 10 Easy Backpack Trips, 150

The Sonoma coast is often so quiet that you can practically hear the pampas grass bending in a light breeze. While you can take your pick of an array of adventures and divine destinations, what you will remember best is the quiet.

You may have forgotten not only the natural beauty of the Sonoma coast, but how fast and easy it is to drive there and capture the enchanted sensations. From SAN FRANCISCO, it's a pretty two-hour cruise and you will be meandering up Highway 1 north of BODEGA BAY . . . past Goat Rock, Fort Ross, Timber Cove, Stillwater Cove, Salt Point, Horseshoe Cove, JENNER, and on up to GUALALA. What you get is a series of beautiful coastal getaways with almost nobody around. And everywhere you go, it's quiet, real quiet.

The drive alone is worth the trip, with coastal panoramas from every bluff. But this stretch of land has excellent, little-used hiking trails, tidepooling, unpeopled beaches for picnicking, a few campgrounds, and, every now and then, small home-cookin' restaurants.

Here is a synopsis of the best:

The Drive

It is not a high-speed cruise, but a go-at-your-own-pace jaunt with lots of twisties, cliffs, canyons, coves, and ocean views. The fastest route is to drive north on U.S. 101 to PETALUMA, then turn west and head to BODEGA BAY, a pretty drive through foothilled dairyland. At Highway 1, just turn right and continue north along the coast.

One summer, I remember getting jammed up behind a couple of Winnebagos taking Highway 1 at 10 miles per hour and refusing to pull over. After about 20 minutes, I finally got by them and all was free and clear. A few minutes later I noticed an incredible coastal lookout, so I pulled over and parked for a photograph—and while loading some film, I looked up and saw those Winnebagos passing by. When I got back on the road, they blocked my way again for another 20 minutes.

Sound familiar? You ain't lyin'. That is why the off-season, especially fall, is the best time to make the trip. The staring-at-the-rear-of-a-Winebago scenario is extremely rare in September and October.

Hiking

You'll find about two dozen hikes near the Sonoma coast. My favorites are described in detail in the Foghorn Press book *California Hiking*. My number one short walk in this area is at Stockhoff Creek at Stillwater Cove Regional Park, and my favorite long hike is at Salt Point State Park.

Stillwater Cove Park is located between Salt Point and Fort Ross. As a county park, it gets less use than state facilities. The trailhead for the Loop Trail is at the day-use parking area; from there, you can walk a one-mile loop that takes about an hour. In the process, you head through redwoods, then down along Stockhoff Creek to Stillwater Cove, a pristine setting. (While the hike is officially called the Loop Trail, many people know it as the Stockhoff Creek Loop.) For information, phone the park at (707) 847-3245.

For a more ambitious romp, Salt Point State Park offers a good prospect, from Fisk Mill Cove on north to the Horseshoe Point Overlook, about a four- or five-mile round-trip. Much of the trail travels on the headlands along the park's north shore, providing great lookouts almost the whole way. The goal should be Horseshoe Point, where you'll be rewarded with a fantastic view of the Sonoma coast. For information, phone the park at (707) 847-3221.

Tidepooling

Always try to time your trip during a big minus low tide, which is the best time to explore the rocky tidal basins along the coast and view all the wonderful little sea critters that live there.

There are many tidal basins on the rocky portions of the Sonoma coast, but the most accessible are at Salt Point State Park, a popular abalone diving spot, and along the "Lost Coast" between Fort Ross and Russian Gulch. (Note: Do not confuse this Lost Coast with the more notable Lost Coast in Humboldt County, described on page 160.) Sonoma's Lost Coast is a very craggy five-mile stretch of coastline, an awesome setting at the base of cliffs, and is best accessed from a long, rugged trail that starts at Fort Ross State Historic Park. For information, phone park headquarters at (707) 847-3286 or fax (707) 847-3601.

Camping

In my travels, I've located half a dozen campgrounds near Highway 1 between Bodega Bay and Gualala. North to south, they are Gualala Point at Sonoma County Regional Park, Salt Point State Park, Ocean Cove Private Camp, Stillwater Cove Regional Park, and Bodega Dunes and Wrights Beach at Sonoma Coast State Beach. They are detailed in my book *California Camping*.

My personal favorites are the six walk-in campsites at Gualala Point, all first come, first served. Walk-in sites here cost only $3 per night and provide a dramatic spot on the ocean near the mouth of the Gualala River. A trail is routed from the bluff down to the ocean. The only downer is summer fog, but hey, it's better in the fall anyway.

Lodging/Restaurants

You'll find 11 inns and lodges that provide accommodations, but relatively few restaurants, just six. After all, there's not many folks around these parts—that's why it's so quiet.

Best Time of Year

My favorite time here is the fall, especially October. With a peaceful backdrop, you can enjoy the Sonoma coast's best weather of the year. The arrival of October brings sunny skies, warm temperatures, and no wind, with the old sea looking like a green velvet carpet, just kind of lapping away at miles of coastal outcrops and untouched beaches. The out-of-staters are long gone, back in Iowa and wherever else they come from during summer, leaving Highway 1 a free and easy drive, where you just mosey around corner after corner. Then, the roads and coastal views are clear, as are the minds of all who visit.

Contact: For a list of lodges and restaurants, including those in the Bodega Bay area, write the Sonoma Coast Visitor Center, P.O. Box 750, Bodega

Bay, CA 94923, or phone (707) 875-2868. **Locator:** (D0).

• FEATURED TRIP •

SOUTHERN PLUMAS COUNTY

Rated: The Top 6 Destinations in Plumas Wonderland, 346

From my canoe at Sardine Lake, I scanned across the back wall of the high mountain crest, topped by the spike-topped Sierra Buttes, and thought of how few places can even come close to matching such great natural beauty.

Unless, that is, you consider the view from the front door of the canvas tent cabins at small but pristine Salmon Lake, where you can stand with arms outstretched, palms up, taking it all in, the small emerald green lake nestled in a mountain cirque and backed by a snowcapped ridge. You might also consider this recent scene at Davis Lake big, full, and pretty, with trout rising to hatching caddis and snowcapped Eureka and Smith peaks looming in the background.

The irony is that these examples are but a sliver of the overall beauty in southern Plumas County, one of California's greatest vacation destinations—yet one that is largely overlooked in the face of TAHOE, YOSEMITE, MONTEREY, MAMMOTH, SHASTA, and Disneyland. The region is located northwest of TAHOE, covers over a million acres, and has more than 100 lakes, 1,000 miles of streams, 40 campgrounds, 30 properties with cabins—and only 22,000 residents and just one stoplight (in QUINCY) in the entire county.

It is distant enough from SAN FRANCISCO, requiring about a five-hour drive (with no direct route), that it will always stay this way, cherished by nearly everyone who takes the time to visit. Cherished not only for the beauty, but for the great adventuring this is possible, especially hiking, boating, camping, fishing—as well as horseback riding and golf.

I recently spent three days poking around here, and then came up with this synopsis of the best it has to offer:

Cabins: There are 23 lakes within a three-mile radius of the cabins at Elwell Lakes Lodge, the best headquarters for day hikes anywhere in California. Meanwhile, from your porch at Sardine Lake, you have a view of lake frontage and the Sierra Buttes, one of the prettiest places on Earth. Bucks Lake Lodge puts you within minutes of a dock, boat rentals, and good fishing for trout. In all, there are 30 properties with cabin rentals of one kind or another in the region. Most have space available throughout much of the summer. However, two very special lodges, one at Sardine Lake and the other at Salmon Lake, are booked years in advance and require hopeful waits on cancellation lists. The selections are Bucks Lake Lodge, Elwell Lakes Lodge, Gold Lake Lodge, Graeagle Lodge, Lassen View, Layman Resort, Packer Lodge, Plumas Pines, Salmon Lake Lodge, Sardine Lakes Lodge.

Lodging: Some 90 destinations offer lodging, including cabins (see above), resorts, bed-and-breakfasts, and vacation home rentals. An example of what is possible is White Sulphur Springs Ranch, a gorgeous restored home from the 1800s near the town of Clio, featuring wonderful food and a great view of a huge mountain meadow that fronts the back wall of the Sierra. It also has a swimming pool filled with natural mineral waters. The selection includes Bidwell House, Chester; Feather Bed, Quincy; High Country Inn, Sierra City; New England Ranch, Quincy; Paxton Lodge, Feather River Canyon; 20 Mile House, Cromberg.

Hiking: The view from Mount Elwell (elevation 7,812 feet) can make you feel as if you are being baptized by mountain beauty. To be so blessed requires a climb of 1,100 feet over the course of three miles, after which you are rewarded with a spectacular view of the Lakes Basin, a landscape of granite, pine forest, and lakes strewn about like one gem after another. This is one of many stellar hikes in the region. The easiest hike with a big payoff is the one-mile round-trip walk to Frazier Falls; the most dramatic is to the Sierra Buttes lookout (from the Packsaddle Campground trailhead), which includes walking up stairs that jut out over thousands of feet of open air. The selections are Elwell Lakes, Eureka Peak, Frazier Falls, Lakes Basin Recreation Area, Pacific Crest Trail, Sand Pond Interpretive Trail, Sierra Buttes, Upper Sardine Lake.

Lakes: The trademark of the Lakes Basin Recreation Area is its pristine mountain lakes set in rock basins, where the water is pure, clear, and often full of trout, and the size is ideal for owners of small boats. There are also much bigger lakes available, the largest being Davis Lake is and Lake Almanor, ideal for powerboating, sailing, skiing, and fishing for big trout. In all, 15 lakes can be reached by car and nearly 100 are accessible by trail. The selections are to the drive-to lakes: Almanor, Antelope, Bucks, Butt, Crystal, Davis, Eureka, Frenchman, Gold, Little Grass Valley, Madora, Round Valley, Silver, Snake, Three Lakes.

Golf courses: I don't play golf, but if I lived here, I might learn (well, on the other hand . . .) because there are eight golf courses available. Most are in high mountain meadow settings with great views, lush greens, and a reputation for players who appreciate the beauty. The feature course is Whitehawk Ranch, located five miles south of the town of Graeagle; the highlight is the views of the Sierra Buttes. The selections are Graeagle Meadows, Feather River Inn, Feather River Park, Lake Almanor Country Club, Lake Almanor West, Mount Huff, Plumas Pines, Whitehawk Ranch.

Horseback riding: Consider that 75 percent of Plumas County is public land managed by the U.S. Forest Service, covering nearly 2,000 square miles. That translates to hundreds of destinations for horseback riding. The best summer trip is out of Gold Lake Stables, where riders have a choice of day or overnight trips; in either case, you can visit dozens of hidden backcountry lakes. The selections are Bucks Lake Stables, Gold Lakes Stables, Graeagle Stables, Plumas Pines Stables (Lake Almanor), Western Adventures (Portola).

Contact: For a travel packet (specify your interests), phone (800) 326-2247, or write to the Plumas County Visitors Bureau, P.O. Box 4120, Quincy, CA 95971.

Locator: (C3).

• FEATURED TRIP •

✶ TOMALES BAY

Rated: The Top 50 Parks, 7; The Top 10 Spots for a First Kiss, 180

TOMALES BAY STATE PARK is an ideal example of a quiet, secluded area within close range of millions of Bay Area residents. While thousands of weekenders might descend on POINT REYES, MUIR WOODS, or STINSON BEACH, nearby TOMALES BAY remains relatively undisturbed by anything except the small waves lapping against the shore.

The wide sandy beaches are a prime attraction for family picnics, and during minus tides, clamming is often outstanding. Hiking, surf fishing for perch, and cross-country running are also popular. Cartop boats can be launched in the quiet surf.

The state park is on the Point Reyes Peninsula on the west side of TOMALES BAY, with more than 1,000 acres within park boundaries. The retreat seems much larger, however, since it is bordered by the POINT REYES NATIONAL SEASHORE.

Here's a good secret to know: Inverness Ridge acts as a blockade to much of the wind and fog that hammers away at the Pacific coast. So when POINT REYES is buried in a rolling, 10 mph fog, TOMALES BAY can be warm and sunny.

The best hike here is on the Jepson Trail, a 6.5-mile trek that crosses through one of the largest remaining virgin stands of Bishop pine trees in California. About 70 percent of the park is filled with pine, oak, and madrone. In this habitat, you can see foxes, raccoons, badgers, weasels, and mule deer.

Clamming is another option. Bring a shovel and pick a good minus tide. When the tide goes out, you will see acres of prime clam beds loaded with cockles. Two of the best spots are south of Heart's Desire Beach and north of Indian Beach. Be certain to have a fishing license and a measuring device, and adhere to the limit of 50 cockles. Wardens commonly cite clammers for not having licenses, which usually results in a fine of $50 to $300; the exact amount depends on the mood of the Marin County judge. You can get a fishing license at the fishing department of sporting goods stores and at most tackle shops.

On high and incoming tides, perch fishing can spice up an otherwise lazy day at the beach. Because of the relatively calm surf in the bay, giant surf rods are not necessary, although long, medium-weight rods can certainly help in attaining long casts.

If you choose to launch a cartop boat from the beach, it is not advisable to head out to the mouth of TOMALES BAY. Just south of the black buoy there, the water is quite shallow and can become very choppy with just a 15-knot wind.

Most folks, however, are content to explore the wooded areas or soak up the sun in relative isolation. That's how it is when you discover a place that seems to be one of the Bay Area's best-kept secrets.

Directions: From San Francisco, drive north on U.S. 101 to San Rafael. Take the Sir Francis Drake Boulevard exit and head west. Continue on Sir Francis Drake Boulevard five miles past Inverness to Pierce Point Road. Turn right to enter the park. **Trip tip:** If you want to fish or clam, check tides carefully; high, incoming tides are best for perch, and minus tides are best for clamming. Dogs are not allowed on the beach or the trails. **Fees:** A $5 per vehicle state park access fee is charged. **Contact:** Tomales Bay State Park, Star Route, Inverness, CA 94937; (415) 669-1140. California State Parks, Marin District, (415) 893-1580. **Locator:** (E1a).

• FEATURED TRIP •

ALCATRAZ ISLAND

Rated: The Top 25 Hikes, 2; The Top 4 Islands, 176; The Top 5 Bay Boat Tours, 208

My name ain't Al Capone, but on one winter afternoon, I turned into an outlaw at ALCATRAZ.

Instead of *Escape from Alcatraz,* we undertook our own raid, to capture and leave with a piece of history. On a cold, still day, the kind where coots bob around like little black corks on the surface of SAN FRANCISCO BAY, we moored a boat just off the southeastern shore of ALCATRAZ, then paddled ashore in a small raft. After hiding the raft, we scrambled up the slope, then bushwhacked around to the south side of the island, which has long been off-limits to all, including Capone's ghost.

Perched on a clifftop, the bay rolling below us, we scanned what has to be the most awesome city skyline in the world. Framed on each side by the GOLDEN GATE BRIDGE and the BAY BRIDGE, fronted by water and wharves, backed by hills and high-rises, this was like visiting another world.

It turns out that nearly the same route my outlaw partner and I took years ago in our secret invasion is now the newest trail in the Bay Area, opened in 1995 by the Golden Gate National Recreation Area. Known as the Agave Trail, it opens one-third of the island previously closed even to legal visitors, and provides some of the greatest views of any of the 15,000 miles of hiking trails in the Bay Area.

The trip starts with a ferryboat ride with the Red and White Fleet from Pier 41 in SAN FRANCISCO. The cost is $7.75, which includes the ride, access to the prison, and entrance to what had long been the forbidden zone. For $11, you are also provided with a headset and cassette tape for an audio tour of the island. Discounts are available for children and seniors. Note that they always pitch the $11 price as if it were the standard rate, but you can beat it.

The trip is pretty enough that you might even forget Al Capone's shadow force is somewhere haunting the island—but not quite. The fact that ALCATRAZ was once the assigned hell for America's most heinous criminals, and the fact that many of them died here, are always just a thought away, as is the abandoned prison.

That is why an excursion to ALCATRAZ ISLAND can provide an eerie walk through history, along with the rewards of a ferry ride, great views, good bird-watching, and memories that stay with you. The old prison is always a feature, of course, with Capone's ghost casting a spell over some visitors, but this new trail provides another compelling reason to come.

The Agave Trail starts at the ferry landing, located on the east side of ALCATRAZ, then traces the rim of the island to its southern tip, shielded by trees and seemingly distant from the cell block. The trail is quite wide, with a few benches and some bulletproof concrete picnic tables providing sweeping views of both the East Bay and San Francisco. The trail was named after the agave plant, which is common here.

If you visit during a low tide, you can explore further and discover some relatively little-known tidepools at the southwest corner of the island. This part of the island also has an abundance of bird life, including a population of night herons, friendly little fellows that look like their heads are sitting right on their shoulders. For pure cuteness, they're right up there with chipmunks and baby ducks.

From its southern tip, the trail is routed back to the historic parade ground atop the island, with some masterpiece sculpture work that includes 110 stone steps. The parade ground is a nesting spot for birds, so this area is closed to the public from February to August each year so the birds will not be disturbed.

The prison is located at the center of the island, with other buildings sprinkled along the eastern shore and the northern tip. After reaching Alcatraz at the ferry dock, the first building you see is Building 64, the second largest structure on the island after the main prison cell block.

In time, the northern tip of the island will also likely be opened to visitors for the first time. Several improvements may be funded by visitor fees. Right now, there is an old, abandoned power plant and bakery, and two prison buildings in relatively decent shape.

Fees: The ferry ride costs $7.75 for adults, $4.50 for children 5 to 11, and $6 for seniors 62 and over. **Audio tour:** The cost is $11 for adults, $5.75 for children 5 to 11, and $9.25 for seniors 62 and over. This includes the round-trip ferryboat ride and a Walkman headset with cassette tape for an audio tour of the cell house. **Charge by phone:** To charge tickets by phone, for an additional service charge, call (415) 705-5555. **Ferry departures:** From Pier 41 in San Francisco with the Blue and Gold Fleet, departing daily at 9:30 a.m. and every half hour thereafter to 4:15 p.m. Late tours ($17.75 per adult) can be scheduled on Thursdays through Sundays. **Contact:** Blue and Gold Fleet, (415) 705-5555; National Park Service Information Line, (415) 556-0560. **Locator:** Alcatraz Island (E1b).

• Featured Trip •

Fisherman's Wharf

Rated: San Francisco's Biggest Tourist Draw; The Top 9 Places to Bird-Watch, 252; The Top 10 Places to View Wildlife, 257; The Top 14 Places to Fly Kites, 389

San Francisco's once-legendary Fisherman's Wharf is now running a distant second to Monterey in terms of cleanliness and class. But it's nothing that can't be fixed.

Fisherman's Wharf in San Francisco is one of the biggest tourist draws on the West Coast, and a center for sport and commercial fishing. It still has just enough sizzle to keep it ranked near the top, but enough problems to make it a second-class experience compared to that at Monterey.

The best thing going at the wharf is the smell of crab, that sweet aroma that can stay with you for days after taking in a few deep breaths of it. The next best thing is the taste of San Francisco's sourdough bread, which just plain can't be duplicated anywhere. The two in combination, crab and bread, give the wharf a special character no visitor ever forgets. With its views of SAN FRANCISCO BAY, ALCATRAZ, and the GOLDEN GATE BRIDGE, its great restaurants, and bay cruises, "THE WHARF" will always be a premier attraction for newcomers.

Though parking can be expensive (I paid $21 one day from 5:30 a.m. to 5:30 p.m.), the main parking garage here has worked out a system of discounts for customers who validate their tickets at fishing boats or wharf-side retail shops. For instance, people who arrive early to go fishing then leave before 5 p.m. are charged only $4.

Other nice touches are the recent additions to the nearby south at Pier 39, including Underwater World, and the crisp paint jobs of the adjacent stores.

Underwater World is unusual enough to make it an attraction in itself, a submerged aquarium with acrylic tunnels that allow visitors to walk through 700,000 gallons of San Francisco Bay. That gives you a seal's-eye view of all kinds of fish and marine creatures. Admission is $12.95 for adults, with a family ticket for four available for $29.95.

The sharp look at Pier 39 stands in stark contrast to the stores adjacent to the main wharf area. Saying it looks tacky is being kind, as the predominant storefronts are a series of vapid-looking shops, one after another, selling mostly trinkets and T-shirts. There are no fishing shops of any kind.

FISHERMAN'S WHARF needs a lot more "Fish" in the "Fisherman." Off-loading of catches, for example, can be a dramatic affair for tourists, kind of like feeding time at the zoo. At other ports, such as in San Diego, the arrival of the boats after a day at sea is a gala event, but here it's more like a period at the end of a sentence. For the most part during the day, the wharf looks like a bunch of boats tied up and most visitors have no idea of the spectacle that awaits when the fishermen return with their catch in the afternoon.

Some repair work is also needed. Along the back row of the boats, there is a horrific 30-foot broken-off section of wooden walkway with water below that has been fenced off like a condemned building. Like most of the problems at the wharf, this could be fixed easily.

We arrived at dawn for the opening of salmon season and were greeted by the sight of trash everywhere. Along the wharf area alone, there were a dozen trash cans that were either overflowing from not being emptied or had been dumped on the street by bums looking for food. At one spot, just across from the boat docking area, there was even a guy sitting on the curb next to a big trash pile, picking through all the garbage, while arriving fishermen pretended not to notice.

By afternoon, when the winds out of the west started to swirl, small piles of paper trash were blown all about the wharf area, not just along the main drag, but even aside some of the great restaurants and along the piers and boat landings. In general, it looked cheap and dumpy, while in comparison, Monterey's Fisherman's Wharf is as clean as my mom's polished kitchen floor.

While trash is the most glaring eyesore, it is also the most easily solved. A city crew could have the wharf washed, scrubbed, and cleaned up by the weekend, and nightly trash bin pickups could keep it that way. Many of the problems could be solved just as easily.

When I left FISHERMAN'S WHARF, the strongest memories should have been the smell of crab, the beauty of the bay, the fish I had caught, and the taste of sourdough bread. Instead I keep remembering the sight of a man sitting on the curb, going through a mound of trash dumped on the street, with a line of trinket shops in the background.

Directions: Fisherman's Wharf is located off of Jefferson Street and the Embarcadero, west of Pier 45, between Taylor and Jones Streets. **Locator:** SAN FRANCISCO (E1b).

• FEATURED TRIP •

HALF MOON BAY

Rated: The Top 25 Hikes, 2; The Top 5 Places to Beach Camp, 108; The Top 10 Spots to Go on a Date, 182; The Top 22 Water Adventures, 311; The Top 12 Windsurfing Locations, 315; The Top 7 Deep-Sea Fishing Trips, 330

Done right, this is a place for exceptional adventuring, hiking, beachcombing, fishing, boating, and eating. Done wrong, though, and you might as well stay tied up at home and get out the Alpo.

To make it work, all you have to do is one little thing: Get there early on weekends and beat the Highway 1 traffic, which has a way of gumming up by late morning and hampering the trip. To make it work great, you just have to do one more little thing: Make a reservation at a restaurant. Do neither, and you will be caught in traffic and then have to wait an hour to get a table—leaving you feeling as if someone just snapped "Bad dog!" and forced you to sit in the corner for a couple hours with no bone.

Rather than getting a bone, the highlight here is the continued rebirth of Pillar Point Harbor, once a dump of a place and now a stellar destination. There are also several beautiful beach walks, PURISIMA CREEK REDWOODS just south of town, and a mélange of adventures and restaurants. But make no mistake, the traffic problems on the roads leading here, Highway 1 from SAN FRANCISCO and Highway 92 from the Peninsula and HAYWARD, inspire the wise few to set out early on Saturday or Sunday, or during noncommuter times on weekdays, to avoid facing a trip that feels more like being locked in a dog kennel.

The harbor at PRINCETON has become the prime destination, of course, with most people attracted to the restaurants and the harbor views. I've eaten at all the restaurants here, and though several have stunning settings and beautiful accommodations, the best calamari in town is at this little hole-in-the-wall called Barbara's Fish Trap, where on weekends there is typically a large crowd waiting outside to get in (and that's not even counting all the cats).

My favorite beach walk in the Bay Area is near here, on the northwest side of the harbor. The parking area and trailhead are located below the giant satellite radar station at Pillar Point, on the left side of the station's access road. After parking, you stroll on a bluff overlooking the most secluded section of the harbor, with a quiet beach and lots of grebes, pelicans, cormorants, and other birds, and head out to the north jetty. Here you turn right and discover a beautiful, hidden beach, with seals often playing in the nearby kelp beds. You can continue all the way out to the point, rock-hopping your way on boulders in tide waters.

The renovation of Pillar Point Harbor is one of the Bay Area's best success stories. In the 1980s, it was a disaster, filthy from some careless commercial fishermen, with only a few slow old boats available for party boat fishing and the nearshore fisheries largely cleaned out from gillnetting. The line for the little boat ramp often extended for a mile on Saturday mornings, and there was no place to park.

All that has changed. The place has been cleaned up, and when afternoon sunlight sends silvers across the water, it practically shimmers like an old trophy polished bright. The handful of problem commercial guys were either arrested for whatever and shipped to the dog pound, or replaced by individuals with a higher sense of ethics. All gillnetting was banned and the fisheries have come back. But there's more.

The harbor was completely overhauled and now features a great six-lane boat ramp, hundreds of new dock slips, an inner jetty to keep ocean surge to a minimum, and a large parking area. As fisheries rebounded from the ban on gill nets, new captains and boat operators arrived, bringing with them a dozen first-class sportfishing boats, fast and clean; now a wide variety of trips are offered, including shallow-water specials where anglers can use light tackle for maximum excitement. Whale watching has become a sensational attraction as well.

Even the ability to get reliable fishing information has changed, with a shop called the Marine Warehouse offering the best free fishing hot line in California (650) 728-0627.

The harbor naturally attracts quite a few people, especially on Sunday afternoons, but it is possible to enjoy a hike or visit to a more remote, solitary area, followed up with a dinner at one of the harbor restaurants, thereby getting the best of both worlds.

The best option for seclusion is PURISIMA CREEK REDWOODS OPEN SPACE PRESERVE, located just south of the town of HALF MOON BAY. It features 2,633 acres of parkland, much of it redwoods, ferns, and sorrel, with a pretty creek in the canyon. To get there, from Highway 1, turn east on Higgins Purisima Road and drive four miles to the parking area. In just a few minutes, the change that occurs can be a stunner for newcomers, with the road crossing a field, entering a valley, winding into a canyon, then suddenly arriving in a redwood grove. This is where you park, with a signed trailhead and small hiking maps available.

Just strolling in from here for 15 minutes on the Whittemore Gulch Trail can be very satisfying, walking along the creek in a fern grotto shaded by a redwood canopy. If you prefer a real hike, just keep going. The trail climbs 1,600 feet over the course of 2.2 miles to Skyline Boulevard, rising out of the redwood-filled canyon for occasional breathtaking views of the ocean and Pillar Point Harbor.

Other options? You might head to the FITZGERALD MARINE RESERVE in MOSS BEACH, or to the northern end of MONTARA at MCNEE RANCH STATE PARK. If you want someone else's feet to do the work, horse rentals are available just north of HALF MOON BAY, on the west side of Highway 1.

Depending on which eye you look out of, the San Mateo County coast can provide something you might be searching for. Out of one eye, you might see the HALF MOON BAY coast as something of an anachronism, with its small town, dirt streets, cowboys on horseback, and sprawling fields of Brussels sprouts. It may seem like you've stepped into an earlier time. But out the other eye, you could see quite a different picture: expensive seaside restaurants, crowded roads, and on sunny days, beaches packed with folks.

Because HALF MOON BAY can satisfy people with opposite interests, it has become one of the most popular places for a weekend visit.

Directions: From San Francisco, drive south on Interstate 280 for 19 miles to the Highway 92 cutoff. Drive west on Highway 92 to Half Moon Bay. **Fishing:** Deep-sea and salmon fishing trips are offered at Pillar Point Harbor by Huck Finn Sportfishing, (650) 726-7133, and Captain John's Sportfishing, (650) 726-2913. Trips cost in the $30 to $45 range. **Parks:** The Fitzgerald Marine Reserve is located in Moss Beach, with a well-signed turnoff on Highway 1. Access is free. For information, phone (650) 728-3584. **Horseback Riding:** Rent horses at Sea Horse Ranch and Friendly Acres, (650) 726-9871 or (650) 726-9903. **Camping:** Campsites are available on a first-come, first-served basis through Half Moon Bay State Park. **Contact:** Half Moon Bay State Park, (650) 726-8819; Half Moon Bay Chamber of Commerce, (650) 726-8380. **Locator:** HALF MOON BAY (E1b).

• FEATURED TRIP •

★ THE PHLEGER ESTATE

Rated: The Newest Public Land

Imagine this scene: A bobcat stalking a cottontail creeps through the high grass. In a nearby meadow, a dozen deer graze in silence, the only sound in the air being the chattering of squirrels playing tag nearby on a 150-year-old oak. A red-tailed hawk circles overhead, using rising thermals to stay aloft without a wing beat. Along an adjacent dirt path, little birds hiding under bushes make crunch-crunch sounds as they hop around on old leaves.

A small stream pours crystalline water down the center of a densely wooded canyon, with refracted sunlight sifting through the branches of madrones, oaks, and redwoods. You take a deep breath and taste the pureness, you smell the scent of woods and water, and before long, every cell in your body starts to feel alive.

These are my recollections of an early summer day spent exploring in some beautiful off-limits Peninsula wildlands to which I was fortunate enough to have been granted access. It turns out, however, that this area recently was opened to the public when it became part of the Golden Gate National Recreation Area.

Known as the PHLEGER ESTATE, it is located in the WOODSIDE foothills on the San Francisco Peninsula, just a minute's drive from Interstate 280 near Edgewood and Cañada Roads. The land covers 1,257 acres of forest and watershed from Skyline to 280, long considered a forbidden paradise for travelers scanning it from the highway.

Its conversion to parkland completed the missing link of unbroken Peninsula greenbelt from SOUTH SAN FRANCISCO to SAN JOSE. Hiking north to south, it is now possible to walk from SWEENEY RIDGE above SAN BRUNO all the way to Portola Valley; hiking east to west will get you from Edgewood Park in Redwood City all the way to the outskirts of Half Moon Bay at Purisima Creek Redwoods.

In the process, a small group of conservationists is proving once and for all that a great way to protect unique natural areas such as this is to buy them. That has been the strategy of the Peninsula Open Space Trust, an organization with about 3,000 members. The group is headed by Audrey Rust, a persistent woman who understands the financial realities of conservation.

When Mary Phleger died in December of 1991, she left behind this vast wonderland. You don't need to be a developer with a cash register for a brain to figure out that subdividing it into 50 25-acre parcels, then building homes worth $4 million on each one, could offer a developer the chance to clear $100 million or so in a few years. But before she died, Phleger and her family asked the Peninsula Open Space Trust to make a competitive bid against three commercial real estate outfits; a little while later, the Phleger family selected a bid of $25 million from the trust. Key cooperation has come from private donations, the trust's revolving land acquisition fund, a grant from the Save the Redwoods League, the sale of the property's mansion, and funding by the U.S. Congress. As a result the property was able to join the Golden Gate National Recreation Area as public parkland.

For most of the 1900s, this piece of property has remained hidden and protected behind a massive stone gate. While no longer a secret, it appears it will always remain protected.

"Keeping the western hillsides and coastal plains in open space is not just for human enjoyment," Rust told me before the land was opened to the public. "We are also meeting the very real needs of the wild inhabitants who share this special place with us. The purchase of the Phleger property will accomplish two missions. It will create a corridor for people trails, and it will increase the total number of protected wild acres that support a myriad of creatures."

"We are only a few, but we try hard to do what we do," she said. "It is very satisfying to know we are protecting beautiful, wild places forever. You can go out and kick the dirt and know you had something to do with protecting it."

Anyone who has driven Interstate 280 in the Peninsula foothills has likely gazed at this piece of land and wondered what it is like. In the summer, you can watch from a distance as wisps of fog slip down the slopes, working their way across the miles of treetops. It is impressive from an airplane, where the solid band of humanity on the Bay Area flatlands gives way to less populated foothills, then to virtual wilderness, with woodlands, creeks, and lakes hidden in canyons.

It is by foot, though, that you really start to discover the magic of the place. A redwood forest has a feel like no other; it's a place for old souls who like old things. Below the giant forest canopy are cradles of ferns, beds of crunchy old redwood leaves, three-leafed clover, mushrooms, and banana slugs. It is a cool, quiet place, where you can find pleasure in just sitting against the trunk of a tree and letting nature's artistry sink in while your cares drift away.

Out here there are no winners and

no losers, no heroes and no bums, only visitors who share a pristine environment, then leave it as they found it.

Directions: From San Francisco, take Interstate 280 south and exit at Edgewood Road. Turn west and continue to the end of the road. **Contact:** For a map and brochure, contact the Peninsula Open Space Trust, 3000 Sand Hill Road, Building 4, Suite 135, Menlo Park, CA 94025; (650) 854-7696. For information, call the Golden Gate National Recreation Area, (415) 239-2366. **Locator:** MENLO PARK (E1b).

• FEATURED TRIP •

THE PRESIDIO

Rated: The Top 4 Walks in San Francisco, 23; The Top 10 Spots to Go on a Date, 182; The Top 9 Doggy Getaway Ideas, 196

Whether viewed by air or by car, or explored on foot or bike, it is easy to see that the PRESIDIO is a piece of land like no other and that it gives SAN FRANCISCO a dimension like no other big city in the world.

I started a tour of SAN FRANCISCO with an overflight, taking my little plane across its western edge, 2,000 feet over the GOLDEN GATE BRIDGE, scanning across The City with its rows of buildings, hills, and high-rises, waterfront, and bridges. What stands out most, however, are the two swaths of greenery, the long strip that makes up Golden Gate Park and the 1,500 acres at the PRESIDIO on the San Francisco Headlands.

From the air, the Presidio looks like an island of greenery, bordered by ocean and bay to the west and north, and houses and asphalt to the east and south. The idea that 750,000 people can live virtually minutes from such a wild and beautiful place is another factor that makes SAN FRANCISCO singular among the big cities of the West.

By car, the contrast is just as striking. On one visit, I was stuck in a line of cars heading to the GOLDEN GATE BRIDGE on Lombard Street, when looking straight ahead, above the cars, the dense cypress and eucalyptus forests on the hills of the PRESIDIO came into view. It only took a few minutes to leave that line of traffic on Lombard, park, and start wandering amid that forest, hiking with my puppy.

My idea of comfort is a pair of old Levi's, a pickup truck, and a mutt that loves me. I'd rather read about Jesse James than Jesse Helms. So when the debate started over whether or not to convert the PRESIDIO from an army base to a national park, my first reaction was "Who cares?" Now that I've explored the place, turns out that I do.

I have a lot of favorite places at the PRESIDIO, spots for heart-stopping views of SAN FRANCISCO BAY, hidden picnics, great hikes with my dog, or cruising on a bike. Tourists and newcomers are often more attracted to the historical monuments such as the two awesome bronze cannons that are some 300 years old, or the old military buildings.

Since the PRESIDIO was handed over from the military to the National Park Service, it has not changed much visually. The bigger changes are in administration, a much-improved visitor center, with most of the future plans centering around how to manage the buildings and office space.

Newcomers should stop first at the visitor center, where you can get a small park map that details the location of the Presidio's historical attractions, trails, and roads.

The Park Service offers guided tours on the main Post Walk, a one-mile trip that takes about an hour. It makes 12 stops, highlights 200 years of history and architecture, and comes with an excellent 10-page guidebook that details the history and attractions of each featured site. This is one of the best introductions you could ask for to the PRESIDIO. It starts with a vision of the PRESIDIO land of 200 years ago, when grizzly bears still bounded down to the beachfront, and ties the architecture to the land's continuing evolution, the bronze cannons dating from the late 1600s at the original Spanish Presidio . . . a cannonball embedded in the west-facing wall of the blockhouse . . . the barracks where Indian fighters were housed after the Civil War.

Seeing these once can be enough, however, and for a return trip the views, picnic spots, hikes, and beauty are much more inspiring. One of the best examples of a great hidden spot at the PRESIDIO is a picnic site located a quarter-mile uphill from Fort Point. You walk up a dirt path that enters a cypress grove and continues to the picnic site on the edge of a bluff, from which there are postcard views of SAN FRANCISCO BAY.

The best-known part of the PRESIDIO is its shoreline frontage, from Crissy Field to Fort Point, which has become one of the most popular jogging courses in America, running along on Golden Gate Promenade. There's an excellent par course available here as well.

Here's a great trip: Park at the Fort Point Administrative Office, then walk along the shore of the bay, absorbing the remarkable beauty: the GOLDEN GATE BRIDGE, SAN FRANCISCO BAY, passing ships, and across the water to ALCATRAZ, MARIN, and SAUSALITO. When you're ready, tromp up the hill to find that surprise picnic spot and enjoy the views some more.

What is even lesser known are the easy and pretty walks routed amid the Presidio's miniature forest, in all, 11 miles of hiking trails and 14 miles of bike routes. They can be simple or extensive. On one visit, for instance, after parking adjacent to the Presidio Golf Course, I went for a walk with my little bear cub of a doggy, about a 45-minute loop, dropping into the forest, looping down into a grassy opening, then returning uphill. Many giant cypress, annual spring greenery, a few blooming poppies, and a pretty garden filled with blooming flowers (located adjacent to the tennis court) make this a first-class way to spend an hour.

This is a favorite dog walk, and friendly doggies that can be controlled by command are allowed to run free, off leash. This is also a destination of choice for San Francisco's resident professional dog walkers, and if you are lucky, you might even see a half dozen or so pups running free, so happy to be outside, literally having a field day.

Two other excellent walks are the Lover's Lane/Ecology Trail and the Coastal Trail. The Lover's Lane/Ecology Trail is a popular hike because it starts next to the Presidio Museum, so many people come upon it by accident. It is pretty, routed through eucalyptus trees, then heading past Inspiration Point before looping back to the museum. A picnic site near the trailhead is a bonus.

The Coastal Trail is famous among San Francisco hikers, a walk that extends along coastal bluffs between the GOLDEN GATE BRIDGE and Baker Beach, passing half a dozen military batteries and providing great views. I've hiked this in both directions, and my preference is to park at Baker Beach, then head north. On clear days, the GOLDEN GATE BRIDGE can feel so close it's as if you could open your arms and gather it all in.

Out here, it can seem like you are a million miles away from the asphalt of a big city. The PRESIDIO is my favorite place in SAN FRANCISCO.

Directions from Marin: Drive over the Golden Gate Bridge to SAN FRANCISCO on U.S. 101 and take the Marina exit. Stay to the right as it feeds into Richardson. In about half a mile, turn right on Lombard Street. Drive up two blocks and enter through the Lombard Gate of the Presidio, where the road becomes Lincoln Boulevard. Follow Lincoln to Montgomery at the Main Post. The visitor center is at Building 102.

Directions from the East Bay: Drive over the Bay Bridge to San Francisco on Interstate 80. Take U.S. 101 north and follow it into the city, past Van Ness Avenue to the next street, Franklin. Turn right on Franklin and drive about 20 blocks to Lombard Street. Turn left on Lombard, stay in the left lane, and drive to the Lombard Gate of the Presidio, where the road becomes Lincoln Boulevard. Follow Lincoln to Montgomery at the Main Post. The visitor center is at Building 102.

Directions from the Peninsula: Take Interstate 280 into San Francisco to 19th Avenue. Follow 19th through San Francisco toward the Golden Gate Bridge. Just before the bridge—be sure to be in the far right lane—take the Marina exit onto Richardson. In about half a mile, turn right on Lombard Street. Drive two blocks and enter the Lombard Gate of the Presidio, where the road becomes Lincoln Boulevard. Continue on Lincoln to Montgomery at the Main Post. The visitor center is at Building 102.

By bus in San Francisco: The San Francisco Muni bus line runs a regular route (43 Masonic) that stops at Letterman Army Medical Center, about a half-mile walk from the Presidio Visitor Center. For information, call, (415) 673-MUNI/6864.

Contact: Presidio Visitor Center (open daily 10 a.m. to 5 p.m.; an excellent map is available here), (415) 561-4323. **Locator:** SAN FRANCISCO (E1b).

• FEATURED TRIP •

ANTHONY CHABOT REGIONAL PARK

Rated: The Top 50 Parks, 7; The Top 10 Strolls, 40; The Top 6 Lakeshore Camps, 116; The Top 10 Spots for a First Kiss, 180; The Top 16 East Bay Lakes, 205; The Top 16 Places to Rent Boats, 305; The Top 22 Water Adventures, 311; The Top 43 Lakes to Fish, 333

Okay, so you don't have anything to do this weekend. If you venture over to Chabot Regional Park, you'll find something better to do than watching Bonanza reruns.

This park covers 5,000 acres, with 31 miles of hiking trails and a fish-filled lake with nine miles of shoreline. Want more? There is also horseback riding, boating, camping, a marksmanship range for target practice, bicycling, and picnic activities such as horseshoes and volleyball.

Chabot is in the East Bay hills above CASTRO VALLEY, a few miles east of Interstate 580. Some folks pronounce Chabot so it rhymes with "habit," but the right way is "shuh-BOWE," after Anthony Chabot. He was a pioneer California philanthropist who created Lake Chabot in the 1890s by building a dam across San Leandro Creek. Some 100 years later, the lake is still the centerpiece of the park. It provides a close-to-home fishing hole and receives special stocks of rainbow trout.

You can rent an aluminum boat with an electric motor and head over to Vasco, Indian Point, or Coot Landing, the best fishing spots in the area. Honker Bay is another good spot, especially for crappie.

If you just want to paddle around the lake, rowboats and canoes are available for rent at the marina. If that isn't enough for you, there are lots of other options.

One of the better deals is the Lakeside Trail, which starts at the marina and traces much of the shoreline. It is paved, so it is accessible to bicyclists and wheelchair users.

If your idea of hiking isn't walking on pavement, then take a look at the Chabot map that details 31 miles of hiking trails. The park is distinguished by a long, grassy valley, bordered both to the east and west by ridges. Select one of the 16 trails, head off up a ridge, and you'll get a workout and some seclusion. If you want to do some real tromping, the East Bay Skyline National Trail runs the length of the park and connects northward to a network of six other regional parks. Up along the ridge-line, the cities in the East Bay flats seem quite distant.

If you want to get the feeling of isolation without doing all the legwork yourself, horse rentals are available. If you're new to the saddle, don't worry. Inexperienced riders will find that most of the rental horses are really tame and seem to go on automatic pilot. When the hour is almost up, an inner alarm clock goes off and back they go to the barn. They know where the hay is, and it sure as heck isn't out there on the trail.

Most people who go to Chabot Park do so for an afternoon or evening picnic and parlay fishing, hiking, or horseback riding into the trip. But you can do it one better, because Chabot has a nice campground with 75 spacious sites that provide plenty of elbow room, even when they are filled.

At the campground, 63 of the sites are for tents and 12 have full hookups for RVs. Piped water, fireplaces, and tables are provided at each site, and toilets and showers are available. It's one of the few Bay Area campgrounds that has a lake nearby.

Unexpectedly pleasant things happen at this park. A few years ago, for instance, a 17-pound, two-ounce bass was caught here. It was the biggest bass caught in Northern California history.

Directions: Take Interstate 580 to San Leandro, then head east on Fairmont Drive, which goes over a ridge and merges with Lake Chabot Road. **Fees:** A $3 parking fee is charged. The fishing permit fee is also $3. Campsite fees vary depending on the type of site. **Fishing:** A California fishing license is required, along with a one-day Chabot fishing permit, which is used to purchase future fish stocks. Kids under 16 don't need either. **Boat rentals:** Aluminum boats with electric motors are available for rent. For more information, phone Lake Chabot Marina, (510) 582-2198. **Hiking:** Maps are available at the Lake Chabot Marina Coffee Shop, or you can phone the East Bay Regional Park

District, (510) 635-0135 extension 2200. **Camping:** Reservations can be made through the park; phone (510) 562-2267. **Horseback riding:** Horse rentals are available for ages 13 and up. Phone the Chabot Equestrian Center, (510) 569-4428. **Marksmanship range:** Access for shooting sports is available for ages 17 and up. For hours and fees, phone the Chabot Gun Club, (510) 569-0213. **Contact:** For general information, call the East Bay Regional Park District, (510) 635-0135 extension 2200. **Locator:** LAKE CHABOT (E1c).

• FEATURED TRIP •

LAKE TAHOE

Rated: The Top 50 Base Camps, 110; The Top 16 Lakes with Cabin Rentals, 177; The Top 2 Places to Mountain Bike at Tahoe, 282; The Top 4 Places for Kids to Ski, 294; The Top 25 Lakes, 307

The natural laws of gravity don't seem to apply at the casinos at LAKE TAHOE. Although the gaming tables are perfectly level, your money always seems to slip out of your hands and into the grasp of a blackjack dealer. Those wary of this phenomenon know that the best bet you can make at TAHOE is to minimize your time at the casinos and instead take your chances with the fishing, boating, and hiking.

The excitement, adventure, and remarkable natural beauty of LAKE TAHOE make this the number one weekend vacation destination for Californians. Just make sure you come home with your shirt; a lot of people don't.

TAHOE is, as Mark Twain called it, "the Lake in the Sky," a natural wonder set amid miles of national forest at an elevation of 6,000 feet. A true gem, it is colored the deepest blue of any lake in the state. A definite tinge of mystery surrounds the lake. Just how deep is it? Scientists claim TAHOE is 1,648 feet deep, yet some old-timers say it is bottomless. The fact that boats and airplanes have disappeared in the lake, never to be seen again, seems to support the latter theory.

When it comes to fishing, there is a lot less mystery. Big Mackinaw, rainbow, and brown trout, along with kokanee salmon, attract anglers from throughout the Pacific Northwest. However, newcomers to TAHOE are usually quite surprised at the techniques used to catch these monsters.

The big fish, the Mackinaws, are deep at TAHOE, and sportfishing boat skippers use downriggers to troll 180 to 260 feet down. Your fishing line is clipped to a separate reel of wire line and a 10-pound weight, and both lines descend to the trolling depth. When you get a strike, your line pops free of the release clip on the weighted line and you fight the fish free of any lead weight. Skippers troll just off the edge of the underwater shelf, using lures such as J-plugs. Be on the water at first light, because the bite is often kaput by 10 a.m., or fish when the moon is in its dark cycles.

Some locals in small boats score with rainbow and brown trout by trolling near the surface in coves. They use Rapala minnows or a flasher/night crawler combination. But for the big trout, you have to go deep, way deep.

Timber Cove Marina, which is closer to the Stateline area, offers boat tours and scuba diving, in addition to fishing trips.

A tremendous number of campgrounds, motels, and resorts ring the lake, but reservations are still a must in the summer.

If you want to break free from the crowds, visit in the fall. I love the darn place in the fall. The traffic is sparse, the lake is its deepest cobalt blue of the year, and you can have some of the most scenic hiking trails in the world virtually to yourself. In addition, from mid-September until late November (when the ski parks open) is considered the off-season here. Visitors can get the best rates of the year at cabins, hotels, and casinos, even rock bottom for TAHOE if you stay at least two nights, Sunday through Thursday.

No lake on Earth is prettier than TAHOE in early autumn. Yeah, there are some fall colors thanks to a sprinkling of aspens, mountain alders, and willows mixed in a pine forest, but the lake itself seems to have magical qualities with its cobalt hues. Because stream runoff into the lake is at a minimum, the water clarity is at a year's peak, and in turn, LAKE TAHOE never appears a deeper blue. Often there is no wind in the fall, so the lake looks soft and inviting, at times without a ripple for miles.

There's just one catch about visiting TAHOE in the fall: what locals call the "brisk" morning. Brisk? What they consider brisk is 27 degrees at daybreak at SOUTH LAKE TAHOE, and 21 degrees in TRUCKEE. Brisk? More like butt cold. Try to enjoy a morning bike ride and the bottoms of your ears will turn numb and blue, water will stream out of your eyes like a fountain, and your entire body will become a block of ice.

But fall in the mountains often sees huge temperature swings, and by 10 a.m. it starts to warm up significantly. By noon, it's in the 60s, ideal for exploring, hiking, and biking.

In fall, all the things that make TAHOE hell in summer are gone, namely the out-of-staters who clog up the roads, hiking trails, bike routes, and overnight facilities. In summer, just driving the beautiful shoreline highway around the lake, or at least partway, say from SOUTH LAKE TAHOE to Kings Beach, is like being stuck in a one-lane procession of lame hamsters. All it takes is one slowpoke Winnebago from Iowa to jam up everyone for miles. But not in the fall, when the shoreline drive is the most beautiful cruise in the world, from the narrow hairpin turn above Emerald Bay, a drop-dead gorgeous lookout, on past Eagle Falls and beyond, with that giant azure pool literally lapping near the highway.

Like the drive, many of the very activities I specifically avoid in the summer are among the most compelling attractions in the fall. Especially the best day hikes and bike rides. My favorite three hikes here are all at the southwest region of the Tahoe Basin.

The Rubicon Trail at D. L. Bliss State Park, located at the lake's southwest shore, is one of the stellar hikes in America. The trail contours along the edge of the lake for several miles with continually stunning views; it's the kind of trail where you can stretch out your palms at any moment and soak it all in, then turn and head back whenever you want. In the summer, this trail is jammed up worse than the roads, and you may start to feel like you really are a hamster. But in the fall with fewer people out, you actually get some privacy, and every step is an exhilarating joy. Good-bye hamsterhood.

A short option on the Rubicon Trail

hike is the one-mile spur route called the Lighthouse Loop. This one is simply incredible, featuring a section where you hike along the edge of a cliff, with a straight drop of about 150 feet to water's edge (for safety, there's a little metal cord railing at the most severe drop-offs).

For the ambitious few, hiking to the top of Mount Tallac may provide a chance for the most striking moments of all. This is a serious climb, an all-day traipse, best taken from the Glen Alpine Trailhead, which provides a moderate grade to the top (another, steeper route is available). It's a 12-mile round-trip, starting at 6,500 feet, then climbing 3,235 feet to the summit at 9,735 feet. The view from here inspires comments such as "magical," "eye-popping," and "divine" as you look across 12 miles of Tahoe's serene blue waters backed by an alpine rim.

The bike rides at TAHOE are great, too. The best on the southwest shore starts at Richardson's Resort, a bike trail that runs three miles, then loops around by the lake for another three miles, with almost all of it perfectly flat for an easy trip. Depending on your level of fitness, you can extend the ride on dirt trails in adjoining Eldorado National Forest.

Another scenic ride is at the lake's northwest shore, a paved recreation bike trail, separate from the highway, that starts near Tahoe Vista and follows along the lakeshore. The route passes in and out of pine and fir trees, but is largely flat, making it perfect for families. Ironically, this is a terrible trip in the summer, because the route requires you to cross the nearby two-lane highway a few times, and it can be frustrating to wait for a gap in the cars so you can get across. Not so in the fall.

The same is true with lodging: no crowds, no waits, and the best deals at most of the best spots.

Another alternative to crowds in the summer is to visit TAHOE NATIONAL FOREST, which borders the north shore of the lake. It provides good backpacking trails, as well as access to wilderness. And out here you don't have to worry about unfriendly blackjack dealers either.

Trout anglers have two good rivers in the area. To the north is the TRUCKEE RIVER, a fine trout stream with excellent access, and to the south is the CARSON RIVER. If your idea of breaking free is not camping, well, some fine motels can be found in the Tahoe Basin. If you want to stick to your car instead of hoofing it on a trail, it takes about three hours to complete the loop drive around the entire lake, about 70 miles on a two-laner.

Just don't spend too much time at the casinos. Never forget that the blackjack tables have their own special laws of gravity.

Campgrounds: Five campgrounds are operated by the California State Parks system, two by the U.S. Forest Service. State park campsite reservations are available by phoning (800) 444-7275. To reserve a Forest Service site, phone (800) 280-CAMP/2267. For information on privately operated campgrounds, contact the Tahoe Chamber of Commerce or refer to my book *California Camping* (Foghorn Press). **Tahoe National Forest:** For information or permits (for the Desolation Wilderness), call the Truckee Ranger District, (530) 587-3558. **Boat tours:** A wide variety of cruises are available. For the M.S. *Dixie II*, call (702) 588-

3508; for the *Tahoe Queen,* call Hornblower Cruises of Lake Tahoe, (530) 541-3364. Many marinas around the lake rent small boats. **Lodging:** Lake Tahoe Visitors Authority at South Lake Tahoe, (800) AT-TAHOE/288-2463; North Lake Tahoe Resort Association, (800) TAHOE-4U/824-6348. **Contact:** Tahoe Chamber of Commerce, 3066 Lake Tahoe Boulevard, South Lake Tahoe, CA 96150; (530) 541-5255. **Locator:** LAKE TAHOE (D4).

• FEATURED TRIP •

Bodie Ghost Town

Rated: California's No. 1 Ghost Town

Stolen artifacts from a California ghost town are suddenly being returned by people who believe the objects are hexing them with a curse.

"I believe in the hex," said Mark Pupich, a ranger at Bodie State Historic Park. "I don't dare take anything and neither should anybody else. I've seen enough letters, talked to enough people about what can happen. People take something then have all this bad luck. There's been some really sad cases."

The returned artifacts include old square nails, pieces of glass, shoes, even a jawbone, accompanied 90 percent of the time with letters from people explaining how a terrible curse has vexed them since they took the objects. One woman believed a series of serious illnesses in her family was caused by the artifacts they had taken, another a death in the family.

BODIE GHOST TOWN is located in the high mountain desert country in remote Mono County near the Nevada border, 135 miles south of Reno. It was established in the 1860s as a mining town for silver and gold, with about 2,000 various buildings constructed by the 1880s. It was abandoned in the 1940s when all mining ended, then taken over in 1962 as a ghost town by the California State Department of Parks, with 170 buildings remaining. Since then, the town has been maintained in "arrested decay," which means that stabilization work is done, such as adding the occasional new roof to hold a building together. Otherwise the town looks much the same as when it was deserted.

That means that most of the artifacts are still at the town site, rather than behind glass in a museum. Thus visitors can be tempted to steal small items. But not only has the hex largely kept that from occurring, it has resulted in items being sent back to the park virtually every month since news of the curse started spreading in the 1990s.

The park has more than 50 letters of regret on file accompanying recently returned items. Here are excerpts from a few:

"AHHHHH! Enough already—here's your nail back—MERCY!"

"During holidays in 1990 we visited Bodie. We saw that nail on the ground and had the feeling we have to take it with us back to Germany. Now after these years of bad luck, we decided to send the nail back to the ghost town, in hope our luck comes back."

"I am SORRY! One year ago around the Fourth of July I was visiting the Ghost Town. I had been there many times before but had always followed the regulations about collecting. This trip was different. I collected some items here and there and brought them home. I was a visitor again this year, and while I was in the museum I read the letters of others who had collected things and had bad luck. I started to think about the car accident, the loss of my job, my continuing illness, and other bad things that have haunted me for the past year since my visit and violation. Please find enclosed the collectibles I 'just couldn't live without' and ask the spirits to see my regrets."

"Please find enclosed one weather-beaten old shoe. My trail of misfortune is so long and depressing, it can't be listed here. I urge anyone tempted to take a souvenir from Bodie to look and DON'T TOUCH!"

"I did something I've never done before. I took something from the land and buildings, pieces of bottles and some nails. Though I wasn't brought up this way, and taught my own children that stealing is wrong, I still did it myself. Since that last trip, we have experienced more tragedies and bad luck than anyone we know. I realize sending these things back won't rid us of any future misfortune, but hopefully they won't be so severe. Please accept my apology for not practicing what I preached."

"I have reached a point of desperation where I'm willing to admit that there may be some truth (to the legend of the Bodie curse). I don't fully believe this could be possible, but I haven't been able to get it off my mind since finding the bone I am returning. I have been haunted by my thoughts since finding this thing and have come to the conclusion that there may be some mysterious truth to the myth. Please accept it back with my sincerest apologies for having removed it from its final resting place."

Ranger Pupich said nothing surprises him anymore when rangers pick up the mail at the eastern Sierra town of BRIDGEPORT. "This has been going on for many years," he said, adding that the park gets about 200,000 visitors a year, but very few of them are now willing to risk the hex by taking something or keeping something they took in the past.

As news of the hex has circulated, rangers have received many items that were taken even in the 1940s and 1950s, prior to when Bodie became a state park, including a coronet, ledgers, a water heater, and stock certificates.

"The buildings were wide open back then, and people would take things without thinking about it," Pupich said. "Now they're thinking about it and they're returning them. We're constantly getting things back."

Rather than mail the items, some people make the long drive to Bodie, about six hours from SAN FRANCISCO and eight hours from Los Angeles, to ensure the items are returned exactly from where they were taken. They often search out a ranger for a personal apology, perhaps hoping that restoration and confession will exorcise any possible curse.

It is illegal, of course, to take or disturb anything from a California state park, but this is the only park with an alleged built-in penalty system. The only other well-known park where visitors are said to be cursed by taking objects is Hawaii Volcanoes National Park in Hawaii, which receives rocks in the mail daily from people claiming horrible bad luck since they removed them from the mountain.

Directions: Bodie Ghost Town is located in the high mountain desert country in remote Mono County near the

Nevada border, 135 miles south of Reno. From the Bay Area, take Highway 120 east through YOSEMITE and over Tioga Pass to U.S. 395. Drive north on U.S. 395 about 30 miles to Highway 270. Turn and go east about 10 miles on paved road, then three miles on dirt road, to the park entrance directly ahead. Note: Check road conditions in winter, when Tioga Pass is sometimes closed. **Contact:** To receive a brochure, send $1.50 to Bodie State Historic Park, P.O. Box 515, BRIDGEPORT, CA 93517. For information, call (760) 647-6445. **Locator:** BODIE GHOST TOWN (E5).

• FEATURED TRIP •

✶ MAMMOTH LAKES/ EASTERN SIERRA

Rated: The Top 50 Base Camps, 110; The Top 10 Camps for Kids, 120; The Top 4 Hike-to Lakes in the High Sierra, 158; The Top 10 Overnight Locations, 185; The Top 4 Places for Kids to Ski, 294; The Top 25 Lakes, 307; The Top 10 Swimming Holes, 395

Children smile an average of 450 times a day, according to one study, but adults only about 15 times. There's a unique place in California where the score can be evened.

In the southeastern Sierra Nevada, nature has carved out high mountain peaks and canyons, then sowed the West's most pristine lakes and streams, meadows and valleys. It is one of the few places in America where there are no limits to the scenic beauty and recreation opportunities. The area is Mammoth, named after the mastodons that roamed in the Pleistocene epoch, and much of the surrounding area retains the feel of ancient times. A hundred years ago, whenever John Muir wanted a change of scenery from YOSEMITE, this is where he came. Some 50 years ago, Ansel Adams took many of his prized photographs here. Today, it still offers the public a place to make their own magic.

The greater MAMMOTH area has more than 100 lakes, most of them exquisite, including 20 that are accessible by car. There are 24 drive-to campgrounds, several near trailheads that provide jump-off points into the Ansel Adams Wilderness, the Minarets, and the JOHN MUIR WILDERNESS. The altitudes range to a 12,000-foot ridgeline, all granite and ice, and a bit lower, woods and water. It is in these mountains that Muir counseled with heaven.

The recreational opportunities include everything from fishing, hiking, boating, and biking in the mountains to scenic tours in the nearby desert east of BODIE GHOST TOWN and among the bizarre tufa spires at MONO LAKE. Near MAMMOTH, you can ride on horseback, in a hot air balloon, and on gondolas at a ski area. Devils Postpile National Monument, the world's best example of columnar rock, is practically a sideshow.

You can rough it or you can go first-class. The town of MAMMOTH, population 5,000, has 50 restaurants, 80 rental condos, and 34 hotels and lodges. It is the gateway to the eastern Sierra, but it's a long way from any bustling metropolis, about a seven-hour drive from SAN FRANCISCO. What has the strongest impact on most visitors are the pristine waters, the excellent fishing, and the mountain wildlands.

From tiny drops of snowmelt, this is where the headwaters of the SAN JOAQUIN RIVER are formed. It pours down a canyon—wild, untouched, and absolutely pure, over boulders and into pools, so different from its pesticide-laden condition 200 miles downstream in the back Delta. From the campground at SODA SPRINGS near Devils Postpile, I hiked upstream for a few miles on the John Muir Trail along the SAN JOAQUIN, then stopped to wade the river and cast with my fly rod, drifting a floating caddis into the pocket water.

The stream is not only pure, it is vibrant with all manner of life, including brook trout, rainbow trout, and more rarely, big brown trout, and in the high country, golden trout. When you cast a dry fly, watch it float downstream. The ensuing swirl as a hungry trout takes it down is a sight you'll never forget. In three hours, I caught and released 30 trout. The farther you walk upstream, the better it gets. But you do not need to walk in order to capture this experience.

In fact, you can drive right up to some of the prettiest sights of all, as well as some of the best fishing. Convict Lake, for instance, is a mountain shrine. It is set at 7,583 feet elevation, always full to the brim with clear blue water and framed by a back wall of wilderness mountain peaks. There are so many others. You can reach Lake Mamie, Lake George, Lake Mary, Gull Lake, Silver Lake, Grant Lake, and more than a dozen others by car. They sit in high mountain pockets, carved out by glaciers and then filled over time by snowmelt. Most now have boat ramps, marinas, campgrounds, and the largest trout in the Sierra Nevada. Rainbow trout in the 20-inch class are caught every day at these lakes, and while most range from 10- to 12-inchers, there are also 10- to 12-pounders.

Many of these lakes also provide trailheads to hike into the backcountry. From Silver Lake at 7,600 feet, there is a streamside trail that is routed up past Agnew Lake, Gem Lake, and Waugh Lake to the headwaters of Rush Creek. It may be the prettiest stream in America, and its golden trout are just as beautiful. Another trek departs at Convict Lake, taking you up the trail adjacent to Convict Creek. It starts on the north side of the lake and in just five miles leads into the JOHN MUIR WILDERNESS and to a series of nine lakes. The showpiece of these is Bighorn Lake.

After a few days out here, you begin shedding layers of civilization. Suddenly, money, honors, and possessions seem irrelevant. That's because in such a beautiful place, they are.

Directions: From the Bay Area, the best route is to take Highway 120 through Yosemite and over Tioga Pass to U.S. 395, then drive south to the Mammoth cutoff (Highway 203). Greyhound offers bus service seven days a week from San Francisco. A small airport is also available near Mammoth. **Weather:** In the summer, temperatures average 80 degrees for a high and seldom fall below 40 degrees. On the hottest days, short and spectacular thundershowers can occur in the afternoon. **Fishing information:** Phone guide Gary Hooper or Rick's Sport Center at (760) 934-3416 or fax (760) 934-3484. **Horseback rides:** Phone Red's Meadows at (760) 934-2345. **Mountain biking course:** Phone Mountain Adventure Connection, (888) Mammoth/462-6668, or fax (760) 934-0603. **Hot air balloons:** Phone High Sierra Ballooning, (760) 934-7188. **Gondola rides:** Phone

Mammoth Ski Park, (760) 934-2571. **Golf:** Phone Snow Creek Resort, (760) 934-6633. **Bodie Ghost Town:** Phone Bodie State Historic Park, (760) 647-6445. **Road conditions:** Phone (800) 427-7623 for road conditions. Then, with a touch-tone telephone, enter the highway number. **Contact:** For general information and a free travel packet, contact the Mammoth Lakes Visitors Bureau, P.O. Box 48, Mammoth Lakes, CA 93546; (800) 367-6572. Or visit their Web site: www.visitmammoth.com. Maps are available from Inyo National Forest, (760) 934-2505. **Locator:** MAMMOTH LAKES (E5).

• FEATURED TRIP •

✶ YOSEMITE NATIONAL PARK

Rated: The Top 50 Base Camps, 110; The Top 10 Camps for Kids, 120; The Top 10 Easy Backpack Trips, 150; The Top 13 Covered Bridges, 194; The Top 5 Learn-to-Ski Packages, 290; The Top 25 Lakes, 307

You've heard the stories about YOSEMITE. Too many people, right? Bears raid your food every night, right? Your vacation turns into an endurance test called You Against The World. That's what kept me away for 20 years.

Finally I was forced to go back. You see, some friends and I were hiking the entire John Muir Trail, all 211 miles of it, and from the trailhead at MOUNT WHITNEY it eventually pours right smack into YOSEMITE VALLEY. Either you hit YOSEMITE or you cancel the hike.

With a few shrugs, we decided to take our chances. We headed to the park expecting congestion and confusion, just like many Bay Area residents who avoid the place. But it took only five minutes in YOSEMITE VALLEY to turn our attitudes around 180 degrees, leaving us completely under the spell of the world's greatest natural showpiece.

With a little homework, you can deal with the people and the bears easily enough; that's what this story is all about. But nothing can prepare you for your first look at YOSEMITE VALLEY.

As you drive into the park, you go through a tunnel and then, looking east, suddenly spot sections of high canyon walls. "Is this it?" It's just a start. You go around a bend and suddenly there stands El Capitan, Yosemite's monolith, the largest single piece of granite in the world, rising straight up from the valley floor. The entire valley then comes into view.

It looks as if it had been sculpted. The valley is framed by three-spired Cathedral Rocks and massive El Capitan, with awesome Half Dome near the center. Nothing anywhere can match this sight. The canyon walls are crossed by long, silver-tasseled waterfalls, although sometimes they run a bit thin. On most afternoons, low-hanging clouds that look as if they were created by Ansel Adams dot the sky from rim to rim.

Now don't think you should get in your car right now and head off for the park, although you can reach it from the Bay Area in under four hours. That ambitious, sudden "Let's go!" is just what causes so many problems for people when they visit YOSEMITE. After paying the entrance fee, they suddenly find they don't have a campsite or other place to stay, don't know where to turn, and are just as likely to wind up spending the night in a MARKLEEVILLE hotel room as looking into a nice little campfire along Yosemite Lake.

Instead, first you should obtain a good map of YOSEMITE NATIONAL PARK, then spend a few evenings just gazing at it and planning your trip. The best park map is available from the Yosemite Association, P.O. Box 230, EL PORTAL, CA 95318. Ask for the YOSEMITE NATIONAL PARK and Vicinity topographic map.

With that in hand, you can plan your vacation. Where are you sleeping? Your choices are developed campsites, wilderness camping, and tent cabin rentals. Going for a walk? Choose between premium day hikes out of the valley and backpack trails in the high country. Fishing? The park has 300 lakes, but 60 percent of them have no fish. Horseback riding? Where? How much?

Or you could give up and just lie around. In fact, a lot of people do exactly that along the MERCED RIVER in YOSEMITE VALLEY. But even those folks rest easier if they know where they're spending the night.

The campgrounds in YOSEMITE VALLEY are filled by reservation only and are packed during the summer months. Well, the overpeopled valley is a nice place to visit but you probably wouldn't want to live there. Alternatives include 11 drive-in camps outside the valley that are filled on a first-come, first-served basis.

The largest of the camps is at Tuolumne Meadows, which holds 325 sites. This is also the farthest camp from the valley, and when all else fails, usually has a space available. As you enter the park, a sign noting campground availability is posted next to the entrance. It is wise to heed those words, go and secure a spot, then enjoy your trip. On summer weekends, finding a campsite can be a difficult task. Your effort can be eased greatly by arriving Thursday or Friday morning. Other options include reserving a tent cabin or staying at Yosemite Lodge.

Backpackers have an easier and far less expensive time of it. All you need is a free wilderness permit, a backpack, and a trail to start walking.

To keep people pressure at a minimum, the park has set hiker quotas for each trailhead. Half of those quotas are filled by reservation through the mail (during the winter and spring), while the other half are first come, first served. You can pick up your wilderness permit at one of four permit stations, located at YOSEMITE VALLEY, Tuolumne Meadows, Big Oak Flat, and Wawona Ranger Station. With camping concerns taken care of, you can get on with the business of having a good time. Hiking, fishing, and horseback riding allow you to experience the best of YOSEMITE.

The hikes starting in YOSEMITE VALLEY range from an easy half-mile jaunt to the base of Lower Yosemite Falls to a 17-mile grunt to the top of Half Dome entailing a near 5,000-foot climb, with plenty of other hikes in between. Some may choose to skip the tougher climbs, but most will want to see Yosemite Falls.

YOSEMITE VALLEY sparkles with the most spectacular waterfalls in the world when high country snows begin to melt, filling rivers and streams. As you enter the valley, you round a bend, and there across the pristine meadow is Yosemite Falls, charged full with foaming, spraying water and silver-tassled in the reflected light. At

2,425 feet, it's the tallest waterfall in the United States.

Across the valley is Bridalveil Falls, 620 feet high and perhaps just as beautiful. Head up the Mist Trail and you'll first encounter Vernal Falls, a wide, 317-foot-high free-flowing cascade of silver, then with a steep, stair-step tromp upstream you'll reach Nevada Falls, tumbling 594 feet at the foot of Liberty Dome.

Every rock crevice seems to be filled with trickling water. When the snow melts, the tiny drops of water slide off rocks and join in small crevices and pools. When they overflow, gravity takes the water down into fissures. The chain continues until a small stream has been formed, which then pours into a river and eventually runs from the high wilderness county over the high Yosemite rim. It is these surging waters and waterfalls that bring YOSEMITE to life.

And there are so many, both in the valley and beyond: Ribbon Falls (1,612 feet), Illilouette Falls (370 feet), Silver Strand Falls (1,170 feet), Sentinel Falls (2,000 feet), and Horsetail Falls (1,000 feet). Any of these would be considered a world-class destination, yet they are often overlooked in YOSE MITE because the falls you can see right from your car in the valley are even more dramatic, primarily Bridalveil and Yosemite Falls.

When it comes to fishing, most anglers are terribly disappointed. I have a simple rule for YOSEMITE: If you can drive to it, don't expect to catch anything. The more difficult the access, the better the prospects.

A good primer is the 16-page booklet "Yosemite Trout Fishing," which rates the fishing at the park's 118 lakes that have trout. You see all kinds of crazy fishing methods being tried, but for the most part, you don't need anything complicated. Just use a light spinning rod and reel and small lures such as the gold Z-Ray with red spots, the black Panther Martin with yellow spots, the blue/silver Kastmaster, and the yellow Roostertail.

My brother and I had a great time of it, catching as many as 30 trout apiece in one evening at Lyell Fork, with some to 14 inches at Emeric Lake. With a little homework, it can be done. Note that all trout stocks have been suspended and easy-to-reach lakes are getting fished out.

If you don't like to hike in the backcountry, you can rent a horse to take you there. Stables are located at four places: YOSEMITE VALLEY, Wawona, White Wolf Camp, and Tuolumne Meadows.

Of course, you might be perfectly content to sit in a different kind of saddle, the kind on the valley's sightseeing shuttle. To encourage visitors to park their cars, an open-air tour bus is available, along with a free bus shuttle around the valley floor.

The first explorer to see YOSEMITE had quite a different vantage point. It was Joe Walker, in 1833, whose team reached the valley floor by lowering their horses on ropes. Walker is considered by many to be the West's greatest trailblazer, yet the tombstone at his grave in MARTINEZ reads simply: "Camped in YOSEMITE, November 13, 1833."

Since that date, millions of people from all over the world have visited the park. Ironically, its popularity is just the thing that keeps many Bay Area residents away.

Haven't been to Yosemite in a while? Maybe never? It's the kind of place that's too spectacular to miss.

Campsites: Yosemite National Park has some campgrounds that do not require reservations. Campsites are filled on a first-come, first-served basis. For best success, you should arrive before noon on weekday mornings to secure the best possible spot. Bridalveil Creek: It's set along Glacier Point Road at 7,200 feet elevation and 27 miles from Yosemite Valley, with 110 campsites. Crane Flat: Located along Highway 120 west near the Tioga Road turnoff at 6,200 feet elevation, 17 miles from Yosemite Valley. It has 166 campsites. Porcupine Flat: Set along Highway 120 east, this one is 38 miles from Yosemite Valley and has 52 campsites. Tamarack Flat: Set along Highway 120 east at 6,300 feet elevation, 23 miles from Yosemite Valley. It has 52 campsites. Wawona: Located along Highway 41 in Wawona at the southern end of the park, 27 miles from Yosemite Valley, this camp has 100 sites. White Wolf: A major camp along Highway 120 east at 8,000 feet elevation, 31 miles from Yosemite Valley, this one has 87 sites. Yosemite Creek: Four miles from White Wolf and 35 miles from Yosemite Valley, this camp has 75 sites.

Hikes: Bridalveil Falls: Start at the Bridalveil Falls parking area and walk a half-mile round-trip. (easy). Lower Yosemite Falls: Start at the shuttle stop for Yosemite Falls and walk a half-mile round-trip (easy). Mirror Lake: Start at the shuttle stop for Mirror Lake and hike one mile to the lake. If you want, hike the three-mile loop around the lake (easy). Panorama: Start at Glacier Point and hike to Yosemite Valley, 8.5 miles with a 3,200-foot elevation loss. Four to five hours one way (moderate). Pohono Trail: Start at Glacier Point and hike 13 miles, with a moderate downgrade, 1,300-foot elevation loss, six to eight hours one way. Four Mile Trail: Start at Southside Drive at road marker V18 and climb to Glacier Point, 4.8 miles one way with a 3,200-foot elevation gain. Three to four hours one way (strenuous). Half Dome: Start at Happy Isles and hike 8.5 miles to the top, including 500 feet on permanently mounted cables to make the summit. 17 miles round-trip, 10 to 12 hours with a 4,800-foot elevation gain. Plan to drink four quarts of water (very strenuous). Upper Yosemite Falls: Start at Sunnyside Campground and hike 3.6 miles one way, with a 2,700-foot elevation gain. Six to eight hours round-trip (very strenuous). Vernal/Nevada Falls: Start at Happy Isles, a trailhead for the John Muir Trail. Vernal Falls is 1.5 miles away with a 1,000-foot elevation gain, three hours round-trip. Nevada Falls is 3.4 miles one way with a 1,900-foot elevation gain. Six to eight hours round-trip (very steep and strenuous). **Contact:** Yosemite National Park, (209) 372-0265 or (209) 372-0200 (touch-tone menu). **Locator:** YOSEMITE NATIONAL PARK (E4).

• FEATURED TRIP •

BIG SUR

Rated: The Top 50 Base Camps, 110; The Top 6 Coastal Camps, 115; The Top 10 Camps for Kids, 120;

Visitors to BIG SUR, that magnificent stretch of coast south of MONTEREY, are rewarded with a look at a magical world.

Heading south on Highway 1, you pass by CARMEL and crest a hill, then BIG SUR opens up before you—an awesome rocky coast bordered by plunging mountains, pockets of redwoods, lush green valleys, and a quiet sense that all is right.

Travel anywhere in the hemisphere and you will not find anything that matches it—a waterfall that runs off a cliff and into the ocean, a beach where sea otters play peek-a-boo in a nearby kelp bed, the best winter backpacking in the West at the adjacent Ventana Wilderness, and lodgings that range from inexpensive rental cabins amid redwoods to $600-a-night suites with ocean views from a hot tub on a deck.

You can just drive on down and take it all in, perhaps stopping at an ocean bluff to watch for the spouts of migrating whales passing by. It seems like just about anything is possible here. While eating at Nepenthe's one evening, I watched the sun set into the ocean while a full moon rose over the hills to the east at exactly the same moment. I've never witnessed anything like it.

In Big Sur, the choices are many:

Driving Tour: The drive on Highway 1 from the Carmel Highlands south to Lucia is one of the prettiest cruises anywhere. The route passes ocean bluffs, rocky lookouts, redwood forests, and wide-open, untouched hillsides, then plunges down into deep valleys and across bridged canyons. All the time, the ocean spans as far as you can see to the west, often appearing much calmer and more serene than at points north. **Coastal Waterfalls:** You get redwoods and waterfalls at Julia Pfeiffer Burns State Park, set right along Highway 1. The biggest waterfall pours over a cliff and onto the beach below, then runs into the ocean. A series of smaller waterfalls is found in the park, up a canyon and surrounded by redwoods, requiring a short hike with a moderate climb. **Friendly Sea Critters:** Just park at the sign for Andrew Molera State Beach, then take the pleasant walk to the untouched beach, about a 30-minute trip. At nearby kelp beds, just beyond a very mild surf, you can often see sea otters playing hide-and-seek. They're friendly little fellows. The rangers at the park will provide visitors with a one-page handout detailing the best places to view sea otters. **Wilderness hiking:** The Ventana Wilderness and Los Padres National Forest border Big Sur to the immediate east, providing the best off-season backpacking in California. Several campgrounds are available at trailheads. **Camping:** The easiest-to-reach campground in Big Sur is Ventana Campground, located 29 miles south of Carmel along Highway 1. It is near the center of Big Sur, making adventuring in the area easy. A nearby grocery store is a plus. **Restaurants:** Of the local dining options, Nepenthe's is a favorite, with an ocean view, decent prices, and good grub. If price is no object, a dinner at the Ventana Inn can easily cost you a Ben Franklin, as in the $100 bill, maybe a lot more. But hey, it's great food. **Monterey Side Trip:** If you want to get back into the hustle and bustle, nearby Monterey to the north has the Monterey Bay Aquarium, Cannery Row, shopping at Carmel, whale watching and fishing trips, and a wide array of restaurants. **Contact:** For a free Big Sur travel packet, call the Big Sur Chamber of Commerce, (831) 667-2100; or contact the Monterey Chamber of Commerce, P.O. Box 1770, Monterey, CA 93942; (831) 648-5350. **Locator:** Big Sur (F1).

831-667-2695

• FEATURED TRIP •

MONTEREY BAY

Rated: The Top 5 Places to Beach Camp, 108; The Top 6 Coastal Camps, 115; The Top 7 Deep-Sea Fishing Trips, 330; The Top 5 Places to Clam Dig, 382

MONTEREY is just over 100 miles from SAN FRANCISCO, or about two hours by car. But as a state of mind, it's like driving into a different universe, providing the relief of a mini-vacation that will stay with you for weeks.

MONTEREY is beautiful year-round, with that cobalt blue water lapping the shore, but in late summer and early fall it has the good weather and variety of activities to make it an ideal getaway. When I last visited, I counted a dozen ventures, ranging from the obvious (touring the Monterey Bay Aquarium) to the obscure (viewing giant blue herons at Elkhorn Slough).

I especially like to visit in early fall, when Indian summer arrives in its typical come-and-go fashion, bringing warm, clear weather. Strolling on the beach, you can almost feel as if you'd escaped to Hawaii. What's more, with the summer vacation season over for out-of-staters, there is less congestion on the roads and at major destination sites.

The best bet is to depart the Bay Area by 8 a.m. to beat the weekend traffic. You will arrive in MONTEREY by 10 a.m., with a full day ahead for your chosen pursuits.

Here is a synopsis of the adventure possibilities:

Activities: No aquarium is more spectacular than the one at Monterey, with its towering, glass-encased kelp forests. To keep things fresh, new displays are added every season. In recent years, special shows have featured sharks and jellyfish. Contact the Monterey Bay Aquarium at (831) 648-4888. **Hiking:** If you want quiet and solitude, you can get it quickly by driving to a trailhead in the nearby Ventana Wilderness, then hiking in for a few hours. This is often overlooked, especially in the fall. Other excellent hiking areas near Monterey are Point Lobos State Reserve, which overlooks the Pacific Ocean, and Garland Ranch Regional Park. Contact the Los Padres National Forest and Ventana Wilderness, (805) 683-6711; Garland Ranch Regional Park, (831) 659-4488; Point Lobos State Reserve, (831) 624-4909. **Fishing:** In early fall, the best deep-sea fishing of the year arrives at Monterey Bay, with trips to the edge of the underwater canyon and also "around the corner" at offshore Carmel Bay. Since commercial gillnetting was banned here in 1987, rockfish populations have made a big comeback. Charter boats leave early every morning from Monterey's Fisherman's Wharf. Contact Sam's Sportfishing at (831) 372-0577 and Chris' Sportfishing at (831) 375-5951. **Scuba diving:** There are many fascinating places to dive, the best being adjacent to the inshore kelp forests. For a possibly perfect trip, tour the Monterey Bay Aquarium for reference, then take a dive and note the remarkable similarity in plant, fish, and mammal species. In August and September, you'll find that the water is much clearer, and also much warmer, than along the Bay Area. Contact the Aquarius Dive Shop, (831) 375-1933 or (831) 375-6605; Or the Monterey Bay School of Diving, (831) 656-0454. **Horseback riding:** Outfitters provide a variety of rides, ranging from the horse-on-automatic-pilot style at Big Sur to a wilderness trail ride in the Ventana Wilderness. Sunsets at Monterey are often unforgettable, but are especially enchanting from horseback. Contact the Ventana Wilderness Ranch, (831) 625-8664. **Sea kayaking:** Not for everybody? Says who? You can learn how in less than an hour, then paddle away with unbelievable ease and silence through calm Monterey Bay waters. Contact Adventures by the Sea, (831) 372-1807. **Bird-watching:** Elkhorn Slough, east of Moss Landing, is the area's best sanctuary. As fall arrives, so do giant blue herons, an awesome sight with wingspans up to seven feet. Another commonly sighted feathered creature is the snowy egret, one of some 250 species that use the marsh during the year. Contact Elkhorn Slough at (831) 728-2822. **Bicycling:** If you hate traffic jams, there are several recreation bicycle trails in Monterey and Pacific Grove that are ideal for a Sunday afternoon cruise. Bike rentals are available at two locations, where staff can provide route details. Contact Bay Bikes, (831) 646-9090 or Adventures by the Sea, (831) 372-1807. **Hang gliding:** Crazy? Perhaps. If you have a taste for the wild and transcendent, hang gliding will send you into another orbit. It is best here in the afternoons near the marina, with at least a morning of certificate instruction now mandatory before you can sail off on your own. Contact Western Hang Gliders, (831) 384-2622. **Driving tour:** Pacific Grove's 17-Mile Drive is world famous, but hey, the cruise on Highway 1 from Monterey on south through Big Sur to Lucia may be even more divine. **Golf:** Monterey is known around the world for its golf courses. El Monte is the oldest course in the area, and Poppy Hills at Pebble Beach is one of the most famous; both are open to the public. Contact El Monte, (831) 373-2700; Poppy Hills, (831) 625-1513. **Camping:** The area has 10 campgrounds, ranging from the well-known Pfeiffer Big Sur State Park (217 campsites) to the lesser-known primitive sites in Los Padres National Forest. Beach camping is available at Marine Dunes, Sunset, Seacliff, and New Brighton state beaches. Contact Pfeiffer–Big Sur State Park, (831) 667-2316; Los Padres National Forest, (805) 683-6711 (headquarters). **Lodging/ Restaurants:** Monterey has more than 200 hotels, motels, and inns with overnight accommodations, along with 300-plus restaurants. For a free travel packet, contact the Monterey Chamber of Commerce, 380 Alvarado Street, Monterey, CA 93940; (831) 648-5360. **Locator:** MONTEREY (F1).

• FEATURED TRIP •

★ MORRO BAY

Rated: The Jewel of San Luis Obispo County

Sometimes I feel like Moses in search of travel adventure, roaming around for 40 years in the wilderness. But for all my wandering, I've discovered only a few places that I know I could settle down in and call home.

One of them came as a complete surprise: MORRO BAY and its environs. I found it to be one of the most captivating places in the West, with a beautiful untouched coast, nearby lakes, and an array of recreational offerings, all first-class. It is great for a weekend visit, or perhaps for much longer.

Maybe I ought to move there, at least part-time anyway, and as soon as I can arrange to live in the master suite at Hearst Castle, I will. That's because MORRO BAY and SAN SIMEON to the north are the jewels of San Luis Obispo County. The area is located about a two-hour drive south of SAN JOSE, making it a viable option to a trip to the Mendocino or Sonoma county coasts, and with more to do once you get there.

It is certainly just as pretty, perhaps even more so. California's central coast is a large untouched marine sanctuary extending all the way north to Big Sur, peppered with giant rocks, acres of inshore kelp beds, and sea otters. Outside of the towns of Morro Bay and San Simeon, much of this is untouched and beautiful, and because of the region's southern range, the climate and ocean waters are far warmer than coastal haunts to the north.

The place has just about everything but mountains: pristine beaches, quiet country roads, unsettled foothills, and a mild, sunny climate. Here is a synopsis of what's available.

Lodging: There's a series of great inns, lodges, and hotels in Morro Bay within walking distance of the main strip, and a few others a bit farther away with seclusion and waterfront views. I stayed at the best of them, The Inn at Morro Bay, which came through with their guarantee of "serenity by the seashore." Quiet, yeah, I must have it quiet. For a list of available lodging, phone the San Luis Obispo County Visitors and Conference Bureau, (800) 634-1414. **Camping:** The best campgrounds are in Morro Bay State Park, with a marina and campsites set amid cypress trees, located about two miles south of town, and San Simeon State Park, with developed sites near San Simeon Creek. I tracked down 10 campgrounds in all, including Montana de Oro State Park in Los Osos, which has 50 primitive sites. So even though reservations are always advised, there are enough spots to keep late arrivals from getting stuck without a spot. For descriptions, locations, and phone numbers, guess you'll have to get my book *California Camping*. **Hearst Castle tour:** You'd have to have come from Mars not to know anything about Hearst Castle. Just don't disturb the master suite. For information, call (800) 444-4445. **Fishing:** Some of the best inshore rockfishing is right here, the result of a shallow underwater shelf that supports kelp forests and protects huge numbers of fish (and otters). You often can fish just 60 to 90 feet deep, yet catch state-record quality rockfish. Trips are available out of both Morro Bay and San Simeon through Virg's Sportfishing, (805) 772-1222. **Bay kayaking:** The sheltered waters of Morro Bay and its volcanic rock formations make for some of the best sea kayaking anywhere. Lessons and tours are available for newcomers, while do-it-yourselfers can create some great excursions. For information, contact Kayak Horizons, (805) 772-6444, or Kayaks of Morro Bay, (805) 772-1119. **Harbor cruise:** This one-hour cruise of the Morro Bay harbor is just now catching on. Because of its newfound popularity, dinner tours and Sunday brunch tours with champagne are now offered. For information, contact *Tigers Folly II,* (805) 772-2257. **Golf:** I'm not much for golf, even got thrown off the course the one time I tried it (my hiking boots were leaving waffle marks on the greens), but even I had to admire the beauty of the courses here. The prettiest is Morro Bay Golf Course; set right along the coast, it's similar to the more famous courses in Monterey. For information, contact (805) 772-4560. **Miniature golf:** This is more my style, and yep, the official name is the "World's Most Difficult Golf Course." It comes with two courses, covered for all-weather play, and the inevitable arcade. For information, contact (805) 927-5428. **Bicycling:** Some great rides are available out of the Central Coast, both in the foothills and along the ocean, with bike rentals available in San Luis Obispo. For newcomers, the best bet is joining up with Alamo Bicycling Touring Company and using their wisdom to set up your own route, or to join in on a guided tour. For information, contact (805) 781-3830. **Horseback riding:** The closest ranch with horse rentals is in San Miguel, located five miles north of Paso Robles on U.S. 101. Daily trail rides are the most common, but you can also set up a trip with a barbecue and a sunset ride. For information, contact (805) 467-3362. **Directions:** From San Jose, drive south on U.S. 1/Shoreline Highway for about two hours. **Contact:** Morro Bay Chamber of Commerce, 880 Main Street, Morro Bay, CA 93442; (805) 772-4467 or fax (805) 772-6038. For a free visitors guide, contact the San Luis Obispo Visitor and Conference Bureau, 1037 Mill Street, San Luis Obispo, CA 93401; (800) 634-1414 or fax (805) 543-9498.* E-mail slocvcb@slonet.org. **Locator:** Morro Bay (G2).

6

WILDLIFE WATCHING

• Tom's Ratings •

• Featured Trips •

See last page for Northern California and Bay Area foldout maps.

• TOM'S RATINGS •

THE TOP 6 OPPORTUNITIES TO SEE BALD EAGLES

In Northern California

Dark sky, silent flight. The sight of a bald eagle lifting off at sunrise from a treetop always makes you aware of what true greatness is.

The power from just a few wing beats can propel a bald eagle hundreds of yards, gliding on its six-foot wingspan while keeping a razor-sharp watch for prey. Morning light makes its white head and tail feathers glisten. It's the kind of scene that can stir your spirit.

It is also the kind of scene that is not so quite so rare anymore, especially in California. As winter arrives and the jet stream sends arctic weather into the Pacific Northwest and Canada, the eagles head south, wintering more in the Golden State than anywhere else in the lower 48.

They have their favorite spots, and that's where you come in. From December through March, taking an eagle watching trip can be a uniquely rewarding adventure. It has become typical to see 10 to 20 bald eagles, often more, along with golden eagles and osprey. For most people, the trip provides a rare look at the best the world has to offer.

The best places for sighting bald eagles in California are LAKE SAN ANTONIO in Monterey County and the KLAMATH BASIN NATIONAL WILDLIFE REFUGE in the northeastern part of the state. During the winter, there are usually close to 1,000 eagles in the KLAMATH BASIN and about 60 at LAKE SAN ANTONIO, a significant increase in the past two decades.

While eagles are still not as abundant as the ones on the backs of quarters, it is rare not to see the great bird at these two habitats.

In the Bay Area, the foothill country of remote Alameda and Contra Costa Counties provides enough habitat and open space for a few resident bald eagles, though sightings can be rare.

1. LAKE SAN ANTONIO

Terry Davis of the Monterey County Parks Department helps direct the organized eagle tours at LAKE SAN ANTONIO, the only place in California where such a trip is available. (At the KLAMATH BASIN, it's a do-it-yourself proposition.)

"The increase at LAKE SAN ANTONIO coupled with reports of increases in other parts of the country is a positive indication that the eagle population is again on the rise," said Davis. "Through research, education, restrictions on the use of chemicals, and the establishment of alternative habitats, environmentalists have made a valuable effort to maintain and increase the eagle population."

The tours at LAKE SAN ANTONIO provide a chance for anybody, regardless of their experience in the outdoors, to see bald eagles, and lots of them. LAKE SAN ANTONIO is located in central California near KING CITY. There is a year-round campground, RV hook-ups, and cabin rentals at the lake, with hotels available in KING CITY and PASO ROBLES.

The eagle tours have become quite popular, and reservations are advised. The trip starts with a 30-minute slide presentation, which will put you in the right frame of mind. Then you board the Eagle One, a 56-foot tour boat on pontoons, and are provided with binoculars by park assistants. There is a seat for everybody, but when the eagles come into view, most people are too excited to stay put. The trip is two hours long; the brunch trip runs three hours.

Contact: For information, write Eagle Tours, Monterey County Parks, P.O. Box 5279, Salinas, CA 93915-5279; reservations, (831) 755-4899. **Fees:** A modest fee is charged for tours at Lake San Antonio. Ask about the low group rates, which inspire schools, seniors' organizations, and environmental clubs to make the trip. Special weekend morning brunch tours are also available. **Locator:** LAKE SAN ANTONIO (F1).

2. KLAMATH BASIN

Up in the KLAMATH BASIN, it's a different world.

Modoc County covers an area as large as the Bay Area's nine counties, yet has a population of only 8,600, not counting dogs. Its remoteness is part of the attraction for visitors, as are the eagles, which typically number 950 during the winter. This is an ideal locale for eagles because they have an abundance of waterfowl to feed on. As winter arrives and the jet stream sends arctic weather into the Pacific Northwest and Canada, the eagles head south, wintering more in the Golden State than anywhere else in the lower 48.

No organized eagle watching trips are available here. Instead, you create your own self-guided tour, with rangers tipping you off on the best places to see eagles.

Helpful hints: Come prepared for cold weather and plan to stay overnight in a hotel, not in a tent. The temperature can hover between 15 and 30 degrees through most of the winter, sometimes getting even colder, and unless you plan on hibernating, you're better off in a hotel room for the night than in a sleeping bag.

That done, you can enjoy your days watching the most majestic of American birds, and keep your tootsies warm at night. It's an experience that will stay with you for a long time.

Contact: For a free brochure, write the Klamath Basin National Wildlife Refuge, Route 1, Box 74, Tule Lake, CA 96134; information, (530) 667-2237. For lodging information, contact Shasta Cascade Wonderland Association, 1699 Highway 273, Anderson, CA 96007; (800) 474-2782. **Locator:** KLAMATH BASIN NATIONAL WILDLIFE REFUGE (A3).

Other areas offering good opportunities to see eagles include:

3. EAGLE LAKE

Has 62 eagles. Located near SUSANVILLE.

Locator: EAGLE LAKE (B4). **See featured trip page:** 358.

4. SHASTA LAKE

Has 14 eagles. Located north of REDDING.

Locator: SHASTA LAKE (B2).

Eagles can also be found at the following locations:

5. TRINITY LAKE

Located north of WEAVERVILLE.

Locator: TRINITY LAKE (B1).

6. LAKE BRITTON

Located near BURNEY.

Locator: BURNEY (B3).

• TOM'S RATINGS •

THE TOP 9 PLACES TO BIRD-WATCH

In the San Francisco Bay Area

Birds are light, airy, happy little fellows, and watching them can make you feel the same way.

That is why bird-watching has become one of the most popular activities in the Bay Area, as well as in many parts of the country. The Bay Area is an ideal place for the pursuit because the wide variety of habitats here results in an equally wide variety of birds, including seabirds, songbirds, raptors, and waterfowl—both resident and migratory.

The sport has changed vastly in the past 20 years. In the good ol' days, bird-watchers all seemed to be nice little old ladies wearing giant rubber boots, with huge pairs of binoculars hanging from their necks. This was serious business, a mission, and they carefully noted every bird on their Audubon "Life List."

Well, these days bird-watchers look different. They are as apt to be bikers as little old ladies and include everyone in between. The equipment has changed, too, with small, lightweight, high-optic binoculars, little backpacks to carry guidebooks, and high-tech waterproof hiking shoes.

The discovery has been made, you see, that this is really fun, a way to leave the daily grind behind and share in the world where all seems gentle and joyous. Most people get involved in the sport as a by-product of another adventure, whether walking, boating, fishing, or hunting. You see the birds, watch them, and soon start wondering what they are. If you take the next step and find out, boom: You have become a bird-watcher.

Buying a home bird feeder is the next logical step, and Rubbermaid makes the widest variety of designs. Naturally, you then want to be able to identify the birds. *The Audubon Master Guide to Birding,* a three-part series of books that provides close-up photographs of each species, is the best available. If you want to expand your search, *The Birders Guide to Northern California,* by Lolo and Jim Westrich, details 250 of the area's premium locations.

Another idea is to take part in a nature walk with an expert. These walks are offered most weekends at locations throughout the Bay Area. They include tours at Bothin Marsh north of SAUSALITO, Hawk Hill at the MARIN HEADLANDS, Palo Alto Baylands, PESCADERO MARSH, Hayward Regional Shoreline, and SAN FRANCISCO BAY NATIONAL WILDLIFE REFUGE at both the FREMONT and ALVISO locations. Avid birder Courtney Peddle contributed to this synopsis of the best of Bay Area bird-watching:

1. HAYWARD REGIONAL SHORELINE

Millions of shorebirds spend the winter on SAN FRANCISCO BAY, and a variety of species can be seen on any mudflat, marshland, or bay tideland, and even on some lakes.

A personal favorite is the HAYWARD REGIONAL SHORELINE, always good for shorebirds with the bonus of peregrine falcons either hovering over the marsh or perched on a power pylon. Sometimes, merlins can be seen there. Another plus is the flock of up to 200 American white pelicans.

Locator: HAYWARD REGIONAL SHORELINE (E1c).

2. Arrowhead Marsh

Another good spot in the East Bay is Arrowhead Marsh (Martin Luther King Regional Shoreline) in Oakland, home to some 30 species. Several pairs of blue-winged teal winter there, uncommon in bay waters. At high tide, this area is also a top spot to see rails, which are typically elusive and more often heard than seen.

Locator: Arrowhead Marsh (E1c).

3. Elsie Roemer Shoreline

Nearby is the Elsie Roemer Shoreline, located on Alameda's south shore, which is also an excellent area for rails during high tides. This habitat is ideal for dowitchers and rare red knots; the ratio is about 300 dowitchers to one knot.

Locator: Alameda (E1c).

4. Lake Merritt

Lake Merritt is always good in the winter, with about 10 species of waterfowl, including plenty of Barrow's goldeneyes, rarely spotted elsewhere. Mergansers and scaups are more common, and sometimes you can spot tufted ducks as well.

Locator: Lake Merritt (E1c).

5. Pigeon Point Lighthouse

The mudflats of San Francisco Bay support an abundance of seabirds, but the real spectacles occur during late April and May at Pigeon Point Lighthouse on the San Mateo County coast.

On a good day, you can see 200,000 (that's right, 200,000) loons, scoters, brants, gulls, and terns heading north. On a lucky day, you might see a million shearwaters, literally enough to speckle the ocean black for 15 miles, and plenty of fulmars and kittiwakes, too. There are many other good areas: Point Reyes and Bodega Bay are among the best, particularly in the vicinity of fishing docks for migrating seabirds. In fact, the coastline is alive with shorebirds gaining glorious breeding plumage before they head north

Locator: Pigeon Point (E1d).

6. Mitchell Canyon

A favorite spot in May is Mitchell Canyon on the northeast side of Mount Diablo for rare migrants, including rufous, calliope, and Costa's hummingbirds, along with Hammond's and willow flycatchers and many warblers.

Locator: Mount Diablo (E1c). **See featured trip page:** 93.

7. Fisherman's Wharf

During the first week of July, squadrons of endangered brown pelicans arrive at the coast. Sometimes, they stop to circle and feed on anchovies; otherwise, they fly low-lying lines along the ocean swells, eventually entering San Francisco Bay and visiting the Fisherman's Wharf area. Another real show takes place out at sea, where thousands and thousands of murres congregate in the vicinity of the Farallon Islands, their breeding area. They are joined by a number of well-traveled seabirds.

Locator: Fisherman's Wharf (E1b). **See featured trip page:** 222.

8. Audubon Canyon Ranch

At Audubon Canyon Ranch on the Marin coast, up through early July, huge herons kick their young out of the nest, and you can watch the juveniles make their first attempts at flight. There are an additional 60 species of birds here. The saltwater marshes of the bay also attract several species of herons, along with egrets, cormorants, and the inevitable coot.

Locator: AUDUBON CANYON RANCH (E1a). **See featured trip page:** 260.

9. POINT REYES NATIONAL SEASHORE

The POINT REYES NATIONAL SEASHORE is the feature point in the fall, when a huge variety of both migrating small birds and larger shorebirds arrive. The best spots are the groves of cypress, upland pastures, and ranch feedlots between Pierce Ranch and the Point Reyes Lighthouse. Another option is the long, uninterrupted shore for viewing very special shorebirds.

Locator: POINT REYES NATIONAL SEASHORE (E1a). **See featured trip page:** 67.

• TOM'S RATINGS •

THE TOP 10 WETLANDS

In the San Francisco Bay Area

Easy walks, great natural beauty, and the best chances in the Bay Area to see shorebirds, waterfowl, and other birds are what make visiting wetland habitats so much fun.

Easy? Most marshes are flat, and the trails that access them provide the easiest walking anywhere. Yet there is no sacrifice of natural beauty, for the paths run right in the middle of wildlands, often with great views of San Francisco Bay as a bonus. Other bonuses at the wetlands include free access, guided walks available at many on weekends, and interpretive centers.

Here are my 10 favorite wetlands in the Bay Area, and what you can expect to see when you visit them:

1. ABBOTTS LAGOON

Abbotts Lagoon is a beautiful spot, but a short hill keeps it out of sight (and also out of mind) of the parade of drivers heading up Pierce Point Road to see the nearby herd of tule elk. A trail climbs up and over that hill and drops you down to the lagoon, set in coastal foothills less than a mile from the ocean. Bird-watching is often good here with a mix of coastal shorebirds and migratory waterfowl. Side trips include a chance to see the elk at nearby Pierce Ranch, and the miles of nearby sand dunes and untouched waterfront along the ocean.

Contact: Point Reyes National Seashore, (415) 663-1092. **Locator:** POINT REYES NATIONAL SEASHORE (E1a). **See featured trip page:** 262.

2. BOTHIN MARSH

The Bicentennial Bike Path is a rare place where bikers, joggers, and walkers mix together without confrontation. That's because the great natural beauty here acts as a natural sedative as you pass along the shore of RICHARDSON BAY from SAUSALITO to CORTE MADERA. The route includes two little bridges that provide passage over tidelands where you can sometimes see egrets and night herons in the little waterways, or sandpipers poking around the mudflats by the dozen at low tide. This is a great nature walk, with a good side trip available to the nearby Richardson Bay Audubon Center.

Contact: Richardson Bay Audubon Center, (415) 388-2524. **Locator:** RICHARDSON BAY (E1a). **See featured trip page:** 263.

3. CHINA CAMP STATE PARK

The Shoreline Trail provides the best introduction to CHINA CAMP STATE PARK. It meanders along the shore of SAN PABLO, providing good lookouts across the bay, and then after a mile, crosses a meadow and is routed adjacent to tidal areas, marshes, and wetlands. In the process, you are apt to see a large mix of birds, including resident shorebirds along SAN PABLO BAY as well as migratory waterfowl at the marsh. Other good hikes are available at the park.

Contact: China Camp State Park, (415) 456-0766. **Locator:** CHINA CAMP STATE PARK (E1a).

4. ARROWHEAD MARSH

Some of SAN FRANCISCO BAY'S most valuable wetland habitat is here at Arrowhead Marsh in the Martin Luther King Regional Shoreline, covering 1,220 acres along both San Leandro Bay and San Leandro Creek. A paved trail lessens the experience, but it is still one of the best bird-watching areas in the East Bay, with 30 species commonly seen. High tide seems to bring in rails, typically an elusive sight at other wetlands.

Contact: East Bay Regional Parks, (510) 635-0135 extension 2200. **Locator:** ARROWHEAD MARSH (E1c).

5. COGSWELL MARSH

Cogswell Marsh is the heart of an 800-acre wetland that includes bridged trails, great views of the bay and the BAY BRIDGE, and a chance to view many rare birds. The white pelican is often the main attraction, but falcons, merlins, and many shorebirds also frequent the place. I once saw 200 white pelicans here at one time. It is a great place for an easy nature hike with wonderful views.

Contact: East Bay Regional Parks, (510) 635-0135 extension 2200. **Locator:** HAYWARD (E1c).

6. CROWN MEMORIAL STATE BEACH

A bicycle trail here runs right along the bay's shoreline, leading 2.5 miles south to an overlook of the Elsie Roemer Bird Sanctuary. The views are excellent, and so are the prospects for spotting many species of birds. High tide is the best time to see grebes, ducks, and even loons, while low tide brings out sandpipers and other birds poking about the exposed mudflats for food. It is located along the shore of SAN FRANCISCO BAY just south of Crab Cove.

Contact: East Bay Regional Parks, (510) 635-0135 extension 2200. **Locator:** ALAMEDA (E1c).

7. SAN FRANCISCO BAY NATIONAL WILDLIFE REFUGE

This is a big refuge, covering 23,000 acres, and the Tidelands Trail pours right through the best of it amid salt marsh and South Bay tidewaters. In 30 minutes or less, you can see half a dozen species of ducks, egrets, sandpipers, willets, and herons. The views of the South Bay and surrounding foothills make a dramatic backdrop.

Contact: San Francisco Bay National Wildlife Refuge, Newark, (510) 792-4275. **Locator:** SAN FRANCISCO BAY NATIONAL WILDLIFE REFUGE (E1c). **See featured trip page:** 263.

8. ENVIRONMENTAL EDUCATION CENTER, ALVISO WETLANDS

A little-known portion of the SAN FRANCISCO BAY NATIONAL WILDLIFE REFUGE lies deep in the South Bay near Alviso, and here you can take an easy walk along a dirt path bordering wild tidal marshland. As you stroll north toward the South Bay, you will delve into wilder and wilder habitat, home of the endangered harvest salt mouse, and have a chance to see a dozen or more species of birds. You will also enjoy a sense of remoteness, rare for Santa Clara County.

Contact: San Francisco Bay National Wildlife Refuge, (408) 262-2867 or fax (408) 262-5513. **Locator:** SAN FRAN-

CISCO BAY NATIONAL WILDLIFE REFUGE (E1b).

9. PALO ALTO BAYLANDS

You will discover an old wooden walkway that spans across tidal marshland and crosses under a series of giant electrical towers. After starting at an interpretive center, you can walk about 10 minutes to an observation deck at the edge of the South Bay, or follow a dirt path along the bay's tidewaters. Egrets and coots are common, and there are also good prospects for seeing jackrabbits and ground squirrels.

Contact: Palo Alto Baylands Nature Center, (650) 329-2506. **Locator:** PALO ALTO (E1b). **See featured trip page:** 283.

10. PESCADERO MARSH

Here is one of the few remaining natural marsh areas on the entire central California coast. It covers 600 acres, with a dirt path that leads through pampas grass and bogs. More than 250 species of birds visit here in a year, including the giant great heron, always a spectacular sight as it lifts off with labored wing beats. Highlights of this spectacular setting are Pescadero Creek and its lagoon and the adjacent PACIFIC OCEAN.

Contact: California State Parks, Half Moon Bay District, (650) 726-8819. **Locator:** PESCADERO MARSH (E1d). **See featured trip page:** 268.

• TOM'S RATINGS •

THE TOP 3 PLACES TO WHALE WATCH

In the San Francisco Bay Area

At first all you see is what looks like a little puff of smoke on the ocean surface. Out of the corner of your eye you see it, and your attention becomes riveted to the spot like a magnet on iron. A closer look and there it is again—only it quickly disappears.

You watch, waiting, but the sea is quiet. A row of cormorants glides past, a dozen murres are paddling around, and for a moment you forget why you're out here on the briny blue. Then your daydreams are popped by a giant tail, the size of a lifeboat, breaking the surface of the water.

A moment later, the head and back of a gray whale surge into view.

After you have seen a whale—a real, live friendly sea monster—you will never again look at the ocean in quite the same way. When you see a whale, you often regain the feeling that this world of ours is still a place where great things are possible. That's because a whale is one of those things.

And there are 21,000 of them swimming along the California coast, cruising 50 to 100 miles per day within range of charter boats and many shoreline lookouts. Seeing one not only makes you feel special but can instill the kind of excitement that will stay with you for many years. Every time you look at the ocean, you will remember.

These giant air-breathing creatures average more than 40 feet in length and can weigh over 30 tons. They will often keep pace alongside a boat, spouting, occasionally emerging to show their backs. As they gain confidence, they may fin you, give you a tail salute, and if you're particularly lucky, do a half breech in full view. In one spectacular 20-minute sequence off the HALF MOON BAY coast, I saw 10 or 15 humpback whales leaping completely out of the water in full 180-degree pirouettes. They landed with gigantic splashes on their backs beside the boat, perhaps trying to clean off the barnacles. Now and then, a pair would even crisscross like Wilkinson sword blades in front of our path. This occurred while on a fishing trip, and it was simply luck that we ran into the rare humpbacks.

However, there is little luck involved in spotting gray whales. The gray whale migration is a 5,000-mile trip from Arctic waters to Baja, a migratory route that brings them along the Bay Area coast from January through April. You don't need a boat to see them, but it can help.

Since the whales cruise along the surface, you can see the little "puffs of smoke" from their spouts, as in "Thar she blows."

Some whales seem attracted by the big boats and will play tag with you on the southern route, disappearing and reappearing several times over the course of an hour.

Skippers have learned that most gray whales will follow a migratory course from POINT REYES on southward past the FARALLON ISLANDS near the continental shelf. Most skippers start the day by heading south, hoping to pick up some whales and cruise parallel to them for many miles.

Before boarding a large vessel for an ocean cruise, you'd be well advised to take a seasickness preventative.

An option is to skip the boat ride and drive to a lookout along the coast. However, don't expect to see much of the whales. You will see whales from considerable distances blowing their spout. Still, even from a distance, it's an exciting affair. From the San Mateo County coast at Pigeon Point, I have seen as many as 200 whale spouts before I stopped counting. Binoculars and a clear day can do wonders.

The best lookouts are from these following bluffs:

1. **DAVENPORT**
   Locator: DAVENPORT (E1d).
2. **PIGEON POINT**
   Locator: SAN GREGORIO (E1d).
3. **POINT REYES NATIONAL SEASHORE**
   Locator: POINT REYES NATIONAL SEASHORE (E1a). **See featured trip page:** 67.

For general information or to learn about charters, please see the following:

Contact for all listings: The Oceanic Society in San Francisco, (415) 474-3385. For recorded whale-sighting information, phone (415) 474-0488. **Berkeley:** Dolphin Charters, (510) 527-9622. **Bodega Bay:** *New Sea Angler,* (707) 875-3495. **Half Moon Bay:** *New Capt. Pete,* (650) 726-7133; *Capt. John,* (650) 726-2913. **Monterey:** Sam's Charters, (831) 372-0577. **San Francisco:** Oceanic Society, (415) 474-3385. From December through April, they offer full-day whale watching excursions from San Francisco and half-day trips from Half Moon Bay. **San Francisco's Fisherman's Wharf:** *Wacky Jacky,* (415) 586-9800; *Butchie B.,* (415) 457-8388; *Easy Rider,* (415) 285-2000. **Sausalito:** *Salty Lady,* (415) 348-2107; *New Rayann,* (415) 924-6851.

• TOM'S RATINGS •

THE TOP 10 PLACES TO VIEW WILDLIFE

In the San Francisco Bay Area

For youngsters whose idea of wildlife is a pet stuffed animal on Easter morning, getting close to the real thing can provide a happy shock that will transport them into pure rapture.

Sure, the Easter Bunny can deliver plenty of short-lived excitement, but some young children seem to think the Easter Bunny is that rabbit who beats a drum on the TV commercial for a battery. Seeing real deer, elk, and squirrels, or even cows, chickens, and ducks, is not only a genuine experience but an unpredictable one, which can make the adventure exciting and unforgettable for anybody.

I've created a list of the top 10 places in the Bay Area to see wildlife, but if you want a sure thing, there are four can't-miss prospects: the San Francisco Zoo, the Oakland Zoo (which includes a petting zoo for children), Little Farm at TILDEN REGIONAL PARK in the BERKELEY hills, and Ardenwood Historic Farm in FREMONT. At Little Farm and Ardenwood, visitors can see plenty of furry and feathered creatures such as chickens, ducks, geese, Mr. Cow, and goats. For information, phone the East Bay Regional Park District at (510) 635-0135.

Some predictable destinations made my list, such as POINT REYES (and its extraordinary elk herd), but many may be surprises.

1. Pierce Ranch

This swath of land is home to more than 300 tule elk and a herd of deer, along with rabbits, fox, bobcats, and a mountain lion that is almost never spotted. Often you can see the elk right from the parking lot, without hiking at all, making it ideal for seniors or children. For those who want to walk, a stellar hike is routed up and down the foothills out to Tomales Point, a spectacular setting with the PACIFIC OCEAN off to the west and serene TOMALES BAY to the east.

Contact: Point Reyes National Seashore, (415) 663-1092. **Locator:** POINT REYES NATIONAL SEASHORE (E1a). **See featured trip page:** 132.

2. Grizzly Island Wildlife Area

GRIZZLY ISLAND, along with the adjacent Suisun Marsh, provides the largest nesting habitat for mallard ducks and is home to a growing herd of tule elk that has been used as seed stock for herds all across California. The wild-life area is networked by small roads, sprinkled with wetlands and grasslands, and finding the elk is always a great fortune hunt. It is best to bring binoculars to spot them, then take your time creeping up for closer views.

Contact: Grizzly Island Wildlife Area, (707) 425-3828. **Locator:** GRIZZLY ISLAND WILDLIFE AREA (D1).

3. Waddell Creek Trail, Rancho Del Oso

A hiking and biking trail starts at the coast at Rancho Del Oso, located on Highway 1 south of AÑO NUEVO, and meanders inland across a variety of stunning habitats: marsh, lagoon, stream, riparian, meadow, and forest. In the process, you can see ducks, seabirds, steelhead, deer, and squirrels as you venture through these habitats, respectively. A bonus is that cyclists can lock their bikes at the end of the trail, then make the short hike to Berry Creek Falls.

Contact: California State Parks, Santa Cruz District, (831) 429-2851; Big Basin Redwoods State Park, (831) 338-8860. **Locator:** WADDELL CREEK (E1d). **See featured trip page:** 270.

4. China Camp State Park

The deer seem almost tame here, often bedding down adjacent to the campground parking lot. But it gets even better. A series of trails trace the shoreline, with the best heading out to Jake's Island, providing intimate glimpses of many birds, including egrets, herons, grebes, and during low tides, sandpipers, mud hens, and others. In addition to the opportunity to see wildlife, the views of San Pablo Bay can make the North Bay seem so vast and tranquil that the setting is almost surreal.

Contact: China Camp State Park, (415) 456-0766; California State Parks, Marin District, (415) 893-1580. **Locator:** China Camp State Park (E1a).

5. Palo Alto Baylands

The walk from the interpretive center on out along the slough to the mouth of San Francisquito Creek features scads of ground squirrels playing hide-and-seek, an occasional surprise jackrabbit, along with egrets, avocets, coots, ducks, and other migratory waterfowl. The views of the South Bay are gorgeous on clear days, when it seems as if you could take a flying leap, sail across the water, and land atop Mount Diablo.

Contact: Palo Alto Baylands Center, (650) 329-2506. **Locator:** Palo Alto (E1b).

6. Pillar Point

From a small parking lot at the west side of Pillar Point Harbor, just below the radar station, a great trail skirts the west end of the harbor and is routed out to Pillar Point. Here you will find up to a dozen sea lions playing in the kelp beds, as well as a secluded beach. The walk out is short and easy, and presents a chance to see grebes, gulls, and cormorants, and later in the summer, pelicans, shearwaters, and other migratory seabirds.

Contact: California State Parks, Bay Area District, (415) 330-6300. **Locator:** Princeton (E1b).

7. Arrowhead Marsh

Here is one of the best bird-watching areas on San Francisco Bay, a shoreline/marsh habitat that covers 1,220 acres. Some 30 species of birds are commonly spotted here, including clapper rails, which can be quite elusive at other wetlands. The marsh runs along San Leandro Bay and is part of the Martin Luther King Regional Shoreline, with a paved trail skirting the edge of the marsh. To extend your venture, walk across a bridge at San Leandro Creek and out to Garretson Point.

Contact: East Bay Regional Park District, (510) 635-0135 extension 2200. **Locator:** Martin Luther King Regional Shoreline (E1c).

8. San Pedro Valley Park

This San Mateo County park is best known for beautiful Brooks Falls and the sweeping views of the coast on the Montara Mountain Trail. But the valley floor is filled with wildlife, especially deer, which are best viewed on warm weekday mornings in early spring when few people visit. If you are lucky, you may see other wildlife, even raccoons at dusk, or perhaps a fox. You stand a better chance of seeing rabbits nibbling at the meadow—and the hawks that circle overhead looking for them.

Contact: San Pedro Valley Park, (650) 355-8289. **Locator:** Pacifica (E1b).

9. Fisherman's Wharf

Sometimes it seems as if the sea lions at the wharf were all dogs in a previous life. After all, they have begging down to a science and put on quite an exciting show (especially for youngsters) treading water, ducking, playing tag—anything to get your attention. Just like a dog! As summer arrives, so will endangered brown pelicans, so many that it is hard to believe the species was once almost wiped out. They join gulls, cormorants, and other birds looking for a handout, much like humanoid wildlife frequenting San Francisco.

Locator: Fisherman's Wharf (E1b). **See featured trip page:** 222.

10. Coyote Hills Regional Park

The Baylands Trail is an easy three-mile walk that features views of the South Bay, crosses four Native American shell mounds, and runs adjacent to a marsh that is a wildlife sanctuary for many waterfowl. But that much is predictable. What is not is how the ground squirrels come popping out of the ground, then scurry off, only to disappear into another of their favorite holes. It can be a great show. For a side trip, take the wooden boardwalk out through the North Marsh to see waterfowl.

Contact: Coyote Hills Regional Park, (510) 795-9385; East Bay Regional Park District, (510) 635-0135 extension 2200. **Locator:** Coyote Hills Regional Park (E1c). **See featured trip page:** 283.

• Featured Trip •

Audubon Canyon Ranch

Rated: The Top 50 Parks, 7; The Top 9 Places to Bird-Watch, 252

Audubon Canyon Ranch on the Marin coast is a little niche of paradise for the few people who know of it. It's the premier place on the Pacific coast to view herons and egrets, those large, graceful seabirds, as they court, nest, mate, and rear their young. Hatchlings can be seen discovering the world, some flying for the first time. The ranch also has eight miles of nature trails, routed up the canyon, along streams, and through redwoods. These include lookouts where you can see Bolinas Lagoon and the Pacific Ocean. Ninety species of birds inhabit the ranch, in addition to deer, fox, lots of bunny rabbits, and even bobcats. But the herons are the feature attraction. They have wingspans approaching six feet and build nests on the tops of redwood trees about 100 feet off the ground. From an overlook, you can use spotting scopes (provided by the ranch) to get a unique glimpse of life in a nest. Watch Junior eat. Watch Mom Heron whack Junior in the head. Watch Junior fly. There's nothing else quite like this.

Access is free, but Audubon Canyon Ranch is open on weekends and holidays only, from 10 a.m. to 4 p.m., spring through midsummer. Donations are welcome and are used to bus in schoolchildren who otherwise wouldn't have the opportunity to visit the preserve. Typically, enough donations are made to pay for more than 5,000 youngsters to make the trip each year.

The adventure begins with the drive to the Marin coast, a rural woodland where birds outnumber people. The drive is quite pretty (as long as you don't get stuck behind a Winnebago), taking Highway 1 three miles north of STINSON BEACH. A natural history display and bookstore are available at the ranch headquarters.

From headquarters, you take a short, steep hike, about 20 minutes long with rest benches available on the way, to the canyon overlook. There, use a spotting scope to peer across the valley and zero in on the giant nests atop the redwoods. In May, the eggs start hatching, and by June, there can be as many as 200 hatchlings in the nests. You can see the adult herons flying away—a spectacular sight with their slow, gentle wing beats powering them off to nearby Bolinas Lagoon—then returning shortly thereafter with goodies. The feeding process is unique: Mom and Dad Heron allow Junior to seize their beaks, which causes them to throw up undigested food all over the nest. Junior and his brothers and sisters then gobble it all up. By the way, what's for lunch?

In late June and early July, one of the highlights of the year occurs when the juveniles decide to find out what this flying thing is all about. You will see the youngsters standing in the nest, practicing wing strokes. Sometimes they hop out on a branch, practicing, getting their courage up. Eventually, if they don't take the big plunge, Mom Heron might give them the heave anyway. Since the nests are 100 feet in the air, Junior has about 10 seconds to figure out how his wings work before the ground suddenly arrives.

The three primary species of birds nesting here are the great blue heron, great egret, and snowy egret. When silhouetted, the great blue heron looks something like a pterodactyl, with its long thin body and massive wingspan. The great egret is pure white, quite thin, and stands about four feet tall. As expected, the snowy egret is also pure white, but is smaller than the great egret, about two feet tall.

Early in the spring, viewers have an opportunity to witness a courtship ritual. It consists of the birds offering sticks to each other. If the stick is accepted, the birds will then work together to build a nest, and from there, great things happen.

Volunteer docents are available to answer questions at the overlook area and the parking lots. Maps of the ranch are provided.

During the week, the ranch is closed to the general public and reserved instead as an outdoor classroom for groups of schoolchildren. For some, it is their first time hiking or seeing nature up close. On one recent visit, a youngster refused to hike into the forest.

"I ain't goin' up in them woods," the boy told Skip Schwartz, executive director of the ranch. "Are there tigers up in them woods?"

"No tigers up there," answered Schwartz with a smile. Having worked here since 1975, he is familiar with the fears of youngsters from the city. "The animals we might see are more afraid of you than you are of them."

Eventually, the boy decided to trust him, take a chance, and go on the hike.

"People are afraid of things they aren't familiar with," Schwartz said later. "AUDUBON CANYON RANCH offers a chance for people to learn to love and respect nature."

The first volunteer interpretive guide I met was the late Clerin Zumwalt of Greenbrae, who had been involved with the area for more than 30 years.

"There's a real warmth to this place," he said. "The joy of the kids is very exciting to see. There is an excitement with all these birds out there on the tops of the trees. It's a down-home experience."

Directions: From San Francisco, take Highway 1 north. The ranch is located 3.5 miles north of Stinson Beach. **Fees:** Entrance is free, but donations are requested. **Contact:** Audubon Canyon Ranch, (415) 868-9244. **Locator:** Audubon Canyon Ranch (E1a).

• Featured Trip •

Point Reyes Elk

Rated: The Top 25 Hikes, 2; The Top 50 Parks, 7; The Top 10 Hikes on Point Reyes, 20; The Top 4 Earthquake Trails, 26; The Top 10 Strolls, 40; The Top 5 Walks at Low Tide, 43; The Top 50 Base Camps, 110; The Top 10 Spots for a First Kiss, 180; The Top 10 Wetlands, 254

The strange, warbled bugling sounds are like nothing you've ever heard in the Bay Area. And for many, the elk making those sounds are like nothing they've ever seen.

While the herd of elk at Point Reyes National Seashore has become well known as it gets bigger and bigger, what is still a surprise to many is the fall mating rituals that take place there, complete with bugling calls, sparring, and collecting harems. If you're especially lucky, you might even see them Do It. For youngsters reading this story, that is how big elkies make little elkies.

In the past 15 years, the big elk have mastered this ability, kind of like hamsters. What started as a small herd of about 25, transplanted from the Grizzly Island Wildlife Area near Fairfield, now numbers over 300, according to a recent count. Meanwhile, the action makes this the number one outdoor getaway in the Bay Area for several months in the spring.

It's so much fun that Doug McConnell and I came out here to tape an episode of his TV show, *Bay Area Backroads.*

It's so easy that often all you'll have to do to see the elk is drive to the parking lot at Pierce Ranch near Tomales Point, where they usually hang out within viewing range. You can add in an easy hike and typically count from 25 to 100 elk as you go. If you want a full workout, hike four to eight miles and explore further on game trails, where you might see 200 elk, along with deer, fox, rabbits, and hawks, but no hamsters.

This is always a feature getaway at Point Reyes and is a great venture when combined with viewing the ongoing recovery of the once-burned area from Inverness Ridge on west to Shell Beach (some distance from the elk herd at Pierce Ranch).

The best way to start your trip is by stopping at the Bear Valley Visitor Center at headquarters, located just off Sir Francis Drake Highway on the left side, a well-signed turn. A free brochure with a park map is available there. To best see the rebirth of the land, drive to the Point Reyes Hostel, park at the nearby lot, then hike the Coast Trail for 2.8 miles to Coast Camp, taking in a great view of the recovering burned area on your left, and eventually, the ocean and a beautiful beach on your right.

The elk herd is no secret, and the parking lot is often full by midday on weekends. To avoid this problem, come during the week (only three other cars were here on my recent visit) or arrive before 10 a.m. or after 4 p.m. on weekends. But even when there are a lot of other elk watchers, the elk don't hardly mind. They are far from tame—don't get too close unless you want to be turned into elk shish kebab—but they are definitely adapted to accommodating numerous daily viewers.

Binoculars make wildlife watching a lot easier and keep you from having to get too close. These are tule elk, and while a shade smaller than their cousin the Roosevelt elk, they are still quite giant. A typical male stands five feet at the shoulder with antlers that practically poke holes in the clouds.

The best way to see the most elk is to start hiking the Tomales Point Trail, veering off to the right after 20 to 40 minutes on one of the game trails and tromping to a good lookout at the ridge. From here, you can see down into a valley to the north, where the elk often congregate at a watering hole. I've found that the elk also herd up in two meadows adjacent to deep coves near the shore of Tomales Point.

While rangers encourage elk watching, they note that it is illegal to herd, chase, or harass the animals in any way, and that no mountain bikes or dogs are permitted past the parking area at Pierce Ranch.

The Tomales Point trail is an abandoned ranch road, wide and with a flat walking surface, that traces near the ridge of these coastal foothills, up and down. Hikers go right past a primary watering area for the elk about three miles in. From here, you can extend your trip for another mile, heading out to Tomales Point, a beautiful spot where crashing breakers shower spray over high rocks, with the ocean on one side, and the mouth of TOMALES BAY on the other.

Even on busy weekends, the number of visitors making the eight-mile round-trip to Tomales Point is relatively few. In fact, if a dozen elk are hanging around the parking lot, which isn't at all unusual, many visitors won't even make it 50 yards from their cars.

Directions: From San Francisco, head north on U.S. 101 to San Rafael and take the Sir Francis Drake Boulevard exit. Drive to the town of Olema, turn right on Highway 1, and go north to Bear Valley Road. Turn left onto Bear Valley Road and drive one-half mile. Turn left at the Point Reyes National Seashore sign and proceed to the parking lot at the visitor center. **Contact:** Point Reyes National Seashore, Point Reyes, CA 94956; Bear Valley Visitor Center, (415) 663-1092. **Fees:** Access is free. **Locator:** POINT REYES NATIONAL SEASHORE (E1a). **See featured trip page:** 67.

• FEATURED TRIP •

★ SAN FRANCISCO BAY NATIONAL WILDLIFE REFUGE

Rated: The Top 50 Parks, 7; The Top 7 Shoreline Walks, 46; The Top 10 Spots to Go on a Date, 182; The Top 10 Wetlands, 254; The Top 5 Bike Rides, 278

How many times have you sped in your car along the shores of SAN FRANCISCO BAY on Highway 101, 17, or 237, dodging traffic like Mario Andretti at the Indy 500?

If you hatch out of that metal co-

coon, rub your eyes to a new day, and look just over yonder, you might see a far different world. The shores of our bay offer a perfect environment for a diverse population of little critters, from tiny crabs to rabbits. And the marshlands also act as one of the major rest stops for millions of birds traveling on the Pacific Flyway.

This all adds up to the SAN FRANCISCO BAY NATIONAL WILDLIFE REFUGE, headquartered along the eastern foot of the DUMBARTON BRIDGE. You can't beat the price, with access, brochures and regularly scheduled guided walks all free. It's an ideal adventure, especially for families or groups. It can be explored by trail or boat—but not by car, motorcycle, or bicycle. That means you can go it alone, on land or on water, and get that quiet you deserve.

The diversity of wildlife here is spectacular. Even a handful of bay mud can contain 20,000 tiny living creatures from the primary levels of the marine food chain. There are as many different kinds of birds in this area as almost anywhere else in Northern California. In a given year, more than 250 bird species will find food, resting space, and nesting sites here. Birdlife, particularly waterfowl, is most abundant in the fall when snowstorms across Canada, Montana, and parts of Washington send migratory birds to their wintering sanctuaries by the bay.

On one visit, after just 15 minutes and before I lost track, I scoped six kinds of ducks, along with a pelican, an egret, a sandpiper, and another species I could not readily identify. No problem. A check at the ranger station later provided the answer: It was a willet, so named for its oft-repeated call during the breeding season, "pill-will-willet."

During low tides, the bay will roll back to reveal miles of tidal flats filled with mussels, clams, and oysters. Pollution control since the birth of the "Save Our Bay" campaign of the 1960s has been so successful that the water is cleaner than it has been in over 25 years, and shellfish digging is now permitted in a few areas.

Fishing and hunting (in specified areas) are permitted, and actually can be quite good if you hit the right place at the right time. For fishing, the right time is during a high incoming tide. The right place is at the Dumbarton Pier along the main channel of the bay, a natural fishway. Sharks, rays, perch, and occasional striped bass, jacksmelt, and flounder can be caught, according to season.

Most folks, however, go just for an easy hike along the shoreline. If you follow in their footsteps, you'll find a close-to-home spot that you may have driven past thousands of times yet never looked at closely.

Directions: From San Francisco, drive south on U.S. 101 to the Willow Road–Dumbarton Bridge exit. Continue east and take the first exit (Thornton Avenue) after the toll plaza. At the bottom of the off-ramp, turn right and drive one mile to the refuge entrance on the right. **Mass transit:** It's not convenient at the present time. The Alameda County bus system schedules a stop about a mile away. For information, call AC Transit, (510) 839-2882. **Trip tip:** Bring good walking shoes and binoculars. Dogs are no longer allowed in the wildlife refuge. **Fees:** Access, brochures, and scheduled guided tours are free. **Contact:** San Francisco Bay National Wildlife Refuge, P.O.Box 524, Newark, CA

94560; (510) 792-4275 or (510) 792-0222. **Locator:** SAN FRANCISCO BAY NATIONAL WILDLIFE REFUGE (E1b).

• FEATURED TRIP •

✦ AÑO NUEVO STATE RESERVE

Rated: The Top 5 Places to Clam Dig, 382

One of the more curious adventures in the Bay Area has become one of the most popular—touring AÑO NUEVO STATE RESERVE to see the giant elephant seals.

It is curious because the elephant seals are such peculiar comrades. They spend most of their time sprawled out on the sand dunes, basking in the sun. But every so often they will surprise you. At the least, they are capable of some fast, jerky movements, or even a mini-charge. When the male elephant seals challenge each other, they will rear up and cut loose with a clucking-type roar, then slam their open jaws into their opponent's blubbery neck. It's a ritual out here, and the scars on their necks will prove it.

Watching this spectacle has become a ritual in its own right, one so popular that reservations are required for a spot on a tour group. Crowds are not a problem, however, because rangers keep groups small so the elephant seals will not feel threatened.

It's a pretty ride to the reserve, located about 10 miles south of Pescadero, just west of Highway 1. Actually, AÑO NUEVO is the name of the island here, where elephant seals have been breeding since practically the beginning of time. There are now so many elephant seals that there isn't enough room for all of them on the island, hence hundreds have taken up residence on the mainland, providing the chance for close-up viewing.

In your tour group, you'll walk along roped-off trails, winding your way among the animals. You'll be surprised at the creatures' size and their complete lack of interest in you.

Size? Yeah, they come big. Most elephant seals range in the 2,000- to 3,000-pound class, but the old boars can reach nearly 20 feet long and 5,000 pounds. Definitely heavyweights, and they are born that way. At birth, the pups often weigh about 75 pounds, and within four weeks, will approach 300.

The creatures look like giant slugs and seem content to put up with being viewed from a distance, usually at least 50 feet or more. If you plan on taking photographs, don't plan on a mug shot without a telephoto lens. A 200 mm lens is a good choice. The beasts are soft-hearted enough, but they don't like posing for tourists with an Instamatic at point-blank range.

In fact, after people get accustomed to walking among the sun-baked blobs, they start thinking, "Hey, I can walk right up to one." That is exactly why each tour group is guided by an experienced leader with a careful eye. Mr. Elephant Seal needs his space, and if you get within squirming range, well, how would you like to be squished?

The elephant seals start arriving every year in mid-November, with tours offered daily from December through March. In January, hundreds of pups are born, which is quite a phenomenon to witness. While elephant seals don't reproduce at a rabbit-like pace, they are doing quite a job of repopulating the Pacific coast, with well over 70,000 elephant seals now ranging south to Baja, living primarily on islands.

At the turn of the century, the species was nearly extinct. Whalers turned their sharp harpoons toward them for oil, and just about wiped them out. Great fellows, those whalers. But sanity won out, and elephant seals have long been a protected species, along with other marine mammals. Their comeback is a testimonial that shows how just leaving something alone is often the best wildlife management tactic.

The reward for this policy today is a chance to go for a walk among the elephant seals, where they are willing to share all their idiosyncrasies with visitors. All they ask is that you share their world from a respectable distance. Fair enough.

Directions: From San Francisco, drive south on Highway 1 to Half Moon Bay. Continue south for about 23 miles. The park entrance is located just off the highway and is well marked. **Mass Transit:** SamTrans offers three tour packages per day on Saturday and Sunday. Advance reservations are required. For information, phone (800) 660-4BUS/4287 or (650) 508-6200. **Fees:** Guided tour, $4. Parking fee, $5. **Reservations:** Reservations are required; phone (800) 444-7275. No self-guided tours are permitted until April, when most of the elephant seals have departed. **Length of walk:** The tour is about three miles long. A shorter route is wheelchair accessible. **Contact:** Año Nuevo State Reserve, (650) 879-2025; California State Parks, Bay Area District, (415) 330-6300. **Locator:** AÑO NUEVO STATE RESERVE (E1d).

• FEATURED TRIP •

FITZGERALD MARINE RESERVE

Rated: The Top 50 Parks, 7; The Top 5 Walks at Low Tide, 43; The Top 22 Water Adventures, 311

The closer you look, the better it gets. The problem is, most people don't look close enough. When you go tidepool-hopping, you either look close enough to see all the little sea critters, or you see nothing.

There is no better place to do that than the FITZGERALD MARINE RESERVE in MOSS BEACH, although there are rocky tidal basins all along the Northern California coast.

At this special reserve, you can explore 30 acres of tidal reef during the minus low tides that arrive in late fall and winter. Almost every pool holds all manner of sealife, from little warring hermit crabs to bright blue sea anemones and little sculpins swimming about.

During winter, the minus low tides will cycle in and out of phase on a two-week basis, so arrange your visit with the tides in mind. During a minus tide at FITZGERALD MARINE RESERVE, the PACIFIC OCEAN rolls back, leaving pools, cuts, and crevices filled with a few feet of seawater. You can walk on the exposed rock, probing the tide waters below as you go.

You don't have to worry about a sudden, giant wave hammering you from behind. On the outside edge of the tidal area, about 50 yards from the beach, there is a natural rock terrace that blunts attacks from waves. So you and the critters that live here are protected from a heavy ocean surge.

This is one of the most abundant and diverse marine life regions in California. A ranger here said that there are 200 species of marine animals, 150 of plants, and 125 of gastropods, or mollusks. Just take a close look.

You don't need to be an oceanographer to enjoy it. The easiest critters to recognize are starfish, hermit crabs, rock crabs, sea anemones, sea urchins, and the zillions of different kinds of snails. For instance, in one pool, we saw two hermit crabs trying to pick food from a giant aqua-colored sea anemone. The anemone just flinched its rubbery tentacles, sending the offenders on their way. It's all a lesson in observing detail, seeing the world as a connection of many small living things.

That's why 20,000 kids visit the marine reserve every year. It's become the most popular outdoor classroom in the Bay Area.

One lesson the rangers teach quickly is to look but don't touch. That's hard for kids, particularly when they find a large starfish. The problem is that an adult starfish is on average 15 to 25 years old, and when one is taken, another starfish doesn't magically replace it. Rangers now have the option to cite people (including kids) if they get caught with a starfish or any other marine creature.

But hook-and-line fishing is permitted here because studies have demonstrated that sportfishing has no impact on fish populations in the area. Part of the reason is because of the difficulty of the sport. However, there always seems to be someone attempting to close down Fitzgerald to fishing, so check before you go.

If you show up with your fishing rod and cast out some bait, you will inevitably find yourself snagging on the reef with every single cast, losing your gear and wanting to quit the sport forever.

A better technique is called "poke-poling." You use a long Calcutta pole or its equivalent, like a worn-out CB antenna, and tie a three-inch piece of wire and a 2/0 hook on the end. Then place a small piece of squid bait on the hook and poke the pole in crevices, under ledges, and in any deep holes on the outer edge of the tidal basin.

While other people are snagging, you can catch sea trout, cabezone, lingcod, and eels with this unique method. As with tide pooling, the best fishing is during the minus low tides.

This area is also a favorite for scuba divers, abalone pickers, and plain ol' beach walkers. Just remember to look close—you don't want to miss it.

Directions: From the north, take Interstate 280 or U.S. 101 to Highway 1 and continue through Pacifica over Devil's Slide and into Moss Beach. The turnoff is well signed. From the East Bay, Peninsula, and south, take Highway 92 into Half Moon Bay, then head north on Highway 1 for seven miles to Moss Beach. Note: Because of landslide problems, Highway 1 is sometimes closed at Devil's Slide. If this is the case, use the Highway 92 route. **Fees:** Entry is free. **Best times:** Prime times are during the minus low tides in late fall and winter. **Trip tips:** Dogs are prohibited. Wear good-gripping rubber-soled shoes. **Contact:** Fitzgerald Marine Reserve, (650) 728-3584; San Mateo County Parks and Recreation Department, (650) 363-4020. **Locator:** FITZGERALD MARINE RESERVE (E1b).

• FEATURED TRIP •

Pescadero Marsh

Rated: The Top 50 Parks, 7; The Top 15 Surprise Hikes in the Rain, 28; The Top 10 Wetlands, 254; The Top 10 Scenic Back Roads, 198; The Top 22 Water Adventures, 311

Just east of Highway 1 near Pescadero is a natural marsh area covering 600 acres, with a quiet trail winding through. Called Pescadero Marsh, it may be the best place in Northern California to see the great blue heron. Almost anybody can hike here, yet it is one of the most overlooked wildlife areas in the Bay Area. The kicker is that after your walk, you can have a meal at Duarte's Restaurant, which serves great artichoke soup (a unique concoction) and homemade bread.

Pescadero Marsh is one of the few remaining natural marsh areas on the entire central California coast. For that reason, it is critical that you not wander off the trail and unknowingly destroy any of this habitat. The trail is almost flat, making it an easy walk for almost anyone, and routes you amid pampas grass, pickleweed, and bogs. This is the main stopover for birds on the Pacific Flyway, as well as home for a good population of year-round residents. You will see a surprising variety of birds.

You do not need to be a birdwatcher to enjoy the scene. However, if you have binoculars, bring them. During the year some 250 species of birds use the marsh. The most impressive is the blue heron, a magnificent creature that stands almost four feet tall with a wingspan of seven feet. The sight of one lifting off is a classic picture. They fly with labored wing beats, which makes them appear even bigger. Pescadero Marsh is a prime nesting ground for the blue heron.

Other unique birds sighted here include the snowy egret, a pure white, frail-looking fellow that spooks easily, and the night heron, a short-necked, short-legged, short-billed bird whose feathers seem squeezed together. The distinct appearances of these coastal birds gives each of them a personable character, especially the night heron. After awhile, they seem like old friends.

The marsh is bordered by the Pacific Ocean on one side and Pescadero Creek on the other, resulting in a unique setting that attracts birds who live in both saltwater and freshwater environments.

After your walk, there is no reason to hurry back to the Highway 1 treadmill. Not when you can go to Pescadero's historic Duarte's Restaurant, a place ingrained with a coastal tradition. It all makes for a memorable outing.

Directions: From Highways 280, 92, or 84, head west to Highway 1, then turn south and continue past Half Moon Bay. Pescadero Marsh is located just northeast of the Pescadero turnoff, 17 miles south of Half Moon Bay. **Fees:** Access is free. **Duarte's Restaurant:** Duarte's is located in Pescadero. Reservations are a must; call (650) 879-0464. **Contact:** Half Moon Bay State Beach and Park, (650) 726-8819; California State Parks, Bay Area District, (650) 330-6300. **Locator:** Pescadero Marsh (E1d).

• FEATURED TRIP •

SOUTH BAY DISCOVERY VOYAGES

Rated: The Bay Area's Best Outdoor Classroom

What starts out as a simple boat ride can end up changing your perspective on life. Providing, that is, the name of the boat is the *Inland Seas* and the ride is a four-hour tour of SAN FRANCISCO BAY—with -the chance to see, touch, and experience all the little critters that make the bay's environment click.

The ride is called Discovery Voyages, and it is one of the most unique adventures available anywhere in the West. From the outside, it appears to be a fun, four-hour cruise exploring southern SAN FRANCISCO BAY. From the inside, it is like a Jacques Cousteau expedition, allowing passengers to view the bay in a way they may have never imagined.

The *Inland Seas,* an 85-foot cruiser, departs from REDWOOD CITY and heads out to the bay between the San Mateo and Dumbarton bridges. You don't need seasickness pills. In fact, the bay is often so calm out here that the skipper calls it "San Francisco Lake."

Out on the water, the crew takes charge—with a net trawl for fish, and samples of plankton water and mud from the bay bottom. You see, this boat is a floating marine laboratory and the public is invited along for a special science lesson.

By itself, the boat ride is lots of fun, but the opportunity to explore, question, and observe the inner workings of SAN FRANCISCO BAY will make you feel different about the area as your home.

"Five million people live and work around SAN FRANCISCO BAY," said Bob Rutherford, president of Discovery Voyages. "Few of them realize their quality of life is greatly influenced by it.

"We don't pull any punches and we're not pointing any fingers. We are analyzing the bay with students. It doesn't matter who is aboard. Whether it is someone from an oil company or the salt company, we do the same thing."

Since the first voyage, Rutherford estimates more than 150,000 people have taken the trip. Some go for the boat ride, some to supplement their science education, others to get in touch with the vast body of water that is the center of the Bay Area.

You start with a simple water sample. It is like looking into a crystal ball, because it can tell you the future. In that water you will find plankton, the basis of the marine food chain. A net with tiny openings just 80 microns across is dragged through the water, and after it is retrieved, you follow a scientist to a room inside the boat. Using a specially designed microscope/projector, the image of the plankton is projected onto a screen, where everyone can view it at once.

You see tiny copepods, diatoms, dinoflagellates, and small protozoa, all squiggling around. Without them, there would be no other life in the bay.

"This is the beginning of the marine food chain," said Peter Olds, one of the onboard scientists. "We explain how everything starts with plankton on the bottom of the food chain. And we emphasize the possible effects that man might have on it.

"If there's too much sewage going

into the bay, for instance, there can be an algae bloom. The plankton and algae will rot, and then the decomposition of the plant matter uses up the oxygen in the water. Without enough oxygen, fish cannot survive."

The mud samples are especially fascinating to kids. They seem to like the idea of a scientist playing in mud. But then they discover that all kinds of little critters are living in the mud as the scientist finds and identifies them: tubeworms, oysters, mussels, clams, sponges, little crustaceans, and snails. They find out that there is more to the muck than just muck.

The fish trawl experiment is often the most exciting. A small net called an otter trawl is dragged behind the boat, allowing a wide sampling. Perch—seen in many species—are the most abundant. You are likely to see leopard sharks, brown smooth-hound sharks, and bay rays. Anchovies, sole, halibut, kingfish, jacksmelt, mudsuckers, bullheads, shiners, and sometimes, although rarely, striped bass and sturgeon also are captured. After inspection, the fish are returned unharmed.

You end up having a fun adventure as well as a unique look at SAN FRANCISCO BAY. On the way, you'll begin to understand the chain of life our bay waters, and how people affect it.

Directions: From U.S. 101, take the Sea Port exit in Redwood City and go left onto Chesapeake Drive. At the end of Chesapeake, turn left on Discovery Parkway and follow it around the giant salt pile to the Marine Science Institute. **Schedule:** Charters are available year-round. Public trips are scheduled, but individuals can often join private charters. **Fees:** Boarding passes are $25 per student ages 10 to 18 and $35 per adult. **Contact:** For a brochure or information, contact Discovery Voyages, 500 Discovery Parkway, Redwood City, 94063-4715; (650) 364-2760. **Locator:** SOUTH BAY DISCOVERY VOYAGES (E1b).

• FEATURED TRIP •

WADDELL CREEK

Rated: The Top 50 Parks, 7; The Top 10 Places to View Wildlife, 257

If the only time you see wildlife is on television, there's an easy walk on the outskirts of the Bay Area that can remedy this problem. In the course of an evening stroll here, I saw seven deer, three rabbits, several squirrels, five quail, a pair of grouse, ten ducks, a blue heron, and baby steelhead feeding on an insect hatch, all in just two hours.

Birds and fish are the centerpiece of this beautiful streamside walk that can take you from a lagoon to meadows to redwood forest.

Most hikers call it the Waddell Creek Walk. The trailhead is located on Highway 1 just inside the Santa Cruz County line, about 20 miles south of HALF MOON BAY. It starts at the Rancho del Oso outpost, the western border for BIG BASIN REDWOODS STATE PARK. Technically, the trail is the lower portion of the Skyline-to-Sea Trail.

It is an ideal spot to view wildlife and birds in their native habitat. But it is also just a good place to walk, a near-flat trail that plays peek-a-boo with forest and meadow. The trail is popular with horseback riders and bicyclists. If you choose to ride, please go slowly and quietly, and show courtesy to walkers.

You can also stay here overnight.

There are secluded hike-in campsites available as close as 1.2 miles from the trailhead, with two others within another two miles. Reservations are required. No open fires or barbecues are permitted, so bring a backpacking stove. Camping is permitted at designated sites only.

You start the trip with a nice cruise on Highway 1, which provides continual views of the PACIFIC OCEAN. After passing AÑO NUEVO and entering Santa Cruz County heading south, be on the lookout for the large sign announcing BIG BASIN REDWOODS STATE PARK and Rancho del Oso. That's your calling. Park at the sign for Rancho del Oso.

The first half mile of the trail loops around the Waddell Creek Lagoon to the park's outpost headquarters. Maps are available here, along with information about the park.

In the next four miles, you can see a lot of wildlife. Huge meadows on each side of the trail attract grazing deer, especially during the late afternoon and evening. Photographers with long-range lenses can get classic shots.

In the wooded areas, keep alert for any chattering sound. If you hear one, stop and look around you. Somewhere, likely hopping down the side of a tree and scurrying off to another, will be a gray squirrel.

In areas where the trail is lined with dense bush, walk quietly and keep your eyes focused far ahead. You are apt to see a little brown bush bunny hopping across the trail or playing in the dirt. Often, when they first spot you, the rabbits freeze in their tracks for five or 10 seconds, rather than immediately disappearing into the bush. This allows you to watch the little critters closely, and can teach children the merits of being quiet in the woods. Unlike the rabbits, the deer here seem almost acclimated to passing hikers.

You can see a surprising diversity of birdlife here. Because it is close to a freshwater lagoon, ducks and blue herons nest in the watershed. The most common waterfowl seem to be mallards. The coastal fields between ocean and forest are perfect for nesting quail. I saw a nice covey of them, which included some females that were so close to nesting they were as round as grapefruits.

WADDELL CREEK itself is a pleasant stream that attracts steelhead in the winter. No fishing is permitted, but you can occasionally spot an adult. It is more common to see newly hatched smolts, the three- to five-inch steelhead, darting to the surface for insects during the evening rise. They look like little trout.

The trail is like an old ranch road and is easy on the feet. It continues level for 4.5 miles, until it enters the redwood interior of BIG BASIN STATE PARK. No bicycles are allowed past this point. Here, the trail starts to climb. If you have the spirit for it, you can continue up to Berry Creek Falls, and on (and up) farther to Cascade Falls.

Directions: Drive south on Highway 1 about 20 miles past Half Moon Bay, just inside the Santa Cruz County line. After passing Año Nuevo, look for the signs marking Big Basin Redwoods State Park/Rancho del Oso. **Contact:** For information on Waddell Creek, phone the Rancho del Oso outpost, (831) 425-1218. If the ranger is on patrol, phone Big Basin Redwoods State Park, (831) 338-8860. **Maps:** For maps of Big Basin, contact the Sempervirens Fund, P.O. Drawer BE, Los Altos,

CA 94023; or call (650) 968-4509. **Camping:** For reservations to hike-in campsites, phone Big Basin Redwoods State Park, (831) 338-8860. **Locator:** BIG BASIN REDWOODS STATE PARK (E1d).

• FEATURED TRIP •

★ FARALLON ISLANDS

Rated: The Top 22 Water Adventures, 311; The Top 10 Places to Fish with Kids, 332

At sunrise from the SAN FRANCISCO HEADLANDS, looking out to sea on a crystal-clear day, you can see the pointed, rocky top of SOUTHEAST FARALLON ISLAND poking up from the horizon. It is only 25 miles from land, but for anybody who has seen the FARALLONES up close, this is in another world.

Birds, sharks, and whales rule the FARALLON ISLANDS, and man is an infrequent visitor. Haunted some 100 years ago by egg-raiders and seal-poachers, the FARALLONES are now the crown jewel of U.S. Fish and Wildlife Refuges. Outside of Alaska, it has the largest nesting colony of seabirds in America, 150,000 birds in all—a living science lab for wildlife and natural history.

On a recent trip, in a single sweep of the eye from the Shubrick Point Lookout, there were 20,000 common murres, a marine bird that resembles a miniature penguin. Just offshore, those here beheld another spectacle, 20 blue whales, the largest mammal ever to inhabit the earth, along with seven humpbacks, three grays, and one minke, cruising and finning, feeding on krill. In Mirounga Bay, a pretty, curving cove on the island's southeast flank, a great white shark was witnessed plucking a harbor seal right out of the surf line.

So many baby western gulls were hatching on a flat called Marine Terrace (10,000 in a 250-yard radius) that it seemed as if they were taking over the planet. In a small patch of beach at the bottom of a deep rock crevice, a posse of endangered stellar sea lions were rearing their pups. All the while, five young marine scientists who live here up to three months at a time, isolated from the mainland, chronicled the events in their role as wildlife guardians.

"We're stewards of the island," said Michelle Hester, a lead biologist for the Point Reyes Bird Observatory, which runs a cooperative program with the U.S. Fish and Wildlife Service. "Our job is to monitor and protect the wildlife here."

The FARALLON ISLANDS mark the edge of the richest marine region from Mexico to Alaska. The key is the under-water shelf that extends 25 miles from SAN FRANCISCO to the Farallones, a relatively shallow area that is perfect in spring and early summer for ocean upwelling, which brings cold, nutrient-rich waters to the surface. That causes tiny organisms to be born in great numbers, especially plankton, the building blocks for the marine food chain that supports vast numbers of seabirds, marine mammals, and fish.

Though the Bay Area's 6.5 million residents are so close, relatively few have seen the FARALLONES, and almost no one has set foot on them. The public is allowed to view the Farallon Islands only from a distance, with nature cruises offered by the Oceanic Society out of SAN FRANCISCO the most popular venue.

Permits for nonscientists to set foot

on the island can be nearly impossible to obtain. It took more than a month of phone calls and faxes, including a request to a well-connected insider at Interior Secretary Bruce Babbitt's office, to finally get the cherished permit for *Examiner* photographer Kurt Rogers and myself.

In SAN FRANCISCO we boarded the *New Superfish,* a 63-foot cruiser piloted by Mick Menigoz, who fired up his twin engines and cruised out under the GOLDEN GATE BRIDGE, past Land's End, and headed out to sea, where only the FARALLONES stand between thousands of miles of open ocean. It's roughly a two-hour cruise, and as we neared, the stark islands appeared an awesome sight, almost like moon rock, a towering specter in thin fog.

We bobbed in the swells 300 yards offshore and watched a 13-foot Boston whaler skiff being hoisted by crane and then dropped in the water. Hester was at the stern, making the short run out to pick us up, bobbing in the ocean swells. To get on the island, a circular platform with a cargo net was let down by the crane. With the ocean tossing us up and down, we managed to climb from the skiff to the platform, and then were hoisted ashore like a circus ride.

Upon landing, the noise was unbelievable, a cacophony of squawks from acres of nesting gulls, murres, and auklets. At the foot of the crane were three just-hatched gulls, their cracked-open eggshells sitting aside them. Their mother squawked and hovered, darting up and down, once trying to grab Hester's cap by the bill.

Hester and other biologists spend months at a time out here. Supply boats are scheduled to make the trip to the FARALLON ISLANDS every two weeks, but if the wind is blowing hard and sea conditions are poor, the trip can be canceled and it can be a month or more between visits from other human beings and fresh food. "We got down to rice and beans a few times," Hester said.

But it's not so bad, she said, because the job is so fascinating, and in fact, the world of the island becomes solely theirs, while life back in the Bay Area seems surreal.

"The hardest thing for volunteers is the noise," Hester said, calling attention to the never-ending background of squawking gulls, barking sea lions and elephant seals, pounding waves, and whistling winds. "One guy couldn't handle the gulls. They just drove him batty, and he had to catch a boat back to the mainland."

We hiked on a marked walkway, surrounded on both sides by wall-to-wall gulls, the newly hatched chicks always in groups of three with their mother standing guard nearby. We turned right and walked past an acre of 500 hatch boxes, positioned to help nesting auklets, then scanned offshore and spotted both puffins and tube-nose albatross patrolling along the rocks. A short climb took us to the Shubrick Point Lookout, a small shack perched on one of the FARALLONES' miniature mountaintops.

From our lookout, we peered down and there before us were 20,000 murres, "the best view of murres in North America," Hester said. "We've documented an increase in murres since the 1980s, from 60,000 to about 75,000."

According to historian Peter White, murres numbered 300,000 here in the 1850s, but egg-raiders took as many as 500,000 murre eggs in two months in 1854 alone, and 14 million eggs over the course of 40 years. The recovery of the species was temporarily derailed in the 1980s when thousands of murres were drowned in now-banned commercial gill nets and when many others were killed by an oil spill in 1984. Now they are back on the way- up, and still dominate the landscape.

From here, we explored the southwest side of the island, staying on marked paths and well clear of the north half, which is off-limits even to biologists, and eventually discovered a mother elephant seal with a 600-pound baby. Elephant seals, harbor seals, sea lions, northern fur seals, and stellar sea lions all breed at the Farallones in increasing numbers.

Then, off to one side, photographer Rogers spotted a sea lion with a missing head, apparently bit clean off by a great white shark. "That's unusual," Hester said. "Usually, their food of choice is juvenile elephant seals."

The big sharks come and go to the Farallones and are most common in the fall months. It was October when Peter Klimely of the Scripps Institute tagged three 17-footers, the size of the mechanical shark in the *Jaws* movies, in a 45-minute span. As many as 13 or 14 have been documented at one time here.

During Klimely's research, he was stunned one morning to wake up and venture out to his moored Zodiac to discover that the beloved boat had been bit and sunk by a shark the previous night.

"This is a land of intrigue and fascination", he said, "where it seems that anything is possible."

I remember hiking out one night to Land's End in San Francisco after we returned to the mainland, gazing out to the open ocean, and seeing this solitary flashing light in the darkness, the beacon from the lighthouse atop the SOUTHEAST FARALLON. While millions in the Bay Area chase their schedules, just 25 miles out to sea is a place that runs on its own time.

Oceanic Society Expedition

Eight-hour expeditions led by a qualified naturalist are available on select Fridays, Saturdays, and Sundays from June through November. Reservations should be made four weeks in advance and must be made at least three weeks ahead. Saturday or Sunday tours cost $65 per person; Friday tours are $60 per person. The minimum age is 10.

Whales, Porpoises, and Sharks

Off the starboard bow of our boat, there was a tremendous crash in the open ocean. Instantly, all aboard turned to look, but only in time to see a 50-foot circle of ocean froth.

A moment later, this time in full view, a giant humpback whale came shooting out of the sea, launching airborne in a pirouette, then thundering back down in a colossal splash. The whale was 45 feet long, weighing maybe 90,000 pounds, and it was right in front of us.

Seeing something like this can feel like somebody is grabbing you by the ears and lifting you right off the ground. Not only will you never forget the sight, but it will change the way you feel about the world, a place where the wonderful and the remarkable are possible in any moment.

This is the appeal of Oceanic Society Expeditions, the San Francisco–based adventure company, which runs cruises and sea tours in the Gulf of the

Farallones and exotic locations about the hemisphere. The cost of one-day trips exploring the FARALLON ISLANDS, watching whales, marine mammals, and seabirds, ranges from $60 to $65; participants must be at least10 years of age. Reservations are advised two weeks in advance.

Though the Southeast Farallon Island is just 27 miles west of the GOLDEN GATE, it is actually a world apart from what most people experience in their daily lives.

The birdlife is fantastic, attracted by the extraordinary numbers of krill and giant squid in the area. Acres of murres, shearwaters, pelicans, gulls, terns, auklets, and other seabirds provide a sure-thing sideshow for wildlife viewers. But the whales are the most unforgettable.

In the past few years, there have been record sightings of humpback whales as well as blue whales, the largest creature ever to inhabit the earth. (They even beat the dinosaurs.) The humpbacks are the most acrobatic, often jumping in an attempt to knock the barnacles off their backs when they splash down. But 100-foot blue whales are simply awesome. If you're lucky, one might give you a tail salute.

The FARALLON ISLANDS are actually the tops of an undersea mountain range that has managed to poke a few holes through the ocean surface, creating perfect habitat for the marine food chain. That is why it has always been an ideal breeding ground for murres, stellar sea lions, harbor seals, and elephant seals. In turn, their abundance draws great white sharks to the area.

You can often tell when a great white is cruising for lunch because the sea lions will start jumping out of the water, like greyhounds over hurdles, trying to make it back to the safety of land. People on board Farallon expeditions have twice witnessed great white attacks on sea lions.

"These are rare and incredible events for people to see," Mary Jane Schramm of the Oceanic Society told me. "By contrast, we've only witnessed three other such incidents in the past 10 years."

The boat departs Fort Mason Center in SAN FRANCISCO at 8:30 A.M., with a 7:45 A.M. check-in time, so there is no middle-of-the-night wake up and groggy drive out to the wharf like when you go fishing. The tour boat is the *New Superfish*, a 63-foot cruiser piloted by Mick Menigoz. Naturalists onboard will explain the dynamics of the marine environment, the natural history of the critters you're seeing, and conservation issues—as well as anything else you might ask about.

In winter, the featured trips are to see gray whales. Their population is now up to 21,000, and they migrate from their summer feeding ground in the Arctic on south down the great whale highway to the winter calving lagoons in Baja. That means that virtually every day in winter you can go out with an excellent chance of sighting several of these behemoths, perhaps even cruising alongside a pod of them for 40 minutes to an hour.

Whale watching trips have become so popular that for the past couple of years the Oceanic Society has offered one of the most spectacular expeditions in the outdoors, a whale watching/touching trip to Baja. This is where people in small boats can actually stroke the back of a curious and affectionate gray whale. The early spring trips generally run 9 to 12 days, departing from San Diego.

Natural history expeditions to strange and wondrous places across the hemisphere are also being offered. These include expeditions to the Amazon, Peru, Belize, and the Galapagos Islands, where adventure travel and wildlife viewing are merged.

But it is the trips to the Farallon Islands that are best treasured. They can give a Bay Area resident a completely new, fresh perspective on a familiar homeland.

Directions: Tours depart from the Fort Mason Center. From U.S. 101, take the Marina Boulevard exit and follow Marina Boulevard to Buchanan Street. Turn left into the Fort Mason parking area. **Contact:** For information regarding nature cruises to the Farallones, write to Oceanic Society Expeditions, Fort Mason Center, Building E, San Francisco, CA 94123-1394; phone (415) 474-3385 or fax (415) 474-3395. Reservations are recommended two weeks in advance. The Oceanic Society maintains a hot line with recorded whale-sighting information: (415) 474-0488. **Locator:** FARALLON ISLANDS (E1b).

7
BICYCLING

• TOM'S RATINGS •

• FEATURED TRIP •

See last page for Northern California and Bay Area foldout maps.

• TOM'S RATINGS •

THE TOP 5 BIKE RIDES

In the San Francisco Bay Area

The San Francisco Bay Area is the most beautiful metropolitan area in the world—and if you don't believe me, try seeing it on a bicycle. The best bike routes combine the sensational with the divine, offering both lookouts and pristine surroundings. Some of these routes are well known, others are not. But all are safe, suitable for a family, group, or solo riders, and are easily accessed for great half-day adventures.

Because of the Bay Area's temperate climate, any month is good for biking. November is my favorite, with its fall colors, ideal temperatures, and often no wind at all (between storms, that is). It's key for cyclists to pick a roadway or byway where they won't mix with many cars or hikers, because both are incompatible with bikes. Starting with the best, these five bicycle tours do just that, as well as provide great natural beauty:

1. GOLDEN GATE BRIDGE TO SAUSALITO

This is the classic Bay Area ride. You head north across the GOLDEN GATE BRIDGE (the lane on the west side is reserved for bikes on weekends), then upon reaching land, take the loop under the bridge, ride down to Fort Baker, and from there, pedal right into SAUSALITO for eats. For a good side trip, poke around Fort Baker, where there's a great view of the GOLDEN GATE from Yellow Bluff.

Insider's note: Park your vehicle at the southern foot of the GOLDEN GATE BRIDGE, just west of the toll plaza. To extend this into a longer trip, see the Marin Byway ride on page 279.

Contact: Golden Gate Bridge Highway and Transportation District, (415) 921-5858; Golden Gate National Recreation Area (415) 556-0560. **Locator:** GOLDEN GATE BRIDGE (E1b).

2. DUMBARTON BRIDGE TO COYOTE HILLS

The view from the highest point on the DUMBARTON BRIDGE makes you feel like you could reach out and touch the Bay Area's highest peaks: MOUNT HAMILTON, MOUNT DIABLO, MOUNT TAMALPAIS, and MONTARA MOUNTAIN. You are also circled by the South Bay's tidelands and an open expanse of water, all quite sensational. The bay is the highlight, with the DUMBARTON BRIDGE providing a bike path that separates cyclists from car traffic with a concrete barrier.

Insider's note: The best place to park your vehicle is at the eastern foot of the DUMBARTON BRIDGE. From there, the trip can be extended on either side of the South Bay. At NEWARK, you can explore the SAN FRANCISCO BAY NATIONAL WILDLIFE REFUGE or head farther north to COYOTE HILLS REGIONAL PARK. At East PALO ALTO, a paved bike trail is routed south to the PALO ALTO BAYLANDS and beyond (just south of Ming's Restaurant) to a bike trail that extends all the way to Shoreline Regional Park in MOUNTAIN VIEW.

Contact: U.S. Fish and Wildlife Service, Newark, (510) 792-4275. **Locator:** DUMBARTON BRIDGE (E1c). **See featured trip page:** 263.

3. INSPIRATION POINT TO SAN PABLO RIDGE

On this, one of the Bay Area's great family bicycle trips, the trail is routed four miles along the crest of San Pablo Ridge, the East Bay's best vista. The "trail" is actually a small paved road with a dividing line that is off-limits to cars. The views are beautiful in all directions, especially SAN FRANCISCO BAY and the city skyline to the west, as well as BRIONES RESERVOIR to the east. The route is shared by walkers and joggers, but it works out fine, with most of the foot traffic staying just off the paved portion of the trail. Insider's note: There are no rest rooms along the trail, and just a few benches and picnic tables.

Directions: From San Francisco, drive across the Bay Bridge and take Highway 24 into the East Bay hills. Drive through the Caldecott Tunnel, then take the Moraga Way exit. At the bottom of the off-ramp, turn left at Moraga Way (it goes under the freeway and becomes Camino Pablo). Continue on Camino Pablo for two miles, then turn left on Wildcat Canyon Road. Drive about two miles on the winding road and look for the Inspiration Point parking area at the top of the hill on the right. **Contact:** East Bay Regional Park District, (510) 635-0135 extension 2200. **Locator:** INSPIRATION POINT (E1c). **See featured trip page:** 100.

4. MARIN BYWAY, SAUSALITO TO BOTHIN MARSH

A superb biking/jogging/walking path leads from SAUSALITO on north to San Quentin Prison. Park in SAUSALITO and start pedaling north, where you will pass under the U.S. 101 overpass, then continue on the trail through the Bothin Marsh Open Space Preserve. It borders RICHARDSON BAY and is quite pretty and varied, crossing small bridges over tidal waterways. The area is beautiful both at high tide, when the bay is full of water and vibrant with life, as well as low tide, when little sandpipers and migratory birds poke around in the mud.

Insider's note: It is possible to ride from the GOLDEN GATE BRIDGE all the way to San Quentin Prison on this path, with the route interrupted by town streets on only a few occasions.

Peninsula Byway, SAN MATEO to WOODSIDE.

The centerpiece of this trek is Cañada Road, a back road in the beautiful Peninsula foothills. It borders the San Francisco Fish and Game Refuge, Crystal Springs Reservoir, the Pulgas Water Temple, and the PHLEGER ESTATE, and goes all the way to WOODSIDE, where you can find lunch. An excellent parking area is available along Highway 92 near its junction with Interstate 280. This trip is easy, pretty, and who knows, you might even see a herd of deer on the adjacent wildlands.

Insider's note: "Cañada" Road, by the way, is pronounced so it rhymes with "piñata," not the country. On the first and third Sundays of each month from March through October, the road is closed to all motor vehicle traffic from Highway 92 to Edgewood Road.

Contact: San Mateo County Parks, (650) 363-4021. **Locator:** SAUSALITO (E1a).

5. PENINSULA BYWAY TO WOODSIDE

If you get a flat tire on the BAYLANDS BICYCLE TRAIL, it might actually help you enjoy your trip. That's because the slower you go, the better it is. This sprawling acreage of wild marshlands is tucked away near the edge of south SAN FRANCISCO BAY. There is no charge to visit and it is just minutes from U.S. 101, yet it still retains a spirit independent of the nearby metropolis.

The best place to start the trip is right behind the grandstand of the Baylands baseball park.

The opening part of the trail is built from flat, hard crushed rock. It is bordered by a creek on the left and a golf course on the right. Judging by the golfing ability displayed by the hackers, a football helmet and a suit of armor might be suitable apparel. Soon enough the trail turns from rock to hard-packed dirt, and you will wind your way past the golf course and the Palo Alto Airport, then on to the marshlands.

Even on a bike, you'll find yourself intentionally slowing the pace. The air was so clear on one visit that it looked like you could take a running start, leap clean over the bay, and land on the East Bay hills.

We parked and locked our bikes and decided to hoof it. The tidal marsh here is cut by sloughs and teems with diverse bird and marine life, as well as the plants that support them. The food chain that starts in the marshland supports almost all the fish and wildlife in SAN FRANCISCO BAY and its tidelands. Some 250 species of birds use the bay as either a resting spot or home, including birds only rarely seen elsewhere. We counted some 15 snowy egrets. There are also lots of fast little ground squirrels.

If you want to extend your visit, continue to the Baylands Nature Center, where an old wooden walkway lifts you just above the soggy marsh and leads to the edge of the bay. During low tides, the water will roll back and expose bare mudflats for miles. The walkway is accessible to wheelchairs, and for that matter, so is the rock-built section of the bike trail. The entire trail is not wheelchair accessible, because storms soften the dirt portion.

The marshlands are filled with plants such as pickleweed and cordgrass, and to the developer may look like a good spot to pave over with concrete and condominiums. However, this is actually one of the most productive ecosystems on Earth.

When the plants decay, little bits of decomposed material are carried into the bay by tidal action and consumed by small animals such as clams, crabs, snails, and pile worms. The food web is complete when these critters are in turn eaten by seals, birds, large fish, and other animals. The richness of the area is reflected in the diversity of birdlife and the abundance of ground squirrels.

You can also follow the bike path across a bridge, then head down the trail behind PALO ALTO. It goes practically to the DUMBARTON BRIDGE.

By foot, one to three hours is plenty of time to see the Palo Alto Baylands area. Regardless of your physical conditioning or age, it can be enjoyable, because there are no hills.

Sure, the rubber on a wheel is faster than the rubber on a heel, but on the BAYLANDS TRAIL, you can take your pick.

Directions: Follow U.S. 101 to Palo Alto, then take the Embarcadero east exit. At the second light, across from Ming's Restaurant, turn left at Geng Street and continue to its end. The trail begins directly behind the baseball field and is signed. **Mass Transit:** SamTrans, (800) 660-4BUS/4287, doesn't travel east of U.S. 101 on Embarcadero. From the bus stop, it is about a 15-minute walk to the trailhead. **Trip Tip:** Your best chance of seeing the maximum number of birds and wildlife is to go in the early morning, when the fewest people are there. **Pets:** Dogs must be leashed.

Fees: Access is free. **Contact:** Baylands Nature Center, (650) 329-2506, Wednesday through Friday (2 p.m. to 5 p.m.) or weekends (1 p.m. to 5 p.m.). Palo Alto Recreation Department, (650) 329-2261. **Locator:** BAYLANDS TRAIL (E1b). **See featured trip page:** 283.

• TOM'S RATINGS •

THE TOP 5 AREAS TO MOUNTAIN BIKE

In the San Francisco Bay Area

I hate mountain bikes, and I love mountain bikes. I hate them because when I go hiking, they always seem to be running over me. I love them because they're so much fun when used in the right place.

The key to quality biking in the Bay Area is to use the old, abandoned ranch roads that have been converted to trails in so many parks.

There are places where mountain bikes don't belong. That starts with trails that are signed as closed to mountain bikers, trails that are open but too wet to ride on, and trails where proven and potential trail-use conflicts are unresolvable and hazardous to all users. Mountain bikes have absolutely no place in a designated wilderness area.

Here is a capsule look at some of the quality rides in the Bay Area:

1. SAMUEL P. TAYLOR STATE PARK

This redwood paradise is a great place to take the family, particularly for weekend trips based out of the park's campground. The finest mountain biking in the North Bay can be accessed from here. That includes nearby Bolinas Ridge, several rides on ranch roads at POINT REYES, and two pleasant rides within park boundaries—one to Devil's Gulch, the other a paved route along Papermill Creek.

Contact: Samuel P. Taylor State Park, (415) 488-9897; California State Parks, Marin District, (415) 893-1580. **Locator:** SAMUEL P. TAYLOR STATE PARK (E1a).

2. BRIONES REGIONAL PARK

Beautiful BRIONES RESERVOIR is the centerpiece of this park, which covers 5,300 acres of rolling grasslands and oak woodlands. A challenging loop ride is a route that goes from the Homestead Valley Trail to Sindicich Lagoon, around Briones Peak, and back. Sure, this one is a puffer, but the view from the peak is well worth the grind.

Contact: Briones Regional Park, (925) 229-3020; East Bay Regional Park District, (510) 635-0135 extension 2200. **Locator:** BRIONES REGIONAL PARK (E1c).

3. ANNADEL STATE PARK

This park, located just off Highway 12 southeast of SANTA ROSA, provides a myriad of ranch roads to explore. They crisscross 5,000 acres of rocky terrain, including a route that takes you to a backcountry bass lake. "You can easily spend a full day riding at ANNADEL," Hodgson says. (His favorite destinations are Ledson Marsh and the trail toward Lake Ilsanjo, the Rough Go Trail, and the Spring Creek Trail.

Contact: Annadel State Park, (707) 539-3911; California State Parks, Silverado District, (707) 938-1519. **Locator:** ANNADEL STATE PARK (D1). **See featured trip page:** 51.

4. Monte Bello Open Space Preserve

Some of the best riding terrain on the Peninsula is found in this region. A bonus is that the routes connect to adjacent greenbelts, including the Long Ridge Open Space Preserve, the Saratoga Gap Open Space Preserve, Stevens Creek County Park, and the Skyline Ridge Open Space Preserve. It is possible to connect one continuous loop encompassing all of these parks.

Contact: Midpeninsula Regional Open Space District, (650) 691-1200. **Locator:** Monte Bello Open Space Preserve (E1d).

5. Wilder Ranch State Park

This state park is located two miles north of Santa Cruz, adjacent to Highway 1. It is a historical preserve, but hidden beyond the ranch are several excellent mountain biking trails (mostly jeep roads). The trail system is ideal for beginners, yet still fun for advanced riders.

Contact: Wilder Ranch State Park Visitor Center, (831) 426-0505. **Locator:** Santa Cruz (F1).

• Tom's Ratings •

The Top 2 Places to Mountain Bike at Tahoe

The perfect solution to the trail wars between hikers and mountain bikers has been found. No longer need hikers walk in fear, the nightmare of a speeding bike coming over the next rise always lurking in their thoughts. And no longer do bikers need worry about what may suddenly appear in their path around the next bend.

That is because at Lake Tahoe, the conflict has largely been resolved. Bikes have been banned from the Tahoe Rim Trail, perhaps the prettiest hiking trail in the world. Meanwhile, two ski areas have created mountain biking parks where hikers and horses are banned.

Both Northstar-at-Tahoe and Squaw Valley at North Tahoe have huge tracts of land with trails for mountain bikes.

At Tahoe, visitors can rent a bike or bring their own, ride a lift up the mountain, then take their pick of trails for the trip down—or in some cases, the trip up. It is both a perfect place for a mountain biking demon from hell to get his ya-yas out and a tranquil spot for a serene pedal.

For hikers, the Tahoe Rim Trail typically becomes accessible and relatively clear of snow by early June, and is completely hikable by early July.

1. Northstar-at-Tahoe

Northstar-at-Tahoe, located halfway between Truckee and North Tahoe, has created what may be the number one park for mountain biking in Northern California. There are more than 100 miles of trails for bikes only, both on dirt roads and single-track trails. In addition, there is a technical course, complete with hazards such as logs and sand, but fortunately, no hikers.

The mountain bike park at Northstar is heavily forested, with views of Martis Valley and, over the ridge, of Lake Tahoe. The air is clean but thin (give yourself a day to get acclimated), and the sun can be like a branding iron (sunscreen is a must). Sometimes on hot summer afternoons, there are spectacular thundershowers, so get your biking done in the morning.

At the lift, the elevation is 6,330 feet. The first lift transports bikers (and bikes) up to 7,040 feet. Waiting there is another lift that will carry them up to 7,960 feet, the top of

Lookout Mountain. From there, an easy trail is routed east to the Tahoe Rim, from which you'll get an astounding view of LAKE TAHOE. Drinking water is available at lift staging areas.

One of the best trips from Lookout Mountain is a five-mile ride to Watson Lake, a great spot for a picnic. This is a small alpine lake surrounded by conifers, very cold but pretty and quite isolated.

If this sounds good, that's because it is. Most visitors will buy in to a package deal, according to Judy Daniels of Northstar. The most popular is "The Mountain Bike Getaway." It includes lodging for two nights, bike rental for two days (along with a helmet, water bottle, and trail map), and a multilift ride ticket for two days, all for $163 per person.

Of course, you can custom design your own trip. If you bring a bike and helmet (one is required on all trails), you can buy a lift ticket for a day for $15. This is the most popular attraction for young people from the Bay Area, but the deal can be even cheaper. If you want to bypass the lift—and don't mind pedaling up, up, and up—access to Northstar's trail system is free.

Locator: LAKE TAHOE (D4).

2. SQUAW VALLEY

Squaw Valley, the world-class Olympic ski resort, also boasts an excellent mountain biking course. Squaw has bike rentals, a cable car that carries 150 passengers, and 30 miles of service roads and single-track trails. The highlight: the trail system spans six mountain peaks that overlook both the SIERRA NEVADA and LAKE TAHOE, often from the same spot.

Squaw offers several packages. The best deal costs $25 and includes unlimited rides on the cable car and access to the entire park. All-day bike rentals are $25 (and include a helmet); half-day rentals go for $20. For those who simply want access, without use of the lift or a bike rental, the price is $7 per day.

Of course, just because these mountain bike parks are at ski areas does not mean that you ride down the same runs that skiers use. Those are way too steep. You'll be riding on service roads and special trails designed for mountain biking.

The result is a perfect biking experience, with incredible views—and not a hiker's rear end in sight.

Locator: LAKE TAHOE (D4).

Contact for both listings: U.S. Forest Service, Lake Tahoe Basin Management Unit, 870 Emerald Bay Road, Suite 1, South Lake Tahoe, CA 96150, or phone (530) 573-2600. To obtain a free trail map and travel packet for Northstar, write to Northstar Mountain Adventures/Ski and Snowboard Rental Shop, P.O. Box 129, TRUCKEE, CA 96160, or phone (530) 562-2248. For a free trail map and travel packet on Squaw Valley, phone (800) 545-4350. For a free travel packet on North Tahoe, phone (800) 824-6348. **See featured trip page:** 232.

• FEATURED TRIP •

BAYLANDS TRAIL

Rated: The Top 50 Parks; 7; The Top 10 Strolls; 40; The Top 10 Wetlands; 254; The Top 10 Places to View Wildlife; 257; The Top 5 Bike Rides; 278

If you get a flat tire on the BAYLANDS BICYCLE TRAIL, it might actually help you enjoy your trip. That's because the slower you go, the better it is. This sprawling acreage of wild marshlands is tucked away near the edge of south San Francisco Bay. There is no charge to visit and it is just minutes from U.S. 101, yet it still retains a spirit independent of the nearby metropolis.

The best place to start the trip is right behind the grandstand of the Baylands baseball park.

The opening part of the trail is built from flat, hard crushed rock. It is bordered by a creek on the left and a golf course on the right. Judging by the golfing ability displayed by the hackers, a football helmet and a suit of armor might be suitable apparel. Soon enough the trail turns from rock to hard-packed dirt, and you will wind your way past the golf course and the Palo Alto Airport, then on to the marshlands.

Even on a bike, you'll find yourself intentionally slowing the pace. The air was so clear on one visit that it looked like you could take a running start, leap clean over the bay, and land on the East Bay hills.

We parked and locked our bikes and decided to hoof it. The tidal marsh here is cut by sloughs and teems with diverse bird and marine life, as well as the plants that support them. The food chain that starts in the marshland supports almost all the fish and wildlife in San Francisco Bay and its tidelands. Some 250 species of birds use the bay as either a resting spot or home, including birds only rarely seen elsewhere. We counted some 15 snowy egrets. There are also lots of fast little ground squirrels.

If you want to extend your visit, continue to the Baylands Nature Center, where an old wooden walkway lifts you just above the soggy marsh and leads to the edge of the bay. During low tides, the water will roll back and expose bare mudflats for miles. The walkway is accessible to wheelchairs, and for that matter, so is the rock-built section of the bike trail. The entire trail is not wheelchair accessible, because storms soften the dirt portion.

The marshlands are filled with plants such as pickleweed and cordgrass, and to the developer may look like a good spot to pave over with concrete and condominiums. However, this is actually one of the most productive ecosystems on Earth.

When the plants decay, little bits of decomposed material are carried into the bay by tidal action and consumed by small animals such as clams, crabs, snails, and pile worms. The food web is complete when these critters are in turn eaten by seals, birds, large fish, and other animals. The richness of the area is reflected in the diversity of birdlife and the abundance of ground squirrels.

You can also follow the bike path across a bridge, then head down the trail behind Palo Alto. It goes practically to the Dumbarton Bridge.

By foot, one to three hours is plenty of time to see the Palo Alto Baylands area. Regardless of your physical conditioning or age, it can be enjoyable, because there are no hills.

Sure, the rubber on a wheel is faster than the rubber on a heel, but on the Baylands Trail, you can take your pick.

Directions: Follow U.S. 101 to Palo Alto, then take the Embarcadero east exit. At the second light, across from Ming's Restaurant, turn left at Geng Street and continue to its end. The trail begins directly behind the baseball field and is signed. **Mass Transit:** SamTrans, (800) 660-4BUS/4287, doesn't travel east of U.S. 101 on Embarcadero. From the bus stop, it is about a 15-minute walk to the trailhead. **Trip Tip:** Your best chance of seeing the maximum number of birds and wildlife is to go in the early morning, when the fewest people are there. **Pets:** Dogs must be leashed. **Fees:** Access is free. **Contact:** Baylands Nature Center, (650) 329-2506, Wednesday through Friday (2 P.M. to 5 P.M.) or weekends (1 p.m. to 5 p.m.). Palo Alto Recreation Department, (650) 329-2261. **Locator:** PALO ALTO (E1d).

8
SNOW GETAWAYS

• TOM'S RATINGS •

See last page for Northern California and Bay Area foldout maps.

*The area code for all phone numbers followed by an asterisk (*) will change to 559 as of November 14, 1998.

• TOM'S RATINGS •

THE TOP 10 CHANCES FOR BAY AREA SNOW

MOUNT ST. HELENA is Sonoma County's highest mountain, the peak that often strikes such a memorable silhouette when viewed from points south in the Bay Area.

Every February, its summit is commonly flecked with snow from passing storms, quite a treat for most folks accustomed to rain. When the snow level drops to 3,500 feet, the entire mountaintop can get a good pasting of a foot of snow, occasionally even more.

In fact, the best chance for snow at Bay Area peaks is in mid-February, according to my log, a time when the Arctic jet stream often dips down and then barrels full strength right through Northern California. With it comes the heaviest precipitation of the year, including snow when the temperatures are cold enough—and that's often the case at 10 mountaintops that are accessible either on foot or by car in the nine greater Bay Area counties. A simple formula can be used to figure approximate snow levels when storms arrive. For every 1,000-foot gain in altitude, the temperature drops about 3.5 degrees, and it typically starts snowing at 33 degrees. Of course, there are local anomalies that sometimes skew this, but for the most part, the formula works quite well.

Here, listed from highest to lowest, is a summary of the 10 mountains around the Bay Area that have the best chance of getting snow, as well as the snow-point temperature in SAN FRANCISCO:

1. MOUNT ST. HELENA, 4,343 FEET

The trail to the summit requires a climb of 2,068 feet over the course of 4.5 miles. North winds clear the air, making visibility best at this time, with distant views in all directions. Snow temperature: 48 degrees in SAN FRANCISCO.

Contact: Robert Louis Stevenson State Park, (707) 942-4575; California State Parks, Silverado District, (707) 938-1519. **Locator:** MOUNT ST HELENA (D1). **See featured trip page:** 53.

2. MOUNT HAMILTON, 4,062 FEET

You can drive right to the top of this, the highest point in the immediate Bay Area, though the access road is long and extremely twisty. The excellent views are of the Santa Clara Valley to the west, with hundreds of square miles of wildlands to the east. Snow temperature: 47 degrees in SAN FRANCISCO.

Contact: Grant County Park (located on access road to summit), (408) 274-6121. **Locator:** MOUNT HAMILTON (E1d).

3. MOUNT DIABLO, 3,849 FEET

No matter how fouled up things get, you can't foul up the view from MOUNT DIABLO, one of the best lookouts in California. You can drive right to the top and take a short trail around the summit. Snow temperature: 46 degrees in SAN FRANCISCO.

Contact: Diablo State Park, (925) 837-2525. **Locator:** MOUNT DIABLO (E1c). **See featured trip page:** 93.

4. MOUNT UMUNHUM, 3,486 FEET

From anywhere in the Santa Clara Valley, MOUNT UMUNHUM dominates the western horizon. It's that mountain with the big radar station atop it. The trail here is a half-mile route on MOUNT UMUNHUM Road adjacent to

BALD MOUNTAIN, a hilltop knoll with extensive views of the Almaden Valley and across SAN JOSE. Snow temperature: 45 degrees in SAN FRANCISCO.

Contact: Midpeninsula Regional Open Space District, (650) 691-1200. **Locator:** MOUNT UMUNHUM (E1d).

5. CASTLE ROCK, 3,000 FEET

Castle Rock State Park is well known to rock climbers, who practice their art here on both CASTLE ROCK and Goat Rock, two honeycombed sandstone formations. The park is located on SKYLINE RIDGE, just south of the junction with Highway 9, and provides both easy access and good hiking. Snow temperature: 43 degrees in SAN FRANCISCO.

Contact: Castle Rock State Park, (408) 867-2952; California State Parks, Santa Cruz District, (831) 429-2851. **Locator:** CASTLE ROCK STATE PARK (E1d).

6. BALD MOUNTAIN, 2,729 FEET

BALD MOUNTAIN overlooks the Napa Valley, a feature lookout in Sugarloaf Ridge State Park. But getting there requires an 8.2-mile loop hike with a long climb, the most demanding hike in the park. A great side trip in the winter is a pretty 25-foot waterfall located just downstream of the campground on Sonoma Creek. Snow temperature: 42 degrees in SAN FRANCISCO.

Contact: Sugarloaf Ridge State Park, (707) 833-5712; California State Parks, Silverado District, (707) 938-1519. **Locator:** BALD MOUNTAIN (D1).

7. MONUMENT PEAK, 2,594 FEET

MONUMENT PEAK gets overlooked by many, yet the views nearly rival that of MOUNT HAMILTON, offering far-ranging vistas of the Santa Clara Valley. It is a long, demanding hike to the summit, a climb of 2,300 feet over the course of 3.75 miles. Snow temperature: 41 degrees in SAN FRANCISCO.

Contact: Ed Levin County Park, (408) 262-6980. **Locator:** MILPITAS (E1d).

8. MOUNT TAMALPAIS, 2,571 FEET

MOUNT TAMALPAIS is one of the few places that projects a sense of power, and from its highest point, some say that power flows through you. With a parking lot set at the foot of the Summit Trail, the hike is short (about 15 minutes) but steep, rising 330 feet to the top. Snow temperature: 41 degrees in SAN FRANCISCO.

Contact: Mount Tamalpais State Park, (415) 388-2070; California State Parks, Marin District, (415) 893-1580. **Locator:** MOUNT TAMALPAIS (E1a). **See featured trip page:** 62.

9. MISSION PEAK, 2,517 FEET

You climb from 400 feet at the trailhead to the summit of MISSION PEAK at 2,517 feet over a span of just 3.5 miles, one of the most popular methods of self-torture in the Bay Area. The mountain is located just east of FREMONT, and in the spring it's one of the Bay Area's best wildflower walks. Snow temperature: 41 degrees in SAN FRANCISCO.

Contact: East Bay Regional Park District, (650) 635-0135 extension 2200. **Locator:** MISSION PEAK (E1c). **See featured trip page:** 168.

10. MONTARA MOUNTAIN, 1,894 FEET

On a clear day from the top of MONTARA MOUNTAIN, the FARALLON ISLANDS to the northwest look close enough that you could reach out and pluck them right out of the ocean. From the main access gate to the top it's 3.8 miles, including three killer "ups."

Snow temperature: 39 degrees in SAN FRANCISCO.

Contact: Half Moon Bay State Park, (650) 726-8819. **Locator:** MONTARA MOUNTAIN (E1b). **See featured trip pages:** 74 and 80.

• TOM'S RATINGS •

THE TOP 5 LEARN-TO-SKI PACKAGES

In Northern California

Everybody had been saying for so long that I'd hate downhill skiing that I started believing them.

Same with my buddies Michael Furniss and Jeffrey Patty—until one day when the three of us finally tried the sport and discovered a simple exhilaration that is matchless in the winter months.

Now I wonder: How many other people have denied themselves the great pleasure of this sport based on the wayward opinions of others? It is a lot easier to learn than most nonskiers believe, the sense of freedom as you glide downhill is transcendent, and as for cost, the learn-to-ski packages are the best bargains on the mountain.

Furniss, Patty, and I are longtime comrades, going on 20-plus years now, and we have spent weeks at a time on expeditions, including searching for Bigfoot, hiking the John Muir Trail, and climbing the West's highest mountains. But year after year, we never went skiing. Come winter and we might try a three-day poker game with some steelhead fishing mixed in, but skiing? Hey, everybody said we'd hate it.

Finally, out of curiosity, we went. Our first time down the hill, we fell several times and came up howling in delight. There was a sense of euphoria we didn't expect that comes with the sensation of gliding with scarcely any effort, even at very slow speeds. It is the passion of the mountain experience, something we had to labor long hours for during summer expeditions. With skiing it comes light, airy, and without a struggle.

On one of the first trips, I shared a ride on a chairlift with Wayne Wilson, then 68, of REDDING. I remember how he gazed across the mountains, smiling all the time.

"For all the sourpusses out there, skiing is the perfect antidote," Wilson said. "When you're out here on a beautiful day, breathing this pure mountain air, taking in the perfect views, how could anybody complain? The answer is they can't. Nobody can. It is exhilarating."

He's 100 percent right. As far as learning the sport, it is much easier than a lot of skiers make out; Furniss, Patty, and I all advanced from beginner to intermediate after just three or four days of skiing. As you learn, you will also discover more experienced skiers giving advice from all quarters, and occasionally, some of it will actually make sense:

Start on short skis: Begin by using short skis (150s or 160s), which makes turning a lot easier. At the rental shop, have the bindings set light, so your boots will pop right out when you fall.

Stay warm: Wear long underwear, so you can keep warm without having to wear a lot of bulky outer layers.

It's all in the turn: You can adjust to the steepness of any mountain and control your speed by simply heading across the slope instead of down the slope. That makes skiing just a matter of turning back and forth, a skill that you can perfect by visualizing your outside ski coming around on the turn, then shifting your weight from the inside ski to the downhill ski. Learn to do that and you can ski almost anywhere.

Ski the powder: Follow the sun—that is, ski where the sun is shining on the snow, where the fluffy powder-like snow is abundant. The shaded areas can get icy and slick, particularly in the late afternoon.

Keep your kids happy: If you have children, make absolutely certain they will be warm and dry. In addition, don't try to teach them how to ski, but instead enroll them in an all-day kids' program, where they will be surrounded by other youngsters of the same age and ability.

The best deals at ski areas are always the learn-to-ski packages. That's because if they can lure you up to try the sport just once, they are betting you will like it enough to come back again. The industry standard is a Beginner's Special that includes a two-hour lesson, beginner lift tickets, and equipment rental.

Of the 22 ski areas from YOSEMITE to MOUNT SHASTA, five offer something special that makes them excellent places to learn the sport. Here is a rundown:

1. Mount Shasta Ski Park

The layout here is perfect for beginners because newcomers learn on a different hill than the warp-speed experts. Other pluses are low lodging and lift ticket costs, great views toward Mount Lassen, and friendly help. The Beginner's Special costs $40.

Contact: Mount Shasta Ski Park, (530) 926-8600. **Locator:** MOUNT SHASTA (B2). **See featured trip page:** 162.

2. Boreal Ski Area

This is an easy hill. Of the 41 runs, 30 percent are for beginners and 55 percent are for intermediates. That is why it is such a popular place to learn (it gets crowded on weekends). It's easy to reach, about a 90-minute drive from SACRAMENTO to Donner Summit on Interstate 80. The Beginner's Ski Special costs $43; for snowboarders, the rate is $47.

Contact: Boreal Ski Area, (530) 426-3666. **Locator:** LAKE TAHOE (D4).

3. Kirkwood Ski Resort

The Beginner's Special here is $43. The terrain is 50 percent intermediate and 15 percent beginner, with a special area for beginner lessons. It's a friendly kind of place, excellent for families and completely self-contained.

Contact: Kirkwood Ski Resort, (209) 258-6000.* Web site: www.skikirkwood.com. **Locator:** SOUTH LAKE TAHOE (D4).

4. Badger Pass Ski Area

The Yosemite Ski School is well known as one of the finest in the country. It is a small ski area compared to the Tahoe monsters, with just nine runs (four lifts), but 35 percent of them are rated for beginners, and 50 percent for intermediates. The valley loop with Half Dome and El Capitan, 22 miles from the ski area, is an unparalleled side trip. The Beginner's Special costs $40.

Contact: Yosemite National Park, (209) 372-0200* (touch-tone menu selection). **Locator:** YOSEMITE NATIONAL PARK (E4). **See featured trip page:** 239.

5. Dodge Ridge Ski Area

You either have fun learning how to ski or your money will be refunded. Dodge also runs one of the largest learn-to-ski programs in the country for children ages 3 to 12. The Beginner's Special (ages 13 and up) costs $45.

Contact: Dodge Ridge Ski Area, (209) 965-3474.* **Locator:** Sonora (E4).

• Tom's Ratings •

The Top 16 Nordic Skiing Areas

In Northern California

Cross-country skiing is inexpensive, adventure filled, calming—and even slow, if you want it to be. It is relatively easy to learn and one of the few outdoor sports in which female participants outnumber males, 53 to 47 percent.

"Cross-country skiing is just so very peaceful," said Jacqui James at Royal Gorge Cross-Country Ski Resort. "It's also an escape, getting away from the crowds, faxes, and phones. I've done it for years and I love it. I tried downhill once or twice, but it wasn't for me. I much prefer cross-country. You can set your own pace."

You also don't have to look over your shoulder, something that can be frustrating for downhill skiers on crowded slopes. In fact, the differences between downhill and cross-country skiing are amazing, with no lines, no stress, and no alpine hotdoggers involved in the latter. It's also a lot safer. Note, for instance, that there are usually no ambulances waiting at the end of the trail.

California has about 25 cross-country ski areas, as well as dozens of other locations where this sport is popular. At nordic centers, the groomed ski trails have two grooves, one for each ski. Set one ski in each groove, and you're off. You push along in a walking motion and enjoy the glide. Instead of strapping your boots into a fixed binding, as with downhill skis, you are attached to your skis by just the tips of your boots. Cross-country skis are also longer and narrower than downhill skis and have no cutting edges. After all, the idea is to glide, not to race and make cuts.

In most cases, novices can ski quite a bit of terrain with just a few friendly pointers from a companion. With a lesson and a little practice, you can enjoy most runs in any nordic center. As for expense, rental of boots, skis, and poles is usually about $16.50 to $19.50 a day, and a ski pass goes for about the same. Package deals can usually be found in the $25 to $30 range.

For instance, one of best deals anywhere is at Royal Gorge, the capital of cross-country skiing in the West, located at Soda Springs along Interstate 80 in the Sierra Nevada. For $30 to $40, you get rental skis, boots, poles, a 90-minute group lesson, and a full-day trail pass. For information, phone (530) 426-3871.

Royal Gorge has more than 80 trails that span over 300 kilometers of set tracks, far more than any other cross-country ski area in the West. Other quality areas include Kirkwood, Tahoe-Donner, and Tahoe Nordic, all with 65 to 70 kilometers of set track trails. The trails are usually marked by ribbons tied off of trees poking up through the snow. At the big cross-country areas, the network of tracks can make it look like an elaborate miniature railroad has taken over the area for winter.

The quiet is something else. You will find that once you get used to it, you may never again want to put up with lines, noise, and high prices at one of the big downhill ski parks.

When you first start, cross-country skiing seems to require little physical effort. But after even 20 minutes, you will realize that this is an aerobic workout, great exercise. After a day or two at it, the sport will hone your body like a knife blade on a whet stone. After a few weekends, you will glow from the exhilaration.

1. Royal Gorge Cross-Country Ski Resort

Directions: Near Soda Springs off Interstate 80. **Contact:** (530) 426-3871. **Locator:** Soda Springs (D4).

2. Spooner Lake Cross-Country Ski Area

Directions: South of Incline Village. **Contact:** (702) 749-5349. **Locator:** Lake Tahoe (D4).

3. Bear Valley

Directions: 55 miles east of Angels Camp on Highway 4. **Contact:** (209) 753-2834. **Locator:** Bear Valley (E4).

4. Tahoe Nordic

Directions: Two miles east of Tahoe City off Highway 28;. **Contact:** (530) 583-9858. **Locator:** Tahoe City (D4).

5. Yosemite Mountaineering

Contact: Yosemite Mountaineering, based in Yosemite Valley; (209) 372-8344. **Locator:** Yosemite National Park (E4).

6. Mount Shasta Nordic Center

Directions: Northeast of Redding on Highway 89. **Contact:** (530) 926-8600. **Locator:** Redding (B2).

7. Fifth Season

Contact: (530) 926-3606. **Locator:** Mount Shasta (A3).

8. Kirkwood Cross-Country Ski Area

Directions: South of Tahoe off Highway 88. **Contact:** (209) 258-6000. **Locator:** Lake Tahoe (D4).

9. Clair Tappaan Lodge

Directions: Near Soda Springs off Interstate 80. **Contact:** (530) 426-3632. **Locator:** Soda Springs (D4).

10. Squaw Valley Nordic

Directions: Northwest of Tahoe off Highway 89. **Contact:** (530) 581-6637. **Locator:** Lake Tahoe (D4).

11. Tahoe Paradise Sports

Directions: Near the airport in South Lake Tahoe. **Contact:** (530) 577-2121. **Locator:** South Lake Tahoe (D4).

12. Strawberry Lodge Touring Company

Directions: Eight miles east of Kyburz off U.S. 50. **Contact:** (530) 659-7200. **Locator:** Kyburz (D4).

13. Childs Meadows

Directions: Nine miles southeast of Lassen Volcanic National Park on Highway 36. **Contact:** (530) 595-3383. **Locator:** Lassen Volcanic National Park (B3).

14. Lassen Ski Touring

Directions: At the southwest entrance to Lassen Park on Highway 36. **Contact:** (530) 550-0373. **Locator:** Lassen National Forest (B3).

15. Bijou Cross-Country Ski Area

Directions: In South Lake Tahoe. **Contact:** 530) 542-6055. **Locator:** South Lake Tahoe (D4).

16. NORTHSTAR-AT-TAHOE CROSS-COUNTRY CENTER

Directions: North of Tahoe off Highway 267. **Contact:** (530) 562-1010. **Locator:** LAKE TAHOE (D4).

• TOM'S RATINGS •

THE TOP 4 PLACES FOR KIDS TO SKI

In Northern California

What do you do with your small children when you go skiing? Leave them with a babysitter? Spend your day on the Bunny Hill? An alternative for parents is to enroll youngsters in a carefully designed kids' ski program. Such programs are easy and fun for kids, and have worked so well for families that many ski areas are offering some form of an all-day program for children ages 6 to 12.

The program is called "Ski Wee" at some ski areas, "Junior Program" at others, but regardless of the name, it allows both parents and their children to enjoy a day of skiing on their own, out of each other's way. In the process, many problems are solved.

Youngsters often perform much better without pressure from their parents. They'll enjoy being in a class with other children around their age and level of experience. Parents can have a much better day of skiing without worrying about their children. The program lasts all day and includes lunch.

It's all part of a national instructional program formatted by *Ski Magazine.* Some 50 ski resorts are taking part in the program across the country, including four in the SIERRA.

The nearest to the Bay Area is the Dodge Ridge Ski Area, located east of SONORA on Highway 108. Heavenly Valley at SOUTH TAHOE, Sierra Summit south of YOSEMITE, and June Mountain in the southeast SIERRA also feature the program. A number of other ski resorts have junior programs, but they do not follow the format designed by *Ski Magazine.* At Dodge Ridge, the program costs $50 per day and includes ski rentals, instruction, full-time supervision, lunch, and snacks. If you supply the skis, the price is $43. The junior ski class starts at 10 a.m., when the youngsters are placed in groups of six, all grouped according to age and skiing ability. Most of the instructors are young women with professional experience in teaching children.

First the youngsters are taught how to put on skis and walk on snow. They are then shown some basic skiing techniques. Instead of a traumatic test in front of their parents, any mistakes just become good fun with a group of friends, all of whom are likely making the same mistakes. By the end of the day, the kids will know how to get on and off rope tows and lifts, how to make a straight downhill run, and how to fall down.

For young children, the most difficult part of the lesson is not how to ski, but how to stop. Some just fall down and consider the mission accomplished. However, with a little practice, kids can learn to "snow plow." This position slows down the skier on a downhill run.

When parents return at 4 p.m., the kids are given a progress card, a bag of treats, and a list of ski pointers.

A lot of people think skiing is just for adults. This program is proving that just isn't true. In addition, it solves two problems at once: It frees adults for a day of skiing, and it allows children to learn the sport in a fun, pressure-free environment.

The following ski resorts feature *Ski Magazine's* instructional program:

1. Heavenly Valley

Directions: Located near Lake Tahoe on U.S. 50. **Contact:** (530) 541-1330 or write to P.O. Box 2180, Stateline, NV 89449. **Locator:** Lake Tahoe (D4). **See featured trip page:** 232.

2. Dodge Ridge Ski Area

Directions: Located on Highway 108, 32 miles east of Sonora. **Contact:** (209) 965-3474. A brochure is available by writing to P.O. Box 1188, Pinecrest, CA 95364. **Locator:** Sonora (E4).

3. Mammoth Mountain

Directions: Located near Bishop in the eastern Sierra off U.S. 395. **Contact:** (760) 934-2571 or write to P.O. Box 24, Mammoth Lakes, CA 93546. **Locator:** Mammoth Lakes (E5). **See featured trip page:** 237.

4. Sierra Summit

Directions: Located just south of Yosemite National Park along Highway 168. **Contact:** (209) 893-3316 or write to P.O. Box 236, Lakeshore, CA 93634. **Locator:** Sonora (E4).

• Tom's Ratings •

The Top 12 Snow Parks

In Northern California

When you're young, there is nothing quite so enjoyable as throwing a light, fluffy snowball at the back of your brother's head.

Unless, that is, you're taking a flying leap into a 10-foot mound of light, dry powder snow and are then mistaken for the Abominable Snowman. Or sailing down a snowbank on a metal saucer. Or maybe taking a little adventure on cross-country skis into a forest wonderland.

On second thought, nothing can top nailing your brother with a snowball.

The towering snowfalls of winter in the Sierra Nevada have inspired many a well-aimed throw. They have also inspired many a family to head up to the snow country to play in the stuff, praying they wind up in a good spot. The answer to the prayer method is provided by 19 "Sno Parks," offshoots of California State Parks.

The Sno Parks are actually snow-cleared parking lots, with direct access to snow-play areas, cross-country skiing, and in a few cases, snow-mobiling. They are ideal for families who want winter recreation without the high price of outfitting a family for downhill skiing. You pay a few bucks for a parking permit, which is then used to pay for snowplowing to keep the parking area clear. Speaking of snowplows, if you plan on parking overnight at any of the Sno Parks where it är permitted, it is highly advisable to stake your car with poles (1 in. x 2 in. x 8 ft. is best) on each side exposed to snow-removal equipment. You avoid the risk of having your car damaged by unsuspecting snowplow operators, should fresh snow fall during the night.

To obtain an annual Sno Park pass ($25) or a onetime permit ($5), phone (916) 324-1222 or write to Sno Park Program Manager, P.O. Box 942896, Sacramento, CA 94296-0001. There's a $75 fine for parking without a permit. Note that all parking is on a first-come, first-served basis, and having a parking permit does not guarantee you a spot. The most popular areas are at Donner Summit, Carson Pass, and Lake Alpine, which fill nearly every weekend morning in the winter.

Thus, you need some strategy in selecting your destination. Here is an area-by-area guide to assist in your approach:

1. Cisco Grove

Located on the north side of Interstate 80 at Cisco, Nevada County, at the entrance to Thousand Trails Campground. There's a small snow-play area, good for snowmobiling. No overnight parking is allowed. Guided snowmobile tours are available at Thousand Trails Campground. Capacity: 50 cars.

Contact: Cisco Grove, (530) 426-3362. **Locator:** Cisco Grove (D3).

2. Yuba Gap

Located on the south side of Interstate 80 at Yuba Gap, Nevada County, on the adjacent frontage road. It's excellent for cross-country skiing, with marked trails. No overnight parking is permitted. Guided snowmobile tours are also available. Obtain Sno Park permits at the Snow Flower grocery store. Capacity: 50 cars.

Contact: Sno Park Program Manager, (916) 324-1222. **Locator:** Cisco Grove (D3).

3. Donner Summit

Located on the south side of Interstate 80 just beyond Boreal Inn, in Nevada County at the Castle Peak exit. This very popular cross-country skiing area can be crowded on weekends, often filled to capacity early on weekend mornings. No snow playing is allowed. It's bordered by private property. On steeper slopes in the backcountry, beware of avalanche danger after heavy snowfall. Capacity: 70 cars.

Contact: Sno Park Program Manager, (916) 324-1222. **Locator:** Donner Summit (D4).

4. Donner Lake

Located on the south side of Interstate 80 at Donner Lake, Nevada County, at Donner Memorial State Park off the Donner Lake exit. There's a limited snow-play area (no sledding), but restrictions against snowmobiles keep things quiet. No overnight parking is allowed. Capacity: 35 cars.

Contact: Sno Park Program Manager, (916) 324-1222. **Locator:** Donner Summit (D4).

5. Blackwood Canyon

Located on the west side of Highway 89, three miles south of Tahoe City, Placer County. This is a decent snow-play area for North Tahoe visitors. Cross-country skiers should avoid the steeper terrain on the north side of Blackwood Canyon, as there is serious avalanche danger. Capacity: 30 cars.

Contact: Sno Park Program Manager, (916) 324-1222. **Locator:** Tahoe City (D4).

6. Taylor Creek

Located on the west side of Highway 89 near Fallen Leaf Lake in South Tahoe, El Dorado County, near Camp Richardson. Great cross-country ski trips are available to Fallen Leaf Lake. There's a snow-play area; no snowmobiles are allowed. Capacity: 30 cars.

Contact: Sno Park Program Manager, (916) 324-1222. **Locator:** South Lake Tahoe (D4).

7. Echo Summit

Located on the south side of U.S. 50 at Echo Summit, El Dorado County. Here's one of the best snow-play areas anywhere, but it's no secret and is very popular. No snowmobiles are allowed; there's some cross-country skiing in the area. Capacity: 100 cars.

Contact: Sno Park Program Manager, (916) 324-1222. **Locator:** TWIN BRIDGES (D4).

8. Echo Lake

Located on the road to Echo Lake off U.S. 50, in El Dorado County, one mile west of Echo Summit. Excellent for cross-country skiing, but poor for snow playing. No snowmobiles are allowed. Capacity: 100 cars.

Contact: Sno Park Program Manager, (916) 324-1222. **Locator:** TWIN BRIDGES (D4).

9. Iron Mountain

On Iron Mountain Road (past Iron Mountain Ski Area) off Highway 88, El Dorado County. At this popular snowmobile area, the machines are loud and fast. Get the picture? Capacity: 30 cars.

Contact: Sno Park Program Manager, (916) 324-1222. **Locator:** IRON MOUNTAIN (D4).

10. Carson Pass

On Highway 88 at CARSON PASS, 60 miles east of JACKSON, or 25 miles south of LAKE TAHOE. The parking lot is at CARSON PASS on the south side of the highway. It's an outstanding cross-country skiing spot with a small snow-play area (rated poor); no snowmobiles are allowed, a plus. It often fills early on weekends. Capacity: 50 cars.

Contact: Sno Park Program Manager, (916) 324-1222. **Locator:** CARSON PASS (D4).

11. Lake Alpine

On Highway 4, 50 miles east of Angels Camp, just past the turnoff to the Mount Reba Ski Area. With a beautiful setting and an excellent snow-play area, this place is popular and often crowded. It usually fills up on weekends.

Contact: Sno Park Program Manager, (916) 324-1222. **Locator:** LAKE ALPINE (E4).

12. Meiss Meadows

On Highway 88 at CARSON PASS, 60 miles east of JACKSON or 25 miles south of LAKE TAHOE. Meiss Meadows, once part of the Carson Pass park, is located just one-quarter mile west of that park on the north side of the highway. No snowmobiles and no overnight parking are allowed. Capacity: 50 cars.

Contact: Sno Park Program Manager, (916) 324-1222. **Locator:** CARSON PASS (D4).

THE FOLLOWING ARE ALSO AVAILABLE:

- Balsam Meadows, Tamarack, Coyote, and Eastwood, all in Fresno County off Highway 168; (209) 855-5360.
- Huntington Lake, Fresno County, off Huntington Lake Road; (209) 855-5360.
- Rock Creek, Mono County, off U.S. 395; (760) 935-4239.
- Yuba Pass, Sierra County, located on the south side of Highway 49; (925) 862-1297.

9
BOATING AND WATER SPORTS

• Tom's Ratings •

• Featured Trips •

See last page for Northern California and Bay Area foldout maps.

*The area code for all phone numbers followed by an asterisk (*) will change to 559 as of November 14, 1998.

• TOM'S RATINGS •

THE TOP 5 HOUSEBOATING SITES

In Northern California

Just turn the key, let the engine rumble to life, then point the houseboat toward open water. That is about as difficult as it gets. The rest of your vacation can seem like it is on automatic pilot.

Houseboats are available for rent at four of the state's largest lakes, SHASTA, TRINITY, OROVILLE, and DON PEDRO, as well as at the SAN JOAQUIN DELTA. A houseboat is a floating RV in which you can barbecue from your front porch, fish from your back deck, camp anywhere, and enjoy sun, water, and a complete getaway from working. For many, nothing could be better.

The prices vary greatly according to the size of the boat, how many days rented, whether it includes a weekend, and if it's peak season. In the Delta during the summer, for instance, a houseboat that sleeps six costs $795 for three days, Friday afternoon through Sunday evening. At SHASTA LAKE, it can be over $2,000 for a week.

Even on the high end, however, the cost can be whittled down by sharing the boat with a group of people. At Holiday Harbor at SHASTA LAKE, for example, a houseboat that sleeps 12 rents for $2,520 by the week (in the summer), which is equivalent to $30 a day per person. That is why it is one of the favorite types of vacations for groups of college students—or anybody else for that matter. It is safe, easy, and fun.

Here is a capsule look at the destinations where houseboats are available, listed from north to south:

1. TRINITY LAKE

TRINITY LAKE is located in the mountains of Northern California north of WEAVERVILLE, right at the foot of the TRINITY ALPS.

Because of its location, summer and warmer temperatures do not arrive until mid-June, and that means reservations are easier to come by than at other houseboat destinations. It's a big reservoir, 175 miles of beautiful shoreline, surrounded by national forest. In the cool spring months, fishing for trout and smallmouth bass is often excellent; the state record for smallmouth was caught here. Because it is such a long drive from the Bay Area, there are far fewer vacationers here than at the other spots listed.

Contact: Cedar Stock Resort, (530) 286-2225; Estrellita Marina, (530) 286-2215; Trinity Alps Marina, (530) 286-2282. **Locator:** TRINITY LAKE (B1).

2. SHASTA LAKE

This is the houseboating capital of the West. Giant SHASTA has 1,000 houseboat rentals and plenty of water for them, 365 miles of shoreline in all. It's one of the few places where there is enough room for everybody: anglers, water-skiers, swimmers, and all kinds of boats. With five major lake arms, there are many little secret spots that can be explored only by boat. The fishing is often excellent in the spring and early summer, with abundant trout and bass.

Contact: For a complete list and prices of the seven marinas with houseboat rentals, contact the Shasta Cascade Wonderland Association, 1699 Highway 273, Anderson, CA 96007; (800) 474-2782. Holiday Harbor, (530) 238-2383 or (800) 776-BOAT/2628. **Locator:** SHASTA LAKE (B2).

3. LAKE OROVILLE

The reservoir covers some 15,000 acres, including extensive lake arms, each of which is like a separate lake. Since it is set at 900 feet in the foothill country, warm weather arrives here earlier than at lakes farther north. The fishing for trout and bass is very good from April through early June; then when the water warms up from July through early fall, it becomes ideal for waterskiing and swimming.

Contact: Bidwell Marina, (530) 589-3165; Lime Saddle Marina, (530) 877-2414. **Locator:** LAKE OROVILLE (C3).

4. SAN JOAQUIN DELTA

The Delta is a vast mosaic of waterways, covering more than 1,000 miles of navigable waters. You can scan a map and dream of where you want to go, then spend a week exploring and not even see a fraction of it. There is just so much water. Most of the houseboat rentals are in the Back Delta near King Island (generally near STOCKTON). This area has many quiet sloughs where you can park a boat for the night, fish for catfish, or just sit there and do absolutely nothing except look at the water. Sounds good.

Contact: Herman and Helen's, (209) 951-4634; Paradise Point Marina, (209) 952-1000. **Locator:** SAN JOAQUIN DELTA (D1, E2). **See featured trip page:** 373.

5. DON PEDRO RESERVOIR

The last time you drove to YOSEMITE, you probably went right past DON PEDRO, that big reservoir with the extended lake arms, located right along Highway 49 in the gold country. It's worth a look, especially in the spring when it's fullest. The lake can cover 13,000 surface acres with 160 miles of shoreline. The far-reaching arms provide secluded haunts, both for parking a boat for the night or fishing for bass, bluegill, and catfish. It is set at 800 feet in the foothills 30 miles east of MODESTO, so the weather is very hot in the summer.

Contact: Don Pedro Marina, (209) 852-2369; Moccasin Point Marina, (209) 989-2206. **Locator:** DON PEDRO RESERVOIR (E3).

• TOM'S RATINGS •

THE TOP 18 RIVER RAFTING EXPEDITIONS

In Northern California

Ever wondered what it feels like to get shot out of a cannon? Then you should try rafting the Upper KLAMATH RIVER and tumbling through Hell's Corner Gorge. Rapids such as Satan's Gate, Scarface, and Ambush can make you feel like a human cannonball.

Those who don't want to join the circus should consider a canoe or raft trip down the MIDDLE KLAMATH, from Horse Creek on downriver. There's just enough white water to make the trip exciting, but it's still tame enough for a family outing.

If you have never taken a raft or canoe trip, you may be curious about why people get excited about the sport. You can find the answer on the UPPER KLAMATH. I recommend it for curiosity seekers going solo, experts looking for a challenge, and even for a family outing.

One spring, when the KLAMATH was near flood stage, six of us in three rafts challenged the entire river from its headwaters in Oregon all the way to the PACIFIC OCEAN. We did it in six days, covering as many as 50 miles per day, and tumbled through more than a thousand rapids in the process.

The whole idea about rafting is to get out there on the "edge" and the KLAMATH can get you there. The first rapid you face in the Hell's Corner Gorge is called Caldera. We were roaring downriver when the nose of the raft headed straight into a big wave and the boat completely disappeared underwater. Moments later, the raft popped up in the air, surging forward—and right then a cross wave hit from the right and flipped us. I flew out of the raft like a piece of popcorn.

I went floating down the rapids, the hydraulics of the river pulling me underwater, and then I popped to the surface. The life-saving equipment makes sure of that. You just time your breathing as you go bobbing along until you eventually come to an eddy, where you can paddle over to safety.

A lot of people never flip, but to most it's kind of like a badge of honor. "Yeah, I rafted Hell's Corner Gorge and Branding Iron got us good."

River rapids are rated from Class I to VI, with Class I being a piece of cake and Class VI being suicide. The UPPER KLAMATH has Class IV and V white water, and the MIDDLE KLAMATH has Class II sprinkled with some Class III.

So if you want more of a family-oriented trip, the MIDDLE KLAMATH provides it. By raft or canoe, it's a fun trip.

My preference on the MIDDLE KLAMATH is to go by canoe. You get more speed, faster cuts, faster decisions, and, alas, faster flips.

Many rivers on the slopes of the SIERRA NEVADA run low in the summer. The KLAMATH provides the answer all summer long.

Here's a river-by-river guide, listed by level of difficulty:

EASY TO MODERATE:

1. Lower Klamath River

Beginners are advised to put in below Weitchpec, as the river broadens here and the rapids are not as menacing. Above Weitchpec, particularly near Happy Camp, rafting experience is necessary to safely navigate the dangerous rapids known as the Ikes. Ishi Pishi Falls, however, should be avoided at any cost. It is Class VI and cannot be attempted without risking your life.

Contact: Klamath National Forest, Happy Camp Ranger District, (530) 842-6131; Whitewater Voyages, (800) 488-7238; Turtle River Rafting, (800) 726-3223 or fax (530) 926-3443. **Locator:** KLAMATH RIVER (A1).

2. Trinity River

The 16-mile stretch from LEWISTON to DOUGLAS CITY is a good weekend trip. From BIG SUR to South Fork Junction is 21 miles. It's okay for intermediates.

Contact: Shasta-Trinity National Forest, Big Bar Ranger District, (530) 623-6106; Kimtu Adventures, (800) 562-8475; Turtle River Rafting, (800) 726-3223 or fax (530) 926-3443. **Locator:** TRINITY RIVER (B1). **See featured trip page:** 317.

3. Sacramento River

With 400 miles of river to choose from, there's something for everybody. Above Shasta Dam, the river is difficult, especially for canoeists. Downstream of REDDING, the only real tough spot is Iron Canyon Rapids. From RED BLUFF on down it's 100 miles of easy paddling.

Contact: Shasta Cascade Wonderland Association, (800) 474-2782; Turtle River Rafting, (800) 726-3223 or fax

(530) 926-3443. **Locator:** SACRAMENTO RIVER (C2, D2).

4. Eel River

The section from Dos Rios to Alderpoint (50 miles) is for advanced rafters only, and you should be wary of the waterfall beyond the sharp turn at Island Mountain. From Alderpoint to the South Fork (32 miles), however, it's an easy paddle and an ideal first trip.

Contact: Turtle River Rafting, (800) 726-3223 or fax (530) 926-3443. **Locator:** EEL RIVER (B0, C1).

5. Middle Fork of the Eel River

This is a beautiful run, sitting high in the mountains with picture-postcard scenery. The river is rarely in good shape past June.

Contact: Tributary Whitewater, (800) 672-3846 or (800) 6-RAFTING/672-3846. **Locator:** EEL RIVER (B0).

6. Cache Creek

Here's a six-mile, one-day run that is ideal for the Bay Area rafter; the put-in is upstream of Rumsey. The river is a little over 100 miles from San Francisco. One note: Please remember to pick up your trash.

Contact: For a brochure or information, phone Upper Cache and American River Rafting Trips, (800) 97-RIVER/977-4837. **Locator:** CACHE CREEK (D1). **See featured trip page:** 321.

7. South Fork of the American River

A good put-in is at the Route 193 Bridge, and take-out is at either the picnic area beyond the Marshall Gold Discovery State Historical Park (six miles) or the short road off Route 49. Warning: Do not try to run from Peavine Ridge Road to El Dorado Powerhouse—it's a death trip!

Contact: Adventure Connection, (800) 556-6060. **Locator:** AMERICAN RIVER (D3).

8. East Fork of the Carson River

The river has many good campsites in the 20 miles from Markleeville to Gardnerville. There's one bad set of rapids about halfway through the run. The beauty of this mountain river run is one to remember. By the way, the casino in Gardnerville is a killer.

Contact: Ahwahnee Whitewater, (209) 533-1401, fax (209) 533-1409, or (800) 359-9790. **Locator:** CARSON RIVER (D4).

9. Stanislaus River

This was the second most popular stretch of water in America until it was flooded by the backwaters of the New Melones Reservoir. What's left is a moderate stretch of water with some small rapids from Knights Ferry to the Oakdale bridge (13 miles).

Contact: Stanislaus National Forest, Groveland Ranger District, (209) 962-7825; OARS, (800) 446-RAFT/7238. **Locator:** STANISLAUS RIVER (E3).

10. Kings River

The nine miles of river from Upper Kings Campground to Kirch Flat Campground are okay for intermediates. Warning: Only advanced rafters should try the stretch from Pine Flat Dam to Centerville. It's beautiful water, but lives have been lost here.

Contact: Sierra National Forest, Kings River Ranger District, (209) 855-8321*; U.S. Army Corps of Engineers, (209) 787-2589*; Zephyr Whitewater, (800) 431-3636 or fax (209) 532-4525. **Locator:** KINGS RIVER (F4).

DIFFICULT:

11. Upper Klamath River

The Upper Klamath starts in Oregon and tumbles its way into Copco Lake, with exciting rapids along the way. It's runnable throughout the year because flows are regulated by releases from the John C. Boyle Reservoir in Oregon.

Contact: Wilderness Adventures, (800) 323-7238 or fax (530) 692-2605. **Locator:** Klamath River (A1, A2).

12. Salmon River

Here's a favorite for experts. Many short, quick rapids run from the forks of the Salmon on downstream to where it pours into the Klamath. The scenery is outstanding with high canyon walls bordering the river.

Contact: Wilderness Adventures, (800) 323-7238 or fax (530) 692-2605. **Locator:** Salmon River (A1).

13. South Fork of the Eel River

A good put-in is at Richardson Grove State Park, from where you can float 40 miles through redwoods to Weott. It's a good run that takes three or four days. Warning: Portage around the low-level bridge before Benbow Lake.

Contact: Tributary Whitewater, (530) 346-6812 or fax (530) 346-6499. **Locator:** Eel River (B0, C1)).

14. North Fork of the Yuba River

The preferred stretch of water is the lower portion from Goodyear's Bar to the Route 20 Bridge, but portage around the 10-foot drop-off near Route 49. Warning: Do not try the four miles from Downieville to Goodyear's Bar; it is unrunnable.

Contact: Tributary Whitewater, (530) 346-6812 or fax (530) 346-6499. **Locator:** Yuba River (D3).

15. North Fork of the American River

This is a very popular run from Colfax to the North Fork Dam (18 miles) but is dangerous at a few spots. It is advisable to scout rapids before attempting to run. Warning: Do not try the Giant Gap Run below the dam—it's suicide.

Contact: American River Touring Association (ARTA), (800) 323-2782 or fax (209) 962-7873. **Locator:** American River (D3).

16. Main Tuolumne River

Here's a real heart-thumper. From Lumsden Campground to Ward Ferry Bridge, it's 18 miles of wild beauty. Until flows drop in midsummer, this stretch of water is almost continuous rapids.

Contact: Bureau of Land Management, Folsom Office, (916) 985-4474 or fax (916) 985-3259; Sierra Mac River Trips, (800) 457-2580. **Locator:** Tuolumne River (E3).

17. Merced River

The best water here is from Briceburg to Bagby, 15 miles of Class III and IV rapids. When you portage around the 20-foot waterfall, look out for poison oak. The rapids ease greatly beyond the waterfall.

Contact: Bureau of Land Management, Folsom Office, (916) 985-4474 or fax (916) 985-3259; Mariah Wilderness, (800) 4-MARIAH/462-7424 or fax (510) 233-0956. **Locator:** Merced River (E3).

18. Upper Kern River

The prized section on this river is from Kernville to Lake Isabella, a half-day, five-mile run for advanced paddlers only. Very scenic. Avoid the river above the bridge, which is a very tough run.

Contact: Kern River Tours, (760) 379-4616 or fax (760) 370-2103. **Locator:** KERN RIVER (F5).

• TOM'S RATINGS •

THE TOP 16 PLACES TO RENT BOATS

In the San Francisco Bay Area

Put this in your mental cash register and ring it up: When spring and summer arrive, there is no better time to go boating, even if you do not have a boat. That is because there are 16 places in the greater Bay Area where you can rent a boat, and that includes streams, lakes, the DELTA, and the PACIFIC OCEAN.

1. LAKE BERRYESSA

This is the Bay Area's backyard vacationland, with 750 campsites and seven resort areas, 165 miles of shoreline, and, alas, plenty of people taking advantage of it. The only way to stake out your own personal spot is to do it by boat. My favorite areas are the extreme south end of the lake, from Markley Cove to the Narrows, and the extreme north end of the lake, up the Putah Creek arm. These areas are quieter than the rest of the lake and provide better fishing because of the large number of coves.

Contact: Markley Cove Resort, (707) 966-2134. **Locator:** LAKE BERRYESSA (D1). **See featured trip page:** 359.

2. RUSSIAN RIVER

You either work together with your partner for adventure and triumph on a canoe trip down the RUSSIAN RIVER or you have a series of confrontations and eventually fall in. Spring rains leave the river fresh and lively, and the area's natural beauty can surprise you, especially the 10-mile stretch of redwoods between FORESTVILLE and GUERNEVILLE.

Contact: Burke's Canoes, (707) 887-1222; Trowbridge's Canoe Rentals, (707) 433-7247. **Locator:** RUSSIAN RIVER (D1). **See featured trip page:** 324.

3. LAKE SONOMA

This is a big lake set in the rich foothill country near the RUSSIAN RIVER, with thousands of hidden coves, boat-in campsites, and an adjacent 8,000-acre wildlife area with 40 miles of hiking trails. In spring, it can provide some of the best bass fishing in the state. The conflict between high- and low-speed boaters has been resolved by making two miles of the Warm Springs Creek arm and five miles of the Dry Creek arm off-limits to waterskiing and jet skiing.

Contact: Lake Sonoma Marina, (707) 433-2200. **Locator:** LAKE SONOMA (D1). **See featured trip page:** 322.

4. LOCH LOMOND RESERVOIR

LOCH LOMOND is the prettiest lake in the Bay Area, set in a canyon amid redwoods and Douglas fir, complete with a little island. The trout fishing is decent, but the picnic area and a great loop hiking trail with a view make this a prime spot.

Contact: Loch Lomond County Park, (831) 335-7424. **Locator:** LOCH LOMOND RESERVOIR (E1d).

5. LAKE MERCED

When you're in a boat, perhaps rowing to a favorite fishing spot along the tules in the 200-acre South Lake, you will have launched into a different orbit than the rest of SAN FRANCISCO'S 750,000 residents. MERCED is pretty and peaceful, with a good number of waterfowl keeping you company and fine trout fishing. Windsurfing and rowing are also popular. The biggest trout in MERCED history—17 pounds, 6 ounces—was caught in the smaller North Lake.

Contact: Lake Merced Tackle Shop, (415) 753-1101. **Locator:** LAKE MERCED (E1b). **See featured trip page:** 366.

6. LAKE CHABOT

This 315-acre lake is the centerpiece of a 5,000-acre regional park that includes 31 miles of hiking trails, horeseback riding rentals, and a campground. The trout fishing is best in the springtime. As a mystery wild card, there are some giant bass in the 15-pound class that are often seen, but only rarely hooked.

Contact: Lake Chabot Marina, (510) 582-2198; Chabot Regional Park, (510) 881-1833 extension 2570; East Bay Regional Park District, (510) 635-0135 extension 2200. **Locator:** LAKE CHABOT (E1c). **See featured trip page:** 230.

7. DEL VALLE RESERVOIR

Del Valle sits in a long, narrow canyon, covering 750 acres with 16 miles of shoreline—much larger than most newcomers expect. An adjacent campground and good hiking in the nearby OHLONE REGIONAL WILDERNESS make DEL VALLE one of the best regional parks in the East Bay.

Contact: Del Valle Regional Park, (925) 373-0332; Del Valle Marina, (925) 449-5201. **Locator:** DEL VALLE RESERVOIR (E2).

8. LAFAYETTE LAKE

Because this little lake is only 53 acres, it is often overlooked in favor of SAN PABLO and CHABOT. But this Lafayette watering hole provides more consistent trout fishing, typically 2.5 to 3.2 fish per rod, with the best prospects in the East Cove.

Contact: Lafayette Lake Marina, (925) 284-9669. **Locator:** LAFAYETTE (E1c).

9. LAKE MERRITT

MERRITT, best known as a popular jogging spot, is also the Bay Area headquarters for paddleboats, rowboats, and small sailboats. In fact, it has earned a reputation for one of the best learn-to-sail classes in California. Because the water salinity changes according to season, fishing is terrible.

Contact: Lake Merritt Boathouse, (510) 444-3807. **Locator:** LAKE MERRITT (E1c).

10. SAN PABLO RESERVOIR

SAN PABLO has the best urban fishing program in the country, with more than 200,000 trout stocked each year. It is a large, beautiful lake, 854 acres, and is best visited on a warm weekday evening when the wind is down, the water is calm, and the trout are biting.

Contact: San Pablo Reservoir Recreation Area, (510) 223-1661. **Locator:** SAN PABLO RESERVOIR (E1c). **See featured trip page:** 375.

11. SHADOW CLIFFS LAKE

Once just a squarish hole for a rock quarry, SHADOW CLIFFS has been filled with water and stocked with trout and catfish. Now it's a 143-acre lake and the highlight of a regional park. It has a submerged look, but folks get used to it.

Contact: Shadow Cliffs Marina, (925) 846-3000. **Locator:** SHADOW CLIFFS LAKE (E1c).

12. ANCHOR MARINA

BETHEL ISLAND is on the SAN JOAQUIN RIVER side of the Delta, where catfishing, waterskiing, and plenty of secluded backwater sloughs can make for an ideal weekend getaway.

Contact: Anchor Marina, (925) 684-2182. **Locator:** BETHEL ISLAND (E2). **See featured trip page:** 373.

13. DELTA BAY CLUB

This spot is on the SACRAMENTO RIVER, right where striped bass trolling tends to be good. Nearby BRANNAN ISLAND STATE PARK provides a camping option.

Contact: Delta Bay Club, (916) 777-5588. **Locator:** ISLETON (E2). **See featured trip page:** 373.

14. CAPITOLA WHARF

Rent a skiff, fire up the motor, and take a short ride to spots such as Adams Reef, Soquel Reef, and South Rock, where small rockfish provide decent prospects. My first memories of great success in the outdoors came here while fishing with my dad and my brother some 30 years ago.

Contact: Capitola Wharf, (831) 462-2208. **Locator:** CAPITOLA (F1). **See featured trip page:** 377.

15. PINTO LAKE

Little PINTO LAKE is a horseshoe-shaped lake that is quite pretty, bordered by a parklike setting. Not many people know that the lake has spaces for campers (no tents), or that it is stocked with trout from winter through spring.

Contact: Pinto Lake County Park, (831) 722-8129. **Locator:** PINTO LAKE (F1).

16. SANTA CRUZ WHARF

The best salmon fishing in this area is from mid-March to mid-April. Just rent a boat and you can be right on top of it. High numbers of marine birds are a bonus.

Contact: Santa Cruz Boat Rentals, (831) 423-1739. **Locator:** SANTA CRUZ (F1).

• TOM'S RATINGS •

THE TOP 25 LAKES

In Northern California

Most people have no idea of the number, diversity, and quality of lakes in California that are ideal for summer vacations spent camping, boating, fishing, and hiking. In a survey I completed for my books California Camping and California Fishing, I counted 373 drive-to lakes, 483 hike-to lakes, and 1,531 campgrounds, many of which put you within easy reach of a lake.

Here, listed by county from north to south, is a capsule look at 25 of the best lakes you can reach by car, selecting my favorite lakes for each Northern California county. Here they are, north-to-south.

Note that many of them are close to numerous other lakes and streams that provide additional recreation options.

1. SANGER LAKE

This is a small, hidden, and beautiful lake, set below Sanger Peak (elevation 5,862 feet) in SIX RIVERS NATIONAL FOREST. Primitive camping is available, with fair fishing for small brook trout. A circuitous drive on mountain roads keeps many visitors away.

Contact: Six Rivers National Forest, Supervisor's Office, (707) 442-1721. **Locator:** SIX RIVERS NATIONAL FOREST (A1).

2. KANGAROO LAKE

This small lake is literally nestled in SCOTT MOUNTAIN, at a 6,000-foot elevation. Fishing for brook trout is often excellent, and the lake is wheelchair accessible with a paved trail leading right to the shore. Trails out of camp connect to the Pacific Crest Trail.

Contact: Klamath National Forest, Scott River Ranger District, (530) 468-5351. **Locator:** KLAMATH NATIONAL FOREST (B2).

3. LILY LAKE

Out here in no-man's-land, you get guaranteed solitude, free drive-in camping, and a high desert setting with a few conifers sprinkled about. If the brook trout don't bite, try nearby CAVE LAKE. No motors are allowed on the water.

Contact: Modoc National Forest, Devil's Garden Ranger District, (530) 233-5811. **Locator:** MODOC NATIONAL FOREST (A4).

4. STONE LAGOON

Of the three freshwater lagoons along U.S. 101 north of EUREKA, STONE LAGOON is the best. It's an ideal destination for canoe campers, with a boat-in site at Ryan's Camp. Some large cutthroat trout are a bonus.

Contact: Department of Fish and Game, Eureka, (707) 445-6493; Humboldt Lagoons State Park, (707) 488-2041. **Locator:** EUREKA (B0).

5. LEWISTON LAKE

One of the prettiest lakes in California, LEWISTON offers shoreline camping at Mary Smith Campground and a low-key lakeside resort at Trinity River Lodge. It is set at the foot of the Trinities, with 15 miles of shoreline. Fishing is good for trout below Trinity Dam.

Contact: Shasta-Trinity National Forest, Big Bar Ranger District, (530) 623-6106; Brady's Sportshop in Weaverville, (530) 623-3121; Trinity River Lodge, (530) 778-3791. **Locator:** LEWISTON LAKE (B1). **See featured trip page:** 128.

6. IRON CANYON RESERVOIR

This shaded, emerald green lake has a resident bald eagle and a nearby campground nestled in a forest. The trout fishing is good, and a boat ramp is available. It is just hard enough to reach that it gets bypassed by the Winnebago set.

Contact: Shasta-Trinity National Forest, Shasta Lake Ranger District, (530) 275-1587. **Locator:** IRON CANYON RESERVOIR (B2).

7. MANZANITA LAKE

This is the jewel of LASSEN VOLCANIC NATIONAL PARK, with the park's largest campground nearby, offering easy access to a premium wild trout fishery (two-fish limit, with all catches over 10 inches to be released). No motors are allowed, but the lake is ideal for a canoe or pram.

Contact: Lassen Volcanic National Park, (530) 595-4444. **Locator:** LASSEN VOLCANIC NATIONAL PARK (B3). **See featured trip page:** 209.

8. BUCKS LAKE

With several campgrounds nearby and the highest catch rates for trout in the north Sierra, this place is no secret. It is a premium spot, set at 5,150 feet near Quincy, with a full-service marina and boat rentals.

Contact: Sportsmen's Den, (530) 283-2733; Plumas National Forest, Mount Hough Ranger District, (530) 283-0555. **Locator:** QUINCY (C3).

9. LAKE CLEONE

This is the centerpiece of MACKERRICHER STATE PARK, located just north of FORT BRAGG, an outstanding layover when touring Highway 1. A lot of park visitors are surprised to find this little lake, which provides good trout fishing and fair bass fishing. No motors are allowed. Camping reservations are advised.

Contact: MacKerricher State Park, (707) 937-5804. **Locator:** MACKERRICHER STATE PARK (C0).

10. Blue Lakes

You get lakeside cabins (and campsites) along with decent fishing, yet getting here doesn't require a killer drive. The lakes are long and narrow, and tend to get overlooked because of their proximity to CLEAR LAKE, just 10 miles away.

Contact: Le Trianon Resort, (707) 275-2262; Pine Acres, (707) 275-2811. **Locator:** CLEAR LAKE (D1).

11. Bullards Bar Reservoir

Here is one of the prettier reservoirs in the Central Valley foothill country, set at a 2,300-foot elevation with 55 miles of shoreline, several campgrounds, and good fishing. Good boat-in camps are located near French Point and upstream at Madrone Cove.

Contact: Emerald Cove Resort, (530) 692-2166. **Locator:** OROVILLE (C3).

12. Stampede Reservoir

This is a classic Sierra lake set in the high granite country at 6,000 feet. It is good-sized at 3,400 acres, yet is easy to reach and offers an extended boat ramp and half a dozen campgrounds. Fishing is good for trout, including some giant Mackinaw on rare occasions.

Contact: Tahoe National Forest, Truckee Ranger District, (530) 587-3558. **Locator:** TRUCKEE (D4).

13. Bowman Lake

A sapphire jewel set at 5,568 feet near Emigrant Gap, Bowman Lake has a primitive campground and the area's best fishery for brown trout. There are many other lakes nearby.

Contact: Tahoe National Forest, Nevada City Ranger District, (530) 265-4538. **Locator:** EMIGRANT GAP (D3).

14. Lake Sonoma

The angler versus water-skier war has been resolved here with specific areas set up for each pursuit. Good boat-in camping is available on the north arm. The bass and bluegill fishing can be excellent; field scout Clyde "The Wrench" Gibbs and his family once caught and released 50 fish in one day here.

Contact: U.S. Army Corps of Engineers, (707) 433-9483. **Locator:** LAKE SONOMA (D0). **See featured trip page:** 322.

15. Lake Berryessa

This is the Bay Area's backyard fishing hole, with 750 campsites and 165 miles of shoreline. And everybody knows about it, right? What you may not know is that cabin and condo rentals are available at Steele Park.

Contact: Putah Creek Resort, (707) 966-2116; Steele Park, (707) 966-2123; Markley Cove, (707) 966-2134. **Locator:** LAKE BERRYESSA (D1). **See featured trip page:** 359.

16. Lake Solano

This small, quiet lake lies just below the dam of LAKE BERRYESSA (where all hell breaks loose every weekend). No motors are allowed, making it good for canoes, rafts, and rowboats. A county park campground adds a nice touch.

Contact: Lake Solano County Park, (530) 795-2990. **Locator:** LAKE BERRYESSA (D1).

17. Hell Hole Reservoir

A deep blue lake in the high Sierra, this is a beautiful sight. The drive in is long and winding, and you need a boat to fish it right (for Mackinaw and brown trout). Two camps, including a boat-in site, are located within half a mile.

Contact: Eldorado National Forest, Information Center, (530) 333-4312. **Locator:** ELDORADO NATIONAL FOREST (D3, D4).

18. Lake Tahoe

The prettiest state park campground is at Emerald Bay. And what need be said about Tahoe? Always an inspiring sight, 22 miles long, 1,645 feet deep, and clear enough to see a dinner plate 75 feet below the surface. Dozens of lakes within 20 miles to the west provide side-trip options.

Contact: Lake Tahoe Visitors Authority, (530) 544-5050 or (800) 822-5922; Emerald Bay State Park, (530) 525-7277. **Locator:** LAKE TAHOE (D4). **See featured trip page:** 232.

19. Silver Lake

Set in a classic granite cirque at 7,200 feet, SILVER LAKE was created from the flows of the Silver Fork American River. Two camps and a boat ramp make it easy; fishing for trout (rainbows, browns, Mackinaws) crowns the adventure.

Contact: Eldorado National Forest, Information Center, (530) 644-6048. **Locator:** SILVER LAKE (D4).

20. Blue Lakes (Upper and Lower)

These lakes are often lost in the shadow of giant Tahoe to the north, but they still shine for visitors. The Blue Lakes are set in the high country, at 8,200 feet, with several camps in the vicinity. Lower Blue has the better trout fishing, by boat at the north end, just at the underwater drop-off.

Contact: Pacific Gas & Electric, (800) 743-5000. **Locator:** MARKLEEVILLE (D4).

21. Lake Alpine

Here's the prettiest sight on Highway 4, at 7,320 feet. LAKE ALPINE has good fishing during the evening rise, developed camps, and good hiking in the area. Once scarcely known, it has become popular lately. Little Mosquito Lake, farther up Highway 4, is a good side trip.

Contact: Stanislaus National Forest, Calaveras Ranger District, (209) 795-1381. **Locator:** LAKE ALPINE (E4) **See featured trip page:** 144.

22. Cherry Lake

Located just outside the northwest border of YOSEMITE NATIONAL PARK at a 4,700-foot elevation, this lake has a campground, a boat ramp, and jump-off points for backpackers. Trails are routed north into the Emigrant Wilderness, or east into YOSEMITE, providing access to dozens of backcountry lakes.

Contact: Stanislaus National Forest, Groveland Ranger District, (209) 962-7825. **Locator:** CHERRY LAKE (E4).

23. Convict Lake

Set at 7,583 feet, the lake is framed by a back wall of wilderness mountain peaks and is fronted by a conifer-lined shore. Sounds beautiful? It is. You'll find good fishing, wilderness trailheads, and all facilities available at the lake.

Contact: Inyo National Forest, Mammoth Lakes Ranger Station and Visitor Center, (760) 934-2505; Convict Lake Resort, (760) 934-3803. **Locator:** INYO NATIONAL FOREST (F5). **See featured trip page:** 237.

24. O'Neill Forebay

The state record striped bass (67 pounds) was caught here, and 20-pounders are caught almost daily, though little guys are a lot more likely to fill five-fish limits. Nearby Basalt Camp at SAN LUIS RESERVOIR provides a spot to overnight it. During the summer, expect hot weather all day and high winds in the afternoon.

Contact: San Luis Recreation Area, (209) 826-1196. **Locator:** SAN LUIS RESERVOIR (F2).

25. TENAYA LAKE

This is one of the prettiest lakes in the world, a showpiece of the YOSEMITE NATIONAL PARK high country. Walk-in picnic sites are available, and nearby Tuolumne Meadows provides a camping option. The only downer is the fishing, which is lousy. No boats are allowed.

Contact: Yosemite National Park, (209) 372-0200. **Locator:** YOSEMITE NATIONAL PARK (E4). **See featured trip page:** 239.

• TOM'S RATINGS •

THE TOP 22 WATER ADVENTURES

In the San Francisco Bay Area

Swimming in a secluded coastal pond, a sailboat ride around TREASURE ISLAND, and hiking past a trio of gorgeous lakes are highlights of the Bay Area boating and water recreation scene.

The secret coastal pond is at POINT REYES NATIONAL SEASHORE, sailboat rides are available out of San Francisco and Sausalito, and the hike along LAGUNITAS, BON TEMPE, and ALPINE LAKES is at the northern slope of MOUNT TAMALPAIS. The three activities make up the best of the best in the greater Bay Area when it comes to boating, swimming, hiking near water, fishing, and windsurfing, along with a few wild cards.

Here are my top choices in each category:

• BOATING •

1. SAN FRANCISCO BAY

What could be more spectacular in a boat than sailing past ALCATRAZ, TREASURE ISLAND, and the GOLDEN GATE BRIDGE, with the SAN FRANCISCO waterfront as a backdrop? Nothing, which is why SAN FRANCISCO BAY is the California capital of sailboating. It is little known that sailboats, powerboats, and sea kayaks are available for rent in SAUSALITO, with a captain provided if needed.

Contact: Cass' Marina, Sausalito (sailboat rentals), (415) 332-6789; Rendezvous Charters, San Francisco (sailboat rentals), (415) 543-7333; Capt. Case's Boat Rentals (powerboats), (415) 331-0444; Sea Trek (kayaks), (415) 488-1000. **Locator:** SAN FRANCISCO BAY (E1a).

2. SAN JOAQUIN DELTA

The DELTA is an awesome mosaic of waterways that's bigger than most can imagine, covering 1,000 miles, enough to take a lifetime to fully explore. There are 25 marinas with boat ramps, including many with boat rentals. It is the number one waterskiing area in Northern California, excellent for houseboating. In recent years, the back SAN JOAQUIN DELTA has become outstanding for bass fishing.

Contact: Brannan Island State Recreation Area, Rio Vista area, (916) 777-7701; Korth's Pirate's Lair, Isleton, (916) 777-6464; Eddo's Harbor, near Antioch, (925) 757-5314; Lazy M Marina, Byron, (209) 634-5555. **Locator:** SAN JOAQUIN DELTA (E1c). **See featured trip page:** 373.

3. San Pablo Reservoir

A combination of beauty, good boating, and fishing make San Pablo the number one lake in the Bay Area. It's fairly large, 860 acres, big enough to allow a 25 mph speed limit, with a 5 mph limit near the shore. The marina has fishing boats, rowboats, and canoes available for rent. No waterskiing or jet skiing is permitted.

Contact: San Pablo Recreation Area, (510) 223-1661. **Locator:** San Pablo Reservoir (E1c). **See featured trip page:** 375.

4. Lake Merritt

Lake Merritt is one of Oakland's prettiest settings, as well as a surprisingly good spot for canoes, paddleboats, small sailboats, and sailboards. All four can be rented here. Because of afternoon winds out of the west combined with typically placid waters, this is one of the best places to learn how to sail.

Contact: Lake Merritt Boat Center, (510) 444-3807. **Locator:** Lake Merritt (E1c).

5. Lake Merced

Lake Merced South is always a surprise to newcomers, larger and prettier than most expect. It is an ideal location to learn how to windsurf or sail, as well as for canoeing, rowing, or sculling. Fishing is fair for trout in the spring and summer, though it can be good at neighboring Lake Merced North.

Contact: Lake Merced Boathouse, (415) 753-1101; San Francisco School of Windsurfing, (415) 753-3235. **Locator:** Lake Merced (E1b). **See featured trip page:** 366.

• FISHING •

6. Golden Gate and Beyond

The Gulf of the Farallones off the Bay Area coast is the richest marine region on the entire Pacific coast. It supports great fishing for salmon, halibut, rockfish, and at times, striped bass. In July, it is one of the best places to fish in North America.

Contact: Emeryville Sportfishing Center, (510) 654-6040; Caruso's, Sausalito, (415) 332-1015; Wacky Jacky Sportfishing, San Francisco, (415) 586-9800; Berkeley Marina, (510) 849-2727. **Locator:** San Francisco Bay (E1b). **See featured trip page:** 272.

7. San Pablo Bay

Sturgeon, striped bass, and salmon live in salt water but spawn in freshwater, and San Pablo Bay is the perfect spot to intercept them on their annual migrations. With so much freshwater pouring from the Delta into the Bay lately, sturgeon have been the king, with fish caught measuring up to 8 feet and 250 pounds.

Contact: Loch Lomond Live Bait, San Rafael, (415) 456-0321; *Morning Star,* Crockett, (510) 787-1047; *Happy Hooker,* Martinez, (510) 223-5388. **Locator:** San Pablo Bay (E1a).

8. San Pablo Reservoir

In my survey of Bay Area lakes, San Pablo ranked first. The reservoir provides a great trout fishery where anglers average two to three fish per rod, with enough 15- to 20-inchers in the mix to provide plenty of sizzle. By boat or by bank the results are good, thanks to the highest trout stocks of any lake in California, paid for by a daily $3 fishing permit.

Contact: San Pablo Recreation Area, (650) 223-1661. **Locator:** San Pablo

RESERVOIR (E1c). **See featured trip page:** 375.

9. Half Moon Bay

The 10-year renovation is complete, and HALF MOON BAY now boasts a new boat ramp, marina, inner jetty, and fishing operations. Its location is ideal for salmon fishing from April through early summer, and deep-sea fishing for rockfish from summer through fall. This is one of the Bay Area's best success stories.

Contact: Huck Finn Sportfishing, (650) 726-7133; Marine Warehouse, (650) 728-7725. **Locator:** HALF MOON BAY (E1b). **See featured trip page:** 224.

10. Lake Chabot

Chabot just plains look fishy, and it is, with good trout fishing from late winter to early summer and a sprinkling of gigantic bass. Weekly trout plants make it work, and shore prospects are often as good as for those renting boats. The only downer: No private boats are permitted.

Contact: Chabot Marina, (510) 582-2198. **Locator:** LAKE CHABOT (E1c). **See featured trip page:** 230.

• HIKING •

11. Coast Trail

This is the top overnight hike in the Bay Area, a 15-mile trip one way with a shuttle. It features dramatic panoramas to the west of the ocean and to the east of the reblooming foothills burned in a wildfire in the fall of 1995. Other highlights include camps at ocean bluffs, sculptured rocks and tidepools, secluded beaches, surprise coastal lakes, and breathtaking Alamere Falls.

Contact: Point Reyes National Seashore, (415) 663-1092. **Locator:** POINT REYES NATIONAL SEASHORE (E1a). **See featured trip page:** 67.

12. Lagunitas/Bon Tempe/ Alpine Lakes

A 5.5-mile hike linking a series of trails will take you past Marin's three prettiest lakes: LAGUNITAS LAKE, BON TEMPE LAKE, and ALPINE LAKE. All are full, pretty, and as spring arrives, will clear and turn emerald green. The hike, which requires a map that's available at the entrance station, features an easy romp on the slopes of MOUNT TAMALPAIS.

Contact: Sky Oaks Ranger Station, (415) 459-5267. **Locator:** LAGUNITAS LAKE (E1a).

13. Loch Lomond Reservoir

This jewel of a lake, circled by Douglas fir, is the showpiece of a five-mile loop hike that provides both intimate glimpses as well as sweeping views. The trail meanders along the southern shore for 1.5 miles, very pretty and serene, then turns right and climbs to the ridge for an overlook. Very special.

Contact: Loch Lomond County Park, (831) 335-7424. **Locator:** LOCH LOMOND RESERVOIR (E1d).

14. Fitzgerald Marine Reserve

A shallow 30-acre reef provides the best tidepool hopping in the Bay Area. All you need is a low tide, then take your time and explore hundreds and hundreds of tidal sea pockets and crevices alive with starfish, sea anemones, sculpins, tons of hermit crabs and rock crabs, and plants in many colors.

Contact: Fitzgerald Marine Reserve, (650) 728-3584. **Locator:** FITZGERALD MARINE RESERVE (E1b). **See featured trip page:** 266.

15. Arastradero Lake

You'll walk just 10 minutes from the parking area to this pond, and even though you know it awaits, it is always a pleasant rush when you top the rise and see it. This is a beautiful farm pond circled by tules, with ducks usually paddling around, squirrels looking for nuts nearby, and hawks circling overhead in search of squirrels. You can extend the venture on trails into the adjacent foothill country, but the pond is what makes it work.

Contact: Foothills Park, (650) 329-2423. **Locator:** ARASTRADERO LAKE (E1b). **See featured trip page:** 69.

• SWIMMING •

16. Bass Lake

Here's the perfect Bay Area hideaway for a swim, little Bass Lake, located an hour's walk north of the Palomarin Trailhead near BOLINAS. On clear days, the hike in along the coast is spectacular. Note that in late summer, when the water becomes stagnant, park officials do not advise swimming here.

Contact: Point Reyes National Seashore, (415) 663-1092. **Locator:** BOLINAS (E1a). **See featured trip page:** 166.

17. Del Valle Reservoir, Livermore

Two swimming beaches, complete with lifeguards, make DEL VALLE a little paradise on 100-degree days in the remote Alameda County foothills. This is a long, narrow, and deep lake, 750 acres with 16 miles of shoreline. A campground, boat rentals, and good fishing are bonuses.

Contact: Del Valle Regional Park, (925) 373-0332; East Bay Regional Park District, (510) 635-0135 extension 2200. **Locator:** DEL VALLE RESERVOIR (E2).

18. Pescadero Creek

One of the biggest secrets on the Peninsula is that a temporary dam is put in place every summer on PESCADERO CREEK, creating a swimming lagoon in MEMORIAL COUNTY PARK. It features cold water and two sandy beaches, located both above and below the dam.

Contact: Memorial County Park, (650) 879-0238; San Mateo County Parks, (650) 363-4020. **Locator:** PESCADERO CREEK (E1d).

19. Don Castro Reservoir

This lake covers just 23 acres, but its cool, clear waters and swimming lagoon provide special appeal on HAYWARD's hot weather days from April through fall. A large shallow area is roped off for children, and a changing room is available. The place sometimes gets crowded.

Contact: Don Castro Regional Park, (510) 538-1148; East Bay Regional Park District, (510) 635-0135 extension 2200. **Locator:** HAYWARD (E1c).

20. Shadow Cliffs Lake

Even when every other lake is muddy from storm runoff, this former water hole for a rock quarry remains clear and clean. Park officials have taken advantage of this by building a sandy beach for swimming and a water slide near the park entrance. Grassy picnic sites are a big plus.

Contact: Shadow Cliffs Marina, (925) 846-3000; East Bay Regional Park District, (510) 635-0135 extension 2200. **Locator:** SHADOW CLIFFS LAKE (E1c).

• BIRD WALKS •

21. Pescadero Marsh

The place that has always held special appeal is PESCADERO MARSH, a 600-acre marsh next to the ocean with a stream and a lagoon. It's common to see 20 or 25 species of birds here—the stars being the great blue heron and egrets—and more than 250 species of birds visiting at one time or another over the course of a year. A dirt path is routed amid pampas grass and bogs, and guided walks are available.

Contact: Half Moon Bay State Parks, (650) 726-8819. **Locator:** PESCADERO MARSH (E1d). **See featured trip page:** 268.

• BIRD WALKS •

22. STEAMER LANE

The best place to surf? Not an easy call. But Steamer Lane in SANTA CRUZ gets the top rating, as well as the biggest crowds. Its location near a coastal point causes good waves, with clean breakers often available with just a moderate ocean swell. Other good spots are Ocean Beach in SAN FRANCISCO, the south Princeton Jetty in HALF MOON BAY, and Linda Mar in PACIFICA.

Contact: Cowboy Surf Shop, in Miramar, (650) 726-6968. **Locator:** SANTA CRUZ (F1).

• TOM'S RATINGS •

THE TOP 12 WINDSURFING LOCATIONS

In the San Francisco Bay Area

What starts out as simple curiosity can sometimes turn into a lifelong passion. That's just what tends to happen with windsurfing.

A newcomer's interest can be kindled by the sight of a windsurfer cutting across SAN FRANCISCO BAY, maybe through ocean breakers, or across LAKE MERCED; it looks effortless, fast, and exciting. The vision has a way of sticking in your mind, and before long you say to yourself, "I'd like to try that."

Then comes the awakening. While windsurfing can be fast and exciting, it's anything but easy, and can even be downright humiliating the first time out. But with practice, you can bridge the gap between your initial vision and the reality. Instruction, equipment rental, and quality waters are available in SAN FRANCISCO. The San Francisco School of Windsurfing offers a package deal for novices that includes an eight-hour course and equipment rental. They conduct beginner courses at LAKE MERCED SOUTH, and intermediate and advanced courses at CANDLESTICK POINT STATE PARK.

Those with previous experience who do not want a lesson can rent a sailboard and wet suit at LAKE MERCED. Advanced-level boards are available at Candlestick. "We have good equipment, and there is somebody watching out for you all the time," said Jeff Craft of the School of Windsurfing.

A large number of windsurfers can be seen most afternoons clipping across the water near CANDLESTICK. It's an ideal spot with strong winds and calm water, and the area is a lot better suited for windsurfing than baseball. Yet for experts, one of the ultimate experiences in windsurfing is cutting across SAN FRANCISCO BAY near CRISSY FIELD on a clear summer evening, mastering the wind out of the northwest, whipping across the water like a surface torpedo.

Intermediate-level windsurfers can cruise at 15 to 20 mph with no problem. If the water is choppy, they'll sail along in the wakes of ferryboats to get a smooth, free ride. Advanced-level windsurfers can rip at 30 to 35 mph, and some are now passing the magic 40 mph mark.

It takes practice to reach that level of performance, of course. The first time on a board can be humbling, especially for skilled athletes who come to the sport with high expectations. It usually takes two or three tries before you can manage a decent ride across a lake or lagoon. Once that's accomplished, it's usually exciting enough to encourage participants to take the sport a step further. Eventually many even decide to buy their own equipment.

"You have to be a sharp buyer," Craft said. "You can usually get something of good quality for $400 or $500. It's very important to get a good, thick wet suit, because the water is cold in the bay."

Once you own the equipment, you're only limited by the conditions nature provides and the skills you've mastered.

Over a summer, you can learn all the tricks of the trade, from squeezing every bit of push from a light breeze to cutting a gale down to manageable proportions. In time you will be able to cut through high breakers and rip from CRISSY FIELD in SAN FRANCISCO to SAUSALITO in 10 minutes, averaging 30 to 35 mph.

You can also venture to many other areas, near and far, to enjoy the sport. SAN FRANCISCO BAY and Maui are among the most glamorous windsurfing spots in the country, for example, and LAKE TAHOE in the summer may be the most beautiful. The DELTA is a hot spot; so is DEL VALLE RESERVOIR. Other popular destinations in the Bay Area include PILLAR POINT HARBOR in HALF MOON BAY, SAN FRANCISCO'S LAKE MERCED SOUTH, Foster City Lagoon, Larkspur Landing, Coyote Point, and Sunnyvale Baylands Park. There are many others.

All you need are decent wind and water, both of which California has in abundance. One of the peculiarities of California weather causes 60-degree temperatures, fog, and low barometric pressure on the coast, but 100-degree temperatures and high barometric pressure in the Central Valley. That change from cold to hot creates wind blowing out of the west, and in turn, guarantees the ideal conditions for this sport in the Bay Area.

If you daydream of a sport that will allow you to feel free like the wind, this is the one for you. It's quite a vision: you're cutting across the water's surface, skipping over boat wakes like a flying fish, and hanging on for the ride while the wind takes you yonder.

The fantasy is enough to inspire the curious. After all, someday that just might be you sailing across the Bay.

Contact: San Francisco School of Windsurfing, (415) 753-3235. Events West in MILL VALLEY, (415) 383-9378 or fax (415) 383-0614; E-mail: eventswest@aol.com. American Windsurfing Industries Association, 1099 Snowden Road, White Salmon, WA 98672; (509) 493-9463 or fax (509) 493-9464; E-mail: awia@gorge.net. Vela Windsurf Resorts, 16 East Third Avenue, #16, San Mateo, CA 94401; (800) 223-5443 or fax (650) 373-1111; E-mail:buck@velawindsurf.com.

1. LAKE MERCED SOUTH

Merced's unusual coastal location means it receives onshore breezes each afternoon for months, enough to get novice windsurfers moving across the water. At the same time, the lake's surface is calm, not choppy as in the bay or ocean, which makes learning more of a joy than an ordeal.

Locator: LAKE MERCED(E1b). **See featured trip page:** 366.

2. Candlestick Point State Park
The wind can howl here, shooting the gap from San Bruno Mountain out of the west, and that's why this is a favorite for speed demons. Some sailboarders hit 40 mph, others even faster. A nasty chop on the water makes it uncomfortable for most and impossible for beginners.

Locator: Candlestick Point State Park (E1b).

3. Crissy Field
Only experts need sign up, but the vision of shooting across the Bay from Crissy Field to Sausalito is enough to inspire many to master the sport. Some daredevils even windsurf in the wakes of the afternoon ferryboats heading from San Francisco to Tiburon. Another good spot is near Larkspur Landing.

Locator: Crissy Field (E1b).

4. Lake Tahoe
Locator: Lake Tahoe (D4).

5. The Delta
Locator: San Joaquin Delta (D1,E2).

6. Del Valle Reservoir
Locator: Del Valle Reservoir (E2).

7. Pillar Point Harbor
Giant Pillar Point, the big rock with a radar station at the north end of Half Moon Bay, provides a perfect shield to the tempest north winds that arrive on spring and summer afternoons here. That means you get calm water, not a chop, yet enough of a wind push to move you along, an ideal combination for newcomers to the sport.

Locator: Pillar Point Harbor (E1b).
See featured trip page: 224.

8. Foster City Lagoon
Locator: Foster City (E1b).

9. Larkspur Landing
Locator: Larkspur (E1a).

10. Coyote Point
Locator: Coyote Point (E1b).

11. Sunnyvale Baylands Park
Locator: Sunnyvale (E1d).

12. Davenport
The combination of north winds, a large beautiful beach, and cliffs to the south create a setting for the best windsurfing in California. It's a remarkable sight, with windsurfing masters clipping along behind the breakers while hang gliders hover above like giant pelicans.

Locator: Santa Cruz (F1).

• FEATURED TRIP •

Trinity River: Hupa Raft Tour

Rated: The Best Historical Journey; The Top 18 River Rafting Expeditions, 301

The Trinity River is being turned into a stream of consciousness by the Native Americans through whose land it runs.

A raft is the vehicle that takes visitors on a trek downriver and offers a look into the culture of the Hupa nation. There is nothing else like it in North America, where Native Americans are reaching out to their fellow countrymen of all races to share both a white-water adventure and a history lesson.

This is taking place on the Hoopa Valley Indian Reservation in Northern California, the largest Native American settlement in the state with 4,000 people living on 90,000 acres of land. Suddenly, there is no such thing as an "outsider" anymore.

"What's important is that we're breaking down barriers through these trips," said Linc McCovey, a Hupa guide on my first trip in 1995, pulling at the oars as our raft floated toward a bend in the river. "We welcome visitors. We're trying to show them respect, and hope that they, in turn, will have respect for what they see and hear here."

This program came about through the cooperation of the Hoopa Valley Tribal Council, Kimtu Outdoor Adventures (now Aurora River Adventures), and tribal elders willing to share the tribe's history. The end result is an adventure that includes a visit to ancient village sites and the Hupa Museum, a rafting trip on the TRINITY RIVER, and a lunch of traditional smoked salmon and acorn soup, along with more mainstream fare.

"We've had decades of a defensive posture and now we're changing that," said Dale Risling, then chairman of the Hoopa Valley Tribal Council. "The Hupa tribe is reaching outside of the reservation for friendships that will be beneficial."

The rafting trip tours a mild piece of the TRINITY RIVER, about a five-mile stretch from Tish Tang Camp downstream to the Hupa village. Along the way, you pull up to the shore of an old Native American village called Tsewenaldin, which means "the place of happy meetings." The stretch of water here is an easy float, nothing more formidable than Class II rapids. It is ideal for families or newcomers to the sport. In fact, many people spend much of the trip in the water, not in the raft, wearing their life jackets.

In the course of a few hours on that first trip, Liam Furniss, then 11, turned from a reluctant city slicker into a happy river otter. "I have to admit, before the trip, water scared me a bit," Liam said. "Not any more. I had the best time of my life."

Also available is a two-day trip that starts farther upriver in the Trinity Canyon and covers more ambitious white water with inflatable kayaks.

The TRINITY has always been the lifeblood of the Hupa tribe. It starts from drops of melting snow high in the TRINITY ALPS, joining to form trickles, brooks, creeks, and then pouring down the river canyon. It is very clear—the product of a hard granite base—and in evening light it glows like an emerald.

The Trinity's fertile banks led the Hupas to settle in the valley here. "We could always count on the salmon in the river and the acorns from the oaks," said Jimmy Jackson, a tribal elder. "We didn't have to move around searching for food, like tribes in other parts of the country."

Jackson and museum curator Bill Carpenter opened the tour by guiding visitors through the museum and the sites of an ancient village, ceremonial dances, and burial grounds.

"See that wood knob in the boat," said Jackson, pointing at the interior of a redwood dugout canoe. "That's the heart of the boat. The boat is alive, not dead."

He went on to explain how Hupas made baskets from willow roots and porcupine quills, and dip nets for salmon from the roots of wild irises. "It would take me a year to make a small dip net from wild irises," Jackson said. "Almost as long to make a rope out of horse hair."

Carpenter showed us a rare albino deer skin, used in a ceremonial dance—a dance that was performed some 500 years ago and is still honored by current tribe members.

An increasing number of younger Indian residents are taking an interest in their heritage. Some are learning the Hupa language. The *Hupa Language Dictionary*, written by Jackson and other tribal elders,was first published in 1996 and is already in its second edition. It is the first of its kind for a Native American nation and was received with great anticipation on the reservation.

Among the Hupas infused with the tribe's new energy was McCovey, the rafting guide on my first trip, who once left the reservation but returned with a newfound sense of purpose.

"What I'm doing is coming back to the reservation and respecting what was here for me all along," McCovey said. "My favorite parts of the trip are the areas of religious and ceremonial concerns. It's something I'm just now learning. When I go down the river, I want to be able to feel the same way my ancestors felt. They made the same trip in their dugout canoes."

Rafting with the Hupas offers a unique mix of past culture and present adventuring. It works for visitors and Native Americans alike, shoulder to shoulder.

Fees: Rafting trip rates are $90 per adult and $50 for children ages 7 to 11. This includes gear, lunch, and a historical tour. **Contact:** For a free brochure, contact Aurora River Adventures, P.O. Box 938, Willow Creek, CA 95573; (800) 562-8475. Directions are provided upon making a reservation. To reach guide Charles Carpenter, phone (530) 625-0049. **Locator:** TRINITY RIVER (B1).

A spelling lesson: The Native American tribe name is spelled "Hupa," whereas the town and the reservation are "Hoopa."

• FEATURED TRIP •

TRINITY RIVER: WHITE-WATER THRILLS

Rated: The Least Expensive White-Water Trip

You don't need to strap a saddle on the space shuttle to take a ride into a new orbit. A seat in a white-water raft can do the same thing, and unlike the space shuttle, this trip comes not only easy but cheap.

What you get is pure exhilaration from a sport that is far easier to learn and safer than most people believe. What you put in can be as little as $25 to rent an inflatable kayak for a day on the TRINITY RIVER, which includes all the gear you need and a shuttle ride, with an extra $5 fee to camp at an adjacent U.S. Forest Service campground.

In a survey of rafting companies throughout the West, this trip turned out to be the least expensive among the hundreds of available white-water adventures. Yet you get an experience that will make you glow with joy for weeks, without any compromises in quality or safety.

The TRINITY RIVER is located in Northern California west of REDDING, starting as a trickle in the TRINITY ALPS and flowing westward for 100 miles, eventually joining with the KLAMATH RIVER in its journey to the sea. It is a fountain of beauty, rolling pure through granite gorges and abounding with birds and wildlife. Because flows are controlled by upstream dam releases, white-water rafting levels are guaranteed throughout summer.

Near the one-store town of Big Flat, the TRINITY is a "pool and drop" river, consisting of long deep pools sprinkled with sudden riffles and drops, making it perfect for rafting. Class II and III rapids such as Hell Hole, The Slot, Zig-Zag, Fishtail, Pinball, and others arrive every five minutes or so, providing bursts of pure thrill interspersed with short rests so you can regain your composure. In the lexicon of rafting, a Class I rapid is easy, a Class III is exciting, and a Class V is dangerous; on this section of the Trinity, most of the rapids are Class II.

"It looks really scary, it looks really dangerous, and it gets your adrenaline rushing because it feels like you're going to fly out of your raft," said Moneca Neary, a newcomer to the sport. "Then it turns out it's not dangerous at all. It's really safe. The worst that can happen is you fall in the water. That is why it is the perfect outdoor recreation."

Phil Ford, a retired gent who took the trip on a lark, suddenly discovered himself a new member of Trinity River Swimming Team, freestyle event. In other words, he got caught off balance by a side current, then suddenly tumbled out of his raft and into the water. He popped up a moment later with a big grin on face, paddle still in hand, the water streaming off him.

"Best part of the trip," he said later. "Absolutely euphoric."

One surprise is how safe this sport is. No matter how hard your heart may pound when your raft is flushed out of a surging river hole, the odds of being injured on a rafting trip are 25,000 to 1. Out of 500,000 participant days on guided raft trips last year in America, there were only 20 injuries of any consequence, according to Inside Outside, an outdoors recreation consulting firm.

The biggest new trend in white-water sports is the popular inflatable kayak, which looks something like a rubber bullet. These are perfect for the Trinity. The larger, traditional rafts are also available, either paddle rafts or the big oar boats. The latter require a guide to handle them and ensure that you have virtually zero chance of flipping.

But while rafting grows more popular as a sport, people are discovering that the more you control the boat, the more fun you get. That is why going solo in an inflatable kayak, with a few friends nearby, is becoming the ultimate in water sports.

After arranging the trip, the best strategy is to arrive a day early, then stay overnight at nearby Big Flat Campground, a 10-site U.S. Forest Service camp with piped water; the fee is $5 per site. Another nearby camp, Pigeon Point, is more primitive and has no piped water, but it's free, is set right along the TRINITY RIVER, and has a swimming beach.

Even early in the morning, the summer air warms quickly and you will likely find yourself eager to start the trip. At the little town of Big Flat, you will check in, pay your $25, get fitted for a life vest and a helmet, then take the 6- to 10-mile shuttle ride upstream in a van loaded with equipment. After a safety lesson, you point your boat downstream and off you go, enjoying the quiet ride, letting the flow of the river sweep you along.

On one trip, we rounded a boulder then suddenly came upon several turtles sunning themselves on rocks. We also saw migrating salmon, blue herons and other birds, and deer. The lucky few may even spot otters playing in the swirling eddies.

But the real excitement comes when you meet the white water head-on. It is here where these little boats turn into river rockets. Temperatures often reach the 90s and low 100s, and some people will "fall" into the river on purpose to cool off.

After a few hours, even the shy rafter will be making headlong runs into water chutes, disappearing into river holes, then popping up downstream, paddling away. Some say they feel like salmon darting around the currents.

"Today is the first time I've ever tried one of these things," said John Skrabo. "Now I've got another toy on my list I'll have to buy."

Actually, this is a rare case where renting is cheaper than buying. A quality inflatable kayak costs about $900, equivalent to the cost of 36 trips at $25 apiece down the TRINITY RIVER.

That means you will have plenty of cash left when your vacation is over. Of course, that's not all you will have. You'll take with you the memories of an ecstatic experience, one that will leave you rejuvenated for weeks. It's like taking a shower and washing off a year's worth of dust, all in just a day of paddling.

Contact: For information, phone Trinity River Rafting, (800) 307-4837, or Bigfoot Rafting, (530) 629-2263. For a free directory of all 50 river outfitters in California and the rivers they specialize in, phone (800) 552-3625. **Locator:** TRINITY RIVER (B1).

• FEATURED TRIP •

★ CACHE CREEK RAFTING

Rated: The Top 18 River Rafting Expeditions, 301

Mad Mike is waiting for you. Regardless of where you are reading this—at home, on a bus, on a train—Mad Mike is waiting. If you make a mistake, he'll get you. And if you don't watch it, Big Mother will get you, too. Mad Mike? Big Mother? That's right, these are the names of two pulse-pounding rapids on Cache Creek, the closest river to the Bay Area to provide a classic white-water experience. For beginners and experienced paddlers alike, Mad Mike is a fellow worth tangling with.

"I've dumped three times at Mad Mike," rafting guide Mark Gholson told me. But as rafting goes, if there isn't a chance of dumping, you miss the excitement. The idea is to get out there on the edge, and sometimes, when you go over the edge, you find it's an amazing and exhilarating place to be.

Cache Creek is located north of the Bay Area, below CLEAR LAKE. It is 110 miles from SAN FRANCISCO, about a two-and-a-half-hour drive. For North Bay residents, it's only 65 miles from NAPA.

For one-day trips, a good put-in spot is about 10 miles north of Rumsey. You can cover about eight miles of river, including shooting a trio of Class III rapids (on a scale of I to VI), and use adjacent Highway 16 as your shuttle road. A beginner can float it safely, while still getting the excitement of a quality run. For two-day trips, the local rafting company will take you on a remote four-wheel-drive road off Highway 16 that climbs to 3,000 feet. On a clear day, you can see MOUNTS SHASTA and LASSEN to the northeast, and the Coast Range to the west. You camp streamside at Buck Island, where rafting techniques are reviewed, and you can also watch for wildlife or go fishing. Turtles, tule elk, and even eagles are commonly seen;

for anglers, catfish seem to come in one size—big. A 30-pounder is on display in a little tackle shop in the town of Guinda.

On the two-day trip, you'll cover about 15 miles of river, spending about four hours on the water the first day and about six hours the second. You'll go through many rapids, but the highlights are Mad Mike, Big Mother, and Mario Andretti Bank.

The only items in your boat, which looks something like an inflatable kayak, are you, your paddle, and a waterproof bag holding lunch and drinks. Two-person inflatable kayaks are also available. Don't worry about getting wet; it's welcome in the typical 90-degree summer heat.

"This trip is unique compared to most other river runs in California, because you do not paddle with a guide but with a buddy," said river guide Gholson. "That means you can control your own destiny, as well as take a break when you want. Novices start out scared and tense, but by the end of the first day, they have a great feeling of accomplishment, because they have done it themselves. The next day they're ready for anything."

And it's a good thing, because Mad Mike is waiting.

Directions: Take Interstate 80 north to Interstate 505. Continue north to Highway 16, then head northwest. Highway 16 runs adjacent to Cache Creek. **Camping:** For those who have their own raft, a campground is available at Cache Creek Canyon Regional Park, (530) 666-8115). Sites cost $13–$15 a night and are first come, first served. **Trip tip:** Remember to bring a change of clothes, primary camping equipment such as a sleeping bag, and a stuff sack to pack your clothes. **Contact:** For a brochure, phone Whitewater Adventures at (707) 255-0761 or (800) 97-RIVER/977-4837. Reservations are recommended. **Locator:** CACHE CREEK (D1).

• FEATURED TRIP •

✶ LAKE SONOMA

Rated: The Top 50 Base Camps, 110; The Top 16 Places to Rent Boats, 305; The Top 25 Lakes, 307

LAKE SONOMA is California's mystery spot, but soon the only mystery is going to be why people haven't visited it yet. Sonoma is California's newest lake, created with the construction of Warm Springs Dam, located north of SANTA ROSA.

The creation of this lake provided the government with a chance to do something right, and they have succeeded. It is a perfect lake for camping, fishing, waterskiing (in designated areas), canoeing, and sailing—but it has some other key elements that make it particularly special: boat-in camping, 40 miles of hiking and horseback riding trails, and an 8,000-acre wildlife area.

It takes less than two hours by car to reach the lake from SAN FRANCISCO, and your first stop should be the SONOMA Overlook at the south end of the lake. From there, you get an ideal picture of the adventure ahead of you. The big lake is set in rich foothill country with thousands of hidden coves to be explored by boat or trail.

From the dam, the lake extends nine miles north on the Dry Creek arm, four miles to the east on Warm Springs Creek. Each of the lake arms has several fingers and miles of quiet and secluded shore. The public boat launch is located near the junction of the lake arms.

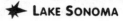

If you don't own a boat, rentals are available from the marina. If you don't want to rent one, but still want a secluded lakeside campsite, there are eight that can be reached by trail.

At some lakes, such as BERRYESSA and SHASTA, for instance, water-skiers and anglers are in constant conflict. At SONOMA, that problem has been solved by providing a large area for water skis and jet skis, and outlawing skiing elsewhere. Two miles of the Warm Springs Creek arm are off-limits to skiing, along with almost five miles on the Dry Creek arm.

As a result, water-skiers can "hit the coves" without worrying about running over folks who are fishing, and anglers can sneak up on quiet shoreline spots and not get plowed under by skiers. Each group has large areas to do their own thing.

As the word gets out, the fishing here is going to attract some excitement. Right now, the bass fishing is quite good, both for anglers casting lures such as the Countdown Rapala, and those using live minnows for bait. Minnows are sold at the Dry Creek Store, located on the approach road south of the lake.

If you are interested in a visit, you should obtain the LAKE SONOMA brochure, which details campgrounds, trails, and posted areas for boating.

The key for good fishing is habitat. When the lake was created, trees were left on the upper stretches of both lake arms. The submerged trees provide an ideal underwater habitat for bass and redear sunfish.

The centerpiece for campers is the Liberty Glen Campground, with 118 developed sites. Each campsite has a tent pad, barbecue grill, picnic table, and developed rest rooms, which include hot running water and showers. Water spigots are spaced about every four or five sites. No electrical hookups for RVs are provided. Reservations are not taken for individual sites. They are available on a first-come, first-served basis, with a maximum 14-day stay. Two large group camps are also available; reservations are required for these.

For a more secluded, lakeside option, 15 primitive shoreline camps are available. Seven can be reached only by boat, while eight are accessible by boat or trail. All are detailed on the LAKE SONOMA map.

For hikers, there are 40 miles of trails on the Warm Springs Creek arm. In addition, an 8,000-acre reserve has been set aside as a wildlife management area. Limited hunting for wild boar is permitted here, but only during special hunts offered by the Department of Fish and Game.

When visitors first see Lake Sonoma, the comparison they most likely will make will be to LAKE BERRYESSA, which is in a similar setting. But when it comes to solving the water-skier vs. fisher conflict, and offering opportunities for secluded camping, boating, and hiking, SONOMA kicks booty on BERRYESSA.

Directions: From San Francisco, drive approximately 75 miles north on U.S. 101 to Geyserville. Turn left on Canyon Road and drive five miles west to the lake. Anglers should take the Dry Creek exit at Healdsburg, about eight miles south of Geyserville, which will route them past the Dry Creek Store, where live minnows are for sale. **Marina:** Boats with motors, canoes, and paddleboats are available for rent. For information, phone (707) 433-2200. **Trip Tip:** A special access point for cartop boats is provided at the quiet north end of the lake from Hot Springs Road. **Camping:** Camping is on a first-come, first-served basis, with a maximum stay of 14 days. The Liberty Glen Campground has 118 developed campsites and opens April 13. The fee is $14 per night with a $2 boat launch fee. There are 15 no-fee boat-in sites, eight of which are also accessible by trail. Two large group camps hold 40 to 100 people each and require reservations; call (707) 433-9483. **Fees:** General day use is free. There is a $2 boat launch fee. **Contact:** Maps and brochures detailing posted lake areas, campgrounds, and trails are available for free from the U.S. Army Corps of Engineers, Lake Sonoma, 3333 Skaggs Springs Road, Geyserville, CA 95441; (707) 433-9483. **Locator:** LAKE SONOMA (D1).

• FEATURED TRIP •

RUSSIAN RIVER CANOE TRIP

Rated: The Top 16 Places to Rent Boats, 305; The Top 4 Places to Rockhound, 392

If you want to find out how well you get along with somebody, just try paddling a canoe together down the RUSSIAN RIVER. By the end of the day, there will be no doubt about it.

Either you will have bonded with your companion or you'll want to jam your paddle down his throat. As you weave your way downriver, you quickly discover that there is no middle ground; you either work together for adventure and triumph, or you don't and fall in—or come mighty close.

The RUSSIAN RIVER in Sonoma County is the best place for such an experiment. It is just an 80-minute drive north of the GOLDEN GATE BRIDGE. In spring and early summer, the river is fresh and lively, rolling green, having been rejuvenated by winter and spring rains. It's quite a change from fall, when the river is reduced to a slow trickle.

The natural beauty of the area comes as a surprise to many newcomers, especially the prime 10-mile stretch between FORESTVILLE and GUERNEVILLE, where redwoods border the river.

Best of all, the trip is easy, because there are two excellent canoe rental services that provide everything at a decent price, including a shuttle ride back to your starting point. Canoe rentals are available at Burke's Canoes in FORESTVILLE, near the most heavily forested section of the stream, and at Trowbridge's in HEALDSBURG, which is right along U.S. 101. Both are easy to reach and are long-established outfitters with excellent reputations. With spring rains, canoes can be rented all summer and into fall, perhaps even through October, depending on sunshine.

One of the best trips, especially for newcomers, is the 10-miler from FORESTVILLE to GUERNEVILLE. It has everything going for it, including the price, in the $27 range, which gets you a canoe for a full day, paddles, and life jackets. Each canoe has two seats, but if you have small children (the minimum age is five), they can fit between the paddlers.

After you shove off from Burke's at FORESTVILLE, you half-glide, half-paddle down the RUSSIAN RIVER. There are no guides, groups, or gawkers (except for your partner) telling you how fast or how slow to go.

That means you move along entirely at your own pace. Typically, the 10-mile trip takes about three and a half hours of paddle time. But virtually everybody loads their canoe with a cooler, beach towels, or fishing equipment, then stops at one of the beaches en route to picnic, swim, sunbathe, or fish.

This is one of the prettiest sections of the river, winding right through the heart of the redwoods. The entire area is green and lush, yet also has many sunny beaches. Another reason it is a favorite is because there is always plenty of water, with no dams to cross. (In the summer, the county places temporary dams in the river to help retain water.)

An ideal departure time from Burke's is about 10 a.m., when the sun usually starts to take over. Most paddlers then mosey their way along, stopping occasionally to loaf, and eventually reach Burke's private beach in GUERNEVILLE. You can arrive there as late as 6 p.m. and still catch a shuttle back to the headquarters in Forestville, where your adventure began.

If you want to end the trip earlier—perhaps to avoid a mutiny and being forced to walk the plank—shuttles depart about every half hour, all day.

Many other trips are available through the canoe rental services on the river. Burke's offers two- and three-day trips, for instance. Trowbridge's in Healdsburg offers some 10 different trips, as well as providing a shuttle service for those who bring their own canoe or kayak.

Both companies advise making advance reservations so that they can have all equipment ready for you on your arrival.

Although it is not a long drive from most parts of the Bay Area, many visitors make an overnighter of the trip. Several campgrounds are available in the area, both public and privately operated.

And let me tell you, if you think you get along well in a canoe, that's nothing compared to a small tent.

Directions to Burke's Canoes: Take U.S. 101 north from San Francisco to the Rohnert Park area, then get on Highway 116 west. Drive 14 miles to Forestville. Turn right on Mirabel Road at the Pit Stop and drive one mile until the road dead ends at the Russian River; Burke's is located right along the river. **Directions to Trowbridge's Canoe Rentals:** Drive north on U.S. 101 from San Francisco for about 70 miles. Take the first Healdsburg exit and turn right on Healdsburg Avenue. Proceed one mile to 20 Healdsburg Avenue. **Campgrounds:** Austin Creek Recreation Area, (707) 869-2015); Faerie Ring Campground, (707) 869-2746); Burke's Canoes, (707) 887-1222; and Mirabel Trailer Park and Camp, (707) 887-2383. **Fees:** One-day canoe rental, paddles, a life jacket, and shuttle service for the 10-mile trip from Forestville to Guerneville costs about $27. **Contact:** Burke's Canoes, (707) 887-1222; Trowbridge's Canoe Rentals, (707) 433-7247. **Locator:** HEALDSBURG (D1).

• FEATURED TRIP •

★ RICHARDSON BAY KAYAKING

Rated: San Francisco Bay's Best Kayaking

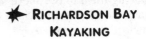

Kayaking on SAN FRANCISCO BAY for the first time is the oddest feeling. It's like you're sitting right in the water but you don't need to sprout a set of gills. Then, with a few easy strokes of a plastic double-ended paddle, you launch about 25 feet forward and at once are enveloped in quiet, smoothness, and excitement.

The first time you push off the shore of SAUSALITO, kayaking headquarters for SAN FRANCISCO BAY, you feel a profound sensation of freedom. Some people just start laughing, or whooping like wild hyenas, because they're too thrilled for words. They find that kayaking is easy and stable, that they are in total control (for the first time in their lives), and they feel a complete release from the daily pressure cooker.

Fall is the best time of the year to kayak here. The spring and summer winds are long gone, leaving serene waters in protected RICHARDSON BAY near SAUSALITO. Your companions include diving terns, harbor seals, and flocks of passing migratory seabirds. Sometimes, a surprise submarine may even pop up in the main channel. No fooling.

Now get this: You can try it on for size—for free! Unbelievable, eh? The first Sunday of the month (May through October) is called Demo Day, and anybody can just show up, hop in a kayak, and paddle around for awhile. (Of course, always call ahead to make sure the event will be staged.) This is an ideal time to bring youngsters with you under the guise of introducing them to the sport, when actually you're the one who's been wanting to give it a try.

Beginning kayakers share the same fear: You are going to tip over, and then while floating around, get eaten by great white sharks. First off, you don't tip over. Sea kayaks are not constructed like tippy river kayaks but are longer, wider, and more stable than a canoe. In addition, the water is calm, so if you don't want to tip over, you won't.

But what if you do? Well, you fall out of the boat and then hold on to it. What about the sharks? There are none, of course. In fact, there has never been a recorded shark attack inside the GOLDEN GATE.

Thousands of people a year are now kayaking on the bay, and it is turning out to be one of the safest outdoor activities available. Watching sunsets may be a little bit safer. But from a kayak, you can do both, or better yet, paddle off to dinner (at Sam's in TIBURON) under a full moon.

The experience in the little boat is unique. Simply floating around can give you a charge, as you sense the power of the water, the tides, and the wind. Just a few hundred yards offshore, you can feel completely alone, even though millions of people are just over yonder.

That is why so many people are deciding to buy into the sport, getting fully outfitted with a kayak, paddle, life jacket, car rack, and waterproof paddling jacket. Going all out will cost you about $800 with a used boat, watching your pennies. If you want the best of everything and want it new, you're looking at the $2,000 range.

A one-person sea kayak typically is about 16 feet long and weighs 45 pounds. That means with a good car rack with a kayak saddle (Yakima makes the best), anybody can pick up the boat and put it on their car for transport. Stowing a kayak at home is not difficult, since the boat does not require a trailer and can be set on end along a wall to take up minimal space.

Who goes? "It is almost 50-50, men and women," Diane Christiansen, cofounder of Sea Trek in SAUSALITO, told me. "It's really a great singles sport, and many couples have met in a double kayak on the water, either on a guided trip or in a class."

Special trips are offered throughout the year and include exploring RICHARDSON BAY and the SAUSALITO waterfront, paddling to ANGEL ISLAND, moonlight kayaking to TIBURON for dinner, and for the advanced, trips to ALCATRAZ, SAN FRANCISCO, and even right around the GOLDEN GATE BRIDGE (don't look up). And it's a lot of fun to just follow the current, paddling a bit, but letting the tidal flows take you wherever. It's a great sensation, one that you will not soon forget.

Typically, this is how things progress: 1) You show up on a Demo Day and go for a test paddle. 2) You like it and decide to take an introductory class. 3) You love it and rent a kayak, heading off wherever your heart desires and your skills can take you.

Like most folks, this is a sport you may never have considered. All it takes, however, is a short time sitting in one of these little boats in the Bay. It may forever change the way you look at the world.

Fees: Demo Days are free, but a fee is charged for subsequent introductory classes and includes equipment and seven hours of instruction. **Contact:** For a free brochure or more information, including dates and directions for Demo Days, phone Sea Trek in Sausalito, (415) 488-1000 or (800) 934-2252. **Locator:** RICHARDSON BAY (E1a).

10
FISHING

• Tom's Ratings •

• Featured Trips •

See last page for Northern California and Bay Area foldout maps.

*The area code for all phone numbers followed by an asterisk (*) will change to 559 as of November 14, 1998. Also, area code 805 is scheduled to split on February 13, 1999. The new area code is yet to be introduced. Call Pacific Bell for a list of prefixes that will receive the new area code.

• Tom's Ratings •

The Top 7 Deep-Sea Fishing Trips

In Northern California

There's a nearby mountain range constructed something like the Sierra Nevada, but you won't find it on any road map. It's buried beneath miles of seawater. Tucked below the ocean surface along the Bay Area coast is a rock ridgeline, complete with craggy peaks and canyons that drop thousands of feet. Just as the Sierra is home to wildlife, this underwater range is perfect for fish.

A huge variety of big rockfish live here along with cabezone and lingcod up to 50 pounds. The best time of the year is in September and

October, when the big lings emerge from the depths of the canyon bottoms to spawn along many of the mountaintops. But the fishing is good as long as the ocean is calm enough to allow it.

The highest peak is 25 miles west of San Francisco, where the Farallon Islands break the surface. The ridgeline extends for about 100 miles, to just north of Bodega Bay. Reefs (south to north) such as the Farallones, Soap Bank, Fanny Shoals, and Cordell Bank attract vast schools of rockfish year-round, and big lingcod every fall.

Fishing for them is a lot of fun for newcomers and experienced hands alike. In any case, you are likely to fill up your freezer. It is common for anglers to bring home burlap bags stuffed with 15-fish limits often weighing 75 to 85 pounds, on trips to these spots. The best lingcod spots are at Soap Bank, which is just south of Cordell Bank, and just offshore of the South Farallon Island.

The *Sea Angler* from Bodega Bay ventures to Cordell Bank daily when seas allow it. On a typical trip in the fall, boatloads of 25 to 35 anglers will catch 30 to 60 lingcod, in addition to the limits of 15 rockfish per rod.

The Soap Bank, a rarely fished spot due to its distance from sportfishing ports, can offer even better action. Lingcod up to 50 pounds are caught every fall. The only sportfishing vessel fast enough to reach the Soap Bank is the *Cobra* out of Richmond Marina, a 96-footer with three engines that hits this spot daily. In many cases, the boat ride takes longer than it does for fishers to limit out.

The rigging is quite simple. Most people buy a shrimp fly rig, that is, a pre-tied leader with three red/yellow shrimp flies. Small strips of squid are baited on the hooks, then dropped to the ocean bottom—usually 200 to 450 feet deep.

The boat does not anchor, but drifts over the reefs, and the speed of the drift is controlled by the intensity of the wind. In turn, this is the variable that decides how much sinker weight is required. It can vary from eight ounces to two pounds, though one-pound weights usually do the job. Instead of lead sinkers, you can add some excitement to your trip by trying a 16-ounce, chrome-plated Diamond jig or Yo Ho jig for a sinker. A chrome jig dangled near the sea bottom is the ticket for big lingcod, which will often smash into it in order to protect the territory they have staked out.

The problem is that these jigs, complete with large treble hooks, can snag up so fast on the bottom that it can seem like the rocks are biting better than the fish. On calm autumn days, when the boat drift is slight and folks have plenty of time to dangle bait over the reef, it is common for everybody aboard to catch two or three fish at a time.

On one trip to the FARALLON ISLANDS, a gent shouted for the gaff—which usually means a big fish is on the line. But when *Sea Angler* skipper Rick Powers looked over the side, he instead saw what looked like a stringer of 15 fish.

"What the heck are you doing using a stringer," Powers said. "This is the ocean. We put them in a burlap bag out here. You put them on a stringer and all you're going to do is attract a bunch of sharks."

The fisherman just grinned. "Look closer," he said.

We all did. It turned out that the man had a custom-tied leader with 15 baits on at once—and he had caught the 15-fish limit in one drop.

1. CAPITOLA

Fishing the edge of inshore kelp beds in shallow water can be productive. Skiff rentals are available.

Contact: Capitola Wharf, (408) 462-2208. **Locator:** CAPITOLA (F1). **See featured trip page:** 377.

2. CORDELL BANK

The *Sea Angler* makes trips daily out of the Boathouse in BODEGA BAY.

Contact: Bodega Bay Sportfishing Center, (707) 875-3495. **Locator:** BODEGA BAY (D0). **See featured trip page:** 212.

3. DEEP REEF

This is the favorite spot for the *Blue Horizon* from Princeton in HALF MOON BAY.

Contact: *Blue Horizon*, (650) 726-2913. Also try the *Queen of Hearts*, (650) 726-7133. **Locator:** HALF MOON BAY (E1). **See featured trip page:** 224.

4. EUREKA

The *Moku* makes two half-day trips out of E-Z Landing RV Park and Marina to Table Rock, or in HUMBOLDT BAY.

Contact: E-Z Landing RV Park, (707) 442-3474 or write to 3458 Utah Street, Eureka, CA 95503. **Locator:** EUREKA (B0).

5. FARALLON ISLANDS

C-Gull II, Huck Finn, and *Rapid Transit* out of EMERYVILLE make regular trips. *Captain John's* from Princeton also makes the run.

Contact: *C-Gull II, Huck Finn,* and *Rapid Transit* at (510) 654-6040 and *Captain John's* at (650) 726-2913 or (800) 391-8787. **Locator:** FARALLON ISLANDS (E1b).

6. FORT BRAGG

The *Trek II* out of Noyo Harbor runs daily to local reefs.

Contact: Noyo Harbor, (707) 964-4550. **Locator:** FORT BRAGG (C0).

The *Holiday* works the MONTEREY underwater canyon. The *Star of Monterey* runs regularly as well.

Contact: The *Holiday*, (408) 375-5951; or Sam's Fishing Fleet (for the *Star of Monterey*), (408) 372-0577. **Locator:** MONTEREY (F1). **See featured trip page:** 244.

7. NEW YEAR ISLAND

Stagnaro's Fishing Charters sends boats here from SANTA CRUZ.

Contact: Stagnaro's Fishing Charters, (408) 427-2334. Or try Shamrock Charters, (408) 476-2648. **Locator:** SANTA CRUZ (F1). **See featured trip page:** 377.

The *Cobra*, the fastest sportfishing vessel in the Bay Area, hits Soap Bank regularly out of SAUSALITO.

Contact: The *Cobra,* (925) 283-6773.
Locator: SAUSALITO (E1a).

• TOM'S RATINGS •

THE TOP 10 PLACES TO FISH WITH KIDS

In Northern California

Youngsters don't just want to do; they want to do well. Thus fishing becomes quite a challenge, a sport that requires logic, persistence, and timing, because the idea isn't just to fish, it's to catch fish.

Which reminds me of a youngster named Justin Stienstra of PALO ALTO, my brother's stepson. Justin has had his share of success, with good grades in school and all-star play on the baseball field, and he tries just as hard with a fishing rod. But over a three-year period in which he made 10 fishing trips, the results did not equal his efforts.

"In that time, I caught two fish," he confided to me. "Make that three, but one got off."

That's all changed now, though.

Many youngsters, and adults, too, can empathize, and plenty quit the sport out of frustration. So the mission of every newcomer to fishing should be to have an adventure in which you'll catch fish—lots of them, one after another, no matter what size—and get a glimpse of the excitement that is possible.

So Justin, my brother Rambob, and I embarked on a crusade in Northern California to catch fish. Not just a few—dozens of them. There are hundreds of lakes, streams, and coastal areas where this is possible.

For example, CLEAR LAKE, along the tules outside of Clear Lake State Park, is an excellent spot to catch bluegill. For yellow perch, try your luck at COPCO LAKE in Siskiyou County. You can't go wrong.

For a wilderness adventure, hike in to COIT LAKE in HENRY W. COE STATE PARK in the Gavilan Mountains and you'll find plenty of bass. Hike in at the Rae Lakes in the JOHN MUIR WILDERNESS, and also at Sapphire Lake in the TRINITY ALPS WILDERNESS, and you'll get plenty of trout. These trips can be extremely grueling for children, however.

There are several streams where you'll be able to catch a lot of fish. The Upper SAN JOAQUIN RIVER, upstream of DEVILS POSTPILE, is a winner for trout, as is the KINGS RIVER near Road's End in KINGS CANYON NATIONAL PARK. Juvenile steelhead are plentiful near ORLEANS on the KLAMATH RIVER in September.

Along the coast, you can find rockfish at shallow-water kelp beds at SAN SIMEON as well as at the FARALLON ISLANDS and at the shallow-water reefs along the San Mateo County coast.

At any of these spots, and dozens of others, you can really haul them in. That chance is all the motivation one requires, and exactly what Justin Stienstra needed to discover.

Our trip took us far north, right to the Oregon border, to COPCO LAKE, where the yellow perch bite like piranhas. On his first cast, Justin caught two perch, one on each hook. In the next three hours, he caught dozens and dozens of them—there's no limit—and the three of us caught close to a hundred. No secret how: All it takes is a little piece of worm, or red yarn, near the boat ramp.

"I never realized this could happen," Justin said.

Well, it can. All you have to supply

to make it happen is the do.

1. Copco Lake

Contact: Shasta Cascade Wonderland Association, (800) 474-2782. **Locator:** Copco Lake (A2).

2. Clear Lake

Contact: Clear Lake State Park, (707) 279-4293; Ferndale Marina, (707) 279-4866. **Locator:** Clear Lake (C1, D1). **See featured trip page:** 362.

3. Farallon Islands

Contact: Huck Finn Sportfishing, Princeton, (650) 654-6040; *Capt. John's*, Princeton, (650) 726-2913; the *Cobra*, Sausalito, (925) 283-6773. **Locator:** Farallon Islands (E1b). **See featured trip page:** 272.

4. San Simeon kelp beds

Contact: San Simeon Landing, (805) 927-4676.* **Locator:** San Simeon (G2).

5. Upper San Joaquin River

Contact: Inyo National Forest, Mammoth Visitor Center, (760) 934-2505. **Locator:** San Joaquin River (F3).

6. Coit Lake

Contact: Henry W. Coe State Park, (408) 779-2728; California State Parks, Four Rivers District, (209) 826-1196. **Locator:** Coit Lake (E1d). **See featured trip page:** 139.

7. Rae Lakes

Contact: Sierra National Forest, Pineridge Ranger District, (209) 855-5360*. **Locator:** John Muir Wilderness (F5).

8. Sapphire Lake

Contact: Shasta-Trinity National Forest, Shasta Lake Ranger District, (530) 275-1587. **Contact:** Trinity Alps Wilderness (B1).

9. Klamath River

Contact: Shasta Cascade Wonderland Association, (800) 474-2782. **Locator:** Klamath River (A1).

10. Kings River

Contact: Sequoia/Kings Canyon National Parks, (209) 565-3341*; Sequoia National Forest, Hume Lake Ranger District, (209) 338-2251.* **Locator:** Kings River (F5).

• Tom's Ratings •

The Top 43 Lakes to Fish

In the San Francisco Bay Area

Daybreak at San Pablo Reservoir brings one of the prettiest scenes in the Bay Area, distinguished by blues and greens, placid water, small boats leaving fresh, white wakes, and happy anglers gathering about the lake, many with nice stringers of trout.

That unique combination of beauty and excitement makes San Pablo the number one lake in my personal survey of the 43 recreational lakes in San Francisco, Santa Clara, Marin, Alameda, Contra Costa, Napa, Solano, and Santa Cruz Counties.

I rated the lakes from best to worst, considering a number of factors including boating, fishing, hiking, camping, and scenic beauty. While San Pablo is the overall winner, other lakes won in individual categories.

Loch Lomond in the Santa Cruz Mountains is the prettiest in the Bay Area, just ahead of Alpine Lake in Marin County. Parkway Lake in Coyote has the highest catch rate for anglers. Bon Tempe Lake in San Anselmo offers the best hiking trails. Del Valle Reservoir south of Livermore provides the best campground and boating access. In addition, several lakes receive special bonus stocks of trophy-size trout: SAN PABLO, LAKE CHABOT, DEL VALLE, MERCED North and South, LAFAYETTE, SHADOW CLIFFS, and PARKWAY.

Also please note that several beautiful lakes don't make the list because public access is forbidden: Crystal Springs, Upper and Lower San Andreas, Pilarcitos, Felt, Searsville, Calaveras, San Antonio, Briones, and Elsman. I also consider BERRYESSA to be out of the Bay Area, so that lake is not rated either.

That leaves 43 lakes, far more than most people imagine are here. A good time can be had at any, regardless of their rating. Now, on with the show:

1. San Pablo Reservoir

SAN PABLO provides a unique combination of beauty, excellent fishing, good access for boats, and a protected area for waterfowl. More trout are stocked here than in any lake in California, about 200,000 per year, joining resident bass, bluegill, and catfish. Boat rentals, a tackle shop, and helpful employees make newcomers feel welcome.

Contact: San Pablo Recreation Information Center, (510) 223-1661. **Locator:** SAN PABLO RESERVOIR (E1c). **See featured trip page:** 375.

2. Del Valle Reservoir

This long, narrow lake has a 100-site campground, a boat launch for powerboats, and an adjacent park for picnics and hikes. The lake is well stocked with trout into early summer, and it also has bluegill for kids, smallmouth bass for know-hows, and some huge striped bass for the persistent few. It's often very hot and dry here in the summer months.

Contact: Del Valle Regional Park, (925) 373-0332; Del Valle Boathouse, (925) 449-5201; East Bay Regional Park District, (510) 635-0135 extension 2200. **Locator:** DEL VALLE RESERVOIR (E2).

3. Lake Chabot

CHABOT just plain looks fishy, and it is, with abundant trout stocks and the biggest largemouth bass in the Bay Area. The largest bass in Bay Area history was documented here—17 pounds, two ounces. Private boats are not permitted, but rentals are available. Picnic sites, hiking trails, and a nearby campground put Chabot right at the top of my list.

Contact: Anthony Chabot Regional Park, (510) 881-1833 extension 2570; East Bay Regional Park District, (510) 635-0135 extension 2200. **Locator:** LAKE CHABOT (E1c). **See featured trip page:** 230.

4. Lake Merced North

If you sit in a boat along the tule-lined shore, you will feel like you are in a different world. That's because you are. This is a place of peace, with the fantastic bonus of a chance of catching a 10-pound rainbow trout. The tackle shop welcomes newcomers by providing a free tip sheet, rod-and-reel rentals, pre-tied leaders, and boats with electric motors.

Contact: Merced Bait Shop, (415) 753-1101. **Locator:** LAKE MERCED (E1b). **See featured trip page:** 366.

5. Loch Lomond Reservoir

LOCH LOMOND is tucked in a canyon in the SANTA CRUZ MOUNTAINS and is circled by redwoods, creating a pristine setting that makes you feel far removed from civilization. On blue-sky days, the lake is often a deeper hue of blue than any other in the Bay Area. Trout stocks start every March, and a resident population of bass adds to the prospects on summer evenings.

Boat rentals, a launch, a shop, and a picnic area are bonuses.

Contact: Loch Lomond Reservoir, (408) 335-7424. **Locator:** LOCH LOMOND RESERVOIR (E1d).

6. LAFAYETTE LAKE

Because of its proximity to SAN PABLO RESERVOIR, LAFAYETTE often gets missed by out-of-towners. But it shouldn't be overlooked, not with boat rentals, regular trout stocks, and some huge but elusive largemouth bass. The catch rates are quite good, with the best spot usually in the East Cove.

Contact: Lafayette Lake Marina, (925) 284-9669. **Locator:** LAFAYETTE LAKE (E1c).

7. BON TEMPE LAKE

This is a pretty lake nestled on the northern slopes of MOUNT TAMALPAIS. It provides a starting point for some outstanding hiking trails, as well as some shoreline baitdunking areas for trout. No boats of any kind are allowed, a big downer, but the plentiful trout stocks make up for that.

Contact: Marin Water District, (415) 924-4600; Sky Oaks Ranger Station, (415) 459-5267. **Locator:** BON TEMPE LAKE (E1a).

8. PINTO LAKE

Little Pinto Lake is often overlooked, despite being one of the few lakes in the Bay Area that provide both a campground and good fishing. Trout are stocked regularly into the summer; then when the warm weather hits, a surprising crappie fishery takes over.

Contact: Pinto Lake County Park, (408) 722-8129. **Locator:** WATSONVILLE (F1).

9. LAKE MERCED SOUTH

If you haven't seen LAKE MERCED lately, you will be surprised at the size and beauty of it. The lake is ringed by tules, provides decent trout fishing, and is best known as an excellent spot to paddle a canoe, row a shell, or sail a dinghy.

Contact: Merced Bait Shop, (415) 753-1101. **Locator:** LAKE MERCED (E1b). **See featured trip page:** 366.

10. ALPINE LAKE

The fishing is lousy, but the remarkable natural beauty of ALPINE LAKE, full to the brim and nestled below MOUNT TAMALPAIS, earns its ranking in the top 10. No boats or water contact are permitted, but the hiking and scenery make this a great destination. Park near the dam for a hike up the Cataract Trail, or at nearby BON TEMPE LAKE, to hike along the far shore.

Contact: Marin Water District, (415) 924-4600. **Locator:** ALPINE LAKE (E1a).

11. UVAS RESERVOIR

UVAS is one of the few lakes in Santa Clara County that usually have plenty of water in them. Typically full to the brim in spring, it is regularly stocked with trout from February through April. From May on, it offers good shoreline bass fishing. A county campground is located nearby.

Contact: Santa Clara County Parks and Recreation, (408) 358-3741. **Locator:** UVAS RESERVOIR (F1).

12. LAKE HENNESSEY

HENNESSEY is a huge lake, 20,000 acres, 12 miles long, and four miles wide. However, it is often lost in the shadow of LAKE BERRYESSA to the east. It is an ideal lake for small boats, with no motors over 10 horsepower permitted. The lake is stocked with trout in the spring and offers fair bass fishing during the summer. Insider's note: The Hennessey Impoundment often has the best trout fishing.

Contact: City of Napa Department of Parks and Recreation, Public Works, and Water, (707) 257-9520. **Locator:** LAKE HENNESSEY (D1).

13. SOULEJULE RESERVOIR

This little-known hike-in lake (park at the base of the dam) provides some of the best shoreline fishing for crappie and bass in the Bay Area. Try it on a warm summer evening.

Contact: Marin Water District, (415) 924-4600; Western Boat, (415) 454-4177. **Locator:** SOULEJULE RESERVOIR (D1).

14. CALERO RESERVOIR

Calero has become so popular that you often need a reservation to launch a boat. This is because the lake is usually kept full, and the catch-and-release fishing can be excellent for bass and crappie. Boating and hiking are prime pursuits here. The lake's appeal is tainted only by the health warning on eating any fish caught in it; still, this remains a popular spot. During the summer, a reservation is required to launch boats.

Contact: Santa Clara County Parks and Recreation, (408) 358-3741. For launch reservations, call (408) 927-9144. **Locator:** COYOTE (E1d).

15. ARASTRADERO LAKE

A 20-minute hike through pretty foothill country will get you to this classic bass pond. No rafts or float tubes are allowed—a major error. This area is part of a 6,000-acre nature preserve, with lots of squirrels, chipmunks, and hawks.

Contact: Foothills Park, (650) 329-2423. **Locator:** ARASTRADERO LAKE (E1b). **See featured trip page:** 69.

16. SANDY WOOL LAKE

Sandy Wool is a small lake, just 14 acres, but is surrounded by parkland with 16 miles of hiking trails. Boating without motors is ideal, and fishing is decent for small planters after a trout stock.

Contact: Ed Levin County Park, (408) 262-6980. **Locator:** MILPITAS (E1d).

17. SHADOW CLIFFS LAKE

SHADOW CLIFFS is a good idea that works. This water hole used to be part of a rock quarry but has been converted into a lake, providing boating and fishing for trout and catfish. At 143 acres, it is decent-sized. It's not exactly pretty, rather like an ugly dog that you learn to love.

Contact: Shadow Cliffs Regional Park, (925) 846-3000. **Locator:** PLEASANTON (E2).

18. DON CASTRO RESERVOIR

Don Castro is the centerpiece of a regional park that doesn't get much attention. No boats are allowed and there are few trout, but prospects are fair during the summer for bass, catfish, and bluegill.

Contact: East Bay Regional Park District, (510) 635-0135 extension 2200. **Locator:** HAYWARD (E1c).

19. COTTONWOOD LAKE

Cottonwood Lake is set in Hellyer Park, just a short hop off U.S. 101. It is a favorite spot for windsurfing and sailing. It also has good picnic sites and six miles of bike trails, and is stocked with trout.

Contact: Santa Clara County Parks and Recreation, (408) 358-3741. **Locator:** SAN JOSE (E1d).

20. LAGUNITAS LAKE

Lagunitas is a living science project, where an attempt to re-create a wild trout fishery is under way. The catch-and-release fishing rates are low, but the scenery is a high.

Contact: Marin Water District, (415) 924-4600; Sky Oaks Ranger Station, (415) 459-5267. **Locator:** SAN ANSELMO (E1a).

21. Parkway Lake

The scenery at Parkway isn't so great, but trout and catfish are large and abundant. The high access fee pays for special stocks of trophy-sized trout.

Contact: Parkway Lake information line, (408) 629-9111; Coyote Discount Bait and Tackle, (408) 463-0711. **Locator:** COYOTE (E1d).

22. Stevens Creek Reservoir

When full, Stevens Creek is quite pretty. It covers 95 acres and can fill quickly during a series of heavy rains. When that happens, the Department of Fish and Game always stocks it with rainbow trout, turning the lake into a respectable prospect. Boating speed limits are often enforced. Check with park headquarters for current regulations.

Contact: Stevens Creek County Park, (408) 867-3654; Santa Clara County Parks and Recreation, (408) 358-3741. **Locator:** CUPERTINO (E1d).

23. Coyote Reservoir

Years ago, this was the Bay Area's best bass lake, until it was drained several times by water manipulations. It can be full in spring, then empty by fall, and nobody seems to know what will happen from one year to the next. A campground along the edge of the lake is a redeeming factor.

Contact: Coyote County Park, (408) 842-7800; Santa Clara County Parks and Recreation, (408) 358-3741. **Locator:** COYOTE RESERVOIR (E1d).

24. Nicasio Reservoir

There are no picnic tables and no trees in the area. It's just this little lake in rolling foothill country. Summer evenings can be good for bass and crappie, but alas, no rafts or float tubes are permitted.

Contact: Marin Water District, (415) 924-4600. **Locator:** NICASIO RESERVOIR (E1a).

25. Contra Loma Reservoir

No motors are permitted here, making Contra Loma ideal for rafts, prams, and rowboats. The trout program is a winner, and striped bass always provide a reason to pray. This is stark country.

Contact: Contra Loma Reservoir, (925) 757-0404. **Locator:** ANTIOCH (E2).

26. Lake Temescal

Temescal is a little lake that responds quickly to trout stocks, but then, so do the cormorants. No boats are permitted. The adjacent hillsides are recovering after being scorched by the terrible OAKLAND hills fire in the fall of 1991.

Contact: East Bay Regional Park District, (510) 635-0135 extension 2200. **Locator:** OAKLAND (E1c).

27. Chesbro Dam

When full, this reservoir covers 300 acres, and also provides some good-sized crappie prospects during the spring. The bass tend to be either very, very small or absolutely giant with a case of lockjaw, so you end up catching midgets or facing a monster. Visiting anglers often leave here amazed by some fish that they saw, but rarely by a fish that they caught.

Contact: Santa Clara County Parks and Recreation, (408) 358-3741. **Locator:** MORGAN HILL (F1).

28. Chabot Reservoir

This lake is adjacent to Marine World, but is accessible through Dan Foley Park. A prime spot for picnics, Chabot

Reservoir is regularly stocked with trout.

Contact: Dan Foley Park, (925) 462-3409; Department of Fish and Game, (707) 944-5500. **Locator:** VALLEJO (E1c).

29. KENT LAKE

The hike to Kent Lake is a pretty one, almost like taking a walk through Tennessee woodlands. While this is a good spot for a picnic, the lake has no facilities, no boating, and no fishing program. Scenic beauty alone earns it a top-30 ranking.

Contact: Marin Water District, (415) 924-4600. **Locator:** KENT LAKE (E1a).

30. PHOENIX LAKE

Improved facilities, access, parking, trout stocks, and boating access (even for rafts) must be implemented in order for Phoenix Lake to move up the list. The Department of Fish and Game stocks it in late winter, providing fair shoreline fishing.

Contact: Western Boat, (415) 454-4177. **Locator:** ROSS (E1a).

31. LAKE ANDERSON

This should be one of the top lakes in the Bay Area. It is big (1,000 acres), has crappie, bluegill, and bass, and there's a 5 mph speed limit to keep the southern end of the lake quiet. Alas, the numbskulls who control the water level here are just as apt to drain it down to the bottom as to keep it full; that hinders the implementation of fishery programs, as well as preventing the lake from becoming a stable site for water sports. During the summer months, a reservation is required for boat launching.

Contact: Santa Clara County Parks and Recreation, (408) 358-3741; for boat launch reservations, call (408) 927-9144. **Locator:** LAKE ANDERSON (E1d).

32. CULL CANYON RESERVOIR

This small lake in the hills gets little attention from anglers, and it's easy to see why with only some dinky catfish to try for. The surrounding parkland nudges up the rating a bit.

Contact: East Bay Regional Park District, (510) 635-0135 extension 2200. **Locator:** CASTRO VALLEY (E1c).

33. CAMPBELL PERCOLATION POND

Easy access is a bonus here; the lake is located just off Highway 17 at Camden Avenue. It's a mere dot of water, just five acres, but it is stocked regularly with trout.

Contact: Santa Clara County Parks and Recreation, (408) 358-3741. **Locator:** CAMPBELL (E1d).

34. CUNNINGHAM LAKE

Trout fishing in an urban setting? That's what you get here. Cunningham Lake is located on Tully Road and the Capitol Expressway, right next to the Raging Waters water slide. The lake covers 50 acres and is surrounded by a small park.

Contact: San Jose Regional Parks, (408) 277-5562. **Locator:** SAN JOSE (E1d).

35. LEXINGTON RESERVOIR

This can be a very pretty lake when it is full of water. With more water, you get a quality reservoir with a boat ramp, trout plants, and a picnic area. Without it, it's a mediocre skunk hole.

Contact: Santa Clara County Parks and Recreation, (408) 358-3741. **Locator:** LOS GATOS (E1d).

36. GUADALUPE RESERVOIR

The fish are contaminated here, and the fact that nobody around these parts seems to care about it accounts for this poor rating. The lake itself covers 75 acres, and is in a pretty setting (in the spring) in the foothills of the Sierra Azul Range. The bass fishing is fair, but don't eat 'em.

Contact: Santa Clara County Parks and Recreation, (408) 358-3741. **Locator:** LOS GATOS (E1d).

37. LAKE ELIZABETH

During the hot summer in the East Bay flats, this is a relatively cool spot, set in Fremont's Central Park. Some small bass, bluegill, and catfish provide a few longshot hopes.

Contact: Lake Elizabeth Central Park, (510) 791-4340. **Locator:** FREMONT (E1c).

38. LAKE VASONA

This is the kind of place you would visit for a Sunday picnic, maybe to play softball. The lake is part of a 150-acre park near the SANTA CRUZ MOUNTAINS. Sailboating and rowing are options, but forget about fishing.

Contact: Santa Clara County Parks and Recreation, (408) 358-3741. **Locator:** LOS GATOS (E1d).

39. LAKE MERRITT

The best thing about LAKE MERRITT is that you can rent a variety of boats, including canoes and paddleboats. You can even take sailing lessons here. It is also good for jogging, and for bird-watching in the spring. Because the water is brackish, there are no resident fish.

Contact: Lake Merritt Marina, (510) 444-3807. **Locator:** LAKE MERRITT (E1c).

40. LAKE ALMADEN

The best thing going for 62-acre Almaden is that a lot of folks bypass it, making this a good picnic site, particularly on weekdays. It is set in the foothill country near some abandoned mines, where mercury runoff has made all fish dangerous to eat.

Contact: Santa Clara County Parks and Recreation, (408) 358-3741. **Locator:** SAN JOSE (E1d).

41. SHINN POND

Once an old gravel pit, Shinn Pond has been filled with water and stocked with bass and bluegill. The pond covers 23 acres, and the fishing is poor.

Contact: East Bay Regional Park District, (510) 635-0135 extension 2200. **Locator:** FREMONT (E1c).

42. LAKE ANZA

The lake itself, just 11 acres, doesn't offer much in the way of fishing, except for a few bluegill and small bass. You will, however, find a nice sandy beach for a Sunday afternoon visit and can explore pleasant TILDEN REGIONAL PARK, which surrounds the lake.

Contact: East Bay Regional Park District, (510) 635-0135 extension 2200. **Locator:** TILDEN REGIONAL PARK (E1c).

43. MERCED IMPOUNDMENT

Of the three lakes that make up LAKE MERCED, this is the one that everybody forgets. It responds quickly to trout plants but dies when not stocked. And it is so small that during low water it can be afflicted with low oxygen levels and high water temperatures, conditions that can cause all stocks to be stopped.

Contact: Merced Bait Shop, (415) 753-1101. **Locator:** LAKE MERCED (E1b). **See featured trip page:** 366.

• TOM'S RATINGS •

THE TOP 8 CITIES WITH DAILY SALMON TRIPS

In the San Francisco Bay Area

The richest marine region from Mexico to Alaska is along the San Francisco Bay coast, a unique area that provides the longest ocean season anywhere for salmon fishing. It is called the Gulf of the Farallones, an underwater shelf that extends 25 miles out to sea before dropping off to never-never land. The plankton-rich waters attract shrimp, squid, anchovies, and herring, and these, in turn, attract hordes of feeding salmon. It means that on any given day of the nine-month season, an angler has the chance to head out on the briny deep and tangle with the king of the coast.

The salmon typically range from four to eight pounds, but there are enough in the 15- to 25-pound class to keep people on edge. The limit is two, with a minimum-size limit of 20 inches, and there are several periods every season when everyone aboard every boat limits out.

One key is finding the baitfish. Do that and you find the salmon. The most popular method of fishing is trolling, which allows anglers to cover the maximum amount of water in the minimum amount of time. The big sportfishing vessels from Bay Area ports fan out across the Gulf of the Farallones like spokes in a wheel. When one finds the fish, the skipper alerts the rest of the fleet and everybody catches fish.

If the baitfish are shallow, tightly schooled, and easy to locate, as is common in midsummer and early fall, a number of anglers will abandon trolling. Instead they'll drift mooch, using light tackle and anchovy-baited Shim jigs, and set the hook on each fish. This technique produces lower catch rates, but the average size of the salmon is much larger.

If you are new to the game, learning how is as easy as tumbling out of bed in time for the 6 a.m. boat departure. A list of full-time sportfishing vessels is included at the end this adventure story to get you pointed in the right direction. Trips include bait, instruction, and a heck of a boat ride under the GOLDEN GATE BRIDGE. Rod rentals are available along with leaders, sinker releases, and sinkers. You should bring a lunch, drinks, warm clothing, and, if you're vulnerable, a seasickness remedy.

Before heading out to sea, the skippers provide brief instructional lessons. They explain that the strategy is to locate a school of anchovies, which are a favorite baitfish of salmon. To attract the salmon, each angler trolls an anchovy as the boat cruises slowly amid the school. A two- or three-pound cannonball sinker is used to get the bait down and is attached to a sinker release. The universal rigging is to tie the sinker release to your fishing line, then use three to six feet of leader from the sinker release to the bait. If you need help, the deckhand will tie your rig for you.

After the cruise to the fishing grounds, the fishermen aboard drop their bait overboard and the trolling begins. Most often, the rods are put in holders, and the angler stations himself or herself nearby. When a salmon strikes, the sinker is released and drops to the ocean floor—and the tip of the pole starts bouncing.

This is where the excitement starts.

You grab the rod and immediately sense the weight of the salmon. I've caught hundreds of salmon, and it still gets to me every time.

The first key is keeping your drag set light, particularly at the beginning of the fight. Many salmon escape in the first few seconds after taking the bait, when the excited angler clamps down too hard on the line. Salmon are too strong for that. Slam the brakes on them and the hook will pull out in a flash.

Instead, take your time and enjoy the fight. Keep a bend in the rod. Give them no slack, but don't muscle them either. It takes an "in-between" touch to land big salmon. Not too tight, not too loose.

When you eventually lead the salmon alongside the boat, the deckhand will provide the crowning touch with the net. If you own your own boat, this should be done with a single, knifelike up-and-down motion. Don't try to reach, scoop, or chase the fish with the net—if you hit the line, it will be adiós.

You can maximize trolling results with a number of additional inside tricks that are particularly effective on private boats. Many people experiment with use of downriggers, plastic planers, dodgers, flashers, and mixing the use of Krocodile and Andy Reeker spoons, hoochies, anchovies clasped in Salmon Rotary Killers, and probing from the surface to the ocean bottom. On a party boat, however, the techniques are straightforward and the catch rates typically high.

Another technique that is gaining in popularity is mooching. Instead of trolling, the skipper turns the engine off and lets the boat drift in the current. Instead of putting the rod in a holder, you keep it in your hands. Instead of a heavy sinker and an anchovy, you use a half-ounce Shim jig and a small chunk of anchovy. My experience with the big salmon is that the best rigging is to fillet an anchovy from its dorsal fin on back to the tail, including the tail in the fillet, then to hook it near the front of the fillet on the jig. You let the line out as the boat drifts.

With rod in hand, you feel every nibble, twitch, and bite. Don't jig it, but keep it steady; the sway of the boat will do the work. You might catch rockfish, kingfish, jacksmelt, mackerel, and even perch along the way, particularly if working inshore reef areas. With the engine off, the ocean is peaceful and quiet. That ends abruptly when a salmon attacks.

When a salmon grabs the bait, there is no doubt about it, and you must be ready. Underwater filming of attacking salmon by my pal Dick Pool shows that they arrive at full velocity from the underside of the bait. As a result, when you get a strike while mooching, you get some immediate slack in the line. If you do not reel down to the fish immediately and remove that slack, the salmon will be one long-gone desperado before you can regain your composure.

Good tackle can help, both for trolling and mooching. For trolling, I like a seven-foot rod with a tip strong enough to withstand the weight of trolling the cannonball sinker. The rod should be matched with a medium-weight, revolving-spool saltwater reel with 20-pound test line.

For drift mooching, you need lighter, more sensitive tips, since you are using just a quarter-ounce or half-ounce weight. One of my favorites is a shorter graphite rod with a stiffer tip, such as the LCI 7.5-foot GBB764. Ed Migale of San Francisco Custom Tackle specializes in making personalized rods built specifically for mooching and trolling. Level-wind reels make good companions for mooching rods, with 10- to 16-pound lines.

Make certain you have your reels filled with fresh, premium line. Salmon, particularly the big ones, can bulldog you and run in erratic spurts. All it takes is one nick on some old line and it breaks. If you rent a rod-and-reel combination on the boat and the line is low and old, demand something better. You deserve it.

Spring is a unique time in the Gulf of the Farallones, because it marks a switch in the feeding pattern of the salmon. In March, salmon feed primarily on shrimp. But with the arrival of April and May comes the migration of huge schools of anchovies from southern waters. The salmon will chase down the baitfish like Jesse James running down a stagecoach.

During this time of year, the schools of bait will often move to inshore areas, along the Marin coast, and also the San Mateo County coast near DALY CITY, PACIFICA, and HALF MOON BAY. The salmon will follow them.

This is your chance. The fish are out there waiting for you. All it takes is a boat ride, a fishing rod, and your bait—and by the end of the day, you will likely be telling the tale of tangling with salmon, king of the Golden Gate fish.

The following list of sport vessels that run daily trips for salmon is provided by the Golden Gate Fisherman's Merchant Association, (415) 626-7070.

1. San Francisco

Contact: *Butchie B,* (415) 457-8388; *Chucky's Pride,* (415) 564-5515; *Fury,* (510) 237-4880; *Hot Pursuit,* (650) 965-3474; *Lovely Martha,* (650) 871-1691; *Miss Farallon,* (415) 352-5708; *New Edibob,* (415) 564-2706; *Wacky Jacky,* (415) 586-9800. **Locator:** SAN FRANCISCO (E1b).

2. Sausalito

Contact: *Flying Fish,* (415) 898-6610; *Ginnie C II,* (415) 454-3191; *Louellen,* (415) 668-9607; *New Merrimac,* (415) 388-5351; *New Rayann,* (415) 924-6851; *Salty Lady,* (650) 348-2107; *Wendigo,* (415) 332-4903. **Locator:** SAUSALITO (E1a).

3. Berkeley

Contact: *El Dorado I,* (510) 758-3474; *El Dorado II,* (510) 223-7878; *New Easy Rider,* (510) 849-2727. **Locator:** BERKELEY (E1c).

4. Emeryville

Contact: *Huck Finn, C-Gull II, New Salmon Queen, New Superfish, Seeker, Captain Hook,* and *Rapid Transit,* (510) 654-6040; *Jubilee,* (510) 881-7622; *New Fisherman III,* (510) 837-5113. **Locator:** EMERYVILLE (E1c).

5. Half Moon Bay

Contact: *Captain John, Outlaw, Blue Horizon,* and *Princeton Special,* (650) 726-2913; *New Capt. Pete, Quite a Lady, Queen of Hearts, Dorothy J, New Mary S, Saint James,* and *Wild Wave,* (650) 726-7133. **Locator:** HALF MOON BAY (E1b).

6. Bodega Bay

Contact: *Dandy,* (707) 875-2787; *Jaws, New Sea Angler, Predator,* (707) 875-3495; *Tracer, Payback,* (707) 875-2323 **Locator:** BODEGA BAY (D0).

7. Santa Cruz

Contact: *Makaira,* (408) 426-4690; *Sea Dancer, New Holiday,* (408) 476-2648; *Stagnaro II, Cottardo Stagnaro,* (408) 427-2334. **Locator:** Santa Cruz (F1).

8. Monterey

Contact: *Capt. Randy, Sur Randy, Randy I,* (408) 372-7440; *Holiday, New Holiday, Checkmate, Tornado,* (408) 375-5951; *Point Sur Clipper, Star of Monterey, Seawolf,* (408) 372-0577; *Top Gun, Magnum Force, Lethal Weapon,* (408) 372-2203. **Locator:** Monterey (F1).

• Tom's Ratings •

The Top 5 Places to Begin a Potluck Trip

In the San Francisco Bay Area

Thousands of tourists, one after another every summer day, pay $16 a pop to take a 45-minute boat tour of San Francisco Bay, cruising around the Golden Gate Bridge and Alcatraz. The views might not be so bad, but the tourists are passing right over the best the bay has to offer with nary a clue. If they only knew. . . .

If only they knew, that is, that just below them in the emerald green waters are striped bass, halibut, salmon, lingcod, cabezone, sharks, and several species of rockfish. Together they make up such a smorgasbord of fishing that bay trips are called "potlucks," and like Friday night church specials, they give anglers a place to practice their own religion. They bring their offerings, then take their pick at the table.

You're invited, too. All the while you are in the center of the most beautiful metropolitan area in the world, ringed by the San Francisco skyline, the Golden Gate Bridge, Mount Tamalpais in Marin, Alcatraz, Angel Island, and the Bay Bridge. It is stunning, even for locals who take such sights for granted. However, it is the fishing, not the views, that provides the excitement.

You send a live anchovy down to the bottom, then start wondering what will grab it. Sometimes you can't even guess. On one trip, I thought I was fishing for striped bass, and in back-to-back drifts, I caught a 17-pound salmon and a 23-pound halibut. Another time, we thought we were fishing for halibut, and my partner Jeff Patty caught the two-fish limit of striped bass on two straight drops to the bottom.

Then there's skipper Chuck "The Wizard" Louie, owner of *Chucky's Pride.* On a recreational trip with his pals, where he got a chance to fish instead of captain his boat, he caught a striper, halibut, salmon, lingcod, cabezone, china rockfish, blue rockfish, bolinas cod, flounder, and shark. That's right, he landed 10 species of fish on one trip. Count 'em.

The season starts in May, when the bay's first schools of striped bass, or what I call "scout fish," start arriving from the Delta, a prelude to the summer fun. Shortly thereafter, halibut start moving in from the ocean. Those two species, striped bass and halibut, join a resident population of rockfish, lingcod, and sharks. June and July are the peak months, and after a short hiatus in August when most of the fish migrate out to the Bay Area coast, they are right back in September, joined this time by salmon migrating upstream through the bay.

"Every day is different, and wondering what will happen next has always kept it fresh for me," said the late skipper Cliff Anfinson, who spent 7,500 days on the bay as captain of the *Bass-Tub* before passing away in 1994. His son Eric now runs the boat, using all the tricks passed down by his dad. Every summer, the stripers and halibut are attracted to SAN FRANCISCO Bay by hordes of anchovies and pods of shiner perch. But unlike in the ocean, where the anchovies roam freely, here they often find themselves trapped by tidal action against ledges, rock piles, and huge pillars. Right then the sportfish, especially striped bass, arrive at these key spots and attack en masse. Aha! Then the potluck boats move into position, drifting over the key habitats, with the anglers aboard dangling live anchovies in front of the fish. It is an offer they can't refuse.

This doesn't mean, however, that all you have to do is toss out a bait, set the hook, and hang on for the ride. It isn't that simple. There are times when you don't get a bite for hours, swear there isn't a fish in the entire bay, then suddenly start catching everything but Moby Dick. Then there are days when you need the Jaws of Life to pry open the fishes' mouths.

Why the crazy fluctuations? The key is that all of the bay's feeding activity is tidal oriented. When the tides are wrong, you might as well pretend you're on a tourist boat and gaze at Coit Tower, or maybe wait for someone to jump off the bridge. Even on good days, when the tides are right, there is usually plenty of slack time broken by two-hour periods when the fish go on the bite.

I remember one late June day when I arrived at Fisherman's Wharf in SAN FRANCISCO at 4 P.M., getting ready for a twilight trip. After all, the tides were projected to be perfect between 5:30 P.M. and 7 P.M., right under the GOLDEN GATE BRIDGE. Well, just as I arrived, a boat returned for the day, and the 18 anglers aboard were mighty glum, having caught only three striped bass among them.

One of the departing unfortunates recognized me, then asked why I was going out. "After all," he said, "there's no fish."

"I guess we'll just have to hope for the best," I responded. But inside, I knew that all the key factors—tides, baitfish, fish migrations, and weather—were perfectly aligned and that evening would bring the chance for greatness.

It turned out to be the best evening of fishing I have ever had in the bay, catching and releasing striper after striper. At one point, I had landed 13 striped bass, bulldogs all. As we fished under the GOLDEN GATE BRIDGE, it became a magical setting: the fog moved in, the golden lights of the bridge cast a glow, the old foghorn blared away, and the 15 anglers aboard shared a little piece of striper heaven.

So the first lesson is that you must match the tides to the spots, or be in close touch with one of the bay's potluck skippers who are already expert at it. The latter is easy enough, just a phone call away; see the list of potluck boats at the end of this piece.

Here are a few rules:

• The best fishing for striped bass is during strong incoming tides at the rock piles between ALCATRAZ and the GOLDEN GATE BRIDGE, and during slow to moderate outgoing tides at the south tower of the bridge, Lime Point, and Yellow Bluff.

• The best fishing for halibut is during slow to moderate tides, especially just after the high tide tops out, at the southwest side of ANGEL ISLAND, along the western shore of ALCATRAZ, and offshore SAN FRANCISCO'S Crissy Field and Baker Beach.

- The best fishing for salmon is always during the first two hours of the outgoing tide, just after a high tide of 5.5 feet or higher has topped out, near Belvedere Point and Raccoon Strait.
- During moderate tides, it is possible to catch the most species.
- Bay fishing is always lousy when there are minus low tides.
- The striper bite dies during slack water or slow tides.
- The halibut bite dies when tides are very strong, especially during minus low tides.

In addition to this information, you must be able to figure whether a tide is weak or strong, and that is easy enough. You simply calculate the difference between two consecutive tides. In the Bay Area, a tidal swing of 4.5 feet or more is a moderate to strong tide, and a tidal swing of 4.5 feet or less is considered a moderate to weak tide. For instance, when a low tide of 0.2 feet is followed by a high tide of 6.6 feet, there is a tidal swing of 6.4 feet, equivalent to a strong incoming tide for SAN FRANCISCO BAY.

This is critical knowledge because it can allow anglers to plan trips far in advance. All you need is a tide book. Without one, it is like planning a trip blindfolded.

Because the tides key the bites, there is usually no reason for a trip to start in the middle of the night. That is why SAN FRANCISCO BAY potluck trips leave the dock fairly late by West Coast standards, usually around 7 a.m. Often there is no rush to reach the fishing grounds either, especially if the skipper has analyzed the tides and knows that the day's bite will start at 10 A.M.

The trip opens with a short instructional lesson and safety review. If you are new to the game, don't be shy; it seems many newcomers are aboard every trip, including tourists from all parts of the country.

The skipper starts by demonstrating the tackle. My favorite setup is the Fenwick 847 rod, the Penn Jigmaster 2/0 reel, with fresh 20-pound monofilament. Then the skipper will explain the three-way swivel concept. It is simple enough: You tie your fishing line from one of the swivels. Then you tie off your sinker from another, using about eight inches of leader for rocky areas, one inch for sandy areas. From the remaining swivel, you tie on three feet of leader to a short-shanked 2/0 live bait hook. The skippers sell pre-tied rigs for a small fee.

Live anchovies and shiner perch are the baits of choice. Anchovies are hooked through the nose vertically, shiners through the nose horizontally.

Once on the bay, the skipper will position his boat at the foot of an underwater ledge, then with the motor still chugging and the tide running past, will allow the boat to move in a controlled drift toward the ledge. Anglers will keep their sinkers near the bottom, then reel in a bit to "walk" the live anchovy up the ledge. This is when you get bit—the tidal action will trap anchovies against the ledge, and sure enough, striped bass, halibut, and other fish will arrive for a picnic.

Except in the end, it is you who partakes of the smorgasbord. On one such trip, I remember a nice old gent, Ron Brawn of SAN FRANCISCO, who was having a great day of it, catching a good-sized halibut and several rockfish. He was a unique fellow, with an old Calcutta fishing rod, the kind that were so popular in the 1950s but are rarely seen anymore.

Then on a drift just north of the Golden Gate Bridge off the Marin coast, the guy hooked something huge. That old rod bent and strained, and the battle went on. Suddenly, the rod snapped right in two. This was one fight it looked like the fish was going to win. There was this poor guy with half a rod and a giant fish on it.

But Ron wouldn't give up. He struggled away, trying to get leverage with the little stub that was left, and after another five minutes, the fish was beat, not Ron. It was a real beauty, a striped bass weighing well over 20 pounds.

Meanwhile, just a few hundred yards away, there was a tourist cruise boat making the rounds. A few tourists aboard that boat had binoculars, and they had apparently witnessed the battle.

With binoculars of my own, I watched them as they tried to explain what they had seen to the other tourists, yet they got little response.

I just smiled. You see, most folks just don't understand what is possible on the bay. If they only knew. . . .

1. San Francisco

Contact: *Bass-Tub,* (415) 456-9055; *Chucky's Pride,* (415) 564-5515. **Locator:** San Francisco (E1b).

2. Berkeley

Contact: *Happy Hooker,* (510) 223-5388. An excellent boat ramp is available at Berkeley Marina. **Locator:** Berkeley (E1c).

3. Emeryville

Contact: *Huck Finn, C Gull II, New Salmon Queen, New Superfish, Seeker, Capt. Hook,* and *Rapid Transit,* (510) 654-6040. An excellent boat ramp is available at Emery Cove Marina. **Locator:** Emeryville (E1c).

4. Point San Pablo:

Contact: *New Keesa,* (510) 787-1720. **Locator:** Point San Pablo (E1c).

5. San Rafael

Live shiners are sold at Loch Lomond Live Bait at Dock A of Loch Lomond Harbor in San Rafael; call (415) 456-0321.

Contact: *Superfish,* (415) 898-6989. A decent boat ramp is available at Loch Lomond Marina. **Locator:** San Rafael (E1a).

• Tom's Ratings •

The Top 6 Destinations in Plumas Wonderland

Every day can be a treasure hunt in Plumas National Forest, the biggest chunk of undiscovered fortune in California.

The area is beautiful, much of it pristine, with 100 lakes, 1,000 miles of streams, and snow-crested mountains covered with pines and firs. There are nearly 2,000 square miles of wildlands, room to wander and be free, whether you are driving or exploring on foot, fishing, hiking, or camping.

To put it in perspective, consider that there is only one stoplight in the entire county. One. The thought of that could put someone from L.A. into paralysis. Even though California has nearly 33 million residents, only 22,000 of them live in Plumas County, despite it being one of America's most beautiful regions. If you get the idea that there is plenty of room, you are right. The deer far outnumber the people. The Gold Lakes Basin, for instance, is very similar to the famous Desolation Wilderness near TAHOE, yet it gets one-tenth of the use.

It's not the 200-mile driving distance from the Bay Area that throws folks off, but rather the complicated route one must take. There's just no direct way to do it. So while TAHOE, CLEAR LAKE, SHASTA, YOSEMITE, and KINGS CANYON are the state's recreation headquarters, PLUMAS remains detached from the rest of the world, and it's for the better.

The county is located between TAHOE and SHASTA, the top two vacation spots in the state. Those who take the in-between route will find a huge variety of lakes, streams, mountains, and meadows to self-style virtually any kind of outdoor vacation. The best place for newcomers in search of solitude and good fishing is PLUMAS NATIONAL FOREST. You can reach 42 campgrounds by car, including many small, hidden spots accessible only by Forest Service roads. A map of PLUMAS NATIONAL FOREST can help you find your own secret camp. Forest Service maps detail all back roads, lakes, streams, and hiking trails.

The best camping spots are those adjacent to streams and lakes. The Middle Fork of the FEATHER RIVER near GRAEAGLE has the best trout fishing, but getting there usually requires some hiking and scrambling down canyons. It is regarded by most outdoorspeople as one of the state's top five trout streams.

The North Fork of the FEATHER is more accessible, with Highway 70 running alongside much of it. The trout fishing is decent, primarily for nine- to 11-inch rainbow trout.

Other streams that provide good trout fishing include Indian Creek, Yellow Creek, and Nelson Creek.

If you prefer lake fishing, PLUMAS offers many opportunities. The most famous are LAKE ALMANOR and DAVIS LAKE. ALMANOR, a big lake set near CHESTER, is the best for powerboaters. DAVIS offers fishing for big rainbow trout.

But there are many other choices. Butte Lake, a few miles from Almanor, has some of the largest rainbow trout in California. Bucks Lake, a short drive from QUINCY, provides some of the most consistent trouting for nine- to 12-inchers in the country.

A good spot for a first trip is Plumas-Eureka State Park. It lies just west of the intersection of Highway 70 and Highway 89 in the historic gold-mining area of JOHNSVILLE. You can either hunker down here, playing at Eureka Lake and taking day hikes in the forest, or set out for something more ambitious, which you can find in the Gold Lakes Basin to the southeast. This is for backpackers only. For those who want to get off the beaten path, there are more than 50 lakes to choose from.

It is primarily granite basin terrain, with a few stands of sugar pine and lakes like deep bowls of water. Since they are natural lakes, they are almost always full, unlike California's reservoirs, which are drained for agricultural use.

As a side trip, you can visit the state's second highest waterfall, Feather Falls, at 640 feet high. The streams here are in the heart of the gold country, and you could get lucky and pay for the trip with a few hours of panning. If you don't like to hike, you might consider renting a horse and visiting the backcountry.

One of my field scouts who knows every inch of this outdoor paradise is Al Bruzza. Bruzza has great enthusiasm and know-how, and has explored this area virtually since he took his first steps on the planet. He has fished 75 of the region's 100 lakes and every main artery of the stream systems in the FEATHER RIVER country, and has hoofed it across the mountains.

"Thank God I'm married to a woman who puts up with this stuff," Bruzza said. His wife, Robin, not only puts up with him, but caught an 11.5-pound trout one day at Bucks Lake.

Bruzza and I got together and ranked the region's current top fisheries. Here are our favorites:

1. Bucks Lake

This place has produced many big Mackinaw trout and brown trout, more than any lake in the county. To do it right, you need to get 40 to 50 feet deep, trolling the old river channel coming out of Mill Creek, or the Rainbow Point area. Use a Macadoo lure, which looks like a crawdad, or a no. 2 J-Plug or no. 9 Rapala.

Locator: QUINCY (C3).

2. Gold Lake

This is the centerpiece of the Gold Lakes Basin. When the weather is warm, the brook trout can be on a great bite. If the wind comes up, no problem, just go over to nearby Sardine Lake, which also has brookies up to 16 inches. No fooling.

Locator: GRAEAGLE (C3).

3. Antelope Lake

The nice campsites here add to a great experience, with a good chance at rainbow trout to 16 inches. The best bet is slow-trolling a no. 6 olive-green Woolly Bugger, giving the rod a jerk every 10 or 15 seconds. The key is getting down 20 feet, right along the underwater shelves.

Locator: ANTELOPE LAKE (C4).

4. Middle Fork Feather River

This is a premium trout stream, but requires hiking and scrambling to reach the best spots. In June, after the hatches start, fly-fishing can be very good. A great trick is to put a single salmon egg on a no. 14 or 16 egg hook with two-pound test line and then drift it into holes. An insider's tip on mountain streams is to use the clear, oil-packed eggs made by Atlas, not the bright red ones.

Locator: MIDDLE FORK FEATHER RIVER (C3).

5. Davis Lake

The damselfly hatch at this lake can be the stuff of legends. When it's on, it inspires some of the best trout fishing in California. Catch-and-release is the way to go, with rainbow trout to 20 inches. Use a float tube, bring waders, or troll using Woolly Buggers. The west side of the lake is the prime area, especially from Eagle Point up to Freeman Creek.

Locator: DAVIS LAKE (C4).

6. Lake Almanor

This is a pretty lake circled by conifers, where the fish come big, although not always easy. Underwater springs and a large population of pond smelt help salmon, rainbow trout, brown trout, and smallmouth bass get big and frisky. The best time of the year to fish is from late April to early June, from dawn to about 9 a.m. Beware of north winds and rough water.

Locator: LAKE ALMANOR (C3).

Directions for all listings: From the Bay Area, take Interstate 80 east to Sacramento. There are two routes from Sacramento: Head north on Highway 99 for about 75 miles, then turn east on Highway 70 and continue up the Feather River Canyon. Or, continue east of Sacramento on Interstate 80 for approximately 105 miles, then turn north on Highway 89 and cruise through the forest country. **Maps for all listings:** For a map of Plumas National Forest, send $4 to: Maps, U.S. Forest Service, 630 Sansome Street, San Francisco, CA 94111. **Contact for all listings:** For a map and brochure, contact the Plumas County Visitors Bureau, P.O. Box 4120, Quincy, CA 95971; (530) 283-6345, (800) 326-2247, or fax (530) 283-5465. Phone Al Bruzza at the Sportsmen's Den, (530) 283-2733. **See featured trip page:** 218.

• FEATURED TRIP •

McCLOUD RIVER PRESERVE

Rated: The Top 5 Drive-to Camps on Streams, 115

Sometimes you wish you could live in an earlier time, a time when deer roamed without fear, when old trees were left standing, and when wild rainbow trout were king of the stream. At the McCloud River Preserve, Californians have the chance to return to such a time. You can experience the wild native wonder of California that trailblazers found when they took their first steps out West.

Hidden southeast of snowcapped MOUNT SHASTA, the McCLOUD RIVER remains in pristine condition. A person can walk among the woods, or fish hip-deep for wild trout, and get the feeling that the area is much as it was 200 years ago, before humans had ever thought of dams and chain saws. And it will always remain this way. The Nature Conservancy, a nonpartisan, nonprofit organization dedicated solely to purchasing and preserving unique wildlands, now manages more than six miles of the McCLOUD watershed. While fishing access is free, it is restricted to no more than 10 rods on the river at any one time. All trout hooked must be released, and anglers must use single barbless hooks or lures.

No hunting, tree cutting, or wood gathering is allowed. When it comes to fishing, the ethic of the Nature Conservancy is clear: A wild trout is too valuable to be caught only once.

The McCLOUD RIVER is unique. Its source for thousands of years has been a huge 44-degree volcanic spring from the underground waterways of nearby MOUNT SHASTA. The surrounding area has never lost its wild character either. Squirrels with giant tails play in the leaves; mountain lions hide in the woods. One morning, I saw a wild turkey running straight up the side of a mountain.

Another time, I came around a bend and saw what looked like two little kittens playing in the dust. They were baby bobcats, like nothing you've ever seen.

A few bald eagles, mink, wild turkeys, and river otters may be seen on the McCLOUD RIVER PRESERVE. A hundred years from now, their descendants will still be here. The chain of wildlife in the preserve will never be broken.

I remember my first morning on the McCloud. My waders were marked to the hip by river water, and I watched insects hatching on the river surface. "Caddis," I thought to myself.

My wrist twitched with the fly rod; I already had a fly patterned after a caddis tied on my fishing line. The late Ted Fay, a fly fishing legend, had tipped me off the previous day. Casting just 25 feet, I laid the fly in a riffle and watched the current take it downstream, the fly tumbling as if no line were attached. Then suddenly—got one! A red flash in the water was at the end of my line, and after a few minutes, it was brought to my side.

It was a wild rainbow trout, about a 12-incher, not a giant by any means, but colored nature's most vivid red. Unhooked, it swam away to freedom.

Trout here are a special breed; they are the Shasta rainbow. According to the Nature Conservancy, it is from the McCloud strain that most hatchery trout in many parts of the world have descended. In 1872, an egg-taking station was situated at the mouth of the river, resulting in the introduction of the fish to places such as New Zealand, where it now provides a world-class fishery. Though the 10-pounders of New Zealand draw anglers from thousands of miles away, there are enough 15- to 30-inchers in the McCloud to entice Bay Area residents to make the 300-mile drive a few times each spring and summer.

However, don't get the false impression that just because they "know" they will be released, the fish are easy to catch. Many anglers get skunked. According to a logbook kept by the Nature Conservancy, the average catch during the morning or evening bite is four to five rainbow trout per angler. Experienced fishers do better, especially for larger trout.

A few key tips can aid your mission. For one, bring chest waders and a wading staff (an old ski pole is fine). The rocks here are coated with a light film of algae and are slippery, particularly the large, flat ones. I once saw an outdoors writer fall in the water three times in a single morning. A good lesson for all. Take your steps with care, avoiding flat rocks and searching for gravel pockets between large rocks.

Another key here is the ability to detect the delicate bite of a trout. Rarely is there a distinct jerk. Usually all you see is a misdirection of your fly line as it drifts downstream with the current. If you see anything peculiar about your line as it drifts downstream, set your hook. Floating strike indicators can be a great help.

Anglers learning this craft usually have to pay their dues. The McCloud River is a little piece of heaven where making these payments comes easy.

Directions: Take Interstate 5 straight up the California Valley, past Redding toward Mount Shasta City, and turn east on Highway 89. Continue to the town of McCloud, turn right on Squaw Valley Road, and drive 10 miles to Lake McCloud. Turn right and take the dirt road along the right side of the lake. At Battle Creek, turn right at the signed turnoff for Ah-Di-Na Campground. **Reservations:** Only 10 rods are allowed on the McCloud River Preserve at a time. To make a reservation, phone the Nature Conservancy, (530) 777-0487. **Guide:** Fishing guide Joe Kimsey can be reached at (530) 235-2969. **Camping:** A $5 camping fee is charged at the primitive Ah-Di-Na Campground. **Hotel:** The nearest lodging is in McCloud. Phone the Stoney Brook Inn, (530) 964-2300; McCloud River Inn, (530) 964-2130; or the McCloud Hotel, (530) 964-2822. **Contact:** For general information on fishing, hotels, directions, and maps, call the Shasta Cascade Wonderland Association, (800) 474-2782, or write to 1699 Highway 273, Anderson, CA 96007. Contact the Nature Conservancy at 201 Mission Street, 4th Floor, San Francisco, CA 94105; (415) 777-0487. **Locator:** McCloud River Preserve (B2).

• Featured Trip •

Lake Almanor

Rated: The Top 50 Base Camps, 110; The Top 10 Camps for Kids, 120; The Top 16 Lakes with Cabin Rentals, 177

The bite in the morning air let's you know that fall is arriving. The bite on your line is all the confirmation you need that fall is the time to be out fishing at Lake Almanor, one of the best lakes in the state to fish during the transition from summer to fall.

Because of its ability to produce big brown trout, Almanor has long been one of my favorite lakes. It is located on the southeastern flank of Mount Lassen in northern Plumas County, and at 4,600 feet elevation, the fall nights are brisk. The fish like nothing better.

Almanor is a big lake, 13 miles long and covering 28,000 acres. Although it is a reservoir, it looks more like a natural lake since the water level is kept high and it is ringed by conifers, mainly Douglas fir and ponderosa pine. In the past, I usually take one day to experiment, to find the fish and figure out how to catch them. The second day we usually catch them.

One year, I fished with guide Mark Jimenez and Rich Roberts, former outdoors editor of the L.A. *Times.* Instead of spending a day figuring out the lake, Jimenez presented it to us on a silver platter. In addition, the chemistry between us was excellent, and it was great fun aboard his boat. Of course, when the fish are biting like crazy, it's easy to have fun.

We were out before daybreak, cruising across the lake to the northeast shore, north of the peninsula adjacent to the mouth of Bailey Creek. We started the day by trolling, with the three of us alternating techniques: trolling a Marabou fly (50 feet of leader, with two colors of lead-core line), trolling a bikini-colored needlefish (also with leader and lead-core line), trolling a pearlescent needlefish with three splitshot for weight (no lead-core line).

At first light, I got a bite right off, but missed the set. In the next 45 minutes, we caught two big brown trout, both about 20 inches, and had two other bites. These are heavy, solid fish with bright red meat, (I smoked them), and both grabbed the Marabou fly like it was the end of time.

Then, as the sun hit the water, the trout bite was over. Mark just smiled, fired up the engine, and headed to the west shore. He had something more up his sleeve besides his arm.

What were we doing? Clue 1: We got out long, light spinning rods, like noodle rods, with four-pound test, then tied on a no. 10 hook and clamped on two tiny splitshot. Clue 2: We hooked on grasshoppers for bait. Clue 3: We flipped the grasshoppers out, let them sink, then kept them barely moving.

Figure it out? Yep, just like when we were kids, we were fishing for smallmouth bass. Every five minutes or so, one of us would hook another. Between Rich, Mark, and me, we caught and released about 25 or 30 smallmouth in a few hours. The biggest landed was a three-pounder that I tussled with for about 10 minutes, but I had a much bigger one, about four pounds, big enough to have the large square body and it broke the line when it dove under the boat.

ALMANOR also has tons of salmon, but most years the majority are small, just 12 or 13 inches. One recent year, though, they averaged three to five pounds. In fact, one day at ALMANOR I caught a five-salmon limit with Dan Barkhimer that weighed 22 pounds.

The fall bite should last at ALMANOR into early November. At that point, the cold weather takes over, and even with good fishing, only the hardy few need apply. Guess what? I'm always ready to sign up.

Directions: From the Bay Area, take Interstate 80 east to Sacramento. There are two routes from Sacramento: Head north on Highway 99 for about 75 miles, then turn east on Highway 70 and continue up the Feather River Canyon. Or, continue east of Sacramento on Interstate 80 for about 105 miles, then turn north on Highway 89 and cruise through the forest country. **Maps:** For a map of Plumas National Forest, send $4 to Maps, U.S. Forest Service, 630 Sansome Street, San Francisco, CA 94111. For another map, send $2 to the Plumas County Visitors Bureau, P.O. Box 4120, Quincy, CA 95971; phone (530) 283-6345 or (800) 326-2247 or fax (530) 283-5465. E-mail: plumasco@psln.com. Web site: www.plumas.ca.us. **Contact:** Mark Jimenez, (530) 596-3072. For a free travel packet, phone Plumas County, (800) 326-2247. **Locator:** LAKE ALMANOR (C3).

• FEATURED TRIP •

BURNEY'S TROUT PARADISE

Rated: Northern California's Fishing Paradise

In the northeastern corner of California is a valley where nature has carved two of the finest trout streams in the western United States. HAT CREEK and the Fall River are not filled by the many trickles of melting snow, unlike most streams along the slopes of California's Sierra Nevada or Oregon and Washington's Cascade ranges, but are spring-fed, each bubbling fresh out of the earth from the underground waterways of nearby MOUNT LASSEN, a volcano that blew its top in 1914.

The area is tucked away near Burney, about 50 miles east of REDDING via Highway 299, and is about a five-hour drive from the San Francisco Bay Area. It is a paradise for fly fishers, but it also offers angling and camping opportunities for anybody who wants to set up a tent and plunk bait in a nearby stream or lake. In addition to HAT CREEK and the Fall River, which have designated Wild Trout sections with special angling restrictions, the area has several prime trout streams and reservoirs that can provide action for all. Upper HAT CREEK, the Pit River, Burney Creek, Baum Lake, and Lake Britton provide a network of trout fishing opportunities just minutes apart.

But the focal points remain the two spring-fed streams, HAT CREEK and the Fall River, where fly fishers find contentment rolling out casts and watching the line settle quietly in the gentle flows.

Rather than being strewn with pebbles, the river bottoms of the Fall River and HAT CREEK are moss-covered, making them ideal homes for insect larvae. When the temperature reaches 60 degrees and warmer, the larvae emerge from the moss and hatch on the surface. At the Fall River, the hatch can be so thick that it looks like San Francisco fog. Locals call it "Hatch Madness." The trout gorge themselves on the insects, with almost every summer day evolving into an all-you-can-eat smorgasbord. A native 14-inch rainbow trout can be considered an average specimen in this haven.

For either the creek or the river, a good fly line is a no. 5. or no. 6. Figure on about nine feet of leader when using nymphs and 12 feet when using dry flies.

HAT CREEK

This is the most popular stream in the area because it offers both a pristine setting and good access. It is a classic chalk stream, and the state Department of Fish and Game has designated the lower 3.5 miles of river as a Wild Trout Stream—no hatchery fish have been planted in eons. The wild trout here average 10 to 16 inches, with an occasional rainbow trout in the 18-inch range. Some particularly elusive monster brown trout also roam the waters.

Highway 299, the two-laner that feeds into the Burney area from REDDING, actually crosses HAT CREEK, providing excellent access. Anglers can arrive from the drive, take a hard look at the river, and then choose whether to hike upstream or downstream. The farther you walk—to reach lesser fished areas—the better the angling can be. Typically, however, fishing is best on HAT CREEK in the evening hours of summer, especially at dusk.

From Powerhouse No. 2 to Lake Britton, Lower HAT CREEK is a designated Wild Trout Stream, where only flies and lures with a single barbless hook are allowed—and a two-fish, 18-inch minimum size limit applies. It is primarily a fly-fishing stream, where anglers use small patterns and two- and four-pound test tippets, very light lines, so the wild trout will not detect their presence. Although the fly patterns vary in size according to season and hatches, in the hot weather from midsummer on, fishers use very small flies, even as small as no. 20. Some of the best patterns are: Adams, Blue Dun, Dark Blue Upright, Quill Gordon, Jerry, Yellow Stone, and Pale Evening Dun.

This area is home to some of the wisest anglers in California. Just a few of the smartest of them are willing to provide up-to-the-minute information on Lower HAT CREEK. One of them is Steve Vaughn of Vaughn's Sporting Goods, 1713 Main Street, Box AV, Burney, CA 96013; (530) 335-2381. If you drop him a stamped, self-addressed envelope, he will be happy to send you his fishing guide map for the Burney Basin.

Four motels are available in BURNEY, with about a dozen in the intermountain area. Reservations are strongly advised. A complete list, along with additional fishing information, can be requested by contacting the Burney Chamber of Commerce, P.O. Box 36, Burney, CA 96013; (530) 335-2111.

Campgrounds are abundant along Highway 89, which intersects Highway 299 about 10 miles east of BURNEY. The U.S. Forest Service operates eight campgrounds, with some specially tailored for RVs. For brochures, write to Lassen National Forest, Hat Creek Ranger District, Fall River Mills, CA 96028. Pacific Gas & Electric also provides campgrounds; for information, contact PG&E, Land Management, P.O. Box 277444, Sacramento, CA 95827; (530) 386-5164. The campsites at McArthur-Burney Falls Memorial State Park are exceptionally popular, and reservations are necessary; phone (800) 444-7275.

UPPER HAT CREEK

A favorite campground here is the Big Pine Camp, operated by the U.S. Forest Service and nestled streamside along the creek. It is an ideal alternative for anglers who want to have a trout barbecue once the trip is completed, instead of releasing everything they hook, as is practiced at Lower HAT CREEK and the FALL RIVER. The stream here is well stocked with hatchery fish, and baitfishing is the favored strategy. The preferred baits are crickets, worms, and salmon eggs. Most of the trout are of the pan-size variety, in the eight- to 11-inch class.

FALL RIVER

Snow-covered MOUNT LASSEN sits above this trout paradise, watching quietly as it has done since its last violent eruption some 85 years ago. If you lose a few big trout on the Fall River, you might blow your stack, too.

When the trout explode in a surface feed, there can be so many pools from rising fish that it can look as if it is raining. And these trout are big, with many measuring 16 to 20 inches, and a few five- to eight-pounders. The water can be so clear during summer months that fly fishers will sometimes even use leaders as long as 15 feet; otherwise the fish might detect the fly line. On some days, you can spot a dime at the bottom of 30 feet of water and reach in the stream with your hand thinking you can pick it up. The FALL RIVER is that clear.

This is a stream that flows so gently that it can be fished in a float tube. On the upper river near GLENBURN, gasoline engines are prohibited and any form of fishing other than with flies is considered sacrilege. The only sound is that of your small craft, either an aluminum boat or canoe, pushing water aside. Electric motors are popular.

The favored fly patterns are the paraduns—olive, tan, or yellow—with a no. 16 as a good starting size. Nymphs such as the Zug Bug, Black AP, Black Leech, and Hare's Ear can also get the desired result. With the wild and varied hatches, this can be an entomologist's dream.

But here is where the problems start. The river is bordered by private land, primarily owned by ranchers, most of whom get their shotguns out at the slightest trace of "another Bay Area trespasser." As a result, access is severely restricted. While this keeps fishing pressure low so the river retains its wild identity, it can also be a source of irritation for anglers. But that factor can be overcome.

One private lodge and one public access point operated by the conservation organization California Trout are the access points an angler can choose from. Rick's Lodge in Dana (near Fall River Mills) is my favorite, providing the best access on the prime upper stretch of river. Anglers can gain fishing access by renting a room for $60 per night, $85 for double occupancy. Boats and electric motors ($50 per day, $35 per half day) are also available, as are advice and customized flies, and a full bar and restaurant. Contact Rick's Lodge at Star Route Glenburn, Fall River Mills, CA 96028; (530) 336-5300.

The only public access point to the prime stretches of the river is at the Island Bridge, where California Trout has constructed a tiny parking lot. The lot will hold only four or five vehicles, and no nearby areas are available for parking. On some summer days, a single RV can take up all the available space. For more information contact California Trout, 870 Market Street, Suite 859, San Francisco, CA 94102; (415) 392-8887.

Cassel Forebay, Baum Lake, Lake Britton, Burney Creek, and the PIT RIVER provide additional angling opportunities in a relatively small area near BURNEY. For more information, call Vaughn's Sporting Goods, (530) 335-2381; Shasta Cascade Wonderland Association, (800) 474-2782; or the Burney Chamber of Commerce, (530) 335-2111. Here's a capsule summary of each:

Baum Lake

This is big fish country, where German and rainbow trout can grow surprisingly large. A 24-pounder was taken in the 1980s, but most trout average one to two pounds. Baum can be fished by boat or bank, but no motors are allowed on the lake. Most people dunk worms or night crawlers; a few others cast flies under a bubble.

Lake Britton

This is a popular lake for vacationers, with campgrounds available on the north shore and also at McArthur-Burney Falls Memorial State Park. It's a take-your-pick fishery, with bass, crappie, bluegill, and trout stocked in the lake.

Burney Creek

Burney Creek is a pretty setting, the river gurgling over rocks polished by centuries of rolling river water. Access is excellent the creek is well stocked, although most fish are small.

Cassel Forebay

Located east of BURNEY, Cassel provides a well-stocked stretch of water with a 10-fish limit. Most anglers use traditional bait like red eggs or crickets, but fly-fishing can be effective as well. A PG&E campground is available at Cassel Park.

Pit River

This is one of the West's most unheralded trout streams despite providing a quality fishing experience. The stretch of river below Pit River Powerhouse No. 3 can be particularly good. One problem is a brushy shoreline, which may present access difficulty to first-timers. A phone call to Vaughn's Sporting Goods or the Burney Chamber of Commerce (see phone numbers below) should be considered mandatory before heading out.

Lodging: For a list of motels in Burney and additional fishing information, contact the Burney Chamber of Commerce, P.O. Box 36, Burney, CA 96013; (530) 335-2111. In the Fall River area, contact Rick's Lodge, Star Route Glenburn, Fall River Mills, CA 96028; (530) 336-5300. **Campgrounds:** For information and brochures, contact Lassen National Forest, Hat Creek Ranger

District, P.O. Box 220, Fall River Mills, CA 96028, (530) 336-5521; or PG&E, Land Management, P.O. Box 277444, Sacramento, CA 95827, (530) 386-5164. For reservations at McArthur-Burney Falls Memorial State Park, call (800) 444-7275. **Fishing information:** Vaughn's Sporting Goods in Burney is an excellent source for current conditions and advice; write to 1713 Main Street, Box AV, Burney, CA 96013, or call (530) 335-2381. **Contact:** For maps and a list of campgrounds, motels, and fishing guides for the entire area, contact the Shasta Cascade Wonderland Association, 1699 Highway 273, Anderson, CA 96007; (800) 326-6944. **Locator:** BURNEY (B3).

• FEATURED TRIP •

DEER CREEK

Rated: Northern California's Best Hidden Trout Stream

If more people knew about places like DEER CREEK, there would be nobody left in the Bay Area during the summer.

This stream starts deep in LASSEN NATIONAL FOREST, then tumbles down the north Sierra slope for some 60 miles toward CHICO. DEER CREEK is pure, clean, and cold, running over boulders, surging into deep, calm pools, and cutting a beautiful swath at the bottom of a forested canyon rimmed by volcanic crags.

A trail runs right along the river for some 12 miles, providing access for hiking, swimming, and trout fishing. There are also three small U.S. Forest Service campgrounds on the river's upper end that can be reached on adjacent Highway 32. For a nearby side trip, the southern entrance station to LASSEN VOLCANIC NATIONAL PARK is only about a 20-mile drive away.

The irony is that there are many places just like this, beautiful streams that are often overlooked. On one visit, as we were driving east on Highway 32 just 20 miles out of CHICO, we saw few other vehicles. California has 185 major streams, most which run down the western slopes of the Sierra Nevada, and so it is with DEER CREEK, fed by both the melting snow of the north Sierra and the 40-degree waters from volcanic springs south of MOUNT LASSEN.

Virtually every east/west highway in the Sierra runs along a stream that offers opportunities for camping, swimming, and fishing, and sometimes rafting or cabin rentals. North to south, they include Highway 299 (near BURNEY, the PIT RIVER and HAT CREEK), Highway 36 (Battle Creek), Highway 32 (DEER CREEK), Highway 70 (FEATHER RIVER), Highway 49 (YUBA RIVER), Interstate 80 (TRUCKEE RIVER), U.S. 50 (AMERICAN RIVER), Highway 88 (BEAR RIVER), Highway 4 (STANISLAUS RIVER), Highway 108 (TUOLUMNE RIVER), Highway 140 (MERCED RIVER), Highway 168 (SAN JOAQUIN RIVER), Highway 198 (KINGS RIVER), Highway 190 (Tule River), and Highway 178 (Kern River).

Each of these streams has qualities that make it special. At DEER CREEK, the most stunning qualities are its natural beauty, lack of people, and ease of access.

From CHICO, you turn east on Highway 32, which starts as a fairly fast road, then becomes more twisty and slow as it gains elevation. At 30 miles in, it rises above the foothill oak woodlands and enters forest, mainly pine, manzanita, and some oak, and the road becomes more twisty. At 40 miles in, you cross a bridge and arrive at the first access point to the river, with parking available at a pullout on the south side of the road.

From here, there is a trail that provides access to several excellent spots, both upriver and downriver, for swimming or fishing. If you hike 1.5 miles downstream, you can see a pretty waterfall and a fish ladder, though a full-on view of the waterfall is not possible due to the giant boulders and a bend in the canyon. This section of Deer Creek is not stocked with hatchery fish, but grows wild trout; special fishing regulations apply, including no fishing at all within 200 yards of the fish ladder.

If you continue driving east on Highway 32, the road becomes very narrow, so narrow in spots that the prospect of two RVs passing each other on opposite sides of the road appears tenuous. The first campground you reach is called Potato Patch (20 sites for tents, 12 for tents or RVs) at 3,400 feet elevation. Heading beyond, you later arrive at primitive Alder Camp at 3,900 feet (five tent sites, no piped water), then at Elam Camp at 4,600 feet (15 sites for tents or RVs). Campsites are available on a first-come, first-served basis, with no reservations available.

Near the campgrounds, the Department of Fish and Game stocks Deer Creek with large numbers of trout—64,000 rainbow trout and 4,000 brook trout, most ranging from 10 to 12 inches. An excellent trail runs along the river here and has little side trails leading down to the best fishing spots, often where miniature rapids pour into deep pools and slicks, with the best fishing prospects from 6 p.m. to dusk.

The best prospects are casting small lures upstream into the tails of the fast water, then retrieving as the lure drifts downstream into the slower-moving pools and slicks. The trout often bite right where the white water disappears into the slick, with the best lure being the 1/16-ounce Panther Martin, yellow spots on a black body, gold blade.

The same fishing spots are also excellent for swimming. However, even with mid-afternoon temperatures in the 90s, perhaps even making a run at the low 100s, a jump in the river is still plenty cold to inspire certain profound anatomical effects on males and females alike. I once guessed the water temperature to be about 55 degrees, and after hiking three miles, a dunk was as refreshing as a cool rain after a hot dust storm.

While you're out and about, Deer Creek can be so entrancing that you forget to take in the surrounding features. They are very unusual. The canyon rims are volcanic, and with rock material having been eroded over time by weather, many weird crags, spires, and pinnacles that jut into the sky have been created. In addition, just 20 miles to the northwest (but with no direct access from Deer Creek) is the Ishi Wilderness, where legend has it the last wild Native American roamed; 20 miles to the northeast (with road access) is Lassen Volcanic National Park.

Directions: From Red Bluff, drive northeast on Highway 36 about 45 miles to the town of Mineral. Continue about 12 miles southeast on the same road. Turn right on Highway 32 and drive south to a pullout on the south side of the road and the first river access point. **Contact:** Lassen National Forest, Almanor Ranger District,

(530) 258-2141 or fax (530) 258-3491. For fishing information, call the Sports Nut in Chester, (530) 258-3327. Always check California Department of Fish and Game regulations prior to fishing. **Locator:** LASSEN NATIONAL FOREST (C3).

• FEATURED TRIP •

EAGLE LAKE

Rated: The Top 16 Lakes with Cabin Rentals, 177; The Top 6 Opportunities to See Bald Eagles, 250

When it comes to big fish, some people will do anything and go anywhere. When it comes to the biggest trout in the West, that is exactly what is required.

Do anything and go anywhere? That can mean an unbelievably long road-grinder of a drive, frigid temperatures and cutting winds, and a chance of getting zeroed despite your best efforts.

This is how it is at Pend Oreille Lake in Idaho, Lake Paulina and Klamath Lake in Oregon, and Twin Lakes in the eastern Sierra, which have produced the biggest trout across the West in the 1990s. And so it is at EAGLE LAKE in Northern California, set at 5,100 feet in remote Lassen County, where the average trout is bigger than that at any of the state's 850 other lakes and streams with trout.

Big? Trout measuring 18 to 20 inches are average, four- and five-pounders are common, and it takes a six-pounder or better to get a local to even raise an eyebrow. Not only that, but the best techniques are simple, with most using a night crawler under a slip bobber, and there are good prospects from shore, that is, for those without boats. The lake also has several excellent campgrounds and cabin rentals.

But all this comes at a price. As we pointed our boat north out of Spaulding Tract, with whitecaps slowing our speed to a crawl, I thought about how disappointed some people could be. For starters, the drive can seem endless, about 320 miles from SAN FRANCISCO (a check of a lodge registry showed that most of the visitors were from the Bay Area), and the wind typically howls by noon, with a frigid bite to the air that can petrify the soul. But people put up with this for a chance at the biggest trout of their life. Many get it.

To get out of the wind, we anchored our boat behind a shoreline point, ducking in amid some tules in just six feet of water. We then followed the prescribed procedure for catching the big trout here: You rig by placing a tiny plastic bobber stop on your line, adding a red bead and a slip bobber, then tie on a no. 4 hook, adding a splitshot about 12 inches above the hook. You then use a night crawler for bait, hooking it with a worm threader so it lies perfectly straight in the water, as natural looking as possible. For those new to the game, the operators at the lake's shops and marinas will demonstrate this rigging.

I then cast along the tules, the bobber floating about. The big trout like the tules, and sometimes they will cruise in and out along the edge of them looking for food.

About 20 minutes passed, and I started thinking about how cold it can get at EAGLE LAKE—so cold that even with its immense size, 100 miles of shoreline and 27,000 surface acres, the lake usually freezes over solid by Christmas. But the best fishing is when the cold weather arrives, from mid-October through early December, so anglers put up with it.

Suddenly, the bobber started dancing for a few seconds, then a moment later, was pulled under the surface. In a flash, I reeled the slack out of the line, then set the hook hard: Got him!

The trout ran off on a curving arc to the left, about 40 feet, and I just hung on and listened to the reel clicker as the line was pulled out. A good fish, to be sure, a big one. I managed a few cranks on the reel, but then the fish tore off again, this time straight out, about a 10-second run. In my mind, I began asking myself: Good knot? New line? Strong hook? How well hooked?

The answers came in the next five minutes, as the fish was slowly brought near the boat, only to take off on yet another run, but everything held. The fight was a good one, the sensation absolutely mercurial. Then, with the fish near the boat again, it zigged instead of zagged and darted right toward us. With a knifelike jab, my partner John Korb netted it. We had it: a trout measuring 22 inches and weighing a shade under five pounds.

Believe it or not, this is just another typical EAGLE LAKE trout. At the Eagle Lake General Store, they didn't even bother taking a picture of it to post on their wall. After all, a youngster had just brought one in a few minutes earlier that made mine look like a guppy.

It turned out that at the rock jetty at Eagle Lake Marina that morning, there was a 45-minute siege in which just about everybody there caught one as big or bigger, by shore or by boat, according to marina manager Todd Amrein.

There are many good spots at the lake. The tules adjacent to the airport runway and the deep point adjacent to Eagle's Nest are the top spots by boat. By shore, the best choices are the rock jetty at the Eagle Lake Marina and the shore adjacent to Highway 139 at the northwest end.

The best catches are usually made with using night crawlers for bait, but as the very cold weather arrives, some do well trolling bikini-colored needlefish along the many stretches of shore lined with tules. Four of us in two boats tried everything, and in two days, caught five trout, with three going better than 20 inches.

Directions: From Redding, drive 29 miles south on Interstate 5 to Red Bluff. Take the Highway 36 exit and travel 105 miles east. Turn north on County Road A1 (three miles west of Susanville) and drive 15.5 miles, then continue northeast on County Road 201 to the lake. **Contact:** Eagle Lake General Store, (530) 825-2191; Eagle Lake Marina, (530) 825-3454; guide Rich Meyer, (530) 825-3278; guide Val Aubrey, (530) 825-2115; Lassen National Forest, Eagle Lake Ranger District, (530) 257-4188; Eagle Lake Cabins, (530) 825-2131. **Locator:** EAGLE LAKE (B4).

• FEATURED TRIP •

★ LAKE BERRYESSA

Rated: The Top 16 Lakes with Cabin Rentals, 177; The Top 16 Places to Rent Boats, 305; The Top 25 Lakes, 307

I peered over the side of the boat and there, hovering just 10 feet away, were the dark silhouettes of nearly half a dozen bass, big ones all, maybe going up to 10 pounds.

"Look at that, look at that," whispered my companion, guide Jim Munk. "They're all huge."

There was scarcely a breeze on the lake and it was a warm afternoon, but the sight of those big bass sent a chill through me. This was at LAKE BERRYESSA, located east of NAPA on the outskirts of the Bay Area, where the bass fishing can be as good as anywhere in America.

I cast out a plastic worm, let it sink, twitched my rod a bit, then let it sink again, watching it through the clear waters. Right off, three of those bass turned and cruised over to the worm. Suddenly, it disappeared as if by magic. "It's gone," he said. Then he shouted: "One of those bass must have it in his mouth."

There was not even the slightest nibble, but I set the hook, and bingo, I had the bass. I tussled with the fish for a bit, a strong and lively fellow, and persuaded it to the boat. Would you believe? It was only a 13-incher, the smallest of the school of fish roaming right in front of us. "That's OK," Munk said as I released it, "now let's try for his big brothers down there. Look at them. They'll drive you crazy."

This is how it can be at BERRYESSA in the spring, full to the brim with both water and fish, providing a great opportunity for adventure and fishing, enough to drive you crazy. The lake is a beautiful sight, covering 21,000 acres with 165 miles of shoreline, complete with secret coves, islands, and an expanse of untouched shore on the eastern side. The surrounding foothills have greened up and are filled with deer and their newborn fawns, with the songs of dozens of species of birds furnishing background music.

It is Munk who best captures the spring phenomenon at BERRYESSA, as well as at neighboring CLEAR LAKE to the north. Munk, in his mid-30s, started fishing at BERRYESSA at age six; he has become one of California's best bass anglers and is ranked No. 1 in the tournaments sponsored by the American Bass Association. But rather than be secretive about his fishing wiles, Munk has done just the opposite, offering guided trips to the public, always willing to show anybody his favorite spots and the techniques he uses.

According to Munk's logbook, in his past 25 trips he has taken 43 people fishing who have caught 375 bass over 12 inches, and another 300 under 12 inches. And though there is no such thing as an average day when it comes to fishing, those numbers figure to an average of 27 bass per trip. In his best streak, he had eight customers in five days who caught 155 bass, including 75 over 12 inches, a largemouth bass that weighed 10 pounds, and a smallmouth bass that weighed 5 pounds.

As word has circulated about Munk's fish-catching abilities, people from all across the West have started booking trips with him at BERRYESSA and CLEAR LAKE, including many father-son teams. He charges $250 for the day, the standard guide fee in California, yet there is nothing standard about the trip. His boat is a new Ranger 488 powered by a 200-horsepower Mercury, worth about $30,000 and capable of speeds over 65 mph, and his tackle features the finest Quantum rods and reels.

Munk also logs all of his trips into a computer database, tracking how water temperature and clarity, season, weather, and barometric pressure changes affect fishing conditions and techniques. "I have about 350 trips logged now just for BERRYESSA and CLEAR LAKE," Munk said. "Even though I've fished my whole life, I'm really starting to see how it really works out here, how everything is connected to everything else, and it's really helping the results."

It has worked so well that many people will book an introductory trip at BERRYESSA to catch lots of bass and learn Munk's techniques, then book a later trip to CLEAR LAKE, known best for its huge Florida bass, in order to use those techniques to catch a real monster.

That is exactly what I did, arriving at BERRYESSA with a trip planned in June for CLEAR LAKE. At dawn, we were launching his boat at the north end of the lake, then zoomed up the Putah Creek arm, and by 6:30 a.m., we were making our first casts, with the cackles of wild turkeys in the distance. By 6:37 a.m., I had my first bass, and as I released it, it became clear that I had discovered something special.

We fished the lake inlet for smallmouth bass, then protected coves for largemouth, using primarily white flukes, which resemble a large, flat-sided plastic worm with a forked tail, along with Zara Spook surface lures.

"Cast it out, let in sink, then barely twitch it so the fluke rises and falls in the water," Munk demonstrated. "See how it flutters? I call it 'Walking the dog.' It drives 'em crazy."

Right then, there was a scarcely discernible tightening in the line, maybe just two or three inches. I set the hook, and wham! Just like that, had another, going about 14, 15 inches. Just plain fish galore.

Later, we pulled into a cove and suddenly, there aside the boat in eight feet of water, were these dark blue outlines, all giant. Munk, a friendly, affable sort, became so excited at the sight of these giant bass that for a moment I thought he might become the first guide in history whose head would explode.

I cast out my fluke, twitched it as instructed, and then it suddenly disappeared from view as a huge bass, maybe a 10-pounder, inhaled it. "Now! Now!" Munk shouted. "He's got it! He's got it!"

Well, it was like 110 volts going through me, and yeah, I tried to set the hook so hard that it pulled right out of the mouth of that big bass, and the lure actually shot up of the water and almost hit me. I practically expected to see a pair of lips on the hook. I had missed out on the big one.

Munk just smiled. "Maybe next time." Then he cast out, and within seconds, had another one, a three-pounder. "There are fish all over the place."

Then he smiled again. Yes, it was a magic time at BERRYESSA.

Directions: From San Francisco, travel east on Interstate 80 toward Sacramento. At Cordelia Junction, turn north on Suisun Valley Road and proceed to Highway 121. Continue north on Highway 121 about five miles. Turn left (west) on Highway 128 and drive five miles to Turtle Rock (look for the restaurant and bar). Turn right (north) onto Berryessa-Knoxville Road and continue north to the lake. **Lodging:** Putah Creek Resort, (707) 966-2116; Steele Park, (707) 966-2123; Markley Cove, (707) 966-2134. **Boat Rentals:** Markley Cove Resort, (707)

966-2134. **Contact:** To receive a guide brochure, contact Jim Munk at P.O. Box 1506, Lower Lake, CA 95457; (707) 995-0438. For general information, contact the U.S. Bureau of Reclamation, Lake Berryessa, (707) 966-2111. **Locator:** LAKE BERRYESSA (D1).

• FEATURED TRIP •

CLEAR LAKE

Rated: The Top 16 Lakes with Cabin Rentals, 177; The Top 10 Overnight Locations, 185; The Top 10 Places to Fish with Kids, 332; The Top 4 Places to Rockhound, 392

One of the most beautiful sights in America during springtime is Northern California's CLEAR LAKE, big and full to the brim, ringed by lush, green foothills, with an occasional puffy cumulus cloud dotting an azure blue sky.

CLEAR LAKE is becoming one of the top vacation destinations in the West. In the spring, the great natural beauty of the lake approaches that of LAKE TAHOE, only the water is warm, not cold. Like TAHOE, CLEAR LAKE is a natural lake, not a reservoir, so it is not drained in the summer to provide water for agriculture. As a result, it has a completely different look and feel from most other lakes in California, and with old Mount Konocti standing near the western shoreline, it also has a sense of history.

State park camps are set at lakeside, and the fishing can be so good that it is rated the number one bass lake in America, with prospects best from April through June. It is also one of the few lakes in California to have shoreline cabins, campsites, and boat rentals.

If you haven't visited CLEAR LAKE for a while, recent changes have significantly improved the quality of the place. New entertainment possibilities, an improved information service, and much better fishing make it a first-class destination.

The centerpiece of the renovation is Konocti Harbor Resort, set in a big cove just below Mount Konocti. The change started when Greg Bennett, who used to book music acts in Southern California, took over the resort and started a music program. Featured performers are often legends, such as B. B. King and Waylon Jennings. At capacity, the concert hall holds 400.

"I really liked playing here," Waylon told me after one show. "With the big crowds at football stadiums and giant auditoriums, the music can get lost. Here you feel real close to the crowd, and sense them more into the music, not just the event. I like to pick out individuals in the crowd, look right at them, and play for them. You can do that here."

Another aspect of the renovation at CLEAR LAKE is the quality of lodging. At one time, it seemed as if many of the available accommodations were run-down. There has been enough new money invested here in the past few years that the general level of quality is up, although a few hole-in-the-wall establishments still exist. Virtually all the resorts have lake views.

The fishing, boating, and waterskiing provide outstanding recreation. Catch rates for bass are very high, among the top five lakes in California, and the chance of catching a four- or five-pounder over a weekend is very good. In addition, there are probably more big catfish and crappie here than in any lake in the state.

Comparing the fishing to LAKE TAHOE, CLEAR LAKE has the edge. The reason is because TAHOE is a pristine, clear water habitat with few nutrients, with 95 percent of the fish in only 5 percent of the lake. Clear Lake, on the other hand, is loaded with nutrients, which start the aquatic food chain. The result is an abundant fishery throughout the lake.

CLEAR LAKE is located 132 miles from SAN FRANCISCO, 96 miles from SACRAMENTO, and is the largest natural freshwater lake within state borders, covering nearly 45,000 acres. It is surrounded by wildlands, including the vast MENDOCINO NATIONAL FOREST to the north, with mountain peaks to 7,000 feet. There are a dozen free boat ramps.

The best time to visit is from April through June, when the average high temperature is in the 80s. In the summer, it really bakes here, with typical daily highs running 95 degrees, which makes it great for waterskiing. Until Memorial Day weekend, there just aren't many folks here. The campgrounds are almost empty, resorts have only a light sprinkling of visitors, and only a few boats are leaving their fresh white wakes in the emerald green waters.

During the summer, CLEAR LAKE STATE PARK is among the most popular campgrounds in the state, with reservations required virtually every day of the vacation season.

There are many routes to the lake, the most popular being Highway 29 from the south and Highway 20 from the west or east. If you don't mind the narrow, twisty road, the two-laner from HOPLAND is a great trip. After topping the summit, you look down and at the center of the panorama is CLEAR LAKE, a beautiful sight from that distance: an aqua pool amid green hills. It is one of the great natural treasures of Northern California.

It is no accident that CLEAR LAKE provides some of the best fishing in the country. In fact, about the only accidents that happen here are when you catch fish without even trying.

That's what happened to me. Dave Zimmer and I were paddling our canoe into position to make a few casts along the shoreline near the state park, while our ignored, unattended lures were just bobbing a little on the surface right next to the boat. Wham! A bass hammered that lure, and I dropped my paddle and managed to grab the rod just in time to keep it from being pulled into the lake.

These kinds of things have a way of happening at CLEAR LAKE. There can be 50-fish days in April and May, catching and releasing, of course, but you get the picture: you catch fish. Fishing at CLEAR LAKE is not an act of faith, a scientific expedition, or a matter of having a charmed life. It's a matter of being there. And the results are no accident.

You see, the fisheries are not funded or managed by the Department of Fish and Game. Rather, a unique program is directed by the county, which understands the value of a quality fishery and how many recreation dollars it can bring to the local economy.

The program, funded by a hotel and homeowners' tax, is called "Lakebed Management." Some 50,000 Florida bass and 17,500 black crappie are stocked each spring; in addition, rules are enforced to protect the aquatic habitat from lakeside homeowners. When a newcomer from L.A. removed the tules along the shore near his lakefront home in LUCERNE in order to create a beach, the county immediately made him replant the tules. Tules, of course, provide breeding and nursery habitat for bass, crappie, and bluegill, as well as nesting areas for ducks and other birds.

"We rely on the Department of Fish and Game for advice, but not for money or decisions," said guide Terry Knight, a member of the management group. "We're not involved in any way with the state bureaucracy. That allows us to get things done that need to be done, and get them done quickly. This is clearly the best-managed lake in California."

The results are in the catches. To document it, Knight directed a local program in which he honored anglers who caught large fish. In a year, he awarded 200 certificates for bass over eight pounds, 100 certificates for crappie over two and a half pounds, and 400 certificates for catfish over 15 pounds. That is more big fish documented than at any other lake in California.

Professional bass fishers across the country have voted CLEAR LAKE the number one lake in America. The reasons are many: catch rates are good; about one of every four bass is a four-pounder; and the fish tend to be in the top three to four feet of water, not down deep like at reservoirs. Because it is a natural lake, the water level is always near the brim, and with Mount Konocti looming overhead, the area has great beauty.

In addition, the success here is a testimonial to catch-and-release fishing, providing perpetual benefits for anglers. At all bass tournaments, participants keep their fish in a live well on the boat, then after weigh-in, release them. At CLEAR LAKE, however, they go one step further. The fish are placed in a special "bass truck" before release. The bass truck is actually a pick-up truck with an oxygen-flooded water tank, where the bass are resuscitated before release.

"We haven't lost a fish in two years," said Skip Simkins, who helps run the truck.

Keys to success here are the high nutrient and algae levels, which create an abundant aquatic food chain from minnows to bass. Another key is that in the past 10-plus years, the county has phased out northern largemouth bass and white crappie, which rarely grow to large sizes. Florida bass and black crappie have been stocked instead, causing the sudden boom in giant fish in the past few years.

Fishing here makes for a wonderful experience. From a boat, you move along, casting along the shore as you go. Tules are abundant, as are old docks, pilings, and rockpiles, creating an ideal fish habitat. It's almost impossible not to catch a bass or crappie.

At CLEAR LAKE, fishing is kind of like riding a bicycle. The only way you fall down is if you stop pedaling.

Directions: From the Bay Area, take Interstate 80 north over the Carquinez Bridge, then turn north on Highway 29, continue through Vallejo and Napa (jogging left just after Napa College), and proceed on Highway 29 through the Napa Valley, past Middletown to the town of Lower Lake. From **Sacramento**, take Interstate 5 north to Williams, then turn west on Highway 20 and continue to the town of Nice. From the North Coast, take U.S. 101 to Calpella (17 miles south of Willits), then turn east on Highway 20 and go to Highway 29, or continue on Highway 20 to Nice. **Fees:** Access to the lake is free. Campsites, cabins, and room rentals are available at reasonable rates. **Boat ramps:** Public boat ramps are available at no charge at the following locations: in Clearlake, at Rosebud County Park; in Kelseyville, at Lakeside County Park; in Lakeport, at First Street, Third Street, Fifth Street, Clear Lake Avenue, and at the junction of Lakeshore Boulevard and Crystal Lake Way; in Lucerne, at Lucerne Harbor County Park; in Nice, at H. V. Keeling County Park, Nice Community Park, and Hudson Avenue. **Contact:** For general information and a free travel packet, contact the Lake County Visitor Information Center, 875 Lakeport Boulevard, Lakeport, CA 95453; (707) 263-9544 or (800) 525-3743 (in California); or call Clear Lake State Park at (707) 279-4293. For fishing conditions or lodging information, phone Konocti Harbor Inn, (707) 279-4291 or (800) 660-LAKE/5253. Reach guide Terry Knight at (707) 263-1699. **Locator:** CLEAR LAKE (D1).

• FEATURED TRIP •

★ HALF MOON BAY

Rated: The Top 25 Hikes, 2

Wouldn't you love to catch 15 largemouth bass in a day, especially when they're all two- to six-pounders and there's a good chance of getting something bigger? That is why shallow-water rockfishing with tackle designed more for freshwater bass than saltwater rockfish provides some of the most fun you can have from mid-August through mid-October.

It is also why I made a trip on the *Top Cat* out of HALF MOON BAY, and tested a variety of rods, reels, lines, lures, and riggings to find the best way to pull it off. While most people aboard were using the standard three shrimp flies baited with squid, dropping them to the bottom, I tried everything imaginable. And what the heck, I ended up winning the pot with a six-pound vermilion and caught about 25 rockfish, keeping about 10 and releasing the rest.

The reason it works is that late-summer/early fall conditions are ideal to inspire rockfish and lingcod to leave their deepwater haunts of spring and summer and migrate to shallow reefs. The inshore surge is largely gone, allowing the fish a comfortable home in the shallows, and most rockfish and lingcod spawn in the shallows in the fall and early winter.

I always bring a lot of equipment, and what worked best for this trip was a 71/2-foot Loomis graphite rod with a stiff tip action, a Quantum level-wind reel (the one with six ball bearings), and 30-pound test Fenwick IronThread, which has the diameter of 10-pound line.

This is why: The problem with using graphite rods with soft tips when ocean fishing is that they are not sturdy enough to handle and cast three- and four-ounce jigs, and when you get a strike, they don't do a sure-thing job of getting the hook set. As for the reel, level-winds need to operate super smooth when fighting ocean fish, and nothing is smoother than a reel with six ball bearings. Lastly, when setting the hook, you want no stretch at all in the line; the IronThread, similar to what we called braided Dacron in the 1960s, provides that.

I tried a ton of lures, and what worked best is the blue-green Point Wilson Dart, the blue-green Excell jig, and a twist-tail green Scampi. Tady jigs also work well. At one point with the Excell, with a treble hook too small to catch anything, I had 17 strikes in three casts, as exciting as any bass fishing I've done in a lake.

This rig is perfect for making casts underhand, out of the way of other people aboard. The best technique is to flip-cast underhand about 50 to 70 feet out, free-spool the lure down near the bottom, then use a twitch retrieve, alternating one twitch and two twitches for each two turns of the reel handle. Halfway in, I drop the jig back down to the bottom and repeat the process.

This way you get the best of both worlds: reef-haunting rockfish, including a chance at a big lingcod, cabezone, black rockfish, chinas, reds, vermilions, coppers, and widows, as well as the midwater schoolfish, primarily blues and yellows.

Let me tell you, I love all fishing, but doesn't this sound a lot more fun than dropping three shrimp flies down about 10 miles and needing a winch to bring up your catch with a fight somewhat similar to fighting a downrigger weight?

Instead, each fish strikes, runs, and fights, just like bass fishing. I caught the six-pound vermilion in 40 feet of water, and it actually had three power bursts of 20 to 35 feet, really exciting stuff, practically like getting pricked with a cattle prod compared to what it feels like to hoist a similar fish from the bottom of 350 feet of water on winch gear.

You can't shallow-water rockfish year-round, only when the ocean temperatures are warm and inshore surge disappears. Anybody who loves bass fishing will find the catches easier and just as exciting using similar techniques under those conditions at shallow-water reefs.

Directions: From San Francisco, drive south on Interstate 280 for about 19 miles to the Highway 92 cutoff. Turn west on Highway 92 and proceed to Half Moon Bay. **Contact:** Marine Warehouse, (650) 728-7725. **Locator:** HALF MOON BAY (E1b).

• FEATURED TRIP •

LAKE MERCED

Rated: The Top 16 Places to Rent Boats, 305; The Top 22 Water Adventures, 311; The Top 12 Windsurfing Locations, 315; The Top 43 Lakes to Fish, 333

The trout program at SAN FRANCISCO'S LAKE MERCED makes this one of the nation's top urban fisheries. MERCED is stocked every week year-round, for a total of nearly 250,000 trout. Those fish include 400 to 500 trout per week that range from three to 15 pounds. The program works because both the Department of Fish and Game and a private concessionaire make regular plants. Add it up and SAN FRANCISCO anglers have a chance at quality, close-to-home fishing.

Anglers at LAKE MERCED pay a $2.50 day-use fee, with 70 percent of the money turned back to purchase more and larger rainbow trout—a higher percentage than at any time in the lake's 100-year-plus history.

Dave Lyons of SAN FRANCISCO, 78, a veteran LAKE MERCED fisherman, can tell you firsthand about the lake's revival. On 46 of 50 trips, he caught his legal limit (five fish per day), often catching and releasing 10 to 15 trout per visit.

"My best went about 22 inches," Lyons said. "I only fish a few hours during the evening, yet they tell me the fishing here is going to get even better."

The lake has some other unique

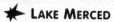

advantages, particularly during the winter-to-spring transition. Because the lake is spring-fed, it is often clean in the late winter, even when most other lakes in California are turbid from heavy storm runoff. In addition, it provides a good spring alternative to fishing in SAN FRANCISCO BAY and the PACIFIC, which have the roughest water conditions of the year from February through May. Then in the summer, the region's coastal breezes and fog keep the waters cool enough to sustain a top trout fishery.

Although MERCED sits within a few miles of SAN FRANCISCO'S 750,000 residents, it seems to have carved out its own niche far removed from the city's concrete and skyscrapers. The lake is located just half a mile from the PACIFIC OCEAN, adjacent to the Harding Golf Course and the San Francisco Zoo. It's a pretty place tucked amid rolling green hills with tules surrounding the water.

LAKE MERCED is actually two lakes separated by a sliver of land, along with a third body of water, a pond named the Impoundment. The lakes cover 386 surface acres and are surprisingly rich in marine life. In 1956, aquatic biologist Bill Johnson of the California Fish and Game Commission called MERCED "the richest trout lake in the state." Forty-two years later, it is much the same. The lakes are filled with freshwater shrimp, a natural feed for the trout, along with perch, bullhead, catfish, and largemouth bass.

As a result, survival rates of stocked fish are high, and they often seem stronger than trout stocked at more barren reservoirs. The trends here have become clear: people using boats out-catch shore fishers by as much as three-to-one; the North Lake produces larger rainbow trout than the South Lake, but results are sporadic; and the South Lake has a steady catch rate for trout, usually averaging two to three per rod, but the fish are smaller—rarely longer than 20 inches. The South Lake also has some big largemouth bass hiding along the tules, but they are difficult to catch.

If you want the closest thing to a guarantee at MERCED, or want to get a kid turned on to fishing, then rent a boat and fish the South Lake. If you want a chance at catching a trophy-sized rainbow trout, like one of those 10-pounders, then the North Lake is your best bet.

Either way, all anglers over age 16 are required to have a California sport-fishing license in their possession.

Boat ramps are available for both lakes, but no gas engines or boats with gas motors are permitted. Canoes, prams, and small boats set up for rowing or rigged with electric motors are ideal. There is a small launch fee.

Some anglers prefer to fish from shore. The favorite spots are the beach on the North Lake and the bridge on the South Lake.

Best results, however, come to boaters who are willing to explore the tule-lined shore. Dave Lyons suggests tying up your boat along the tules, then casting 10 to 30 feet from them.

Since the trout here have so much natural forage at their disposal, they often are reluctant to strike spoons, spinners, or plugs. Instead, bring a variety of baits, including Power Bait, night crawlers, salmon eggs, cheese, and marshmallows. Over the course of a few hours, Lyons will use them all, often in combination, such as salmon eggs with Power Bait on one hook, a night crawler with a small marshmallow on another.

A light-duty spinning rod is the best outfit for fishing here. The simplest and most effective setup is a two-hook rigging. On the bottom hook, thread half a night crawler partially on the hook so it will lie straight and have a natural appearance in the water.

Another strategy is to inflate the worm like a little balloon by using a worm inflater (a small plastic bottle with a hollow needle). With an inflated worm, the bait will float off the bottom of the lake, just where the big trout swim. The same effect can be achieved by topping off the night crawler with a small marshmallow.

After you cast out and let the bait sink to the bottom, you must be alert for even the most subtle signs of a nibble. On a windless day, simply watch where the line enters the water—if it twitches even an inch, you're getting a pickup. A technique suggested by Lyons is just to lay down your rod, leave the bail of your spinning reel open, and place the line under the light plastic lid of a worm tub.

"There's virtually no resistance, so it doesn't spook the fish," Lyons said. "But when the line gets pulled out from under the lid, I know darn well what's going on down there."

What's going on most likely is a rainbow trout on the prowl—thanks to the premium stocking program. MERCED receives approximately 80,000 to 100,000 trout per year, a good number when compared to most other lakes. Bon Tempe Lake in Marin County, for instance, gets about 15,000 trout per year. The difference is that in addition to stocks from the state Department of Fish and Game, special trout plants are made with the funds accrued from the sale of fishing permits. So as more anglers try their luck, the trout stocks improve at the same rate.

In a typical year, 60,000 people will average 1.5 fish per rod here. The largest fish documented was a 17-pound rainbow trout landed in the North Lake by Will Rose of SAN FRANCISCO. In 1987 an eight-pound, 10-ounce largemouth bass was caught in the South Lake by Mike Rainey, also of SAN FRANCISCO.

Since Merced was converted to a reservoir in 1877, a number of fishing programs have been attempted. Many have failed. In 1891, carp were stocked, but the water roiled up so much that 19 sea lions were trapped and put in the lake to clean them out. Two years later, 90,000 muskies were stocked and never heard from again. Officials next tried largemouth bass, but few anglers could figure out how to catch them. It wasn't until 1944 that trout were planted, but because of the lake's infestations of carp, hitch, and squawfish, sportfishing didn't have much of a chance to get established. Finally in 1949, the lake was poisoned with rotenone to clear out the trash fish, then restocked with rainbow trout and reopened to fishing in 1950.

But not until the past few years has anything like the present trout fishing program been attempted. So before you head to some far-off place in search of quality rainbow trout fishing, try SAN FRANCISCO's backyard hole, Lake Merced.

Rigging for big trout: The simplest way to rig your outfit for big trout is to slide a small barrel sinker over your line, then tie on a snap swivel. From there, tie on three feet of leader and a no. 8 or 10 hook.

But you can take it a step further. Midway up your leader, tie a small dropper loop, then add a second hook. This gives you the ability to double your chances; after a hungry trout has stolen the bait off one hook, you still have a shot at catching it on the other.

For an advanced lesson, use no weight at all. A night crawler for bait will provide enough casting weight. Hungry trout are easily spooked by the sensation of any unnatural weight attached to a baited hook. Dave Lyons, MERCED'S fishing master, is happy to show people how to rig their lines. He's available at the Merced Bait Shop.

Directions: From Interstate 280 west of Daly City, take John Daly Boulevard west. Turn right at Skyline Boulevard and continue to the lake. **Fishing permits:** A special daily permit is required for all anglers over age 16, with separate prices for each lake. An annual pass can be purchased for South Lake fishing access. Kids under 16 do not need a permit to fish at South Lake; at North Lake, they are allowed to share a permit with another angler. Obtain permits at the Merced Bait Shop. **California state fishing license:** Anglers age 16 and over must have a state fishing license in their possession. Annual licenses and one-day permits are available; for information, contact the California Department of Fish and Game at (707) 944-5500. **Boat rentals:** Rowboats, canoes, motorboats, rods, and reels are available for rent at the lake. There is a fee for boat launching. Limits: A five-fish limit is in effect for trout or bass, 10 for catfish. Any trout or bass over three pounds wins a free whopper button from the Merced Bait Shop. The largest trout caught each month wins a quality spinning rod-and-reel combination. **Contact:** Merced Bait Shop, 1 Harding Road, San Francisco, CA 94123; (415) 753-1101. **Locator:** LAKE MERCED (E1b).

• FEATURED TRIP •

PACIFICA PIER

Rated: The most temperamental fishing spot

When it comes to fishing, some days you're the windshield and some days you're the bug. At PACIFICA PIER, fishing can make you feel more like a prisoner of hope than anything else, waiting for the annual arrival of salmon, and with it, the best fishing of the year from any public pier in America.

In a high fog, with calms seas beneath, schools of anchovies start migrating inshore, marked by gulls and pelicans, circling, diving, and feeding. Birds never lie, you know, and most people figure the salmon can't be far behind, chasing and corralling the anchovies.

"Fishing at the pier is like playing the stock market," says Jim Klinger, a field scout and PACIFICA resident. "One day it's all limos and Lear jets; the next day you want to be perched on a window ledge on the 30th floor."

One happy July, 300 salmon were caught at the pier in a few hours, a maniacal but joyful scene. Word circulated overnight around the Bay Area, and the 1,000-foot pier became jammed with 800 fishermen the following day. At daybreak, the salmon charged inshore again, and more than 600 were landed by afternoon; the next day, more than 1,000 were caught, with hundreds of others hooked and lost. It lasted for five days, then, after settling down to 50 to 100 salmon per day, another siege ensued for a week, with 300 to 400 fish caught daily. Peaks and valleys, it went up and down like this through August.

To some extent, this happens every year, just after the Fourth of July, but nobody knows exactly when the salmon will arrive and nobody knows exactly how many fish will show or when they will bite. And that's when fishers start thinking about prayer.

"From day to day, even hour to hour, it can be so unpredictable that you never know what's going to happen next," Klinger said. "Everything seems so temperamental and finicky. It can be the greatest day of your life or the biggest disappointment."

Over the years, the scene at PACIFICA PIER has become a microcosm of urban life in the United States. Cost is a factor in recreation these days, and not only is fishing at the pier free, but a fishing license is not required. People can stand shoulder to shoulder here, and despite huge differences in backgrounds, mainly language and culture, they learn to work together anyway. Whether it be loaning a crab net to land and hoist up a big fish, or dipping under and over lines while playing a salmon to avoid tangles, people discover that you get results by cooperating, just as in urban life.

And just like life elsewhere, everybody can be happy, excited, and tense over what is possible on some days, yet surly, closed, and grumpy over what seems impossible on others.

PACIFICA PIER is located about 10 miles south of SAN FRANCISCO, and with access from Highway 1 out of The City and also from Sharp Park/Westborough Boulevard off Interstate 280 from the Peninsula, it is within close, easy reach of thousands. Like the fish, the people come in waves. When the bite is on, every spot is filled along the railing, both sides. When someone finally turns their back on the fish and goes home, the spot is quickly taken by a newcomer. With lights posted and night fishing permitted, it can be the fishing pier that never goes to sleep.

Though salmon are the most sought-after catch, striped bass often frequent the nearby surf, with kingfish, sharks, and perch also common. Though rare, sturgeon, barracuda, and bonito have also been caught here, and several years ago, a 60-pound white sea bass was landed. But like Klinger said, you never know what might happen next.

Neil Giffen, a longtime PACIFICA resident and angler, lost a fish here when it wrapped his line around a piling—and when he looked down, he spotted a baby sea lion that had crawled up on one of the angled pilings.

"Everybody was saying, 'Look at the poor little guy, he looks scared, maybe he's hurt,'" Giffen said.

But right then, a 15-foot great white shark appeared out of nowhere, cruised right beneath the baby sea lion, eyeing it as if considering dinner.

"That baby seal stayed lodged there for hours," Giffen said with a laugh. "That was one smart little seal."

A few smarts are also required to fish here, but nothing that can't be learned quickly. The standard rigging is called the "trolley rig," named after a fishing system unique to PACIFICA PIER.

You start with a four- to eight-ounce pier sinker, which looks like a four-legged spider, tying it to your line, then make a short underhand cast, with the sinker grabbing the bottom and holding tight despite the ocean surge. You then attach a pier bobber, about the size of an apple, to the line with a snap swivel, along with six feet of leader and a size 5/0 hook. After hooking a whole anchovy for bait, you let the bobber and bait "trolley" down the line to the water. You end up with that giant bobber floating on the surface, a whole anchovy for bait below it, and you wait for that bobber to get tugged under, perhaps when a giant salmon has taken the bait.

Because the fish are often large, with 10- to 20-pound salmon typical, crab nets are dropped down and positioned under the fish, then hoisted up to the pier deck to land the fish.

A small bait and tackle shop at the foot of the pier has terminal tackle, and during downtime, an employee can often demonstrate how to rig. A pre-tied trolley rig costs $4.25, and a pier bobber costs $1.98.

When the pier is full of anglers, it actually helps the fishing, because all those anchovies in the water for bait are like chum line, drawing the fish right in.

Everything is perfect for such a scene to unfold in summer when the water temperature is about 55 degrees, ideal for salmon, and the first migrating anchovies arrive. The water is tinted green like a champagne bottle, a color that Klinger says often brings the best prospects, especially compared to the murky browns of winter. The water is then filled with a vibrant essence of life, with birds, baitfish, and the first salmon of the year.

Most of the people at the pier are helpful to their neighbors, but just like in the big city, there are exceptions.

"One day at the pier, this guy was just plain making life miserable for everyone around him," Klinger said. "He was bumping into people, hitting people with his rod, and finally, when things settled down and we got back to fishing, his bobber goes bye-bye. We knew he had a huge fish on, and sure enough, he started to fight it, reeling, his rod doubled over, but the guy got all screwed up and before long, his line started getting tangled with several people.

"He looks over at us and says, 'What do I do now?'

"And the guy next to him says, almost automatically, 'Cut your line.'

"So the guy pulled out his knife, cuts his line, and proceeds to lose one of the biggest salmon you could ever dream of."

Directions: From San Francisco, head south on Interstate 280 to Daly City. Turn south on Highway 1 and continue to the town of Pacifica. In Pacifica, turn right on Paloma Avenue and drive west toward the ocean. Paloma Avenue becomes Beach Boulevard. From Beach Boulevard, you will see the pier on the right. **Contact:** Pacifica Pier, (650) 355-0690; Coastside No. 2 Bait and Tackle, (650) 359-9790. **Locator:** PACIFICA PIER (E1b).

• FEATURED TRIP •

BERKELEY PIER

Rated: The Most Uncomplicated Fishing Spot

Some Bay Area folks complain of feeling like a hamster on a treadmill after a few years of the daily commute and the grind at work. One way to snap out of that mood is to take a slow stroll down BERKELEY PIER, with or without a fishing rod.

At BERKELEY PIER, you discover that waiting, the thing people hate most about city life, is the very heart of pier fishing, and it's a medicine that should be taken in regular doses. Tension has a way of eating at you, but out here you find yourself unworried, and that tight spring within begins to uncoil slowly. This historic structure extends 3,000 feet into SAN FRANCISCO BAY, in the midst of some awesome landmarks that people travel around the world to see. You haven't looked lately? You're not alone.

Straight to the west is the GOLDEN GATE BRIDGE, a classic panoramic view. During the next few hours, you will see giant tankers come and go through the GOLDEN GATE. If you watch a sunset here, you will discover how the GATE got its name. It looks different out here than when you're burning up the road—especially if you bring along a loaf of French bread and some cheese, plus something to wash it down with, and maybe a fishing rod as well.

Hanging out at BERKELEY PIER has been a favorite way to spend a day in the Bay Area since 1937, when the pier was converted to a fishing pier. Since then, it has provided a place to spend a day on the bay for everyone from old pros who want some peace and quiet to young anglers out for excitement.

Perch, jacksmelt, flounder, sharks, stingrays, and bat rays are the most common catch here. Even the grand prizes of bay fishing—striped bass, halibut, and salmon—are occasionally caught during their respective migrations, in spring, early summer, and fall. For decking the larger fish, it is essential to bring along a crab net, which can be dropped by a rope and then scooped under the fish. Anglers attempting to land a fish by hoisting it up by fishing line have lost some beauties.

A fishing shop for bait, tackle, and, most importantly, advice, sits at the foot of BERKELEY PIER. Even if you don't need any tackle, you should always check here first for the latest information.

Don't get the idea that this is a complicated adventure. BERKELEY PIER is 3,000 feet long, so walking to the end takes an average of about 20 minutes. Many of the best perch fishing spots require a short walk, however. Most folks just hook on their bait—either grass shrimp, pileworm, or a chunk of anchovy—flip it in the water, take a seat, and watch their line trailing out into the bay in little curls. Sometimes they get a bite, sometimes they don't. Somehow, it doesn't really seem to matter.

Directions: From Interstate 80 in Berkeley, take the University Avenue exit and follow the signs to the Berkeley Marina. The pier is at the foot of University Avenue, just past the bait shop and marina. **Trip tip:** A Department of Fish and Game regulation allows anglers to fish with two lines here—either two fishing rods, or a fishing rod and a crab trap simultaneously. **Fees:** Access to the pier is free. Since Berkeley Pier is a municipal facility, no fishing license is necessary. **Contact:** Berkeley Marina Sports, (510) 849-2727. **Locator:** BERKELEY PIER (E1c).

• FEATURED TRIP •

THE DELTA

Rated: The Top 5 Houseboating Sites, 300; The Top 16 Places to Rent Boats, 305; The Top 22 Water Adventures, 311

If you are losing your zest for life, some doctors prescribe looking at everything as if you were seeing it for the first time. THE DELTA is the perfect place to take the cure. Because there is so much to explore, everything you see can literally be for the first time, every day, for the rest of your life. All you need is a boat.

"I've been exploring this son-of-a-gun my whole life and I still haven't seen all of it," Tony Addimando of LIVERMORE told me. "I'm 60 and I'm going to keep at it the next 60 years just to find out how much I can see. But you know, we'll never see it all. There's just too much out there."

THE DELTA is one of America's largest recreation areas for all kinds of activities. For boaters, it's likely the best. The only comparable waterway is the Okefenokee Swamp, which runs over the state line between Georgia and Florida, a tangled bayou web where the public is barred without a guide and a permit.

The public is welcome at THE DELTA, on the other hand, and there is room to play for pleasure boaters, anglers, water-skiers, and houseboaters alike. It seems to have no end, with 1,000 miles of navigable waters, 46 boat launches, and 44 public and private campgrounds.

If you don't own a boat, there are many options. Houseboat rentals are available at 16 locations, skiffs are rented at five marinas, and one- and two-day trips on tour boats are available out of STOCKTON, BRENTWOOD, ISLETON, SACRAMENTO, and OAKLAND.

THE DELTA is located about 60 miles from SAN FRANCISCO, but when you are on the water, it can feel like you're a million miles away from any city. Access routes by car include Highways 4, 12, and 160, which gives you an idea of THE DELTA'S vast size.

It is fed by two of the West's largest rivers, the SACRAMENTO and the SAN JOAQUIN, along with many big feeder rivers—the MOKELUMNE, STANISLAUS, TUOLUMNE, MERCED, and KINGS. All of them start as little trickles from melting snow high in the mountains, but eventually join at THE DELTA and then rumble as one to SAN FRANCISCO BAY.

When viewed from the air, the mosaic of smaller connecting rivers, sloughs, and islands makes THE DELTA look like the product of intricate masonry work. By boat, it can look like paradise.

The first thing you notice is that no matter where you go, you are shadowed by that big mountain, MOUNT DIABLO. At 3,849 feet, it isn't so tall when compared to peaks in the Sierra Nevada, but since it is surrounded by the Bay Area and THE DELTA virtually at sea level, it is visible for hundreds of miles.

On the water, old DIABLO gives you a reference point, a connection to something familiar, something strong and still amid stirring waters. It also provides a backdrop for spectacular sunsets in the fall, when orange sunlight refracts through cumulus clouds and across the slopes of DIABLO and THE DELTA'S waterways.

"I love this old delta," said Jay Sorensen of STOCKTON. "I've lived here since I was 10 months old, and in the past 40 years, I've been on the water five days a week. One time I was out

30 straight days, just on my own.

"I just plain love being on the water. We catch a lot of fish, but a few days you just don't get 'em. A lot of people don't mind, because they're out here on THE DELTA. There's a special feeling to this place."

Musician David Crosby even recorded a song called "The Delta" on a Crosby, Stills & Nash album, an album that was awarded a gold record for sales.

The gold for boaters and anglers, however, is the variety of fisheries that THE DELTA supports.

The biggest attraction is the striped bass, which arrive in their annual fall run. Also in the fall, salmon migrate through THE DELTA, headed upriver to spawning grounds on the upstream rivers. Resident fish that live here year-round include catfish, black bass, bluegill, and, of course, the giant sturgeon.

How big do the sturgeon get? Well, consider the tale of Bill Stratton, who was fishing for striped bass in the lower DELTA one November day. It was warm out, but when "something huge" took his bait, a cold tingle went down his spine. Several hours later, when the fish was finally brought alongside the boat, it looked like some kind of whale.

That's because it was over eight feet long and weighed 390 pounds. It was a world record for 30-pound test line. (A six-foot maximum size limit is now the law.) He had been fishing for stripers, like most of the others who are attracted to THE DELTA during fall and winter. Stripers have been severely impacted by state and federal water projects, but they still number about 750,000, according to Fish and Game estimates. It is a viable fishery.

Sometimes it is better than viable. In one recent winter season, guide Barry Canevaro and his customers caught 1,300 stripers, releasing many—remarkable numbers by any standards. Some years are not as productive. Weather, water flows, and fishing skills are key determinants.

During November, the first sprinkling of striped bass arrive here. The big school locates in SAN PABLO BAY, where it awaits rain and freshened-up waters before heading home. From fall to spring, several traditional spots attract fish: Big Break, San Andreas Shoals, the mouth of the False River, and the mouth of the MOKELUMNE on the SAN JOAQUIN RIVER; Sherman Lake, the southern tip of Decker Island, just upriver of the Rio Vista Bridge, and the shoal at the river bend between RIO VISTA and ISLETON, on the SACRAMENTO RIVER.

You don't have to fish to have a good time on THE DELTA. You can go houseboating for a week, or take a two-day tour boat ride from SACRAMENTO to SAN FRANCISCO'S Fisherman's Wharf. Or just show up on a hot Indian summer weekend and water-ski all your willies away.

Or maybe you could just pick out your own spot and watch the water go by. No extra pushing needed.

Directions: The Delta is crossed by Highways 4, 12, and 160, all of which are accessible from the Bay Area via Interstate 80. A detailed map of the Delta can be obtained for a small fee from any area tackle shop or by mail; forward $3.75 to Hal Schell, Delta Map, P.O. Box 9140, Stockton, CA 95208; (209) 951-7821. **Boat rentals:** Paradise Point Marina at King Island, (209) 952-1000; Rainbow Resort at Brannan Island, (916) 777-6172; Korth's

Pirate Lair on the Mokelumne River, (916) 777-6464; and Herman and Helen's Marina, (209) 951-4634. **Boat launches:** Available at Collinsville, Rio Vista, Brannan Island, Antioch Bridge, west tip of Sherman Island, Bethel Island, Walnut Grove, Terminous, and Del's near Clifton Court Forebay, West Stockton. **Camping:** Brannan Island State Park is the most popular public area with 32 boat slips that include either a walk-in campsite or drive-in RV site. These are available on a first-come, first-served basis. There are also 102 sites for tents or RVs, and a boat launch. For information, phone (916) 777-6671, or call California State Parks, Brannan Island Delta Center at (916) 777-7701. Private campgrounds are shown on Delta maps and are detailed in my book California Camping (also published by Foghorn Press). **Fishing:** Hap's Bait in Rio Vista, (707) 374-2372; Delta Bait and Tackle in Bethel Island, (925) 684-2260; and Tony's Tackle in Livermore, (510) 443-9191. **Fishing guides:** Two excellent fishing guides are Barry Canevaro, (916) 777-6498, and Jay Sorensen, (209) 478-6645. **Houseboating:** There are 16 Delta houseboat agencies that can be reached through the Chambers of Commerce for Antioch, (925) 757-1800, and Stockton, (209) 547-2770. **Tour boats:** One- and two-day deluxe tours on large double-decker boats are available out of Oakland by calling (510) 834-3052. **Locator:** San Joaquin Delta (E2).

• FEATURED TRIP •

San Pablo Reservoir

Rated: The Top 50 Parks, 7; The Top 16 East Bay Lakes, 205; The Top 16 Places to Rent Boats, 305; The Top 22 Water Adventures, 311; The Top 43 Lakes to Fish, 333

In my survey of the Bay Area's 43 lakes, I rated San Pablo Reservoir number one. Every spring and summer, it has a chance to show why.

It is the only lake in the Bay Area that provides first-class beauty, boating, fishing, and bird-watching, along with opportunities for hiking and biking. It's got everything except a campground for overnight use.

When spring arrives, the surrounding hills turn lush green, sprinkled with wildflowers, and the lake becomes a divine sight, filled with emerald waters. At the same time, the trout fishing is also coming to life, boosted by more stocks than any lake in Northern California, often reaching 125,000 to 150,000 fish per year.

San Pablo Reservoir is a large lake, covering 850 acres in an East Bay canyon between Orinda and San Pablo, near the town of El Sobrante. Because it is closed to the public each winter, its wildlife habitat gets an annual rest from public pressure. When it reopens again in the spring, the trout have to learn all over again about the hooks of anglers. You'll see many nesting waterfowl that have hatched their eggs and are raising their chicks.

Daybreak is often gorgeous at San Pablo. As the sun rises above the hills to the east, it sends yellows and oranges across the water. Minute by minute, the scene changes, with various blues and greens finally emerging and boats cutting fresh, white wakes. At times like this it can be difficult to believe that San Pablo Reservoir is so close to 5.5 million Bay Area residents.

The prospect of good trout fishing

attracts most visitors here for the first time, and the natural beauty and complete outdoor experience keeps them coming back for more.

While there are no guarantees in the world of fishing, SAN PABLO often comes close. The concessionaire, Urban Parks, designed the model fishing program where anglers pay a $3 fee for a permit, which is then used to purchase rainbow trout; there is also a $5 entry fee per car. The result is that 6,000 to 10,000 trout are stocked each week, more than at any lake in the western United States. This program, using funds from day-use permits to buy trout, has been copied at dozens of lakes across America.

So there is good trout fishing, both for shoreliners and boaters. In addition, the headquarters store at the Main Rec Area not only has all necessary bait and tackle available—it also can provide detailed how-to and where-to tips to put visitors on to fish.

A first-class boat launch as well as boat rentals are also available. The launch opens each day at 6 a.m., and with a 25 mph speed limit on the open lake, it is one of a handful of Bay Area lakes that offers good boating access. Small, low-speed boats fit in as well. A 5 mph speed limit is enforced along the shore, as well as at the southern end of the lake at the Waterfowl Area.

That is why boat rentals are popular here, including 14-foot aluminum boats with eight-horsepower engines, rowboats, and patio boats. The cost ranges from a low of $21 half day for a rowboat to a high of $43 for a boat and motor for a full day.

The lake's several unique areas are best explored by boat. Scow Canyon, located directly across from the Main Rec Area, extends for nearly a mile north into foothill so remote that you can often feel like you are the only person in the world. The Waterfowl Area is another distinctive spot, where low-speed boats (no gas motors permitted) and low-noise people are the rule, and where ducks and coots breed. This is one of the better birdwatching areas at a Bay Area lake.

Though the lake is best known for boating and fishing, there are also opportunities for picnicking, hiking, and biking.

There are excellent picnic sites with lake views at both the boat launch and the Main Rec Area, with enough room to handle 500 people. Of course, typically visitors have plenty of room, especially during the week when the lake gets far less use than on weekends.

While there is no network of hiking trails at SAN PABLO, there is a good route the extends from the dam all the way along the western shoreline to the boat ramp. It covers about seven miles one way and passes such spots as the Main Rec Area and Berkeley Tower.

While no bikes are permitted on that trail, they are allowed on all paved routes around the lake. The best bike route starts at the dam and extends four miles on a paved road to Berkeley Tower. There it links up to a fire road and continues another three miles to the boat ramp.

The only drawback at SAN PABLO in the spring are occasional winds, which often burst upon the scene in early afternoon. They can turn a placid lake into a dangerous howler, complete with waves and whitecaps. Many visitors often call the Main Rec Area to get a wind report prior to heading out. Others will show up at the boat launch at daybreak, typically well before there is any sign of wind.

After all, it is daybreak when this lake seems so pristine, so distant from the nearby urban rush. And that is the greatest attraction of all.

Directions: From Interstate 80, exit on San Pablo Dam Road. Head right, toward Orinda, and drive six miles to the main park entrance. **Fees:** There is a $5 parking fee. A one-day fishing access permit costs $3 The reservoir is closed every year from mid-November through mid-February. **Pets:** Pets are allowed on leash in picnic areas, but are not allowed anywhere along the reservoir shoreline. **Contact:** San Pablo Reservoir, (510) 223-1661. **Locator:** SAN PABLO RESERVOIR (E1c).

• FEATURED TRIP •

CAPITOLA WHARF

Rated: The Top 16 Places to Rent Boats, 305; The Top 8 Deep-Sea Fishing Trips, 330

Time has a way of changing every day, and truth has a way of changing all the time. But when it comes to fishing at MONTEREY BAY, more than 35 years seem to have flashed by in a day or two. Little appears to have changed here.

It was back in 1962 that my dad first took my brother and me to CAPITOLA. While fishing, we'd listen to the Giants game on the radio; Willie Mays was hitting the left field wall, Billy Pierce was hitting the corners, and we were having the time of our lives, catching rockfish like crazy on the quiet waters of MONTEREY BAY.

Years later, Willie Mays is long gone and Barry Bonds now patrols Candlestick (3Com) Park. And at CAPITOLA, the good times remain for the few people who know of the angling attractions here.

CAPITOLA WHARF is one of the few places on the West Coast where you can rent a small boat for a day of fishing. Hence, an adventure is waiting for any angler yearning for one. It is the perfect place for a father and son fishing trip. Just ask my Dad.

At 7 a.m. or so, we'd arrive at CAPITOLA, which is a relatively short drive (under two hours) from SAN FRANCISCO. After hopping aboard a rental skiff, it is just a five-minute ride to the prime fishing grounds, situated at the edge of the nearby kelp beds. Spots such as Adams Reef, Surfers Reef, and South Rock all produce outstanding fishing.

With rod in hand, you allow your bait to descend to the shallow sea bottom. Squid-baited shrimp flies, strips of mackerel, or cut anchovy chunks entice a surprising variety of rockfish. A bonus is that very little weight is required to reach the bottom, often just a few ounces.

Most folks use light saltwater rods, with line rated at 12- to 20-pound test. Rod rentals are available at Capitola Pier for a few dollars.

In the fall, MONTEREY BAY gets its quietest water of the year, as well as its best rockfishing. If you'd like to tussle with some heavyweights, autumn also brings with it a good number of blue sharks. For folks with even bigger plans, long-range trips are made this time of year in search of albacore and tuna. If you just want to stick to the pier, crabbing and fishing for mackerel can be fairly productive.

Finding a common ground for a father and son can be difficult, but a fishing trip from CAPITOLA can provide that rare space, and in the process, some special memories.

Maybe time doesn't have to change

every day after all.

Directions: From San Francisco, take either Interstate 880 to Highway 17 or Highway 1 south to Santa Cruz. Continue south to Capitola and take the 41st Avenue exit. Turn left on Capitola Road and go through three stop signs. Continue west to the wharf; parking areas are available nearby. **Fees:** Access to the wharf is free, but fees are charged for the rental of skiffs, rods, and reels. **Contact:** For tips on fishing, weather, and sea conditions, call the Capitola Wharf, (831) 462-2208. **Locator:** CAPITOLA WHARF (F1).

11
BONUS GETAWAYS

• TOM'S RATINGS •

• FEATURED TRIPS •

See last page for Northern California and Bay Area foldout maps.

*The area code for all phone numbers followed by an asterisk (*) will change to 559 as of November 14, 1998. Also, area code 805 is scheduled to split on February 13, 1999. The new area code is yet to be introduced. Call Pacific Bell for a list of prefixes that will receive the new area code.

• TOM'S RATINGS •

THE TOP 10 CAVE EXPLORATIONS

In Northern California

Caves, caverns, and tunnels are full of mystery and secrets, and there are many such perfect places in Northern California that make great weekend getaways.

This feeling of mystery, inspired by entering the earth's darkened interior, is brought to life when you shine a flashlight beam on stunning crystalline formations, towers, stalagmites, and dark tunnels that seem to lead to never-never land.

The best series of caves and caverns is in Calaveras County in the Sierra foothills, home to three of the West's most dramatic caverns. Here, both guided walking tours and more daring "discovery tours" involving rope descents are available.

The only cave in the greater Bay Area is actually a mine shaft, the Prospect Tunnel at Black Diamond Mines Regional Preserve near ANTIOCH, where no guide is needed. Many people are surprised to learn that Northern California has many hidden caves created from lava flows and caverns formed of limestone, including two at SHASTA LAKE.

Here are the 10 best caves and caverns:

1. SAMWEL CAVE

A hidden gem is locked away at famous SHASTA. The name "Samwel" comes from a Wyntu word meaning holy place. The cave opens out from a limestone crag overlooking SHASTA LAKE, then enters the mountain, extending into an erratic series of multiple levels. The main attraction, one that's quite dangerous and eerie, is a 75-foot pit that drops off to the bottom level—where an anthropologist once discovered a human skeleton. You can access the cave by boat, or on a short hike off Gilman Road (off Interstate 5). But note: There is a locked gate at the cave entrance; a key is available for free (with a $10 deposit) from the Shasta Lake Visitor Center.

Contact: Shasta-Trinity National Forest, Shasta Lake Ranger District, (530) 275-1587. **Locator:** SHASTA LAKE (B2).

2. SHASTA CAVERNS

There is no place on Earth like the Shasta Caverns. Once inside, you'll see multicolored fluted columns; magnificent stone draperies; symmetrical folds, stalactites, and stalagmites studded with brilliant crystals; milky-white flowstone; and miniature waterfalls. It's as pretty as any limestone marble cave in America. The caverns are the hidden jewel of SHASTA LAKE, set high in a limestone wall on the east side of the MCCLOUD RIVER arm. Guided tours are available year-round; they typically spend about one hour in the caverns with a 15-minute boat ride there and back from O'Brien Inlet.

Fees: Adults, $14; children, $7. **Contact:** Shasta Caverns, (530) 238-2341 or (800) 474-2782. **Locator:** SHASTA LAKE (B2).

3. ICE CAVES

Here you will find a series of very strange-looking caves, some of them actually shallow, gouged-out hollows in volcanic rock. The caves are more like lava grottoes than tunnels or caverns. This is remote country in northern Siskiyou County, located near MEDICINE LAKE amid lava flows adjacent to LAVA BEDS NATIONAL MONUMENT.

Contact: Modoc National Forest, Tule Lake Ranger District, (530) 667-2246; Lava Beds National Monument, (530) 667-2282. **Locator:** MODOC NATIONAL FOREST (A3).

4. SUBWAY CAVE

This hidden surprise is located just off Highway 89, marked only by a small sign along the road. The cave, created in a gouged-out lava flow, extends about 40 feet. It's best seen as a side trip while en route to the Medicine Lake Highlands.

Contact: Modoc National Forest, Tule Lake Ranger District, (530) 667-2246. **Locator:** MODOC NATIONAL FOREST (B3).

5. SUBWAY CAVE (HAT CREEK)

People often discover 1,300-foot-long Subway Cave by accident while camping and fishing at Hat Creek along Highway 89. For many, it turns out to be the highlight of a trip. When you first enter, you step into a massive cavern, Devil's Doorway; from that point on you'll need a big flashlight. The cave meanders to the right, where you will begin seeing Native American petroglyphs on the wall. Along the way you'll stop at Lucifer's Cul-De-Sac and Lavacicle Lane. You exit the cave at a different point after about 45 minutes of exploration. Note that you'll need good shoes because the floor is made of bumpy, cooled lava flows. The whole venture is like taking a walk through geological history.

Contact: Lassen National Forest, Hat Creek Ranger District, (530) 336-5521. **Locator:** LASSEN NATIONAL FOREST. (B3).

6. PROSPECT TUNNEL, BLACK DIAMOND MINES

Bring a flashlight with fresh batteries and you have the chance to explore 200 feet of mountain tunnel. This is the feature attraction of Black Diamond Mines Regional Preserve. The best destination is the Prospect Tunnel, which bores 400 feet in the side of MOUNT DIABLO, with half of it accessible to the public. To get there, take the Stewartville Trail for 1.5 miles. The Prospect Tunnel was drilled out in the 1860s by miners in search of black diamonds, that is, coal.

Contact: East Bay Regional Park District, (510) 635-0135 extension 2200. **Locator:** MOUNT DIABLO (E2).

7. CALIFORNIA CAVERNS

The delicate limestone formations are spectacular, especially the stalactites that hang like chandeliers and branch out—a sight you won't see anywhere else. The walking tour lasts 80 minutes, a mostly level trek into the earth, extending through a maze of rooms, some of them quite large. The more ambitious discovery tour, or Downstream Circuit Trip, starts where the walking tour ends, continuing for four hours through a maze of underground tunnels, drops, and chambers, with some rooms over 100 feet tall.

Fees: Walking tour, $8; introductory trip, $58; Downstream Circuit Trip, $75. **Contact:** Calaveras County Visitor Center, (209) 736-2708* or (800) 225-3764 extension 211. **Locator:** SAN ANDREAS (E3).

8. MERCER CAVERNS

A small opening in limestone rocks leads into a series of stunning caverns and extensive hidden passageways. The adventure features an enormous variety of unusual crystalline formations of all sizes, textures, and shapes. These include columns and towers, where visitors are dazzled by superb artistry in a subterranean wonderland. All tours are guided, run 45 minutes, and explore 161 feet deep into the earth.

Fees: $7. **Contact:** (209) 728-2101* or (800) 225-3764 extension 212. **Locator:** MURPHYS (E3).

9. Moaning Caverns

When you enter the earth here you will discover a huge cavern, 180 feet deep, with a spiral staircase that allows you to descend to its base. This portion of the cavern is lighted, so you can see a fantastic array of stalactites (formations that hang from the rock ceiling) and stalagmites (columns extending up from the rock floor), as well as pieces of ancient skeletons intact from unfortunate souls who made wrong turns. You can take an Adventure Trip, for which you are provided all equipment and instruction, descend 165 feet by rope, then explore deeper into linked caves for three hours using headlamps for light. You'll feel as if you are jumping off the edge of the world.

Fees: Walking tour, $7.75; introductory tour, $35; Adventure Trip, $75. **Contact:** Calaveras County Visitor Center, (209) 736-2708* or (800) 225-3764 extension 211. **Locator:** ANGELS CAMP (E3).

10. Bear Gulch Cave

The PINNACLES is a fascinating place, a miniature mountain range in the San Joaquin Valley with two surprise cave systems. The Bear Gulch Cave is approximately four-tenths of a mile long, and the Balconies Cave extends for three-tenths of a mile. These are not subterranean tunnels, like the old mines, but talus caves. They were created in canyons and crevices where rocks have slipped or fallen, and over time, where rain removed volcanic material. The result is a series of completely enclosed spaces in a rock canopy. All the cave walks are self-guided; you are advised to bring an extra set of batteries for your flashlight (though no skeletons have been discovered recently).

Contact: Pinnacles National Monument, (831) 389-4485. **Locator:** PINNACLES NATIONAL MONUMENT (F2). **See featured trip page:** 147.

• TOM'S RATINGS •

The Top 5 Places to Clam Dig

In the San Francisco Bay Area

Clamming is an ideal family adventure because everyone's on equal terms, youngsters and adults alike. Techniques vary widely. On a single beach, one might see such tools as garden hoes, shovels, and cultivators, or long, narrow clammer's shovels and clam guns. I've even seen kids use a piece of abalone shell to dig for cockles, and after finding one, look up at Dad as if he was the king of the world.

But if you don't know when to go, you won't find clams, only lots of sand. During minus outgoing tides, the prime clamming grounds up and down the coast are unveiled. With a little preparation, you can be ready.

Horseneck and Washington clams are available for the taking, depending on where you go. Don't expect to find clams on long, exposed stretches of sandy beach. Clams need protection. Ideal clam habitats are available at certain parts of BODEGA BAY, TOMALES BAY, HALF MOON BAY, south of Pigeon

Point, and in Elkhorn Slough at MOSS LANDING.

Cockles are my favorite, and are especially popular at TOMALES BAY, HALF MOON BAY, and AÑO NUEVO. These little fellows will bury themselves in a rock and sand mix, usually just three or four inches below the surface. A three-pronged garden cultivator, used as if one were weeding a patch of lettuce, can produce the limit of 50 on a good day. Children prefer using a small hand shovel and the hands-and-knees technique. The minimum size cockle legally taken is 1.5 inches in diameter, and participants must have a measuring device and a state fishing license in their possession when digging.

Cockles are choice morsels when steamed and dipped in garlic butter sauce, a simple preparation. Horseneck and Washington clams, on the other hand, require a fairly extensive beating to soften them up for eating. But their size makes up for the work. They get big, though state law requires any horseneck or Washington clam dug must be kept until the bag limit is reached, regardless of size or condition.

To find horsenecks, you should be out during the minus tide, scanning the tidal flats, searching for the telltale sign of a small siphon hole in the sand. The hole is actually the clam's neck hole, through which they feed. If you spot the bubbling hole, dig and dig fast. The clam will withdraw its long neck, leaving no sign of its whereabouts. But rest assured, somewhere below where that small hole appeared will be a clam.

The favored tool for these larger specimens is the clammer's shovel, a long, slender device engineered to dig a narrow, deep hole as fast as possible.

Though adults may savor the tranquility of a day on the coast, youngsters want action. Clamming is one way to make sure that everybody gets what they want.

Here are some great places to go clamming:

1. BODEGA BAY

During a minus tide, the harbor will completely drain except for the channel, leaving acres of prime spots exposed, particularly on the western side. Horseneck clams are most abundant.

Contact: State Health Department's Shellfish Information Line, (800) 553-4133. **Locator:** BODEGA BAY (D0). **See featured trip page:** 212.

2. DILLON BEACH

This has become one of the most popular clamming spots around. You can camp here for $12 a night.

Contact: Lawson's Landing (any day but Wednesday), (707) 878-2443. **Locator:** TOMALES BAY (D0).

3. HALF MOON BAY

Just inside the south and north ends of the harbor, or rock jetty, are popular spots for locals and tourists alike.

Contact: Half Moon Bay, (650) 726-8819. **Locator:** HALF MOON BAY (E1b).

4. AÑO NUEVO

The rock and sand mix that cockles need is abundant in this area, but be careful not to actually dig on the AÑO NUEVO STATE RESERVE, where it is prohibited. You can dig north of the reserve between Pigeon Point and Franklin Point. To make sure you know the correct boundaries, call the number below.

Contact: Año Nuevo State Reserve, (650) 879-2025. **Locator:** Año Nuevo State Reserve (E1d). **See featured trip page:** 265.

5. Elkhorn Slough

Located just 20 miles south of Santa Cruz at Moss Landing, this area has a legendary reputation for its horseneck and Washington clams.

Contact: Department of Fish and Game, (831) 649-2870. **Locator:** Moss Landing (F1). **See featured trip page:** 244.

• Tom's Ratings •

The Top 12 Forests to Collect Firewood

In Northern California

You bring the great outdoors indoors every time you light a match to firewood that you have cut and split yourself. Part of the appeal is the sweet smell. As your fire burns, the mountain scent of acres of pines, firs, cedars, and madrones is captured in your living room. Then you notice a different kind of heat than what you get from a thermostat, a penetrating warmth that gives your home the feel of a cozy log cabin.

Toss another log on the fire and you get the satisfaction of seeing and feeling the results of your own labor, from that nice stack of wood out back to a quiet night in front of the fireplace.

From forest to fireplace, cutting your own firewood can be easy, fun, and save you hundreds of dollars in the process. (It costs only $10 to $20 to buy a firewood permit from the U.S. Forest Service, which allows you to cut two cords of wood from trees that are dead or down.) It can also add a special dimension to a weekend camping/fishing trip, even if you spend just a few hours at it, like in the middle of the day when the fishing goes flat. You end up bringing home a stack of firewood as well as memories of good times.

Fall is the ideal time to cut, because timber companies are putting the wraps on their summer logging operations. This means there are plenty of slash piles—logs judged unusable for building purposes—where you can cut a load of firewood. But no matter the time of year, it all makes for time well spent in the miles of mountain country that comprise our national forests.

In California, there are 95 ranger districts in the national forests—mountain land that is owned and used by the public. These forests are far different from national parks, such as Yosemite. A national park is considered something of a nature preserve, while a national forest is there to be used—to be fished, hunted, hiked, and to some extent, logged.

The national forests closest to the Bay Area are Mendocino (east of Ukiah), Tahoe (east of Marysville), Eldorado (east of Placerville), and Stanislaus (east of Sonora). They are close enough that you can combine a weekend camping trip with a session of firewood cutting and come up a winner.

If you plan on visiting more distant forests, such as Shasta-Trinity or Klamath, it is wise to finagle an extra day or two for your trip. Otherwise, you'll spend too much time driving and not enough time in the forest. Instead of fun, it will seem like work.

You should take your time, decide which national forest you want to visit, then buy a map for it. For maps, write to the U.S. Forest Service, Office of Information, 630 Sansome Street, San Francisco, CA 94111. These maps detail all backcountry roads, as well as hiking trails, streams, and lakes that you previously may not have known existed.

The next step is to call the district office and ask about firewood availability. In areas where a timber sale has been completed, dead and downed logs are often lying around, waiting to be cut up. In other spots, it can be slim pickings.

You must show up at the district office in person to purchase your firewood permit. While you're at it, the information officer will usually tell you precisely where to go. On the firewood trips I've taken, the Forest Service even provided free locator maps to pinpoint the best spots.

On one trip, it took little over an hour to fill my pickup truck, which left plenty of time to hike, fish, and explore the area.

If you don't have a pickup truck, you'll have to team up with somebody who does, rent one, or limit the size of your load. Occasionally, some Bay Area neighbors share in the cost of renting a large flatbed truck, head to the mountains as a team, and pool their permits, then cut, split, and stack enough wood for everyone involved.

Wood is measured by the cord, which describes a well-stacked pile that measures four by four by eight feet. You can fit a cord of wood in a standard-size pickup truck bed, but only if it is carefully stacked. Most people will settle for about half a cord, since a cord can weigh a lot, especially when wet.

With a wood-burning stove or fireplace insert, two to three cords is usually enough to get you through a winter in the Bay Area. People living in mountain areas use about six cords per year.

The savings? Your permit will get you two cords of firewood—which would cost anywhere from $250 to $450 in the Bay Area. In mountain areas, the price is about half that. The cost of hardwoods, such as oak or madrone, is usually 25 percent higher than softwoods like pine or cedar, because hardwoods burn hotter and longer. Mixing hardwoods and softwoods can make for the ideal fire—the pine will keep your flame, but the oak will throw off more heat and burn all night long.

You don't need much equipment, but you'll be lost without a few essentials. A good chain saw, of course, is a prerequisite, and most cost in the $200 range. Some rental companies have them available. My preference is for a chain saw with a 20- to 24-inch bar. Smaller ones, with 12- to 14-inch bars, are designed for limbing, not logging. The 36-inch saws are heavy and powerful, designed for professional tree fallers, and can be dangerous in the hands of a novice.

Homelite, McCulloch, Stihl, Echo, and Husquavarna are the most popular brands. I own two kinds, and members of my family own two other brands. All have performed well. *Consumer Reports* has completed an excellent safety study on them, describing how manufacturers have changed design to virtually eliminate kickback.

By state law, you must have a fire extinguisher and a shovel; it is also wise to wear heavy boots and leather gloves. A few wedges and a maul or sledge can be critical if you get your chain saw stuck in a log. They can also be used by a friend to split the logs while you're cutting rounds off a fallen tree.

The most important safety factor is to always make the trip with a friend and to alternate cutting and loading. Otherwise, fatigue gradually sets in and the cutter becomes vulnerable to a serious accident.

The most common error, which increases as fatigue mounts, is to look directly down at your cut. If the saw were to jam on a knot or kick back, your face would be directly in the path of the chain. Instead, always keep your head out of the plane of the chain saw. This is where a companion, watching for any errors, can keep the cutter out of trouble. Alone, you may not even be aware of the mistake.

Kickback, which occurs when a dull saw hits a tough spot or knot, is the most dangerous element of woodcutting. The best prevention is to keep your chain saw razor sharp.

You should split the logs with either a maul or a sledge and wedge, so the wood will dry and make a perfectly sized package for your fireplace. Cedar, pine, and fir can often be split in one swing of the maul, with no wedge necessary. After splitting, the wood will be cured as soon as two to four months, but burns best after sitting for a year. If the tree has been dead and down for a considerable amount of time, the wood may be ready to burn immediately.

It's a good team project—with one person cutting, another splitting, and another loading. In only an hour, you can have enough firewood cut, split, and stacked for many nights of warm fires.

Cutting with a group will also simplify your trip. Instead of problems, you will have solutions. Instead of work, getting a load of firewood will be a fun diversion on a weekend camping outing.

Contact: Obtain the U.S. Forest Service brochure on firewood cutting and a detailed map of the national forest you want to visit by writing to the U.S. Forest Service, Office of Information, 630 Sansome Street, San Francisco, CA 94111. Phone (415) 705-2874 for map prices. **Where to cut:** Stop in at the ranger district office, purchase a cutting permit, then receive directions pinpointing areas to cut your firewood. **What to bring:** A chain saw, gas, a can of two-cycle oil, 30-weight oil for the chain, sturdy boots, gloves, a fire extinguisher, and a shovel are mandatory. If your saw jams in a tree, a maul and a few wedges can get you free. If you flood the engine, a spark-plug wrench will come in handy. **Law of the land:** Cut only trees that are dead and down.

1. Eldorado National Forest

Location: East of Placerville. **Contact:** 100 Forni Road, Placerville, CA 95667. (530) 644-6048. **Locator:** Eldorado National Forest (D3).

2. Klamath National Forest

Directions: West of Yreka. **Contact:** 1312 Fairlane, Yreka, CA 96097. (530) 842-6131. **Locator:** Klamath National Forest (A1).

3. Lassen National Forest

Directions: East of Redding. **Contact:** Eagle Lake Ranger District, 477-050. Eagle Lake Road, Susanville, CA 96130; (530) 257-4188. Supervisor's Office, 55 South Sacramento Street, Susanville, CA 96130; (530) 257-2151. **Locator:** Lassen National Forest (B3).

4. Los Padres National Forest
Directions: South of Monterey. **Contact:** 6144 Calle Real, Goleta, CA 93111; (805) 683-6711.* **Locator:** Los Padres National Forest (F1).

Kirk Creek Campground #15, 17, 19, 22

5. Mendocino National Forest
Directions: Northeast of Ukiah. **Contact:** 875 North Humboldt Avenue, Willows, CA 95988; (530) 934-3316. **Locator:** Mendocino National Forest (C1).

6. Modoc National Forest
Directions: In the northeast corner of the state. **Contact:** 800 West 12th Street, Alturas, CA 96101; (530) 233-5811. **Locator:** Modoc National Forest (A3, B3, B4).

7. Plumas National Forest
Directions: Northwest of Lake Tahoe. **Contact:** P.O. Box 11500, Quincy, CA 95971; (530) 283-2050. **Locator:** Plumas National Forest (C3).

8. Shasta-Trinity National Forest
Directions: North and west of Redding. **Contact:** 2400 Washington Avenue, Redding, CA 96001; (530) 246-5222. **Locator:** Shasta-Trinity National Forest (B1).

9. Sierra National Forest
Directions: South of Yosemite National Park. **Contact:** 1600 Tollhouse Road, Clovis, CA 93611; (209) 487-5155.* **Locator:** Sierra National Forest (E4).

10. Six Rivers National Forest
Directions: Between Eureka and Crescent City. **Contact:** 1330 Bayshore Way, Eureka, CA 95501; (707) 442-1721. **Locator:** Six Rivers National Forest (A0).

11. Stanislaus National Forest
Directions: East of Sonora. **Contact:** 19777 Greenley Road, Sonora, CA 95370; (209) 532-3671.* **Locator:** Stanislaus National Forest (D4).

12. Tahoe National Forest
Directions: Northwest of Lake Tahoe. **Contact:** 631 Coyote Street, Nevada City, CA 95959-2250; (530) 265-4531. **Locator:** Tahoe National Forest (D4).

• TOM'S RATINGS •

The Top 5 Airports Offering Flying Lessons

In the San Francisco Bay Area

I looked down the runway and discovered I could barely breathe. I was just too excited. I thought I heard cannons going off in the cockpit, then I realized it was my heart pounding.

"Push the throttle forward all the way, and then when I tell you, pull back on the yoke."

It was flight instructor Rusty Ballinger assigned to my "orientation flight," where newcomers to aviation are provided with a demonstration flight in small airplanes in the hope that they will be tempted to try for a private pilot's license.

"Go ahead," Ballinger said with a smile. "Do it now."

I did as directed. The engine roared and the airplane began moving down the runway at San Carlos Airport, slowly at first, then faster and faster. I noticed how easy it seemed to use the rudder pedals to keep the plane pointed down the center line. But for a moment, it looked as though the runway wasn't long enough. The cannons fired again in my chest. Suddenly the airplane started flying seemingly all by itself. We lifted off, and in seconds we were above the jammed traffic on U.S. 101.

By now, I couldn't breathe at all. Breathe? Hey, I was gripping the yoke too hard to worry about breathing.

"See, the airplane wants to fly," Ballinger said. "It's not so difficult. Let it climb up to 800 feet, then head on over toward the DUMBARTON BRIDGE."

"Take control, take control," I ordered Ballinger.

"Why?" he asked. "What's the matter?"

"I have to breathe."

Finally, with Ballinger flying the plane, I took my first genuine breath of air since climbing into the cockpit. I looked at my hands and there were large, red creases in each from the death grip I had on the yoke. But then, after a few deep breaths, I gazed down over the South Bay, and it didn't seem so dangerous after all. Within a few minutes, I was breathing almost normally and took the yoke again.

"You see, flying gives you a new perspective on the world and it's safe," Ballinger said. "I have over 12,000 hours in the air. The most dangerous part of flying is driving to the airport."

Orientation flights such as this are offered at several general aviation airports around the Bay Area as a way to introduce people to flying. The flight generally lasts about an hour, costs around $35, and is available at small airports in SAN CARLOS, PALO ALTO, NOVATO, HAYWARD, and LIVERMORE.

Anybody can do it by simply making a phone call and setting up an appointment. Even if you decide not to continue on toward a pilot's license, that first flight is an exhilarating experience.

A week later, participants often find that they are telling so many people about it that they decide to do it again. And again. And again. Until suddenly they discover they are reading flight books, studying aviation law, scanning charts, and dreaming of flight destinations. That's what happened to me. A year after my orientation flight, I was handed my private pilot's certificate after passing written and oral tests and a flight check with an inspector from the Federal Aviation Administration.

The cost of flying can be very expensive or very cheap, depending on how you go about it. Obtaining a private license often requires $3,000 to $4,000 in plane-rental fees and an additional $1,000 in private tutoring fees. But it can cost a lot less. The most economical way is to take a ground class in flying at a community college, available in evening sessions once a week. In these courses, the final exam is the FAA written test. That done, when you start flying you won't be paying top-dollar fees to learn basics that are covered in the low-cost ground school.

The plane-rental fee can also be reduced to next to nothing. Instead of renting a plane for $40 to $50 an hour, it's become increasingly common for several student aviators to pool their funds and buy a small trainer for $12,000 to $18,000. After getting their licenses, they sell the plane to another pool of students for the same price and recoup their entire investment.

Those who take a ground-school course at a community college and join forces with other students to buy a trainer, can earn a pilot's license for just over $1,000 in instructor (no solos until checked off) and insurance fees.

In return, you get a wonderful view of the world and a fast way to travel.

From a pilot's seat, the Bay Area looks like a band of connected cities on the flats, surrounded by mountain wilderness. Lakes are everywhere—there are more than 60, including at least a dozen large, beautiful reservoirs that are off-limits to visitors. The bay itself looks like the Mediterranean Sea, speckled with half a dozen islands.

And fast? From SAN CARLOS, you can fly to LIVERMORE in just 15 minutes. It's worth the trip just to look down on the traffic jams on Interstate 580 as you sail by at 120 knots. And get this: even in the slowest plane, you can reach MONTEREY in about 45 minutes.

To keep it safe, student pilots are only allowed to perform skills they have mastered with an instructor aboard, and they also must demonstrate a knowledge of aviation law and associated subjects before they move on to each successive step in the process.

On my first flight, we flew out over the East Bay hills, checking the water levels at DEL VALLE, CALAVERAS, and SAN ANTONIO reservoirs. Then we practiced a few basic turning maneuvers, a meager attempt to coordinate aileron and rudder control. Finally, we headed back over the bay, getting clearance from the SAN CARLOS control tower to put the plane in sequence in the landing pattern.

"Tell me," Ballinger said, "Isn't flying the greatest feeling in the world?"

"Well, not really," I replied. "It's actually the second greatest feeling in the world."

"Then what's the first?" he asked.

"That's easy," I answered. "Landing."

1. SAN CARLOS AIRPORT
Contact: West Valley Flying Club, San Carlos Airport, (650) 595-5912. **Locator:** SAN CARLOS (E1b).

2. PALO ALTO AIRPORT
Contact: Palo Alto Flying Club, Palo Alto Airport, (650) 494-6946. **Locator:** PALO ALTO (E1b).

3. NOVATO AIRPORT
Contact: North Bay Aviation, Gnoss Field, Novato, (415) 899-1677. **Locator:** NOVATO (E1a).

4. HAYWARD AIRPORT
Contact: California Airways, (510) 887-7686, or Flightcraft, (510) 785-5511. **Locator:** HAYWARD (E1c).

5. LIVERMORE AIRPORT
Contact: Ahart Aviation, Livermore Airport, (925) 449-2142. **Locator:** LIVERMORE (E2).

• TOM'S RATINGS •

THE TOP 14 PLACES TO FLY KITES

In Northern California

Some might figure I'm the last guy in the world who would write a story about kite flying. After all, I'd be more apt to fish on SAN FRANCISCO BAY, search out a secret waterfall, or climb MOUNT WHITNEY, right? Of course. The End. Right?

Wrong. Actually it's just the beginning. You see, when I was eight years old (when I first grew my beard and climbed Half Dome), I got a kite so high that it showed up on FAA radar scopes in OAKLAND and I was nearly arrested for flying an unauthorized aircraft. That's right, champion kite flyer.

I remember this every April because there is no better time to fly a kite in the Bay Area, when winds come hurtling down across the North Pacific and get sucked right through the GOLDEN GATE as well as through the gaps in foothill ridges. It's a once-a-year chance to put a kite practically in orbit.

There are some tricks to getting a kite to fly right, as well as a little local knowledge needed to learn the best spots.

If you are willing to settle for nothing special, there are no secrets. Just buy your typical kite, put on a knotted four-foot tail from a rag strip, get some light string, and send it up on your typical windy April afternoon.

But if you are not willing to settle, a whole new experience awaits you.

If you really want to send a kite into orbit, the wind needs to howl. Your best chance for that is to pick one of the spots suggested at the end of this story.

The next thing you need is to make sure your kite is very sturdy, not a cheap one made out of thin paper. And note that in high winds, you will need to attach a longer tail to keep the kite steady as she blows. If you ever see a kite doing dive-bombs and up-shoots, that's usually because the tail is too short. But that much is easy.

You can take it a step further and buy a bigger kite, the best being the big box-style versions. They look something like a box on each end of four skinny balsa-wood dowels. For my first foray into unmanned aviation, I built a giant custom double-box kite that was nearly five feet high (taller than I was). The problem with the bigger kites is that on an average day, especially in the morning, there isn't enough wind to get them off the ground.

With a big kite or very windy conditions, you will quickly notice that once the kite is airborne, the pull of it is strong enough to make a small person feel like they are about to be flown to the moon. In addition, the tiny diameter kite string can stretch to the limit and can seem very sharp to the touch—or worse, flat-out break and ruin the day.

Even at age eight, I started experimenting with alternatives. What ended up working best was to use a large fishing rod and an ocean reel loaded with 350 or 400 yards of fishing line. There seemed no limit to how high the kite might fly in the sky.

On the day the federal authorities came looking for me, I had my big box kite out more than 1,000 feet. As they approached, that little eight-year-old with a beard figured out he was in trouble, so naturally he cut the line. Then they asked him what he was doing.

"Fishing, of course," I answered.

"Fishing!" an official guy responded. "Fishing for what?"

"Why, for flying fish, of course," I said. "I had a big one on, but right when you came up, it broke the line and got away."

I learned my lesson that day at PACIFICA: kites should be kept 500 feet or lower, and not be flown near airports. That's to keep them clear of airplanes, which are permitted to fly no lower than 500 feet above the ground in most areas.

But getting a kite way up there, so far that it looks like nothing but a tiny speck in the sky, is what makes it so much fun.

Kites used to be quite cheap, made out of paper and balsa rods. While the cheapest still cost under $5, the good ones, the diamond or box kites, can run over $20. They're constructed of rip-stop nylon these days, and if the string breaks while flying one of these, a kid is out a small fortune instead of milkshake money.

The best spots for kite flying are places where you can run in any direction to get it started, where the wind is strong and the surroundings are pretty.

1. Marina Green

Marina Green in San Francisco is the capital of kite flying in the western world. It's pretty with expansive Bay views, and gets great winds right through the Golden Gate.

Contact: Golden Gate National Recreation Area, Fort Mason, (415) 556-0560. **Locator:** San Francisco (E1b). **See featured trip page:** 222.

2. Milagra Ridge

Contact: Golden Gate National Recreation Area, Fort Mason, (415) 561-4323 or (415) 556-0560. **Locator**: Pacifica (E1b).

3. Sweeney Ridge

Contact: Golden Gate National Recreation Area, Fort Mason, (415) 561-4323 or (415) 556-0560. **Locator:** San Bruno (E1b). **See featured trip page:** 85.

4. Russian Ridge Open Space Preserve

Contact: Midpeninsula Regional Open Space District, (650) 691-1200. **Locator:** Woodside (E1b). **See featured trip page:** 82.

5. Windy Hill Open Space Preserve

Contact: Midpeninsula Regional Open Space District, (650) 691-1200. **Locator:** Palo Alto (E1b). **See featured trip page:** 82.

6. Shoreline Regional Park

Contact: Shoreline Regional Park, City of Mountain View, (650) 903-6392. **Locator:** Mountain View (E1d).

7. Hawk Hill

Contact: Golden Gate National Recreation Area, Marin Headlands, (415) 331-1540. **Locator:** Marin Headlands (E1a). **See featured trip page:** 59.

8. Bolinas Ridge

Contact: Golden Gate National Recreation Area, Fort Mason, (415) 663-1092. **Locator:** Bolinas Ridge (E1a). **See featured trip page:** 60.

9. Inverness Ridge

Contact: Point Reyes National Seashore, Bear Valley Visitor Center, (415) 663-1092.**Locator:** Point Reyes National Seashore (E1a). **See featured trip page:** 67.

10. O'Rourke's Bench

Contact: Mount Tamalpais State Park, (415) 388-2070. **Locator:** Mount Tamalpais State Park (E1a). **See featured trip page:** 62.

The East Bay hills hold many good spots, virtually any ridge or gap between hills where the wind whistles past from onshore breezes out of the west. The best are:

11. Franklin Ridge

Contact: East Bay Regional Parks District, (510) 635-0135 extension 2200. **Locator:** Martinez (E1c). **See featured trip page:** 89.

12. San Pablo Ridge

Contact: East Bay Regional Parks District, (510) 635-0135 extension 2200. **Locator:** Tilden Regional Park (E1c). **See featured trip page:** 100.

13. Pleasanton Ridge Regional Park

Contact: East Bay Regional Parks District, (510) 635-0135 extension 2200. **Locator:** Pleasanton (E2).

14. Coyote Hills Regional Park

Contact: East Bay Regional Parks District, (510) 635-0135 extension 2200. **Locator:** Dumbarton Bridge (E1c).

Of course, most any beach can be a great spot to pick up coastal winds. The paradox at the beach, however, is that with a wind out of the west, the kite will fly over land rather than the ocean, which seems backward for the location. Maybe in heaven, that will be turned around.

• Tom's Ratings •

The Top 4 Places to Rockhound

In Northern California

One Christmas 30 years ago, my dad announced that he had a special family present. Suddenly, he had the immediate attention of five kids and Mom, something of a miracle in itself.

The present was then opened by several of us, and we discovered, at first to our collected chagrin, a box with the words "Rock Polisher." My brother figured it was some kind of a joke, that a different gift was inside the box, but no, inside was this little barrel-like unit with a small motor to make it turn. Yep, a rock polisher, to our disbelief, and no, it was not intended as a joke.

The next thing we knew, all seven of us, was that we were suddenly going out on rock-finding expeditions. We discovered that the Bay Area can be an excellent setting for such an adventure. That is because there are several places where, with a little bit of detective work, most people can collect some fascinating samples—primarily nonprecious stones that can be cut and polished to look like gemstones. Thirty years later, many of us still keep an eye out for unusual rocks while hiking.

Right from the beginning, my dad's favorite was poppy jasper, a brilliant, shining stone, usually brown and often with many tints of gold and red, that looks like it's embedded with a small flower.

Other nonprecious gemstones in the Bay Area that make great finds include different kinds of quartz, agate, cinnabar, and limestone with small embedded seashells. Outside of the Bay Area, you are likely to find varieties of obsidian and arrowheads in volcanic areas near Mount Lassen and Mount Shasta, quartz in gold mining areas in the Sierra foothills, and all manner of glacially sculpted granite in the high Sierra range.

The Bay Area can be such a good place for rockhounding because of the region's ancient geologic history. Even as an 11-year-old, I can remember my dad explaining this:

"First, you've got all of these earthquake fault lines here," he told the group of five youngsters, all of us actually listening. "The faults have moved tremendous amounts of earth, literally miles over eons. That has placed a lot of different kinds of material in our local area.

"Not only that, but the Bay Area has been below sea level and under water several times," he explained. "We can go to the Peninsula foothills and see evidence that it was under water, such as the small shells of all kinds of sea creatures embedded in limestone, which used to be the sea-bed. So when you think of the Bay Area, and you think of rocks, you have to think of what has been here over millions of years, not just in modern times."

Some 30 years since those first instructions, my dad still keeps an eye out for unusual rocks on his hikes, especially during the rainy season. That is because the best time to make a discovery is after a good hard rain. The storm runoff will wash away loose dirt material, unveiling hidden rocks. This is especially true at areas in the foothills where there have been road cuts and hiking trails (that have been recently cut), along streams and in gullies.

1. Jasper Ridge

My dad's favorite spot is called Jasper Ridge, located in the foothills of PALO ALTO on Stanford land, with access off of the Foothill Expressway. From a distance, it looks like nothing more than hilly grasslands with a few oaks sprinkled about. But close up, a different world becomes evident.

"You have to keep your eyes open, hike around, and look for where there has been a recent wash, where rain has removed the soil and exposed fresh rock," he says. "Sure, there's a lot of average stones out there, but jasper will catch your eye because of its color. It's striking—usually reddish brown."

The best way to become a rock hound is simply to start visiting the Bay Area's 250 parks, keeping a lookout for unusual rocks while you hike. That is how most people get hooked on the adventure. All it takes is one find and you'll be looking for life.

Locator: PALO ALTO (E1b).

2. Clear Lake

At CLEAR LAKE, one hiker actually found rare crystals that resembled diamonds.

Locator: CLEAR LAKE (D1). **See featured trip page:** 362.

3. Jamestown

Near JAMESTOWN, another hiker found a giant gold nugget. My dad, however, is happy whenever he finds some jasper. One reason for that is because jasper, as with agate, the two most common finds, can shine up so brilliantly.

Doing so is easy with a rock polisher. You simply put the rock in the barrel, add polishing grit, and turn it on. It's a three-stage process that takes a few weeks (though it can seem like an eternity), where you use different grades of polishing grit, almost like sharpening a knife, and then end up with a beautiful nonprecious gemstone. The polishing action is much like that of a mountain stream, which repeatedly turns over rocks. Hence, stream gravel is so smooth.

If you find a large rock, big enough to make into several articles, you can find rock shops in the Bay Area that will cut up large pieces of raw material to specific sizes for jewelry or even split a big chunk into bookends. In addition, maps, books, and classes are available.

However, sometimes the best way to make a find is to just go hiking and find gems by accident. That is exactly the strategy used by my dad.

Locator: JAMESTOWN (E3).

4. Russian River

"I was walking along the banks of the RUSSIAN RIVER near CLOVERDALE, when I looked down and saw a shiny color, red, about the size of a quarter, right where the water was lapping at the shore," he said. "It looked like jasper. I started digging and it got bigger and bigger and bigger. The piece ended up being two feet across, weighed more than 100 pounds, and took two loggers to lift it and put it in a wheelbarrow."

It was the find of a lifetime. He turned a piece of that jasper into a beautiful glimmering heart that my mom still wears on a silver chain.

Locator: RUSSIAN RIVER (D0). **See featured trip page:** 324.

• TOM'S RATINGS •

THE TOP 4 PLACES TO SKY WATCH

In the San Francisco Bay Area and Beyond

There have been nights when I've seen the sky look like a spectacle from Star Wars, other nights when the shooting stars resembled snowflakes. It was the Perseids meteor shower, and the first time I saw it, there was a shooting star every 30 to 40 seconds for two hours, sometimes even bursts of them, one after another.

Ever since then, I've kept track of the significant meteor showers and I often schedule my camping trips during them. In the Bay Area, the best places to see shooting stars are mountaintops that put you above the glare of lights, including:

1. MOUNT DIABLO

Locator: MOUNT DIABLO (E1c). **See featured trip page:** 93.

2. MONTARA MOUNTAIN

Locator: MONTARA MOUNTAIN (E1b). **See featured trip page:** 74.

3. MOUNT HAMILTON

Locator: MOUNT HAMILTON (E2).

4. MOUNT TAMALPAIS

Locator: MOUNT TAMALPAIS (E1a). **See featured trip page:** 62.

Outside of the Bay Area, any mountain ridge or dark hilltop will do, as long as you can view the sky free of obstructions and without lights reducing your night vision.

The most active time period for meteor showers is often after midnight in the summer, but I've learned that the show will sometimes start at 10 p.m. and be simply astonishing an hour later.

Here are the best meteor showers, which appear each year on the same dates, though they can vary dramatically in strength from year to year:

January 1–6, peak date January 3. The Quadrantids shower is best viewed from midnight to dawn. There are 40 to 150 meteors per hour, sometimes more than twice that. Usually medium speed, blue, with long silver trails. Look to the north.

APRIL 18–25

Peak date April 22. The Lyrids shower is best viewed at 4 a.m. There are 10 to 20 meteors per hour. Usually medium-swift speed, rich in faint meteors, with some bright ones that leave long trails. Look to the northeast.

APRIL 21–MAY 12

Peak date May 4. The Et Aquarids shower is best viewed from 2 a.m. to dawn. There are 10 to 40 meteors per hour. Very swift, some yellow with long, glowing tails. Look to the south.

JULY 5–AUGUST 12

Peak dates July 8, 16, and 26, and August 2. The Capricornids shower is best viewed from midnight to dawn. There are five to 30 meteors per hour.

Slow, sparse, but bright yellow with fireballs. Look to the south.

July 15–August 20

Peak date July 29. The Delta Aquarius shower, with its meteors overhead at 2 a.m. There are 10 to 35 per hour, often yellow, some bright, medium to medium-slow. Look to the south.

July 23–August 20

Peak date August 12. This is one of the best of the year. The Perseids shower, with meteors increasing in intensity toward dawn. There are 50 to 100 per hour, swift with some fireballs. Faint ones are white or yellow, bright ones are green, orange, or red, with one-third leaving sometimes-spectacular trails. Look to the northeast.

October 7–10

Peak date October 9. The Draconids shower is best viewed from 9 p.m. to midnight. There are zero to 10,000 meteors per hour, with medium-slow comets. In 1946 it was one of the most astonishing meteor showers of the century. Look to the north.

October–November 7

Peak date October 20. The Orionids shower, with meteors overhead at 4 a.m. There are 10 to 40 per hour, very swift, some bright, mostly faint. About 20 percent are fireballs that leave trails. Look to the south.

November 3–13

Peak date November 5. The Taurids shower is usually overhead at 1 a.m., with five to 15 meteors per hour. All are slow and bright, with many fireballs, some fragments and multiples. Rises in the east.

November 14–20

Peak date November 17. The Leonids shower is overhead at 6 a.m. but good from midnight to dawn. There are five to 20 per hour in normal years, but in 1966 some 250,000 were seen in one hour—the greatest shower in modern history. These are the fastest known meteors, many bright, some fireballs, greenish or blue, half of them leaving trails. Look to the east.

December 4–16

Peak date December 13. The Geminids shower is overhead at 2 a.m., good from dusk to dawn. It's a favorite, with 50 to 100 per hour; medium speed, bright, some fireballs, mostly white, 25 percent yellow and a few blue, orange, red, or green. The show is more colorful before midnight. Rises from due east.

December 17–24

Peak date December 22. The Ursids shower has about 10 to 15 per hour, medium speed, mostly faint. Shows out of the Little Dipper to the north.

• Tom's Ratings •

The Top 10 Swimming Holes

In the San Francisco Bay Area

A small leap and a big splash into a lake or stream in the great outdoors is the fastest way known to wash away every curable care.

It's nothing like jumping into a swimming pool. When you take the plunge, the cool, fresh water envelops you in a sea of bubbles, quickly transporting most swimmers to a state of euphoria. The water is clean and free of chemicals, the bottom may be off in never-never land, and as for temperature, it can vary wildly, even in the same lake or stream.

There are dozens of lakes and streams that are perfect for swimming, including many in the Bay Area. My top 10 include a remote hike-to pond, a little-known river with a temporary dam, and several small, warm lakes. Regardless of where you go, you'll experience the same phenomenon.

When swimming in a lake, you will discover that the water temperature can vary, even from foot to foot. You can be relaxing in cool water, then take a few strokes and suddenly discover a pocket of very warm water. The surprise changes can be weird but wondrous. One time at Hot Creek in MAMMOTH it was quite warm at my shoulders, almost scalding hot at my chest, cool at my hips, and icy cold at my feet—an overall bizarre sensation.

In the Bay Area, the temperature of the water changes according to weather, shade, and wind conditions. Of course, water in sunny, shallow coves is warmer than in shaded, deep canyons. In the mountains, water temperature can also depend on elevation and whether or not it receives direct snowmelt. In rivers below reservoirs, it can also depend on whether water is released from the top (warm) or bottom of dams (cold).

Anyone swimming in lakes or streams should first take safety precautions. Make absolutely certain the depth of water is safe prior to jumping in; in my many years as an outdoors writer, I have heard too many terrible stories of people who jumped head first into shallow pools and broke their necks, rendering them paralyzed for life.

In addition, always keep a float cushion with you or wear a life vest. Sometimes it is fun to wear a life vest and just float around like a cork. Remember that compared to what you are likely accustomed to, you will be expending more energy, in colder water, and perhaps at a higher elevation. When you get tired, a float cushion or life vest will give you a chance to rest without sinking. In addition, parents should never allow children to swim in lakes or streams without careful guidance and never, absolutely never, without a life vest, float cushion, or air mattress.

That said, here are the best places to take a flying leap at ecstasy. Note that if the lake is in a park, an entrance fee is usually charged.

1. Lake Sonoma

Of the lakes on the outskirts of the Bay Area, this is by far the best for swimming. The Dry Creek arm extends nine miles north, where there are boat-in campsites and speed limits to keep the water quiet. Temperatures are hot and the water is warm, but you can cool off just the same.

Contact: Lake Sonoma Marina, (707) 433-2200; U.S. Army Corps of Engineers, (707) 433-9483. **Locator:** LAKE SONOMA (D0). **See featured trip page:** 322.

2. Bass Lake

This little coastal pond is a perfect hideaway for swimming. Reaching it requires hiking an hour or so north from the Palomarin Trailhead, located northwest of BOLINAS. It is largely undiscovered, warm in August and September.

Contact: Point Reyes National Seashore, (415) 663-1092. **Locator:** POINT REYES NATIONAL SEASHORE (E1a). **See featured trip pages:** 67 and 166.

3. Cull Canyon Reservoir

This little, narrow lake covers just 18 acres and gets less use than the other lakes available for swimming in the East Bay. But the water is warm and a

1.5-acre swimming lagoon is available, ideal for families with small children. A snack bar, a changing area, and a picnic area are available.

Contact: Cull Canyon Regional Park, (510) 537-2240; East Bay Regional Park District, (510) 635-0135 extension 2200. **Locator:** CASTRO VALLEY (E1c).

4. Del Valle Reservoir

DEL VALLE is a big lake, 750 acres with 16 miles of shoreline. It features two swimming beaches, complete with lifeguards. This is also one of only five of the Bay Area's 44 lakes with a campground.

Contact: Del Valle Regional Park, (925) 373-0332; Del Valle Marina, (925) 449-5201; East Bay Regional Park District, (510) 635-0135 extension 2200. **Locator:** DEL VALLE RESERVOIR (E2).

5. Don Castro Reservoir

HAYWARD can feel like the hottest place on Earth, that is until you jump into Don Castro. At 23 acres, this is a small but pretty lake that attracts swimmers to its lagoon and clear, warm blue waters. A large shallow area is roped off for children; a snack stand and changing rooms are available.

Contact: Don Castro Regional Park, (510) 538-1148; East Bay Regional Park District, (510) 635-0135 extension 2200. **Locator:** HAYWARD (E1c).

6. Lake Anza

Lake Anza is nestled just over the hill from BERKELEY in TILDEN REGIONAL PARK, where the afternoons are hot and the water is just right. The ridge keeps the lake sheltered from bay breezes, yet open to the sun. Ample parking and picnic grounds are nearby.

Contact: East Bay Regional Park District, (510) 635-0135 extension 2200. **Locator:** TILDEN REGIONAL PARK (E1c). **See featured trip page:** 100.

7. Lake Temescal

This little lake features warm water, a sandy beach, and a roped-off area for children. It is conveniently located near the intersection of Highways 13 and 24. Facilities include a concession stand and a changing room.

Contact: East Bay Regional Park District, (510) 635-0135 extension 2200; Lake Temescal Regional Park, (510) 635-0135 extension 2581. **Locator:** OAKLAND (E1c).

8. Shadow Cliffs Lake

This 80-acre lake is a former pond for a rock quarry, so the water quality is quite good. Though the lakeshore is steep on two sides, there is a sandy beach near the park entrance and, for a bonus, a water slide is available. There are also grassy picnic sites.

Contact: Shadow Cliffs Marina, (925) 846-3000; East Bay Regional Park District, (510) 635-0135 extension 2200. **Locator:** PLEASANTON (E1c).

9. Pescadero Creek

A little-known tidbit is that PESCADERO CREEK north of LA HONDA has a temporary dam every summer, creating a swimming lagoon in Memorial County Park. It features cold water and two sandy beaches, one above and one below the dam. A bonus is that the park has a campground (first come, first served—always full on weekends) and good hiking trails.

Contact: Memorial County Park, (650) 879-0238; San Mateo County Parks, (650) 363-4020. **Locator:** PESCADERO CREEK (E1d).

10. Hot Creek

There is no place anywhere quite like Hot Creek, located on the eastern SIERRA just south of MAMMOTH. Hot Creek is actually quite cold, but is heated up by boiling hot springs. That allows you to wade in and float about, feeling the strange shifts in water temperature as hot merges with cold. The turnoff is located near the Mammoth Airport on U.S. 395, with a large parking area at the hot springs.

Contact: Mammoth Lakes Visitors Bureau, (800) 367-6572. **Locator:** MAMOTH (E5). **See featured trip page:** 237.

• FEATURED TRIP •

★ Big Bend Hot Springs

Rated: Northern California's Cheapest Hot Springs

Ninety-five percent of the people go to 5 percent of the recreation areas in California, and my mission is to help some of them join the 5 Percent Club—that is, the five percent of us who explore the state's hidden and beautiful spots.

Find some place way out there that nobody knows about. Make sure there's something real special about it. And make sure it's pretty, maybe with a lake or a stream, maybe a campground nearby. That's my job. Nice work, eh?

Well, my ramblings took me to the town of BIG BEND, population 200, "including dogs," set in remote eastern Shasta County.

Nobody knows about BIG BEND, right? Yet it has one of the most spectacular hot springs in America, with three-tiered pools overlooking the beautiful PIT RIVER. In addition, a small, private campground operates near the hot springs, and the adjacent PIT RIVER is one of the 10 best trout streams in California. Just seven miles away is Iron Canyon Reservoir, an outstanding trout fishing lake, which offers a free campground and the company of a few bald eagles and osprey that go on patrol every evening.

It's a long drive to get here, but hey, I'm just following orders. From SAN FRANCISCO, you drive 221 miles to REDDING, then turn east on Highway 299. From there, drive 40 miles (past the area burned by the huge forest fire a few years back), then turn north on Big Bend Road and continue 17 miles to town.

Town? When you reach BIG BEND, your first reaction will probably be, "Is this it?" On arrival, it doesn't look like much: Set in oak woodlands, it's got a small market, a U.S. Forest Service ranger station, a trailer park, and a few dogs. That's it. Driving through town takes about 20 seconds.

But the adventure starts upon a left turn at the little wood sign for Big Bend Hot Springs. The hot springs are on a bluff overlooking the river, a beautiful setting. The tubs are made of rock and concrete, designed in tiers so the water flows in miniature waterfalls from tub to tub before tumbling to the river. The hot mineral water is tapped from a deep lava tube, entering the tubs at 175 degrees. It is then cooled to your exact comfort level by separate water piped in from adjacent Indian Springs Creek.

Swimsuits are required, and no alcohol or drugs are permitted. But there is no limit to the pleasurable sensations available if you soak in the tubs for 15 or 20 minutes, letting the 105-degree mineral water permeate your body, then suddenly jump into the nearby 45-degree PIT RIVER.

A bonus is that just a quarter mile away, right beside the river, there are four more "tubs," actually shallow pools dug out in a boulder field, just two to 10 feet from the stream. One is so close that you can literally roll out of the pool and into the river. No water temperature adjustments are possible here, of course. While the water is tolerable during morning or evening, in the afternoon it is practically hot enough to cook a lobster.

The climate is more tolerable, typically hovering around 85 or 90 degrees in the afternoon, 50 at night. It is perfect for camping, boating, and fishing. Nearby Iron Canyon Reservoir is available for that.

Iron Canyon is a fine trout lake, producing good catches of rainbow and brown trout. Deadlun Campground, named after Deadlun Creek, sits at the west end of the lake in a dense forest. Campsites are free, but no piped water is available. For campers with trailers or RVs, a small trailer park with hookups is in BIG BEND.

Another option is fishing the PIT RIVER, a beautiful freestone stream where dozens of trout thrive in every pool. It is a particular favorite for fly fishers during the evening rise, with easy access near the Big Bend Bridge, which crosses the stream.

If you want to join the 5 Percent Club, BIG BEND is one of the places where you can sign up.

Directions: To Big Bend: From San Francisco, drive 221 miles up Interstate 5 to Redding. Turn east on Highway 299 and drive 40 miles. Turn north on Big Bend Road and drive 17 miles. The turnoff for Big Bend Hot Springs is on the left side, adjacent to the town's market. To reach Iron Canyon Reservoir from Big Bend, continue over the Big Bend Bridge and travel seven miles, then turn left at either the sign marking the turnoff for the boat ramp, or one mile later, at the sign marking the turnoff for Deadlun Camp. **Campgrounds:** A private campground is available at Big Bend Hot Springs. The fee includes unlimited use of the hot springs. The Pit River Trailer Park is located in Big Bend. A free camp (Deadlun), with no piped water provided, is available at Iron Canyon Reservoir. **Contact:** For a free brochure, contact Big Bend Hot Springs, P.O. Box 186, Big Bend, CA 96011; (530) 337-6680. For information about the Pit River Trailer Park, phone (530) 337-6254. For information about Deadlun Campground, phone the U.S. Forest Service, Shasta Lake Ranger District, (530) 275-1587. For general information about the area, try the Shasta Cascade Wonderland Association, (800) 474-2782. **Locator:** BIG BEND (B3).

• FEATURED TRIP •

★ CALISTOGA MUD BATHS

Rated: Northern California's Best Hot Springs

The first time you imagine taking a mud bath, you are apt to get all kinds of crazy ideas about what it's like. Then when you go to CALISTOGA and actually do it, you find out that most of them are true. As you slowly sink into the hot black ooze, you feel like you are being enveloped by a giant sponge. Your body submerges deeper, then an attendant covers you right up to your Adam's apple. There are several immediate sensations: the 100-degree heat, the weight of 100 pounds of muck, the smell of peat, and a generally strange feeling of euphoria.

After five minutes, your body has a strange glow from the heat and you might start to feel light-headed. Two minutes later, you might become a little short of breath as the toxins begin leaving your body and sweat pours from your forehead. Ten minutes into the process, you start thinking you can't take it anymore—you need to escape. Your breathing is short; the heat is all-encompassing.

Finally, you surrender. Then you find out this strange journey has only begun.

After the mud bath, comes the rejuvenating treatment called "The Works," 10 minutes in a tub full of 106- to 108-degree mineral water, a sit in the steam room, a towel wrap, and a massage. At that point, what you will probably need is somebody to cart you away in a wheelbarrow, because after all of this, you will feel like a happy, amorphous blob. It's a good feeling.

This is the treatment at Dr. Wilkinson's Hot Springs, one of the oldest mineral spas in CALISTOGA. Your first visit might be out of curiosity, the need for stress relief, or a search for a cure for rheumatism. Regardless of what gets you here, you'll leave feeling like you are starting a whole new life. And the glow stays with you for days.

"People originally came here looking for relief from rheumatic ailments," said Dr. John Wilkinson, founder and owner of the spa. "Nowadays, the main reason they come is because of stress." They return because they find the treatment works pretty well.

CALISTOGA, located at the north end of the NAPA wine valley, is the nation's headquarters for mud baths and hot springs. Why here? Because submerged in the earth under this small town are several boiling cauldrons of mineral water. The mineral spas tap that water, and in turn, are able to offer its unique powers to the public.

"It's like a giant tea kettle under this building," Wilkinson said. "Imagine a boiling pool of 250-degree water. That's what it's like down there. Our biggest problem is cooling it down before we use it."

A large mineral spa with 103- or 104-degree bubbling mineral water is available. But when you sign up for "The Works," the water goes into the tub much hotter, around 107 or 108 degrees. Two larger pools are also available at Wilkinson's, one that makes you feel like you're soaking in a big bathtub, the other set at swimming pool temperature.

At the least, just soaking in mineral water will take the fight out of you. At the most, it will leave you feeling like a new person. Most folks walk out feeling somewhere in between.

According to Wilkinson, soaking in hot mineral water helps rid your skin of toxins. The effect is compounded in the mud bath, in which the "mud" is actually composed of Canadian peat and Calistoga volcanic ash mixed with hot mineral water. Topping it off with a session in the steam room seems to purify your entire body. Although you sweat out fluids profusely during the experience, cold carbonated mineral water is provided so you won't get dehydrated.

"The Works" has become so popular that a reservation is usually required, even on weekdays.

Ironically, sometimes it is not the

mud bath or mineral spa that ends up as the most memorable feature. Instead, the towel wrap often has the greatest impact. You are wrapped in a towel and blankets, with an ice cold towel on your forehead—just after having finished the mud bath, mineral spa, and steam room. As you lie there, you feel as if you are in the midst of some phenomenal sensory experience. It's because you are.

The mud bath itself is a relatively small, square tub filled with dark, bubbling goo. As you start sinking into the stuff, it feels kind of like wallowing in warm, shallow quicksand. Then, when submerged to your neck, you gain a sense of weightlessness, as if there are no sides or bottom to the tub and you are floating in space, suspended in hot mud.

If you think it might be a strange experience to find yourself sitting in the stuff, well, you're right. But if you want to feel like a whole new person, this is one of the best ways there is to do it.

Directions: Take Interstate 80 north to the Highway 29 cutoff to Napa. Turn north on Highway 29 and continue past St. Helena to Calistoga. **Spas:** Dr. Wilkinson's Hot Springs, (707) 942-4102; International Spa, (707) 942-6122; Lavender Hill Spa, (707) 942-4495; Roman Spa, (707) 942-4441; Calistoga Spa and Hot Springs, (707) 942-6269; Village Inn and Spa, (707) 942-0991; Pine Street Inn and Eurospa, (707) 942-6829; Golden Haven Hot Springs, (707) 942-6793; Indian Springs, (707) 942-4913; Nance's Hot Springs, (707) 942-6211; Lincoln Avenue Spa, (707) 942-5298; Mount View Hotel and Spa, (707) 942-5789. **Fees:** Packages typically include a mud bath, mineral whirlpool bath, mineral steam room, and blanket wrap. Massages can be added for an extra charge. Phone individual spas for price lists. Mud bath packages range from $30 to $100. **Contact:** Calistoga Chamber of Commerce, (707) 942-6333. If you have time (allow three weeks), ask them to send you a free visitors guide to Calistoga. **Locator:** CALISTOGA (D1).

• FEATURED TRIP •

✶ HALF MOON BAY HORSEBACK RIDES

Rated: The Top 25 Hikes, 2; The Top 5 Places to Beach Camp, 108; The Top 10 Spots to Go on a Date, 182; The Top 13 Covered Bridges, 194

If you dream of the days when people roamed the open rangeland watching sunsets from a saddle, there's a horse waiting for you in the coastside town of HALF MOON BAY. You can slip a cowboy boot in a stirrup, saddle up, and literally ride off into the sunset.

You don't have to be JOHN WAYNE, and even if you have never ridden before, the cowfolk at Sea Horse and Friendly Acres Ranches will find a horse to match your ability. For small children, they provide a special pony corral, where youngsters can spend 15 minutes with Old Paint. Should your child start to have visions of the Grand National, a few bucks will get him or her 15 more minutes.

Horseback riding is popular in HALF MOON BAY, where dirt streets, hometown post offices, and vast farms give the coast its special brand of country. One way to share in this experience is to hop in the saddle and trot down to the beach. With 200 horses and ponies to pick from, the hired hands here will be able to find a relatively fresh and well-mannered horse to match your size and experience.

One Sunday afternoon, I climbed aboard Moon, a big, strong horse. Ol' Moon and I trotted on out to the beach and watched the sun sink clean into the PACIFIC OCEAN, the light refracting for miles across the water.

Behind us, an orange hue was cast across MONTARA MOUNTAIN. I expected Waylon Jennings to come by singing, "Mama, don't let your babies grow up to be cowboys" at any moment. Well, I've always felt you shouldn't let your cowboys grow up to be babies. Then Moon suddenly decided that with the sun down, it was time to return to the barn. Over yonder, a buddy of mine, Gus Zimmer, was experiencing a similar phenomenon, his horse heading hell-bent for leather for the barn. "Slow doooown!" he yelled at the horse. Gus was hanging on to the big saddle horn with both hands, the reins flapping loosely. "I'm outta control," he shouted, disappearing around the bend.

Up until this point, the relationship between Moon and me had been something like that of the Lone Ranger and Silver. I mean, whenever Moon would pull his ears back and snort, I would pat him on the neck and say, "Good horsey," and he would behave.

But after the sun went down and my buddy disappeared, no amount of "good horseys" had any effect. With a snort, Moon decided the hour was up and he was heading for the barn as well. He knew there was some hay waiting for him and that it was time for me to get a little shut-eye.

Directions: From the north, take Highway 1 past Princeton Harbor. From the east, take Highway 92 to Half Moon Bay, then head north on Highway 1 for one mile. Sea Horse Ranch and Friendly Acres Ranch are on the west side of Highway 1, between the city of Half Moon Bay and the town of Miramar. Note: Because of landslide problems, Highway 1 is sometimes closed at Devil's Slide. An alternate route is to take Interstate 280 to Highway 92 in San Mateo. Turn west and drive to Highway 1 and Half Moon Bay. Turn right and travel one mile to the ranches on the left side of the road. **Trip tip:** Get a horse that matches your riding ability, and remember always to treat the animals with respect. **Contact:** Sea Horse Ranch and Friendly Acres Ranch, (650) 726-9903. Fees: Horses and ponies can be rented at reasonable rates. **Locator:** HALF MOON BAY (E1b). **See featured trip page:** 224.

• FEATURED TRIP •

SANTA CRUZ STEAM TRAIN

Rated: The San Francisco Bay Area's Best Train Ride

Spending a day touring the SANTA CRUZ MOUNTAIN redwoods by train and by foot is like venturing back into history.

Roaring Camp Train Rides offers two unique trips, one that putts from FELTON to SANTA CRUZ, another that meanders up to Bear Mountain. Potential side trips include the Santa Cruz Boardwalk and Henry Cowell Redwoods State Park near FELTON, both of which are within short walking distance of the train's two staging areas. The adventure is based near FELTON in the SANTA CRUZ MOUNTAINS. This region has the Bay Area's largest stand of redwoods, the pretty SAN LORENZO RIVER, and several little restaurants in an area where the motto is still "good grub—cheap."

An old steam train on a narrow gauge track attracts most of the publicity to this area. It should. The old mare huffs and puffs, then takes you on a unique scenic tour of Bear Mountain. We're not talking about the Silver Bullet. This train just kind of goes, pretzeling its way through the redwoods on a six-mile round-trip that lasts about an hour and 15 minutes. There are both open and closed passenger cars, including a special observation car that is open on the sides and closed on top. Riding in that car adds a nice dimension to the experience, allowing you to smell the redwoods, hear the old steam belcher, and feel in close touch with your surroundings.

The other train ride is routed between FELTON and SANTA CRUZ. The route roughly parallels Highway 9, running along the SAN LORENZO RIVER, over a trestlework bridge, through a tunnel, and into SANTA CRUZ. The train features open-air and old-fashioned parlor cars, with seating both inside and out.

This train, too, is no speed demon. It runs on a broad gauge track and is powered by an old diesel. Perfect, eh? It takes an hour and 15 minutes for the trip to SANTA CRUZ, one way, traveling just under five miles per hour. The train meanders. It moseys. It ambles. But it gets there.

Depending on your starting point, the destination of this train is either the Santa Cruz Boardwalk or Henry Cowell Redwoods State Park in FELTON. The staging area in SANTA CRUZ is adjacent to the boardwalk, and the staging area in FELTON is about 30 steps from the entrance to the state park. Both destinations provide quality side trips. The city of SANTA CRUZ deserves some credit for cleaning up the boardwalk. A while back, it was getting run down, but the place has been spruced up and is once again great for a family outing.

The other option is Henry Cowell State Park. The park has 20 miles of hiking trails. You can route trips to a lookout where you will see the PACIFIC OCEAN (when the fog isn't in), or through redwoods and to the SAN LORENZO RIVER. If you want to stay overnight, a campground is available, though reservations are necessary during the summer.

When you add it all up—an old-style train ride, a hike through redwoods, maybe a tour of the boardwalk, topped off by dinner at a good restaurant—this is one of the top single-day destinations in this part of the state.

Directions: From the Peninsula, take Interstate 280 south to Highway 17. Follow Highway 17 south toward Santa Cruz, then take the second Scotts Valley exit, Glen Canyon/Mount Hermon Road. Take Mount Hermon Road through Scotts Valley and continue until it dead ends at Graham Hill Road. Turn left, drive a half mile, and look for Roaring Camp on the right. From the coast, take Highway 1 south to Santa Cruz, then turn north on Highway 17. Take the Scotts Valley/ Big Basin turnoff, which will lead to Mount Hermon Road. Continue until it dead ends at Graham Hill Road, then turn left, drive a half mile, and look for Roaring Camp on the right.
Contact: For a brochure and schedule information, phone Roaring Camp Train Rides, (831) 335-4484. **Fees:** Steam train rides cost $13; prices are slightly higher for the Santa Cruz tour.
Locator: SANTA CRUZ (E1).

• FEATURED TRIP •

★ Gold Panning on the South Fork Tuolumne River

Rated: The Most Enticing Adventure

Gold flecks glittered in the morning sun, sparkling amid a bed of black sand, and yes, I figured I was rich.

I was kneeling on the banks of the SOUTH FORK TUOLUMNE RIVER, deep in STANISLAUS NATIONAL FOREST east of Sonora, and as I looked into that gold pan it was like peering into a crystal ball to see my future. "What will I do with my riches from all the gold?" I wondered. Well, for starters, no more Denison's canned chili for lunch.

Right then, my partner, Ed Dunckel, let out a roar. "My pan is filled with gold," he said. "Best I've ever seen."

Ed Dunckel looks like what an old, grizzled goldpanner is supposed to look like, even though some people think he's about 150 years late. He's 70, with a big white beard, a Snuffy Smith hat, a scar on his face, one glass eye, and an eagle-sharp look in the other eye like he might pull a Colt six-shooter on anybody making a grab for his gold pan.

Dunckel, who has been panning for gold for 30 years, is one of thousands who believe that years with heavy snowmelt are the best for gold panning. Riches were mine.

What happened is that the New Year's Flood of 1997 reshaped rivers across California, digging, scouring, and clearing unbelievable tons of silt and gravel from riverbeds, often right down to the bedrock. That unveiled new gold finds from spots never before mined, as well as sprinkle gold on the banks of many rivers in the SIERRA foothills.

So many rivers have been reshaped that Dunckel says it's as if nature has reinvented the sport. This theory is supported by logic, according to scientist Michael Furniss, a specialist in soil science and hydrology.

"The earth's core is a pressurized molten mass, and it emerges where it can find cracks and fissures in the surface," Furniss said. Over time, the gold rises to the surface where it can find these fissures, he explained, and the floods then scour the rivers down to the bedrock. "That brings new gold to existing feeder streams and river canyons."

That explains why California's gold belt runs roughly from MARIPOSA north to DOWNIEVILLE, where there's a series of canyons and fissures from the valley foothills on up to roughly 4,500 feet elevation. It also explains why streams such as the FEATHER, AMERICAN, YUBA, MOKELUMNE, TUOLUMNE, and STANISLAUS, which cross this gold belt, can produce so much gold.

So I chose the SOUTH FORK TUOLUMNE. That is where Dunckel owns a remote parcel with a primitive cabin, and where gold was so abundant in the 1850s that three lucrative mines were dug within a mile.

I arrived at the cabin in darkness, late enough for Dunckel to be in a grouchy mood about it. But after a few minutes, I discovered that he actually was just edgy for us to set out and get all that gold. He broke out into a huge gold miner's smile, thinking of the riches that awaited us.

"Let me tell you what happened one afternoon," he said, tugging on his beard. "One day some friends were visiting me and this young girl went for a walk down by the river. She looks down and sees this nugget, so she just reaches down and picks it up, then later shows it to me. It was as big as a fingernail, the biggest on my property in 30 years. Because of the flood, there could be hundreds more out there."

Dunckel flashed a "We're-going-to-get-rich" smile at me and then started talking strategy.

The reason gold panning works, he explained, is because gold is heavier than other material. "The whole key is developing the skill to separate the silt and worthless fool's gold from the real gold."

The best way to do this, he said, was to find a comfortable rock or log to sit on along the stream, scoop some material into the pan, then swish it in a circular motion and from side to side. "You dip the pan just barely underwater from time to time," Dunckel said, now all business. "That lets the flow of the water lift the lighter material out of the pan."

Then he smiled that 24-karat smile again. "Pretty soon all you'll have left is the heavy black sand and gold flecks, and if we're really lucky, something bigger."

Don't try to pick the gold out of the pan along the stream, he advised, but instead put the contents of the pan in a large container. "Later, we'll spread it out on a white cloth under a bright light, then pick out all the gold." This is easy, using a magnifying glass to make sure you miss nothing, a moistened toothpick for the flecks, and a pair of tweezers for the bigger chunks, what we call the "picker outers."

The next morning, we were out on the river. Its new contours were extraordinary to see for the first time. Just across from Dunckel's cabin, the flood had wiped out a meadow 50 yards across and cut a 15-foot-deep cliff on one side. We worked our way down, and once we located suitable rocks to sit, started our mission.

The water was cold and clear, and as I swished the material about in the pan, I noticed that while no gold nuggets were apparent, there did indeed seem to be flashes of gold. Within 20 minutes, I had mastered this art and had only a layer of fine black sand and gold flecks in my pan. Just like Dunckel said, I thought.

By mid-morning we had collected enough material that we decided to wait no more, and we were off to his cabin to pick out all the gold. The black sand was sprinkled on a bright white cloth, spotlighted by a bright, battery-powered beam (after all, Dunckel has no electricity). In the next hour, we picked out fleck after fleck with our toothpicks, placing them in a small bottle.

Finally, we were done. Dunckel then weighed the bottle. By subtracting the weight of the bottle, we were able to calculate that the weight of the contents—the gold flecks—weighed a total of roughly one-tenth of an ounce. At the price of $349 per ounce, that means we had each worked 10 hours to earn $17.45.

Then I noticed I was getting hungry. "Got anything for lunch?" I asked.

"How about some Denison's chili?"

Locator: SOUTH FORK TUOLUMNE RIVER (E4).

12
RESOURCES

PARKS AND RECREATION AREAS

NATURE PRESERVES

MIDPENINSULA REGIONAL OPEN SPACE PRESERVE

See last page for Northern California and Bay Area foldout maps.

PARKS AND RECREATION AREAS

CALIFORNIA STATE PARKS

The greater Bay Area has close to 20 state parks that provide hiking opportunities, along with 15 state beaches. These range from ANGEL ISLAND in the center of SAN FRANCISCO BAY to the redwood forests of BIG BASIN, BUTANO, and HENRY COWELL parks in the SANTA CRUZ MOUNTAINS.

Contact: For a brochure, write to the Publications Office, Department of Parks and Recreation, P.O. Box 942896, Sacramento, CA 94296-0001, or phone state headquarters at (916) 653-6995.

To contact individual district offices: Bay Area District, (415) 330-6300; Marin District, (415) 893-1580; Monterey District, (408) 649-2836; North Coast Redwoods, (707) 445-6547; Russian River–Mendocino District, (707) 865-2391; Santa Cruz District, (408) 429-2851; Sierra District, (530) 525-7232; Silverado District, (707) 938-1519.

EAST BAY REGIONAL PARK DISTRICT

The East Bay Regional Park District manages more than 50 parks that cover 75,000 acres in Alameda and Contra Costa Counties. Over 1,000 miles of trails cut through all kinds of settings, and an additional 100 miles of trails connects the parklands.

Contact: For information and free maps, contact the East Bay Regional Park District, 2950 Peralta Oaks Court, P.O. Box 5381, Oakland, CA 94605-0381; (510) 635-0135* extension 2200.

GOLDEN GATE NATIONAL RECREATION AREA

Redwood forests, grassy hillsides, and ocean bluffs make this a spectacular attraction in Marin County. Some of the best spots are MUIR WOODS, TENNESSEE VALLEY, the MARIN HEADLANDS, and MOUNT TAMALPAIS. A network of trails connects the various parks.

Contact: For a free map and brochures, call the Golden Gate National Recreation Area at (415) 556-0560, or write the National Park Service, Building 201, Fort Mason, San Francisco, CA 94123.

MIDPENINSULA REGIONAL OPEN SPACE DISTRICT

This is one of the best-kept secrets on the San Francisco Peninsula, with some 50,000 acres of open land sprawling across 30 preserves—most of them set along the peninsula ridgeline at Skyline Boulevard.

Contact: For maps, contact the Midpeninsula Regional Open Space District, 300 Distel Circle, Los Altos, CA 94022; (415) 691-1200.

POINT REYES NATIONAL SEASHORE

In one day you can see tule elks, a waterfall that flows onto the beach, and whale spouts on the ocean, together in this diverse spot. The terrain varies from grasslands and chaparral ridges to ocean bluffs and forest.

Contact: For information and a free brochure, contact Point Reyes National Seashore, Point Reyes, CA 94956; (415) 663-1092.

OTHER OPTIONS

Many Bay Area counties also manage their own parks, and you can get information by calling them directly. To obtain maps for prime hikes outside of the Bay Area, contact the U.S. Forest Service, which manages 16 national forests in California.

Contact: A guide sheet to national forests is available for free by writing USDA-Forest Service, Office of Information, Pacific Southwest Region, 630 Sansome Street, San Francisco, CA 94111. Maps of individual forests, which detail all hiking trails and lakes, cost $4; write to the same address. For information, call (415) 705-2874.

NATURE PRESERVES

The Quiet America. It is land unencumbered by concrete, stoplights, and miles of cars and people. It is a delicate place where you can retain the belief that you, one person in a vast world, are still important. It is a retreat where you can slink away from the masses and focus on the life immediately around you.

An organization called the Nature Conservancy is committed to preserving habitats in their natural state. In Northern California alone more than 10 areas have been bought by or donated to the Conservancy, which offers free access to all. Each preserve offers something special, like the mystical attraction of BISHOP PINE PRESERVE near INVERNESS.

The number of people allowed on a preserve varies from as few as two per day to as many as 30, depending on the fragility of the environment. Access is free, but you must make a reservation—which is easily arranged by calling the Conservancy at (415) 777-0487. Camping is not allowed on the preserves themselves, but all are situated near campgrounds.

The goal of the Nature Conservancy is to preserve rare and threatened lands. The group does not take political stands like other environmental organizations, but instead works by acquiring land and offering a special and quiet place to be enjoyed by all. A nationwide organization, the Conservancy owns more than 1.5 million acres, operates 670 preserves, and has projects in all 50 states.

Exploring the remote reaches of California has become so popular that no matter where you go, it's often difficult not to come upon a party of hikers. On a preserve, your solitude is guaranteed—call it The Quiet America.

Here's a breakdown of the preserves available in Northern California, listed from north to south:

LANPHERE–CHRISTENSEN DUNES PRESERVE

Just a few people per day are allowed in this fragile area, which is situated along the Pacific coast just north of HUMBOLDT BAY near EUREKA.

The dunes were formed by the accumulation of sand washed ashore by waves, then blown inland by sea winds. A beach pine forest is found farther inland, where dense stands of trees tower over ferns and mosses and offer an undisturbed home for the wild.

Camping is allowed at PATRICKS POINT, PRAIRIE CREEK REDWOODS, and REDWOOD STATE PARKS, where trails tunnel through lush vegetation.

MCCLOUD RIVER PRESERVE

Here's your chance, fly-fishers. Rainbow and brown trout are native to this river, where catch-and-release fishing with flies and lures and single barbless hooks is the rule. Ten rods per day are allowed on the preserve, five by reservation.

MCCLOUD sits in a steep, forest-lined canyon that's home to ring-tailed cats, black bears, mountain lions, and black-tailed deer. More than 85 species of birds, including bald eagles, have been seen on the preserve.

NORTHERN CALIFORNIA COAST RANGE PRESERVE

This is the oldest and largest preserve in Northern California, where some 8,000 acres were protected in 1958. Black bears, deer, mountain lions, and other mammals are still found in a wild state here, unaccustomed to the presence of humans. Virgin Douglas fir forests in Northern California have been cut extensively for wood products, but here, in one of the few remaining stands, you can still experience the tranquil life that has been unchanged for centuries.

It is situated between LAYTONVILLE on U.S. 101 and WESTPORT on Highway 1. Camping is offered on the coast at RUSSIAN GULCH and VAN DAMME STATE PARKS.

BOGGS LAKE PRESERVE

BOGGS LAKE is nestled in the mountains between KELSEYVILLE and COBB VALLEY in Lake County, just eight miles south of CLEAR LAKE, where campsites are plentiful.

It offers an unusual combination of vernal pool and pond that sit in a basin of volcanic rock. As the lake dries in the summer, wildflowers bloom in concentric rings in the shallow water. The animal life consists of natives common to the area: deer, raccoons, skunks, and an occasional bobcat, mountain lion, or fox. Five to 10 people per day are allowed access to this area.

FAIRFIELD OSBORN PRESERVE

The preserve consists of 150 acres of oak, evergreen forest, freshwater marsh, ponds, and streams high on the slopes of the SONOMA MOUNTAINS, 60 miles north of San Francisco.

Copeland Creek crosses the preserve, which helps support deer, foxes, weasels, quail, and owls. As many as 20 people per day are allowed. Campsites are available at Sugarloaf Ridge State Park and Sonoma Coast State Beach.

SACRAMENTO NATIONAL WILDLIFE PRESERVE

John Muir described these woodlands as "forests of tropical luxuriance." The dense foliage of oaks, cottonwoods, ash, and willows provide habitat for a wide variety of wildlife, such as beavers, mule deer, river otters, ringtailed cats, mink, and wildcats. No other terrestrial habitat in the state supports so large a number of bird species, including the very rare yellow-billed cuckoo.

The preserve is located near the Sacramento River southwest of CHICO, and nearby camping is available at Woodson Bridge State Recreation Area and Colusa–Sacramento River State Recreation Area.

BISHOP PINE PRESERVE

Bishop Pine is a 400-acre area in Marin County about 35 miles north of SAN FRANCISCO. It sits on the Point Reyes Peninsula, overlooking TOMALES BAY near INVERNESS. The Samuel P. Taylor State Park and the POINT REYES NATIONAL SEASHORE offer nearby camping spots.

The preserve is named after the stand of Bishop pines that grows within the dense mixed evergreen forest. Deer, coyotes, squirrels, chipmunks, and bobcats live there. A spring-fed stream flows through the center of the preserve and empties into TOMALES BAY at Willow Point.

SPINDRIFT POINT PRESERVE

Spindrift serves as a viewing area for the migrating gray whales that breach as they pass by the rocks at the tip of the point. The preserve is graced with meadows that provide elaborate wildflower displays and are home to a variety of wildlife.

It's a summer haven for kingfishers, hawks, gulls, and California brown pelicans, among many other birds. It's located along the Marin coast near the community of MUIR BEACH, just a short drive from SAN FRANCISCO. Camping is available at the POINT REYES NATIONAL SEASHORE. Access is limited to five people per day.

ELKHORN SLOUGH PRESERVE

Elkhorn Slough is the second largest salt marsh in California, and one of the last major undisturbed estuaries on the coast. It opens into MOSS LANDING, between SANTA CRUZ and MONTEREY, and contains a seven-mile tidal channel. The preserve covers 441 acres. Some excellent clamming is available at low tides (in the minus one-foot range) just west of the preserve. You can camp at Fremont Peak.

BIG CREEK PRESERVE

Big Creek is located about 45 miles south of CARMEL and, at sea level, includes nearly four miles of rock coast centered in the California Sea Otter Refuge. The preserve's land rises from the ocean to an elevation of 4,000 feet at its eastern boundary with Santa Lucia Mountain.

The preserve is home to mountain lions, black-tailed deer, bobcats, and endangered sea otters. Plus, 125 bird species have been observed here, including hawks, owls, and myriad shorebirds.

Big Creek is also one of the last central coastal areas that supports a vigorous run of steelhead.

Up to 20 people per day may access the preserve. Camping is available at Julia Pfeiffer Burns State Park and Andrew Molera State Park.

MIDPENINSULA REGIONAL OPEN SPACE DISTRICT

The public is a lot smarter than some people (er, politicians) think. For one thing, they had the wisdom to create the Midpeninsula Regional Open Space District.

The district was established in a 1972 ballot vote that also provided for annual funding to purchase open-space lands on the Peninsula. There are now 27 preserves covering more than 35,000 acres, much of it among the most pristine hiking terrain in the Bay Area.

This is part of a trend that has attracted the attention of metropolitan centers across the country. Question: How do you preserve the Bay Area's natural aura from urban sprawl? Answer: Buy open space, then preserve it forever.

That has been the solution in the East Bay with the East Bay Regional Park District, in the North Bay with the Marin Water District and the GOLDEN GATE NATIONAL RECREATION AREA, and more recently, on the peninsula.

The first preserve bought by the Midpeninsula Regional Open Space District was the Foothill Preserve, 210 acres adjacent to Page Mill Road in the PALO ALTO foothills. That was in June of 1974, and since then some 50,000 acres have been purchased, preserved, and opened to the public with free access. They are located in San Mateo County, Santa Clara County, and in a small portion of Santa Cruz County.

The following is a synopsis of the open-space preserves:

COAL CREEK

This preserve is known for its rolling meadows, historic barn, and in the spring, blooming wildflowers.

Notes: 490 acres located on Skyline Boulevard, north of Page Mill Road.

El Corte de Madera Creek

Thirteen miles of trails make excellent hiking in this heavily forested area. There are also fascinating sandstone formations.

Notes: 2,800 acres located on Skyline Boulevard, south of Kings Mountain Road.

El Sereño

This is primarily chaparral foothill country, but with exceptional views of Lexington Reservoir and the South Bay.

Notes: 1,080 acres located in the Saratoga/Los Gatos foothills.

Foothill

Here is the oldest preserve in the system, featuring woodlands and ravines, knolls and lookouts.

Notes: 210 acres located on Page Mill Road in the Palo Alto foothills.

Fremont Older

A historic home is the centerpiece, surrounded by 4.5 miles of trails.

Notes: 740 acres located in the Cupertino foothills.

La Honda Creek

This area is made up of open grasslands with hilltops offering spectacular views of the San Mateo County coast, and lots of wildlife. A permit is required for access.

Notes: 840 acres near La Honda.

Long Ridge

You get views of the coastal redwoods with an excellent 7.5-mile loop hike available that includes connections to Monte Bello Preserve and Skyline Ridge Preserve.

Notes: 980 acres on Skyline Boulevard, just north of the intersection with Highway 9.

Los Trancos

It features the San Andreas Fault Trail, which traces an earthquake faultline for more than a mile.

Notes: 270 acres located on Page Mill Road near Skyline above Palo Alto.

Monte Bello

Great hiking is available here, with 13 miles of trails in all, including the three-mile loop hike on the Stevens Creek Nature Trail.

Notes: 2,600 acres located on Page Mill Road, opposite the Los Trancos Preserve.

Pulgas Ridge

A new favorite, this one offers cool canyons and ridgetop views of the adjacent San Francisco watershed lands and its lakes.

Notes: 290 acres located off Interstate 280 and Edgewood Road.

Purisima Creek Redwoods

This is a gorgeous area with redwoods and superb views of the coastal foothills and the ocean. Wheelchair access is available, along with rugged hiking.

Notes: 2,500 acres located on Highway 35 south of Highway 92.

Rancho San Antonio

Deer Hollow Farm—a small working demonstration farm, including animals—is the main attraction.

Notes: 970 acres located in the Cupertino foothills.

Ravenswood

This area is set along the South Bay, with tidelands, marshlands, and lots of birds. Trail construction is planned for the future.

Notes: 370 acres located adjacent to East Palo Alto.

Russian Ridge

With a 2,500-foot lookout summit providing views of Monterey Bay to the west and MOUNT DIABLO to the east, this is one of the best. It also offers six miles of trails.

Notes: 1,500 acres located on Alpine Road, near Skyline Boulevard.

SARATOGA GAP

You get exceptional views of the Santa Clara Valley here, along with good hiking with lots of rock outcrops.

Notes: 615 acres located on Highway 35 and Highway 9.

SIERRA AZUL I

This includes densely wooded canyons, old orchards, and a 3.5-mile trail routed through both.

Notes: 1,310 acres located east of Highway 17 near Kennedy Road.

SIERRA AZUL II

MOUNT UMUNHUM and other classic peaks are the highlights, though public access is currently sharply limited. There are high hopes for the future.

Notes: 6,000 acres located above Los Gatos, south of Highway 17.

SKYLINE RIDGE

Highlights include eight miles of trail, two beautiful farm ponds with lots of wildlife and birds and access to the adjacent RUSSIAN RIDGE PRESERVE.

Notes: 1,250 acres located on Skyline Boulevard south of Alpine Road.

STEVENS CREEK SHORELINE

A birder's paradise, this nature study area on the South Bay has waterfowl, shorebirds, and trails along a levee.

Notes: 55 acres located in Mountain View, off U.S. 101 on Shoreline Boulevard.

ST. JOSEPH'S HILL

A prime spot for hiking and horseback riding, with meadows, wildflowers, and the remains of an old vineyard.

Notes:360 acres located south of Los Gatos near Lexington Reservoir.

INDEX

C

D

G

N

O

Q

R

U

V

ABOUT THE AUTHOR

Tom Stienstra has made it his life work to explore the West—hiking, camping, fishing, and boating—searching for the best of the great outdoors and writing about it.

He is the outdoors writer for the *San Francisco Examiner,* which distributes his column on the New York Times News Service, and an associate editor for *Western Outdoor News.*

In the 1990s, he was twice named National Outdoor Writer of the Year (newspaper division) by the Outdoor Writers Association of America, and three times named California Outdoor Writer of the Year.

His books with Foghorn Outdoors are the best-selling outdoor guidebooks in the nation. They include:

California Camping
California Hiking (with Ann Marie Brown)
California Fishing
California Boating and Water Sports
Pacific Northwest Camping
Easy Camping in Northern California
Epic Trips of the West: Tom Stienstra's 10 Best

CREDITS

Editor in Chief	Kyle Morgan
Editor	Karin Mullen
Senior Research Editor	Janet Connaughton
Production Coordinator	Jean-Vi Lenthe
Production Assistant	Mark Aver

HOW TO USE THIS BOOK

Tom Stienstra's Outdoor Getaway Guide for Northern California has several features designed to help the reader navigate through its contents and zoom in on useful information.

1. Tom's Ratings: Thumbnail descriptions of the top 5, top 12, top 50 (etc.) locations or activities in the different categories (e.g. hiking, camping, fishing).

Example:

• TOM'S RATINGS •

THE TOP 6 OPPORTUNITIES TO SEE BALD EAGLES

2. Featured Trips: Longer descriptions of locations or activities, following a starburst.

Example:

• FEATURED TRIP •

CAPITOLA WHARF

3. Ratings for Featured Trips: These refer the reader to Tom's Ratings throughout the book—*if* the reference has a page number after it.

Example:

Rated: The Top 50 Parks, 7

If there is no page number, it does ***not*** refer to one of **Tom's Ratings.** It stands alone.

Example:

Rated: The Prettiest Land in the Western United States

4. Reference sections with contact information, fees, directions, locators, and Featured Trip references: Offset from the main text so the reader can cut to the chase.

Example:

Contact: Drakesbad Guest Ranch, (530) 529-1512; Shasta Cascade Wonderland Association, (800) 474-2782. **Locator:** LASSEN VOLCANIC NATIONAL PARK (B3). **See featured trip page:** 209.

a. Locators: In the reference section a name of the nearest city, park, or other geographical locator appears in small caps.

Example:

Locator: HUMBOLDT REDWOODS STATE PARK (B0).

b. Map grid numbers after the locators: The letter and number refer to the horizontal and vertical-grids on the maps at the back of the book.

Example:

Locator: HUMBOLDT REDWOODS STATE PARK (B0).

c. Featured Trip references (*only* in the Tom's Ratings sections): Directs the reader to one or more of the Featured Trips for an in-depth description.

Example:

See featured trip pages: 78, 224, and 401.

5. In-text locators: Small caps throughout the text indicate towns, rivers, parks, etc. printed on the maps.

Example:

In the SANTA CRUZ MOUNTAINS my favorite is BERRY CREEK CANYON, deep in BIG BASIN REDWOODS STATE PARK.